HANDBOOK OF COMP
SOCIAL SCIENCE, V

The *Handbook of Computational Social Science* is a comprehensive reference source for scholars across multiple disciplines. It outlines key debates in the field, showcasing novel statistical modeling and machine learning methods, and draws from specific case studies to demonstrate the opportunities and challenges in CSS approaches.

The Handbook is divided into two volumes written by outstanding, internationally renowned scholars in the field. This first volume focuses on the scope of computational social science, ethics, and case studies. It covers a range of key issues, including open science, formal modeling, and the social and behavioral sciences. This volume explores major debates, introduces digital trace data, reviews the changing survey landscape, and presents novel examples of computational social science research on sensing social interaction, social robots, bots, sentiment, manipulation, and extremism in social media. The volume not only makes major contributions to the consolidation of this growing research field but also encourages growth in new directions.

With its broad coverage of perspectives (theoretical, methodological, computational), international scope, and interdisciplinary approach, this important resource is integral reading for advanced undergraduates, postgraduates, and researchers engaging with computational methods across the social sciences, as well as those within the scientific and engineering sectors.

Uwe Engel is Professor at the University of Bremen, Germany, where he held a chair in sociology from 2000 to 2020. From 2008 to 2013, Dr. Engel coordinated the Priority Programme on "Survey Methodology" of the German Research Foundation. His current research focuses on data science, human–robot interaction, and opinion dynamics.

Anabel Quan-Haase is Professor of Sociology and Information and Media Studies at Western University and Director of the SocioDigital Media Lab, London, Canada. Her research interests include social media, social networks, life course, social capital, computational social science, and digital inequality/inclusion.

Sunny Xun Liu is a research scientist at Stanford Social Media Lab, USA. Her research focuses on the social and psychological effects of social media and AI, social media and well-being, and how the design of social robots impacts psychological perceptions.

Lars Lyberg was Head of the Research and Development Department at Statistics Sweden and Professor at Stockholm University. He was an elected member of the International Statistical Institute. In 2018, he received the AAPOR Award for Exceptionally Distinguished Achievement.

The European Association of Methodology
(EAM) serves to promote research and
development of empirical research methods
in the fields of the Behavioural, Social,
Educational, Health and Economic Sciences
as well as in the field of Evaluation Research.
Homepage: http://www.eam-online.org

The purpose of the EAM book series is to advance the development and application of methodological and statistical research techniques in social and behavioral research. Each volume in the series presents cutting-edge methodological developments in a way that is accessible to a broad audience. Such books can be authored, monographs, or edited volumes.

Sponsored by the European Association of Methodology, the EAM book series is open to contributions from the Behavioral, Social, Educational, Health and Economic Sciences. Proposals for volumes in the EAM series should include the following: (1) Title; (2) authors/ editors; (3) a brief description of the volume's focus and intended audience; (4) a table of contents; (5) a timeline including planned completion date. Proposals are invited from all interested authors. Feel free to submit a proposal to one of the members of the EAM book series editorial board, by visiting the EAM website http://eam-online.org. Members of the EAM editorial board are Manuel Ato (University of Murcia), Pamela Campanelli (Survey Consultant, UK), Edith de Leeuw (Utrecht University) and Vasja Vehovar (University of Ljubljana).

Volumes in the series include

SMALL SAMPLE SIZE SOLUTIONS
A Guide for Applied Researchers and Practitioners
Edited by Rens van de Schoot and Milica Miočević

ADVANCED MULTITRAIT-MULTIMETHOD ANALYSES FOR THE BEHAVIORAL AND SOCIAL SCIENCES
Edited by Jonathan Lee Helm

HANDBOOK OF COMPUTATIONAL SOCIAL SCIENCE, VOLUME 1
Theory, Case Studies and Ethics
Edited by Uwe Engel, Anabel Quan-Haase, Sunny Xun Liu and Lars Lyberg

HANDBOOK OF COMPUTATIONAL SOCIAL SCIENCE, VOLUME 2
Data Science, Statistical Modelling, and Machine Learning Methods
Edited by Uwe Engel, Anabel Quan-Haase, Sunny Xun Liu and Lars Lyberg

For more information about this series, please visit: https://www.routledge.com/European-Association-of-Methodology-Series/book-series/LEAEAMS

HANDBOOK OF COMPUTATIONAL SOCIAL SCIENCE, VOLUME 1

Theory, Case Studies and Ethics

Edited by Uwe Engel, Anabel Quan-Haase,
Sunny Xun Liu and Lars Lyberg

Routledge
Taylor & Francis Group

LONDON AND NEW YORK

First published 2022
by Routledge
2 Park Square, Milton Park, Abingdon, Oxon OX14 4RN

and by Routledge
605 Third Avenue, New York, NY 10158

Routledge is an imprint of the Taylor & Francis Group, an informa business

British Library Cataloguing-in-Publication Data
A catalogue record for this book is available from the British Library

Library of Congress Cataloging-in-Publication Data
Names: Engel, Uwe, 1954– editor. | Quan-Haase, Anabel, editor. |
Liu, Sunny Xun, 1977– editor. | Lyberg, Lars, editor.
Title: Handbook of computational social science : theory, case studies and ethics / edited by Uwe Engel, Anabel Quan-Haase, Sunny Xun Liu and Lars Lyberg.
Description: Abingdon, Oxon ; New York, NY : Routledge, 2022. |
Series: European association of methodology | Volume 1. Handbook of computational social science / edited by Uwe Engel, Anabel Quan-Haase, Sunny Xun Liu and Lars Lyberg. | Includes bibliographical references and index.
Identifiers: LCCN 2021014136 (print) | LCCN 2021014137 (ebook) |
ISBN 9780367456535 (hbk) | ISBN 9780367456528 (pbk) |
ISBN 9781003024583 (ebk)
Subjects: LCSH: Social sciences—Data processing. | Social sciences—Methodology. | Social sciences—Mathematical models.
Classification: LCC H61.3 .H36 2022 (print) | LCC H61.3 (ebook) |
DDC 300.72/7—dc23
LC record available at https://lccn.loc.gov/2021014136
LC ebook record available at https://lccn.loc.gov/2021014137

ISBN: 978-0-367-45653-5 (hbk)
ISBN: 978-0-367-45652-8 (pbk)
ISBN: 978-1-003-02458-3 (ebk)

DOI: 10.4324/9781003024583

Typeset in Bembo
by Apex CoVantage, LLC

Lars E. Lyberg

December 1, 1944–March 1, 2021

Lars E. Lyberg had a passion for methods and statistics and made many contributions to these fields. During his career, he was a prolific writer and active member of the research community, working across disciplines including statistics, sociology, public opinion, and survey methodology, but his recent contributions to computational social science made him an innovative and much-respected scholar. In May 2018, Lars Lyberg received the American Association for Public Opinion Research (AAPOR) Award for Exceptionally Distinguished Achievement. This award is given for outstanding contribution to the field of public opinion research. We quote from this laudation to appreciate once again Lars' many outstanding contributions to the field of survey methodology and statistics.

"For more than five decades, Lars Lyberg has made significant and important contributions to the field of survey research. Lars' career started at Stockholm University where he earned a doctorate in statistics. In 1966, Lars began his professional work career at Statistics Sweden where he spent more than 40 years, culminating in his appointment as Head of the Research and Development Department."

Lars was the founder of the *Journal of Official Statistics* and served as its chief editor for more than 25 years. Lars was a prolific author, having written or edited many books and numerous journal articles in top journals, including *Survey Methodology*, *Public Opinion Quarterly*, and *Survey Research Methods*. Lars was an elected member of the International Statistical Institute, past president of the International Association of Survey Statisticians, and a fellow of the Royal Statistical Society and American Statistical Association.

Lars is co-editor of the present *Handbook of Computational Social Science* and therein a co-author of a chapter on a changing survey landscape. On March 1, 2021, Lars passed away. We dedicate Volume 1 of this Handbook to the memory of Lars E. Lyberg, a pioneer in statistics, survey methodology, and computational social science.

On the occasion of the 2018 AAPOR Award, Steve Everett produced a video that is publicly available at www.youtube.com/watch?v=Gi_P86lf3IY. The video starts with Lars talking about himself, his life, his career, continues with showing the moment he receives the award, and ends with a speech by Lars to commemorate the occasion. The video provides an opportunity to remember Lars, and his many personal and academic accomplishments.

March 15, 2021   Uwe Engel, Anabel Quan-Haase, Sunny Xun Liu

CONTENTS

Contents

Contents

CONTRIBUTORS

Michael Adelmund is a PhD student at the Department of Social Sciences, University of Bremen, and the University of Hildesheim. He is a social scientist and works as an analyst in the administration of the federal state of Bremen, Germany. His research interest focuses on right-wing extremism in the social network Facebook.

Séraphin Alava is a tenured researcher in educational sciences at the EFTS Joint Research Unit and member of the MSH Toulouse CNRS "Radicalities and Regulations". He leads the UNESCO world report on the links between radicalization and social media. He is at the head of three European networks of researchers to better understand the processes of radicalization and the stakes of radical desistance. He has developed a mechanism for evaluating the impact of counter-discourse aimed at preventing radicalization (Radicalization Awareness Network). He is a member of the UNESCO Chair for the Prevention of Radicalization and Violent Extremism. https://orcid.org/0000-0001-9286-8648

Elizabeth Arredondo is a writer focused on created compelling characters for television and interactive media. She is currently designing the personality, backstory, and conversations for a robotic wellness coach named Mabu. Mabu is the latest effort in social robotics from Cory Kidd, formerly of MIT's Media Lab. After earning her MFA in writing for screen and TV from USC's School for Cinematic Arts in 2005, Elizabeth received a feature film writing fellowship and participated in NBC's "Writers on the Verge" program. Elizabeth worked as a staff writer on the prime-time CBS drama Cold Case. She has also worked with a network to develop an original pilot.

Ho-Chun Herbert Chang is doctoral student at the Annenberg School for Communication and Journalism. He studies democratic movements and sociotechnical systems through computational social science and machine learning. His work has appeared in the *New Journal of Physics*, *Knowledge-Based Systems*, and the *Harvard Misinformation Review*. He holds an MSc in artificial intelligence from the University of Edinburgh and a BA in mathematics, quantitative social science, and a senior fellowship from Dartmouth College. https://orcid.org/0000-0002-0056-2527

Emily Chen is a doctoral student in computer science at the Information Sciences Institute at the University of Southern California. Prior to her time at USC, Emily completed her BS in computer engineering at the University of Illinois Urbana–Champaign in 2017. She is currently working under the supervision of Dr. Emilio Ferrara, and her research interests lie in machine learning, computational social sciences, and human behavior analysis. https://orcid. org/0000-0003-2363-9889

Wenhong Chen is Associate Professor of Media and Sociology and the Founding Co-Director of the Center for Entertainment and Media Industries at the University of Texas at Austin. Her research has focused on digital media industries and entrepreneurship. Dr. Chen's current project examines how U.S. and Chinese AI policies affect tech and media entrepreneurship. E-mail: wenhong.chen@austin.utexas.edu https://orcid.org/0000-0003-0521-2267

Yimin Chen is a PhD candidate in library and information science in the Faculty of Information and Media Studies at the University of Western Ontario. His research examines the communicative practices of online communities and cultures, with a focus on internet trolling behaviors and the controversy surrounding them. His previous work has ranged from fake news and deception detection, to library automation, to the impact of political memes on social media. Yimin is currently investigating the circulation and cultural impact of wholesome memes in hopes of finding clues towards a kinder, gentler internet. https://orcid. org/0000-0002-0924-3661

Claudio Cioffi-Revilla holds doctoral degrees from the University of Florence's Cesare Alfieri School of Social and Political Sciences and the State University of New York at Buffalo. He is University Professor (emeritus), George Mason University, where in 2002 he founded and directed the first PhD program on computational social science in the United States and the Center for Social Complexity. He is a Jefferson Science Fellow of the U.S. National Academy of Sciences, an Honorary Elected Fellow of the American Association for the Advancement of Science, co-founder and first president (2009) of the Computational Social Science Society, and author of the comprehensive textbook *Introduction to Computational Social Science* (Springer, 2017, 2nd ed.). His research interests are in agent-based models, disaster science, conflicts, and origins and development of social complexity. In applied mathematics, he has a special interest in the analysis of hybrid functions of continuous and discrete variables using the new nabladot operator calculus, which he created. He has served in senior science advisory government roles in the United States and other countries. He has authored numerous books and over 100 peer-reviewed papers, primarily on aspects of mathematical models and computational social science theory and applications. https://orcid.org/0000-0001-6445-9433

Nicole Coomber received her master of arts criminology degree from Wilfrid Laurier University. Her research interests include police use of social media and community policing. She is now a practitioner in the field of criminal justice.

Andrea Corradi is a PhD candidate in the Department of Criminology at Pennsylvania State University and has completed a graduate certificate in security studies from the Penn State School of International Affairs. She is a university graduate fellow and studies mechanisms of social control, security, artificial intelligence, and terrorism. Her dissertation studies the influence of gender, race, and mental health status on the criminal justice outcomes of extremists and terrorists. Ongoing research interests also include the use of artificial intelligence and machine learning to identify unknown perpetrators of terrorism. https://orcid. org/0000-0003-4612-2292

Lena Dahlhaus is a lecturer at the University of Bremen, where she teaches statistical data analysis using R to undergraduate level sociology students. Following a bachelor's degree in sociology, she received a master's degree in social research with distinction from the University of Bremen in 2020. Previously, Lena has worked at the Social Science Methods Centre and the Working Group Statistics and Social Research at the University of Bremen, where she was involved in research projects about the role of artificial intelligence in society. Her research interests include survey methodology, natural language processing, research ethics, and integrating traditional and new forms of data. https://orcid.org/0000-0003-4244-5545

Mark Elliot has worked at University of Manchester since 1996, mainly in the field of confidentiality and privacy. He is one of the key international researchers in the field of statistical disclosure and collaborates widely with non-academic partners, particularly with national statistical agencies, where he has been a key influence on disclosure control methodology used in censuses and surveys and where the SUDA software that he developed in collaboration with colleagues in computer science at Manchester is used. In 2012, he led the UK Anonymisation Network (www.ukanon.net), which has 600 members and provides advice, consultancy, and training on anonymisation. Aside from confidentiality, privacy, and disclosure, his research interests include data science methodology and its application to social science. He is director of the University of Manchester's new interdisciplinary MSc in data science and the doctoral program in data analytics and society. https://orcid.org/0000-0002-3142-4493

Uwe Engel is Professor Emeritus at the University of Bremen (Germany), where he held a chair in sociology from 2000 to 2020. In 2007, he founded the Social Science Methods Centre of Bremen University and has directed this institution since then. Prior to that, he held a professorship in social sciences at the University of Potsdam and an assistant professorship at the Department of Philosophy, Religious Studies, and Social Sciences at the University of Duisburg. From 2008 to 2013, Uwe coordinated the Priority Programme 1292 "Survey Methodology" of the German Research Foundation (DFG). His research focuses on survey methodology, data science, longitudinal and multilevel modeling, and field research (experiments, surveys). Sociological interests include human-robot interaction, artificial intelligence, and opinion dynamics. Uwe is a founding member of the European Association of Methodology (EAM) and the Bremen International Graduate School of Social Sciences (BIGSSS). He earned a doctorate in sociology at Leibniz University of Hannover in 1986 with a PhD thesis on multivariate data analysis in status inconsistency research. http://orcid.org/0000-0001-8420-9677

Emilio Ferrara is Associate Professor of Communication & Computer Science jointly at the USC Annenberg & Viterbi Schools of Communication and Engineering, Associate Director of Undergraduate and Master's Programs in Data Science, Research Team Leader at the USC Information Sciences Institute, and Principal Investigator at the USC/ISI Machine Intelligence and Data Science (MINDS) center. Dr. Ferrara was recently named Director of the Annenberg Networks Network (ANN) center and Chair of the Web Science Trust Networks (WSTNet). Ferrara's research uses AI and network science to study human behavior in techno-social systems and information networks. Ferrara has published over 170 articles on social networks, machine learning, and network science; appeared in venues like Proceeding of the National Academy of Sciences, Communications of the ACM, and Physical Review Letters; and his research has been featured on all major news outlets. He was named 2015 IBM Watson Big Data Influencer and he received the 2016 Complex Systems Society Junior Scientific Award, the 2016 DARPA Young Faculty Award, and the 2018 DARPA Director's Fellowship. As PI, he received over $20M in research funding from DARPA, IARPA, AFOSR, and the Office of Naval Research. https://orcid.org/0000-0002-1942-2831

Jeremy Freese is Professor of Sociology at Stanford University. He conducts research on a variety of topics, including public opinion, health disparities, social response to innovation, diffusion of knowledge, and social science genomics. He is Co-Principal Investigator of the General Social Survey (GSS) and of Time-Sharing Experiments in the Social Sciences (TESS), two ongoing infrastructural projects of the National Science Foundation that have been pioneering in their data-sharing practices. With Garret Christensen and Ted Miguel, he is the co-author of *Transparent and Reproducible Social Science Research: How to Do Open Science*, published by the University of California Press. https://orcid.org/0000-0002-9451-6432

David Garcia has been Professor for Computational Behavioral and Social Sciences at the Graz University of Technology since 2020 and group leader at the Complexity Science Hub Vienna and the Medical University of Vienna since 2017. David leads the Computational Social Science Lab, where an interdisciplinary team analyzes human behavior through digital traces and computational models. His research is funded by the Vienna Science and Technology Fund (WWTF) through a Vienna Research Group grant. David holds computer science degrees from Universidad Autonoma de Madrid (Spain) and ETH Zurich (Switzerland). David did a PhD and Postdoc at ETH Zurich, working at the chair of systems design. His main work revolves around the topics of emotions, polarization, inequality, and privacy, combining statistical analyses of large datasets of online interaction with computational models. His thesis, "Modeling Collective Emotions in Online Communities", provides an example of how agent-based modeling can be used to construct an integrated approach to collective emotional phenomena in cyberspace. His postdoctoral research on opinion polarization and online privacy has been funded by the Swiss National Science Foundation and the ETH Risk Centre. http://orcid.org/0000-0002-2820-9151

Stephanie Geise is (interim) Professor of Communication and Media Studies with a focus on Digital Communication at ZeMKI Centre for Media, Communication and Information Sciences, at the University of Bremen. Dr. Geise's research focuses on political communication, media effects and empirical methods, with a special emphasis on the analysis of the visual and multimodal communication. She headed the research project, "Still Images Moving People" until 2019; currently, she leads the research project "Remixing Multimodal News Reception" founded by the Deutsche Forschungsgemeinschaft (German Research Association, DFG). As an expert in experimental research and observational computational methods, she headed the Center for Advanced Internet Research (CAIS), Germany, working group on Computational Social Sciences in 2018. From 2011 to 2015, she was Chair of the Visual Communication Section of the Deutsche Gesellschaft für Publizistik und Kommunikationswissenschaft (German Association for Journalism and Communication Science, DGPuK). https://orcid.org/0000-0003-4553-4762

Mathieu Génois is Maître de Conférence (tenured lecturer) at the Aix-Marseille University and has been a researcher at the Centre de Physique Théorique (CPT) in France since 2018. Dr. Génois defended his PhD in theoretical physics of complex systems from the University Paris Diderot in 2013. His first postdoc at the CPT focused on the study of face-to-face contacts and its application to digital epidemiology. During his second postdoc at GESIS–Leibniz Institute for the Social Sciences in Cologne, Germany, he has pushed his research further into the empirical analysis and modeling of human interactions. His current work is at the intersection of statistical physics, complex networks, and sociology, in particular the study of the mechanisms of human interactions in the physical space. https://orcid.org/0000-0001-5492-8750

Jeff Hancock is founding director of the Stanford Social Media Lab and is a professor in the Department of Communication at Stanford University. Professor Hancock is well known for his research on how people use deception with technology, from sending texts and emails to detecting fake online reviews. His TED Talk on deception has been seen over 1 million times, and he's been featured as a guest on "CBS This Morning" for his expertise on social media. His research has been published in over 80 journal articles and conference proceedings and has been supported by funding from the U.S. National Science Foundation and the U.S. Department of Defense. His work on lying and technology has been frequently featured in the popular press, including the *New York Times*, CNN, NPR, CBS, and the BBC.

Peter Hedström is Professor of Analytical Sociology at Linköping University. He is an internationally recognized authority in the area of analytical sociology, with publications such as *Dissecting the Social: On the Principles of Analytical Sociology* (Oxford 2005). He received his PhD from Harvard University and has held professorial appointments at the University of Chicago, Stockholm University, University of Oxford, Singapore Management University, NYU–Abu Dhabi, and Linköping University. He is a member of several academies, including the Royal Swedish Academy of Sciences. https://orcid.org/0000-0003-3536-8449

Steven G. Heeringa is a senior research scientist and associate director of the Survey Research Center (SRC) at the University of Michigan Institute for Social Research (ISR). He is a member of the Faculty of the University of Michigan Program in Survey and Data Science and the Joint Program in Survey Methodology. He is a fellow of the American Statistical Association and elected member of the International Statistical Institute. He is the author of many publications on statistical design and sampling methods for research in the fields of public health and the social sciences. He is the lead author of *Applied Survey Data Analysis, 2nd Edition* (Chapman & Hall, 2017), a comprehensive new text on methods for the statistical analysis of complex sample survey data. Steve has over 40 years of statistical sampling experience in the development of the SRC National Sample design, as well as research designs for ISR's major longitudinal and cross-sectional survey programs. Since 1985, Steve has collaborated extensively with scientific colleagues in the design and conduct of major studies in aging, psychiatric epidemiology, and physical and mental health. He has been a teacher of survey sampling and statistical methods to U.S. and international students and has served as a sample design consultant to a wide variety of international research programs based in countries such as Russia, the Ukraine, Uzbekistan, Kazakhstan, India, Nepal, China, Egypt, Iran, the United Arab Emirates, Qatar, South Africa, and Chile. https://orcid.org/0000-0002-3920-8074

William Hollingshead is a PhD student in the Department of Sociology at Western University. He received an honours bachelor of arts degree in sociology from Trent University and a master of arts degree in sociology from Queen's University. His doctoral research aims to examine the nature and expression of anti-immigrant sentiment on social media. https://orcid.org/0000-0001-8450-0077

Benjamin F. Jarvis is Senior Lecturer at the Institute for Analytical Sociology at Linköping University. His research links the dynamics of inequality and segregation to processes of social and geographic mobility. His methodological interests include the application of discrete choice models to mobility data and the implementation of empirically calibrated simulations for linking micro-level mobility to macro-level outcomes. His current projects use Swedish register data to understand how social networks influence residential mobility and segregation and how internal migration relates to patterns of social mobility in the United States. https://orcid.org/0000-0001-8127-4051

Florian Keusch is Professor (interim) of Statistics and Methodology at the University of Mannheim, Germany, and Adjunct Assistant Professor at the Joint Program in Survey Methodology (JPSM), University of Maryland, USA. He received a PhD in social and economic sciences (Dr. rer.soc.oec.) and an MSc in business (Mag.rer.soc.oec.) from WU, Vienna University of Economics and Business. His research focuses on nonresponse and measurement error in (mobile) web surveys and digital trace data collection. (E-mail: f.keusch@uni-mannheim.de) https://orcid.org/0000-0003-1002-4092

Marc Keuschnigg is Professor of Sociology at Leipzig University and Associate Professor at the Institute for Analytical Sociology at Linköping University. His research interests include peer influence and opinion dynamics, cooperation and normative change, as well as spatial inequality and urban-rural divides. Much of his work centers around how people use social cues to guide their choices and how these behaviors interact to bring about hard-to-predict collective outcomes. Recent work has appeared in *Sociological Methods & Research*, *Sociological Science*, *Science Advances*, and *PNAS*. (E-mail: marc.keuschnigg@liu.se) https://orcid.org/0000-0001-5774-1553

Frauke Kreuter is Chair of Statistics and Data Science for the Social Sciences and Humanities at the Ludwigs-Maximilians-University in Munich (LMU), Germany; and Professor in the Joint Program in Survey Methodology (JPSM) at the University of Maryland, USA. She is also co-director of Data Science Centers at the University of Maryland and the University of Mannheim, co-founder of the Coleridge Initiative and the International Program in Survey and Data Science (IPSDS), and co-host of the German podcast digdeep.de. Her recent textbooks include *Big Data and Social Science: A Practical Guide to Methods and Tools* and *Practical Tools for Designing and Weighting Survey Samples*. (E-mail: frauke.kreuter@lmu.de) https://orcid.org/0000-0002-7339-2645

Jennifer Lavoie is an associate professor of psychology and criminology at Wilfrid Laurier University, Brantford, Ontario, Canada. Dr. Lavoie conducts nationally funded research focused on police interactions with people in mental health crisis. Her program of work explores the effectiveness of police de-escalation and crisis response training models, the use of co-response models, and police decision-making during encounters with citizens in mental health crises. She also investigates how people with lived experience of mental illness and family carers perceive police encounters during crisis. Jennifer is currently the lead investigator on a research project that examines the feasibility and efficacy of virtual reality scenario-based training for frontline police officers.

Sunny Xun Liu is a social science research scientist and associate director at Stanford Social Media Lab. Liu earned her PhD in mass communication and media from Michigan State University. Her research focuses on the social and psychological effects of social media and AI, social media and well-being, and how the design of social robots impacts psychological perceptions. Before joining Stanford, she was an associate professor at California State University, Stanislaus. She has won top three faculty paper awards from ICA and AEJMC and published in communication and psychology journals. Her research has been funded by Google Research and Stanford HAI.

Jan Lorenz is a computational social scientist at Jacobs University Bremen. He obtained a doctoral degree in mathematics from University of Bremen in 2007 working on models and simulation of opinion dynamics. He worked on the general dynamics of complex socioeconomic systems at ETH Zurich until 2009. Since then, he has published in the social sciences. https://orcid.org/0000-0002-5547-7848

Niklas M Loynes is an early career researcher in computational social science and a data engineer. He received his PhD in political science from the University of Manchester in 2021, focusing on methodologies for Twitter-based public opinion research. Beforehand, Nik was a research assistant at the University of Manchester's Personal Social Services Research Unit, working on health economics and social care research. From 2017 to 2020, he was a research fellow at New York University's Social Media and Political Participation (SMaPP) Lab, where he developed an integrated software pipeline for geo-locating Twitter users for social science research. In 2020, Nik founded the research and engineering company Corridor Labs and currently leads it as its CEO, where he is focused on developing software for the common good and collaborating with traditional research institutions. Current projects include work with Indiana University on COVID-19 misinformation and vaccine uptake or how information emerging on Facebook influences UK MPs' behavior.

For more than five decades, **Lars Lyberg** has made significant and important contributions to the field of survey research. Lars' career started at Stockholm University, where he earned a doctorate in statistics. In 1966, Lars began his professional work career at Statistics Sweden, where he spent more than 40 years, culminating in his appointment as head of the Research and Development Department. Lars was the founder of the *Journal of Official Statistics* and served as its chief editor for more than 25 years. Lars has written or edited numerous books and is author of numerous journal articles. Lars was an elected member of the International Statistical Institute, past president of the International Association of Survey Statisticians, and a fellow of the Royal Statistical Society and American Statistical Association. In 2018, he received the AAPOR Award for Exceptionally Distinguished Achievement of the American Association for Public Opinion Research.

Hannah Mieczkowski is a graduate student in the Department of Communication at Stanford University. Mieczkowski is interested in the connections between language and technology use, such as perceptions of affect in texting or the content of messages across social media platforms.

Goran Muric is a postdoctoral researcher at the USC Information Sciences Institute. His research falls at the intersection of social computing, machine learning, agent-based simulations, and network theory. Dr. Muric studies complex machine-to-machine, machine-to-human, and human-to-human interactions and addresses societal problems leveraging the online and offline data. https://orcid.org/0000-0002-3700-2347

Rasha Nagem is a doctoral student at the University of Toulouse. She is working on the measurement of the psychological and psycho-sociological impact of counter-discourses for the prevention of radicalization. She is also a manager of European security and justice projects and a researcher specializing in the prevention of radicalization and cyber-radicalization. She is a member of the UNESCO Chair for the Prevention of Radicalization and Violent Extremism and an expert in Islamology. She is a trainer for the prevention of radicalization leading to violence at the Inter-ministerial Committee for the Prevention of Delinquency and Radicalization.

Marcos Oliveira is a scientist interested in understanding real-world complex systems using data-driven approaches focusing on cities, human dynamics, and self-organizing mechanisms. In particular, Dr. Oliveira is interested in uncovering how urban crime emerges and exhibits regularities in cities. His research also involves understanding the mechanisms behind inequality in urban areas and social contexts such as face-to-face situations. He also investigates how self-organizing interactions drive intelligence in swarm intelligence algorithms. He is a lecturer in city science and analytics with the Department of Computer Science at the University of Exeter, UK, and affiliated with the Computational Social Science department at GESIS–Leibniz Institute for the Social Sciences in Cologne, Germany. https://orcid.org/0000-0003-3407-5361

Max Pellert is a PhD candidate at the Section for Science of Complex Systems at the Medical University of Vienna, affiliated with the Complexity Science Hub Vienna and Graz University of Technology. Max studied economics (and psychology) at the University of Vienna and obtained a master's degree in cognitive science from the University of Vienna and the University of Ljubljana, Slovenia. In his master thesis, entitled "Collective Dynamics of Multi-Agent Networks: Simulation Studies in Probabilistic Reasoning", he showed the superiority of a probabilistic version of inference to the best explanation (IBE) over standard Bayesian strategies of inference making in coin tossing experiments. Max is part of the WWTF research group "Emotional Well-Being in the Digital Society", led by David Garcia. He has used digital traces to study emotion dynamics in social media and to build a real-time monitor of affective expression in online communities. https://orcid.org/0000-0002-6557-7607

James F. Popham, PhD, is an assistant professor, Department of Criminology, at Wilfrid Laurier University. His research focuses on two distinct areas: community-based knowledge development and digital criminology. During his career, he has worked as a community scholar, conducting program evaluations and strategic policy development for agencies and communities throughout Canada. He has also recently contributed as an expert advisor to the United Nations Office on Drugs and Crime's Education for Justice (E4J) cybercrime module. He is the co-editor of a volume on technology and social control, available through Fernwood Press in 2020, and a forthcoming textbook that focuses on cybercrime in Canada, under development with Oxford University Press. Dr. Popham is also author or co-author on more than 30 publications. https://orcid.org/0000-0003-3485-009X

Anabel Quan-Haase is a full professor of sociology and information and media studies at Western University. Dr. Quan-Haase is the coeditor of *The Handbook of Social Media Research Methods* (Sage, 2017), coauthor of *Real-Life Sociology* (Oxford University Press, 2020), author of *Technology and Society* (Oxford University Press, 2020), and coeditor of the *Handbook of Computational Social Science* (Routledge, forthcoming). https://orcid.org/0000-0002-2560-6709

Byron Reeves received a BFA in graphic design from Southern Methodist University and his MA and a PhD in communication from Michigan State University. Prior to joining Stanford in 1985, he taught at the University of Wisconsin, where he was director of graduate studies and associate chair of the Mass Communication Research Center. He teaches courses in mass communication theory and research, with particular emphasis on psychological processing of interactive media. His research includes message processing, social cognition, and social and emotion responses to media, and he has been published in books of collected studies as well as such journals as *Human Communication Research, Journal of Social Issues, Journal of Broadcasting, and Journalism Quarterly.* He is co-author of *The Media Equation: How People Treat Computers, Television, and New Media Like Real People and Places* (Cambridge University Press). His research has been the basis for a number of new media products for companies such as Microsoft, IBM, and Hewlett-Packard in the areas of voice interfaces, automated dialogue systems, and conversational agents. He is currently working on the applications of multi-player game technology to learning and the conduct of serious work.

Johann "Wanja" Schaible is a computer scientist and leads the team Knowledge Discovery in the Computational Social Science department at GESIS–Leibniz Institute for the Social Sciences in Cologne, Germany. Dr. Schaible's dissertation examined the use of linked data to recommend an appropriate schema when building knowledge graphs (2017). His current research focuses on spatio-temporal analysis of sensor-based human interaction data, specifically face-to-face interactions and human mobility. In addition, Johann Schaible extends his research in the living lab-based evaluation of retrieval and recommendation approaches to enhance reproducibility in the area of information retrieval. https://orcid.org/0000-0002-5441-7640

Holger Schultheis holds a diploma in computer science and in psychology from Saarland University (2004). He received his PhD (2009) and habilitation (2017) in computer science from the University of Bremen, where he was a senior researcher before recently starting to lead AI and Data Science projects at neusta software development West. His research aims to bridge the gap between natural and artificial intelligence. By combining insights from cognitive science and methods from artificial intelligence, he works towards more sophisticated artificial agents and a deeper understanding of human cognition. Among other things, he applies the insights gained from his basic research to build intelligent tutoring and cognitive assistance systems that flexibly adapt to the current needs of the human user. https://orcid.org/0000-0001-6892-1656

Simon Schweighofer joined the Media & Communication Department of Xi'an Jiaotong-Liverpool University, Suzhou, P. R. China, in 2020 as Assistant Professor for Quantitative Research and Analysis. Simon was postdoctoral researcher at the Medical University of Vienna and the Complexity Science Hub Vienna. He holds a PhD in computational social science from ETH Zurich, an MSc and BSc in psychology, and an MA and BA in sociology from the University of Salzburg. He previously taught at the Paracelsus Medical University Salzburg. Simon has published in renowned journals, such as *Policy and Internet, Chaos,* and *EPJ Data Science* and presented his research in various international conferences, among them the International Conference on Computational Social Science (IC2S2), the Conference of the International Society of Research on Emotion (ISRE), and Complex Networks. His research focuses on online data (especially text), social networks, and the roots of political polarization. http://orcid.org/0000-0002-8679-0052

Juan Luis Suárez got his PhD in philosophy at the University of Salamanca in 1996 and a PhD in Hispanic literatures at McGill University (2000). He became Full Professor at Western University in 2007. In 2014, he completed his global executive MBA at I.E. Business School. Professor Suarez has authored 4 books, co-authored 7 monographs, and published over 80 articles. Since 2010, he has run the Canada Foundation for Innovation-funded CulturePlex Lab (new.cultureplex.ca) at Western University, a multidisciplinary lab on digital transformation that works with banks, technology start-ups, and other organizations in designing and implementing their digital future.

Daniel Varona received a BSc in computer sciences from the University of Informatic Sciences UCI, Cuba, 2008. He is experienced in the software engineering field as practitioner and educator, including several managerial levels in both industry and academy, and currently conducts artificial intelligence research as part of the CulturePlex Laboratory in Western University, Canada, where he is a PhD candidate. He has been awarded Emerging Leaders American Program (ELAP) 2010, MITACS Accelerate 2019, and Voucher for Innovation and Productivity 2020 from the Ontario Center of Excellence scholarships to solve practical problems applying artificial intelligence in partnership with local enterprises and start-ups. His scientific production consists of several academic papers on software engineering, artificial intelligence, and applied modeling in top international journals and conference proceedings. His current research interests include social and ethical implications of artificial intelligence. He can be reached at dvaronac@uwo.ca, and further information about him can be found at www.danielvarona.ca. https://orcid.org/0000-0003-2992-527X

Jan G. Voelkel is a PhD student in the Department of Sociology at Stanford University, a member of the Polarization and Social Change Lab, a graduate fellow at the Immigration Policy Lab, and a PhD fellow at the Center on Philanthropy and Civil Society. Jan studies political persuasion, group conflicts, and meta-science. He is interested in (a) why different political and ideological groups fight with each other, (b) under which circumstances people have constructive and effective discourse about moral and political issues, and (c) what the best ways are to conduct research and make scientific progress. Methodologically, Jan uses experiments as well as text analyses and is currently running his first mass collaboration project. https://orcid.org/0000-0003-4275-9798

Annie Waldherr is Professor of Computational Communication Science in the Department of Communication at the University of Vienna. She specializes in digitized public spheres and computational methods. With her team, she analyses how public issues emerge, from which perspectives they are publicly debated and interpreted, and how these processes have changed under the conditions of digitalization and datafication. For her work on the dynamics of media attention, Annie Waldherr obtained her PhD in media and communication studies from Freie Universität Berlin in 2011. After visiting the Network Science Institute at Northeastern University in Boston in 2016, she worked as Assistant Professor in the Department of Communication at the University of Münster from 2017 to 2020. https://orcid.org/0000-0001-7488-9138

Maria Zens is a researcher at GESIS–Leibniz Institute for the Social Sciences, Cologne, Germany. She has a background in social sciences, international politics, and literary studies, with degrees from the Universities of Bonn (Germany) and Aberystwyth (Wales, UK). Maria has extensive experience as a science journalist and has worked as a journal editor and publisher for several years. Joining GESIS in 2007, she was part of the Department of Computational Social Science on its foundation in 2013 and did her first RFID sensor study in 2016. Her academic publications include works in cultural history, information science, and social sciences and often benefit from interdisciplinary perspectives. https://orcid.org/0000-0001-7461-8231

Meiqing Zhang is a doctoral candidate at the Annenberg School for Communication and Journalism, University of Southern California. Her research interests lie in political attitudes, opinion dynamics, and computational social science. https://orcid.org/0000-0002-3722-1865

PREFACE

Digitization has revolutionized society, including the realm of social science. We are currently in the midst of a digital paradigm where digital technology evolves at unprecedented rates and impacts ever more domains of life. With the seamless integration of digital technology from mobile phones to AI into the rhythms of everyday life, there is also greater generation and accumulation of related behavioral data of prime interest to the social sciences. Digitization is changing the object of social science research. Public life and human behavior increasingly take place in digital environments both within and beyond social media. Robots, autonomous vehicles, and conversational agents are gaining considerably in importance. Advances in data science and artificial intelligence create behavioral opportunities but also challenge privacy protection, ethical norms, and common ways of life. In short, social science is changing because digitization is changing its focus.

Digitization is also changing the very methods of social research. If life takes place in digital environments, novel methods are needed for reaching target populations. Similarly, different kinds of data need different methods of data collection, processing, and analysis. The past decade has seen continued efforts toward the development and application of computational methods to let social science follow people to where they are – in digital environments ranging from social media to video gaming to AI. Computational social science (CSS) has become the umbrella term for all such efforts. CSS is both a rapidly developing field and a field in need of professional and institutional consolidation. This concerns its theoretical and methodological foundations, issues of research ethics and data policy, and further development of statistical and computational methods.

While the dynamic development of CSS observed in recent years is largely due to the digitization of society, it is important to remember that the roots of CSS are in mathematical sociology, statistical modeling, and social simulation. The field is much broader than the efforts around the study of popular digital trace data lets us assume. Furthermore, CSS represents a genuinely interdisciplinary field of study, not just a subfield of social science.

Against this background, the *Handbook of Computational Social Science* aims to make a major contribution to the consolidation of CSS whilst also moving it in new directions. The editors developed the idea of the handbook at the Digital Traces Workshop, which took place in 2018 at the University of Bremen, Germany. The three-day workshop was organized by the University's Social Science Methods Centre and funded by the German Research Foundation

(DFG), the federal state of Bremen, and the Bremen International Graduate School of Social Sciences (BIGSSS). During the workshop, an interdisciplinary group of scholars shared recent advancements in CSS research and established new transatlantic research collaborations. Forty-four participants from Canada, the United States, and eight countries in Europe took part in the invited talks on key debates in the field, showcasing novel statistical modeling and machine learning methods and also drawing from specific case studies to demonstrate the opportunities and challenges in CSS approaches. While not all the authors of the present handbook were a part of the initial workshop, the idea for the handbook was born out of this event.

Computational social science is a field at the intersection of different disciplines, such as social science, computing, and data science. The editors thus deliberately invited authors to contribute from diverse disciplines and fields of study to showcase the interdisciplinary nature of computational social science research. We very much appreciate that so many colleagues accepted this invitation: they carefully drafted and revised their chapters and participated in the peer-review process. This is a particularly impressive achievement, as the COVID-19 pandemic has created new work-life balance challenges for many academics. We would also like to express our sincere thanks to Lucy McClune, editor in psychology at Routledge, Taylor & Francis Group, and her assistant, Akshita Pattiyani, for their encouragement and continued support. A big thanks goes also to Silke Himmel at the University of Bremen for her invaluable assistance in the organization of the Digital Traces Workshop and her invaluable administrative assistance in this handbook project.

We end this preface with a heavy heart. On March 1, 2021, our co-editor Lars Lyberg passed away. Lars was a lead participant in the Digital Traces Workshop in 2018 and has been a valued collaborator in shaping the direction of the handbook. With his parting, the field of computational social science loses an influential scientist and visionary. We mourn a friend.

March 15, 2021
Uwe Engel, Anabel Quan-Haase, Sunny Xun Liu

1

INTRODUCTION TO THE *HANDBOOK OF COMPUTATIONAL SOCIAL SCIENCE*

Uwe Engel, Anabel Quan-Haase, Sunny Xun Liu, and Lars Lyberg

We write the introduction to the two-volume *Handbook of Computational Social Science* with excitement and awe. The Handbook brings together a considerable corpus of research and insight, with 22 contributions for Volume 1, "Theory, Case Studies and Ethics", and 22 contributions for Volume 2, "Data Science, Statistical Modelling, and Machine Learning Methods". Over 90 experts contributed from a wide range of academic disciplines and institutions to provide a mosaic of the diversity of CSS scholarship. They lay out the foundation for what CSS is today and where it is heading, outlining key debates in the field, showcasing novel statistical modeling and machine learning methods, and also drawing from specific case studies to demonstrate the opportunities and challenges presented by CSS approaches.

Our goal with the Handbook is to reach a wide readership by taking a multidisciplinary and multimethod approach. The Handbook includes foundational chapters for up- and- coming scholars and practitioners who are interested in consolidating their understanding of key terms, methods, and means of data interpretation as well as more advanced analytical approaches that serve as a learning resource for current experts in CSS. The Handbook is aimed at a wide range of scholars with backgrounds in technical fields such as statistics, methods, and computer science, as well as scholars in the social and behavioral sciences, the latter notably including psychology, cognitive science, sociology, communication, new media studies, and political science, among others. The Handbook also allows practitioners and policymakers who are tasked with analyzing a specific dataset to adopt a set of best practices to guide their research efforts.

Computational social science is an exciting field of research that is growing rapidly and in diverse directions. In 2018, Springer started the publication of its dedicated journal, *the Journal of Computational Social Science*, which is broad in scope and interdisciplinary in nature and aims "to understand social and economic structures and phenomena from a computational point of view". For example, its volume 3, issue 2, special issue was on "Misinformation, Manipulation and Abuse in the Era of COVID-19", bringing together top modeling and simulation experts on the topic. This demonstrates how CSS is having a direct impact on our understanding of pressing societal research questions and advancing novel methodological approaches. Computational social science research has an important role to play in society by providing unique and policy-relevant insights through its capability to apply computational approaches to large datasets. Besides, many special issues with a CSS focus are being proposed, such as the 2021 call

DOI: 10.4324/9781003024583-1

for papers by the journal *Chinese Sociological Review*. The call requests manuscripts that "offer important theoretical and empirical insights to advance our understanding of the development in CSS and help move forward the field in Chinese societies". This shows that there is an invisible college of the kind that Diana Crane (1972) described in her earlier work forming around the topic, with a rapid "proliferation of conferences, workshops, and summer schools across the globe, across disciplines, and across sources of data". (Lazer et al., 2020, p. 1060). As the field grows, CSS collaborations and research clusters are emerging globally. The field is not only growing but also consolidating, and our handbook represents an important step forward in this process.

The chapters in the two-volume Handbook provide a deep understanding of theory as well as methodological opportunities and challenges. The main aims include:

- *Theoretical debates*: Key theoretical debates are presented from different perspectives to show how the field is gaining strength and evolving.
- *Showcasing novel statistical modeling and machine learning methods:* The chapters describe cutting-edge methodological developments and their application to a range of datasets.
- *Ethical debates and guidelines*: The chapters demonstrate the dimensions of data ethics and the need for guidelines and appropriate pedagogy.
- *State-of-the-art artificial intelligence*: The chapters highlight the use of various AI systems as methodological tools, datasets, and a combination of both.
- *Demonstrating cross-disciplinary applications of CSS*: The chapters promote the development of new interdisciplinary research approaches to answer new and pressing research questions.
- *Computational methods of data collection and data management:* The chapters support our understanding and application of such methods in the field.

Computational social science and the digitization of everyday life

Computational social science (CSS) is an interdisciplinary field of study at the intersection of data science and social science which pursues causal and predictive inference as its main objective. With historical roots in mathematical modeling and social simulation, the recent digitization of all aspects of everyday life has turned CSS into a dynamically developing and rapidly growing research field. With the seamless integration of digital technology from mobile phones to AI into the rhythms of everyday life, there is also a greater generation and accumulation of related behavioral data of prime interest to the social sciences. Because most of these data are digital, CSS calls for computational methods of data collection, data management, data processing, and data analysis (Lazer et al., 2020). Computational social science is, thus, an evolving field with a mix of big-data, computational-methods, and data-science facets, as will be further detailed in this handbook (Engel, Volume 1: Chapter 9).

While it is true that computational methods are becoming increasingly relevant to the social sciences, it is equally true that the social sciences have participated in the development of a range of computational methods from the outset: some examples include statistical data analysis, social simulation, and mathematical modeling. For example, Coleman's (1964) seminal book *Introduction to Mathematical Sociology* constitutes one of the precursors of contemporary analytical sociology by explaining the unique challenges in attempting to quantify social behavior: "Because behavior is usually expressed in qualitative terms, any mathematical language which can serve for social science must in some fashion mirror this discrete, nonquantitative behavior" (p. 102). Also included in these early developments was Columbia University's Bureau of Applied Social Research (Barton, 1979), with its pioneering work on multivariate analysis, measurement, the analysis of change, and multilevel methodology. Additionally, we can also highlight the contributions to CSS made in the area of social simulation and its multilevel approach toward social complexity (Cioffi-Revilla, 2017). Hox (2017, p. 3) similarly identifies the social simulation branch as critical in the development of CSS as a unique field of study when reviewing "three important elements" of CSS, listing: "big data, analytics, and simulation".

The very interdisciplinary nature of CSS and its diverse historical roots make this field difficult to define and delimit. While some scholars narrow the scope of CSS to "big data", harvested through computational methods from social media platforms – often referred to as digital trace data – this narrow approach is perhaps questionable (Cioffi-Revilla, Volume 1: Chapter 2; Lorenz, Volume 1: Chapter 10). "Big data" are not only available through social media data extraction; many other sources of "big data" are available, including location-based data collected via mobile phones, bank transaction data, e-health records, and e-commerce transactions. Another important point is that the development of artificial intelligence (AI) and its integration into daily life through robotics. Smart speaker assistants (SSA) is another source of data for CSS. As SSAs like Google Home and Amazon Echo (Alexa) support a range of activities from e-commerce to information provision, they also generate increasing amounts of data (Brause & Blank, 2020). As our society advances toward sensor-rich computational environments in the future, data from smartphones, smart offices, and smart city devices will also be a primary data source.

Another approach to delimiting the field of CSS is by looking at its relation to data science. Hox (2017, p. 3), for instance, regards CSS as an interdisciplinary field that combines mathematics, statistics, data science, and social science. In this view, data science is a central tool, among others, in CSS. Some proponents of data science go as far as to subsume CSS under data science, in which case it is regarded as a "new interdisciplinary field that synthesizes and builds on statistics, informatics, computing, communication, management, and sociology . . . to transform data to insights and decisions" (Cao, 2017, pp. 43, 8). In contrast, Kelleher and Tierney (2018, p. 1) move away from any kind of taxonomy and instead stress the commonalities that exist between data science and CSS such as the focus on improving decision-making through a reliance on data. For Kelleher and Tierney, all these concepts are used in the literature interchangeably – data science, machine learning, and data mining – although data science can be broader in scope. While machine learning "focuses on the design and evaluation of algorithms for extracting patterns from data" and "data mining generally deals with the analysis of structured data", data science

> also takes up other challenges, such as the capturing, cleaning, and transforming of unstructured social media and web data; the use of big-data technologies to store and process big, unstructured datasets; and questions related to data ethics and regulation.
>
> (Kelleher & Tierney, 2018, p. 1f)

Hence, these terms are often used interchangeably, and, as our discussion shows, how they relate to each other remains a subject of debate.

If CSS is regarded as an emerging scientific field, this trend should be reflected in suitable indicator variables. Here, we look only at one such indicator, the number of publications making explicit reference to CSS. This represents only one such indicator; a few others are covered in later chapters (see Engel & Dahlhaus, Volume 1: Chapter 20, Bosse et al., Volume 2: Chapter 3). Figure 1.1 draws a rough picture of the trends in CSS in recent years, as reflected in the *Web of Science* Core Collection for the period 2010 to 2020. Figure 1.1 displays

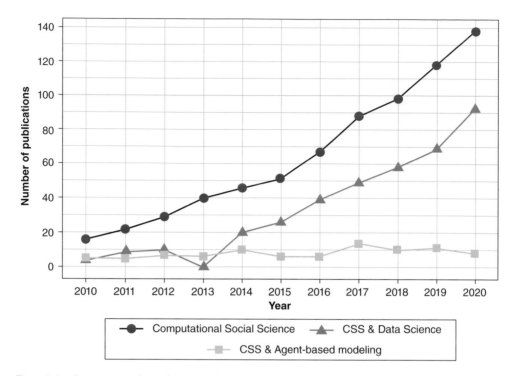

Figure 1.1 Computational social science, data science, and agent-based modeling

the results of three separate searches: the number of publications in response to a search for (1) "computational social science", (2) "data science" *in conjunction with* "computational social science", and (3) "agent-based modeling" (considering both spellings: modeling and modelling) in conjunction with "computational social science". It is noteworthy that a search for "data science" and "agent-based modeling" reveals considerably higher numbers *if each is used alone* as a search term. This simply indicates that both appear to also be of great importance far beyond the narrower field of CSS.

Figure 1.1 demonstrates an increasing interest in core CSS questions as well as in combination with data science. The lack of publications combining CSS and agent-based modeling is noteworthy, the latter taken as an example of a prominent approach in the simulation branch of CSS. Also of great importance is the advancement of research that combines agent-based modeling with empirical research (Lorenz, Volume 1: Chapter 10; Bosse, Volume 2: Chapter 13).

Balanced scope, modeling perspectives, and a basic multilevel orientation

We asked a group of notable scientists to delineate the scope and boundaries of CSS in relation to theory and methodology. First, *Claudio Cioffi-Revilla* outlines the scope of CSS (Volume 1: Chapter 2), which, for him, is understood as a field that integrates the study of humans and groups at all scales through the formal methodology of computational and mathematical models. The chapter aims to offer a balanced view of CSS, not slanted toward a version "driven by 'big data' from social media, and progress in algorithms from computer science, eschewing theory, mathematical models, and computational simulations".[1] Instead, Cioffi-Revilla specifies the scope of CSS as "theoretically and methodologically guided by theory, enriched by analytical models, and enabled by computer simulations; all three drawing on empirical data, be it big or small".

A key advantage of the interdisciplinary nature of CSS is its connections with theoretical terrains in multiple areas. Analytical sociology involves three defining characteristics: a basic multilevel orientation towards the modeling of social processes and a methodological realism which rejects "as-if" explanations and instead pursues a mechanism-based explanation of aggregate outcomes (Keuschnigg, Lovsjö, & Hedström, 2018). Against this background, *Benjamin F. Jarvis, Marc Keuschnigg*, and *Peter Hedström* highlight and discuss the relationship between CSS and analytical sociology (Volume 1: Chapter 3). They "highlight the ways in which analytical sociologists are using CSS tools to further social research" using "agent-based modelling, large-scale online experiments, digital trace data, and natural language processing" to identify "how large-scale properties of social systems emerge from the complex interactions of networked actors at lower scales". The authors also discuss how computational social scientists can, conversely, take advantage of analytical sociology.

Sociological explanations of aggregate outcomes assign an elementary role to the individual human agent (Coleman, 1990). Individuals act and interact and that way intentionally or inadvertently produce the phenomena we observe at the aggregate level. The behavior of agents represents accordingly an essential part of the micro-foundations of aggregate outcomes and should, thus, be understood properly. This is the starting point of the chapter on cognitive modeling (Volume 1, Chapter 4) in which *Holger Schultheis* presents computational cognitive modeling as an approach to a deeper understanding of the individuals involved in social processes.

A vital discussion concerns the issue of whether social science should target prediction or explanation (Hofman, Sharma, & Watts, 2017). Cautiously worded, practicing social science unguided by theory is presumed unimaginable to many social scientists. This places an emphasis on explanation. On the other hand, data science lays much stress on just the opposite pole, prediction. A balanced concept of CSS should accordingly strive for a solution to the explanation vs. prediction debate, too. As *Uwe Engel* sets out in his chapter on causal and predictive

Table 1.1 Overview of topics covered in Volume 1 "Theory, Case Studies and Ethics"

Volume 1			
Scope		*Ethics/policy*	*Case studies*
Methodology and research		*Self-commitments*	*Subject areas*
Topics			
The Balanced scope of CSS	Cognitive modeling	Open computational science	Face-to-face interaction
Analytical sociology	Agent-based modeling	Privacy	Affective science
Causal and predictive modeling	Survey Landscape	Big data regulations	Political Sentiment
Communication science	Digital trace data	Principled AI framework	Bots and social media
			Social robots
			Propaganda and extremism

modeling (Volume 1: Chapter 9), one such solution is offered by taking advantage of CSS being a *computational* science which translates an abstract debate into precise models, with the inclusive choice of exploiting the complete causal–predictive modeling spectrum.

Social science may be conceived of as an umbrella term for disciplines such as sociology, political science, and communication science. *Stephanie Geise* and *Annie Waldherr* devote their chapter to an overview of one such subfield of CSS, computational communication science (CCS) (Volume 1: Chapter 5). Based on lessons from working group sessions with experts, the chapter addresses recent challenges of CCS while reflecting upon its future development and expansion.

Survey research

The textual and digital trace data collected in social media represent an undoubtedly extremely relevant source for social research. However, even though such data have gained considerable importance in recent years and even though CSS research uses social media as a major data source, it would be misleading to regard survey research as a field outside of CSS and decoupled from its dynamic development. The digitization of life has changed the opportunity structure *for both* research branches. To this can be added the observation that both are exposed to similar threats to data quality and the combined use of their data in integrated research designs. The handbook, thus, covers relevant survey aspects as well.

First, *Lars Lyberg* and *Steven G. Heeringa* draw a picture of a changing survey landscape (Volume 1: Chapter 6). They start with the "golden age of survey research" and continue by providing an insight into the changes survey research underwent since that golden age. The exposition includes the "new data sources such as types of big data, administrative data, Paradata, and other process data", highlights the role of model-assisted surveys and survey-assisted models, and, among others, draws attention to combinations of probability and non-probability sampling and the enrichment of traditional survey work by artificial intelligence and machine learning.

Other chapters take up the sampling topic as well. *Rebecca Andridge* and *Richard Valliant* (Volume 2: Chapter 11) set out the statistical foundations for inference from probability and nonprobability samples. They review the fundamentals of probability sampling, describe two main approaches to inference for nonprobability samples, and provide examples of nonprobability samples that have worked and others that have failed. Second, *Jelke Bethlehem* centers on the challenges of online non-probability surveys (Volume 2: Chapter 12). He draws attention to the fact that the lack of proper sampling frames causes many surveys to be de facto self-selection surveys. In this connection, he also addresses the role of online panels if taken as sampling frames. The chapter compares online surveys recruited using random sampling with those based on self-selection. Some simulations and examples show the perils of non-probability-based online surveys. Third, *Camilla Zallot*, *Gabriele Paolacci*, *Jesse Chandler*, and *Itay Sisso* address crowdsourced samples in observational and experimental research using the Amazon Mechanical Turk (MTurk) as an example of "what has become the most popular sampling frame in the social sciences" (Volume 2: Chapter 10). The chapter asks how MTurk samples compare to traditional samples in survey and experimental research, highlights the ethical concerns involved, and asks what challenges researchers can expect to face on this platform.

Digital trace data

"Digital traces left by individuals when they act or interact online provide researchers with new opportunities for studying social and behavioral phenomena". *Florian Keusch* and *Frauke Kreuter* (Volume 1: Chapter 7) review digital trace data and the variety of technical systems such data come from. The authors point to the fine-grained nature of such data and the virtue of enabling observations of individual and social behavior at high frequencies and in real time. The authors also draw attention to a feature similarly addressed in other chapters, in fact, a non-intrusive measurement in which "the data collection happens without the observed person having to self-report". While the original definition of digital trace data is limited to data that are found, that is, "data created as a by-product of activities not stemming from a designed research instrument", the authors argue "that digital traces can and should sometimes be collected in a designed way to afford researchers control over the data-generating process and to expand the range of research questions that can be answered with these data".

Data collection

Digital trace data come from a variety of technical systems. *Florian Keusch* and *Frauke Kreuter* (Volume 1: Chapter 7) provide a non-exhaustive list: business transaction systems, telecommunication networks, websites, social media platforms, smartphone apps, sensors built in to wearable devices, and smart meters. Several chapters address accordingly related forms of data collection. *Stefan Bosse*, for instance, covers crowdsensing for large-scale agent-based simulation in his concept of fusing real and virtual worlds by "creating augmented virtuality by using mobile agents and agent-based simulation technologies" (Volume 2: Chapter 13). Social media data take center stage in chapters on data collection via application programming interfaces (APIs) and web mining. First, *Jakob Jünger* traces a brief history of APIs and discusses the opportunities and limitations of their use for online research (Volume 2: Chapter 2), while the subsequent chapter focuses more on a demonstration of how to access data practically using an API (Volume 2: Chapter 3). In this chapter, *Dominic Nyhuis* discusses the value of APIs for social research and provides an overview of basic techniques for accessing data from web interfaces. Then, *Stefan Bosse, Lena Dahlhaus*, and *Uwe Engel* draw attention to web data mining (Volume 2: Chapter 4). The chapter highlights the steps involved and threats to data quality; outlines how to extract content from web pages via an alternative method to the use of APIs, namely web scraping; and addresses the legal implications of this method of data collection.

Data quality

Several chapters address the data quality theme by some means or another, including the chapters referred to in the preceding three sections. Two prominent points of origin help in introducing the data quality topic in CSS: the well-known total survey error approach (Biemer & Lyberg, 2003) and the classic concept of unobtrusive measures (Webb, Campbell, Schwartz, & Sechrest, 2000). *Indira Sen, Fabian Flöck, Katrin Weller, Bernd Weiß*, and *Claudia Wagner* present their total error framework for digital traces of humans online (TED), an approach inspired by existing error frameworks in survey methodology, such as the total survey error (TSE) framework (Volume 2: Chapter 9).

A prominent argument assumes that improved data quality is already achievable by passive forms of data collection because "found" data replace error-prone self-reports on behavior by the unnoticed direct observation of this behavior itself. At first glance, this argument appears convincing indeed: if people are not asked for a response at all, neither such a response nor any inadvertent survey-related side effect can occur. This, however, does not preclude the potency of other sources of social influence if opinions are expressed in public contexts where platform-specific terms of service, higher-ranking legal rules, and the potential fear of undesirable personal consequences may shape the way opinions in blogs and discussion lists are expressed.

Michael Adelmund and *Uwe Engel* use the example of public opinion formation on the far right of the political spectrum to discuss this case (Volume 1: Chapter 22). Also, *Lena Dahlhaus* and *Uwe Engel* draw attention to a further factor that may impair the quality of digital trace data, the systematic protection against tracking on the internet (Volume 1: Chapter 20).

Open science

The direction of numerous science fields has been moving toward an open science paradigm. *Stephanie Geise* and *Annie Waldherr* (Volume 1: Chapter 5) describe how CSS researchers from multiple disciplines see both opportunities and challenges for open science practices. For example,

> content and data sharing activities connected with "best practice" exchange also are associated with additional ethical and legal challenges – including the acknowledgement of privacy requirements and terms of service, as well as an increased risk of data misuse by third parties.

In the chapter "Open Computational Science" (Volume 1: Chapter 8), *Jan G. Voelkel* and *Jeremy Freese* set out four principles of open science: open practices, open data, open tools, and open access. These principles have direct relevance for the achievable data quality and validity of scientific inference because the replicability of results may depend strongly on the way these principles are implemented in research practice. The chapter provides theoretical definitions and concrete practical examples for each principle. It describes the main challenges of the implementation of the principles and the computational approaches to address these challenges. *Lars Lyberg and Steven G. Heeringa* (Volume 1: Chapter 6) provide a unique perspective on the open

Table 1.2 Overview of topics covered in Volume 2, "Data Science, Statistical Modeling, and Machine Learning Methods"

Volume 2			
Data collection, management, cleaning	Data quality	Statistical modeling and simulation	Machine learning
Topics			
History of APIs	Total error approach	Crowdsensing and data mining	ML methods for CSS
API use	Crowdsourced samples	Agent-based modeling	Principal component analysis
Web content mining	Inference from probability and non-probability surveys	Subgroup discovery and latent growth modeling	Clustering methods
Online learning for data streams	Challenges	Robust analysis of heterogeneous data	Topic modeling
Handling missing data in large databases			Contextualized word embeddings
Probabilistic record linkage			Automated video analysis

science movement when they discuss the changing landscape of the survey method. They point out that technological innovations, such as the internet and cloud computing, are "influencing not only how significant amounts of survey data are being collected but also the standards and expectations for the transparency, access and usability of survey products". Also, as to the "tools and norms required to formalize transparent, replicable research", especially in "the context of team-based collaborative research", *John McLevey, Pierson Browne,* and *Tyler Crick* (Volume 2: Chapter 8) introduce a principled data-processing framework.

Privacy, ethics, and policy

Ethical considerations are a key part of any research project, and CSS projects have unique challenges when it comes to ethics. First, the many ethical considerations that need to be taken into account are only now becoming more apparent. As these projects are complex, ethics are also complex. Ethical guidelines for conducting survey research and experimental studies are well established and well known, yet guidelines linked to CSS projects are still in their infancy and only slowly emerging. There are, for example, large discrepancies in ethical expectations across disciplines, institutions, and private vs. academic environments. Three chapters in this volume highlight central ethical debates and suggest approaches to better integrate data stewardship in ways that are equitable and just.

The chapter by *William Hollinghead*, *Anabel Quan-Haase,* and *Wenhong Chen* focuses on four major challenges that CSS scholars confront concerning ethical questions and dilemmas: 1) data representativeness, 2) aggregation and disaggregation, 3) research data archiving, and 4) data linkage. One topic the authors highlight is the impact of data representativeness because it is not well understood to what extent the social media user base of any given platform reflects a nationally representative sample or what biases may be present. Drawing on case studies of exemplary research, the authors provide a roadmap for CSS to address these issues. They conclude that what is needed is a commitment to pedagogy, to teaching the principles of ethics in computational social science projects.

To explore ethical dimensions in CSS scholarship further, *James F. Popham*, *Jennifer Lavoie*, *Andrea Corradi*, and *Nicole Coomber* examine the challenges involved in using big data technologies to provide valuable insights for and ultimately inform decision-making in municipalities, based on a case study of public engagement through a symposium Big Data in Cities: Barriers and Benefits, which was held in May of 2017 in Ontario, Canada. From the insights gained from the public engagement, they propose a set of best practices on how to address privacy and ethics, data-sharing protocols, the motives for using data, and how they are used.

The chapter by *Daniel Varona* and *Juan Luis Suárez* looks critically at the use of artificial intelligence, specifically machine learning, in decision-making processes. Through a detailed analysis of existing guidelines for the use of artificial intelligence, the authors propose a regulatory framework that follows the merits of "principled artificial intelligence" to move toward design-based trustworthy artificial intelligence. Through their analysis, they identify potential barriers that could prevent the framework from becoming a methodological reference during the AI project lifecycle, such as references to passive skills. The authors also highlight the digital gap that exists between developed and developing countries in creating trustworthy AI.

Research examples and case studies

A significant advantage of CSS research is its interdisciplinarity. Computational social science can borrow theories, methodologies, and data from multiple disciplines, especially the disciplines that rarely talked to each other beforehand. This interdisciplinary advantage can bring challenges. Grasping a fitting theory, an appropriate computational approach, and an available dataset that best answer a research question is tough, especially for new CSS researchers. Several chapters provide concrete examples to explore this process.

Social media is a popular data source in CSS studies, especially in the fields of psychology, political science, and communication. *Max Pellert, Simon Schweighofer*, and *David Garcia* (Volume 1, Chapter 15) focus on emotional dynamics and summarize methods to collect, classify, quantify, and analyze social media data to trace and measure emotion dynamics, collective emotions, and affective expression in various social and cultural contexts. The chapter presents theoretical thinking on the role, meaning, and functionality of affective expression in social media and practical examples and case studies from previous studies.

Several case studies focus on the applications of CSS in political domains. *Séraphin Alava* and *Rasha Nagem* (Volume 1, Chapter 21) present a detailed roadmap, method descriptions, and modeling toolkit for detecting ISIS extremist discourse online. A few chapters focus on Twitter data. Developments in data mining and machine learning have advanced the approaches we take to use the data to understand and even predict human behavior and important outcomes, such as the state of a pandemic or an outcome of an election. *Niklas M Loynes* and *Mark Elliot* (Volume 1, Chapter 16) attend to a forecasting aspect of Twitter-based public opinion research. They showcase how sentiment analysis was use to predict the U.S. 2016 Democratic presidential primary elections in New Hampshire, South Carolina, and Massachusetts. *Ho-Chun Herbert Chang, Emily Chen, Meiqing Zhang, Goran Muric*, and *Emilio Ferrara* (Volume 1, Chapter 18) summarized recent studies using Twitter data on the COVID-19 pandemic and the 2020 U.S. presidential election. The chapter provides a nuanced analysis of the impact of bots on the manipulation of the issues and describes how a health issue can be confounded with political agendas to distort the public sphere. In the chapter, the authors further provide reflections on a sensible balance between advancing social theory and concrete, timely reporting of ongoing events, which has been the subject of a debate in the CSS community. *Yimin Chen* (Volume 1, Chapter 17) also focuses on bots, but their discussions of trolls and bots are oriented from a broad cultural and historical perspective. The chapter argues that "trolls and bots are products of internet culture, but internet culture is shaped by our broader societal cultures. A kinder, gentler internet can only be achieved through striving for a kinder, gentler society".

Sensing technology and machine learning represent key links to both data analytics and human–robot interaction. The Royal Society (2017) locates machine learning at the intersection of artificial intelligence, data science, and statistics, with applications in robotics. Machine learning in society is a topic of central relevance to CSS because it changes both the object and methods of social science. *Johann Schaible, Marcos Oliveira, Maria Zens*, and *Genois Mathieu* (Volume 1, Chapter 14) provide a review on how to use sensors to study face-to-face interaction and how to align proxies from sensing data with social interaction constructs. The chapter lays out the steps for using sensors to study human interactions: from operationalization of the face-to-face interaction concept, to link the concept with a physical entity that can be detected by sensors, to choose the useful sensors to measure the concept, and finally to work out strategies to resolve the issues related to the collection and quality of the data. *Uwe Engel* and *Lena Dahlhaus* (Volume 1, Chapter 20) set out various theoretical and methodological thinking about data quality and privacy concerns of digital tracing data. The chapter offers empirical findings from a Delphi survey and a population survey in the context of human–robot interactions to further explore the intricate balance between data analytics and human–robot interaction. *Sunny Xun Liu, Elizabeth Arredondo, Hannah Mieczkowski, Jeff Hancock*, and *Byron Reeves* (Volume 1, Chapter 19) present an experimental design study to investigate the effects of social robot characteristics (warm vs. competent) and design features (physical appearance, narratives describing these characteristics, and combinations of appearance and characteristic narratives) on people's perceptions of warmth, competence, job suitability, and overall first-impression evaluations of social robots.

Machine learning methods and statistical and computational advancements

A first point of reference is the popular "big data" concept because it defines the characteristic features data may possess. Often, big data are described in terms of the four Vs of big data: volume (scale of data), velocity (analysis of streaming data), variety (different forms of data), and veracity (uncertainty of data) (IBM, 2012). To this original list, two additional Vs have been added: virtue (ethics) and value (knowledge gain) (Quan-Haase & Sloan, 2017). All these *V*s make great demands on data collection and statistical analysis. *Volume* matters because large datasets can make analysis more complicated. Accordingly, *Martin Spiess* and *Thomas Augustin* cover in their chapter one such complicating factor, the handling of missing data in large databases (Volume 2: Chapter 6). Then, the collection and analysis of streaming data may require special computational tools. Referring to this, *Lianne Ippel, Maurits Kaptein*, and *Jeroen Vermunt* present *online learning* as an analysis method that updates parameter estimates instead of re-estimating them to analyze large or streaming data (Volume 2: Chapter 5).

In CSS, *variety* is a challenge through the simultaneous use of quite different kinds of data, such as the user-generated content in social media and the digital marks people leave when surfing the web. Such textual and digital-trace data complement survey data and make great demands on their separate and combined analysis. In any case, the combination of information from multiple data sources represents a challenge. *Ted Enamorado* discusses in his chapter on probabilistic record linkage in R how "new computational algorithms have reduced the computational resources and time needed to merge large data sets" and illustrates "the power of these new algorithms through a guided example using the open-source R package fastLink" (Volume 2: Chapter 7).

Finally, *veracity* refers to the whole spectrum of data-quality criteria as known in social-science methodology. Statistical advancements in this regard involve, for instance, the sampling topic as covered in the chapter on inference from probability and non-probability samples already referred to by *Rebecca Andridge* and *Richard Valliant* (Volume 2: Chapter 11).

Statistical modeling is taken as a second point of reference to statistical and computational advancements. A first strand refers to the conjunction of simulation and empirical data. *Jan Lorenz* discusses in his chapter how agent-based modeling can be driven by data (Volume 1: Chapter 10). He views the "strength of agent-based modeling" in the "quantitative causal understanding of emergence through complex nonlinear dynamics on the macro level" and raises the query of validation with empirical data. He points out that "agent-based models are to explain real-world phenomena, and thus a useful model should have a reflection in empirical data and the other way round". In a similar vein, *Stefan Bosse* seeks the conjunction of agent-based modeling and crowd-sensing in his exposition of multi-agent systems (Volume 2: Chapter 13). Also, *Fernando Sancho-Caparrini* and *Juan Luis Suárez* (Volume 2: Chapter 14) present a model based on cultural agents, "that is, human-like agents whose main framework of interactions is defined by its belonging to cultural networks".

Advanced statistical modeling in the presence of heterogeneity is the third point of reference taken in the present context. First, *Axel Mayer, Christoph Kiefer, Benedikt Langenberg*, and *Florian Lemmerich* integrate methods of growth curve modeling and state-of-the-art pattern mining techniques to identify unusual developmental trajectories (Volume 2: Chapter 15). Then, *Nazanin Alipourfard, Keith Burghardt,* and *Kristina Lerman* (Volume 2: Chapter 16) cover disaggregation via Gaussian regression for heterogeneous data. They propose a method "that discovers latent confounders by simultaneously partitioning the data into overlapping clusters (dis-aggregation) and modeling the behavior within them (regression)".

Machine learning methods represent an extremely significant point of reference for statistical and computational advancements. *Richard D. de Veaux* and *Adam Eck* give a systematic and detailed overview of this field of advanced methods (Volume 2: Chapter 17). In their chapter, they "introduce two fundamental problems in supervised machine learning – classification and regression" and explain the supervised machine learning process. The authors "also describe and contrast several fundamental types of supervised machine learning models" and "conclude by highlighting both the strengths of the various approaches and popular software resources for utilizing and applying these valuable tools". Following this exposition of supervised methods, two chapters cover the most important unsupervised methods of machine learning. First, *Andreas Pöge* and *Jost Reinecke* (Volume 2: Chapter 18) introduce principal component analysis (PCA) as belonging to a group of statistical procedures "that are used to reduce the complexity of a given set of variables". The authors offer a brief overview of the basic concepts, history, and statistical fundamentals of the original PCA; compare PCA with factor analysis; and list some software programs and packages that offer PCA. Then, *Johann Bacher, Andreas Pöge,* and *Knut Wenzig* (Volume 2: Chapter 19) provide an overview of clustering methods. The chapter covers topics such as the steps toward an appropriate cluster solution, clustering methods, criteria to determine the number of clusters, methods to validate cluster solutions, and relevant computer programs.

Textual data represent a data source of great and growing importance for the social sciences. Such data make high demands on data analysis. *Raphael H. Heiberger* and *Sebastian Munoz-Najar Galvez* (Volume 2: Chapter 20) deal with text mining and a popular tool therein – topic modeling. They point out that "topic models are a popular tool to reduce texts' complexity and find meaningful themes in large corpora". The chapter addresses the methodological challenges the method is faced with, particularly the selection of an appropriate number of topics and its relation to pre-processing decisions. Then, *Gregor Wiedemann* and *Cornelia Fedtke* (Volume 2: Chapter 21) address the research interests that "go beyond topics that are limited to broad discourse-level semantics". They refer to the "interest which arguments, stances, frames, or discourse positions are expressed in what specific contexts and how they emerged in the first place". In their chapter, they "elaborate on how basic text mining and new neural-network-based embedding technologies such as BERT relate to linguistic structuralism as the theoretical and methodological foundation of discourse analysis and many other qualitative research methods".

Video data represent another resource of great importance for the social sciences. *Dominic Nyhuis, Tobias Ringwald, Oliver Rittmann, Thomas Gschwend,* and *Rainer Stiefelhagen* (Volume 2: Chapter 22) cover automated video analysis for social science research. They provide an overview of technical solutions for common classification scenarios in video data, discuss current studies and "a sample application on video footage from a German state-level parliament in greater detail", and close "with a discussion of potentials and challenges for automated video analysis in social science research".

Conclusions

This introductory chapter provides an overview of some of the cutting-edge and innovative work occurring in CSS across disciplines and geographic boundaries. The Handbook makes numerous contributions to consolidating CSS whilst also moving it in new directions. First, the handbook brings together current understandings of what CSS is and the opportunities it provides to scholars and policymakers. The Handbook also showcases novel approaches as they are being developed and tested. State-of-the-art machine learning tools and models have been applied to tackle critical social, political, and health issues, such as misinformation, extremist propaganda, and COVID-19. Computational social science has been applied to study interpersonal interactions, human–robot interaction and various human–AI communications. The Handbook also creates awareness around challenges that CSS confronts moving forward. Computational social science projects cannot be neatly aligned within a single discipline and often require multidisciplinary teams. This multidisciplinary model does not always conveniently align with institutional expectations and resources (Lazer et al., 2020) and thus calls for a rethinking of how academic institutions, funding agencies, and tenure and promotion guidelines work. Another challenge of CSS projects is the role of ethics. Where do data originate? How can we guarantee individuals' data self-determination? The Handbook starts an important debate around how to best implement ethics best practices, but it also shows the need for more work to identify critical questions and develop robust guidelines.

In our aim to be comprehensive, we brought together 90+ experts from 40+ institutions in North America, Europe, and the Middle East. Certainly, there is the opportunity for future projects in CSS to expand the geographic reach and diversity of topics. Furthermore, gender representation in CSS is critical. We call for further analysis of how the interdisciplinary nature of CSS can contribute to greater gender equity in the selection of collaborators and thereby have a lasting effect on the technical fields in a way that impacts *what* is studied and *how*.

Note

1 Quotations refer to the respective chapter abstracts.

References

Barton, A. (1979). Paul Lazarsfeld and applied social research: Invention of the university applied social research institute. *Social Science History*, *3*(3/4), 4–44. https://doi:10.2307/1170954

Biemer, P. B., & Lyberg, L. E. (2003). *Introduction to survey quality*. Wiley.

Brause, S. R., & Blank, G. (2020). Externalized domestication: Smart speaker assistants, networks and domestication theory. *Information, Communication & Society*, *23*(5), 751–763.

Cao, L. (2017). Data science: A comprehensive overview. *ACM Computing Surveys*, *50*(3), 43.1–43.42. https://doi.org/10.1145/3076253

Chinese Sociological Review. *Call for papers on "computational social science"*. Retrieved from https://think.taylorandfrancis.com/special_issues/computational-social-science/

Cioffi-Revilla, C. (2017). *Introduction to computational social science: Principles and applications* (2nd ed.). Springer.

Coleman, J. S. (1964). *Introduction to mathematical sociology*. The Free Press of Glencoe.

Coleman, J. S. (1990). *Foundations of social theory*. Belknap Press of Harvard University Press.

Crane, D. (1972). *Invisible colleges: Diffusion of knowledge in scientific communities*. The University of Chicago Press.

Hofman, J. M., Sharma, A., & Watts, D. J. (2017). Prediction and explanation in social systems. *Science*, *355*(6324), 486–488. https://doi.org/10.1126/science.aal3856

Hox, J. J. (2017). Computational social science methodology, anyone? *Methodology*, *13*, 3–12. https://doi.org/10.1027/1614-2241/a000127

IBM Big Data & Analytics Hub. (2012). *The four V's of big data*. Retrieved December 30, 2020, from www.ibmbigdatahub.com/infographic/four-vs-big-data

Kelleher, J. D., & Tierney, B. (2018). *Data science*. The MIT Press.

Keuschnigg, M., Lovsjö, N., & Hedström, P. (2018). Analytical sociology and computational social science. *Journal of Computational Social Science*, *1*, 3–14. https://doi.org/10.1007/s42001-017-0006-5

Lazer, D. M. J., Pentland, A., Watts, D. J, Aral, S., Athey, S., Contractor, N., . . . Wagner, C. (2020). Computational social science: Obstacles and opportunities. *Science*, *369*(6507), 1060–1062. https://doi.org/10.1126/science.aaz8170

Quan-Haase, A., & Sloan, L. (2017). Introduction to the handbook of social media research methods: Goals, challenges and innovations. In L. Sloan & A. Quan-Haase (Eds.), *The Sage handbook of social media research methods* (pp. 1–9). Sage.

The Royal Society. (2017). *Machine learning: The power and promise of computers that learn by example.* Retrieved from https://royalsociety.org/~/media/policy/projects/machine-learning/publications/machine-learning-report.pdf

Webb, E. J., Campbell, D. T., Schwartz, R. D., & Sechrest, L. (2000). *Unobtrusive measures.* Sage.

SECTION I

The scope and boundaries of CSS

2

THE SCOPE OF COMPUTATIONAL SOCIAL SCIENCE

Claudio Cioffi-Revilla

> It was six men of Indostan
> To learning much inclined,
> Who went to see the Elephant,
> (Though all of them were blind)
> That each by observation
> Might satisfy his mind.
>
> John Godfrey Saxe (transl.), *The Blind Men and the Elephant*

Introduction

Understanding, defining, and reflecting on the scope of computational social science (CSS) could not be more timely, given the rapid and highly dynamic expansion of this fledging field in recent years and current complex crises in our epoch. This chapter provides context for and a description of the scope of CSS based on its history and evolving investigations from the core to the frontiers of the field.

The scope of CSS is diverse, because the subject matter under investigation is vast and its methods are numerous. For example, big data is exceptionally valuable for enriching the core and expanding the frontiers of the field. It can be said that big social data, or big data about social phenomena, is already beginning to play a transformative role as a driver of growth in social knowledge. However, CSS is an interdisciplinary field of social science that integrates individual social science disciplines as well as neighboring disciplines. The purpose of CSS is to advance scientific understanding of society and social dynamics using the computational paradigm of complex adaptive systems – as pioneered by Herbert A. Simon and his contemporaries – and to make advanced use of computation in *all* its functions.

Recently, a more restrictive version of CSS has been proposed, driven mostly by the novelty of "big data" from social media and other sources (e.g., geospatial remote sensing, the Internet of Things [IoT], multimedia and multi-sensor data), leveraging progress in algorithms from computer science, while largely ignoring rigorous theory, models, or computational social simulations – all three of which have provided powerful and lasting contributions.[1] This chapter argues for a comprehensive and balanced scope for CSS, one that is paradigmatically guided by theory ("there is nothing so practical as a good theory", Lewin, 1952, p. 128), enriched by

DOI: 10.4324/9781003024583-3

analytical models, and enabled by computer simulations, all three drawing on data, be they big or small (Kitchin & Lauriault, 2014). The role of data in CSS is fundamental, as it is in astronomy, biology, linguistics, or any other field of empirical and computational science.

The chapter continues as follows: the next section describes two metaphors that shed light on how to define the contemporary scope of CSS. "The Nature of CSS" highlights the scientific nature of CSS and what that entails. "The Scope of CSS" presents the main content by providing a comprehensive and balanced scope for CSS. The last section summarizes the main conclusions.

Two metaphors: on elephants and Italian pasta

Describing the scope of contemporary CSS in light of a plurality of contending descriptions or specifications is challenging and reminiscent of two insightful metaphors. Both metaphors, by analogy, illustrate how parochial or unnecessarily narrow perspectives erroneously claim to represent what in reality is a much bigger and richer reality.

The first and more familiar of the two metaphors is the proverbial parable known as "The Blind Men and the Elephant", cited at the beginning of this chapter.[2] Each blind man examines the elephant in its various constituent components, including tusks, feet, ears, back, tail, and other parts. They then compare notes and conclude that they are in disagreement based on their individual perceptions. But the elephant's sighted owner has a realistic understanding of the whole animal, because his comprehensive perspective is based on direct observation.

The second metaphor is more scholarly and (regrettably) not as well known. Here, a group of scientists from a variety of disparate disciplines take the place of the men in the elephant's metaphor. In this case, the scientists congregate for an Italian pasta meal consisting of *pappardelle alla bolognese* (noodles with delicious meat and tomato sauce from Bologna) accompanied by some hearty *Amarone* red wine.[3] The physicist sees how heat applied to salted water makes the latter boil sooner when cooking the pasta and how torque exerted by his fork gathers each clump of pasta while wondering whether surface tension may attract more sauce. The chemist understands how chewing the pasta begins to break down the grain flour glutens, assisted by the sauce's own acidity (pH $\approx$ 4.2). The management scientist, a former systems engineer, thinks about the complex supply chains that make possible the delicious meal, providing pasta, San Marzano tomatoes, olive oil, ground meat, and all other necessary ingredients for a proper bolognese sauce, not to mention the cheese and other tasty ingredients. The sociologist enjoys her pasta while observing the table manners of her colleagues, two of whom assist their fork with a soup spoon, while another cuts his pasta instead of twisting it unbroken, indicative of their likely socioeconomic status (SES). The chef knows all these (as well as other) perspectives, so he has the most comprehensive and, therefore, most realistic understanding of the whole situation.

Metaphorically speaking, CSS is like all elephants and all pasta dishes. It is a fertile field consisting of several areas of investigation that offer immense and exciting domains and tools for research, such as algorithmic information extraction from big and small datasets, network models, social complexity, and various well-established and novel computer simulation approaches, as described in "The Scope of CSS". Each of these areas within CSS – grounded on computational foundations – can be pursued individually or in combination, depending on the goals of investigation. For one area to claim a monopoly on the whole field is like one of the actors in the two metaphors claiming that theirs is the whole field, ignoring other equally valid perspectives. CSS is immensely exciting in proportion to the variety and power of its foundational concepts, algorithms, data, theories, models, and simulations, especially when leveraged in combination and through creative synergies.

The nature of CSS

We know what astronomy, organic chemistry, and archaeology are about, which helps understand their respective scientific scope. As we approach the scope of CSS, we need to clearly ask and answer the question: What is CSS about? There are three classes of epistemological reasons CSS requires – and in fact demands – inclusion of theories, models, simulations, and other scientific constructs, besides big data and data mining algorithms. These reasons can be summarized in terms of three simple arguments stated in the form of claims, or even testable (i.e., refutable and verifiable) hypotheses:

1   CSS is an empirical science.
2   CSS is a social science.
3   CSS is a computational science.

Each of these claims on the nature of CSS has been documented in what is becoming a whole library of volumes (cf., e.g., Bankes, Lempert, & Popper, 2002; Bennato, 2015; Castelfranchi, 2001; Cioffi-Revilla, 2009, 2010, 2017 [2014]; Conte, Gilbert, Bonelli, & Helbing, 2011, 2012; Epstein, 2006; Gilbert, 2010; Hedström & Bearman, 2009; Kuznar, 2006; Manzo, 2014; Squazzoni, 2008; Torrens, 2010; Trobia, 2001), as well as in thousands of CSS papers in professional journals and conference proceedings.[4] What follows in this section is a summary of "what CSS is about" intended for reference.

CSS is an empirical science: testable knowledge on humans and groups

CSS is part of science, as opposed to the fine arts or humanities, although computational investigations in these two are growing. As an empirical science (as opposed to pure mathematics), this basic fact indicates that the epistemology of CSS has to do with elements such as systematic, testable, and reproducible descriptions, explanations, and predictions (or forecasts) – although the third class is not strictly necessary for CSS to qualify as a science.[5]

Description, a foundational element of CSS *qua* empirical science, requires observation and measurement, the results of which are often formalized in terms of mathematically stated laws that describe *how* phenomena occur. Duverger's law of party systems, Zipf's rank-size law, Pareto's law on income inequality, and Richardson's law of war magnitudes, among many others, are examples (Arrow, 1956; Kemeny & Snell, 1962; Simon, 1957). Although not all scientific laws are stated in mathematical form, those that are provide many advantages, not least of which is the power to generate additional logically valid and often empirically testable deductions for expanding frontiers of knowledge.

Scientific laws that are stated mathematically are commonly referred to as models (Arrow, 1956; Kemeny & Snell, 1962; Lave & March, 1993; Maki & Thompson, 1973; Olinick, 2014), although the term "model" also applies to other objects, not all of them necessarily mathematical – analogous to the term "mechanism" in analytical social science and CSS. For example, a flowchart, a Gantt chart, and any Unified Modeling Language (UML) diagram (class, sequence, state, use case, and others) are also models (Bruschi, 1971). Models provide ways of describing phenomena, sometimes crossing the boundary between description and explanation.

Explanation in science means providing a causal mechanism that accounts for observed phenomena, such as events and other occurrences, features, and laws. A causal mechanism can be deterministic or probabilistic (Eells, 1991; Good, 1980; Salmon, 1980; Suppes, 1984), depending on its causality, where the "or" refers to the Boolean logic inclusive OR, also known as "and/or" in common language. Laws require theoretical explanation, because by themselves they only describe; they do not explain *why* a given pattern holds as a law. A scientific explanation is normally in the form of a process composed of one or more causal mechanisms (e.g., Lave & March, 1993, ch. 1, on how and why the theory of plate tectonics [due to Alfred Wegener and others] is a valid scientific explanation for earthquakes, the intensity of which is described [but not explained] by Richter's well-known power law of seismic magnitude).

Simulations are used in every field of science where there is need to analyze high dimensionality models or theories, because traditional closed form solutions are unavailable or undesirable, for whatever reasons. High dimensionality can be a sufficient condition for using simulations, which enable the deduction of conclusions by running a simulation, assuming computational tractability.

In all science, therefore, *laws describe and theories explain* – paraphrasing S. Toulmin (1960). Laws and theories are constitutive or defining features of science, not optional activities or exotic embellishments created for esthetic purposes (although elegance is a desirable attribute of social theory; Cioffi-Revilla, 2017: ch. 8; specifically applying Lave & March, 1975 to CSS). Simulations are necessary only when scientific analysis requires many variables or parameters that are relevant to the phenomenon under investigation, as are all complex systems and many complicated ones. This is the first reason theories, models, and simulations are part of and necessary for CSS.

The essential role of social theory – that is, the use of theoretical concepts, causal mechanisms, and scientifically viable explanations – in understanding and making sense of big data should be obvious. Consider the use of data mining and dimensionality reduction algorithms for extracting information from big data such as large-scale networks (e.g., Gleich & Mahoney, 2016). A common formalism used in algorithmic information extraction is to compute the Laplacian matrix $\mathbf{L}_{n \times n}$ of a large, weighted network graph G_w (V, E), where $n = |V|$, defined as the difference between the diagonal or degree $\mathbf{D}$ and the adjacency $\mathbf{A}$ matrices of G_w, or $\mathbf{L} := \mathbf{D} - \mathbf{A}$. The common interpretation of $\mathbf{L}$ when applied in data mining is as a network of springs with different tensions, which is impossible to understand without a proper theoretical grasp of such dynamics and how spring-linked networks behave. (By contrast, the mathematical interpretation of $\mathbf{L}$ is as a graph-based gradient equivalent to a field gradient in continuous space, which is not a theory.) Similarly, results from most other complex data mining algorithms cannot be understood without reference to constructs that constitute theoretical models, such as metric spaces, mathematical functions (and functionals), forces, preferences, energy, entropy, and dynamics, among others.

CSS is a social science: the "big five" and all others

Like all sciences, social science is articulated through disciplines. The universe of social science includes many large and well-established disciplines. These are the "big five", which are frequently defined as anthropology, economics, political science, social psychology, and sociology – however, other classifications are also common.[6]

The universe of social sciences also includes rich interdisciplinary fields, such as human geography, management science, linguistics, communication science, and social science history, among others.

CSS is a social science, analogous to the claim that computational astronomy, computational biology, and computational linguistics are part of astronomy, biology, and linguistics, respectively. Any computational science is, by definition, part of some science.

Each social science discipline includes a set of social theories, models, and simulations, more in some disciplines and areas and less in others, albeit some more than others.[7] Social theories from "the big five" and other social sciences are used in CSS to inform the causal mechanisms and processes under investigation. Conversely, CSS contributes to social science by formulating new theories that explain social phenomena.

CSS is a computational science: the value proposition of computing

Social simulations are like computational theories; they are used when models and theories contain too many variables for mathematical or analytical approaches leading to closed-form solutions. This situation is common in many social contexts, given the intrinsic complexity of even (seemingly) simple human phenomena (e.g., aggregating votes, small group behavior, decision-making under risk), as discussed in "Core" in greater detail.

There is no single instrument that is used in science for producing new knowledge. Conversely, no single tool has a monopoly on the production of new science. Every science – natural, social, engineering, pure, or applied – relies on sets or ensembles of specialized instrumental methodologies and methods to investigate its subject matter and achieve progress in the advancement of knowledge. In the natural sciences, initially philosophical methods of inquiry and, subsequently, after many centuries, mathematical, statistical, and computational methods provided such instruments (Casti, 1992), in addition to actual physical instruments. In the social sciences, roughly the same instrumental sequence – philosophical, historiographic, statistical, and mathematical tools – has occurred, albeit with somewhat different priorities (statistics has prevailed over mathematics, and historiographic methods are not used in natural science, except in the field of history of science, which is more akin to history).

Social science became computational after centuries of having used historiographic, statistical, and mathematical methods – somewhat similarly to the natural and engineering sciences – soon after the invention of automatic computing; that is, since the early 1960s (e.g., Guetzkow, Alger, Brody, Noel, & Snyder, 1963; Simon, 1969 [first edition of Simon, 1996]; Deutsch, 1963; Messick, 1963), about a decade after John von Neumann's (1966) pioneering *Theory of Self-Reproducing Automata*. The fact that the term "computational" was not used from the very first day when computers were used to conduct social research does not detract from the fundamental and historically verifiable claim.

As has been observed elsewhere, "Field Theory (Lewin, 1952), Structuralist-Functionalist Theory (Radcliffe-Brown, 1952), Conflict Theory (Richardson, 1952a, 1952b), the Theory of Groups (Simon, 1952), Political Systems Theory (Easton, 1953), as well as Behavioral Decision Theory (Allais, 1953), among others, required new formalisms that could treat conceptual and theoretical complexity of human and social dynamics, beyond what could be accomplished through systems of mathematical equations solved in closed form" (Cioffi-Revilla, 2017, p. 36). Each of these social theories and related models, as well as numerous others, eventually underwent computational implementation and simulation became a new methodology (Benson, 1961; Borko, 1962) before object-orientation was introduced into social research through R, Java, Python, and other programming languages.

Earlier it was stated that a computational approach – including but not limited to simulation modeling methods – is required when encountering problems of high dimensionality, as is the case with many social phenomena. However, the computational approach in social science has a dual nature, encompassing a theory as well as a tool. This is because CSS is both a field of science enabled by computing as well as a field of social science informed by a computational paradigm.

The methodological aspect of CSS is well known, obviously, due to the fact that, by definition, computing requires data processing hardware and software. Less appreciated or understood, but far deeper from a scientific perspective, is the computational paradigm of CSS introduced by Herbert A. Simon (1996 [1969]) and others (Augier & March, 2004; Batty, 2006; Gilbert & Troitzsch, 2005; Holland, 1975, 1995; Miller & Page, 2007). This aspect of CSS relies on the interdisciplinary theory of complex adaptive systems and the role played by information processing at all scales of human and societal behavior (Cioffi-Revilla, 2017, pp. 331–334; Simon, 1996). This computational paradigm also includes a specific theory of artificial systems that explains how and why social complexity originates and evolves. Recent developments of the same computational and information processing paradigm include the canonical theory of social complexity (Cioffi-Revilla, 2005, 2014, pp. 214–220, 2017, pp. 335–341), which aims to explain the genesis and evolution of coupled and complex systems-of-systems that include human, artificial, and natural entities.

Again, big data also plays a major role at this computational level any time that large amounts of information are necessary for numerous reasons that may range from creating new theories and simulations to testing hypotheses and models of social systems and processes.

The scope of CSS

The scope of any field can be described or specified in two ways: intensively or extensively, similar to the way in which the definition for a given concept is constructed (Collier & Gerring, 2009; Goertz, 2006; Hempel, 1952). Here we will approach the scope of CSS in both ways, because each perspective elicits complementary information and jointly increases overall clarity. The last part of this section illustrates the scope of CSS by considering what is required to investigate and understand the subject of complex crises, which are replete with challenging human and social dynamics.

For heuristic purposes, we shall describe the scope of CSS as consisting of a core, composed of five areas, surrounded by boundaries and borderlands.

Core

The core of contemporary CSS consists of the following five main areas of investigation: computational foundations, algorithmic information extraction, networks, social complexity, and social simulations. Each of these interrelated areas contains additional components – in terms of key concepts, principles, and applications – such that the entire core constitutes a system-of-systems (Ackoff, 1971; Cioffi-Revilla, 2017, with bibliographies for each area of the CSS core). The five areas are conceived in roughly ordinal sequence, as in an ordered set, because it is often the case that each area depends on or can be enriched by one or more of the previous areas (as in a Likert scale), and, conversely, each area can be investigated without recourse to subsequent areas (e.g., computational research on social networks, or on social complexity, without reference to simulations).

Area 1: Computational foundations in CSS consist of ideas common to all computing systems and programs and their basic characteristics and relevance for humans and social systems. These include elementary notions familiar to all computer scientists (computers, operations, memory, programs, languages, abstraction, data structures, algorithms, and heuristic tools such as UML; Ambler, 2005) and Systems Modeling Language (SysML) (Freidenthal, Moore, & Steiner, 2015), especially *how these apply to humans and social systems* (Cioffi-Revilla, 2017, ch. 2). In other words, CSS foundations include all the building blocks of the field which define the computational paradigm (not upper constructs). This is therefore different from other formal or even mathematical approaches to doing social science. This first, foundational area within the CSS core is conceptual, methodological, procedural, and theoretical, consistent with the information processing and complex adaptive systems approach of Herbert A. Simon and founders of the field. Concepts, principles, and methods from computational foundations are used in all other areas of CSS.[8]

Area 2: Automated (or algorithmic) information extraction is the second area within the core of CSS (Cioffi-Revilla, 2017, ch. 3). This field concerns the use of algorithms, data structures, and associated methods (e.g., visualization, sonification) to extract information from social data, be it in the form of large or small datasets. This is often seen as today's "home of big data", with all its diversity (textual, digital, numerical, audio, graphical, geospatial, sensor data, as well as other forms).[9] Research in this area requires an understanding of principles of linguistics and content analysis, semantic dimensions of meaning, and data mining in a technical sense. In general practice, data mining takes on the framework of a process whereby there is an initial corpus (or corpora) of input data pertaining to some human or social phenomena (events, transactions, interactions, and other directional data, but it can also be attributes, such as geospatial features) and the automated information extraction proceeds through various stages which include but are not limited to data preparation, algorithmic selection and preparation, the actual running of algorithms, data collection, and, finally, analysis and dissemination. These procedures often involve sequential spirals, similar to a learning process, so they are not always as linear as they may sound. Multidimensional cognitive spaces are used in this area of CSS (e.g., so-called "sentiment analysis", among others), as well as behavioral theories – such as affect control theory (Heise, 1987), including Osgood's foundations and Hoey's current developments (e.g., Hoey et al., 2013) – that explore and extend such spaces. Results from automated information extraction are sometimes used in other areas of CSS, such as in social network investigations, in research on social complexity, or in simulations.

Area 3: Social networks are the third area of the CSS core (Cioffi-Revilla, 2017, ch. 4). Fundamental concepts and principles in this area include basic network ideas as they apply to human and social science, as well as metrics, mathematical models, and associated theories. Although social network analysis dates to the 1950s (i.e., prior to the availability of computers), an interesting and telling reason this area of CSS did not take off until the advent of computational methods in social science is because it often requires the manipulation of large, non-sparse matrices (for specifying adjacency, distance, or other networks of social relations). For example, in the case of everyday social transactions, such large matrices have dimension defined by $N \times N$ actors, requiring large and computationally expensive processes, which – for all intents and purposes – are impractical or sometimes simply not feasible to analyze other than computationally. Not until the advent of computers, especially current fast computers within the past 10–20 years, did social scientists gain access to such tools. This core area has numerous applications in domains that range from individual-level human cognition and belief systems to global networks in the world system. Any given investigation in the area of social networks may be self-contained, or it may relate to one or more of the other areas: social data mining, social complexity, or simulation.

Area 4: Social complexity is the fourth area in the core of CSS (Cioffi-Revilla, 2017, pp. 5–7; Simon, 1965). This area is so extensive that it is often divided into three subareas of learning and investigation: (a) origins and measurement of social complexity (lines of evidence, indicators, organizational structures), (b) laws of social complexity (both empirical and mathematical patterns), and (c) theories of social complexity (explaining and understanding the origin and long-range development of social complexity). From a temporal perspective, the computational science of social complexity covers the social history of the past 12,000 years, since the earliest phase transitions from kin-based, simple societies of hunter–gatherers to the first socially complex human communities (simple chiefdoms), which first occurred during the late Upper Paleolithic (ca. 9000–7000 BC) in Anatolia and adjacent regions of west Asia. This long-range formative phenomenon (origin of social complexity) occurred independently as the first archaic state-level polities formed in separate parts of the world (west Asia, followed by east Asia, South America, and Mesoamerica), and throughout the millennia it has evolved to the current aggregate and highly interdependent system of the world community of countries (nation-states) and organizations that exhibit diverse forms of social complexity. Measuring, describing, and explaining social complexity is similar to cosmology, only focused on social as opposed to physical (and much later biological) systems (Bellwood, 2018; Cangelosi & Parisi, 2012; Christian, 2004; Mithen, 2004). Computational theories of social complexity are informed by both archaeological and environmental data, as well as by formal theories based on mathematical models.

Area 5: Computational social simulations constitute the fifth area of the CSS core. Beginning with pioneering investigations in the 1950s, this area contains numerous concepts, principles, methodologies, and types of simulation models. This area is divided into (a) simulation methodology (motivation, design, verification, validation, and analysis of simulation models [the so-called MDIVVA methodology of simulation development], which is independent of the specific type or simulation), (b) variable-oriented models (system dynamics models, queueing models, microsimulations), (c) object- oriented models (cellular automata, agent-based models), (d) learning and evolutionary models, and (e) hybrid models that combine modules of different kinds (e.g., system dynamics combined with agent-based modules or any of these augmented by learning or evolutionary algorithms). Social simulation models are created in native code or using a modeling environment such as Stella, Vensim, or Wolfram SystemModeler (for system dynamics models) and MASON (Luke et al., 2019), Netlogo (Laver, 2020; Wilensky & Rand, 2015), or Repast (for agent-based models), among others.[10]

Not surprisingly, these five areas of the CSS core also constitute its modern academic curriculum. The whole core is often taught in a single course (often called Introduction to Computational Social Science), whereas each area is subsequently amplified by ad hoc courses. After mastering the core, students are further trained in additional topics, such as geospatial science, data visualization, evolutionary computation, epidemiology, or other related topics discussed in the next section.

Boundaries and borderlands

Beyond the core of CSS lie its boundaries and borderlands, where CSS meets other fields and disciplines. While avoiding distraction by nominal categories and classifications, it is useful to clarify the boundaries of CSS. To begin, consider the CSS core as the principal scientific territory of the field (its "turf", similar to mechanics being within the turf of physics or genetics within biology), with "provinces" constituted by the five core areas just described. Based on the nature and scope of CSS, at the boundaries, we see other disciplines and fields from neighboring natural sciences and engineering sciences – since social complexity is always lodged within some natural environment or ecosystem. Artifacts ("artificial systems", in the sense of H. Simon [1996]) provide the interface between society and nature. In addition, the borderlands of CSS contain complexity science, applied mathematics, operations research, systems engineering, and artificial intelligence, among other fields.

Borderlands, which straddle the boundaries of CSS, are fascinating because they witness the interactive flow of people, information, energy, and other resources – tangible and intangible, natural and engineered. The borderlands of CSS are populated by researchers and ideas from CSS ("CSS natives", so to speak) and by researchers and ideas from neighboring disciplines ("collaborative foreigners" or partners). Examples of borderlands include complexity science applications in CSS, any number of areas from applied mathematics used in CSS (e.g., queuing theory, dynamical systems, stochastic processes), and optimization problems encountered in CSS, among many others.

Scientific interactions among core areas and borderlands generate CSS investigations and new frontiers with increasingly universal scope, as follows:

Disciplinary CSS: The most narrowly focused work refers to single-discipline-based CSS, such as is the case for computational archaeology, computational economics, computational geography, computational linguistics, computational political science, computational social choice, or computational sociology. Each of these draws on concepts and principles within the confines of a specific social science discipline or specialization.

Multidisciplinary CSS: A higher level of universality refers to CSS that is constituted by two or more social science disciplines, such as political sociology, social psychology, human geography, and communication science, or by one or more social sciences plus one or more natural or engineering disciplines, such as socionatural systems, human factors, computational conflict science, or cognitive neuroscience. The distinctive feature of these is that these disciplines are aggregated without much intent to integrate in a unified sense; that is, the unity of science is not the primary intent or result in multidisciplinary research.

Interdisciplinary CSS: This is the version of CSS which seeks the highest degree of scientific integration across disciplines and fields, based on unifying concepts and principles. Complexity science, network science, systems theory, and information science, as well as applied mathematics, are often essential in supporting interdisciplinary CSS.

Complex crises

The scope of CSS just presented is well illustrated by considering the nature and scientific research demands of complex crises. While the core, boundaries, and borderlands of CSS describe its spatial scope on the scientific landscape, complex crises occur also in time, such that they represent a uniquely challenging and currently active subject of CSS investigation. Not all crises are complex (Hermann, 1990; McClelland, 1961; Snyder & Diesing, 1977). However, all crises are space-time defined by a large and partially interrelated set of interesting features. Every crisis has the following phenomenology:

Initiating event(s): One or more specific historic event always initiates a crisis, although it may take a while to recognize such events. Initiating events are frequently sudden or unexpected (e.g., the 9/11 terrorist attacks, the 1962 discovery Soviet missiles directed to Cuba, the 2019 COVID-19 outbreak in Wuhan, China [Chang, Harding, Zavhreson, Cliff, & Propopenko, 2020; Enserink & Kupferschmidt, 2020; Jager, 2020], and similar "triggers"),[11] but they may also occur gradually (e.g., human migrations, climate change, substance abuse epidemics, depletion of nonrenewable resources, increasing illiteracy in science, decreasing technology skillsets).

Branching process: The lifecycle of a crisis involves a branching process, where the root of the tree is given by the initiating event(s), branches are represented by the various sequences of events that follow the initiation, and the leaf events define an outcome space that is highly contingent or path dependent. The probability of each outcome is determined by the probability of all prior events, according to the tree's structure – by probabilistic causality.

Phase transitions: The branching process of a crisis includes transition from pre-crisis normality, to the crisis itself (in a narrow sense), to the crisis aftermath. This strictly ordered sequence of phase transitions is another universal characteristic in the phenomenology of crises. The timing of ordered phase transitions is often unpredictable, although the necessary or sufficient conditions associated with each transition may be known or predictable.

Uncertainty increase: Uncertainty increases in a crisis, because the variety and number of possible outcomes in the outcome space – including some hazardous subspaces – is high relative to normal, non-crisis conditions. Increases in uncertainty (entropy) are known to naturally cause stress in humans, whereas a decrease in variety or number of outcomes can decrease stress.

Possible extreme outcomes: While some outcomes of a crisis may be beneficial (e.g., win-win resolution outcomes), others frequently generate calamities with a range of negative payoffs. The (ordinal) level of calamity ranges from emergency (relatively minor consequences well within management's resources), to disaster (significant but manageable consequences with available resources), to catastrophe (unmanageable consequences beyond all available resources), to extinction (societal collapse).[12]

Time pressure: Stress experienced by crisis participants and stakeholders has the effect of reducing the perceived time available to make decisions. Scientifically valid information can reduce such stress by adding verifiable information, realism, and comparative perspective to the situation.

High stakes: Low stakes are inconsequential, by definition, so it takes high stakes to produce a crisis. High stakes can be generated by skewed distributions of events as well as other sources of extreme values or realizations, such as cultural values, features of complexity (discussed in the following) and other sources. High stakes may not be the same for all actors, so relative comparisons can clarify a crisis and sometimes facilitate its resolution.

Game structure and evolution: Every crisis is formally characterized by some game structure in terms of actors, strategies, outcomes, payoffs, and situational information such as communication, perceptions of length of game, and other characteristics. Often the crisis game structure is some combination of elementary 2×2 game in the sense of Rapoport. However, the game structure of a crisis is typically nonstationary, since it evolves through several forms from the onset phase to termination, and is not always known in real time (because it depends on assessments and estimates of actors' strategies, preferences, and other defining features of the crisis game).

While the previous are universal features of all crises, the subset of *complex crises* have the following additional characteristics:

Many actors: The simplest crises occur between two actors. Complex crises involve three or more actors or components (i.e., high cardinality). An analogy in natural science would be the so-called *n*-body problem in astronomy, where the future trajectory of three or more bodies in a gravitational field is impossible to obtain in closed form but can be rigorously analyzed via a computational model.

High dimensionality: Numerous variables and parameters (both continuous and discrete) are necessary to model and understand a complex crisis, making it more difficult and frequently impossible to derive closed-form solutions. Formally, actors and entities in a complex crisis encapsulate numerous attributes (and operations/methods), more so than in a simple crisis.

High heterogeneity: The diversity of entities in the ontology of a complex crisis is higher than in a simple crisis. Classes of heterogeneous actors, multiplex network relations (each relation, in turn, having multiple attributes and dynamics), time scales (from short to long, depending on strategies considered, spanning several orders of magnitude), and other heterogeneous entity categories are examples.

Large outcome space: While simpler crises may have a relatively small outcome space, a complex crisis always has a larger outcome space, based on the previous features. Outcome space size grows exponentially with cardinalities, so in a complex crisis, the size of the outcome space can easily be orders of magnitude greater. Due to these challenging counting problems, regions of such outcome spaces are often unknown or even unknowable, especially in real (i.e., actionable) time. Metastability – the possibility of or potential for transitioning to other states – is a related feature of a complex crisis.

Networked interdependence: Connectivity among actors and other entities in a complex crisis is manifested through interdependence.[13] While game theory provides some assistance in understanding this aspect, there are myriad other aspects of networked interdependence that remain analytically intractable in closed form, which calls for computational simulation methods.

Nonlinearity: Finally, numerous relations and, therefore, many effects are not linear but rather exponential, hyperbolic, periodic, stochastic, or of other forms. Nonlinearity can be a source of surprise and uncertainty, adding to overall stress. Hierarchies, feedback loops, bifurcations, tipping points, and phase transitions are manifestations of nonlinearity.

While the theoretical analysis of crises for cases that have minimal, reduced form – such as in 2-actor 2×2 games and, more recently, mean field games – real-world complex crises are more analytically tractable via increasingly powerful approaches provided by CSS. Climate change, epidemics ranging from local to global pandemics, increasingly challenging urban and critical infrastructure systems, and the challenges of spacefaring civilization, among others, provide examples of contemporary complex crises that are being investigated in collaboration with other fields – at the CSS core, the borderlands, and beyond.

Conclusions

Computational social science is an empirical science, a social science, and a field similar to other computational sciences where computing plays a dual and defining role, both as a theoretical paradigm and a methodological instrument. The former regards the fundamental role of information processing for describing, explaining, and understanding social phenomena, in this case through human cognition and decision-making at the micro level that generates societal phenomena at the macro level. The latter regards the role of the computer as an enabling instrument allowing us to reach and investigate frontiers of knowledge far beyond what is possible through historical, statistical, or even mathematical methods. Both aspects define the character of CSS.

Today, theories, models, and data (both "small" and "big") make up the complex landscape and rich ecology of CSS. The only difference in terms of big data is that its sheer size and rate of growth (first and second derivatives, respectively) present major and exciting challenges to the other components. Theories and models are challenged and enabled by big data, and vice versa. Computational social simulations use and also create new demands for big data.

There is good reason to think that "the science of the twenty-first century will be computational" (Denning, 2007). Such a big CSS perspective includes big data, algorithms, theories, models, and simulations, among other scientific constructs and instruments. Denning's insightful prediction (and conjecture) is arguably becoming increasingly true of social science, as for most other domains of science. In the future, social science will prosper if it adopts the computational approach with more robust understanding of its historical origins and rich diversity, even more so if CSS leverages more formal approaches from applied mathematics, just as during the twentieth century, the social sciences learned how to apply statistics. This is also necessary with the addition of virtual worlds and robots (Parisi, 2014) to the domain of social science investigations (Bainbridge, 2007; chapters by Engel & Dahlhaus and Liu et al. in this volume). The synergy of current statistical approaches, long-range historical and comparative perspectives, enhanced variety of mathematical approaches (beyond differential equations and game theory), and the full spectrum and scientific power of computational approaches cannot but generate an explosive abundance of new discoveries and deeper understanding of social phenomena, both simple and complex.

> So oft in theologic wars
> The disputants, I ween,
> Rail on in utter ignorance
> Of what each other mean,
> And prate about an Elephant
> Not one of them has seen!
> J. G. Saxe (transl.), *The Blind Men and the Elephant*

Computational social scientists should work together to describe, explain, and scientifically understand the whole elephant of social science.

Acknowledgments

Dedicated to the late Rosaria Conte (1954–2016), interdisciplinary computational social scientist *per eccellenza*. The earliest and shorter version of this chapter was presented at the panel on "Computational Social Sciences: A Bricolage of Approaches", 8th International ACM Web Science Conference (WebSci'16), Hanover, Germany, May 22–25, 2016, chaired by Paolo Parigi. An expanded version was presented at the 2016 Lipari International Summer School in Complex Systems and Computational Social Science, Lipari, Italy, directed by Alfredo Ferro. The author would like to thank panel chair Paolo Parigi for the invitation to write and present this paper, and Robert Axtell, Joshua Epstein, Nigel Gilbert, Dirk Helbing, David Masad, J. Daniel Rogers, Larry Kuznar, Vahab Mirrokni, Chris Rouly, Flaminio Squazzoni, and Klaus G. Troitzsch for comments and discussions. The final version of this chapter was presented and developed for the Digital Traces Workshop, University of Bremen, Germany, November 8–10, 2018, at the kind invitation of Professor Uwe Engel. This work was originally funded by NSF CDI Type II grant no. IIS-1125171 and by the Center for Social

Complexity at George Mason University. The author is solely responsible for the views and opinions expressed in this paper.

Notes

1 Controversies over the proper scope of CSS would be entirely unnecessary were it not for the fact that several recent publications by a number of accomplished scholars have presented a description of CSS focused entirely on the new big data (a sort of "Big Data CSS"; e.g., Alvarez, 2016; Lazer et al., 2009, 2020). By well-established scientific and epistemological standards, such a view is incomplete, short-sighted, biased, and less productive as a viable description of CSS, because it excludes other exciting constituent components of the emerging field, such as theories, mathematical models, simulations, and new analytical methods.

2 See www.wordfocus.com/word-act-blindmen.html for John G. Saxe's English translation of the parable of *The* Blind *Men and the Elephant*. On the same website, it is observed that "the story is also used to teach tolerance for other cultures. We only 'see' the culture in which we are immersed". Wise advice for computational social scientists of all persuasions.

3 My summary version is adapted from McCain and Segal (1988). I am grateful to Nancy McGlen, who many years ago at the University of Buffalo brought this amusing and deeply insightful little book to my attention.

4 A small representative sample of CSS journals includes *Computational and Mathematical Organization Theory* (CMOT), founded by Herbert A. Simon, arguably the leading CSS theoretician of the founder's generation, the *Journal of Artificial Societies and Social Simulations* (JASSS), *Social Science Computer Review* (SSCR), and others in areas of applied computing, network science (*Social Networks*), complexity science (*Advances in Complex Systems*), applied physics (*Physical Reviews E*), and simulation modeling (*International Journal of Modelling and Simulation*). The *Journal of Computational Social Science* (JCSS Springer) and IEEE's *Transactions on Computational Social Systems* are among the newest periodical journals specifically focused on CSS.

5 The argument that CSS is part of science remains valid regardless of whether prediction or forecasting are viewed as required features of science.

6 For example, at the U.S. National Science Foundation, the Directorate of Social, Behavioral and Economic Sciences comprises two divisions, each containing a myriad of disciplines.

7 If anything, it could be argued that a fundamental problem in social science is the proliferation of unviable theories lacking in testability or falsifiability, as well as the survival of demonstrably inferior, flawed, or false theories. CSS can play a useful role in this area by demonstrating or exposing logical or empirical errors in putative social "theories" – that is, debunking faulty theories.

8 The historical origins by founders of each area of CSS are summarized by chronological tables at the beginning of each chapter in Cioffi-Revilla (2017).

9 In practice, however, social simulation (Area 5) generates just as much volume of data from running models, so social media alone does not have a monopoly on "big data", as mentioned in the following.

10 A useful resource in this area of CSS is the SIMSOC listserv

11 Another term used in the crisis literature is "precipitating event". In the case of international relations crises, the initiating event is generally a compound event consisting of other events (Cioffi, 1998, pp. 160–163; Snyder & Diesing, 1977, p. 15). Such compound events frequently encapsulate an underlying complex structure that can be challenging to understand and model.

12 This is a simplified version of the ordinal scale of calamity used in the area of disaster research and emergency management.

13 The interdependence of states is known as "entanglement" in quantum science.

References

Ackoff, R. L. (1971). Towards a system of systems concepts. *Management Science*, 17(11), 661–671.

Allais, M. (1953). Le comportement de l'homme rationnel devant le risque, critique des postulats et axiomes de l'ecole Americaine [Rational human behavior under risk: Critique of postulates and axioms of the American school]. *Econometrica*, 21, 503–546.

Alvarez, R. M. (2016). *Computational social science: Discovery and prediction*. Cambridge University Press.

Ambler, S. W. (2005). *The elements of UML 2.0 style*. Cambridge University Press.

Arrow, K. J. (1956). Mathematical models in the social sciences. *General Systems: Yearbook of the Society for General Systems Research, 1*, 29–24.

Augier, M., & March, J. G. (Eds.). (2004). *Models of a man: Essays in memory of Herbert A. Simon*. The MIT Press.

Bainbridge, W. S. (2007). The scientific research potential of virtual worlds. *Science, 317*(5837), 472–476.

Bankes, S. C., Lempert, R. J., & Popper, S. W. (2002). Making computational social science effective: Epistemology, methodology, and technology. *Social Science Computer Review, 20*(4), 377–388.

Batty, M. (2006). *Cities and complexity: Understanding cities with cellular automata, agent-based models, and fractals*. The MIT Press.

Bellwood, P. (2018). Agricultural origins. *International Encyclopedia of Anthropology*, 1–9.

Bennato, D. (2015). *Il computer come macroscopio [The computer as a macroscope]*. Franco Angeli.

Benson, O. (1961). A simple diplomatic game. In J. N. Rosenau (Ed.), *International politics and foreign policy* (pp. 504–511). Free Press.

Borko, H. (Ed.). (1962). *Computer applications in the behavioral sciences*. Prentice-Hall.

Bruschi, A. (1971). *La Teoria dei Modelli nelle Scienze Sociali [The theory of models in the social sciences]*. Il Mulino.

Cangelosi, A., & Parisi, D. (Eds.). (2012). *Simulating the evolution of language*. Springer Science & Business Media.

Castelfranchi, C. (2001). The theory of social functions: Challenges for computational social science and multi-agent learning. *Journal of Cognitive Systems Research, 2*, 5–38.

Casti, J. (1992). *Reality rules, picturing the world in mathematics, volumes 1 (the fundamentals) and 2 (the frontiers)*. Wiley.

Chang, S. L., Harding, N., Zavhreson, C., Cliff, O. M., & Propopenko, M. (2020). *Modelling transmission and control of the COVID-19 pandemic in Australia*. arXiv, March 24, 2020. Preprint.

Cioffi-Revilla, C. (1998). *Politics and uncertainty: Theory, models and applications* (1st ed.). Springer-Verlag.

Cioffi-Revilla, C. (2005, April–June). A canonical theory of origins and development of social complexity. *Journal of Mathematical Sociology, 29*, 133–153.

Cioffi-Revilla, C. (2009). *On social complexity: A manifesto for computational social science*. Presidential Address. Annual Conference of the North American Association of Computational Social and Organizational Sciences, Phoenix, Arizona.

Cioffi-Revilla, C. (2010). Computational social science. *Wiley Interdisciplinary Reviews (WIREs): Computational Statistics, 2*(3), 259–271.

Cioffi-Revilla, C. (2014). *Introduction to computational social science: Principles and applications* (1st ed.). Springer-Verlag.

Cioffi-Revilla, C. (2017 [2014]). *Introduction to computational social science: Principles and applications* (2nd ed.). Springer.

Collier, D., & Gerring, J. (2009). *Concepts and method in social science*. Routledge.

Conte, R., Gilbert, G. N., Bonelli, G., Cioffi-Revilla, C., Deffaunt, G., Kertesz, J., . . . Helbig, D. (2012). Manifesto of computational social science. *European Physical Journal Special Topics, 214*, 325–346.

Conte, R., Gilbert, G. N., Bonelli, G., & Helbing, D. (2011). FuturICT and social sciences: Big data, big thinking. *Zeitschrift fur Soziologie, 40*(5), 412–413.

Christian, D. (2004). *Maps of time: An introduction to big history*. University of California Press.

Denning, P. J. (2007). Computing is a natural science. *Communications of the ACM, 50*(7), 13–18.

Deutsch, K. W. (1963). *The nerves of government*. Free Press.

Easton, D. (1953). *The political system: An inquiry into the study of political science*. Alfred A. Knopf, Inc.

Eells, E. (1991). *Probabilistic causality* (Vol. 1). Cambridge University Press.

Enserink, M., & Kupferschmidt, K. (2020). With COVID-19, modeling takes on life and death importance. *Science, 367*(6485), 1414–1415.

Epstein, J. (2006). *Generative social science: Studies in agent-based computational modeling*. Princeton University Press.

Freidenthal, S., Moore, A., & Steiner, R. (2015). *A practical guide to SysML: The systems modeling language*. Elsevier.

Gilbert, N. (Ed.). (2010). *Computational social science*. Sage.

Gilbert, N., & Troitzsch, K. (2005). *Simulation for the social scientist*. Open University Press.

Gleich, D. F., & Mahoney, M. W. (2016). Mining large graphs. In P. Bühlmann, P. Drineas, M. Kane, & M. van der Laan (Eds.), *Handbook of big data* (pp. 192–215). CRC Press.

Goertz, G. (2006). *Social science concepts: A user's guide*. Princeton University Press.

Good, I. J. (1980). Some comments on probabilistic causality. *Pacific Philosophical Quarterly*, *61*, 301–304.

Guetzkow, H., Alger, C. F., Brody, R. A., Noel, R. C., & Snyder, R. C. (Eds.). (1963). *Simulation in international relations: Developments for research and teaching*. Prentice Hall.

Hedström, P., & Bearman, P. (Eds.). (2009). *The Oxford handbook of analytical sociology*. Oxford University Press.

Heise, D. R. (1987). Affect control theory: Concepts and model. *Journal of Mathematical Sociology*, *13*(1–2), 1–33.

Hempel, C. G. (1952). *Fundamentals of concept formation in empirical science*. University of Chicago Press.

Hermann, C. F. (1990). International crisis as a situational variable. In J. A. Vasquez (Ed.), *Classics of international relations*. Prentice-Hall, Inc.

Hoey, J., et al. (2013). *Bayesian affect control theory*. 2013 Humaine Association Conference on Affective Computing and Intelligent Interaction, IEEE.

Holland, J. H. (1975). *Adaptation in natural and artificial systems*. University of Michigan Press.

Holland, J. H. (1995). *Hidden order: How adaptation builds complexity*. Addison-Wesley.

Jager, W. (2020). Predictions on the spread of COVID-19 bear many uncertainties. *Elephant in the Lab*. https://doi.org/10.5281/zenodo.3724048

Kemeny, J. G., & Snell, J. L. (1962). *Mathematical models in the social sciences*. The MIT Press.

Kitchin, R., & Lauriault, T. P. (2014). Small data in the era of big data. *GeoJournal*, *80*(4), 463–475.

Kuznar, L. A. (2006). High-fidelity computational social science in anthropology. *Social Science Computer Review*, *24*(1), 15–29.

Lave, C. A., & March, J. G. (1993 [1975]). *An introduction to models in the social sciences*. Harper and Row.

Laver, M. (2020). *Agent-based models of social life: Vol. 1 (fundamentals), vol. 2 (polarization and ethnocentrism)*. Cambridge University Press.

Lazer, D., Pentland, A., Adamic, L., Aral, S., Barabasi, A. L., Brewer, D., . . . Alstyne, M. Van. (2009). Computational social science. *Science*, *323*(5915), 721–723.

Lazer, D. M. J., Pentland, A., Watts, D. J., Aral, S., Athey, S., Contractor, N., . . . Wagner, C. (2020). Computational social science: Obstacles and opportunities. *Science*, *369*(6507), 1060–1062. https://doi.org/10.1126/science.aaz8170

Lewin, K. (1952). *Field theory in social science: Selected theoretical papers*. University of Chicago Press.

Luke, S., et al. (2019). The MASON simulation toolkit: Past, present, and future. *Proceedings of the MABS (multi-agent-based simulation XIX) workshop, AAMAS, Stockholm, Sweden, 2018*. Springer.

Maki, D. P., & Thompson, M. (1973). *Mathematical models and applications: With emphasis on the social, life, and management sciences*. Prentice-Hall, Inc.

Manzo, G. (Ed.). (2014). *Analytical sociology: Actions and networks*. Wiley.

McCain, G., & Segal, E. M. (1988). *The game of science* (5th ed.). Brooks and Cole Publishing Co.

McClelland, C. A. (1961). The acute international crisis. *World Politics*, *14*(1), 182–204.

Messick, S. J. (1963). *Computer simulation of personality: Frontier of psychological theory*. American Psychological Association.

Miller, J. H., & Page, S. E. (2007). *Complex adaptive systems: An introduction to computational models of social life*. Princeton University Press.

Mithen, S. (2004). *After the ice: A global human history, 20,000–5000 BC*. Harvard University Press.

Olinick, M. (2014 [1978]). *An introduction to mathematical models in the social and life sciences*. Reading, MA: Addison-Wesley.

Parisi, D. (2014). *Future robots: Towards a robotic science of human beings*. John Benjamins Publishing Company.

Radcliffe-Brown, A. R. (1952). *Structure and function in primitive society*. Free Press.

Richardson, L. F. (1952a). Is it possible to prove any general statements about historical fact? *British Journal of Sociology*, *3*(1), 77–84.

Richardson, L. F. (1952b). Contiguity and deadly quarrels: The local pacifying influence. *Journal of the Royal Statistical Society*, Series A, *115*(Part II), 219–231.

Salmon, W. C. (1980). Probabilistic causality. *Pacific Philosophical Quarterly*, *61*, 50–74.

Simon, H. A. (1952). A formal theory of interaction in social groups. *American Sociological Review*, *17*(2), 202–212.

Simon, H. A. (1957). *Models of man*. John Wiley & Sons.

Simon, H. A. (1965). The architecture of complexity. *Proceedings of the American Philosophical Society*, *106*, 467–482.

Simon, H. A. (1996 [1969]). *The sciences of the artificial* (3rd ed.). The MIT Press.

Snyder, G. H., & Diesing, P. (1977). *Conflict among nations: Bargaining, decisionmaking, and system structure in international crises*. Princeton University Press.

Squazzoni, F. (2008). A (computational) social science perspective on societal transitions. *Computational and Mathematical Organization Theory, 14*(4), 266–282.

Suppes, P. (1984). *Probabilistic metaphysics*. Basil Blackwell.

Torrens, P. M. (2010). Geography and computational social science. *GeoJournal, 75*(2), 133–148.

Toulmin, S. (1960). *The philosophy of science: An introduction*. Harper and Row.

Trobia, A. (2001). *La Sociologia Come Scienza Rigorosa: Modelli simulativi, intelligenza collettiva, forme del mutamento [Sociology as a rigorous science: Simulation models, collective intelligence, and patterns of change]*. Franco Angeli.

von Neumann, J. (1966). *Theory of self-reproducing automata* (A. W. Burks, Ed.). University of Illinois Press.

Wilensky, U., & Rand, R. (2015). *An introduction to agent-based modeling: Modeling natural, social, and engineered complex systems with NetLogo*. The MIT Press.

3

ANALYTICAL SOCIOLOGY AMIDST A COMPUTATIONAL SOCIAL SCIENCE REVOLUTION

Benjamin F. Jarvis, Marc Keuschnigg, and Peter Hedström

Acknowledgments: We thank Martin Arvidsson, Miriam Hurtado Bodell, Dorottya Kisfalusi, Etienne Ollion, and Christian Steglich for valuable comments. We are grateful for financial support through the Swedish Research Council (2016–01987, 2018–05170, and 445–2013–7681) and Formas (2018–00269).

Introduction

The emerging fields of computational social science (CSS) and analytical sociology (AS) have been developing in parallel over the last two decades. The development of CSS has been largely technological, driven by enormous increases in the power and availability of computational tools, the increasing digitization of contemporary life, and the corresponding broadening and deepening of data describing that life (Lazer et al., 2009, 2020). This explosion in computing capabilities and social data has inspired an interdisciplinary assortment of social and computational scientists to grapple with and mine these data for new insights into the social world (Conte et al., 2012; Watts, 2013; Ledford, 2020). The development of AS, meanwhile, has been spurred by an underlying substantive and theoretical interest in producing mechanistic explanations of collective dynamics (Hedström & Ylikoski, 2010; Keuschnigg, Lovsjö, & Hedström, 2018). By collective dynamics, we mean the emergence and transformation of system-level properties of social collectivities. AS is premised on the idea that the explanation of collective dynamics can only be achieved by understanding the social mechanisms that bring those dynamics about. This means analyzing the activities of individual actors; uncovering the social, institutional, and environmental contexts and cues that influence their actions; and demonstrating how their interdependent behaviors accumulate into macro-level social patterns and collective change (Hedström & Bearman, 2009). Drawing on this underlying philosophy, analytical sociologists have sought to achieve deeper understandings of collective phenomena such as inequality, segregation, market success, and political change.

As CSS and AS have matured, obvious connections between them have emerged. Both are keenly interested in complexity and emergence, whereby "the behavior of entities at one 'scale' of reality is not easily traced to the properties of the entities at the scale below" (Watts, 2013, p. 6; see also Anderson, 1972). And both build models that view emergence as driven by the interactions of socially embedded, interdependent actors. CSS and AS have also come to share some methodological tools, including simulation approaches like agent-based modeling. But despite these connections, there remains a distinct gap between these two fields. While analytical sociologists have often used computer simulations for theoretical purposes, it is mainly within the last decade that they have begun to adopt other CSS techniques and research designs, like computational text analysis and online experiments, for empirical work. Even then, AS is often playing catch-up with the most cutting-edge CSS tools. Meanwhile, CSS research, while often making gestures to the importance of scale and emergence in social systems, all too often falls short in offering empirical confirmation of postulated behaviors at lower scales and in demonstrating how these behaviors aggregate up to real, observed patterns at larger scales.

The purpose of this chapter is to describe and strengthen the nascent connections between CSS and AS. In the process, we consider how CSS methods and perspectives have been used to augment and advance the analytical sociology project and how an analytical sociology perspective can improve the practice of CSS. We begin by offering a primer on the analytical sociology tradition. We then highlight how different CSS approaches, including empirically calibrated agent-based models, large-scale online experiments, broad and deep digital datasets, and natural language processing, fit into AS research designs. Along the way, we highlight several points for analytical sociologists to consider when incorporating CSS approaches into their research. This includes assessing the scale at which potential CSS techniques provide research insights, discerning how these tools enhance the explanatory power of AS research designs, and determining whether and how to synthesize CSS methods in AS research. Finally, we suggest how an AS perspective can guide the development of CSS and improve CSS research designs in ways that will uncover and elucidate key social mechanisms that drive collective dynamics.

Analytical sociology: a primer

This section presents core features of analytical sociology. At the same time, we distinguish its intellectual project from traditional quantitative sociology. Of course, the exact details of what analytical sociology is and how it should be practiced are not entirely settled (see, e.g., Hedström, 2005; Hedström & Bearman, 2009; Hedström & Ylikoski, 2010; Manzo, 2010, 2014; León-Medina, 2017). With that said, there is agreement that the key aspects of AS are a commitment to clarity and precision in developing mechanism-based explanations, a concern with bottom-up social processes, and an interest in achieving realism in sociological theory building.

How social systems come to evince particular patterns and how those patterns change over time or vary across contexts are main concerns for many sociologists. Much of the quantitative sociological tradition has examined these long-standing interests by focusing on "factors" rather than the interdependent behaviors of "actors" (Macy & Willer, 2002). Largely, although not exclusively, this has meant applying statistical models that identify and describe associations, or even causal relationships, between time-ordered social variables, categories, or events but with insufficient attention paid to the concrete activities, relations, and patterns of mutual influence among the social actors involved in key social processes (Sørensen, 1998). What is more, micro-level data, typically collected and analyzed based on a premise of statistical independence, came to dominate empirical social analysis (Boelaert & Ollion, 2018). This tradition has yielded at times revelatory insights into the social world, but it has rarely provided scientifically satisfying answers to questions about *how* certain social phenomena come about or *how* associations emerge between certain variables, categories, or events.

Analytical sociology distinguishes itself from this tradition by addressing these *how* questions. Analytical sociologists intend to produce mechanism-based explanations of social phenomena and their dynamics (Hedström, 2005; Hedström & Ylikoski, 2010). By a mechanism-based explanation for a social phenomenon, we mean the identification of "entities and activities organized in such a way that they are responsible for the phenomenon" (Illari & Williamson, 2012, p. 120; see also, Glennan & Illari, 2017). From the AS perspective, it is insufficient to establish a predictive relationship, even a causal one, between antecedent and subsequent variables, categories, and events. Proper explanation of a social phenomenon is achieved by specifying who the relevant actors are, theorizing the social behaviors and relations that are expected to bring about the phenomenon, and, critically, demonstrating how these "nuts and bolts [and] cogs and wheels" produce the social phenomenon in question (Elster, 1989, p. 3).

Mechanism-based explanation is premised on an ideal-typical distinction between the micro and macro levels, or scales, of a social system (Coleman, 1986). At the macro level are observed aggregate social patterns such as inequality, network density, segregation, population prevalence, and so on. These are the social phenomena to be explained. At the micro level are the actors who make up the social system and their inter-relations. In many research cases, the actors are individual persons, but in other cases, those actors may be aggregations, like families, firms, or political parties. AS researchers usually subscribe to some version of methodological individualism (Coleman, 1986, 1994; Udehn, 2002). As such, AS assigns explanatory primacy to these micro-level entities, because they – not variables, categories, or events – are capable of social action. This means that AS explanations of social processes necessarily proceed from the bottom up.

The micro and macro levels of the system are coupled. Changes in macro properties may redound to social actors at the micro level by, for example, shaping their opportunity structures, altering decision rules, shifting incentives, or channeling information. Changes in the local circumstances or thought processes of actors can lead to behaviors that, in turn, influence macro-level social patterns. This is especially likely when people are interconnected such that the actions of some will influence the actions of others, leading to domino effects. One classic example of this kind of micro-macro link is the Schelling segregation model, which shows how a population that tolerates intergroup mixing nonetheless achieves a state of near complete segregation through a process of neighborhood "tipping" induced by chains of interdependent moves (Schelling, 1971, 1978).

Finally, analytical sociologists are keenly interested in achieving realism in their research. AS aims to explain social dynamics in the real world, not in abstract, fictive social systems. Few analytical sociologists would be content to demonstrate that one particular mechanism *might* be implicated in the production of an aggregate social phenomenon. Instead, the goal is to identify actually operating mechanisms in empirically observed social systems and to demonstrate how these mechanisms, taken together, bring about the social phenomenon to be explained. This contrasts with the tendency in traditional quantitative approaches in the social sciences, most notably perhaps in economics (Friedman, 1953), to elide the often messy, heterogeneous cognitive and social processes guiding individual behavior in favor of reductive, analytically tractable models. To meet the empirical prerequisites of realistic theory building, analytical sociologists are increasingly turning to CSS methods.

New tools for sociology

Up until recently, most quantitative sociology has been limited to the conventional statistical analysis of survey data. The survey-research model and its attendant analytical tools largely rely on the sampling of independent observations. This reliance on statistical independence has often precluded the analysis of large-scale social phenomena produced by interconnected actors (Coleman, 1986). This has driven a wedge between sociological theory, primarily interested in larger-scale phenomena emerging from networked social systems, and quantitative practice, which has often narrowed its ambitions to the prediction of individual-level outcomes as functions of various temporally prior psychological and sociodemographic attributes. In short, the survey-research paradigm has steered quantitative sociology's research aims, shifting attention from the "social processes . . . shaping the system's behavior to psychological and demographic processes shaping individual behavior" (Coleman, 1986, p. 1315).

Thanks to the rise of CSS, the data and tools for realigning sociology's empirical attention with its long-standing theoretical interests are either presently or nearly at hand. Producing mechanism-based explanations of system-level properties and dynamics is predicated on an ability to access or collect datasets describing the interactions of thousands or even millions of individuals and analyzing those data to uncover the complex processes that may drive social change or maintain stability. The observations in these data are necessarily statistically dependent. With abundant computing resources and the increasing digitization of social life, not only is it now possible to gather these data, but also it is now within the realm of possibility to properly analyze them and the interdependent behaviors they describe. This has brought sociology to the cusp of transcending the survey-research paradigm and truly putting quantitative tools to work in service to sociological theorizing.

In the remainder of this section, we discuss CSS tools that analytical sociologists are using to build and investigate social theories. We discuss some of the current applications of these tools, provide suggestions for how these can be applied fruitfully in research, and suggest some potential opportunities for combining these tools. We place a particular emphasis on empirically calibrated agent-based models which have played a crucial role in developing the AS paradigm over the past two decades. Conventional agent-based models (ABMs) have occupied a niche space in sociology for several decades now (Schelling, 1971; Sakoda, 1971), but increasing computing power and programming sophistication are making it possible to apply ABMs in ways that recreate, in simulations, real-world populations and social processes. We then highlight the role of large-scale online experiments for sociological theory building. We subsequently turn to the increasing availability of broad and deep digital datasets covering networked populations and their digital traces, like those generated on social media platforms, and the potential for these datasets to revolutionize observational studies. Finally, we discuss computational text analysis, which is opening up vast, text-based troves of data describing both collective and individual sentiments, ideologies, and bodies of knowledge. We argue that CSS approaches to data collection and analysis are well suited to sociological interests in explaining the dynamics of systems populated by interdependent actors, and we consider ways in which these different approaches overlap and might be combined.

Empirically calibrated agent-based models

Empirically calibrated agent-based models (ECABMs) are becoming a key tool for demonstrating how micro-level behaviors produce macro-level outcomes not only in theory but also in real empirical settings (Bruch & Atwell, 2015). In some cases, ECABMs remain largely theoretical tools that attempt to overcome the limitations of more abstract, conventional ABMs. Building ABMs has typically involved constructing hermetically sealed, digital social worlds in which micro behaviors and the structure and form of agent interactions are entirely fabricated by the model implementer. Arbitrary assumptions coded into these models throw their real-world relevance into question. "Low-dimensional realism" ECABMs (Bruch & Atwell, 2015, p. 187), in contrast, tether some portion of the model to real data, substituting empirical findings for arbitrary assumptions. Ideally, this can yield theoretical models that are more pertinent to understanding processes in existing social systems. ECABMs are also used to achieve "high-dimensional realism" (Bruch & Atwell, 2015, p. 187). Such models integrate data about individual behaviors and aggregate outcomes so as to reproduce, as closely as possible, the collective dynamics in the observed system. The highly calibrated models can then be used to perform *in silico* experiments to judge how an intervention – possibly a policy intervention – affects a target macro-level outcome. High-dimensional-realism models are of particular interest when experimental intervention in a social system is precluded by ethical dilemmas, exorbitant costs, or practical feasibility. Programming this class of ECBMs involves thoroughly grounding the agent behaviors, characteristics, and structural positions in empirical data, the more the better. This yields greater realism but potentially at the expense of unmanageable complexity that may render opaque the ultimate mechanisms producing a macro-level phenomenon (León-Medina, 2017). And programming detailed ECABMs is no small feat: because the models are populated by many thousands, if not millions, of agents, each making dozens, hundreds, or even thousands of decisions, special care must be made to program the models efficiently and to optimize for distributed computing platforms (Deissenberg, van der Hoog, & Dawid, 2008; Collier & North, 2013). Both the low-dimensional and high-dimensional realism approaches to ECABMs have their place, and both can align with the AS desire to achieve realistic, mechanism-based explanations.

Up until now, empirically calibrated models have rarely been used in sociology. Some prominent exceptions include studies of segregation (Bruch & Mare, 2006; Xie & Zhou, 2012; Bruch, 2014), network dynamics (Snijders, 2001; Snijders, van de Bunt, & Steglich, 2010; Stadtfeld, 2018), and noncontagious disease spread (Liu & Bearman, 2015). Many applications of ECABMs have fallen on the "low-dimensional realism" side of the ECABM complexity scale. But in fields such as epidemiology, urban planning, natural resource management, and computational economics, ECABMs of the "high-dimensional realism" variety have gained wider acceptance, in part because of their utility in performing policy analyses and generating predictions (e.g., Zhang & Vorobeychik, 2019). Two prominent examples are the UrbanSIM model (Waddell, 2002) of urban land use, utilized by numerous city-planning departments, and the Global Scale Agent Model of disease transmission developed by the Brookings Institution (Epstein, 2009; Parker & Epstein, 2011) and used to study pandemics.

There are two main techniques for incorporating empirical data into ABMs: either by using micro-level data about human decision-making to calibrate agent behaviors or by fitting the full ABM model to distributional data describing the target population. Calibrating the micro-level behaviors of agents is typically done by fitting statistical models or applying machine learning algorithms to data about the relevant behaviors – such as consumption, mobility, or tie formation – to extract the parameters or decision rules that guide action (Bruch & Atwell, 2015). The identified micro-level behaviors and their parameters are then directly programmed into the ABM. In the analytical-sociology tradition, this micro-level calibration approach has been deployed most notably in studies of segregation (Bruch & Mare, 2006; Xie & Zhou, 2012; Bruch, 2014; Jarvis, 2015).

When data about micro-level behaviors are lacking or incomplete, an alternative is to directly fit an ABM to empirical data describing a self-contained social system. To do this sort of fitting, an analyst must make assumptions about micro-level agent behaviors, specify a parameterized micro-level model that links agent contexts and attributes to their behaviors, and then tune the micro-level parameters until they reproduce, in simulation, relevant macro-level statistics describing the observed system. Most prominently in sociology and network science, this approach has spawned stochastic actor-oriented models (SAOMs) for network analysis (Snijders et al., 2010). The SAOM approach to network analysis uses longitudinal network data in conjunction with assumptions about the micro-level tie-formation process to generate estimates of behavioral parameters determining tie formation and dissolution. The estimates are produced such that simulated networks match selected network-level statistics observed in the real data (e.g., degree distributions) but not to exactly reproduce the observed network. Not only can SAOMs be used to study network evolution, but also they can uncover how social influence leads to changes in distributions of node-level outcomes and behaviors, like academic achievement, alcohol consumption, and tobacco use (Steglich, Snijders, & Pearson, 2010; although see Daza & Kreuger, 2019; Ragan, Osgood, Ramirez, Moody, & Gest, 2019). For example, adams and Schaefer (2016) use this approach to examine how smoking behavior is both a cause and consequence of friendship ties in schools and to understand the implications of this endogeneity for school-level smoking prevalence. Their study illustrates the power of the SAOM approach: because the same machinery is used for both estimation and simulation, the models can account for endogenous micro-level processes during the parameter estimation stage while simultaneously providing tools for answering "what if" questions about the trajectories for the analyzed social system as a whole.

Both kinds of ECABMs – those using the independent calibration approach and those, like SAOMs, calibrated directly to data about a social system – achieve the micro-macro link in mechanistic explanation by offering a platform for performing counterfactual experiments. During counterfactual experiments, an analyst manipulates features of the model, that is, the mechanistic cogs and wheels, and examines the impact of those manipulations on aggregate outputs (Manzo, 2011; Marshall & Galea, 2015). With empirical calibration comes not only an ability to assess whether a given mechanism or set of mechanisms is capable of producing some macro-social pattern in a broad sense, as is the case with conventional ABMs, but also to analyze – using precise, quantitative measures – whether and to what degree the mechanisms in the model produce the empirically observed phenomena. This ability to simulate the social world under different conditions is one way to unpack how a social mechanism works and sort out which behaviors and structural components are needed to produce a given macro outcome. Importantly, data derived from these simulations can be used to explore whether and how those components interact as social processes unfold.

Performing a counterfactual experiment with ABMs involves either adjusting behavioral parameters and rules or altering the attributes, resources, or social contexts of agents populating the system. To begin, one can ask whether suppressing, enhancing, or otherwise modifying an aspect of the micro-level behaviors leads to changes in observed macro-level outcomes. This is typically done by modifying parameters attached to those behaviors (e.g., Snijders & Steglich, 2013). In the segregation literature, this can involve changing ethnic preferences of one or more groups and examining what different levels or patterns of segregation are realized as a result (e.g., Jarvis, 2015). In the case of network dynamics, one can alter popularity and transmission effects related to certain behaviors and trace the resulting effects on behavioral adoption (Schaefer, adams, & Haas, 2013; Lakon, Hipp, Wang, Butts, & Jose, 2015; Fujimoto, Snijders, & Valente, 2018). An alternate counterfactual approach is to modify the agent population structure, covariate distributions, or social relations without altering behavioral rules or parameters. This approach can be used to answer questions like: How does network structure shape the diffusion of social behaviors (adams & Schaefer, 2016)? How does between- and within-group inequality affect patterns of segregation (Bruch, 2014)? And how does adding or switching network ties influence mobility and segregation (Arvidsson, Collet, & Hedström, 2021)?

Both counterfactual approaches have their advantages and disadvantages. The first approach of adjusting agents' behavioral parameters is useful for understanding whether and to what degree particular behaviors contribute to macro outcomes. For example, by manipulating group preferences in a model of segregation, it should be possible to attribute the degree of segregation attained at equilibrium to the preferences of one group or another or to the interactions between these preferences. This sort of attributional exercise is of some intellectual value but may have less practical value in terms of guiding policy making or in understanding the dynamics of actually existing social systems. This is because directly modifying underlying behavioral parameters like preferences or beliefs may be tremendously difficult in practice. The second approach – adjusting variables representing relations, distributions, or other social structures – is potentially more promising for understanding policy interventions and the behavior of real social systems. This is because these interventions are more plausible – they take people as they are rather than as we might like them to be – and consider how people would behave with slightly different resources, incentives, or social influences.

Deciphering why and how a particular ABM model produces a particular macro phenomenon under some counterfactual conditions but not others is a mounting challenge in the AS and ABM community. There are increasing calls to open up ABM "black boxes" to uncover the precise chains of behavior that bring about the macro outcomes of interest (León-Medina, 2017). There are no easy solutions to these problems, but other CSS techniques may offer avenues for further exploration. Pattern recognition approaches, like sequence analysis (Cornwell, 2015; Ritschard & Studer, 2018), might be fruitfully applied not only to empirical data but also to the outputs of agent-based models to understand the sequences of events that account for macro-level outcomes that differ between *in silico* counterfactual experiments. Using these approaches might allow AS to move beyond identifying the relative importance of different "cogs and wheels" that bring macro outcomes about and towards a fuller account of how these parts fit together in causal chains of transformative social action.

Large-scale web-based experiments

Increasingly, sociologists make use of web-based experiments not only to study behavior among participant groups that are more diverse than those sustained by traditional laboratory pools (e.g., Bader & Keuschnigg, 2020; Schaub, Gereke, & Baldassarri, 2020) but also, importantly, to elicit behavior of larger groups of interacting population members (Salganik & Watts, 2009; Centola, 2018). This type of experiment – introduced to the analytical sociology toolbox in 2006 by a study of music downloading in artificial cultural markets (Salganik, Dodds, & Watts, 2006) – focuses on the social processes arising from behavioral interdependencies, and it tackles questions about the "social production" of macro phenomena that cannot be addressed using the more individualistic perspectives taken in small-group experiments. This design breaks with the older experimental traditions by randomizing participants into separate "social systems", or "multiple worlds", that each serve as a unit of analysis.

During the experiment, entire miniature social systems are populated by real users, with each miniature system varying in the conditions guiding social interactions and user choices. By manipulating conditions in theoretically informed ways, it can be determined which interactive mechanisms produce system-level outcomes. Interpreting each social system, rather than each experimental subject, as a unit of analysis shifts the focus from individual action towards macro phenomena. Participants in an experimental run learn about the others' decisions either through direct interaction – such as on a social media-like platform that signals network contacts' adoptions of certain behaviors (Centola, 2010, 2011) – or through statistics that summarize the aggregate behaviors of other participants – such as a popularity ranking derived from past participants' choices (Salganik et al., 2006; Macy, Deri, Ruch, & Tong, 2019). Experimental runs start on an all-to-all network and are left alone to evolve endogenously, or they start from predefined worlds, for example, by placing participants on a network with a certain number of homophilic contacts. Each run then resembles a realization of a social process in a population of interconnected individuals, and it provides controlled data on the social interactions that lead to a specific collective outcome.

Observing larger groups of interacting individuals in such "macrosociological" experiments (Hedström, 2006) acknowledges that collective properties, such as status hierarchies, the diffusion of products and ideas, the strength of social norms, or network segregation, are not defined by the micro-level characteristics of the population members alone. As argued previously, many macro-level outcomes do not result from a linear aggregation of individual preferences and individualistic choices but often depend on critical masses and tipping points of contingent behaviors. Understanding how such social dynamics unfold is important because they have the capacity to construct highly path-dependent, and arbitrary, realities. In Salganik et al.'s prominent study, where participants could listen to and download songs of unknown artists in parallel "cultural markets", it became highly arbitrary which artists were most often downloaded once participants were exposed to a popularity ranking summarizing other participants' choices, and different artists led the popularity rankings in the parallel social systems (Salganik et al., 2006; see also Macy et al., 2019 on the polarization of arbitrary policy stances across political affiliations in the United States).

There is a potentially strong link here between ECABMs and large-scale web experiments. ABMs are increasingly used by experiment designers to target mechanisms for experimental manipulation, generate hypotheses, and extrapolate experimental results (e.g., Frey & van de Rijt, 2020; Stein, Keuschnigg, & van de Rijt, 2021). Typically, experiments are designed to collect detailed information about participants' micro-level behaviors. These data can then be used to (1) fit micro-level behavioral models that yield estimates of key behavioral parameters and (2) generate macro-level predictions using ECABMs that capture the empirically observed micro behaviors. The predictions can be produced as an internal consistency check to confirm that the experimentally observed micro behaviors indeed produce the macro phenomenon as hypothesized. The behavioral parameters estimated from experimental data might also be used to propose additional "virtual" interventions in the experimental platform or to scale up findings to understand the system behaviors among larger populations (e.g., Analytis, Stojic, & Moussaïd, 2015).

Digital trace data

Many sociological research questions defy randomized experimentation, and there are often other reasons, not least the transportability of empirical findings to the real world, to instead rely on observational data collected in real social environments. In the last decade, digitization has provided a plethora of sociologically relevant observational data from sources such as social-media platforms, online retail sites, mobile apps, administrative records, and historical archives. A particularly active research field investigates the behavioral mechanisms (e.g., confirmation bias) and situational mechanisms (e.g., network segregation) underlying political polarization on platforms such as Twitter and Facebook (e.g., Bakshy, Messing, & Adamic, 2015; Boutyline & Willer, 2017). These studies make particular use of the relational data provided by users following and maintaining ties to other individuals (e.g., friends, politicians) and organizations (e.g., media outlets, political parties). Analyses of co-following graphs on Twitter (Shi, Mast, Weber, Kellum, & Macy, 2017) further reveal that political polarization extends to other domains of social life, most notably cultural consumption, with conservative and liberal Twitter users (as indicated by their following of Republican or Democratic members of Congress) following different musical artists, restaurants, sports teams, and universities.

Typically, observational data from digital traces are not only wide – capturing, in the extreme, entire populations – but also deep in terms of granularity and the sheer number of variables available. The high dimensionality of many online datasets allows researchers to construct new measures of latent characteristics and to describe local social environments in detail, including network structures, homophily levels, and information flows (Golder & Macy, 2014; Bruch & Feinberg, 2017; Salganik, 2018; Edelmann, Wolff, Montagne, & Bail, 2020). These types of data differ in both size and kind from those typically used in the social sciences, and this has prompted interest in new methods emanating from the vibrant field of machine learning. Social scientists are using machine learning to distill new measures of hard-to-quantify constructs and to refine methods of causal inference from observational data, in contrast to the mainly predictive uses of machine learning in computer science and the emerging field of data science (Grimmer, 2015; Molina & Garip, 2019). Legewie and Schaeffer (2016), for example, study millions of geo-coded service and complaint calls made to New York City's 311 service to better understand neighborhood conflict in ethnically diverse settings. The authors use computer vision algorithms applied to census data to locate boundaries between racially and ethnically dissimilar areas of the city. They find that poorly defined rather than crisp and polarized boundaries between ethnic and racial groups act as drivers of neighborhood conflict.

In a recent study using Spotify data, Arvidsson, Hedström, and Keuschnigg (2020) estimate the causal effect that exposure to new music through a friend has on individuals' listening behavior. The user data contain information about who follows whom as well as musical tastes, characterized by fine-grained digital traces of users' listening habits. The difficulty of isolating social influence from confounding factors – homophily among interconnected individuals (e.g., friends like the same music) and common exposure to external stimuli (e.g., the like-minded receive similar algorithmic recommendations) – makes such analyses of social influence challenging (Aral, Muchnik, & Sundararajan, 2009; Shalizi & Thomas, 2011). The Spotify study uses the granular data on users' tastes to substantially improve the statistical matching of "treated" and "untreated" users and arrives at estimates of peer influence with substantially reduced confounding biases. Rather than matching on sociodemographic variables that correlate with adoption behavior, their procedure allows matching directly on music taste, a main driver of adoption behavior, tie formation, and exposure to music outside of Spotify. Importantly, the matching is performed after pre-processing individuals' playlist data. Playlists follow strong thematic patterns such that song co-occurrences in playlists indicate musical similarities. Inferring relational structures from co-occurrences is a central task in natural language processing. The study uses probabilistic topic models (Blei, Ng, & Jordan, 2003; see discussion in the following section) to map artists and their songs onto genres. The topic model allocates artists with different probabilities to different topics, capturing graded memberships in musical genres (Hannan et al., 2019). Replacing millions of songs contained in the individuals' playlists by their inferred genre preferences, the study arrives at a lower-dimensional representation of users' music tastes. The pre-processing makes sparse and granular data tractable for traditional matching models, such as propensity score matching and coarsened exact matching (Stuart, 2010), which have been developed for relatively low-dimensional settings where observations markedly outnumber variables.

Computational text analysis

For much of their disciplinary history, quantitative social scientists have found it difficult to study text. Lexical approaches that rely on word counts came to dominate, and with them attempts to infer meaning from word frequencies (Lasswell, Lerner, & de Sola Pool, 1952; Riffe et al., 2014). This tradition received renewed attention with the increasing availability of digitized text and the vast number of documents that can be searched in automated ways (Michel et al., 2011; Lorenz-Spreen, Mønsted, Hövel, & Lehmann, 2019). Related lexicon-based methods have also been used in analyses of sentiment expressed in text which, with the surge in human-annotated as well as machine-generated sentiment lexica, have been substantially refined in recent years (e.g., Pang & Lee, 2008; Pennebaker, Boyd, Jordan, & Blackburn, 2015). A particularly interesting design combines sentiment measures (e.g., from Twitter posts interpreted as "social sensors" over time) with a natural experiment (an exogenous variation of environmental conditions) such as policy changes or terrorist attacks in order to draw conclusions on their causal impact on public sentiment (Flores, 2017; Garcia & Rimé, 2019).

Advances in machine learning revolutionized the use of text as data (Grimmer & Stewart, 2013; DiMaggio, 2015; Mohr, Wagner-Pacifici, & Breiger, 2015; Evans & Aceves, 2016). Combined with ever larger corpora of digitized text, these tools offer new ways to measure what people think, feel, and talk about – on the level of a whole society. Traditional approaches to revealing such patterns of social behavior through text analysis required qualitative deep reading and time-consuming hand-coding which restricted analyses to small- and medium-sized collections of text (Franzosi, 2010; Riffe, Lacy, Fico, Lacy, & Fico, 2014). The abundance of text data now available makes the limited scalability of traditional approaches more apparent (Mützel, 2015), and the use of keywords to restrict analyses to important parts of a corpus, for example, has been shown to lead to biased results (King, Lam, & Roberts, 2017). At the same time, procedures based on hand- or automated-coding that rest on predefined classifications have been criticized as ill equipped to identify underlying cultural meanings and the context of social text (Biernacki, 2012; Guo, Vargo, Pan, Ding, & Ishwar, 2016). Fortunately, a collection of machine-learning methods developed for analyzing vast quantities of text data – often subsumed under the *natural language processing* label – have emerged in the last two decades (Jurafsky & Martin, 2009; Hirschberg & Manning, 2015).

Natural language processing offers new ways to describe both the macro-level properties of social systems and the characteristics of individual actors. In terms of macro properties, computational text analysis offers a lens through which to view relationships between words and, perhaps most interestingly for sociologists, the shared understandings of terms prevalent in a given population. On the micro level, text-analytic tools provide new measures of individuals' beliefs, sentiments, and tastes which in the past had to be collected using costly and difficult-to-administer survey instruments.

There is a classic distinction between supervised and unsupervised methods of computational text analysis. Supervised machine-learning algorithms can extrapolate hand-coded annotations from small subsets of documents to vast digitized corpora, making them available to large-scale quantitative analyses. Training computers to classify content opens up avenues for a broader and more representative study of vast bodies of digitized text, and "[i]nstead of restricting ourselves to collecting the best small pieces of information that can stand in for the textual whole. . ., contemporary technologies give us the ability to instead consider a textual corpus in its full hermeneutic complexity and nuance" (Mohr, Wagner-Pacifici, & Breiger, 2015, p. 3).

Unsupervised machine-learning algorithms for the analysis of text require no prior coding but recognize words that frequently occur together. A prominent approach is probabilistic topic modeling (Blei et al., 2003) which distills themes or categories from texts. Each corpus consists of multiple such "topics", and each document (e.g., online post, newspaper article, political speech) exhibits these topics in different proportions. From the viewpoint of the social sciences, topic models can reveal the "hidden thematic structure in large collections of documents"

(DiMaggio, Nag, & Blei, 2013, p. 577). Although topic models capture documents as "bags-of-words", ignoring syntax and word location, their coding of a corpus into meaningful categories often yields plausible readings of the texts, demonstrating what DiMaggio et al. (2013) describe as high levels of "substantive interpretability". The text-analytic concept of studying word co-occurrences connects to sociological ideas about how people create meaning and make sense of the social world by relating terms to other words and concepts (Goffman, 1974; DiMaggio, 1997; Mohr et al., 2020). Word co-occurrences are thought to capture such sociocultural associations, providing indications of schemata of interpretation and cultural frames more generally (Bail, 2014; DiMaggio, 2015). Correspondingly, topic models are increasingly used in sociology to operationalize relationality and meaning structures (e.g., DiMaggio et al., 2013; Lindgren, 2017; Nelson, 2020).

Another class of unsupervised algorithms, word embedding models (Mikolov, Yih, & Zweig, 2013; Pennington, Socher, & Manning, 2014), accounts for semantic structures by letting a sliding window pass through documents, recording the frequency with which words occur in a narrow context of other words. Word embeddings capture relations between words as distances between vectors in a high-dimensional space, allowing the inference of social meanings attached to words based on their positioning relative to other words. Because the dimensions of the identified vectors are largely uninterpretable, however, it is often unclear why words are predicted to be related. Important methodological developments thus focus on the interpretability of word embeddings. Hurtado Bodell, Arvidsson, and Magnusson (2019) and Kozlowski et al. (2019), for example, propose novel methodologies to study the meaning of individual words in relation to predetermined dimensions of interest (e.g., sentiment, gender, social status). An alternative to word embeddings builds on the older approach of co-occurrence networks where words – as nodes – are linked to their nearest neighbors, and a target term will associate with different close words over time, capturing the fluidity of meaning (Leskovec, Backstrom, & Kleinberg, 2009; Rule, Cointet, & Bearman, 2015; Bail, 2016). Such methodological developments strengthen the applicability of natural language processing to social science research questions, and they can deepen our understanding of how and why the cultural associations of words change over time.

It is also worthwhile to consider text-analytic models as a non-parametric way to conduct research using complex categorical data that are not typically thought of as corpora. The world is filled with detailed, linguistically delineated categories such as ethnicities, occupations, industries, and music genres. In many cases, the universe of categories runs into the dozens, if not hundreds or thousands. Sociologists often want to describe aggregations of people (e.g., neighborhoods, firm employees) or activities (e.g., cultural consumption, opinion expression) according to their compositions along these different categorical axes. In conventional statistical analyses with finite samples, it is rarely feasible to use all of the detailed categorical information at one's disposal, and often substantial simplification is necessary. Models derived from natural language processing can be used to induce, in a non-parametric way, salient regularities in compositional data rendered in full detail. To refer to a previous example, Arvidsson et al. (2020) apply topic models to Spotify playlists (i.e., documents) and their constituent artists (i.e., words). This use of topic models yielded condensed but nuanced descriptions of users' listening habits, which could then be employed in a causal analysis of social influence. Similar approaches could be taken to describe, for example, the ethnic mix of neighborhoods, the industrial mix of cities, or the mix of educational credentials in firms. Text-analytic models like topic models are especially appealing because they explicitly assume that any "document" (e.g., playlist, neighborhood, firm) is a mixture of topics. This allows for ambiguity and mixtures in classification, unlike many clustering methods which algorithmically assign analytical units to single categories.

While text-analytic models, on their own, stand to contribute novel insights for analytical sociologists, even greater insight may be unlocked by combining them with other CSS methods. The possibility of combining text analytic methods with ABMs is one largely unexplored avenue of research. Most ABMs, for practical reasons, postulate agents that think, perceive, and act in terms of numeric quantities or stark categorical distinctions. But language – its production and comprehension – is the basis for many human interactions, whether face to face or online. Combining ABMs with text analysis is an opportunity to leverage the dual interpretive and generative nature of some text-analytic models, like topic models, to understand social dynamics that are mediated by language. Agents in ABMs could be programmed to receive and interpret messages based on a text-analytic model and generate new messages based on the same discursive model. They could then take other actions, such as forming or dropping network ties or engaging in mobility, based on interpretations or classifications of messages received (e.g., Mordatch & Abbeel, 2018; Karell & Freedman, 2020). These kinds of agent-based models could be particularly helpful for modeling social processes in digital trace data, understanding not just the evolution of network ties but also, potentially, the evolution of the discourse itself.

Discussion

The dual growth in the power of computational tools and availability of digital trace data has pushed quantitative sociology to the brink of a new "watershed" moment, similar in significance to the introduction of representative population surveys and the tools for their statistical analysis in the middle of the twentieth century (Coleman, 1986; McFarland, Lewis, & Goldberg, 2016). Now the question is whether sociologists will take advantage of these new tools and evolve their empirical practice to live up to sociology's theoretical ambitions. Doing so requires transcending the tendency to limit quantitative analysis to the prediction of individual-level outcomes using psychological and sociodemographic variables contained in survey data. The new tools of computational social science present sociologists generally, and analytical sociologists in particular, with the chance to identify the complex social mechanisms that cause macro-level social patterns to emerge from the behaviors of networked, micro-level actors.

In this chapter, we have examined CSS methods that offer promise for analytical sociology's aim to understand and explain collective dynamics. In particular, we have shown how empirically calibrated agent-based models have made it possible to perform *in silico* counterfactual experiments in cases where *in situ* experimentation is virtually impossible, thereby identifying micro mechanisms that generate macro-level phenomena. We have discussed how large-scale web-based experiments make it possible to treat social systems, rather than individuals, as units of analysis in experimental tests of social mechanisms. And we have discussed how digital trace data, in combination with computational techniques of dimensionality reduction, including the tools of natural language processing, are opening up new data frontiers for quantifying difficult to measure concepts and observing related micro-level behaviors.

Our presentation has perhaps given the impression that the intellectual avenues connecting CSS and analytical sociology run one way: first, computational scholars in CSS create methods for their own purposes, and then sociologists adapt those methods to fit their substantive and theoretical interests. This is not our intent. We believe that AS has important contributions to make to CSS. Primarily, we believe an AS influence would lead CSS scholars to shed a preoccupation with producing aggregate-level descriptions of digital trace, text, and other "big" data that lack explanatory depth. We also believe that an AS influence would encourage CSS scholars to divert energy away from producing black-box predictive models and in the direction of developing tools to identify social mechanisms and assess their influence on macro-level social phenomena.

CSS techniques have greatly increased the ability of social scientists to collect data about complex social systems, to detect empirical regularities across these social systems, and to make predictions about individual and macro outcomes (Watts, 2013; Salganik, 2018). However, CSS scholars have too often rested at providing evidence of an empirical regularity and using a highly abstract mathematical or simulation model to propose a simple mechanism capable of producing that regularity. This theoretical work often lacks explanatory depth because it ignores empirical evidence at the micro level or gives little consideration to other mechanisms capable of producing similar empirical patterns. Examples of this tendency include the literature on urban scaling (Bettencourt, Lobo, Helbing, Kühnert, & West, 2007; Bettencourt, 2013) and research on the prevalence and emergence of power law distributions and scale-free networks (Barabási & Albert, 1999; Mitzenmacher, 2004). To summarize the critiques of these literatures (e.g., Stumpf & Porter, 2012; Keuschnigg, Mutgan, & Hedström, 2019), exclusive reliance on macro-level data to attribute a given regularity to a particular micro-level behavior is difficult, all the more so when multiple mechanisms are theoretically implicated (Young, 2009).

The antidote to the neglect of micro mechanisms is not to abandon explanatory ambition and resign ourselves to constructing complex prediction algorithms. Certainly, data scientists and other CSS researchers have made strides in making precise predictions for human behaviors, and the new innovations are increasingly finding their way into the social sciences (Molina & Garip, 2019; Edelmann et al., 2020; although see Salganik et al., 2020). However, we should recognize that the digital machinery used to, say, accurately predict a Netflix user's movie ratings or predict epidemics as a function of internet search terms is not necessarily conducive to understanding how aggregate social patterns like the distribution of box office revenues or the spread of global pandemics come about. For one, the digital machines used for prediction are typically black boxes. In the worst case, this raises serious questions about their reliability and reproducibility (Hutson, 2018). But even in the best case, these black boxes make it difficult to connect a prediction's inputs to its outputs, and in so doing may even hamper our ability to identify social mechanisms (Boelaert & Ollion, 2018; Wolbring, 2020). Machine learning models and artificial intelligence algorithms may provide more accurate predictions of human action than conventional statistical models, but ambiguity in linking this action to particular motivations, cognitive biases, or social influences poses a challenge for connecting micro behaviors to macro outcomes.

One potential solution is to employ theory to avoid the explanatory pitfalls that come from relying on aggregated digital data or micro-level predictive models. CSS should give fuller consideration to the many micro mechanisms that can produce a macro pattern of interest and explicitly investigate how these mechanisms combine and interact. Failure to articulate and demonstrate the social mechanisms driving a particular social phenomenon creates doubt about the practical implications of CSS research and hamstrings the research community's ability to generalize its findings. We are left with shallower understanding and greater uncertainty about effective policy responses to remedy perceived social problems (Martin & Sell, 1979; Deaton, 2010; Hedström & Ylikoski, 2010). A theory-driven approach that strives to identify mechanisms would improve the causal analysis of social systems, yielding insights that can be ported to other research cases covering different social domains.

A concern with social mechanisms should translate into a good-faith effort to incorporate mechanistic thinking into CSS research designs and analytic techniques. This means more than paying lip service to social mechanisms or relying on post-hoc, common-sense explanations of empirical findings (Kalter & Kroneberg, 2014; Watts, 2014). Instead, it requires CSS scholars to think more carefully about applying existing methods, or developing new tools, to explicitly locate and elucidate generalizable social mechanisms. In some cases, this may require thinking more carefully about heterogeneity and the importance of variation and randomness to the processes under study (Macy & Tsvetkova, 2015). To address this, machine learning algorithms might be deployed not only to produce precise predictions but also to sort through dense empirical data to identify behavioral "ecologies", making behavioral variation and its role in system-level dynamics the object of study (Arthur, 1994; Molina & Garip, 2019).

In other cases, understanding how a mechanism works requires identifying sequences of interrelated actions that bring about large-scale phenomena of interest. The point here is to see how the mechanistic cogs and wheels fit together and set each other in motion. To take an example, Schelling's (1971) work on segregation is still appreciated today not only because it connected micro-level behaviors to equilibrium patterns of segregation but also because Schelling delved into his model's unfolding micro-level dynamics to understand how chains of mobility created cascades towards segregation (Hegselmann, 2017). In Schelling's case, the micro-level dynamics were accessible because he acted as the computational engine: Schelling implemented his model by manually moving physical pieces around on a board. But more complex models, implemented *in silico*, may offer resistance when researchers attempt to pick out the chains of events that precipitate the emergence of macro properties. CSS techniques may help here. Pattern recognition algorithms designed for ordered events, like sequence analysis (Cornwell, 2015; Ritschard & Studer, 2018), could be strategically applied to real and simulated data alike to identify sequences of interconnected actions that generate macro outcomes. Similar care in examining micro-level dynamics can also be applied to the analysis of text data. Adopting a longitudinal perspective that explicitly acknowledges the relational and temporally contingent nature of discourse can provide insight into how cross-temporal social influence works and can even be used to imagine counterfactual patterns of discourse (Gerow, Hu, Boyd-Graber, Blei, & Evans, 2018). In general, there remains ample room for technical innovation in this space. As our generative models become more complex, social scientists will likely need complementary computational tools to help with unpacking the dynamic processes connecting micro behaviors to macro outcomes in these models.

CSS scholars do not have to act alone in introducing mechanistic thinking into their research. They can invite analytical sociologists, and social scientists more generally, to join their research projects from inception. And social scientists should consider returning the favor. Encouraging greater collaboration between AS and CSS is perhaps the most likely way to improve social explanation and technological practice in both (Watts, 2013; Subrahmanian & Kumar, 2017). However, extensive interdisciplinary collaboration between analytical sociologists and computational social scientists remains elusive. Perhaps a philosophical disconnect stemming from very different objects of research in the originating disciplines – physical systems rather than social systems – is the main stumbling block. CSS researchers, who often hail from computer science, statistics, and physics, typically emphasize predictive power rather than mechanistic explanation, whereas accurate prediction is a lesser concern, if it is even a realistic possibility, in the social sciences (Lieberson & Lynn, 2002; Salganik et al., 2020). It is also possible that more practical obstacles related to publication strategies, career expectations, and target audiences are impeding collaboration. These barriers separating CSS from analytical sociology will only be overcome with concerted effort. CSS scholars and analytical sociologists alike must invest in interdisciplinary activities and outlets, like journals and conferences, to build the lasting professional relationships that can cement ties between these disciplines. New models of research, communication, and publication that satisfy the intellectual and career needs of both CSS and AS researchers will need to be forged through dialogue and, eventually, collaboration. By building a shared intellectual community, the potential of CSS and analytical sociology to produce profound insights into the social world can be more fully realized.

References

adams, jimi, & Schaefer, D. R. (2016). How initial prevalence moderates network-based smoking change: Estimating contextual effects with stochastic actor-based models. *Journal of Health and Social Behavior.* https://doi.org/10.1177/0022146515627848

Analytis, P. P., Stojic, H., & Moussaïd, M. (2015). *The collective dynamics of sequential search in markets for cultural products* (SFI Working Paper No. 2015–06–023). Sante Fe Institute.

Anderson, P. W. (1972). More is different. *Science, 177*(4047), 393–396. https://doi.org/10.1126/science.177.4047.393

Aral, S., Muchnik, L., & Sundararajan, A. (2009). Distinguishing influence-based contagion from homophily-driven diffusion in dynamic networks. *Proceedings of the National Academy of Sciences, 106*(51), 21544–21549. https://doi.org/10.1073/pnas.0908800106

Arthur, W. B. (1994). Inductive reasoning and bounded rationality. *American Economic Review, 84*(2), 406–411.

Arvidsson, M., Collet, F., & Hedström, P. (2021). The Trojan-horse mechanism: How networks reduce gender segregation. *Science Advances, 7*(16), eabf6730. https://doi.org/10.1126/sciadv.abf6730

Arvidsson, M., Hedström, P., & Keuschnigg, M. (2020). *Social influence and the emergence of the unexpected: How novel music spreads on Spotify* (Working Paper). Norrköping: Institute for Analytical Sociology.

Bader, F., & Keuschnigg, M. (2020). Bounded solidarity in cross-national encounters: Individuals share more with others from poor countries but trust them less. *Sociological Science, 7*, 415–432. https://doi.org/10.15195/v7.a17

Bail, C. A. (2014). The cultural environment: Measuring culture with big data. *Theory and Society, 43*(3), 465–482. https://doi.org/10.1007/s11186-014-9216-5

Bail, C. A. (2016). Combining natural language processing and network analysis to examine how advocacy organizations stimulate conversation on social media. *Proceedings of the National Academy of Sciences, 113*(42), 11823–11828. https://doi.org/10.1073/pnas.1607151113

Bakshy, E., Messing, S., & Adamic, L. A. (2015). Exposure to ideologically diverse news and opinion on Facebook. *Science, 348*(6239), 1130–1132. https://doi.org/10.1126/science.aaa1160

Barabási, A.-L., & Albert, R. (1999). Emergence of scaling in random networks. *Science, 286*(5439), 509–512. https://doi.org/10.1126/science.286.5439.509

Bettencourt, L. M. A. (2013). The origins of scaling in cities. *Science, 340*(6139), 1438–1441. https://doi.org/10.1126/science.1235823

Bettencourt, L. M. A., Lobo, J., Helbing, D., Kühnert, C., & West, G. B. (2007). Growth, innovation, scaling, and the pace of life in cities. *Proceedings of the National Academy of Sciences, 104*(17), 7301–7306. https://doi.org/10.1073/pnas.0610172104

Biernacki, R. (2012). *Reinventing evidence in social inquiry: Decoding facts and variables.* Palgrave Macmillan. https://doi.org/10.1057/9781137007285

Blei, D. M., Ng, A. Y., & Jordan, M. I. (2003). Latent Dirichlet allocation. *Journal of Machine Learning Research, 3*(Jan), 993–1022.

Boelaert, J., & Ollion, É. (2018). The great regression. *Revue Française de Sociologie, 59*(3), 475–506. https://doi.org/10.3917/rfs.593.0475

Boutyline, A., & Willer, R. (2017). The social structure of political echo chambers: Variation in ideological homophily in online networks. *Political Psychology, 38*(3), 551–569. https://doi.org/10.1111/pops.12337

Bruch, E. E. (2014). How population structure shapes neighborhood segregation. *American Journal of Sociology, 119*(5), 1221–1278. https://doi.org/10.1086/675411

Bruch, E. E., & Atwell, J. (2015). Agent-based models in empirical social research. *Sociological Methods & Research, 44*(2), 186–221. https://doi.org/10.1177/0049124113506405

Bruch, E. E., & Feinberg, F. (2017). Decision-making processes in social contexts. *Annual Review of Sociology, 43*(1), 207–227. https://doi.org/10.1146/annurev-soc-060116-053622

Bruch, E. E., & Mare, R. D. (2006). Neighborhood choice and neighborhood change. *American Journal of Sociology, 112*, 667–709. https://doi.org/10.1086/507856

Centola, D. (2010). The spread of behavior in an online social network experiment. *Science, 329*(5996), 1194–1197. https://doi.org/10.1126/science.1185231

Centola, D. (2011). An experimental study of homophily in the adoption of health behavior. *Science*, *334*(6060), 1269–1272. https://doi.org/10.1126/science.1207055

Centola, D. (2018). *How behavior spreads*. Princeton University Press.

Coleman, J. S. (1986). Social theory, social research, and a theory of action. *American Journal of Sociology*, *91*(6), 1309–1335. https://doi.org/10.1086/228423

Coleman, J. S. (1994). *Foundations of social theory*. Belknap Press of Harvard University Press.

Collier, N., & North, M. (2013). Parallel agent-based simulation with repast for high performance computing. *Simulation*, *89*(10), 1215–1235. https://doi.org/10.1177/0037549712462620

Conte, R., Gilbert, N., Bonelli, G., Cioffi-Revilla, C., Deffuant, G., Kertesz, J., . . . Helbing, D. (2012). Manifesto of computational social science. *The European Physical Journal Special Topics*, *214*(1), 325–346. https://doi.org/10.1140/epjst/e2012-01697-8

Cornwell, B. (2015). *Social sequence analysis: Methods and applications*. Cambridge University Press. https://doi.org/10.1017/CBO9781316212530

Daza, S., & Kreuger, L. K. (2019). Agent-based models for assessing complex statistical models: An example evaluating selection and social influence estimates from SIENA. *Sociological Methods & Research*. https://doi.org/10.1177/0049124119826147

Deaton, A. (2010). Instruments, randomization, and learning about development. *Journal of Economic Literature*, *48*(2), 424–455. https://doi.org/10.1257/jel.48.2.424

Deissenberg, C., van der Hoog, S., & Dawid, H. (2008). EURACE: A massively parallel agent-based model of the European economy. *Applied Mathematics and Computation*, *204*(2), 541–552. https://doi.org/10.1016/j.amc.2008.05.116

DiMaggio, P. (1997). Culture and cognition. *Annual Review of Sociology*, *23*(1), 263–287. https://doi.org/10.1146/annurev.soc.23.1.263

DiMaggio, P. (2015). Adapting computational text analysis to social science (and vice versa). *Big Data & Society*, *2*(2), Article 2053951715602908. https://doi.org/10.1177/2053951715602908

DiMaggio, P., Nag, M., & Blei, D. (2013). Exploiting affinities between topic modeling and the sociological perspective on culture: Application to newspaper coverage of U.S. government arts funding. *Poetics*, *41*(6), 570–606. https://doi.org/10.1016/j.poetic.2013.08.004

Edelmann, A., Wolff, T., Montagne, D., & Bail, C. A. (2020). Computational social science and sociology. *Annual Review of Sociology*, *46*(1), 61–81. https://doi.org/10.1146/annurev-soc-121919-054621

Elster, J. (1989). *Nuts and bolts for the social sciences*. Cambridge University Press. https://doi.org/10.1017/CBO9780511812255

Epstein, J. M. (2009). Modelling to contain pandemics. *Nature*, *460*(7256), 687–687. https://doi.org/10.1038/460687a

Evans, J. A., & Aceves, P. (2016). Machine translation: Mining text for social theory. *Annual Review of Sociology*, *42*(1), 21–50. https://doi.org/10.1146/annurev-soc-081715-074206

Flores, R. D. (2017). Do anti-immigrant laws shape public sentiment? A study of Arizona's SB 1070 using Twitter data. *American Journal of Sociology*, *123*(2), 333–384. https://doi.org/10.1086/692983

Franzosi, R. (2010). *Quantitative narrative analysis*. Sage.

Frey, V., & van de Rijt, A. (2000). Social influence undermines the wisdom of the crowd in sequential decision making. *Management Science*. https://doi.org/10.1287/mnsc.2020.3713

Friedman, M. (1953). The methodology of positive economics. In M. Friedman (Ed.), *Essays in positive economics* (pp. 3–43). University of Chicago Press.

Fujimoto, K., Snijders, T. A. B., & Valente, T. W. (2018). Multivariate dynamics of one-mode and two-mode networks: Explaining similarity in sports participation among friends. *Network Science*, *6*(3), 370–395. https://doi.org/10.1017/nws.2018.11

Garcia, D., & Rimé, B. (2019). Collective emotions and social resilience in the digital traces after a terrorist attack. *Psychological Science*, *30*(4), 617–628. https://doi.org/10.1177/0956797619831964

Gerow, A., Hu, Y., Boyd-Graber, J., Blei, D. M., & Evans, J. A. (2018). Measuring discursive influence across scholarship. *Proceedings of the National Academy of Sciences*, *115*(13), 3308–3313. https://doi.org/10.1073/pnas.1719792115

Glennan, S., & Illari, P. (2017). Introduction: Mechanisms and mechanical philosophy. In S. Glennan & P. Illari (Eds.), *The Routledge Handbook of Mechanisms and Mechanical Philosophy* (pp. 1–7). Taylor & Francis. https://doi.org/10.1007/978-3-030-10707-9_1

Goffman, E. (1974). *Frame analysis: An essay on the organization of experience*. Harvard University Press.

Golder, S. A., & Macy, M. W. (2014). Digital footprints: Opportunities and challenges for online social research. *Annual Review of Sociology*, *40*(1), 129–152. https://doi.org/10.1146/annurev-soc-071913-043145

Grimmer, J. (2015). We are all social scientists now: How big data, machine learning, and causal inference work together. *PS: Political Science & Politics*, *48*(1), 80–83. https://doi.org/10.1017/S1049096514001784

Grimmer, J., & Stewart, B. M. (2013). Text as data: The promise and pitfalls of automatic content analysis methods for political texts. *Political Analysis*, *21*(3), 267–297. https://doi.org/10.1093/pan/mps028

Guo, L., Vargo, C. J., Pan, Z., Ding, W., & Ishwar, P. (2016). Big social data analytics in journalism and mass communication: Comparing dictionary-based text analysis and unsupervised topic modeling. *Journalism & Mass Communication Quarterly*, *93*(2), 332–359. https://doi.org/10.1177/1077699016639231

Hannan, M. T., Mens, G. L., Hsu, G., Kovács, B., Negro, G., Pólos, L., Pontikes, E., & Sharkey, A. J. (2019). *Concepts and categories: Foundations for sociological and cultural analysis*. Columbia University Press.

Hedström, P. (2005). *Dissecting the social: On the principles of analytical sociology*. Cambridge University Press. https://doi.org/10.1017/CBO9780511488801

Hedström, P. (2006). Experimental macro sociology: Predicting the next best seller. *Science*, *311*(5762), 786–787. https://doi.org/10.1126/science.1124707

Hedström, P., & Bearman, P. (Eds.). (2009). *The Oxford handbook of analytical sociology*. Oxford University Press.

Hedström, P., & Ylikoski, P. (2010). Causal mechanisms in the social sciences. *Annual Review of Sociology*, *36*(1), 49–67. https://doi.org/10.1146/annurev.soc.012809.102632

Hegselmann, R. (2017). Thomas C. Schelling and James M. Sakoda: The intellectual, technical, and social history of a model. *Journal of Artificial Societies and Social Simulation*, *20*(3), 15. https://doi.org/10.18564/jasss.3511

Hirschberg, J., & Manning, C. D. (2015). Advances in natural language processing. *Science*, *349*(6245), 261–266. https://doi.org/10.1126/science.aaa8685

Hurtado Bodell, M., Arvidsson, M., & Magnusson, M. (2019). Interpretable word embeddings via informative priors. In K. Inui, J. Jiang, X. Wan (Eds.), *Proceedings of the 2019 Conference on Empirical Methods in Natural Language Processing and the 9th International Joint Conference on Natural Language Processing (EMNLP-IJCNLP)* (pp. 6323–6329). Association for Computational Linguistics. https://doi.org/10.18653/v1/D19-1661

Hutson, M. (2018). Artificial intelligence faces reproducibility crisis. *Science*, *359*(6377), 725–726. https://doi.org/10.1126/science.359.6377.725

Illari, P. M., & Williamson, J. (2012). What is a mechanism? Thinking about mechanisms across the sciences. *European Journal for Philosophy of Science*, *2*(1), 119–135. https://doi.org/10.1007/s13194-011-0038-2

Jarvis, B. F. (2015). *Matching residential mobility to raced-based neighborhood preferences in Los Angeles: Implications for racial residential segregation*. University of California Press. http://escholarship.org/uc/item/9174793s

Jurafsky, D., & Martin, J. H. (2009). *Speech and language processing: An introduction to natural language processing, computational linguistics, and speech recognition*. Prentice Hall.

Kalter, F., & Kroneberg, C. (2014). Between mechanism talk and mechanism cult: New emphases in explanatory sociology and empirical research. *Kölner Zeitschrift für Soziologie und Sozialpsychologie*, *66*(1), 91–115. https://doi.org/10.1007/s11577-014-0272-7

Karell, D., & Freedman, M. (2020). Sociocultural mechanisms of conflict: Combining topic and stochastic actor-oriented models in an analysis of Afghanistan, 1979–2001. *Poetics*, *78*, 101403. https://doi.org/10.1016/j.poetic.2019.101403

Keuschnigg, M., Lovsjö, N., & Hedström, P. (2018). Analytical sociology and computational social science. *Journal of Computational Social Science*, *1*(1), 3–14. https://doi.org/10.1007/s42001-017-0006-5

Keuschnigg, M., Mutgan, S., & Hedström, P. (2019). Urban scaling and the regional divide. *Science Advances*, *5*(1), eaav0042. https://doi.org/10.1126/sciadv.aav0042

King, G., Lam, P., & Roberts, M. E. (2017). Computer-assisted keyword and document set discovery from unstructured text. *American Journal of Political Science*, *61*(4), 971–988. https://doi.org/10.1111/ajps.12291

Kozlowski, A. C., Taddy, M., & Evans, J. A. (2019). The geometry of culture: Analyzing the meanings of class through word embeddings. *American Sociological Review*, *84*(5), 905–949. https://doi.org/10.1177/0003122419877135

Lakon, C. M., Hipp, J. R., Wang, C., Butts, C. T., & Jose, R. (2015). Simulating dynamic network models and adolescent smoking: The impact of varying peer influence and peer selection. *American Journal of Public Health*, *105*(12), 2438–2448. https://doi.org/10.2105/AJPH.2015.302789

Lasswell, H. D., Lerner, D., & de Sola Pool, I. (1952). *The comparative study of symbols: An introduction*. Stanford University Press.

Lazer, D. M. J., Pentland, A., Adamic, L., Aral, S., Barabási, A.-L., Brewer, D., . . . Alstyne, M. V. (2009). Computational social science. *Science, 323*(5915), 721–723. https://doi.org/10.1126/science.1167742

Lazer, D. M. J., Pentland, A., Watts, D. J., Aral, S., Athey, S., Contractor, N., . . . Wagner, C. (2020). Computational social science: Obstacles and opportunities. *Science, 369*(6507), 1060–1062. https://doi.org/10.1126/science.aaz8170

Ledford, H. (2020). How Facebook, Twitter and other data troves are revolutionizing social science. *Nature, 582*(7812), 328–330. https://doi.org/10.1038/d41586-020-01747-1

Legewie, J., & Schaeffer, M. (2016). Contested boundaries: Explaining where ethnocidal diversity provokes neighborhood conflict. *American Journal of Sociology, 122*(1), 125–161. https://doi.org/10.1086/686942

León-Medina, F. J. (2017). Analytical sociology and agent-based modeling: Is generative sufficiency sufficient? *Sociological Theory, 35*(3), 157–178. https://doi.org/10.1177/0735275117725766

Leskovec, J., Backstrom, L., & Kleinberg, J. (2009). Meme-tracking and the dynamics of the news cycle. In J. Elder, F. S. Fogelman, P. Flach, & M. Zaki (Eds.), *Proceedings of the 15th ACM SIGKDD International Conference on Knowledge Discovery and Data Mining* (pp. 497–506). Association for Computing Machinery. https://doi.org/10.1145/1557019.1557077

Lieberson, S., & Lynn, F. B. (2002). Barking up the wrong branch: Scientific alternatives to the current model of sociological science. *Annual Review of Sociology, 28*(1), 1–19. https://doi.org/10.1146/annurev.soc.28.110601.141122

Lindgren, S. (2017). *Digital media and society*. Sage.

Liu, K., & Bearman, P. S. (2015). Focal points, endogenous processes, and exogenous shocks in the autism epidemic. *Sociological Methods & Research, 44*(2), 272–305. https://doi.org/10.1177/0049124112460369

Lorenz-Spreen, P., Mønsted, B. M., Hövel, P., & Lehmann, S. (2019). Accelerating dynamics of collective attention. *Nature Communications, 10*(1), Article 1759. https://doi.org/10.1038/s41467-019-09311-w

Macy, M. W., Deri, S., Ruch, A., & Tong, N. (2019). Opinion cascades and the unpredictability of partisan polarization. *Science Advances, 5*(8), eaax0754. https://doi.org/10.1126/sciadv.aax0754

Macy, M. W., & Tsvetkova, M. (2015). The signal importance of noise. *Sociological Methods & Research, 44*(2), 306–328. https://doi.org/10.1177/0049124113508093

Macy, M. W., & Willer, R. (2002). From factors to actors: Computational sociology and agent-based modeling. *Annual Review of Sociology, 28*(1), 143–166. https://doi.org/10.1146/annurev.soc.28.110601.141117

Manzo, G. (2010). Analytical sociology and its critics. *European Journal of Sociology, 51*(1), 129–170. https://doi.org/10.1017/S0003975610000056

Manzo, G. (2011). Relative deprivation in silico: Agent-based models and causality in analytical sociology. In P. Demeulenaere (Ed.), *Analytical sociology and social mechanisms* (pp. 266–308). Cambridge University Press. https://doi.org/10.1017/CBO9780511921315.014

Manzo, G. (2014). Data, generative models, and mechanisms: More on the principles of analytical sociology. In G. Manzo (Ed.), *Analytical sociology* (pp. 1–52). John Wiley & Sons. https://doi.org/10.1002/9781118762707.ch01

Marshall, B. D. L., & Galea, S. (2015). Formalizing the role of agent-based modeling in causal inference and epidemiology. *American Journal of Epidemiology, 181*(2), 92–99. https://doi.org/10.1093/aje/kwu274

Martin, M. W., & Sell, J. (1979). The role of the experiment in the social sciences. *Sociological Quarterly, 20*(4), 581–590. https://doi.org/10.1111/j.1533-8525.1979.tb01237.x

McFarland, D. A., Lewis, K., & Goldberg, A. (2016). Sociology in the era of big data: The ascent of forensic social science. *American Sociologist, 47*(1), 12–35. https://doi.org/10.1007/s12108-015-9291-8

Michel, J.-B., Shen, Y. K., Aiden, A. P., Veres, A., Gray, M. K., Team, T. G. B., . . . Aiden, E. L. (2011). Quantitative analysis of culture using millions of digitized books. *Science, 331*(6014), 176–182. https://doi.org/10.1126/science.1199644

Mikolov, T., Yih, W., & Zweig, G. (2013). Linguistic regularities in continuous space word representations. In L. Vanderwende, H. Daumé III, & K. Kirchhoff (Eds.), *Proceedings of the 2013 Conference of the North American Chapter of the Association for Computational Linguistics: Human Language Technologies* (pp. 746–751). Association for Computational Linguistics. https://aclanthology.org/N13-1090/

Mitzenmacher, M. (2004). A brief history of generative models for power law and lognormal distributions. *Internet Mathematics, 1*(2), 1385. https://doi.org/10.1080/15427951.2004.10129088

Mohr, J. W., Bail, C. A., Frye, M., Lena, J. C., Lizardo, O., McDonnell, T. E., . . . Wherry, F. F. (2020). *Measuring culture*. Columbia University Press.

Mohr, J. W., Wagner-Pacifici, R., & Breiger, R. L. (2015). Toward a computational hermeneutics. *Big Data & Society*. https://doi.org/10.1177/2053951715613809

Molina, M., & Garip, F. (2019). Machine learning for sociology. *Annual Review of Sociology*, *45*(1), 27–45. https://doi.org/10.1146/annurev-soc-073117-041106

Mordatch, I., & Abbeel, P. (2018). Emergence of grounded compositional language in multi-agent populations. *ArXiv:1703.04908*. http://arxiv.org/abs/1703.04908

Mützel, S. (2015). Facing big data: Making sociology relevant. *Big Data & Society*, *2*(2), Article 2053951715599179. https://doi.org/10.1177/2053951715599179

Nelson, L. K. (2020). Computational grounded theory: A methodological framework. *Sociological Methods & Research*, *49*(1), 3–42. https://doi.org/10.1177/0049124117729703

Pang, B., & Lee, L. (2008). Opinion mining and sentiment analysis. *Foundations and Trends in Information Retrieval*, *2*(1–2), 1–135. https://doi.org/10.1561/1500000011

Parker, J., & Epstein, J. M. (2011). A distributed platform for global-scale agent-based models of disease transmission. *ACM Transactions on Modeling and Computer Simulation*, *22*(1), Article 2 https://doi.org/10.1145/2043635.2043637

Pennebaker, J. W., Boyd, R. L., Jordan, K., & Blackburn, K. (2015). *The development and psychometric properties of LIWC2015*. University of Texas. https://repositories.lib.utexas.edu/handle/2152/31333

Pennington, J., Socher, R., & Manning, C. (2014). GloVe: Global vectors for word representation. In A. Moschitti, B. Pang, & W. Daelemans (Eds.), *Proceedings of the 2014 Conference on Empirical Methods in Natural Language Processing (EMNLP)* (pp. 1532–1543). Association for Computational Linguistics. https://doi.org/10.3115/v1/D14-1162

Ragan, D. T., Osgood, D. W., Ramirez, N. G., Moody, J., & Gest, S. D. (2019). A comparison of peer influence estimates from SIENA stochastic actor-based models and from conventional regression approaches. *Sociological Methods & Research*. https://doi.org/10.1177/0049124119852369

Riffe, D., Lacy, S., Fico, F., Lacy, S., & Fico, F. (2014). *Analyzing media messages: Using quantitative content analysis in research*. Routledge. https://doi.org/10.4324/9780203551691

Ritschard, G., & Studer, M. (Eds.). (2018). *Sequence analysis and related approaches: Innovative methods and applications*. Springer.

Rule, A., Cointet, J.-P., & Bearman, P. S. (2015). Lexical shifts, substantive changes, and continuity in State of the Union discourse, 1790–2014. *Proceedings of the National Academy of Sciences*, *112*(35), 10837–10844. https://doi.org/10.1073/pnas.1512221112

Sakoda, J. M. (1971). The checkerboard model of social interaction. *Journal of Mathematical Sociology*, *1*(1), 119–132. https://doi.org/10.1080/0022250X.1971.9989791

Salganik, M. J. (2018). *Bit by bit: Social research in the digital age*. Princeton University Press.

Salganik, M. J., Dodds, P. S., & Watts, D. J. (2006). Experimental study of inequality and unpredictability in an artificial cultural market. *Science*, *311*(5762), 854–856. https://doi.org/10.1126/science.1121066

Salganik, M. J., Lundberg, I., Kindel, A. T., Ahearn, C. E., Al-Ghoneim, K., Almaatouq, A., . . . McLanahan, S. (2020). Measuring the predictability of life outcomes with a scientific mass collaboration. *Proceedings of the National Academy of Sciences*, *117*(15), 8398–8403. https://doi.org/10.1073/pnas.1915006117

Salganik, M. J., & Watts, D. J. (2009). Web-based experiments for the study of collective social dynamics in cultural markets. *Topics in Cognitive Science*, *1*(3), 439–468. https://doi.org/10.1111/j.1756-8765.2009.01030.x

Schaefer, D. R., adams, jimi, & Haas, S. A. (2013). Social networks and smoking: Exploring the effects of peer influence and smoker popularity through simulations. *Health Education & Behavior*, *40*(1_suppl), 24S–32S. https://doi.org/10.1177/1090198113493091

Schaub, M., Gereke, J., & Baldassarri, D. (2020). Does poverty undermine cooperation in multiethnic settings? Evidence from a cooperative investment experiment. *Journal of Experimental Political Science*, *7*(1), 72–74. https://doi.org/10.1017/XPS.2019.19

Schelling, T. C. (1971). Dynamic models of segregation. *Journal of Mathematical Sociology*, *1*(2), 143–186. https://doi.org/10.1080/0022250X.1971.9989794

Schelling, T. C. (1978). *Micromotives and macrobehavior*. W. W. Norton & Company.

Shalizi, C. R., & Thomas, A. C. (2011). Homophily and contagion are generically confounded in observational social network studies. *Sociological Methods & Research*, *40*(2), 211–239. https://doi.org/10.1177/0049124111404820

Shi, Y., Mast, K., Weber, I., Kellum, A., & Macy, M. (2017). Cultural fault lines and political polarization. In P. Fox, D. McGuinness, L. Poirier, P. Boldi, & K. Kinder-Kurlanda (Eds.), *Proceedings of the 2017*

ACM on Web Science Conference (pp. 213–217). Association for Computing Machinery. https://doi.org/10.1145/3091478.3091520

Snijders, T. A. B. (2001). The statistical evaluation of social network dynamics. *Sociological Methodology*, *31*(1), 361–395. https://doi.org/10.1111/0081-1750.00099

Snijders, T. A. B., & Steglich, C. (2013). Representing micro–macro linkages by actor-based dynamic network models: *Sociological Methods & Research*, *44*(2), 222–271. https://doi.org/10.1177/0049124113494573

Snijders, T. A. B., van de Bunt, G. G., & Steglich, C. (2010). Introduction to stochastic actor-based models for network dynamics. *Social Networks*, *32*(1), 44–60. https://doi.org/10.1016/j.socnet.2009.02.004

Sørensen, A. B. (1998). Theoretical mechanisms and the empirical study of social processes. In P. Hedström & R. Swedberg (Eds.), *Social mechanisms: An analytical approach to social theory* (pp. 238–266). Cambridge University Press. https://doi.org/10.1017/CBO9780511663901.010

Stadtfeld, C. (2018). The micro–macro link in social networks. In *Emerging trends in the social and behavioral sciences* (pp. 1–15). John Wiley & Sons, Inc. https://doi.org/10.1002/9781118900772.etrds0463

Steglich, C., Snijders, T. A. B., & Pearson, M. (2010). Dynamic networks and behavior: Separating selection from influence. *Sociological Methodology*, *40*(1), 329–393. https://doi.org/10.1111/j.1467-9531.2010.01225.x

Stein, J., Keuschnigg, M., & van de Rijt, A. (2021). *Network segregation and the propagation of misinformation* (Working Paper) Florence: European University Institute.

Stuart, E. A. (2010). Matching methods for causal inference: A review and a look forward. *Statistical Science*, *25*(1), 1–21. https://doi.org/10.1214/09-STS313

Stumpf, M. P. H., & Porter, M. A. (2012). Critical truths about power laws. *Science*, *335*(6069), 665–666. https://doi.org/10.1126/science.1216142

Subrahmanian, V. S., & Kumar, S. (2017). Predicting human behavior: The next frontiers. *Science*, *355*(6324), 489–489. https://doi.org/10.1126/science.aam7032

Udehn, L. (2002). *Methodological individualism: Background, history and meaning*. Routledge.

Waddell, P. (2002). UrbanSim: Modeling urban development for land use, transportation, and environmental planning. *Journal of the American Planning Association*, *68*(3), 297–314. https://doi.org/10.1080/01944360208976274

Watts, D. J. (2013). Computational social science: Exciting progress and future directions. *The Bridge: Linking Engineering and Society*, *43*(4). https://nae.edu/106118/Computational-Social-Science-Exciting-Progress-and-Future-Directions

Watts, D. J. (2014). Common sense and sociological explanations. *American Journal of Sociology*, *120*(2), 313–351. https://doi.org/10.1086/678271

Wolbring, T. (2020). The digital revolution in the social sciences: Five theses about big data and other recent methodological innovations from an analytical sociologist. *Soziale Welt, Special Issue*, *23*, 52–64.

Xie, Y., & Zhou, X. (2012). Modeling individual-level heterogeneity in racial residential segregation. *Proceedings of the National Academy of Sciences*, *109*(29), 11646–11651. https://doi.org/10.1073/pnas.1202218109

Young, H. P. (2009). Innovation diffusion in heterogeneous populations: Contagion, social influence, and social learning. *American Economic Review*, *99*(5), 1899–1924. https://doi.org/10.1257/aer.99.5.1899

Zhang, H., & Vorobeychik, Y. (2019). Empirically grounded agent-based models of innovation diffusion: A critical review. *Artificial Intelligence Review*, *52*(1), 707–741. https://doi.org/10.1007/s10462-017-9577-z

4

COMPUTATIONAL COGNITIVE MODELING IN THE SOCIAL SCIENCES

Holger Schultheis

There has been a growing awareness in the social sciences that a more accurate and complete understanding of social processes may profit from a deeper understanding of the individuals involved in the social processes (e.g., Jager, 2017; Palmer & Smith, 2014). This chapter is devoted to a method for providing such a deeper understanding of individuals, which seems particularly useful for research in the computational social sciences: computational cognitive modeling. In the following, I first provide an overview of computational cognitive modeling and models before elaborating on the merits of this method for the computational social sciences.

Computational cognitive modeling. . .

A cognitive model is a formalization of information representation and processing in the human mind. If this model is realized as an executable program in a precisely specified computer language, it is called a *computational cognitive model*.

Such models have proven a useful means for investigating human cognition and behavior. Implementing assumptions about human information processing as executable computer programs is associated with a number of advantages for theorizing in the cognitive sciences (Cooper, 2002; Sun, 2008a). First, the computational implementation makes assumptions explicit, which allows one to more easily and clearly communicate these assumptions. Second, the need to explicitly and in detail specify the workings of the model helps uncover areas in which (too) little is known about human cognition – modeling highlights promising areas for further research. Third, computational models facilitate a formal analysis of one's assumptions and, fourth, also allow simulating human behavior that arises from these assumptions. Comparing a model's predictions of human behavior to the actually observed behavior provides evidence regarding the model's quality as well as the possibility to explore the importance and impact of specific assumptions realized in the model.

Note that computational cognitive models are commonly modeling circumscribed cognitive abilities and skills such as decision-making (in moral judgment) or spatial information processing (during wayfinding and navigation), for example. Models are also traditionally focused on individual cognition and behavior in the sense that little research investigates cognitive skills in the scope of interactions between individuals. Within this focus on specific abilities of individuals, computational cognitive models aim to uncover the general workings of the human mind;

DOI: 10.4324/9781003024583-5

that is, a model is meant to formalize representations and mechanisms that are common to (almost) all humans.

The remainder of this section is devoted to a more detailed discussion of the nature of these models and the process of creating them. Figure 4.1 illustrates four major steps commonly involved in computational cognitive modeling and their relation to each other. The process starts with conceptualizations of the representations and processes assumed to underlie the modeled cognitive skill. Based on these conceptualizations, a concrete model is implemented, run to generate model behavior, and finally evaluated. Based on the evaluation results, the cycle may start anew with a re-consideration and re-conceptualization of the assumed representations and processes. Each of the four steps will be detailed in turn in the following.

Conceptualize mechanisms

The first step involves developing and conceptualizing one's assumptions about the representations and processes, that is, the *mechanisms*, that give rise to the cognitive ability under investigation. There are no established "standard" methods, recipes, or algorithms for this step; it is left to the modeler what mechanisms are assumed and on which basis. Assumptions may, for example, be derived from introspection or the modeler's intuition or be based on existing

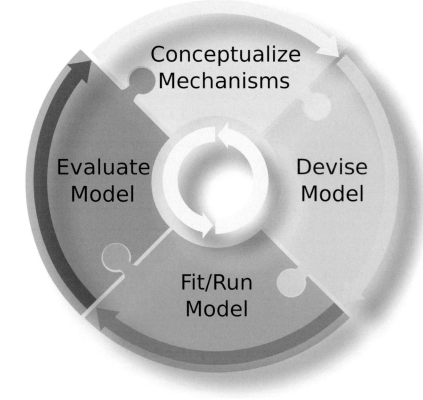

Figure 4.1 Four main steps of computational cognitive modeling

theorizing related to the ability. Often conceptualization will result from a mix of these and further influences.

Devise model

The second step involves realizing a suitable instantiation of the conceptualized mechanisms as an executable computational model. This means first devising the model and then implementing it in a programming language of one's choice. There are a number of different ways of devising models that have been distinguished in cognitive modeling research. I will call these different ways *modeling paradigms*. Different paradigms take different assumptions on how to best view and formalize human cognitive mechanisms. Existing modeling work suggests that each paradigm has a specific strength in readily lending itself to successfully model certain cognitive abilities but not others. Accordingly, each of the paradigms can be conceived as a different window on the human mind, and it currently seems that all these different windows may be needed to gain a deeper understanding of the human mind in its entirety. The most commonly employed modeling paradigms are the symbolic, the connectionist, the dynamic, the Bayesian, and the architectural paradigms.

Symbolic. One basic building block of a symbolic model are propositions, also called *symbols*. These symbols are formal objects that represent knowledge of facts, which may be expressed in natural language. For example, the symbol smarter (Anna, John) may represent the fact that "Anna is smarter than John". Each symbol constitutes a piece of knowledge, and the collection of symbols in a symbolic model represents the factual knowledge of the modeled individual. The second basic building block are means, often called *rules*, for manipulating symbols (creating new symbols, modifying existing symbols, etc.), and application of the rules changes the set of symbols entertained in the model. Typical representatives of symbolic models are production system models (Davis & King, 1985) and formal logic models (Bringsjord, 2008). Importantly, the symbolic modeling paradigm assumes that human cognition can completely and accurately be described as representation and manipulation of symbols (Newell & Simon, 1976). Accordingly, the symbolic paradigm posits that it is possible to understand and model human cognition without taking into account the properties of the hardware from which cognition arises (i.e., the brain).

Connectionist. The connectionist paradigm is motivated by the aim to more closely take the structure and workings of the brain into account than symbolic models (McClelland & Cleeremans, 2009). Connectionist models comprise a set of simple computing units that are connected to each other by weighted connections. At each point in time, each unit has an activation value, and through the weighted connections, the activation value of one unit influences and is influenced by the activation values of other units. Knowledge is represented by patterns of activations, and this knowledge is processed by the units' mutual influence on each other's activations. A fact such as "Anna is smarter than John" is usually represented by an activation pattern across several units instead of a single entity of representation such as a symbol. In particular, individual unit activation usually does not represent anything that is easily interpreted; it represents only part of a symbol (e.g., only part of the proposition "Anna is smarter than John"). Therefore, connectionist models have also been called *subsymbolic models*.

Dynamic. The assumption underlying the dynamic paradigm is that human cognition and behavior instantiate and can be understood as (several) dynamic systems (van Gelder, 1998). A system is a collection of interdependent variables, where each variable represents aspects relevant to the modeled cognitive ability (e.g., memory for the location of a previously perceived stimulus). The variables are interdependent, because change in one variable depends on the other variables and vice versa. The state of a system is the value of its variables at a certain point in time. What renders the system dynamic is that the system's behavior is governed by a quantitative relationship between change in state, elapsed time, and current state. This relationship is expressed in the form of ordinary or stochastic differential equations. Although it shares some ideas with the symbolic (system variables can be symbolic in representing interpretable entities) and the connectionist paradigm (multiple variables in quantitative mutual interaction), the dynamic paradigm provides its own view on human cognition that puts particular emphasis on the following aspects: (a) change of the system vs. the state of the system, (b) the timing of cognition and behavior, and (c) processes are conceived as ongoing (not adopting the traditional input-processing-output model).

Bayesian. The Bayesian paradigm is associated with two main assumptions. The first assumption maintains that uncertainty is at the core of most, if not all, cognitive abilities. In language, for example, uncertainty arises and needs to be addressed on phonological (e.g., extracting words from noisy auditory streams), lexical (e.g., the word "bank"), syntactic, and semantic (e.g., interpretation of the sentence "Visiting relatives can be boring") levels. Accordingly, a major aspect of (human) cognition consists of successfully addressing and handling such uncertainties. The second assumption maintains that the cognitive mechanisms enabling humans to cope with these uncertainties can appropriately and accurately be formalized as Bayesian probabilistic inference (Chater, Oaksford, Hahn, & Heit, 2010; Griffiths, Kemp, & Tenenbaum, 2008). One corollary of these assumptions is that humans are rational Bayesian agents within the constraints of their cognitive resources (Lieder & Griffiths, 2020): Human cognition and behavior is governed by the most probable Bayesian inference and the actions that have the highest Bayesian probability of success given the available data. In this sense, the Bayesian paradigm assumes that human cognition and behavior are optimal.

Architectures. Starting with Newell (1973), some researchers have argued that it is problematic to try to achieve a comprehensive understanding of human cognition by building isolated computational models. Instead of building models in isolation, all models should be realized within the same framework, and this framework has been termed a *cognitive architecture*. Specifically, an architecture is meant to formalize the fixed and invariant mechanisms and structures of human cognition, that is, those mechanisms and structures that permeate all of human cognition. To model a particular cognitive ability still requires adding ability-specific knowledge to the architecture, but all models are realized within the same architecture by drawing on the same mechanisms and structures that are provided by the architecture. Two popular and successful architectures are adaptive control of thought–rational (ACT-R, Anderson, 2007) and Soar (Laird, 2012).

For the sake of exposition, the paradigms have been described as separate categories. This may raise the impression that a model follows either one or the other paradigm, but, in fact, many models are hybrid models that combine ideas and techniques from several paradigms. For example, connectionist and symbolic paradigms have often been combined to draw on the complementary advantages of both paradigms.

Run/fit model

After the model has been devised, it can be run by executing the computer program that implements it. This step is less trivial than it may seem, because most models have one or more so-called *free parameters*, which influence model behavior: The model may behave quite differently depending on how these parameters are set. Such parameters are "free" in the sense that there is no a-priori basis for fixing the value of the parameters, though there may be a range of theoretically reasonable values. The two major reasons for free parameters are (a) not enough is known about human cognition to set the parameter value or (b) the parameter is associated with an aspect of human cognition that is known to vary between individuals. For example, in a model addressing human working memory, memory capacity (how much information can be maintained at a time) may be a free parameter, because previous research suggests that different people have different capacities.

Because different parameter settings can lead to quite different model behavior, the question arises which parameter values to employ for running the model and investigating its behavior. The common procedure in computational cognitive modeling is to investigate the model's behavior in its best possible parameterization, at which the model's behavior is as similar as possible to human behavior. Finding the best possible parameterization is called *fitting* the model. Model fitting is an optimization problem and thus can, in principle, be addressed by methods developed in research on optimization (e.g., Muñoz, Sun, Kirley, & Halgamuge, 2015). Popular methods in cognitive modeling have been grid search, in which all possible parameter values lying on an equidistant grid in parameter space are tested and the best selected, and the Nelder-Mead method (Nelder & Mead, 1965). For more complex models, whose behavior is governed by non-determinism and non-linearities, more complex optimization methods such as Markov Chain-Monte Carlo with simulated annealing (Madras, 2002) may be required and have been applied.

The outcome of fitting and running the model is both a set of optimal parameter values and the model's behavior with this optimal parameter set.

Evaluate

A straightforward means to assess the quality of a model is to use the result of the run/fit step: If the model's behavior does not mirror human behavior well despite optimized parameters, this raises serious doubt about the validity of the model. Accordingly, a good fit of the model's behavior to human behavior is a necessary requirement to consider the model a good model. A good fit is, however, not a sufficient requirement. Even if the model fits well, further considerations are important to judge its value. One important criterion is *plausibility*, the extent to which the assumptions realized in the model are consistent with established findings. A good model should also be *falsifiable*; that is, potential observations proving the model wrong should exist. A third criterion is *interpretability*, which has sometimes been termed the "no magic doctrine". It needs to be clear how (good) model performance comes about, that the components of the model are understandable and linked to known processes.

There is a further reason that renders the interpretation of a model's good fit problematic (Roberts & Pashler, 2000). Even if a model is falsifiable, interpretable, and plausible, a good fit may be a misleading indicator of the model's ability to explain human behavior (Pitt & Myung, 2002). The reason is that human behavior and observations thereof are noisy. For example, if your task is to press a button as quickly as possible as soon as you perceive a certain stimulus and you repeat the task, your time to respond will vary across the different button presses. These (small) variations are considered noise, because they are assumed not to be related to the cognitive mechanisms under investigation (the mechanisms that allow you to press the button when perceiving the stimulus). Put differently, observed human behavior is assumed to be the combination of effects related to the mechanisms under investigation and noise. Ideally, the model should capture the relevant mechanisms but not the noise. However, simply considering how well a model fits observed data does not indicate to what extent the good fit arises from a good fit to the relevant mechanisms or from a good fit to the noise. In response to this problem, a number of methods have been proposed that aim to assess how well a model accounts only for the relevant mechanisms. These methods are thought to measure model *generalizability*, because a model will only generalize well to new data (from new situations) if it captures the mechanisms and not the noise.

One class of methods is simulation based, using repeated and extensive model fits/runs to gauge a model's generalizability. Among these are the cross-fitting method (Wagenmakers, Ratcliff, Gomez, & Iverson, 2004), parameter-space-partitioning (Pitt, Kim, Navarro, & Myung, 2006), model flexibility analysis (Veksler, Myers, & Gluck, 2015), and the simple hold out (Schultheis, Singhaniya, & Chaplot, 2013). Other methods such as the minimum description length (Grünwald, 2000) and the Bayes factor (Kass & Raftery, 1995) are theory-based but originally only applicable for a small subclass of models (models that can be described in terms of probability density functions). More recently, simulation- and theory-based methods have been combined in an approach called *approximate Bayesian computation* (Palestro, Sederberg, Osth, Van Zandt, & Turner, 2018) that allows extending the use of theory-based evaluation methods to models that are not described in terms of probability density functions.

If the evaluation provides evidence for the merit of the model, the modeling process may be terminated after this step. If the evaluation reveals problems with the model, revision or redesign of the model may be approached. Depending on the nature of the problems with the model, revision may begin at any of the previous three steps.

Cross-talk and feedback

The description so far has painted a somewhat idealized picture of the modeling process. Neither are the different steps as separate as it may seem, nor does feedback influence model development only after evaluation is complete. Often aspects of subsequent steps will influence work during the current step. For example, conceptualizing the mechanisms (first step) may be influenced by the considerations of how (and in which paradigm) the model would be devised (second step). Sometimes the two first steps may actually proceed in parallel and in mutual interaction such that ideas on mechanisms influence implementational choices which in turn lead to new ideas about possible mechanisms. Likewise, choice of fitting techniques and procedures (step 3) may be affected by the desired means of evaluation (step 4) and, generally, fitting and evaluation are closely intertwined (e.g., Kangasrääsiö, Jokinen, Oulasvirta, Howes, & Kaski, in press).

. . . in the social sciences

As detailed in the previous section, computational cognitive models are commonly devoted to capturing the general mechanisms underlying *individual* cognition, not societal phenomena. This may raise the question to what extent computational cognitive models are of relevance to the social sciences: Why should social scientists be interested in such models? In this section, I will discuss the relation between computational cognitive modeling and (computational) social science and will argue for the advantages of combining both.

The first thing to note is that societal phenomena can often be conceived as arising from or being substantially influenced by the joint and interactive behavior of individuals. For example, Palmer and Smith (2014) have argued that a proper understanding of climate change dynamics requires factoring in the behavior of individuals. Similarly, risk and crisis management has been shown to profit from considering individuals' behavior (Jumadi, Malleson, Carver, & Quincey, 2020). Consequently, to understand societal phenomena, it can be helpful to consider the involved individuals and their interactions.

One approach to do this is to use a rather abstract notion of the individual. In the social force model (Helbing & Molnár, 1995), for instance, movement of crowds is assumed to (partly) rely on attracting and repelling forces between individuals. No particular assumptions about the individuals are made except for their mutual influence on each other. The forces working between the individuals are assumed to arise from some process at work within each individual, but these processes are not spelled out; the social force model abstracts away from them. Another, less abstracting, approach to consider individuals is by detailing their inner processes that are assumed to give rise to the social phenomena under investigation. Regarding the movement of crowds, for example, this may involve explicating assumptions about which and how inner processes influence the individuals' motions (see later for an example). Including assumptions about individuals' inner processes in social science theorizing seems necessary whenever the nature and dynamics of social processes under investigation arise from individual behavior in a way that cannot or cannot readily be captured on the macro level that abstracts from inner processes of individuals. Specifically, abstraction can work well when the properties of the individuals can be assumed to be constant: If behavior is not substantially different for different individuals and behavior of single individuals does not change substantially over time, it is reasonable to neglect inner processes and to treat individuals as abstract parts/entities of a larger system. With increasing difference between individuals, changes within individuals and, in particular, if one assumes that inner processes mediate a non-trivial interaction between changes of individuals' behavior and social processes, a more detailed consideration of the inner processes become more important (Gilbert, 2005; Jager, 2017; Sun, 2006b). For example, taking into account inner processes is crucial when one wants to investigate how the behavior of (groups of) people may be changed. An abstracted macro-level consideration may reveal how the individual behavior needs to change to yield the desired macro-level phenomena, but it provides no insight on what is required to bring about the desired change in the individual(s). To identify the most promising course of action to change people's behavior, it is necessary to consider how the effect of one's actions is mediated by the inner processes of individuals. Consequently, consideration of inner processes can be of high applied relevance in guiding decisions of governments and policy makers, for instance.

The success of including assumptions on individuals' inner processes obviously depends on the validity of these assumptions, and this is where computational cognitive models can play an important role. Given that models are means for both validating such assumptions and formalizing validated assumptions, they offer a number of merits, which will be detailed in the following.

Merits of cognitive modeling

Computational cognitive modeling has at least three merits for social science research that wants to take into account inner processes of individuals. First, existing cognitive models constitute a hoard of precisely specified insights about how the human mind works. If social scientists are looking for validated assumptions about human individual cognition, computational models and the associated theorizing provide a rich source, spanning a wide variety of cognitive abilities, to draw from. Second, as explained previously, computational modeling is a useful tool to investigate and validate one's hypotheses about cognitive processes. If existing work should not provide the right or all necessary information on the desired cognitive processes, modeling can help to investigate and validate one's intuitions before employing them to examine social processes. Third, computational cognitive models naturally lend themselves to extend social simulation with a computational and executable formalization of individuals' inner processes. Given this handbook's focus on computational social science, the remainder of this section discusses this last advantage in more detail.

Social Simulation. This chapter can only provide a rough characterization of social simulation; the reader is referred to Chapter 14 (Vol. 1) as well as 16 and 17 (Vol. 2) of this handbook for a more in-depth treatment on agent-based social simulation. In a nutshell, *social simulation* aims to explore and understand social processes by means of computer simulation: As cognitive models formalize individual cognition in executable form, social simulation formalizes social processes in executable form. To the extent that social simulation involves considering individuals' inner processes, a computational formalization of these processes is required.

In the remainder of this section, I will highlight the merits of computational cognitive modeling in social simulation. Using selected examples of previous work, I will explain that and how (a) modeling can improve explanation and understanding of group behavior, (b) modeling can be helpful for understanding social processes, and (c) it can be advantageous to "plug" existing cognitive models into social simulation.

Group Behavior. Kielar and Borrmann (2016) investigate the behavior of pedestrian groups and, in particular, how pedestrians' time within a certain environment (e.g., a transportation hub, a job fair) is distributed across different locations within this environment. The simulation used to examine this issue is a formalization of the individual pedestrian with three main components. The strategic component determines which location the individual visits. The tactical component, which is based on Dijkstra's algorithm (1959), determines the route to the chosen location. The operational component realizes the individual's behavior en route and in coordination with other pedestrians using a social force approach (see previously). This work is of interest for the current considerations for two main reasons: First, for the strategic component, Kielar and Borrmann (2016) develop a computational cognitive model, which is strongly rooted in previous experimental and computational work in the cognitive sciences. Specifically, the model formalizes the individual pedestrian's interest for the different locations in the environment and how this interest changes over time and in response to actions of the individual (e.g., visiting a certain location). Second, Kielar and Borrmann (2016) explicitly evaluate the merit of the cognitive model by comparing the predictive performance of two pedestrian simulations differing only in the strategic component: One simulation includes the cognitive model, whereas the other employs a not cognitively motivated origin-destination matrix. The simulations revealed that inclusion of the cognitive model in the strategic component led to considerably more accurate prediction of pedestrian behavior during a student career fair. Accordingly, the study by Kielar and Borrmann (2016) provides evidence for the advantages of including computational cognitive models in simulations of group behavior.

Social Processes. Note that in the pedestrian simulation, the cognitive model does not address social aspects. The model formalizes how an individual's interest for different locations rises and falls over time. Although the overall group behavior certainly depends on this individual interest in locations, influences of interactions between individuals seem only to be taken into account in the operational component by a social force model and, thus, the cognitive model itself does not address social aspects. Against this background, it seems interesting to consider to what extent cognitive models of social cognition can contribute to social simulation. An architecture that takes social cognition into account is the Consumat approach (Jager, Janssen, De Vries, De Greef, & Vlek, 2000). Besides other components such as needs and abilities of individuals, the Consumat approach assumes that individual decision-making constitutes a crucial influence on social processes. Depending on an individual's satisfaction and informational uncertainty, decision-making is modeled as being of one of four types: (a) *repetition* of previous decisions, when uncertainty is low and satisfaction is high; (b) *imitation* of individuals in one's social network, when both uncertainty and satisfaction are high; (c) *deliberation* of options, when both uncertainty and satisfaction are low; and (d) *inquiring* about options in one's social network, when uncertainty is high and satisfaction is low. Consequently, in contrast to the pedestrian simulation considered previously, the individual decision-making model in the Consumat approach takes into account social cognition and processes. Social simulations building on the Consumat approach have successfully been applied in a number of domains (Schaat, Jager, & Dickert, 2017). Work by Kangur, Jager, Verbrugge, and Bockarjova (2017), for example, has employed the Consumat architecture to investigate determinants of the diffusion of electric cars. Roughly 3000 modeled individuals were initialized based on a representative sample comprising the same number of Dutch car owners. Behavior of these individuals was simulated over 2 years in weekly cycles with respect to which cars are used and bought. The results of this simulation were compared with the actual usage and market data in the Netherlands. Simulation outcomes corresponded well to the observed data, thus supporting the validity of the model. The validated model was then employed to examine how certain measures (e.g., taxing fuel cars, subsidizing electric cars, expanding charging networks) influence diffusion of electric cars. This revealed a number of unexpected and important relations between measures and adoption of electric cars (e.g., that joint measures can be overadditive in their effect).

The two examples considered so far indicate that modeling of individual cognition can improve the accuracy and utility of social simulation both when social aspects are not and when they are taken into account in the cognitive models. The two example simulations also both develop their own computational cognitive models. The models are motivated from previous work in the cognitive sciences but developed particularly for the social simulation in which they are employed. This has been argued to be necessary because of the lack and vagueness of formalization of relevant theorizing (e.g., Jager, 2017). At the same time, the use of simulation-specific computational cognitive models has also been deemed problematic (Balke & Gilbert, 2014; Conte & Giardini, 2016; Sun, 2009). If different social simulations include different cognitive models on similar cognitive abilities and skills such as decision-making, it is questionable whether all of them can be assumed to accurately capture the modeled abilities. Furthermore, given the effort that is required to develop and evaluate computational cognitive models (see earlier), it is not immediately clear that models developed ad hoc for social simulations will yield very accurate and valid accounts of the modeled abilities. The more the outcome of the social simulation depends on the accuracy of the employed cognitive model, the more desirable it is that the model have high validity.

Existing Cognitive Models. A promising way to avoid the problems of ad-hoc models in social simulation is to employ established computational cognitive models instead. As described previously, cognitive models aim at formalizing the structures and processes underlying the modeled ability generally: Considerable emphasis in evaluating the models is put on the model's ability to apply across individuals and to generalize well to new situations. Given that the models are also already specified in executable form, it should be comparatively easy to include them in one's social simulation; they certainly are precisely enough formalized to do so. Even if interfacing the model and the social simulation may not be trivial, it seems preferable to ad-hoc models, because (a) an established model promises higher validity and (b) interfacing seems more feasible than developing a cognitive model of comparable validity from scratch. The merit of employing an established cognitive model is illustrated by the work of Wolf, Schröder, Neumann, and de Haan (2015). The design and purpose of this simulation were similar to the one of Kangur et al. (2017). By modeling individual consumers and their interaction, adoption of electric vehicles and its determinants were investigated. Individual models were parameterized and validated based on survey data of a representative sample of 675 citizens of Berlin, Germany. In contrast to Kangur et al. (2017), however, Wolf et al. (2015) employ an established cognitive model, the HOTCO model (Thagard, 2006), to formalize the decision-making of individuals. In social simulations including this model, different measures meant to influence adoption of electric vehicles were then investigated with respect to their effectiveness. These simulations revealed, among others, that certain measures will be more effective generally, while the effectiveness of particular measures can be quite different for different (types of) individuals. Accordingly, this work and the work of Kangur et al. (2017) highlight the utility of cognitive modeling-based social simulation in guiding policy decisions.

Social simulation including existing models seems to be the exception; most simulations develop their own cognitive model. This is particularly surprising with respect to cognitive modeling of and the role of decision-making in social simulation. Decision-making is among the most important abilities that need to be and are explicitly modeled in social simulations that consider inner processes of individuals (Balke & Gilbert, 2014; Schlüter et al., 2017). At the same time, individual decision-making has been a topic of intense debate and research for decades in the cognitive sciences (e.g., Brown & Heathcote, 2008; Busemeyer & Wang, 2018; Ratcliff, Smith, Brown, & McKoon, 2016; Usher & McClelland, 2001), with sequential sampling models emerging as an accurate general characterization of human decision-making processes (Busemeyer, Gluth, Rieskamp, & Turner, 2019). It is not clear why there has been so little transfer of cognitive modeling results to social simulation research. One reason may be that cognitive modeling work tends to focus on individuals and not on groups of people in a social context. However, the proposed decision-making mechanisms are general enough to be applicable to social processes: There is no in-principle problem to include social factors, assumed to drive decisions, in the models. It seems that the potential of integrating established computational cognitive models in social simulation has not been fully exploited so far.

Merits for cognitive modeling

Up to this point, the exposition has focused on the advantages that computational cognitive modeling offers to the (computational) social sciences and, in particular, social simulation. In fact, including cognitive models in social simulation is not only beneficial for the latter but also holds merit for the former. Inclusion of models in social simulations can help to counterbalance the usual focus on individual cognition present in current modeling work (Schröder & Wolf, 2017; Sun, 2009). Although such focus can be helpful to isolate, pinpoint, and understand selected cognitive abilities, it also neglects that these abilities are embedded in and express themselves in social interactions and networks. Accordingly, the extent to which a model performs well in the scope of rich social interactions should be considered another quality criterion of models: If the model also yields reasonable behavior and predictions when embedded in social networks, this provides additional evidence for the validity of the model. As models lend themselves to easily equip social simulations with individual cognition, social simulations lend themselves to easily examining the suitability of a computational cognitive model when embedded in social interactions. Indeed, agent-based social simulation has recently been argued to constitute a instrumental tool for tuning model parameters, validating model predictions, and fostering model development (Madsen, Bailey, Carrella, & Koralus, 2019). Consequently, computational cognitive modeling and social simulation constitute a mutually beneficial pair of techniques that, if employed jointly, can shed light on both cognitive abilities of individuals and social processes and phenomena.

Conclusion and further reading

Computational cognitive modeling with its focus on individual cognitive processes and computational social science with its focus on groups of individuals and related social processes seem to address separate topics. Closer inspection, however, reveals the complementary nature of the two research fields and the connections between them. While social processes and social phenomena ultimately depend on individual cognition and behavior, individuals' cognition can most comprehensively be understood in the context of the social interactions and networks in which it normally expresses itself. Consequently, only the joint consideration of cognitive and social processes will lead to a more complete and accurate understanding of the mechanisms underlying both cognitive and social phenomena.

Integrating existing computational cognitive models into social simulations seems like a particularly promising approach to achieve this, because, from a practical point of view, their respective computational realization renders their combination comparatively easy and, from a theoretical perspective, it allows combining established and well-validated insights from both fields. It seems as if this potential has so far not been exploited to a desirable extent. Future research in computational cognitive modeling and computational social science would profit from a closer interaction facilitating exchange between the fields by raising mutual awareness of both existing methodologies and results.

This chapter can only provide a brief summary of computational cognitive modeling and its possible role in computational social science. For more in-depth discussions on these topics, the reader is referred to the following books and collections: Cooper (2002), Farrell and Lewandowsky (2018), and Sun (2008b) provide an excellent overview of modeling methodology as well as the theoretical underpinnings and role of modeling in the cognitive sciences. The collections of Sun (2006a) and Sun (2011) assemble a comprehensive set of contributions discussing the interfaces between and mutual merits of computational cognitive and social science for each other.

References

Anderson, J. R. (2007). *How can the human mind occur in the physical universe?* Oxford University Press.

Balke, T., & Gilbert, N. (2014). How do agents make decisions? A survey. *Journal of Artificial Societies and Social Simulation, 17*(4), 13. doi:10.18564/jasss.2687

Bringsjord, S. (2008). Declarative/logic-based cognitive modeling. In R. Sun (Ed.), *The Cambridge handbook of computational psychology*. Cambridge University Press.

Brown, S. D., & Heathcote, A. (2008). The simplest complete model of choice response time: Linear ballistic accumulation. *Cognitive Psychology, 57*(3), 153–178. doi:10.1016/j.cogpsych.2007.12.002

Busemeyer, J. R., Gluth, S., Rieskamp, J., & Turner, B. M. (2019). Cognitive and neural bases of multi-attribute, multi-alternative, value-based decisions. *Trends in Cognitive Sciences, 23*, 251–263. doi:10.1016/j.tics.2018.12.003

Busemeyer, J. R., & Wang, Z. (2018). Hilbert space multidimensional theory. *Psychological Review, 125*(4), 572–591. doi:10.1037/rev0000106

Chater, N., Oaksford, M., Hahn, U., & Heit, E. (2010). Bayesian models of cognition. *WIREs Cognitive Science, 1*(6), 811–823. doi:10.1002/wcs.79

Conte, R., & Giardini, F. (2016). Towards computational and behavioral social science. *European Psychologist, 21*(2), 131–140. doi:10.1027/1016-9040/a000257

Cooper, R. P. (2002). *Modelling high-level cognitive processes*. Lawrence Erlbaum Associates Publishers.

Davis, R., & King, J. J. (1985). The origin of rule-based systems in AI. In B. G. Buchanan & E. H. Shortliffe (Eds.), *Rule-based expert systems*. Addison-Wesley.

Dijkstra, E. W. (1959). A note on two problems in connexion with graphs. *Numerische Mathematik, 1*, 269–271. doi:10.1007/BF01386390

Farrell, S., & Lewandowsky, S. (2018). *Computational modeling of cognition and behavior.* Cambridge University Press. doi:10.1017/CBO9781316272503

Gilbert, N. (2005). When does social simulation need cognitive models? In R. Sun (Ed.), *Cognition and multi-agent interaction: From cognitive modeling to social simulation* (pp. 428–432). Cambridge University Press. doi:10.1017/CBO9780511610721.020

Griffiths, T. L., Kemp, C., & Tenenbaum, J. B. (2008). Bayesian models of cognition. In R. Sun (Ed.), *The Cambridge handbook of computational psychology.* Cambridge University Press.

Grünwald, P. (2000). Model selection based on minimum description length. *Journal of Mathematical Psychology, 44*(1), 133–152. doi:10.1006/jmps.1999.1280

Helbing, D., & Molnár, P. (1995). Social force model for pedestrian dynamics. *Physical Review E, 51*(5), 4282–4286. doi:10.1103/PhysRevE.51.4282

Jager, W. (2017). Enhancing the realism of simulation (EROS): On implementing and developing psychological theory in social simulation. *Journal of Artificial Societies and Social Simulation, 20*(3). doi:10.18564/jasss.3522

Jager, W., Janssen, M., De Vries, H., De Greef, J., & Vlek, C. (2000). Behaviour in commons dilemmas: *Homo economicus* and *Homo psychologicus* in an ecological-economic model. *Ecological Economics, 35*(3), 357–379. doi:10.1016/S0921-8009(00)00220-2

Jumadi, J., Malleson, N., Carver, S., & Quincey, D. (2020). Estimating spatio-temporal risks from volcanic eruptions using an agent-based model. *Journal of Artificial Societies and Social Simulation, 23*(2). doi:10.18564/jasss.4241

Kangasrääsiö, A., Jokinen, J. P. P., Oulasvirta, A., Howes, A., & Kaski, S. (in press). Parameter inference for computational cognitive models with approximate Bayesian computation. *Cognitive Science, 43*(6), e12738. doi:10.1111/cogs.12738

Kangur, A., Jager, W., Verbrugge, R., & Bockarjova, M. (2017). An agent-based model for diffusion of electric vehicles. *Journal of Environmental Psychology, 52*, 166–182. doi:10.1016/j.jenvp. 2017.01.002

Kass, R. E., & Raftery, A. E. (1995). Bayes factors. *Journal of the American Statistical Association, 90*(430), 773–795.

Kielar, P. M., & Borrmann, A. (2016). Modeling pedestrians' interest in locations: A concept to improve simulations of pedestrian destination choice. *Simulation Modelling Practice and Theory, 61*, 47–62. doi:10.1016/j.simpat.2015.11.003

Laird, J. E. (2012). *The soar cognitive architecture.* The MIT Press.

Lieder, F., & Griffiths, T. L. (2020). Resource-rational analysis: Understanding human cognition as the optimal use of limited computational resources. *Behavioral and Brain Sciences, 43*. doi:10.1017/S0140525X1900061X

Madras, N. N. (2002). *Lectures on Monte Carlo methods.* American Mathematical Society.

Madsen, J. K., Bailey, R., Carrella, E., & Koralus, P. (2019). Analytic versus computational cognitive models: Agent-based modeling as a tool in cognitive sciences. *Current Directions in Psychological Science, 28*(3), 299–305. doi:10.1177/0963721419834547

McClelland, J. L., & Cleeremans, A. (2009). Connectionist models. In T. Byrne, A. Cleeremans, & P. Wilken (Eds.), *Oxford companion to consciousness.* Oxford University Press.

Muñoz, M. A., Sun, Y., Kirley, M., & Halgamuge, S. K. (2015). Algorithm selection for black-box continuous optimization problems: A survey on methods and challenges. *Information Sciences, 317*, 224–245. doi:10.1016/j.ins.2015.05.010

Nelder, J. A., & Mead, R. (1965). A simplex method for function minimization. *The Computer Journal, 7*(4), 308–313.

Newell, A. (1973). You can't play 20 questions with nature and win: Projective comments on the papers of this symposium. In W. G. Chase (Ed.), *Visual information processing.* Academic Press.

Newell, A., & Simon, H. A. (1976). Computer science as empirical inquiry: Symbols and search. *Communications of the ACM, 19*(3), 113–126.

Palestro, J. J., Sederberg, P. B., Osth, A. F., Van Zandt, T., & Turner, B. M. (2018). *Likelihood-free methods for cognitive science.* Springer.

Palmer, P. I., & Smith, M. J. (2014). Earth systems: Model human adaptation to climate change. *Nature, 512*(7515), 365–366. doi:10.1038/512365a

Pitt, M. A., Kim, W., Navarro, D. J., & Myung, J. I. (2006). Global model analysis by parameter space partitioning. *Psychological Review, 113*(1), 57–83.

Pitt, M. A., & Myung, J. (2002). When a good fit can be bad. *Trends in Cognitive Sciences, 6*, 421–425.

Ratcliff, R., Smith, P. L., Brown, S. D., & McKoon, G. (2016). Diffusion decision model: Current issues and history. *Trends in Cognitive Sciences*, *20*(4), 260–281. doi:10.1016/j.tics.2016.01.007

Roberts, S., & Pashler, H. (2000). How persuasive is a good fit? a comment on theory testing. *Psychological Review*, *107*, 358–367.

Schaat, S., Jager, W., & Dickert, S. (2017). Psychologically plausible models in agent-based simulations of sustainable behavior. In A. Alonso-Betanzos, N. Sánchez-Maroño, O. Fontenla- Romero, J. G. Polhill, T. Craig, J. Bajo, & J. M. Corchado (Eds.), *Agent-based modeling of sustainable behaviors* (pp. 1–25). Springer International Publishing.

Schlüter, M., Baeza, A., Dressler, G., Frank, K., Groeneveld, J., Jager, W., . . . Wijermans, N. (2017). A framework for mapping and comparing behavioural theories in models of social-ecological systems. *Ecological Economics*, *131*, 21–35. doi:10.1016/j.ecolecon.2016.08.008

Schröder, T., & Wolf, I. (2017). Modeling multi-level mechanisms of environmental attitudes and behaviours: The example of carsharing in Berlin. *Journal of Environmental Psychology*, *52*, 136–148. doi:10.1016/j.jenvp.2016.03.007

Schultheis, H., Singhaniya, A., & Chaplot, D. (2013). Comparing model comparison methods. In M. Knauff, M. Pauen, N. Sebanz, & I. Wachsmuth (Eds.), *Proceedings of the 35th annual conference of the cognitive science society*. Cognitive Science Society.

Sun, R. (2006a). *Cognition and multi-agent interaction: From cognitive modeling to social simulation*. Cambridge University Press.

Sun, R. (2006b). Prolegomena to integrating cognitive modeling and social simulation. In R. Sun (Ed.), *Cognition and multi-agent interaction: From cognitive modeling to social simulation* (pp. 3–26). Cambridge University Press. doi:10.1017/CBO9780511610721.002

Sun, R. (2008a). Introduction to computational cognitive modeling. In R. Sun (Ed.), *The Cambridge handbook of computational psychology*. Cambridge University Press.

Sun, R. (2008b). *The Cambridge handbook of computational psychology*. Cambridge University Press.

Sun, R. (2009). Cognitive architectures and multi-agent social simulation. In D. Lukose & Z. Shi (Eds.), *Multi-agent systems for society* (pp. 7–21). Springer.

Sun, R. (2011). *Grounding social sciences in cognitive sciences*. The MIT Press.

Thagard, P. (2006). *Hot thought: Mechanisms and applications of emotional cognition*. The MIT Press.

Usher, M., & McClelland, J. L. (2001). The time course of perceptual choice: The leaky, competing accumulator model. *Psychological Review*, *108*(3), 550–592. doi:10.1037/0033-295x.108.3.550

van Gelder, T. (1998). The dynamical hypothesis in cognitive science. *Behavioral and Brain Sciences*, *21*(5), 615–628. doi:10.1017/S0140525X98001733

Veksler, V. D., Myers, C. W., & Gluck, K. A. (2015). Model flexibility analysis. *Psychological Review*, *122*(4), 755–769.

Wagenmakers, E.-J., Ratcliff, R., Gomez, P., & Iverson, G. J. (2004). Assessing model mimicry using the parametric bootstrap. *Journal of Mathematical Psychology*, *48*, 28–50.

Wolf, I., Schröder, T., Neumann, J., & de Haan, G. (2015). Changing minds about electric cars: An empirically grounded agent-based modeling approach. *Technological Forecasting and Social Change*, *94*, 269–285. doi:10.1016/j.techfore.2014.10.010

5

COMPUTATIONAL COMMUNICATION SCIENCE

Lessons from working group sessions with experts of an emerging research field

Stephanie Geise and Annie Waldherr

We live in a world full of digitized communication: Search engines such as Google; social networking sites such as Facebook, Twitter and Instagram; mobile applications and digital news portals are integral parts of our lives. The ubiquity of digital communication facilitates our living, keeping us informed and vividly in touch with our peers. At the same time, digital media generates a wealth of sensitive information about ourselves, our social connections and communicative relationships and our media usage behavior, with which we leave a dense network of individual digital traces. These digital traces open up new opportunities for communication research, particularly to explore social communication phenomena that arise from the use, appropriation and impact of digital technology and media. These phenomena range from questions of private communication in the mediatized home and issues connected to the collection of individual messages and the sharing of health and fitness data to the critical analysis of the digitized formation of public opinion such as potential filter bubbles, fake news and hate speech – to name but a few current examples.

It is therefore only logical that communication and media studies have increasingly focused their knowledge and analytical interest on phenomena of and around digitization. But current developments in communication science are not only promoted by a growing interest in substantive questions related to digitization: Driving forces also include technological advancements in computing capacities, the rise of machine learning and the ubiquity of artificial intelligence. These trends open up new opportunities for communication researchers to access existing datasets and collect vast amounts of structured and unstructured data "on the side", while at the same time new computational approaches for data analysis are developing, which also facilitate the content-related examination of the data. Accompanied by an incorporated paradigm shift from "traditional" empirical research to potentially large-scale computational methods, the research field of computational communication science (CCS) has emerged, responding to the demand to adapt repertoires of analysis and methods to the changing conditions of increasingly digital media and digitized communication (e.g., Hilbert et al., 2019; Niemann-Lenz et al., 2019; Van Atteveldt & Peng, 2018).

Yet, the speed at which computational social science (CSS) is expanding should not hide the fact that it is still a fragmented field in much need of consolidation. Embedded in the broader "computational turn" in the social sciences, the changes in our field not only offer new

DOI: 10.4324/9781003024583-6

opportunities but also bring new methodological, data-analytical and research-ethical challenges with them. Particularly, the application of advanced, often machine-driven approaches implies serious challenges of this kind (see, for example, Berinsky, Huber, and Lenz (2012) on Amazon's Mechanical Turk), which empirical communication research must face.

The ongoing implementation of computational methods has also been criticized for being data driven and deficient in theoretical positioning, and valid criticism has been made particularly regarding the reliability, validity and reproducibility of computational methods (e.g., Mahrt & Scharkow, 2013; Waldherr, Geise, & Katzenbach, 2019). Especially because of their novelty and their potential to expand the visibility of communicative processes, CCS explicitly needs to be subject to a critical and reflected debate within the social sciences itself.

Aiming to contribute to this discourse, this chapter provides an overview of CCS as an emerging and exemplary subfield of computational social science. Based on lessons from working group sessions with 34 experts, we address recent challenges and desiderata that CCS researchers from communication and political science, informatics, computer science, linguistics, sociology and other related research fields see while reflecting upon its development and future expansion. We summarize and further discuss four major fields of action these experts have put particular focus on: First, challenges related to a reflected but integrated CCS methodology; second, challenges related to a further elaboration on theoretical perspectives on CCS; third, challenges related to the formation and further institutionalization of CCS as fundamental basis for further discourse, quality control and scientific progress; and fourth, further ideas as to how the challenges discussed can be tackled and implemented by empirical communication research and which concrete decisions should prove to be relevant in this context.

The computational turn of communication science and its characteristics

At the heart of the digitalization of society is digitized communication. Communication scholars have been quick to point out that major parts of the digital traces available in digitized information environments are factual communication data (Shah, Cappella, & Neuman, 2015) – such as text messages in chats and social media posts, memes, podcasts or audio-visuals – or data on media use and exposure – such as tracking, log or search data. Consequently, with the key role communication plays in the increasing digitalization of contemporary societies, CCS has emerged as one of the most vibrant subfields of CSS. It therefore makes sense to take a closer look at CCS as an exemplary – and at the same time increasingly important – research field of computational social science.

With Hilbert et al. (2019, p. 3914), we understand CCS "as an application of computational science to questions of human and social communication". Although the rapid development of the field has certainly been triggered and catalyzed by the massive availability of digital traces (Hilbert et al., 2019; Shah et al., 2015), big data is only one of the defining instances of CCS. Another defining characteristic of CCS is its strong orientation towards computational methods to investigate social communication phenomena. This has been driven by quickly growing computing capacities enabling powerful methods for modeling large and complex data. Over the last decade, communication scholars have increasingly taken advantage of computational approaches such as automated content analysis, network analysis or computer simulation to answer fundamental questions about human behavior, interaction and communication. From a topical perspective, CCS researchers focus primarily, but not exclusively, on interactive computer-based phenomena and the associated technologies, structures and processes of computer-mediated reception, information processing and communication, as well as their social consequences.

The powerful combination of big data and computational methods has led scholars to predict an "unprecedented boost to progress" for communication science (van Atteveldt & Peng, 2018, p. 82). In recent years, this development has gained momentum. Several programmatic articles on the potentials of computational methods in communication research have been published (Choi, 2020; Hilbert et al., 2019; Niemann-Lenz et al., 2019; Van Atteveldt & Peng, 2018). In 2016, a new interest group on computational methods in the International Communication Association (ICA) was founded, which only four years later would be established as a proper division of the association. In 2019, the first issue of a new open-access journal, *Computational Communication Research*, was published.

Apart from these first instances of institutionalization on an international level, CCS is still in its formative stage, and a lot of open questions merit a thorough discussion. For example, while the potential of computational methods for data analysis is obvious, the role of theory in this emerging field is still rather unclear and underrepresented (Waldherr, Geise, Mahrt, Katzenbach, & Nürnbergk, 2021). It seems that the rapid development of computational methods has not been accompanied by an equally strong emphasis on theoretical developments within the scholarly community. Which theories and theoretical concepts are available that can enrich the methodological discussion on CCS? How can theory development inspire further methodological advances? What are the main challenges and core issues to be addressed in the further development of CCS?

Working group sessions with experts: line-up and learning

All of these questions were taken up and openly discussed in the context of an interdisciplinary working group, "Computational Communication Science 'en route': theory, methodology & research ethics", funded by the German Center for Applied Internet Studies (CAIS). The 34 invited experts in this working group came from the research fields of communication and political science, computer science, informatics, linguistics, sociology and other related research areas. During the funding period of around one year, we met regularly in collaborative workshops, reflecting on the development of CCS, intending to assess its future advancement and potential ways of improvement. Guided by our key questions and conceptual impulses, the discussions revolved around the interplay between subject-related interests and their underlying driving research questions, and the partly highly specific theoretical and methodological perspectives of CCS, its possible interfaces with established social theories and the methodological questions and advances that arise from them.

Methodologically, the group sessions were conceptualized as a combination of explorative expert interviews and dialogue-oriented, transdisciplinary workshops (Bergmann et al., 2010; Defila & Di Giulio, 2014; Dexter, 1970; Niederberger, 2014). The aim was to encourage the invited experts to engage in an open, collaborative exchange in order to inquire about their expert knowledge, assessments, experiences, ideas and development perspectives, and to involve them in a further constructive dialogue (Defila & Di Giulio, 2014; Dexter, 1970) about the future of CSS/CCS. At the same time, the invited experts were themselves part of the social field of action of CSS/CCS we aimed to explore.

From our perspective, there were three arguments in favor of establishing a workshop series that was situated in the field of communication science but was equally open to neighboring disciplines in the social sciences: First, collaborative expert workshops are particularly well suited for exploring and eliciting lines of development and potential problem areas, as well as the resulting requirements and solution approaches, because they stimulate an interactive and creative exchange of multi-faceted expert experience (Defila & Di Giulio, 2014; Niederberger,

2014). Second, although straight methodological guidelines to systematize the elicitation process of experts are rare (Defila & Di Giulio, 2014; McDonald, Bammer, & Dean, 2009), the involvement of experts in social science research is becoming increasingly important (Niederberger, 2014). In our case, the principal motivations for our workshop approaches were to reduce the complexity of the research process, improve the quality of the results and address some of the major issues often experienced by computational researchers. Third, at the national level, or rather in German-speaking countries, researchers working with computational methods often are regarded as "lone wolves", because institutional opportunities for interdisciplinary networking are still lacking. With the establishment of the working group as well as with this chapter, we thus not only aim to gain in-depth knowledge but to extend the expert discussions to the larger CSS/CCS community, finally intending to contribute to its further institutionalization.

Having these lofty goals, we conducted a series of guided collaborative CCS/SSS-expert workshops, thematically ranging from 1) challenges related to a reflected but integrated CCS *methodology*; 2) challenges related to a further elaboration of specific *theoretical perspectives* on CCS and potential interfaces to established social science theories; and 3) challenges related to the *formation and further institutionalization* of CCS as fundamental basis for further discourse, quality control and scientific progress. Focusing the discussions along the lines of an exemplary thematic field of research – namely the digitization of public opinion formation – we 4) further discussed ideas as to how the identified challenges could be tackled and implemented by empirical communication research and which concrete decisions should prove relevant in this context. In the following, we give an overview of the results of these experts' workshops and integrate them into the existing CCS research landscape.

Learning 1: contours of an expanding field of research

In our kick-off workshop, we aimed at developing a common understanding of the research area, orientation and objectives of CSS and CCS. The experts agreed that CSS is not yet a social-scientific discipline on its own but may be characterized as a "fluid network" or "movement" within the social sciences. Some experts also suggested that CSS – in its specific orientation – could serve as "auxiliary science" for the social sciences, just like statistics, and some even noted that CSS is a "buzzword" or "label" that might be used strategically to position researchers and institutions in competition for resources, sometimes even without having any substantial meaning.

In the discussion, we did not follow this last thought but identified three components we deemed essential for defining the field of CSS: 1) the analysis of social processes 2) with (big) digital data on these processes and 3) the use of computer-based methods that allow a high degree of automation of the research process. Later, we specified these dimensions as "driving forces" of CCS (Waldherr et al., 2021). Just as in the social sciences in general, the big (communication) data deluge and powerful computing capacities have been main catalysts for the computerization and algorithmization of communication research (Hilbert et al., 2019). Although digital data and computational methods can be applied to any research question in communication, a third driver of CCS we and others have identified are often highly complex research problems of human communication which newly emerge in digitized societies and which call for developments in theories as well as methodological toolkits (Niemann-Lenz et al., 2019), thinking, for example, of phenomena such as filter bubbles, Twitter storms, flash mobs, cyberbullying and so on (so-called "wicked problems"; see subsequently).

CSS in general is a highly interdisciplinary field. Yet, the impression of our experts was that CSS is currently dominated by the technical disciplines such as computer science, engineering, mathematics and physics. Consequently, the field is experienced as highly method and data driven. For example, a number of interdisciplinary conferences have a pronounced bias towards computer science (e.g., social informatics, complex networks, ICWSM, IC2S2) or a strong focus on one specific method (NetSci, Sunbelt, ESSA). Social scientists and their theoretical approaches as well as methodological standards thus do not appear to be represented equally and "have come late to the party", as one of our experts phrased it.

This is partly also true for the specific field of CCS. However, communication researchers quite early opened up to computational approaches themselves, engaged in further developing computational methods for their purposes and started scholarly discussions in forums quite central to their discipline (e.g., in the computational methods division of the ICA and in several special journal issues addressing the field; Domahidi, Yang, Niemann-Lenz, & Reinecke, 2019; Theocharis & Jungherr, 2021; Van Atteveldt & Peng, 2018). Thus, the computational turn in communication science by now appears to be well embedded in the overall discipline, although "far from being normalized" or "mainstreamed". From our perspective, CCS can really profit by having trained communication researchers who are skilled in computational approaches but also savvy in communication theories. This potentially is an advantage compared with other social-scientific disciplines, for example, political science, where scholars have observed that internet research and data science is still regarded as a "playground of cute nerds" (Jungherr, 2017, p. 301).

Learning 2: theories in CCS

In the context of the euphoria in the early development stage of CCS, some colleagues have argued that the availability of large datasets and computational methods would make theories obsolete (Anderson, 2008; Mayer-Schönberger & Cukier, 2013). This positivist view was widely criticized (Driscoll & Walker, 2014; Mahrt, 2018; Mahrt & Scharkow, 2013; Vis, 2013) – and we also took it as a pointed starting point for a further discussion of the role of theory in CCS to which we devoted the second two-day expert workshop. Starting from an exploration of potentials of a theoretical "common ground" of CSS and its major challenges, the aim of the theory workshop was to elaborate on existing or imaginable theoretical references and interfaces of CCS research as well as to identify requirements of appropriate theories that can inspire and advance it.

Our analytical interest was guided by three main considerations we initially carved out in the workshop: First, like other scholars before, the invited experts shared the belief that even exploratory pattern detection is necessarily driven by numerous theoretical assumptions that are reflected in how data are collected, analyzed and interpreted (Andrejevic, 2014; Crawford, 2013). Second, and interconnected, the invited experts agreed that research that lacks sufficient theoretical reflection of the studied phenomena risks producing methodological and/ or data-analytical artifacts instead of meaningful findings about social reality (Bright, 2017; Kitchin, 2014; Ruths & Pfeffer, 2014). CCS scientists have thus, and third, demonstrated that computational methods in many respects are ideally suited to empirically test both long-term social theories (González-Bailón, 2017) as well as medium-term communication theories such as agenda-setting (e.g., Vargo, Guo, & Amazeen, 2018), and computational methods have also been used to inductively develop and advance theories in a computational grounded theory approach (Choi, 2020).

However, in our view, a discussion about CCS and theory, a larger reflection of how theories, particularly meta-theoretical frameworks, can serve CCS scholarship, is widely missing. But how can social science theories advance CSS/CCS? And which theories are particularly suitable for empirical theory-based CSS/CCS research? To discuss these questions, in the second workshop stage, we conducted a "CCS theory roadshow", for which each of the invited CCS experts had prepared a theory input, which was then presented and discussed in a round table format. For this input, the invited experts a priori selected theories they believed highly suited for research in the field of CSS and prepared "theory profiles" guided by the following evaluation scheme: 1) short description of the theory/theoretical framework (including basic ideas, core assumptions, central concepts and premises), 2) disciplinary setting and previous application (e.g., in which fields of research, for the analysis of which phenomena, in the context of which research contexts), 3) gain in knowledge and/or analytical potential for CSS/ CCS (e.g., specific theoretical perspectives, new questions, sensitization for otherwise unilluminated structures, processes or phenomena), 4) challenges and ambiguities (e.g., premises theoretically worthy of discussion, empirical verifiability of central assumptions, contradictions), 5) possible interrelations and/or conflicts with other established theories relevant to CSS/CCS.

On that basis, we worked out inspiring theoretical grounds and interconnections of the different approaches, identified explicit and implicit premises of CCS research guided by theory and derived general requirements that theories should meet in order to provide further insights for CCS research (see Table 5.1). Along these criteria, we discussed the potential of five theoretical frameworks in greater depth and intensity: 1) structuration theory, 2) actor-network theory, 3) complexity theory, 4) mediatization and 5) theories of the public sphere. The discussion found that the selected theories can indeed constructively inform and inspire CCS research – although the different concepts naturally involve different emphases, challenges and limitations.

We then summarized our findings and reflections at a higher level. Here, it became clear that CCS experts saw particular benefit in applying *macro frameworks* to the analysis of CCS/CSS phenomena. Even though macro-theoretical frameworks may not directly point computational scientists to any particular research questions or hypotheses, they do have a lasting impact on their research: Theoretical frameworks strongly influence what types of questions we ask, what types of hypotheses we formulate and what (computational or traditional) methods we consider appropriate and useful to investigate them. A conscious foundation of our thinking and

Table 5.1 Premises of CCS research and requirements for theories in CSS

Conceptual premises of CCS research	Requirements for theories
Conclusions about social reality can be drawn from digital traces.	Consideration of *digitization and media change*
Media change and digital technologies influence social reality.	Analysis of the *interdependencies between social structures, individuals and technology*
Networks describe and explain social structures.	Connection of several levels of analysis
Human-machine interactions are a central subject of CSS/CCS research.	Options to model *dynamic processes*
Findings lay claim to truth, objectivity and completeness.	Raising *awareness of hidden bias* in the data and normativity of research
CSS/CCS helps to find technical solutions for social problems.	*Application for empirical analysis* with computational methods

of (computer-aided) communication research through macro-theoretical frameworks forces us to make explicit and reflect the epistemological basic assumptions of our work (Resnyansky, 2019). In addition, macro-theoretical frameworks inspire us to answer critical questions, such as: How do we as CCS researchers understand the world? How do we try to decipher meaning and significance in this world? What is our research interest (explanation, description, standardization or criticism)? Which actors and/or structures do we consider relevant to explain social communication processes based on the computerized collection and/or analysis of (digital) data?

The reproduction of the complete theory discussion would go beyond the scope of this book chapter. However, our considerations are documented elsewhere: In a first theory paper, we devoted ourselves more intensively to the discussion of the potentials and possible applications of the actor network theory (ANT), revisiting the framework as a helpful concept for theorizing and inspiring CCS scholars' research agendas (Waldherr, Geise, & Katzenbach, 2019). Based on a literature review, we showed that ANT has already been used to study a variety of questions in (computational) media and communication research and identified three key contributions of an ANT perspective in CCS: First, by focusing on the role of technology in communication and the relationships between nonhumans and humans guided by ANT, the frameworks help us to open our discipline to new questions and perspectives of communication research. Second, from a meta-perspective, the framework suggests to further reflect on the emergence, development and inscriptions of computational methods in CCS, as they are not only shaped by technological and scientific innovations, but they also influence how we do communication science now and in the future. And third, this meta-perspective motivates an even further step of self-reflection, pushing researchers to deliberate about their roles in the research process as well as the normative and ethical assumptions guiding them. Taken together, as we illustrate in the chapter in more detail, the outlined theoretical considerations open up potential future perspectives of ANT-informed CCS.

In addition to this contribution devoted to a specific theoretical conception, we dedicated a second article to the added value of *macro-theoretical perspectives* – such as, for example, *complexity theory*, *theories of the public sphere* and *mediatization theory* – in establishing a meta-theoretical underpinning of CCS research (Waldherr et al., 2021). With the help of three analytical dimensions – 1) interdependencies between varieties of entities and actors on different levels of hierarchy and organization, 2) the consideration of normativity and 3) multi-level dynamics in the research process, we argue that CCS scholars can benefit from connecting their empirical, often highly innovative work to established macro-theoretical frameworks: Particularly because these frameworks make explicit how computational research foci (and blind spots) and designs are shaped by (implicit or explicit) theoretical underpinnings and how these significantly impact computational research questions, hypotheses and methods, the integration of macro-theoretical perspectives can inspire and advance future CCS scholarship.

Learning 3: methods of CCS

In the third expert workshop, we took two days for in-depth discussions of several selected computational methods. When choosing the methods of interest, we aimed for a broad variety of approaches. Besides methods of digital trace data analysis, which are already well established in communication research – such as network analysis, text classification, web scraping, web tracking and bot detection – we also discussed methods that have not been at the center of development so far but in our view add important perspectives to CCS, namely agent-based modeling as well as computational observation methods such as eye tracking and automated facial emotion recognition. Of course, this set of methods is also by no means exhaustive and represents only a small selection of the current toolbox of CCS. Yet, all of these methods are computational in that sense that they are able to analyze and/or generate large amounts of digital data and enable a high degree of automation of the research pipeline (Jünger & Schade, 2018). In addition, they belong to the realm of communication science, as they are used to study processes of human communication.

On the basis of short methodological profiles, the CCS/CSS experts had prepared in advance, we discussed the specific insights gained by each method as well as the methodological and ethical challenges of the methods, which were perceived as central in the current debates by the experts. The essence of these discussions is summarized in Table 5.2.

Independently of the methods discussed in each case, nearly all of our experts reported challenges concerning the *representativeness* of CCS data. At the heart of this challenge is the question of how well the data or the model "represent the real social world" and how safe it is to draw conclusions based on this data or model. Issues under discussion ranged from questions of boundary definition and drawing representative samples from social networks to technical and social biases in data.

Technical biases might occur, for example, due to access restrictions (through APIs and their terms of service or bot blockers on web pages) or technical disruptions in data collection (e.g., through interrupted internet connections or other technical issues). Another form of technical bias is the automated production of social media content through bots. Depending on the research question, detecting and filtering out bot-produced content is essential to prevent biased conclusions. Social biases arise particularly for all research relying on social media data, as these platforms are known to underrepresent certain demographic groups (e.g., gender and educational biases on Twitter and Facebook; Barberá & Rivero, 2015; Mellon & Prosser, 2017). Another challenge to representativeness occurs with very demanding forms of data collection such as web tracking or eye tracking which for different reasons often result in very small samples, but with large amounts of fine-grained individual-level data (Möller, Van de Velde, Merten, & Puschmann, 2020; Geise, Heck, & Panke, 2020).

Another common theme in the expert discussion was the *validity* of CCS methods. The core question with regard to validity is matching the measurements with the theoretical constructs under study. While computational methods often produce massive amounts of data, it is not always clear what these data really mean substantively and what conclusions might be drawn or not drawn from them. For example, there are multiple algorithms for community detection, which are able to identify subgroups in large-scale networks. As Stoltenberg, Maier, and Waldherr (2019) have shown, each of these algorithms generates possibly different results

Table 5.2 Challenges of CCS methods and desiderata for the CCS community

Challenges of CCS methods	Desiderata for CCS community
Representativeness: drawing samples, access to data, technical and social biases	Ensure access to data, establish data infrastructure
Validity: substantive meaning of measures, defining gold standards and ground truths	Systematic and comparative methods research, definition of best practices
Hypothesis testing: Violation of distributional assumptions, meaningfulness of significance tests with large-scale data	Develop standards for hypothesis testing with large-scale online data
Ethics and privacy: sensitive and private user data, difficulties of secure anonymization	Define common ethical standards and techniques for secure data sharing

in such a way that it is important to make theoretically informed choices on which theoretical types of communities in the theoretical sense researchers want to measure (e.g., based on similarity, ideological association or strategic alliance of actors). In automated text analysis and classification tasks, pressing questions of validity are developing the right gold standards and ground truths for training algorithms (Song et al., 2020), especially when dealing with ambiguous categories.

Comparable challenges arise in the computational observation of sensory behavioral data, as is typically applied in eye tracking and computer-based biometric emotion measurement. Here, too, the measurement and automated classification of the data is determined by the algorithms used to detect the measured constructs. In eye tracking, for example, a so-called fixation filter is set, so that the processing script is technically able to identify eye movements that should be grouped together as foveal fixations or saccades. While such a fixation filter is a common and necessary technological requisite, the fixation–classification algorithms used can affect data precision (Hessels, Kemner, van den Boomen, & Hooge, 2016). It is also common practice here to subsequently define so-called "areas of interest" – specific areas of the received stimuli, over which the eye tracking data are then compared (Geise et al., 2020; Hessels et al., 2016). Such methodological decisions should critically reflect the fact that standards for setting this technological pre-structuring are only slowly established – but the resulting data and findings are rarely questioned later (Geise, 2014).

The question of ground truth becomes particularly virulent when it is socially and politically consequential, such as in bot identification. While detecting and filtering out bots from social media datasets might increase the representativeness and validity of the results, bot detection algorithms such as botometers are prone to producing false positives (Keller & Klinger, 2019). Because bots constantly evolve and are a "moving target", it is also hard to define a reliable ground truth against which to test the algorithms. Finally, in computational modeling, the validity of basic assumptions and parameter choices as well as finding an appropriate level of abstraction is key (Sun et al., 2016). Particularly, strategies of empirical validation are an issue of ongoing scholarly debate (Gräbner, 2018).

Digital trace data generally are a lot more messy than the data gathered in classical empirical research (Waldherr, Maier, Miltner, & Günther, 2017). For example, online data, particularly network data, tend to produce highly skewed distributions and nonlinear relationships (Adamic & Huberman, 2000; Broido & Clauset, 2019), which prohibits the unreflected use of statistical modeling based on normal distributions and linearity assumptions (such as ordinary least square regressions). This makes *hypothesis testing* complicated, requiring rather complex techniques of analysis (such as exponential random graph modeling in network analysis; Lusher, Koskinen, & Robins, 2013). Because this considerably raises the analytical bar for communication scholars (and reviewers), this often leads to rather descriptive and exploratory studies. Additionally, the mere scale of data produced in CCS studies often makes the use of inferential statistics and significance tests obsolete – an issue which has also been discussed for the large amounts of data generated in computer simulations (Troitzsch, 2016).

The fourth and final set of challenges the invited experts highlighted centered on questions of *ethics*, particularly *privacy*. When working with fine-grained individual-level data, such as in web tracking studies, highly sensitive user data are generated. This requires comprehensive privacy protection protocols, ensuring not only informed consent before installing tracking apps but also that only necessary data are collected (e.g., by defining white- and blacklists of URLs for data collection) and that data be securely anonymized (Möller et al., 2019). Of course, meeting these standards is impossible if researchers work on problems such as bot detection and misinformation, where it is essential to collect data without users' consent and also where access to data deleted by users would be helpful.

Based on the discussions of these challenges, we derived desiderata for the development of CCS methods and the CCS community. It was suggested to create systematic overviews of research questions and adequate computational methods and software packages (e.g., in the form of a handbook or an electronic tool collection). The development of best practice standards and more methodological research in the form of systematic comparisons of methods and instruments was also highlighted as necessary. For the community, a regular and institutionalized interdisciplinary exchange was proposed, and problems of equal data access, establishing data infrastructures and protocols for data and code sharing were addressed.

In sum, it is reassuring that the major CCS challenges largely correspond to those of classical empirical research. However, they come in new qualities so that long established solutions cannot simply be adopted. This implies a high potential to make CCS research frustrating, because researchers first need to solve very basic methodological problems before they can turn to answering their primary research questions. However, the expert discussions made clear that one of the biggest CCS desiderata is precisely this: advance systematic, comparative methodological research, and develop common standards for data collection and data analysis.

"CCS en route": central challenges and future perspectives for an emerging research field

The last workshop aimed at an integrative synthesis of the previous findings, on the basis of which we wanted to work out the question of future perspectives and challenges of CCS research. We proceeded in two steps: In step 1, we summarized our findings from the previous three workshops in a few bullet points, condensed the central arguments and, together with the invited experts, specified which desiderata arise with regard to method and theory development in CCS. On this basis, in step 2, we worked out which next steps should necessarily result from our analysis of the current status quo and how and where we, as CCS researchers, can contribute to the implementation, further professionalization and institutionalization of CCS research and scholarship. Our central learnings can be condensed into four conceptual statements the experts agreed with, which we summarize in the following.

The virtue of disciplinary openness and interdisciplinary collaboration

From the very beginning, our collaborative expert workshops were based on disciplinary and thematic openness. Leading to multi-faceted, inspiring and highly interesting discussions, the workshop series again highlighted that we, as communication scholars, can immensely profit from disciplinary openness and interdisciplinary collaboration, particularly with, for example, political science, sociology, computer science and linguistics. All experts emphasized that an interdisciplinary approach in small workshop groups proved a particularly effective format and should be maintained in subsequent projects.

The benefit of sharpening the CCS focus

At the same time, it became apparent that we achieved particular analytical depth when the questions and discussions became very specific and case related. For this reason, the invited experts advocated a content-based focus and interdisciplinary bundling of the discussion – this can be interpreted as a commitment to the further establishment and institutionalization of a specified CCS, whereby all experts expressed the wish for a "home" under the umbrella of the larger CSS. Keeping a focus on specific topics, problems and examples seemed to ease further progress in the discussion and work on specific solutions.

To give an example, the opportunities and challenges of CCS were unfolded in a prototypical way with the example of forms, functions and processes of digitized opinion formation, which is becoming increasingly relevant in times of ongoing digital media change. This leads us to the conviction that computational research in communication science is particularly promising, where researchers share their research questions and their analytical framework, as well as their examples of application. For future work, we therefore suggest a focus on more concrete research problems (particularly on "wicked problems"; see subsequently) in order to discuss and develop specific theoretical and methodological solutions for concrete theoretical and methodological problems at hand.

The potential of a stronger theoretical grounding of CCS

One of the recurring questions the experts raised in the workshops was how we – as social scientists – can add value to the further development of the research field. What contribution can communication scientists make to the debate of an expanding computational research at large? What can the field really profit from in its further development? In view of the discussions about the lack of theory in CSS/CCS research and the frequently observed strong application orientation in the field, the strengthening of the theoretical foundation crystallized as an important developmental step to which CCS experts in particular can contribute meaningfully.

The need for institutionalization

All participants agreed that a focused, interdisciplinary collaboration is easier, more interactive and more productive in small groups and expressed the wish for a continuation and perpetuation of the exchange that had begun with our workshop series. At the same time, it became apparent that the institutionalization of CCS research is experienced as both potentially one of the biggest drivers as well as one of the biggest obstacles to further development – especially if the hitherto low level of institutionalization is not further expanded and promoted. In order to create an opportunity for cross-locational and topic- and task-related exchange and thus promote further development of CCS research, the establishment of CCS scholars' networks seems an effective next step to proceed with. The importance of stronger networking for the exchange of experience was substantiated by the experts, among other things, by the example of shared tools, methods and procedures of analysis but also with regard to an overarching "best practice" platform to facilitate interdisciplinary cooperation and to increase the reproducibility, replicability and generalizability of findings.

In these considerations, it is already indicated that the invited experts strongly appreciated the development towards an open science – considerations that have been the subject of intensive science policy discussions, particularly in recent times (e.g., Dienlin et al., 2020; Niemann-Lenz et al., 2019; Nosek et al., 2015). At the same time, the experts were very much aware that many content- and data-sharing activities connected with "best practice" exchange are also associated with additional ethical and legal challenges – including, for example, the acknowledgment of privacy requirements and terms of services, as well as an increased risk of data misuse by third parties. As in similar contexts (Niemann-Lenz et al., 2019), the experts pointed out that the additional effort required to comply with the necessary ethical and legal standards of open CCS research (e.g., complete anonymization of very large amounts of data) could, in the worst case, outweigh the (individual) benefits (e.g., reproducibility). There was agreement, however, that the community should create appropriate framework conditions that promote an overarching "open science" exchange, as this would ultimately benefit the entire development of the research field.

Wicked problems as incubators for CCS research

To conclude, one of the key insights we gained from our workshop series is that "wicked problems" serve as inspiring incubators for CCS (and CSS alike). We borrow the term from public policy research (Rittel & Webber, 1973; Weber & Khademian, 2008) to signify complex and unstructured problems entailing myriad and highly interdependent subproblems which are impossible to solve without generating multiple threads of follow-up problems. It is exactly this type of problem that many CCS scholars set out to study: big, highly complex and wicked social problems where communication technology might be the cause and/or solution.

For example, many phenomena which might be subsumed under the term digitized opinion formation and which have gained much scholarly attention in recent years (Bennet & Pfetsch, 2018; Quandt, 2018) are certainly "wicked", such as misinformation, fragmentation, propaganda, conflict or radicalization. Tackling these challenges is a strong motivation for researchers to build interdisciplinary collaborations and overcome methodological obstacles, and it is in these contexts where we observe and expect the most cutting-edge advancements in CCS. Thus, our most important lesson is that we should use this momentum and further connect the different research groups working on similar substantial problems to learn from each other, join efforts on methods development and eventually help solve the big issues of our digitized times.

Acknowledgments

We would like to thank the CAIS – Center for Advanced Internet Studies (Bochum, Germany) for the generous support, the competent guidance through our funding period and the great hospitality that we and all invited experts enjoyed at the CAIS in Bochum. Without the personnel, organizational and financial support of the CAIS, we would not have been able to realize the described workshop series this chapter is based on. We would also like to thank all the experts – listed in the appendix – who discussed the diverse development perspectives of CCS with us intensively and with great passion. Our project would not have been possible without your constructive, cooperative and always inspiring exchange: Many thanks to you!

Appendix
LIST OF PARTICIPANTS

1   Gioele Barabucci, Fellow at the CAIS
2   Matthias Begenat, CAIS
3   Ralf Benzmüller, G DATA SecurityLabs
4   Laura Burbach, RWTH Aachen University
5   Anja Dieckmann, GfK Nuremberg
6   Emese Domahidi, TU Ilmenau
7   Frederik Elwert, Ruhr University Bochum
8   Uwe Engel, University of Bremen
9   Christoph Engemann, Fellow at the CAIS
10 Lena Frischlich, WWU Münster
11 Volker Gehrau, WWU Münster
12 Stephanie Geise, WWU Münster, Workshop Organizer
13 Andreas Jungherr, University of Constance
14 Christian Katzenbach, Alexander von Humboldt Institute for Internet and Society Berlin
15 Melih Kirlidog, Fellow at CAIS
16 Ulrike Klinger, Freie Universität Berlin
17 Iris Lorscheid, TU Hamburg-Harburg
18 Seraphine Maerz, University of Freiburg
19 Merja Mahrt, HHU Düsseldorf
20 Dennis Michels, University Duisburg-Essen
21 Judith Möller, University of Amsterdam
22 Linda Monsees, Fellow at CAIS
23 Christoph Neuberger, LMU Munich
24 Christian Nuernbergk, LMU Munich
25 Cornelius Puschmann, Hans Bredow Institute Hamburg / University of Bremen
26 Hermann Rotermund, Fellow at the CAIS
27 Andreas Scheu, WWU Münster
28 Armin Scholl, WWU Münster
29 Geeske Scholz, University of Osnabrück
30 Tatjana Scheffler, University of Potsdam

31   Annie Waldherr, WWU Münster, Workshop Organizer
32   Katrin Weller, GESIS Cologne
33   Martin Welker, HMKW University for Media, Communication and Economy, Cologne
34   Gregor Wiedemann, University of Hamburg

References

Adamic, L. A., & Huberman, B. A. (2000). Power-law distribution of the world wide web. *Science, 287*(5461), 2115. https://doi.org/10.1126/science.287.5461.2115a

Anderson, C. (2008). The end of theory: The data deluge makes the scientific method obsolete. *Wired.* Retrieved from www.wired.com/2008/06/pb-theory

Andrejevic, M. (2014). The big data divide. *International Journal of Communication, 8*(1), 1673–1689. Retrieved from https://ijoc.org/index.php/ijoc/article/view/2161

Barberá, P., & Rivero, G. (2015). Understanding the political representativeness of Twitter users. *Social Science Computer Review, 33*(6), 712–729. https://doi.org/10.1177/0894439314558836

Bennet, W. L., & Pfetsch, B. (2018). Rethinking political communication in a time of disrupted public spheres. *Journal of Communication, 68*(2), 243–253. https://doi.org/10.1093/joc/jqx017

Bergmann, M., Jahn, T., Knoblauch, T., Krohn, W., Pohl, C., & Schramm, E. (2010). *Methoden transdisziplinärer Forschung. Ein Überblick mit Anwendungsbeispielen.* Campus.

Berinsky, A. J., Huber, G. A., & Lenz, G. S. (2012). Evaluating online labor markets for experimental research: Amazon.com's Mechanical Turk. *Political Analysis, 20*(3), 351–368.

Bright, J. (2017). "Big social science": Doing big data in the social sciences. In N. G. Fielding, R. M. Lee, & G. Blank (Eds.), *The Sage handbook of online research methods* (pp. 125–139). Sage.

Broido, A. D., & Clauset, A. (2019). Scale-free networks are rare. *Nature Communications, 10*(1), 1017. https://doi.org/10.1038/s41467-019-08746-5

Choi, S. (2020). When digital trace data meet traditional communication theory: Theoretical/methodological directions. *Social Science Computer Review, 38*(1), 91–107. https://doi.org/10.1177/0894439318788618

Crawford, K. (2013). The hidden biases in big data. *Harvard Business Review Blog.* Retrieved from www.hbrianholland.com/s/05-The-Hidden-Biases-in-Big-Data-Crawford.pdf

Defila, R., & Di Giulio, A. (2014). Methodische Gestaltung transdisziplinärer Workshops. In M. Niederberger, & S. Wassermann (Eds.), *Methoden der Experten- und Stakeholdereinbindung in der sozialwissenschaftlichen Forschung* (pp. 69–93). Springer VS.

Dexter, L. A. (1970). Elite and specialized interviewing. In J. A. Robinson (Ed.), *Handbooks for research in political behavior.* Northwestern University Press.

Dienlin, T., Johannes, N., Bowman, N. D., Masur, P. K., Engesser, S., Kümpel, A. S., . . . Huskey, R. (2020). An agenda for open science in communication. *Journal of Communication.* https://doi.org/10.1093/joc/jqz052

Domahidi, E., Yang, J., Niemann-Lenz, J., & Reinecke, L. (2019). Outlining the way ahead in computational communication science: An introduction to the IJoC special section on "computational methods for communication science: Toward a strategic roadmap". *International Journal of Communication, 13*, 3876–3884.

Driscoll, K., & Walker, S. (2014). Working within a black box: Transparency in the collection and production of big Twitter data. *International Journal of Communication, 8*(1), 1745–1764. Retrieved from https://ijoc.org/index.php/ijoc/article/view/2171

Geise, S. (2014). Eyetracking in media studies. Theory, method and its exemplary application in analyzing shock-inducing advertisements. In F. Darling-Wolf (Ed.), *The international encyclopedia of media studies. Research methods in media studies* (pp. 419–444). Blackwell.

Geise, S., Heck, A., & Panke, D. (2020). The effects of digital media images on political participation online: Results of an eye-tracking experiment integrating individual perceptions of "photo news factors". *Policy & Internet.* https://doi.org/10.1002/poi3.235

González-Bailón, S. (2017). *Decoding the social world: Data science and the unintended consequences of communication.* MIT Press.

Gräbner, C. (2018). How to relate models to reality? An epistemological framework for the validation and verification of computational models. *Journal of Artificial Societies and Social Simulation, 21*(3), 8. https://doi.org/10.18564/jasss.3772

Hessels, R. S., Kemner, C., van den Boomen, C., & Hooge, I. T. C. (2016). The area-of-interest problem in eye tracking research: A noise-robust solution for face and sparse stimuli. *Behavior Research Methods, 48*(4), 1694–1712. https://doi.org/10.3758/s13428-015-0676-y

Hilbert, M., Barnett, G., Blumenstock, J., Contractor, N., Diesner, J., Frey, S., . . . Zhu, J. J. H. (2019). Computational communication science: A methodological catalyzer for a maturing discipline. *International Journal of Communication, 13*, 3912–3934.

Jünger, J., & Schade, H. (2018). Liegt die Zukunft der Kommunikationswissenschaft in der Vergangenheit? Ein Plädoyer für Kontinuität statt Veränderung bei der Analyse von Digitalisierung. *Publizistik, 63*(4), 497–512. https://doi.org/10.1007/s11616-018-0457-6

Jungherr, A. (2017). The Internet in political communication: State of the field and research perspectives. *Politische Vierteljahresschrift, 58*(2), 284–315. https://doi.org/10.5771/0032-3470-2017-2-284

Keller, T. R., & Klinger, U. (2019). Social bots in election campaigns: Theoretical, empirical, and methodological implications. *Political Communication, 36*(1), 171–189. https://doi.org/10.1080/10584609.2018.1526238

Kitchin, R. (2014). Big data, new epistemologies and paradigm shifts. *Big Data & Society, 1*(1). https://doi.org/10.1177/2053951714528481

Lusher, D., Koskinen, J., & Robins, G. (2013). *Exponential random graph models for social networks: Theory, methods, and applications.* Cambridge University Press.

Mahrt, M. (2018). Big data. In P. M. Napoli (Ed.), *Mediated communication* (pp. 627–642). Mouton De Gruyter.

Mahrt, M., & Scharkow, M. (2013). The value of big data in digital media research. *Journal of Broadcasting & Electronic Media, 57*(1), 20–33.

Mayer-Schönberger, V., & Cukier, K. (2013). *Big data. A revolution that will transform how we live, work, and think.* Murray.

McDonald, D., Bammer, G., & Dean, P. (2009). *Dialogue tools for research integration.* ANU E Press, The Australian National University.

Mellon, J., & Prosser, C. (2017). Twitter and Facebook are not representative of the general population: Political attitudes and demographics of British social media users. *Research & Politics, 4*(3), 2053168017720008. https://doi.org/10.1177/2053168017720008

Möller, J., van de Velde, R. N., Merten, L., & Puschmann, C. (2020). Explaining online news engagement based on browsing behavior: Creatures of habit? *Social Science Computer Review, 38*(5), 616–632. https://doi.org/10.1177/0894439319828012

Niederberger, M. (2014). Methoden der Experteneinbindung. In M. Niederberger & S. Wassermann (Eds.), *Methoden der Experten- und Stakeholdereinbindung in der sozialwissenschaftlichen Forschung* (pp. 33–47). Springer VS.

Niemann-Lenz, J., Bruns, S., Hefner, D., Knop-Huelss, K., Possler, D., Reich, S., . . . Klimmt, C. (2019). Crafting a strategic roadmap for computational methods in communication science: Learnings from the CCS 2018 conference in Hanover. *International Journal of Communication, 13*, 3885–3893.

Nosek, B. A., Alter, G., Banks, G. C., Borsboom, D., Bowman, S. D., Breckler, S. J., & Yarkoni, T. (2015). Promoting an open research culture. *Science, 348*(6242), 1422–1425. https://doi.org/10.1126/science.aab2374

Quandt, T. (2018). Dark participation. *Media and Communication, 6*(4), 36–48.

Resnyansky, L. (2019). Conceptual frameworks for social and cultural big data analytics: Answering the epistemological challenge. *Big Data & Society, 6*(1). https://doi.org/10.1177/2053951718823815

Rittel, H. W. J., & Webber, M. M. (1973). Dilemmas in a general theory of planning. *Policy Sciences, 4*, 155–169.

Ruths, D., & Pfeffer, J. (2014). Social media for large studies of behavior. *Science, 346*(6213), 1063–1064. https://doi.org/10.1126/science.346.6213.1063

Shah, D. V., Cappella, J. N., & Neuman, W. R. (2015). Big data, digital media, and computational social science: Possibilities and perils. *The ANNALS of the American Academy of Political and Social Science, 659*(1), 6–13. https://doi.org/10.1177/0002716215572084

Song, H., Tolochko, P., Eberl, J.-M., Eisele, O., Greussing, E., Heidenreich, T., . . . Boomgaarden, H. G. (2020). In validations we trust? The impact of imperfect human annotations as a gold standard on the quality of validation of automated content analysis. *Political Communication*, online first. https://doi.org/10.1080/10584609.2020.1723752

Stoltenberg, D., Maier, D., & Waldherr, A. (2019). Community detection in civil society online networks: Theoretical guide and empirical assessment. *Social Networks, 59*, 120–133. https://doi.org/10.1016/j.socnet.2019.07.001

Sun, Z., Lorscheid, I., Millington, J. D., Lauf, S., Magliocca, N. R., Groeneveld, J., . . . Buchmann, C. M. (2016). Simple or complicated agent-based models? A complicated issue. *Environmental Modelling & Software, 86*, 56–67. https://doi.org/10.1016/j.envsoft.2016.09.006

Theocharis, Y., & Jungherr, A. (2021). Computational social science and the study of political communication. *Political Communication, 38*(1–2), 1–22. https://doi.org/10.1080/10584609.2020.1833121

Troitzsch, K. G. (2016). The meaningfulness of statistical significance tests in the analysis of simulation results. *International Journal of Agent Technologies and Systems, 8*(1), 18–45. https://doi.org/10.4018/IJATS.2016010102

Van Atteveldt, W., & Peng, T.-Q. (2018). When communication meets computation: Opportunities, challenges, and pitfalls in computational communication science. *Communication Methods and Measures, 12*(2–3), 81–92. https://doi.org/10.1080/19312458.2018.1458084

Vargo, C. J., Guo, L., & Amazeen, M. A. (2018). The agenda-setting power of fake news: A big data analysis of the online media landscape from 2014 to 2016. *New Media & Society, 20*(5), 2028–2049. https://doi.org/10.1177/1461444817712086

Vis, F. (2013). A critical reflection on big data: Considering APIs, researchers and tools as data makers. *First Monday, 18*(10). https://doi.org/10.5210/fm.v18i10.4878

Waldherr, A., Geise, S., & Katzenbach, C. (2019). Because technology matters: Theorizing interdependencies in computational communication science with actor – network theory. *International Journal of Communication, 13*, 3955–3975.

Waldherr, A., Geise, S., Mahrt, M., Katzenbach, C., & Nürnbergk, C. (2021). Towards a stronger theoretical grounding of computational communication science: How macro frameworks shape our research agendas. *Computational Communication Research*. Retrieved from https://osf.io/rpa98/

Waldherr, A., Maier, D., Miltner, P., & Günther, E. (2017). Big data, big noise: The challenge of finding issue networks on the web. *Social Science Computer Review, 35*(4), 427–443. https://doi.org/10.1177/0894439317690337

Weber, E. P., & Khademian, A. M. (2008). Wicked problems, knowledge challenges, and collaborative capacity builders in network settings. *Public Administration Review, 68*(2). https://doi.org/10.1111/j.1540-6210.2007.00866.x

6

A CHANGING SURVEY LANDSCAPE

Lars Lyberg and Steven G. Heeringa

The data needs of government, business, science and human society in general are constantly evolving. Many of those data needs are met by conducting surveys of target populations of interest, and the scientific survey method as we know it today is the product of the continual change that has operated over time. This chapter aims to trace the path that survey design and methods have followed over the past century, placing its primary focus on how recent dramatic changes in the survey landscape are impacting survey designs, methods and the process of integrating survey data with other sources of data to produce estimates and make valid inferences concerning study populations.

The chapter begins with a brief overview of the past century's development of the survey method. "Challenges in Today's Survey Landscape" discusses five major challenges that current survey programs are facing, followed in "New Sources and Types of Data in the Survey Landscape" by a description of new types and sources of data that are available to survey producers working in official agencies, business and academia. Statistical integration of traditional survey designs and data with new data sources is the subject of the fourth section. The chapter concludes in "Facing the Future" with the authors' perspectives on how the ongoing process of change will affect the future of the survey method.

One hundred years of survey research

The concept of a survey as a tool for meeting evolving data needs is now so imbedded in modern societies' programs of official statistics, scientific research, opinion polling and marketing research that we can easily forget that the foundations of the scientific survey method were laid down only a little more than a century ago. If we go back to the late 19th and early 20th century, there was intense debate among official statisticians over the question of how to select samples that could provide useful and generalizable data for entire populations (Kiaer, 1897). The debate over the merits of the "representative method" and the primacy of probability samples was settled for the most part by seminal publications by Neyman (1934, 1937) and extensive development of survey applications during WWII and the following years. Most of the foundational texts and publications on sampling theory and methods were published in the post-war period spanning the late 1940s to the mid-1960s. The 20-year period from 1960–1980 has been described by some authors as the "golden age of survey research",

DOI: 10.4324/9781003024583-7

(Kalton, 2019). It was a period of major expansion for survey applications in official statistics and social research and advances related to survey design, data collection and data analysis. During this period, response rates for in-person household surveys were high, and the real and perceived quality of the data produced by the new survey programs justified the major financial outlays needed to support them. Although these years may in retrospect appear "golden", it was not a benign period. The advent of computerized data processing, the onset of telephone surveys, the introduction of stand-alone and networked systems of microcomputing and the arrival of the Internet dramatically altered the survey landscape of the last two decades of the 20th century.

During this same period, another change occurred. It affected not only how surveys were designed and conducted but also reoriented the expectations of the survey user community. The global quality movement that began in the 1980s also entered the survey landscape (Morganstein & Marker, 1997). As discussed in the following, accompanying the quality movement was a new focus on the needs of the customer. The introduction of the total survey error (TSE) paradigm (Groves, 1989) in the late 1980s gave survey data producers and users a unified framework for simultaneously considering all major sources of survey error. As a matter of fact, the TSE paradigm was really a reintroduction of the U.S. Census Bureau Survey Model developed in the late 1950s and early 1960s by Morris Hansen and colleagues. The survey model was, however, incomplete in the sense that it covered mainly sampling and measurement errors (Hansen, Hurwitz, & Bershad, 1961; Bailar & Dalenius, 1969). Under TSE, the optimal survey design achieves minimum total survey error for a given budget or total cost. Survey methodologists and practitioners were quick to adopt the TSE paradigm but also recognized that it focused primarily on the survey as a process that began with design and ended with analysis of the data. As a result, by the early 2000s the broader concept of a total survey quality (TSQ) framework gained in popularity (Biemer & Lyberg, 2003). The TSE goal of achieving accuracy in survey results by minimizing the total survey error is one of the primary dimensions of the TSQ framework, but the latter recognizes additional dimensions of quality, including credibility, compatibility, usability, relevance, accessibility, timeliness, completeness and coherence (Brackstone, 1999; Biemer, 2010). These added dimensions ensure that the products of the survey program are truly "fit for use" or, in the words of Deming (1944), "useful in the sense of providing a rational basis for action". National statistical institutes had endorsed TSQ since at least 1980, but the additional dimensions could vary between producers depending on what users were most interested in (Lyberg, 2012).

Challenges in today's survey landscape

Today's survey programs face major challenges in meeting total survey quality standards. The decline in survey participation rates is certainly not a new challenge but has intensified in the past three decades. As response rates have declined, there has also been a rapid increase in the cost of traditional survey methods such as in-person and telephone data collection. Ironically, as response rates have declined and costs have risen, the demand for survey data has never been stronger (Groves, 2011). Most survey programs that produce nonproprietary data serve a very broad community of stakeholders in government, industry, academia and general society, and these "survey users" are all asking survey producers to meet varied needs for data that are "wider, deeper and better" while at the same time doing it more "quickly and cheaper". Furthermore, technology changes and competition from new data sources and approaches to data delivery are other challenges for today's survey programs.

It is impossible to discuss each of these challenges in isolation, since they are by no means independent of one another, and strategies for addressing these challenges must take account of these interdependencies.

Response rates

Nonresponse issues have been the concern of survey researchers for many years. The decline in response rates to traditional surveys conducted in person or by telephone has been a global phenomenon (Groves & Couper, 1998; deLeeuw & de Heer, 2002). Until the late 1980s, response rates for U.S. household surveys conducted by field interviewers generally exceeded 80%. Focusing on the past 25 years, Williams and Brick (2018) present data that show a clear pattern of steadily declining response rates for five major repeated cross-sectional studies of U.S. household populations. For example, the response rate to the monthly Current Population Survey (CPS) declined from 90% in 1990 to approximately 76% in 2014. Over roughly this same period, deLeeuw, Hox, amd Luiten (2018) analyzed response rate trends in the labor force surveys for 25 countries, including European labor force survey data collection agencies, New Zealand, Australia, Canada and the United States. After accounting for country to country heterogeneity in base response rates, their analysis suggested a population-average decline in response rates of approximately 0.73% for each additional year.

Telephone sample frames, random digit dialing (RDD) and computer-assisted telephone interview (CATI) data collection methodology entered the survey landscape in the late 1970s and early 1980s, and by 1990, telephone surveys were firmly established as a leading mode for collecting marketing, polling and scientific data in the United States (Groves & Kahn, 1979). Response rates for surveys conducted by telephone have always been lower than those for in-person interview surveys; however, in the early years, scientific telephone surveys such as the University of Michigan Survey of Consumer Attitudes were able to achieve response rates that exceeded 65%. Paralleling the trend seen for in-person surveys, telephone response rates declined steadily over the period 1990 to the present (Curtin, Presser, & Singer, 2005). Accelerating the decline in telephone response rates has been the shift from household landline phones to individual mobile phones. For example, average response rates for the Pew Center's nonpartisan telephone polls have declined from 37% in 1997 to a low of 6% in 2018 (Kennedy & Hartig, 2019).

For many survey data collections, self-administered web surveys or web panels based on probability samples now provide a very cost-effective alternative to RDD telephone surveys. While web surveys have many desirable features, a high response rate is not one of them (Couper, 2008).

Survey costs

Compounding the challenge that declining survey participation poses to survey practitioners are the rising costs of traditional survey data collection methods. Much of the increase in costs of in-person or telephone data collection can be attributed to economic factors such as rising labor costs, increased travel costs and general inflation of related expenses that survey producers cannot directly control. However, the rising costs of surveys can also be attributed to changes in data collection protocols that survey producers feel are needed to address the steady decline in response rates. These include the costs associated with extended callbacks and refusal conversion efforts as well as incentive payments to encourage survey participation.

Today's surveys are also more costly because stakeholders expect much more from the survey products. With few exceptions, today's survey programs are operating under a far more demanding set of expectations than they were three decades ago. Due to the increased financial outlay needed to field surveys, advances in information technology and the increased data-dependence of our societies, survey programs are now challenged to produce data that is wider (broader content), deeper (more detailed and higher spatial resolution) and more timely and transparent (more quickly available and usable by stakeholders). At the same time they must deal with these challenges, survey producers are expected to achieve better quality and do so cheaply (Holt, 2007).

Technological effects on modes of data collection

The Internet and related technological innovations have had a transformative effect on the survey landscape, influencing not only how significant amounts of survey data are being collected but also the standards and expectations for the transparency, access and usability of survey products.

Until roughly 1980, the capacity to design and field large population-based surveys belonged to government agencies and large academic and other research organizations. Development of probability-based telephone surveys in the 1980s allowed smaller research units – many formerly survey users – to participate directly as survey producers. The advent of 2G digital cellular service in the 1990s and SMS messaging was a significant technological change. As the population of cell phone users grew in the United States, the proportion of "cell only" members of the population – those with no complementary landline service – was small, and most survey producers relied only on the RDD landline frame for sample selection. However, as time passed, the proportion of "cell only" households continued to rise as young adults formed new households and established households abandoned landline service. By roughly 2015, most U.S. RDD telephone surveys had shifted entirely to sampling from frames of cellular numbers (Lavrakas et al., 2015). Household landlines typically serve families or individuals at their residential addresses, but cell phones are personal devices that generally accompany the owner throughout their day. For many reasons (including respondent safety while driving or engaged in other activities, restricted use at work, lack of privacy in public places and highly selective call screening) successful contacts and interviews with RDD cell phone samples are more difficult and have higher costs per completed case than traditional landline RDD samples. Response rates to cold contacts via cell phone are extremely low. Although RDD telephone surveys are still being conducted in the United States in 2020, many survey producers are considering abandoning the telephone survey method and shifting their survey data collections to multi-mode web/mail surveys or transitioning to data collection with established web panels (Olson et al., 2019). This is also the trend in other countries where telephone surveys are conducted in traditional ways (Eurostat, 2014).

With the introduction and widespread adoption of 3G (and eventually 4G and 5G) cellular service, the new smart phones and other enabled devices (iPads, tablets) could now connect to the internet. Web surveys, which previously had to be completed on a desktop or laptop computer, could now be accessed and completed on individual smart phones. Today, most well-designed web surveys can be completed on a range of devices, including laptops, tablets and smart phones.

Today's direct and efficient internet communication with sample populations via e-mail, web portals and user-friendly survey software has provided the smallest research units the capability to design, author and administer a survey data collection. Web survey panels capable of on-demand data collection for omnibus survey content have been developed and are widely used in today's polling, marketing and attitudinal survey research. To optimize the cost and error tradeoff of various modes of data collection (in-person, telephone, mail and web), today's major survey programs are frequently turning to sequential or adaptively designed multi-mode data collection protocols in which self-administered web surveys are the preferred mode.

Expectations of survey funders and user communities

Survey programs of official statistical agencies, academic institutions and not-for-profit research organizations have long supported open sharing of survey results with their stakeholders in government, business, academia and the public. A half-century ago, data sharing typically took the form of printed reports prepared by the survey producers. During the 1970s and early 1980s, advances in electronic data storage, mainframe computing and statistical software enabled survey producers to begin to share disclosure protected microdata files with stakeholders who had computer capacity and statistical capability to perform their own analysis of the survey data. The advent of microcomputing in the mid-1980s had a major impact on both survey producers and survey users. Initially this effect took the form of personal workstations with microcomputer versions of survey software, followed quickly by networks of workstations for computer-assisted telephone interviewing and, by the early 1990s, stand-alone laptops and software for computer-assisted personal interviewing (CAPI). As these developments in computing technology took over the survey landscape, they brought new opportunities to directly share micro-level data with the survey users. Advances in compact data storage and file transfer protocols made it much easier for survey producers to share data and greatly facilitated survey users' ability to access survey data and perform their own analysis.

Hot on the heels of the microcomputing developments came the introduction of the world wide web/Internet. It is hard to overstate the effects that the Internet has had on the survey landscape. The Internet and electronic mail rapidly accelerated communication and information exchange through all stages of the survey life cycle – from design and planning, to production management and secure data transfer from data collection systems, to the dissemination of final survey data and documentation.

As these and other advances in information technology have broken down barriers to our ability to store, access and share information, they have enabled survey producers to meet greater quality standards for data access and transparency. By the same turn, stakeholders' expectations for data access and transparency with respect to survey designs, methods and the data themselves have risen sharply.

The result of these technical, statistical and scientific advances is that there has been a shift in how survey programs must prioritize internal data analysis and reporting activities vs. collecting and providing access to data that others will analyze. Many of today's survey programs operate in an environment where traditional reporting and summarization of findings is no longer their primary responsibility. Instead, the focus has been redirected to supporting a diverse community of government, business and scientific data users who will conduct secondary analyses of the data. As discussed in more detail in the following, these statistical and data science user communities are increasingly performing analysis and modeling activities that integrate data from multiple sources.

Competition from alternative data sources, big data and data science

Declining survey response rates, rising costs and demands for data that are accessible and "wider, deeper and cheaper" have caused many in government, business and academia to look for new sources of data. For example, government survey programs worldwide that conduct "market basket" surveys to supply data to derive consumer price indices (CPIs) are using transactional data routinely captured at supermarket and retail store checkouts as an alternative or supplemental data source. This application is probably the most common current implementation of big data use in statistics production (Japec & Lyberg, 2020). "Big data" and "data science" have certainly challenged policy makers, scientists, statisticians and others to rethink the role that traditional surveys may play in meeting future data needs (Japec et al., 2015). Early on, some futurists in social scientific fields held out limited prospects for the future of surveys, as reflected in the following quote from Savage and Burrows (2007).

> where data on whole populations are routinely gathered as a by-product of institutional transactions, the sample survey seems a very poor instrument.

The popular press went even further, predicting the demise not only of designed data collections but the entire scientific method (Anderson, 2008). Fortunately, strong proponents with extensive experience in the field presented a counterargument (Groves, 2011; Couper, 2013) that survey practitioners should not view big data as a threat but as stimulus to adapt to opportunities that these new sources of data provide.

> Survey research is not dying, it is changing. . . . The challenge to the survey profession is to discover how to combine designed data with organic data, to produce resources with the most efficient information-data ratio.
>
> Groves (2011)

Nonprobability sampling

"New Sources and Types of Data in the Survey Landscape" briefly reviews many of the new and alternative forms of data that may be statistically integrated with data from surveys, including other survey data, administrative data, geographic information system (GIS)/global positioning systems (GPS) geospatial data, data from biomonitoring and sensors and many new forms of organic or "found" data such as web content or social media. Many of these new or alternative data sources are characterized by the fact that they arise through automatic, voluntary or participatory processes that may be highly selective in representing populations of interest. As noted in the introduction, for almost 100 years, probability sampling or the "representative method" and design-based methods for estimation and inference have been adopted by most government, business and academic researchers as the gold standard for achieving unbiased or nearly unbiased inference in population-based research. Survey statisticians of the authors' generation have worked most of their careers assuming that the debate over probability sampling vs. nonprobability sampling had been put to rest by 1950. For reasons of timing, cost or practicality, quota sampling, convenience sampling, volunteer samples and other nonprobability or pseudo-probability means of gathering population data have certainly continued to be used in marketing, polling and other specialized data collection activities. Even strong advocates of model-based inference acknowledged the advantage of working with data collected under probability sample designs (Rubin, 1984).

Over the past decade, the statistical literature has reflected a renewed interest in population estimation and inference from nonprobability data sources (Baker et al., 2013). There are several potential explanations for the renewed interest in the treatment of data from nonprobability methods. First and foremost, with the exception of a few large, national administrative data systems that have almost universal population coverage, most of the "big data" that governments, businesses and other researchers hope to utilize in their statistical programs are obtained from selective, convenient, volunteer or other nonrandom segments of the target population. Second, increased needs for studies of rare, highly specialized or "hard to survey" populations cannot be cost-effectively met using traditional probability sampling methods, and nonprobability techniques or network sampling techniques such as respondent driven sampling (RDS) are necessary to shed some light on these hard to survey populations. Finally, recent advances generally associated with data science and the big data movement have de-emphasized design of data collection and promoted the use of models – possibly trained or calibrated – for population estimation and prediction. The following quote illustrates the current divide between traditionalists and modelers.

> However, self-selection dramatically departs from the traditional, so-called gold standard approaches of targeted enrollment to scientific studies and sampling frame-based surveys. Traditionalists argue that we must adhere to the values of planned accrual and follow-up for all studies and identification of a sampling frame for surveys and possibly also for epidemiological and other such studies. Others propose that we should stop worrying about it and open up accrual, using modern approaches (covariate adjustments, find instrumental variables, "big data") to make the necessary adjustments.
>
> Keiding and Louis (2016)

For an overview of the debate, see Cornesse et al. (2020), who also outline paths for continued research regarding the use of nonprobability sampling in surveys. See also Volume 2, Chapter 12 (Andridge & Valliant) and Volume 2, Chapter 13 (Bethlehem), in this publication.

New sources and types of data in the survey landscape

"Data! data! data!" he cried impatiently. "I can't make bricks without clay."
Arthur Conan Doyle, *The Adventure of the Copper Beeches*

If Sherlock Holmes were engaged today in an investigation – criminal, statistical or otherwise – he would find himself awash in data. As Groves (2011) noted almost a decade ago, survey research is undergoing rapid change, and survey producers must adapt to the new landscape and the many new types of data that governments, businesses and science are demanding and our advanced technologies and information capture systems are providing.

Statistical data integration

Statistical data integration is a relatively new term that we will use in this chapter. It refers to the theory and methods of combining multiple sources of data (Allen, 2017). The Australian Bureau of Statistics (ABS) website defines statistical data integration as

> combining data from different administrative and/or survey sources, at the unit level (i.e., for an individual person or organization) or micro level (e.g., information for a small geographic area), to produce new datasets for statistical and research purposes. This approach leverages more information from the combination of individual datasets than is available from the individual datasets separately.

Statistical data integration that incorporates survey data occurs in different ways. The first of these, which Allen (2017) labels "multi-view", occurs at the micro or individual level and merges data from multiple sources (e.g., survey questionnaires, administrative records, biomarkers such as genetic data derived from saliva or blood samples) for the purpose of conducting joint analysis of the multivariate data. The Adolescent Brain Cognitive Development (ABCD) study funded by the U.S. National Institute of Drug Abuse (NIDA) is a good example of this form of statistical integration in which baseline and longitudinal survey measures on children's medical history, family, school life and self-reported activities are integrated with testing data, administrative data (school and medical records), geographically linked environmental data, genetic and genomic information and extensive neuroimaging data on brain morphology and function (Garavan et al., 2018).

Even more challenging forms of statistical data integration are those in which distinct sets of survey and nonsurvey data are brought together to develop pooled statistical estimates and inferences. The simplest of these are well-established procedures for cumulating data from repeated surveys to increase the sample size and precision for analyses of rare subpopulations or smaller geographic domains (Kish, 1987). Combining independent surveys of varying sample size and content can serve to enhance precision of population estimates or to calibrate estimates from one survey (Schenker & Raghunathan, 2007). A detailed survey based on a probability sample may serve as the training dataset for statistical modeling of larger administrative data systems or as a tool for evaluating coverage and selection biases in "found" or "organic data" sets with unknown sampling or error properties (see survey-assisted modeling in the following). Finally, although theory and methods are still under development, in an ad hoc form of "meta-analysis", population estimates from sample survey data may be combined with independent estimates from other data sources to inform decisions by policy makers and businesses. Sometimes this ad hoc form is called, somewhat improperly, borrowing strength.

The earliest examples of statistical data integration by survey producers involved data from administrative data systems. For at least half of the past century, administrative data systems have served as frames for selecting samples of target populations. Through legislation or direct consent of the surveyed units, it naturally became more common to augment the micro-level survey data with linked data from administrative data systems. Official statistical agencies have been the leaders in the integration of surveys and administrative data systems. Many of these agencies are actively engaged in research and testing the feasibility of relying more heavily on both public- and private-sector sources of administrative data as the primary source of data for many of their official statistics. Examples of official administrative record systems that are commonly being used or considered for use in integrated applications with survey data include tax records, pension and employment system records, business licensing, medical insurance and medical payment systems. Quite a few countries have replaced their traditional enumeration censuses with administrative record censuses. Also, in some countries, entire statistical programs are based on administrative records (Wallgren & Wallgren, 2014). Advances in electronic monitoring, scanning and tracking of sales and flows of commodities and services are new sources of data for economic and financial statistics programs that traditionally have relied heavily on surveys.

Geographic information system software; global positioning systems; and satellite, aerial and other geo-imaging tools

These tools, such as Google Earth and Street View, now play major roles in probability sample designs for populations as well as a geospatial reference for integrating many forms of nonsurvey data. Historically, innovative spatial sampling and estimation methods based on geographic coordinate systems have been widely used in the fields of agriculture (https://landsat.usgs.gov/), geology, natural resources and wildlife population dynamics (Thompson, 1992). Precursors to today's sophisticated software tools such as ArcGIS (www.arcgis.com) enabled sample designers to use these digitized map resources in combination with census and other geographic data to visualize spatial distributions of populations and to improve the efficiency of sample stratification and sample allocation in multi-stage area probability sample designs (Heeringa, Haeussler, & Connor, 1994). The sophistication and usability of commercially available geographic information system software and global positioning systems advanced rapidly in the 1990s. The U.S. government turned off "selective availability" to GPS satellites in May of 2000, enabling further rapid advances in civilian applications for GPS and related GIS technology. The advent of Google Earth in 2001 was one such advance. Google Earth integrated overlapping satellite images with the global GPS coordinate system, enabling users to locate and visualize areas of the Earth's surface with a high degree of resolution – a resolution fine enough to locate and assign coordinates to individual structures as small as a typical dwelling unit. See, for example, Eckman, Himelein, and Dever's (2019) application of multiple GIS tools to handle problems associated with countries where traditional sampling designs are not possible.

Biomonitoring data

Despite debate over the need for external validity in some forms of epidemiological research (Keiding & Louis, 2016), there is no question that probability sample surveys remain important tools in studies of disease prevalence and general health-related characteristics of target populations. In the United States, the National Health Interview Survey (NHIS) and the National Health and Nutrition Examination Survey (NHANES) provide critical longitudinal data series on the health of U.S. adults and children. Similar national health survey programs in countries around the globe are fielded independently by national health ministries or as part of multinational programs of coordinated health surveys. Historically, epidemiological and other health studies relied on self-reports of symptoms or a diagnosis by a medical professional, such as "Have you ever been told by a doctor that you have diabetes or high blood sugar?" Today's survey programs routinely combine traditional survey interviews with biomarker samplings (blood spots, whole blood, saliva) that are used in turn for direct diagnosis of conditions such as diabetes, hyperlipidemia and physical stress as well as for advanced studies in genetics and genomics. Epidemiological survey programs are also expanding to include testing of population attributes such as educational achievement, mental health and cognitive functioning. Researchers in the neurosciences are now routinely fielding population-based studies that combine survey-based assessments with neuroimaging to study brain morphology and function. Internationally, in response to the 2020 COVID-19 pandemic, governments, businesses and academic researchers have launched extensive population studies that will combine survey measures of recent health status with testing for active coronavirus infections or serology testing for viral exposure and immune response.

Sensor technology and networks

Technological advances in sensor technology and networks (the Internet of Things) have enabled researchers in agricultural, environmental sciences and medical research to combine detailed point-in-time survey observations with continuous streams of monitoring data from sensors and internet-enabled devices such as smart phones and watches and wearable devices.

Internet access to public web sites for government agencies, business enterprises and non-profit organizations provides statistical programs with an alternative avenue to compile data that historically may have relied exclusively on sample surveys. Social media services such as Twitter, Facebook and many others are a natural "big data" source of information on population behaviors, expectations, trends and attitudes (Foster, Gahni, Jarmin, Kreuter, & Lane, 2016). Data accessed anonymously from social media and web sources are often used directly as a standalone source, but they may also be linked to survey data. Survey researchers in the social sciences, education and health research often ask participants for consent to link their survey responses to information that is abstracted from their social media accounts.

In summary, today's survey programs may no longer simply collect data using traditional survey questionnaires. Instead, the survey protocols are increasingly serving as a platform for collecting multiple types of data (questionnaires, tests and assessments, biomarkers, geographic information, consent for linkage to administrative record systems and personal social media accounts), all with the aim that these data will be integrated in analyses that support diverse study goals.

Statistical data integration and statistical inference in today's world: where does the survey method fit?

As described previously, today's statistical programs are increasingly challenged to meet stakeholder needs for data that are timely and detailed with respect to the types of data that are supported and the demographic, socioeconomic and geographic specificity. Effective application of statistical integration of surveys and nonsurvey sources of data begins at the design stage and continues through the analysis phase that produces the statistical outputs – estimates and inferences – that are the ultimate objective for combining data sources. In designing a new integrated statistical program, it is necessary to identify and evaluate all available sources of data that are fit for purpose. The decision of whether to include a data source must follow a total error paradigm rather than a TSE paradigm and balance errors and costs (Biemer & Amaya, 2020). It makes no sense in today's world to design and field a costly national survey program when most of the key variables of interest may be available from, say, administrative or transactional data sources. By the same token, relying on a nonsurvey data source that is subject to high noncoverage and missing or poorly measured variable items simply because it is low cost is not a suitable approach.

Adapting survey designs, estimation and inferences to the information content of available data sources

Figure 6.1 illustrates how today's approaches to statistical data integration relate to the availability of existing data sources. In the setting represented by the apex of the triangle, where existing sources of population data on a variable of interest (Y), covariates (Z) or their relationships, $f(Y \mid Z)$ do not exist or are out of date, we continue to rely on robust survey methods and design–based estimation to yield estimates and inferences for the population statistics. Moving from the apex to the base of the triangle, we next encounter settings and problems that are richer in available data that can be employed both in design and in statistical estimation. A good example of this data landscape would be the business statistics programs of official statistics agencies where established registries are often rich in historical observations on the variables of interest, Y, as well as current covariate information (Z) from administrative processes such as licensing, taxation or mandated reporting. Here, even when new survey data are required, the existing data support model-assisted survey design and calibration of survey estimates to ancillary totals for the study population (Särndal, Swensson, & Wretman, 1992).

Moving further down the information triangle, we encounter statistical problems for which existing nonsurvey data sources are the primary inputs for statistical modeling of population characteristics and processes. Existing sources of data (big or small) may provide detailed data on population characteristics and events. Information on multivariate distributions for population characteristics and conditional distributions for some selected outcomes – both cross-sectional and longitudinal – may also be available. Here, survey data collections may play a supporting role in the modeling process but are no longer the sole or dominant basis for statistical estimation and inference. We label this "survey-assisted modeling". The survey assistance to the statistical model building can serve several purposes. A probability sample survey may be used to derive a dataset used to provide timely information on model form and estimates of model parameters relating outcomes of interest to the covariate information in the big data systems. The survey may assist in refining and validating the model, providing more complete information on multivariate associations, mediating and moderating effects and chronological/spatial variation in the big data models. An "assisting survey" may be designed to provide compensation for known problems such as noncoverage, nonobservation or item missing data in existing nonsurvey inputs to a statistical model or more generally to develop a better understanding of the total error profile of the nonsurvey data sources that will serve as input to a population model.

At the base of the information triangle, we find the world that some imagine as the end of the line for the survey method or, as quoted previously, "where data on whole populations are routinely gathered as a by-product of institutional transactions, the sample survey seems a very poor instrument". The assumption is that the existing and new nonsurvey sources of data including administrative records and other big data are sufficient to meet the statistical objective. There no longer is a role, even a supporting one, for survey designs. Estimates and inferences will be based exclusively on statistical or algorithmic models fitted to the

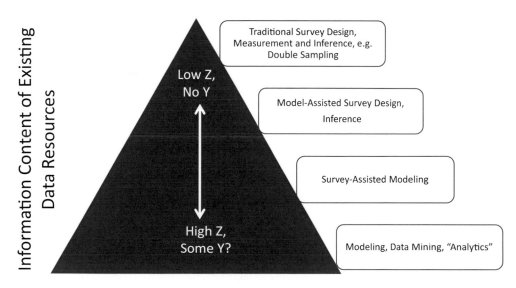

Figure 6.1 Integrating survey data and administrative data. Adaptation to information content of available data.

available nonsurvey data sources. Some authors emphasize that there has been a paradigm shift to increased use of nonparametric and algorithmic models in modern statistical practice (Efron & Hastie, 2016) and also in production of official statistics (Buelens, Boonstra, van den Brakel, & Daas, 2012; Buelens, Burger, & van den Brakel, 2018.). These new tools certainly have applications in statistical programs, but care should be taken to avoid creating yet another schism based on what Breiman (2001) labeled "data modeling" as distinct from "algorithmic modeling" – the former referring to approaches that depend on a probability model for the data-generating mechanism and the latter seeking the highest predictive accuracy with less concern for ability to explain or interpret the model. Without question, there will be statistical aims in government, business and academia that can be met solely by fitting models to available secondary data sources such as administrative record systems, transactional databases or organic sources such as social media. However, as described in the following section, most applications will require a more involved approach to estimation and inference than simply applying the latest sophisticated statistical modeling software or computation algorithms to an available dataset. Effective applications of pure modeling approaches will require both in-depth substantive expertise and a detailed understanding of the mechanisms that generated the actual data inputs.

Increasing importance of statistical models

Considerable debate has occurred in the statistical literature over the relative merits of design-based and model-based approaches to estimation and inference (Hansen, Madow, & Tepping, 1983; Brewer, 2013). To some extent, in recent years, this debate has been clouded by lack of a concise definition for what is meant when we say we are employing models in our statistical practice.

Statistical models (either explicitly defined or implicit in the assumptions underlying our methods for estimation and inference) underlie almost all of survey statistics. Even under design-based theory where π_i are inclusion probabilities for population elements, we assume a model in which, over repeated sampling from the population, the expanded quantities $y_i^* = y_i / \pi_i$ are exchangeable conditional on parameters θ_y in the true population model for a random variable Y regardless of which Y is of interest. More realistically, when design-based estimation and inference incorporate modeled weighting adjustments for nonresponse, we practice what Little (2012) labels "quasi-design based" inference. Here we work with the weighted quantities $y_i^{**} = (y_i / \pi_i) \cdot W_{NR} = y_i^* \cdot \left[p(I \mid Z, \phi) \right]^{-1}$ that again assume the y_i^* are exchangeable conditional on the parameters θ_y but also that the response mechanism with indicator (I) is missing at random (MAR) conditional on observed covariates Z and that ϕ_y and θ_y are independent for all Y. In model-assisted estimation and inference, a probability model $p(Y \mid Z, \theta)$ is employed to "assist" or calibrate the weighted design-based inference, for example, $y_i^{***} = y_i^{**} \cdot W_{GREG}$ for the generalized regression estimator (Särndal et al., 1992). Under the model-assisted approach, the calibration model $p(Y \mid Z, \theta)$ can be chosen to be specific to individual Ys. In practice, it often is not, and a single model relating the Ys to the available Zs is assumed in the calibrated weighting.

In a sense, then, all of us as practitioners have been dealing with implicit or explicit models in estimation and inference whether we realize it or not. Whatever theoretical schism remains, current and future statistical practice will require more careful attention to explicit models for both the data itself but also the "inclusion process" that generates the data to be analyzed. This is particularly true given the trend toward employing administrative and "found" data along with traditional survey sample data in the production of statistics.

Regardless of how explicitly the "statistical model" is specified, as we transition to greater usage of statistical data integration, the elements of a working model that should always be recognized and taken into account are:1) the population model/likelihood for the data, $p(Y \mid Z)$; 2) prior information, training (empirical) data to inform estimation of model parameters, θ_y; 3) informative features of the data collection design (e.g., stratification, clustering of population elements); and, importantly, 4) a model of the inclusion probability of the observed data, $p(I \mid Y, Z, \varphi)$, taking into account potential noncoverage and selection bias due to nonresponse, item missing data or measurement inconsistencies and errors. To formalize our thinking on a model-based approach to official statistics, Little (2012, 2015) and others (Box, 1980; Rubin, 1984) advocate a "calibrated Bayes" approach to estimation and inference.

An important benefit of using statistical models in statistical data integration is that the model provides a unified, explicit (transparent) approach to statistical analyses of data from multiple sources (surveys, administrative data, found data). In integrated modeling, data obtained through use of probability samples improves the ignorability of the inclusion mechanism, while the selective or nonignorable inclusion probabilities of nonprobability samples or "found data" are explicitly incorporated into the inferential model. Estimation and inference under a correct form of the model are statistically efficient, and computational resources and software tools needed to apply models (including Bayesian methods and algorithmic machine learning tools) are now available. Modeling methods and tools for statistical data integration are at the forefront of new innovations in statistics, and there will likely be major advances in the coming years. Guidance on some of the latest developments can be found in Zhang and Chambers (2019), Buskirk, Kirchner, Eck, and Signorino (2018), Kern, Klausch, and Kreuter (2019) and Savitsky and Srivastiva (2018).

A more formal model-based approach to statistical estimation and inference does bring some disadvantages and can add additional costs and training demands. The approach requires a more explicit dependence on model choice for Y, which may add an element of subjectivity. But such subjective assumptions are explicit and hopefully testable. Severe mistakes in model misspecification lead to bias. Therefore, greater subject matter expertise is needed for deep understanding of the data, model specification and model evaluation. Valid estimates and inferences under the model presented previously rely on accurate assessment of the inclusion probabilities, $p(I \mid Y, Z, \phi)$. Even when covariate information, Z, is available for all elements of the population, modeling the nonignorable inclusion mechanisms (e.g. for a nonprobability data source) is a complex statistical task and may not be fully effective in addressing selection biases in the data inputs to the model. Also, the covariates, Z, should be monitored over time to check if they are still relevant.

Facing the future

The past 100 years have taught us that we should expect the survey research landscape to be constantly changing and that adaptation is essential. Most will agree that the past two decades have been a period of accelerated change in the form of major new challenges to the way that we have traditionally used surveys, but we also recognize that this same period has produced opportunities for expansion and innovation in the application of population survey methods.

It is impossible to paint a clear picture of the future, but we can speculate on how survey research will evolve in response to the ongoing change in the survey landscape. Survey participation rates are now at all-time lows. Although reversing the response rate trends of the past two decades is probably not an attainable goal, innovations in survey data collection methods (e.g., incentives and effective motivational tools, mixed modes, adaptive and responsive design) may be able to halt the decline and possibly gain back some fraction of the loss in participation. Survey programs that rely heavily on in-person data collection with large population samples will continue to face inflationary cost pressures, and we expect the current trend toward using mixed modes and lower-cost online, self-administered data collection will continue. Lower-cost, multi-mode data collection is already the standard for large-scale data collection such as population censuses or major survey programs such as the American Community Survey (ACS).

The next decade holds promise for real advances in statistical data integration approaches that combine survey and nonsurvey data sources. Regarding big data and predictions that it would supplant future needs for surveys or other forms of statistical data collections, on the life cycle profile of technology adoption, we have passed the period of "inflated expectations". We are instead in a period of mature learning where we recognize the limitations of the various sources and forms of big data and how they may be optimally integrated with other survey and non-survey data to meet statistical program goals. To that end, total error and total quality paradigms and tools that have been developed and applied in survey programs are readily transferrable to the evaluation of big data and other alternative data sources, all of which bring their own costs and errors in the form of selectivity due to noncoverage and nonresponse, measurement errors and processing errors for key constructs and obsolete or missing data for important variables. Eurostat, which is in charge of the European Statistical System, has been very active during recent years in an attempt at defining and handling quality in an era of big data and its role in official statistics (Eurostat, 2020a, 2020b). In the same vein, the United Nations (2020) wants to implement a new role for official statistics in times of expanded possibilities.

Statistical data integration and optimal use of all data sources that are "fit for use" will require major new developments in statistical methods. Data scientists and statisticians have contributed major advances in software and methods for statistical and algorithmic modeling and machine learning. As described by Buskirk et al. (2018), machine learning algorithms and artificial intelligence methods are tools that can be applied in survey design, data collection, data processing and analysis. In statistical data integration, these advanced tools are important for many forms of data modeling and necessary for others; however, the tools themselves are not sufficient to ensure a reasonable total quality of a data product. Developments in the area of model fitting must also be accompanied by continued improvements in data management and data prepara-tion processes, including tools for data standardization and record linkage, de-duplication and fraudulent data detection (e.g., in social media data), imputation software and procedures for handling missing data, as well as software for text processing, coding and editing.

Statistical data integration is clearly a feature of the future survey and statistical landscape, and many applications will fall under the label of "survey-assisted modeling" that we defined in "Statistical Data Integration and Statistical Inference in Today's World: Where Does the Survey Method Fit?" Here, new theoretical and applied work is needed to effectively blend data from probability and nonprobability sources in estimation and inference (Citro, 2014; Elliott & Valli-ant, 2017; Lohr & Raghunathan, 2017; Dever, 2018; Rao, 2020). Little's (2012, 2015) sugges-tion to employ calibrated Bayes models to simultaneously reflect the probability likelihood for the model of interest, prior information on model form and parameters and, importantly, the data inclusion likelihood provides one theoretical framework for deriving estimates and making inferences from combinations of probability and nonprobability data sources. Little recom-mends that producers of official statistics embrace calibrated Bayes as the inferential paradigm to use. A major challenge in all of this exciting new work will be to establish how best to assign inclusion probabilities to observations in the integrated data structure. Here, again, smaller-scale, efficiently designed survey data collection will be one solution to addressing the problem of modeling inclusion probabilities for data from other nonrandom sources.

In conclusion, we can echo Groves (2011) and say with confidence that "survey research is not dying, it is changing", adding the corollary that change has always been a property of the survey landscape, and survey methodologists and practitioners have and must continue to address the challenges and take advantage of the opportunities that this change presents.

References

Allen, G. I. (2017). Statistical data integration: Challenges and opportunities. *Statistical Modelling*, *17*(4–5), 332–337.

Anderson, C. (2008). The end of theory. The data deluge makes the scientific method obsolete. *Wired Magazine: 16:07*.

Australian Bureau of Statistics (undated). Retrieved from https://statistical-data-integration.govspace.gov.au/about-3/process-map-for-data-integration-projects

Bailar, B., & Dalenius, T. (1969). Estimating the response variance components of the U.S. Bureau of the census survey model. *Sankhya, Series B, 31, 341–360*.

Baker, R., Brick, J. M., Bates, N. A., Battaglia, M., Couper, M. P., Dever, J. A., . . . Tourangeau, R. (2013). Summary report of the AAPOR task force on non-probability sampling. *Journal of Survey Statistics and Methodology*, *1*(2), 90–143.

Biemer, P. (2010). Total survey error: Design, implementation and evaluation. *Public Opinion Quarterly*, *74*(5), 817–848.

Biemer, P., & Amaya, A. (2020). Total error frameworks for hybrid estimation and their applications. In C. Hill, P. Biemer, T. Buskirk, L. Japec, A. Kirchner, S. Kolenikov, & L. Lyberg (Eds.), *Big data meets survey science: A collection of innovative methods* (Chapter 4, pp. 133–162). John Wiley & Sons.

Biemer, P., & Lyberg, L. (2003). *Introduction to survey quality*. John Wiley & Sons.

Box, G. E. P. (1980). Sampling and Bayes inferences in scientific modeling and robustness (with discussion). *Journal of the Royal Statistical Society, Series A, 143*, 383–430.

Brackstone, G. (1999). Managing data quality in a statistical agency. *Survey Methodology*, *25*(2), 1–23.

Breiman, L. (2001). Statistical modeling: The two cultures. *Statistical Science*, *16*(3), 199–215.

Brewer, K. (2013). Three controversies in the history of survey sampling. *Survey Methodology*, *39*(2), 249–262.

Buelens, B., Boonstra, H. J., van den Brakel, J., & Daas, P. (2012). *Shifting paradigms in official statistics. From design-based to model-based to algorithmic inference*. Statistics Netherlands, Discussion paper.

Buelens, B., Burger, J., & van den Brakel, J. (2018). Comparing inference methods for non-probability samples. *International Statistical Review*, *86*(2), 322–343.

Buskirk, T., Kirchner, A., Eck, A., & Signorino, C. (2018). An introduction to machine learning methods for survey researchers. *Survey Practice*, *11*(1), 1–10.

Citro, C. F. (2014). From multiple modes for surveys to multiple data sources for estimates. *Survey Methodology*, *40*, 137–161.

Cornesse, C., Blom, A., Dutwin, D., Krosnick, J., . . . Wenz, A. (2020). A review of conceptual approaches and empirical evidence on probability and nonprobability sample survey research. *Journal of Survey Statistics and Methodology*, *8*(1), 4–36.

Couper, M. P. (2008). *Designing effective web surveys*. Cambridge University Press.

Couper, M. P. (2013). Is the sky falling? New technology, changing media and the future of surveys. *Survey Research Methods*, *7*(3), 145–156.

Curtin, R., Presser, S., & Singer, E. (2005). Changes in telephone survey nonresponse over the past quarter century. *Public Opinion Quarterly*, *69*(1), 87–98.

deLeeuw, E., & de Heer, W. (2002). Trends in household survey nonresponse: A longitudinal and international comparison. In R. M. Groves, D. A. Dillman, J. L. Eltinge, & R. J. A. Little (Eds.), *Survey nonresponse* (pp. 41–54). John Wiley & Sons.

deLeeuw, E., Hox, J., & Luiten, A. (2018). International nonresponse trends across countries and years: An analysis of 36 years of labour force survey data. *Survey Insights: Methods from the Field*. Retrieved from http://surveyinsights.org/?p=10452

Deming, E. (1944). On errors in surveys. *American Sociological Review*, *9*, 359–369.

Dever, J. A. (2018). *Combining probability and nonprobability samples to form efficient hybrid estimates: An evaluation of the common support assumption*. Proceedings of the 2018 Federal Committee on Statistical Methodology (FCSM) Research Conference.

Eckman, S., Himelein, K., & Dever, J. (2019). Innovative sample designs using GIS technology. In T. Johnson, B.-E. Pennell, I. Stoop, & B. Dorer (Eds.), *Advances in comparative survey methods* (Chapter 4, pp. 67–92). John Wiley & Sons.

Efron, B., & Hastie, T. (2016). *Computer age statistical inference. Algorithms, evidence and data science.* Cambridge University Press.

Elliott, M. R., & Valliant, R. (2017). Inference for nonprobability samples. *Statistical Science, 32,* 249–262.

Eurostat. (2014). *Data collection for social surveys using multiple modes.* Final report, ESSnet DCSS.

Eurostat. (2020a). *ESSnet Big Data II. Work Package K, methods and quality.* Deliverable K6. Quality report template, Final version 28 February.

Eurostat. (2020b). *European Statistical System. Handbook for quality and metadata reports.* 2020 edition.

Foster, I., Gahni, R., Jarmin, R. S., Kreuter, F., & Lane, J. (Eds.). (2016). *Big data and social science: A practical guide to methods and tools.* Chapman and Hall and CRC Press.

Garavan, H., Bartsch, H., Conway, K., Decastro, A., et al. (2018). Recruiting the ABCD sample: Design considerations and procedures. *Developmental Cognitive Neuropsychology, 32,* 16–22.

Groves, R. M. (1989). *Survey errors and survey costs.* John Wiley & Sons.

Groves, R. M. (2011). Three eras of survey research. *Public Opinion Quarterly, 75*(5), 861–871.

Groves, R. M., & Couper, M. (1998). *Household Survey nonresponse.* John Wiley & Sons.

Groves, R. M., & Kahn, R. (1979). *Surveys by telephone: A national comparison with personal interviews.* Academic Press.

Hansen, M. H., Hurwitz, W., & Bershad, M. (1961). Measurement errors in censuses and surveys. *Bulletin of the International Statistical Institute,* 32nd Session, *38,* Part 2, 359–374.

Hansen, M. H., Madow, W. G., & Tepping, B. J. (1983). An evaluation of model-dependent and probability-sampling inferences in sample surveys (with discussion). *Journal of the American Statistical Association, 78,* 776–793.

Heeringa, S. G., Haeussler, J., & Connor, J. (1994). *The 1990 Survey Research Center National Sample.* Ann Arbor: Survey Research Center, Institute for Social Research, University of Michigan.

Holt, D. T. (2007). The official statistics Olympic challenge. *The American Statistician, 61*(1), 1–8.

Japec, L., Kreuter, F., Berg, M., Decker, P., et al. (2015). Big data in survey research: AAPOR task force report. *Public Opinion Quarterly, 79*(4), 839–880.

Japec, L., & Lyberg, L. (2020). Big data initiatives in official statistics. In C. Hill, P. Biemer, T. Buskirk, L. Japec, A. Kirchner, S. Kolenikov, & L. Lyberg (Eds.), *Big data meets survey science: A collection of innovative methods* (Chapter 9, pp. 275–302). John Wiley & Sons.

Kalton, G. (2019). Developments in survey research over the past 60 years: A personal perspective. *International Statistical Review, 87*(51), S10–S30.

Keiding, N., & Louis, T. A. (2016). Perils and potentials of self-selected entry to epidemiological studies and surveys. *Journal of the Royal Statistical Society, Series A, 179,* 319–376.

Kennedy, C., & Hartig, H. (2019, February 27). Response rates in telephone surveys have resumed their decline. *Facttank.* Pew Research Center.

Kern, C., Klausch, T., & Kreuter, F. (2019). Tree-based learning methods for survey research. *Survey Research Methods, 13*(1), 79–93.

Kiaer, A. (1897). The representative method of statistical surveys. *Kristiania Videnskapsselskabets Skrifter, Historisk-filosofiske Klasse, 4,* 37–56 (in Norwegian).

Kish, L. (1987). *Statistical design for research.* John Wiley & Sons.

Lavrakas, P. J., Benson, G., Blumberg, S., Buskirk, T., Flores-Cervantes, I., Christian, L., et al. (2015). *The future of U.S. general population telephone research* (Report of the AAPOR Task Force). The American Association for Public Opinion Research.

Little, R. J. (2012). Calibrated Bayes, an alternative inferential paradigm for official statistics. *Journal of Official Statistics, 28,* 447–462.

Little, R. J. (2015). Calibrated Bayes, an alternative inferential paradigm for official statistics in the era of big data. *Statistical Journal of the IAOS, 31*(4), 555–563.

Lohr, S. L., & Raghunathan, T. E. (2017). Combining survey data with other data sources. *Statistical Science, 32,* 293–312.

Lyberg, L. (2012). Survey quality. *Survey Methodology, 2,* 107–130.

Morganstein, D., & Marker, D. (1997). Continuous quality improvement in statistical agencies. In L. Lyberg, P. Biemer, M. Collins, E. deLeeuw, C. Dippo, N. Schwarz, & D. Trewin (Eds.), *Survey measurement and process quality* (pp. 475–500). John Wiley & Sons.

Neyman, J. (1934). On the two different aspects of the representative method: The method of stratified sampling and the method of purposive selection. *Journal of the Royal Statistical Society*, *97*, 558–625.

Neyman, J. (1937). Outline of a theory of statistical estimation based on the classical theory of probability. *Philosophical Transactions of the Royal Society of London, Series A, Mathematical and Physical Sciences*, *236*(767), 333–380.

Olson, K., Smyth, J. D., Horwitz, R., Keeter, S, Lesser, V., et al. (2019). *Report of the AAPOR task force on transitions from telephone surveys to self-administered and mixed mode surveys*. The American Association for Public Opinion Research.

Rao, J. N. K. (2020, April 3). On making valid inferences by combining data from surveys and other sources. *Sankhya B*. https://doi.org/10.1007/s13571-020-00227-w

Rubin, D. B. (1984). Bayesian justifiable and relevant frequency calculations for the applied statistician. *The Annals of Statistics*, *12*, 1151–1172.

Särndal, C.-E., Swensson, B., & Wretman, J. (1992). *Model assisted survey sampling*. Springer-Verlag.

Savage, M., & Burrows, R. (2007). The coming crisis of empirical sociology. *Sociology*, *41*(5), 885–889.

Savitsky, T. D., & Srivastiva, S. (2018). Scalable Bayes under informative sampling. *Scandinavian Journal of Statistics*, *45*, 534–556.

Schenker, N., & Raghunathan, T. E. (2007). Combining information from multiple surveys to enhance measures of health. *Statistics in Medicine*, *26*, 1802.

Thompson, S. K. (1992). *Sampling*. John Wiley & Sons.

United Nations. (2020). *Implementation of the new role of national statistical offices at the time of expanded possibilities*. Economic and Social Council, Economic Commission for Europe, Conference of European Statisticians, ECE/CES/2020/10.

Wallgren, A., & Wallgren, B. (2014). *Register-based statistics: Statistical methods for administrative data* (2nd ed.). John Wiley & Sons.

Williams, D., & Brick, M. (2018). Trends in U.S. face-to-face household survey nonresponse and level of effort. *Journal of Survey Statistics and Methodology*, *6*(2), 186–211.

Zhang, L.-C., & Chambers, R. L. (2019). *Analysis of integrated data*. CRC Press.

7

DIGITAL TRACE DATA

Modes of data collection, applications, and errors at a glance

Florian Keusch and Frauke Kreuter

Introduction

Digital traces, often defined as "records of activity (trace data) undertaken through an online information system (thus, digital)" (Howison, Wiggins, & Crowston, 2011, p. 769) or "behavioral residue [individuals leave] when they interact online" (Hinds & Joinson, 2018, p. 2), provide researchers with new opportunities for studying social and behavioral phenomena. These data come from a variety of technical systems, among others, business transaction systems, telecommunication networks, websites, social media platforms, smartphone apps, sensors built in wearable devices, and smart meters (Stier, Breuer, Siegers, & Thorson, 2019). Their analysis is a core part of computational social science (Edelmann, Wolff, Montagne, & Bail, 2020; Lazer et al., 2009). The excitement about digital trace data mainly stems from the fine-grained nature of the data that potentially allows researchers to observe individual and social behavior as well as changes in behavior at high frequencies and in real time. In addition, their measurement is non-intrusive; that is, the data collection happens without the observed person having to self-report. Removing human cognition and social interactions from the data collection process can mitigate their well-documented negative impacts on the quality of self-reports (e.g., Tourangeau, Rips, & Rasinski, 2000). However, the true potential of digital trace data to answer a broad range of social science research questions depends on the features of the specific type of data, that is, how they were collected and from whom. The original definition of digital trace data is limited to data that are found, that is, data created as a by-product of activities not stemming from a designed research instrument. We argue that digital traces can and should sometimes be collected in a designed way to afford researchers control over the data generating process and to expand the range of research questions that can be answered with these data.

Readers of this chapter will quickly realize that the use of digital trace data is in its early stages. We share the enthusiasm of many researchers to explore the capabilities of digital trace data, and enhance and systematize their collection. However, there is more research needed to tackle problems of privacy, quality assurance, and a good understanding of break-downs in the measurement process.

In this chapter, we introduce digital trace data and their use in the computational social sciences ("Use of Digital Trace Data to Study Social and Behavioral Phenomena"). In order to successfully use digital trace data, research goals need to be aligned with the available data, and

DOI: 10.4324/9781003024583-8

researchers need to recognize that not all data are suitable to answer the most relevant questions ("What Is the Research Goal?"). Data quality also needs to be evaluated with the research goal in mind ("Quality Assessment – Quality Enhancement"). To ensure reproducibility and replicability, documentation of digital trace data collection and processing is necessary, and creating sufficient transparency might be even harder than it already is with traditional data sources ("Transparency and Reporting Needs").

Use of digital trace data to study social and behavioral phenomena

Digital trace data allow researchers to study a variety of social and behavioral phenomena and can be organized in a number of ways. Given the fast-paced development of digital technology and the concomitant emergence of novel forms of digital trace data, a mere taxonomy of the types of digital trace data (e.g., social media data, Internet search data, geolocation data from smartphones) might become outdated quickly. Instead, we organize this section along dimensions of their use in computational social science (i.e., what type of phenomenon is studied?) and the type of observation used when collecting the data (i.e., how obtrusive is the observation?). This broader perspective might help social researchers to detect new sources of digital trace data and assess properties of digital trace data that already exist and data sources that will emerge in the future.

Type of phenomenon to be studied

We use two dimensions to describe the types of phenomena that can be studied with digital trace data (see Figure 7.1). First, we differentiate between phenomena that pertain to *individual behavior* and those that represent *social interactions* involving multiple individuals. Second, we distinguish between digital and analog phenomena, building on and extending the classification of mobile sensing data by Harari, Müller, Aung, and Rentfrow (2017). Digital phenomena are types of behaviors and interactions that happen while using a digital device, such as browsing the Internet, posting a comment on a social media platform, or making a video call. These behaviors and interactions are inherently digital, as they could not happen without the use of digital technology. Analog phenomena are behaviors and social interactions that people encounter in their everyday lives and that existed well before the age of digital technology, including face-to-face communication, physical activity, mobility, and sleep. While the phenomena themselves happen without the use of digital technology, the ubiquity of smartphones, wearables, sensors, and other digital devices leaves a digital trace about them that researchers can leverage.

The combination of these two dimensions creates four broad categories of phenomena that can be measured using digital trace data: digital individual behavior (e.g., browsing the Internet, typing a query into an online search engine, using an app), analog individual behavior (e.g., sleeping, working out, doing chores), digital social interactions (e.g., video calling, text messaging), and analog social interactions (e.g., face-to-face conversations). While it is helpful to organize phenomena along these four categories, we acknowledge that there can be overlap between the groups. In particular, behaviors and interactions that used to be primarily analog have become increasingly digital over time. Consider, for example, driving; driving is inherently an analog individual behavior that does not necessarily require digital technology. However, increasingly, cars rely on a combination of traditional mechanics and digital technologies for navigation, safety, and autonomous driving (Horn & Kreuter, 2019), changing driving from a primarily analog behavior to a digital behavior in the near future.

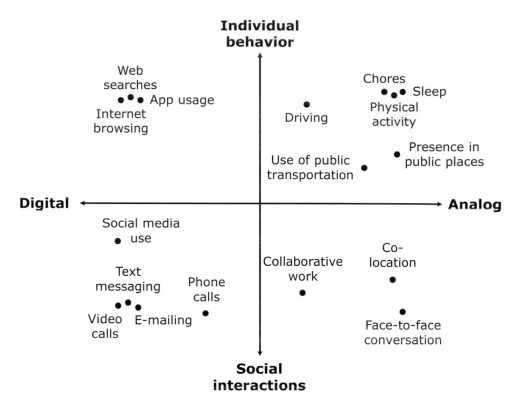

Figure 7.1 Examples of analog and digital behaviors and interactions that can be studied using digital trace data

Similarly, while individuals have always worked together on projects even without the help of digital technologies, collaborative work is increasingly done via platforms, such as Dropbox, Google Docs, and GitHub. Other phenomena can be considered as muddling the boundaries between individual behavior, social behavior, and social interaction. For example, while posting something on a social media platform is at first an individual behavior (in particular if the site is private and there are no followers), the post might trigger a conversation with other users, leading to social interactions. Figure 7.1 plots examples of analog and digital behaviors and interactions that can be measured using digital trace data in a two-dimensional space along our two dimensions.

One important piece that we will discuss in "What Is the Research Goal?" in more detail is the absence of digital trace data in all of these quadrants for certain people and certain behaviors through selective use of digital devices. It is very easy to get blindsided by the vast amount of data available and to overlook what is not there. Results of research projects can be easily biased.

Type of observation

Similar to traditional observational methods in the social sciences, the observation of aforementioned individual behaviors and social interactions using digital trace data can be more or less obtrusive, depending on how aware the individuals are of the fact that they are being observed and that their data are used for research. For example, a form of unobtrusive collection of digital trace data happens when private companies utilize technologies such as cookies and browser fingerprinting to collect information about the browsing behavior of Internet users (Lerner, Simpson, Kohno, & Roesner, 2016). Data brokers (e.g., Acxiom, LexisNexis Risk Solutions, Experian) provide vast amounts of these data back to interested parties, mainly with the goal to infer user attributes (e.g., sociodemographics, personal and political interest) from the contents visited for targeted marketing and political campaigning (Duhigg, 2012; Kruschinski & Haller, 2017; Nickerson & Rogers, 2014).

As a consequence of the introduction of the EU General Data Protection Regulation (GDPR) in May 2018, website providers have started asking Internet users to agree to the terms and conditions and accept cookies upon entering their website. However, only a small fraction of users seem to be actively reading and understanding what information they are agreeing to share with the website and third parties (Obar & Oeldorf-Hirsch, 2020). While in some contexts, for example, when using an online shop such as Amazon, users might expect their data to be used for various purposes, in other cases, for example, when scientists and researchers use the platform ResearchGate[1] to share papers, users might be surprised about the amount of data that is collected about them and with whom they are shared.

Digital trace data can also be collected in an unobtrusive manner from social media platforms where users post comments, share content, and interact with each other. These data can usually be scraped or accessed via an application programming interface (API). While APIs are usually not primarily designed for a research purpose but for software systems to communicate with each other, social scientists have explored the use of, for example, Twitter data to study political communication (Jungherr, 2015); Reddit data to measure strength of attitudes on politics, immigration, gay rights, and climate change (Amaya, Bach, Keusch, & Kreuter, 2020); and Facebook data to study friendship networks (Cheng, Adamic, Kleinberg, & Leskovec, 2016; Ugander, Karrer, Backstrom, & Marlow, 2011). While posts, for example, on Twitter are public by default, only few users are aware that their tweets are used by researchers (Fiesler & Proferes, 2018).

Several other forms of unobtrusive digital trace data have been used to study behavior and other social phenomena, for example:

- Researchers have used aggregated data from online search engines and the queries users post there to study consumer trends (Vosen & Schmidt, 2011), tracking of disease outbreaks such as influenza (Ginsberg et al., 2009), tracking of economic crises (Jun, Yoo, & Choi, 2018), political polarization (Flaxman, Goel, & Rao, 2016), and migration (Böhme, Gröger, & Stöhr, 2020; Vicéns-Feliberty & Ricketts, 2016).
- Blumenstock, Cadamuro, and On (2015) used anonymized mobile phone metadata from cellular network operators to predict poverty and wealth in Africa.
- Göbel and Munzert (2018) studied how German politicians enhance and change their appearance over time based on traces of changes to biographies on the online encyclopedia Wikipedia.
- Edelman, Luca, and Svirsky (2017) used Airbnb postings to understand racial discrimination.
- The Billion Price Project scrapes online prices to measure consumption and inflation across countries (Cavallo & Rigobon, 2016).
- Przepiorka, Norbutas, and Corten (2017) studied reputation formation in a cryptomarket for illegal drugs using price and buyers' ratings data of finished transactions.
- Philpot, Liebst, Levine, Bernasco, and Lindegaard (2020) analyzed bystander behavior, that is, whether and how individuals intervene during an emergency when in the presence of others or alone, using footage from closed-circuit television (CCTV) in public spaces.

- Social epidemiologists increasingly use electronic health record data to study, for example, the impact of built and social environment, for example, poverty rates in certain geographic areas, on health outcomes (Adler, Glymour, & Fielding, 2016).
- Several large-scale projects have deployed connected environmental sensors (Internet of Things [IoT]), measuring, for example, temperature, humidity, air quality, noise levels, and traffic volume, in so-called "smart cities" allowing researchers access to urban measurements with greater spatial and temporal resolution (Benedict, Wayland, & Hagler, 2017; Catlett, Beckman, Sankaran, & Galvin, 2017; Di Sabatino, Buccolieri, & Kumar, 2018; English, Zhao, Brown, Catlett, & Cagney, 2020).

In contrast, some collection of digital trace data is much more obtrusive in that the individuals who produce the data are made explicitly aware of the fact that their data are used for research purposes. That is, they have to consent to the data collection and install a designated research app to their smartphone, download a meter and install it as a plugin to their Internet browser, or wear a sensor on their body. Smartphones in particular have become popular data collection tools among social and behavioral scientists (Harari et al., 2016; Link et al., 2014; Raento, Oulasvirta, & Eagle, 2009), because many users carry their phones around with them throughout the day, allowing for real-time, in situ data collection using the growing number of sensors built into these devices (see Figure 7.2). Using designated research apps, researchers can get access to log files that are automatically generated by a device's operating system, enabling the collection of information about the usage of the device for tasks like texting, making and receiving phone calls, browsing the Internet, and using other apps on smartphones (i.e., digital behaviors and interactions). These data allow researchers to study, among others, social interactions (e.g., Keusch, Bähr, Haas, Kreuter, & Trappmann, 2020c), and even infer personality based on how users interact with the smartphone and what apps they use (e.g., Stachl et al., 2020). The native sensors built into smartphones and other wearable devices enable the measurement of users' current situation and their behavior outside of the generic functions of the phone, where the device is merely present in a given context (i.e., analog interactions and behaviors). For example, researchers have collected information about smartphone users' location and movements via global navigation satellite systems (GNSS), Wi-Fi, and cellular positioning, proximity to others using Bluetooth, and physical activity through accelerometer data. In addition, a combination of sensors (e.g., microphone, light sensor, accelerometer) can be used to capture information about the smartphone's and – by extension – the participant's ambient environment, inferring frequency and duration of conversation and sleep (e.g., Wang et al., 2014), as well as levels of psychological stress (Adams et al., 2014).

To provide context to the passively collected sensor and log data, researchers often administer in-app survey questions that inquire about phenomena such as subjective states (e.g., mood, attitudes) that require self-report (Conrad & Keusch, 2018). This combined approach of self-report and passive measurement on smartphones has been used to study, among others, mobility patterns (Elevelt, Lugtig, & Toepoel, 2019; Lynch, Dumont, Greene, & Ehrlich, 2019; Scherpenzeel, 2017), the influence of physical surroundings and activity on psychological well-being and health (Goodspeed et al., 2018; Lathia, Sandstrom, Mascolo, & Rentfrow, 2017; MacKerron & Mourato, 2013; York Cornwell & Cagney, 2017), student well-being over the course of an academic term (Ben-Zeev, Scherer, Wang, Xie, & Campbell, 2015; Harari, Gosling et al., 2017; Wang et al., 2014), integration efforts of refugees (Keusch et al., 2019), job search of men recently released from prison (Sugie, 2018; Sugie & Lens, 2017), the effects of unemployment on daily life (Kreuter, Haas, Keusch, Bähr, & Trappmann, 2020), and how students interact with

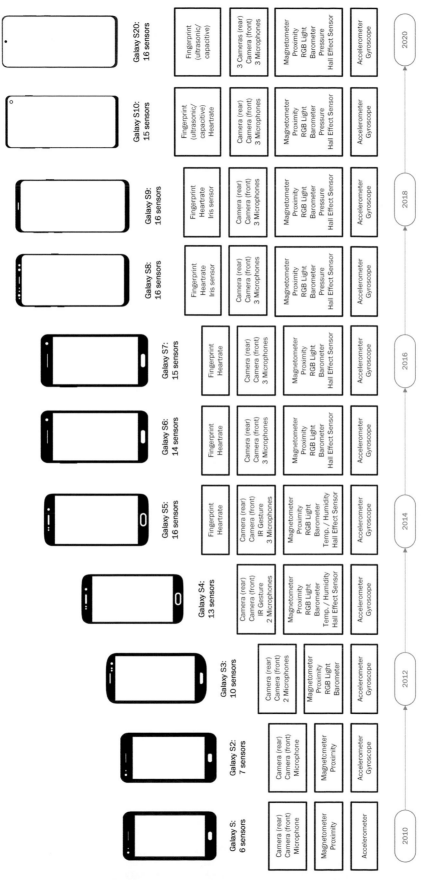

Figure 7.2 The growing number of native smartphone sensors provides researchers access to even more digital trace data (Struminskaya, Lugtig, Keusch, & Höhne, 2020)

each other across a variety of communication channels (Sapiezynski, Stopczynski, Lassen, & Lehmann, 2019; Stopczynski et al., 2014).

Digital traces can also be collected from wearable devices such as wrist- or waist-worn trackers that measure physical activity and, depending on the device type, additional information such as heart rate and geolocation. Some studies have recruited existing users of consumer-grade fitness trackers (e.g., Fitbit, Garmin) and smartwatches (e.g., Apple Watch) to share their data with researchers (Ajana, 2018). For example, over 500,000 German volunteers donated data collected from their fitness wristbands and smartwatches to the Robert Koch Institute (RKI) during the COVID-19 pandemic.[2] Some studies have used platforms such as Fitabase[3] to get access to the wearable data of people recruited into their studies (Phillips & Johnson, 2017; Stück, Hallgrímsson, Ver Steeg, Epasto, & Foschini, 2017). In population studies, another option is to equip all participants with the same research-grade wearable device (e.g., Actigraph, Geneactive) and then collect the devices at the end of the field period (Harris, Owen, Victor, Adams, & Cook, 2009; Kapteyn et al., 2018; Troiano et al., 2008).

Another approach of obtrusive digital terrace data collection is the use of online tracking applications ("meters") that users need to actively install to their Internet browsers and/ or mobile devices to allow the collection of browsing histories and app usage. This approach allows the researcher to trace individual online behavior, for example, news consumption via social media websites (Scharkow, Mangold, Stier, & Breuer, 2020), across time. Linking behavioral meter data with self-reports from web surveys allows researchers to study, for example, the relationship between passively measured online news consumption and self-reported voting behavior (Bach et al., 2019; Guess et al., 2020) or online news consumption and political interest (Möller, van de Velde, Merten, & Puschmann, 2019).

Depending on the design of the study, the measurement might be perceived as being less obtrusive over time because participants forget or get used to the presence of the measurement device. If the only active task for the participant is, for example, to download a research app or a meter that collects data in the background on their smartphone or Internet browser, then participants might soon forget that their behavior is even being observed. However, wearing a research-grade device on the body will potentially serve as a constant reminder that the individual is part of a study. Similarly, if the study design involves a combination of passive measurement of digital traces and repeated collection of self-reports (e.g., ecological momentary assessment [EMA] questions multiple times a day), it will probably make participants more aware of the observational part of the study.

What is the research goal?

Given that digital trace data are often collected incidentally and are reused for research purposes, it helps to take a step back and examine the goal of the research. Different research questions place different requirements on data and might create the need to go above and beyond readily available (digital trace) data. To simplify the discussion, we differentiate between three very general research goals irrespective of the data types: *description*, *causation*, and *prediction*. Of course, any given research project might combine several of these aspects or include variants not spelled out here in detail. This is not the first time we have discussed these issues. Readers interested in our presentations in other contexts can refer to Foster, Ghani, Jarmin, Kreuter, and Lane (2020) for general big data methods and privacy topics and Kohler, Kreuter, and Stuart (2019) for more detailed thoughts on causality and prediction.

When social scientists aim at describing the state of the society or a special population within the society, they typically seek to report a mean, a median, or a graphical distribution of a variable of interest. A first decision has to be made when interpreting the descriptive statistic. Researchers need to be clear if their aim is to describe a population or only report on the data at hand. In the case of a census data collection, where by definition all units of the population are covered, the two aspects overlap. In all other cases, an extra step is needed, which is often difficult when dealing with digital trace data. Say, for example, a researcher is scraping job postings in Germany in the first week of May in a given year. She can then describe the percentage of data scientists sought in her scraped set of posts and only in those. Such restrictions need to be communicated clearly when presenting and publishing the results. A much harder task is to estimate the percentage of data scientists searched for by all German companies in that year with such data at hand.

When data are not available for the entire population but accessed via samples, the goal of inferring to the population is solved by taking a sample with *known* selection probabilities and ensuring that everybody from the population of interest has a *positive selection probability*. Doing so requires a sampling frame that ideally covers the entire population. In the scraping example, this could be achieved by having a complete list of companies and being able to acquire all the job postings of a sample of companies selected from such a frame. In such a setting, standard errors would be used to express uncertainty due to the sampling procedure. When totals are reported (i.e., the absolute number of postings for data scientists), getting the selection probabilities right is particularly important (Lohr, 2009). In practice, one will often face a situation in which not all elements in the sample (companies) post all the data scientist positions, or, if the method of data collection is a survey, they refuse to respond to the survey request. The survey methodology literature has decades of publications on this topic and suggestions for adjustments for situations in which the mechanism leading to the missing values is well understood (see, for example, Bethlehem, Cobben, & Schouten, 2011; Groves & Couper, 1998; Schnell, 1997; Valliant, Dever, & Kreuter, 2018; Willimack, Nichols, Elizabeth, & Sudman, 2002). Starting with a probability sample has the strong advantage that sampling errors can be estimated; nonresponse error can be adjusted for known covariates; and with sufficient information on the sampling frame, the coverage errors are also known.

Of course, even if sampling and nonresponse error are adjusted for, assumptions about the measurement process still have to be made. Mislabeling might occur, for example, if a job is classified as "data scientist" even if the activities do not match the label (false positive) or, conversely, if a job entails what is commonly understood as data science but is not explicitly labeled as such in the ad (false negative).

The issue of overinterpreting the results is not new to digital trace data. We saw and still see this happening in the context of traditional data collections via (sample) surveys. The classic example where a data generating process was not understood or ignored is the Literary Digest poll, which incorrectly called the 1936 election (Squire, 1988). The Literary Digest went for volume and overlooked issues of selective access to phones and magazine subscriptions when assembling its mailing lists. Many of the data collection efforts in the COVID-19 pandemic show a similar tendency (see Kohler, 2020 and the associated special issue). Likewise, using Twitter data as a source to identify areas in need of support after natural disasters (e.g., hurricanes) my misguide policy makers. Resources and attention would likely flow towards the younger population, people with easy Internet access, or those generally well connected (Shelton, Poorthuis, Graham, & Zook, 2014).

When the main research goal is the establishment of a *causal relationship*, the situation is a bit different (Kohler et al., 2019). If a treatment is applied with a proper randomized experiment or a strong non-experimental study design, then statements about such causal relationship can be made for anyone who had a chance to be treated. Knowing the selection probability of the cases is then much less important, though it is very important that all elements have a positive selection probability to be assigned to the treatment and control conditions (Imbens & Rubin, 2015).

One example of an experiment done in a controlled fashion with digital trace data as the outcome is the Facebook emotional contagion study (Kramer, Guillory, & Hancock, 2014), where the number and type of posts seen on the users' wall were manipulated for a random sample of Facebook users. Differences in posting behavior (i.e., number of posts, sentiment) between users who were exposed to the treatment and those who were not can be interpreted as the causal effect of the treatment. Similarly, in a study with 193 volunteer Japanese smartphone owners who downloaded a research app, a random half of participants received on-screen reminders designed to stimulate interaction with communication weak ties during the two-month study period. The researchers compared the average number of phone calls, text messages, and emails from the smartphone log files to estimate the causal effect of the reminder messages (Kobayashi, Boase, Suzuki, & Suzuki, 2015).

Interesting causal claims can also be made in quasi-experimental settings where external shocks create the treatments, and regression discontinuity or similar designs can be used. During the COVID-19 pandemic, digital trace data from mobile devices were used to assess the (causal) effects of lock-down restrictions or other interventions designed to slow the spread of the virus. However, in the digital trace data setting – just as with traditional data collection – detailed knowledge about what is measured always needs to be available to interpret a "treatment" correctly. The Google mobility data in Figure 7.3 show how difficult it can be to differential signal and noise and how much pre-processing and data cleaning is still necessary.

While these examples have internal validity (albeit to different degrees), they lack external validity: inference to the population at large is not possible without further assumptions. In the Google mobility data example, not all units in the population have mobile devices that feed into this analysis. Thus any causal claim made from the data is generalizing to

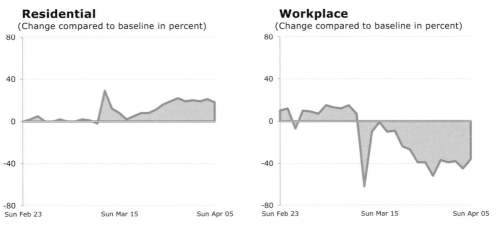

Figure 7.3 Google mobility data. Google points out "March 12 was a widely celebrated public holiday in this region. Workplace and residential changes are a little different from the community's response to COVID-19 but give an idea of the scale of the change. You'll need to apply your local knowledge, but holidays provide a very specific point of comparison" (Adapted from https://support.google.com/covid19-mobility/answer/9825414?hl=en-GB Accessed: 7/21/2020)

the population without mobile devices. In general, should the research question involve a causal claim or causal inference about a larger population than what is covered by the data, then the same issues arise as in the descriptive setting described earlier. The causal relationship will only hold if the causal effect is the same for the people that had the chance to be randomized to the treatment and those that did not (effect homogeneity) or, in the case of the Google mobility data, those for whom measures can be obtained and those for whom they cannot.

Not being able to randomize into treatment and control on a random sample of the population is a known problem in medical research. There the assumption of effect homogeneity has often been made. More recently, medical and public health researchers have increasingly scrutinized these assumptions and created statistical methods that help to generalize causal effects to the general population (DuGoff, Schuler, & Stuart, 2014). We would not be surprised if similar efforts will take place for digital trace data, with researchers thinking hard about the behavior of people not contributing to datasets (at all or at the same rate).

Prediction tasks are common in a data science pipeline when dealing with digital trace data. While social scientists are usually more interested in description of a population or causal effects, in doing either, they use predictions when specific measurements cannot be designed for the covariates of interest. Examples are Fitbit converting accelerometer sensor data into steps, using algorithms that differentiate between different motions, settings, and movements;[4] predicting voting behavior based on online news consumption (Bach et al., 2019); predicting personality traits based on smartphone usage (Stachl et al., 2020); or predicting the level of gentrification in a neighborhoods based on data about business activities from Yelp (Glaeser, Kim, & Luca, 2018). The reason prediction models are popular for such tasks is that they "often do not require specific prior knowledge about the functional form of the relationship under study and are able to adapt to complex non-linear and non-additive interrelations between the outcome and its predictors while focusing specifically on prediction performance" (Kern, Klausch, & Kreuter, 2019, p. 73).

Prediction tasks can work very well when large amounts of data are available, ideally for the exact same situation, person, or setting, and the prediction is made in close temporal proximity to the observation. However, the further the predicted outcome is from the data the prediction is based on, both temporally (e.g., predicting a "like" or "click" three months down the road) and conceptually (e.g., predicting an election outcome) or both (e.g., predicting an election outcome three months down the road), the lower the prediction success.

The potential for (massive amounts) of digital trace data to be used in prediction tasks is undeniable due to its unprecedented scope and variety. However, knowing who is covered by the data, for which settings, and which circumstances or time frames is just as important here as it is in the description and causal inference setting. Without knowing the ins and outs of the data generating process, there are real risks of biases due to unknown or unobserved systematic selection with respect to a given research question. This will increasingly be an issue with automated decision systems used in the societal context. For example, while predictive policing can be used to allocate police resources, it could harm society if the data do not represent the population at large and predictions are biased (Rodolfa, Saleiro, & Ghani, 2020).

Quality assessment – quality enhancement

The quality of digital trace data is relative to the research goal. Or, to put it differently, without knowing the research goal, it is only in very specific circumstances possible to make an overall claim about the quality of the data – or assess the fit of the data for a given research goal. Several frameworks exist that can help characterize data quality (see summaries in Christen, 2012; National Academies of Sciences, 2017). Typical elements are *accuracy, completeness, consistency, timeliness,* and *accessibility*. Ultimately, a researcher has to ask herself whether the data can support the inference she is planning to make. This situation is no different for digital trace data than for any other data source, for example, more traditional survey data (Schnell, Hill, & Esser, 2018).

Klingwort and Schnell (2020) show the difficulty in using digital trace data related to COVID-19 data collection. They convincingly question the use of the volunteer Fitbit app data donations in the previously described Robert Koch Institut effort. Not only was the number of people installing the app insufficient to cover all the variability in the population (as of early May 2020), but it also suffered from sources of nonresponse due to lack of knowledge about the app, privacy concerns, willingness to participate, and regular device use, as well as sources of coverage error due to owning the appropriate device and having the necessary technical skills (see Figure 1 in Klingwort & Schnell, 2020).

In addition, digital trace data can be subject to quality challenges less common in traditional data sources. For example, easily overlooked are problems of de-duplication, with units appearing in found or donated digital trace data multiple times, or records representing multiple units without being noticed as such. Schober, Pasek, Guggenheim, Lampe, and Conrad (2016) describe the former in their assessment of the use of social media data for social research and state that individual posts can represent. The latter is a problem that easily appears when devices such as computers, tablets, or smartphones are used by multiple people (Hang, von Zezschwitz, De Luca, & Hussmann, 2012; Matthews et al., 2016; Silver et al., 2019) and likely occurs more often when data are collected via smart devices in households. Another problem in analyzing social media data is the presence of bots that would be treated as human posters when computing the summary statistics. Data from search engines also illustrate novel challenges to data quality in digital trace data. Search engines might change in terms of how they are designed, who uses them, and how users engage with them over time in ways that are out of the researcher's control (Lazer, Kennedy, King, & Vespignani, 2014).

In a more abstract way, a *design feature* is the possibility to gain access to data in an *organic, found, or ready-made* way (Groves, 2011; Japec et al., 2015; Salganik, 2017). While this distinction between data found in the wild and data collected by design highlights an important feature, the data collection itself (say digital trace vs. survey questions) is independent of the found vs. design distinction.

Designed measurement of digital traces would mean participants are selected into the study and a specific technology such as an online meter, a mobile app, or a wearable specifically designed for a research study is used for data collection. Found data are byproducts of interactions with the world that leave digital traces; or, put differently, they arise organically. With found data, researchers have no control over who provides the data and how. A typical example for found data would be credit card transactions, postings in online search engines, or interactions with and on social media.

In practice, we often see a mix of designed and organic data. Sometimes, when researchers collaborate closely with the primary entities that collect the data, they might have the chance to provide input into what information is captured. For example when working closely with government agencies, researchers might have some input into how the measurement is taken (i.e., fields on a form of digital health records or unemployment insurance notices). Likewise, one can select respondents carefully (design the sample), but collect "found/organic" data that were not designed for the purpose of the research study but metered through already existing devices. An example is the IAB-SMART study (Kreuter et al., 2020), where existing measurement instruments in smartphones (accelerometer, pedometer, GPS) are used, but measurements are taken at specific intervals or in response to an event, bringing a design element into the mix. One major advantage of collecting data through designated research apps is that this allows researchers to specifically design all aspects of the data collection process (e.g., field period, participants' characteristics, particular sensors used) with a specific research question in mind. The controlled environment, potentially in conjunction with a probability sample, allows the researcher to not only to assess coverage (Keusch, Bähr, Haas, Kreuter, & Trappmann, 2020a), nonresponse (Keusch, Bähr, Haas, Kreuter, & Trappmann, 2020b), and measurement error (Bähr, Haas, Keusch, Kreuter, & Trappmann, 2020) but also to address these issues through weighting techniques known from survey research that would allow inference of the results to a larger population.

It can be useful to ask prior to any applied research the following questions:

- Which population is covered by the data? If not, which groups are missing? Is it even known which groups are missing?
- Can the sample represent the population? If not, are certain units entirely missing, or are they just not represented in the proportion needed? Are the reasons they are missing known, and can they be measured (in which case weighting might be an option)?
- Do I know what the measurements represent? Or do I need to generate new features from the digital trace data to answer the research question? How accurate are the attribute values in the data? Are all variables needed for the analysis in the data?
- How timely are the data?
- Are there data available that can be used to assess the quality of the generated features on a small scale? Can the small-scale assessment be generalized to the entire data?

For computational social science to be successful in using digital trace data, we foresee that in most (if not all) cases, data from different sources need to be combined, either to overcome the problem of unknown populations of inference or to overcome the problem of missing covariates and overall unclear measurement properties (Christen, Ranbaduge, & Schnell, 2020; Couper, 2013; Schnell, 2019).

Transparency and reporting needs

As tempting as the use of (easily available) digital trace data is, one has to keep in mind that there is a long path between the raw data and insights derived from the data. Because many of the digital trace data are by-products of processes with a purpose different from the researcher's intent, many pre-processing steps are needed before the analyses can begin. In a complex fast-moving world, where platforms and processes change, digital traces will by definition be inconsistent and noisy (Foster et al., 2020) and be filled with missing data, not the very least because of different terms and conditions for data access and use that the different platforms exhibit (Amaya, Bach, Keusch, & Kreuter, 2019).

How sensitive results are to such preprocessing steps and the accompanying decisions was demonstrated by Conrad et al. (2018) for studies trying to create alternative indicators for consumer confidence and consumer sentiment from Twitter data. The volatility of the results raised skepticism among the authors and prompted them to call for best practices in generating features and documenting results when using Twitter data for these purposes. Such desire for best practices and standards in reporting can be seen in many other communities as well, very prominently among statistical agencies around the world. The United National Statistics Division[5] lists principles governing international statistical activities, including a call for transparency of "concepts, definitions, classifications, sources, methods and procedures employed". Growing adoption of FAIR data principles – Findability, Accessibility, Interoperability, and Reusability – by funding agencies, journals, and research organizations further increases the need to acquire sufficient information about the data generating process, as well as subsequent steps in preprocessing the data. It is important to realize that FAIR principles also apply to algorithms, tools, and workflows generating the analytic dataset, not just to the raw data or, in our case, the raw digital traces.[6] As Wilkinson et al. (2016) state, "all scholarly digital research objects – from data to analytical pipelines – benefit from application of these principles, since all components of the research process must be available to ensure transparency, reproducibility, and reusability" (p. 1).

This said, researchers intending to use digital trace data should be aware that even if data collection is cheap, there are substantial costs associated with cleaning, curating, standardizing, integrating, and using the new types of data (Foster et al., 2020). Novices in using digital trace data might benefit from reading Amaya et al. (2019) to get a sense of challenges and opportunities when working with digital trace data from platforms, in this case Reddit. While specific to Reddit, the paper lists types of information one may seek to acquire prior to conducting a project that uses any type of social media data.

Conclusion

We are, without a doubt, excited about the possibilities digital trace data provide to social science research. The direct and often unobtrusive observation of individual behaviors and social interactions through digital systems produces data in breadth and depth that cannot be generated using traditional methods. However, for digital trace data to become a mainstream data source, there is still a long way to go. The initial hype has leveled off, and more and more research papers appear showing the challenges and limits of using digital trace data. At the same time, research studies that use clever designs to combine multiple data sources are on the rise.

The combination of multiple sources is not without risk. Multiple streams of data from different sources can create detailed profiles of users' habits, demographics, or well-being that carry the risk of unintentionally de-identifying previously anonymous data providers (Bender, Kreuter, Jarmin, & Lane, 2020; Deursen & Mossberger, 2018). We are hopeful that the parallel efforts going on right now with respect to privacy preserving record linkage (Christen et al., 2020) and encrypted computing (Goroff, 2015) will help mitigate those risks. While both areas are heavily dominated by computer scientists and statisticians, we encourage social scientists to inject themselves into this discussion so that the solutions work not just theoretically but also in practice (see Oberski and Kreuter, 2020, for the controversy around the use of differential privacy).

Whether multiple data sources are combined or single sources of digital traces are used, ethical challenges arise when the digital traces are the result of organic processes with a different original purpose (*found data*). As Helen Nissenbaum (2018) clearly lays out in her framework of contextual integrity, one cannot or should not ignore the question of the appropriateness of data flows. Appropriateness is a function of conformity with contextual informational norms. To give a brief example: A bouncer at a nightclub might see a woman's address as he checks her age to allow entrance into the club. If he later shows up at her house using the piece of information acquired during his job, he violates contextual informational norms. Re-purposing of digital trace data can violate contextual informational norms in similar ways. While the unanticipated secondary use constitutes the "crown jewels" of passively collected digital trace data (Tene & Polonetsky, 2013), users are increasingly concerned about the privacy of their data and how much they can control how their personal information is used (Auxiere et al., 2019). For the researcher, the use creates a challenge in how to balance the risk to the participants with the utility of the collected data, the so-called privacy-utility trade-off (Bender et al., 2020).

Notes

1 At the time of writing this chapter, ResearchGate asks the users for permission to share their personal data (e.g., IP address, cookie identifiers) with almost 500 external partners (www.researchgate.net/privacy-policy, June 30, 2020).
2 https://corona-datenspende.de/science/en/
3 https://www.fitabase.com/
4 https://help.fitbit.com/articles/en_US/Help_article/1136
5 https://unstats.un.org/unsd/methods/statorg/Principles_stat_activities/principles_stat_activities.asp
6 Including code leading to data as well as metadata, data describing the data, has already been part of the data management plan requirements of the U.S. National Science Foundation, for example. https://nsf.gov/eng/general/ENG_DMP_Policy.pdf

References

Adams, P., Rabbi, M., Rahman, T., Matthews, M., Voida, A., Gay, G., Choudhury, T., & Voida, S. (2014). *Towards personal stress informatics: Comparing minimally invasive techniques for measuring daily stress in the wild.* Proceedings of the 8th International Conference on Pervasive Computing Technologies for Healthcare, pp. 72–79. https://doi.org/10.4108/icst.pervasivehealth.2014.254959

Adler, N. E., Glymour, M. M., & Fielding, J. (2016). Addressing social determinants of health and health inequalities. *JAMA, 316*(16), 1641–1642. https://doi.org/10.1001/jama.2016.14058

Ajana, B. (2018). Communal self-tracking: Data philanthropy, solidarity and privacy. In B. Ajana (Ed.), *Self-tracking: Empirical and philosophical investigations* (pp. 125–141). Springer International Publishing. https://doi.org/10.1007/978-3-319-65379-2_9

Amaya, A., Bach, R. L., Keusch, F., & Kreuter, F. (2019). New data sources in social science research: Things to know before working with Reddit data. *Social Science Computer Review.* https://doi.org/10.1177/0894439319893305

Amaya, A., Bach, R. L., Keusch, F., & Kreuter, F. (2020). Measuring attitude strength in social media data. In C. A. Hill, P. Biemer, T. D. Buskirk, L. Japec, A. Kirchner, S. Kolenikov, & L. E. Lyberg (Eds.), *Big data meets survey science* (pp. 163–192). John Wiley & Sons, Ltd. https://doi.org/10.1002/97811189 76357.ch5

Auxiere, B., Rainie, L., Anderson, M., Perrin, A., Kumar, M., & Turner, E. (2019). *Americans and privacy: Concerned, confused and feeling lack of control over their personal information.* PEW Research Center. Retrieved from www.pewresearch.org/internet/2019/11/15/americans-and-privacy-concerned-confused-and-feeling-lack-of-control-over-their-personal-information/

Bach, R. L., Kern, C., Amaya, A., Keusch, F., Kreuter, F., Hecht, J., & Heinemann, J. (2019). Predicting voting behavior using digital trace data. *Social Science Computer Review.* https://doi.org/10.1177/0894439319882896

Bähr, S., Haas, G.-C., Keusch, F., Kreuter, F., & Trappmann, M. (2020). Measurement quality in mobile geolocation sensor data. *Social Science Computer Review.* https://doi.org/10.1177/0894439320944118

Bender, S., Kreuter, F., Jarmin, R. S., & Lane, J. (2020). Privacy and confidentiality. In I. Foster, R. Ghani, R. S. Jarmin, F. Kreuter, & J. Lane (Eds.), *Big data and social science* (2nd ed.). Chapman and Hall and CRC Press. https://textbook.coleridgeinitiative.org/

Benedict, K., Wayland, R., & Hagler, G. (2017, November). Characterizing air quality in a rapidly changing world. *Air and Waste Management Association's Magazine for Environmental Managers.* Retrieved from https://cfpub.epa.gov/si/si_public_record_report.cfm?Lab=NERL&dirEntryId=338745

Ben-Zeev, D., Scherer, E. A., Wang, R., Xie, H., & Campbell, A. T. (2015). Next-generation psychiatric assessment: Using smartphone sensors to monitor behavior and mental health. *Psychiatric Rehabilitation Journal, 38*(3), 218–226. https://doi.org/10.1037/prj0000130

Bethlehem, J., Cobben, F., & Schouten, B. (2011). *Handbook of nonresponse in household surveys.* John Wiley & Sons.

Blumenstock, J., Cadamuro, G., & On, R. (2015). Predicting poverty and wealth from mobile phone metadata. *Science, 350*(6264), 1073–1076. https://doi.org/10.1126/science.aac4420

Böhme, M. H., Gröger, A., & Stöhr, T. (2020). Searching for a better life: Predicting international migration with online search keywords. *Journal of Development Economics, 142*, 102347. https://doi.org/10.1016/j.jdeveco.2019.04.002

Catlett, C. E., Beckman, P. H., Sankaran, R., & Galvin, K. K. (2017). *Array of things: A scientific research instrument in the public way: Platform design and early lessons learned.* Proceedings of the 2nd International Workshop on Science of Smart City Operations and Platforms Engineering, pp. 26–33. https://doi.org/10.1145/3063386.3063771

Cavallo, A., & Rigobon, R. (2016). The billion prices project: Using online prices for measurement and research. *Journal of Economic Perspectives, 30*(2), 151–178. https://doi.org/10.1257/jep.30.2.151

Cheng, J., Adamic, L. A., Kleinberg, J. M., & Leskovec, J. (2016). *Do cascades recur?* Proceedings of the 25th International Conference on World Wide Web – WWW'16, pp. 671–681. https://doi.org/10.1145/2872427.2882993

Christen, P. (2012). *Data matching: Concepts and techniques for record linkage, entity resolution, and duplicate detection.* Springer-Verlag. https://doi.org/10.1007/978-3-642-31164-2

Christen, P., Ranbaduge, P., & Schnell, R. (2020). *Linking sensitive data: Methods and techniques for practical privacy-preserving information sharing.* Springer.

Conrad, F. G., Gagnon-Barsch, J., Ferg, R., Hou, E., Pasek, J., & Schober, M. F. (2018, October 25). *Social media as an alternative to surveys of opinions about the economy.* BigSurv18.

Conrad, F. G., & Keusch, F. (2018, October 25). *Emergent issues in the combined collection of self-reports and passive data using smartphones.* BigSurv18, Barcelona, Spain.

Couper, M. P. (2013). Is the sky falling? New technology, changing media, and the future of surveys. *Survey Research Methods, 7*(3), 145–156. https://doi.org/10.18148/srm/2013.v7i3.5751

Deursen, A. J. A. M. van, & Mossberger, K. (2018). Any thing for anyone? A new digital divide in internet-of-things skills. *Policy & Internet, 10*(2), 122–140. https://doi.org/10.1002/poi3.171

Di Sabatino, S., Buccolieri, R., & Kumar, P. (2018). Spatial distribution of air pollutants in cities. In F. Capello & A. V. Gaddi (Eds.), *Clinical handbook of air pollution-related diseases* (pp. 75–95). Springer International Publishing. https://doi.org/10.1007/978-3-319-62731-1_5

DuGoff, E. H., Schuler, M., & Stuart, E. A. (2014). Generalizing observational study results: Applying propensity score methods to complex surveys. *Health Services Research, 49*(1), 284–303. https://doi.org/10.1111/1475-6773.12090

Duhigg, C. (2012, October 13). Campaigns mine personal lives to get out vote – The New York times. *New York Times.* Retrieved from www.nytimes.com/2012/10/14/us/politics/campaigns-mine-personal-lives-to-get-out-vote.html

Edelman, B., Luca, M., & Svirsky, D. (2017). Racial discrimination in the sharing economy: Evidence from a field experiment. *American Economic Journal: Applied Economics, 9*(2), 1–22. https://doi.org/10.1257/app.20160213

Edelmann, A., Wolff, T., Montagne, D., & Bail, C. A. (2020). Computational social science and sociology. *Annual Review of Sociology, 46*(1). https://doi.org/10.1146/annurev-soc-121919-054621

Elevelt, A., Lugtig, P., & Toepoel, V. (2019). Doing a time use survey on smartphones only: What factors predict nonresponse at different stages of the survey process? *Survey Research Methods, 13*(2), 195–213. https://doi.org/10.18148/srm/2019.v13i2.7385

English, N., Zhao, C., Brown, K. L., Catlett, C., & Cagney, K. (2020). Making sense of sensor data: How local environmental conditions add value to social science research. *Social Science Computer Review.* https://doi.org/10.1177/0894439320920601

Fiesler, C., & Proferes, N. (2018). "Participant" perceptions of Twitter research ethics. *Social Media + Society, 4*(1). https://doi.org/10.1177/2056305118763366

Flaxman, S., Goel, S., & Rao, J. M. (2016). Filter bubbles, echo chambers, and online news consumption. *Public Opinion Quarterly, 80*(S1), 298–320. https://doi.org/10.1093/poq/nfw006

Foster, I., Ghani, R., Jarmin, R. S., Kreuter, F., & Lane, J. (Eds.). (2020). *Big data and social science* (2nd ed.). Chapman and Hall and CRC Press. https://textbook.coleridgeinitiative.org/

Ginsberg, J., Mohebbi, M. H., Patel, R. S., Brammer, L., Smolinski, M. S., & Brilliant, L. (2009). Detecting influenza epidemics using search engine query data. *Nature, 457*(7232), 1012–1014. https://doi.org/10.1038/nature07634

Glaeser, E. L., Kim, H., & Luca, M. (2018). Nowcasting gentrification: Using Yelp data to quantify neighborhood change. *AEA Papers and Proceedings, 108*, 77–82. https://doi.org/10.1257/pandp.20181034

Göbel, S., & Munzert, S. (2018). Political advertising on the Wikipedia marketplace of information. *Social Science Computer Review*, *36*(2), 157–175. https://doi.org/10.1177/0894439317703579

Goodspeed, R., Yan, X., Hardy, J., Vydiswaran, V. V., Berrocal, V. J., Clarke, P., . . . Veinot, T. (2018). Comparing the data quality of global positioning system devices and mobile phones for assessing relationships between place, mobility, and health: Field study. *JMIR MHealth and UHealth*, *6*(8), e168. https://doi.org/10.2196/mhealth.9771

Goroff, D. L. (2015). Balancing privacy versus accuracy in research protocols. *Science*, *347*(6221), 479–480.

Groves, R. M. (2011). Three eras of survey research. *Public Opinion Quarterly*, *75*(5), 861–871. https://doi.org/10.1093/poq/nfr057

Groves, R. M., & Couper, M. P. (1998). *Nonresponse in household interview surveys*. John Wiley & Sons.

Guess, A. M., Nyhan, B., & Reifler, J. (2020). Exposure to untrustworthy websites in the 2016 US election. *Nature Human Behaviour*, *4*(5), 472–480. https://doi.org/10.1038/s41562-020-0833-x

Hang, A., von Zezschwitz, E., De Luca, A., & Hussmann, H. (2012). *Too much information! User attitudes towards smartphone sharing*. Proceedings of the 7th Nordic Conference on Human-Computer Interaction: Making Sense Through Design, pp. 284–287. https://doi.org/10.1145/2399016.2399061

Harari, G. M., Gosling, S. D., Wang, R., Chen, F., Chen, Z., & Campbell, A. T. (2017). Patterns of behavior change in students over an academic term: A preliminary study of activity and sociability behaviors using smartphone sensing methods. *Computers in Human Behavior*, *67*, 129–138. https://doi.org/10.1016/j.chb.2016.10.027

Harari, G. M., Lane, N. D., Wang, R., Crosier, B. S., Campbell, A. T., & Gosling, S. D. (2016). Using smartphones to collect behavioral data in psychological science: Opportunities, practical considerations, and challenges. *Perspectives on Psychological Science*, *11*(6), 838–854. https://doi.org/10.1177/1745691616650285

Harari, G. M., Müller, S. R., Aung, M. S., & Rentfrow, P. J. (2017). Smartphone sensing methods for studying behavior in everyday life. *Current Opinion in Behavioral Sciences*, *18*, 83–90. https://doi.org/10.1016/j.cobeha.2017.07.018

Harris, T. J., Owen, C. G., Victor, C. R., Adams, R., & Cook, D. G. (2009). What factors are associated with physical activity in older people, assessed objectively by accelerometry? *British Journal of Sports Medicine*, *43*(6), 442–450. https://doi.org/10.1136/bjsm.2008.048033

Hinds, J., & Joinson, A. N. (2018). What demographic attributes do our digital footprints reveal? A systematic review. *PLoS One*, *13*(11), e0207112. https://doi.org/10.1371/journal.pone.0207112

Horn, C., & Kreuter, F. (2019). *Die digitale Herausforderung: Tipping Points, die Ihr Unternehmen verändern werden* (1. Auflage 2020). Haufe.

Howison, J., Wiggins, A., & Crowston, K. (2011). Validity issues in the use of social network analysis with digital trace data. *Journal of the Association for Information Systems*, *12*(12), 768–797. https://doi.org/10.17705/1jais.00282

Imbens, G. W., & Rubin, D. B. (2015). *Causal inference in statistics, social, and biomedical sciences*. Cambridge University Press.

Japec, L., Kreuter, F., Berg, M., Biemer, P., Decker, P., Lampe, C., . . . Usher, A. (2015). Big data in survey research AAPOR task force report. *Public Opinion Quarterly*, *79*(4), 839–880. https://doi.org/10.1093/poq/nfv039

Jun, S.-P., Yoo, H. S., & Choi, S. (2018). Ten years of research change using Google trends: From the perspective of big data utilizations and applications. *Technological Forecasting and Social Change*, *130*, 69–87. https://doi.org/10.1016/j.techfore.2017.11.009

Jungherr, A. (2015). *Analyzing political communication with digital trace data: The role of Twitter messages in social science research*. Springer.

Kapteyn, A., Banks, J., Hamer, M., Smith, J. P., Steptoe, A., Soest, A. van, . . . Wah, S. H. (2018). What they say and what they do: Comparing physical activity across the USA, England and the Netherlands. *Journal of Epidemiol Community Health*, *72*(6), 471–476. https://doi.org/10.1136/jech-2017-209703

Kern, C., Klausch, T., & Kreuter, F. (2019). Tree-based machine learning methods for survey research. *Survey Research Methods*, *13*(1), 73–93. https://doi.org/10.18148/srm/2019.v1i1.7395

Keusch, F., Bähr, S., Haas, G.-C., Kreuter, F., & Trappmann, M. (2020a). Coverage error in data collection combining mobile surveys with passive measurement using apps: Data from a German national survey: *Sociological Methods & Research*. https://doi.org/10.1177/0049124120914924

Keusch, F., Bähr, S., Haas, G.-C., Kreuter, F., & Trappmann, M. (2020b, June 11). *Participation rates and bias in a smartphone study collecting self-reports and passive mobile measurements using a research app*. AAPOR 75th Annual Conference, Virtula Conference.

Keusch, F., Bähr, S., Haas, G.-C., Kreuter, F., & Trappmann, M. (2020c, July 17). *Social networks on smartphones. Congruence of online and offline networks and their effect on labor market outcomes.* 6th International Conference on Computational Social Science (IC²C²), Virtual Conference.

Keusch, F., Leonard, M. M., Sajons, C., & Steiner, S. (2019). Using smartphone technology for research on refugees: Evidence from Germany. *Sociological Methods & Research.* https://doi.org/10.1177/0049124119852377

Klingwort, J., & Schnell, R. (2020). Critical limitations of digital epidemiology: *Survey Research Methods, 14*(2), 95–101. https://doi.org/10.18148/srm/2020.v14i2.7726

Kobayashi, T., Boase, J., Suzuki, T., & Suzuki, T. (2015). Emerging from the cocoon? Revisiting the tele-cocooning hypothesis in the smartphone era. *Journal of Computer-Mediated Communication, 20*(3), 330–345. https://doi.org/10.1111/jcc4.12116

Kohler, U. (2020). Survey research methods during the COVID-19 crisis. *Survey Research Methods, 14*(2), 93–94. https://doi.org/10.18148/srm/2020.v14i2.7769

Kohler, U., Kreuter, F., & Stuart, E. A. (2019). Nonprobability sampling and causal analysis. *Annual Review of Statistics and Its Application, 6*(1), 149–172. https://doi.org/10.1146/annurev-statistics-030718-104951

Kramer, A. D. I., Guillory, J. E., & Hancock, J. T. (2014). Experimental evidence of massive-scale emotional contagion through social networks. *Proceedings of the National Academy of Sciences, 111*(24), 8788–8790. https://doi.org/10.1073/pnas.1320040111

Kreuter, F., Haas, G.-C., Keusch, F., Bähr, S., & Trappmann, M. (2020). Collecting survey and smartphone sensor data with an app: Opportunities and challenges around privacy and informed consent. *Social Science Computer Review.* https://doi.org/10.1177/0894439318816389

Kruschinski, S., & Haller, A. (2017). Restrictions on data-driven political micro-targeting in Germany. *Internet Policy Review, 6*(4). Retrieved from https://policyreview.info/articles/analysis/restrictions-data-driven-political-micro-targeting-germany

Lathia, N., Sandstrom, G. M., Mascolo, C., & Rentfrow, P. J. (2017). Happier people live more active lives: Using smartphones to link happiness and physical activity. *PLoS One, 12*(1), e0160589. https://doi.org/10.1371/journal.pone.0160589

Lazer, D., Kennedy, R., King, G., & Vespignani, A. (2014). The parable of Google flu: Traps in big data analysis. *Science, 343*(6176), 1203–1205. https://doi.org/10.1126/science.1248506

Lazer, D., Pentland, A., Adamic, L., Aral, S., Barabási, A.-L., Brewer, D., . . . Van Alstyne, M. (2009). Computational social science. *Science, 323*(5915), 721–723. JSTOR.

Lerner, A., Simpson, A. K., Kohno, T., & Roesner, F. (2016). *Internet Jones and the raiders of the lost trackers: An archaeological study of web tracking from 1996 to 2016.* Proceedings of the 25th USENIX Security Symposium, pp. 997–1013.

Link, M. W., Murphy, J., Schober, M. F., Buskirk, T. D., Hunter Childs, J., & Langer Tesfaye, C. (2014). Mobile technologies for conducting, augmenting and potentially replacing surveys executive summary of the AAPOR task force on emerging technologies in public opinion research. *Public Opinion Quarterly, 78*(4), 779–787. https://doi.org/10.1093/poq/nfu054

Lohr, S. L. (2009). Sampling and survey design. In D. Pfeffermann & C. R. Rao (Eds.), *Sample surveys: Design, methods and applications* (pp. 3–8). Elsevier.

Lynch, J., Dumont, J., Greene, E., & Ehrlich, J. (2019). Use of a smartphone GPS application for recurrent travel behavior data collection: *Transportation Research Record, 2673*(7), 89–98. https://doi.org/10.1177/0361198119848708

MacKerron, G., & Mourato, S. (2013). Happiness is greater in natural environments. *Global Environmental Change, 23*(5), 992–1000. https://doi.org/10.1016/j.gloenvcha.2013.03.010

Matthews, T., Liao, K., Turner, A., Berkovich, M., Reeder, R., & Consolvo, S. (2016). *"She'll just grab any device that's closer": A study of everyday device & account sharing in households.* Proceedings of the 2016 CHI Conference on Human Factors in Computing Systems, pp. 5921–5932. https://doi.org/10.1145/2858036.2858051

Möller, J., van de Velde, R. N., Merten, L., & Puschmann, C. (2019). Explaining online news engagement based on browsing behavior: Creatures of habit? *Social Science Computer Review.* https://doi.org/10.1177/0894439319828012

National Academies of Sciences, E. (2017). *Federal statistics, multiple data sources, and privacy protection: Next steps.* https://doi.org/10.17226/24893

Nickerson, D. W., & Rogers, T. (2014). Political campaigns and big data. *Journal of Economic Perspectives, 28*(2), 51–74. https://doi.org/10.1257/jep.28.2.51

Nissenbaum, H. (2018). Respecting context to protect privacy: Why meaning matters. *Science and Engineering Ethics*, *24*(3), 831–852. https://doi.org/10.1007/s11948-015-9674-9

Obar, J. A., & Oeldorf-Hirsch, A. (2020). The biggest lie on the Internet: Ignoring the privacy policies and terms of service policies of social networking services. *Information, Communication & Society*, *23*(1), 128–147. https://doi.org/10.1080/1369118X.2018.1486870

Oberski, D. L., & Kreuter, F. (2020). Differential privacy and social science: An urgent puzzle. *Harvard Data Science Review*, *2*(1). https://doi.org/10.1162/99608f92.63a22079

Phillips, L. A., & Johnson, M. A. (2017). Interdependent effects of autonomous and controlled regulation on exercise behavior. *Personality and Social Psychology Bulletin*. https://doi.org/10.1177/0146167217733068

Philpot, R., Liebst, L. S., Levine, M., Bernasco, W., & Lindegaard, M. R. (2020). Would I be helped? Cross-national CCTV footage shows that intervention is the norm in public conflicts. *American Psychologist*, *75*(1), 66–75. https://doi.org/10.1037/amp0000469

Przepiorka, W., Norbutas, L., & Corten, R. (2017). Order without law: Reputation promotes cooperation in a cryptomarket for illegal drugs. *European Sociological Review*, *33*(6), 752–764. https://doi.org/10.1093/esr/jcx072

Raento, M., Oulasvirta, A., & Eagle, N. (2009). Smartphones: An emerging tool for social scientists. *Sociological Methods & Research*, *37*(3), 426–454. https://doi.org/10.1177/0049124108330005

Rodolfa, K. T., Saleiro, P., & Ghani, R. (2020). Bias and fairness. In I. Foster, R. Ghani, R. S. Jarmin, F. Kreuter, & J. Lane (Eds.), *Big data and social science* (2nd ed.). Chapman and Hall and CRC Press. https://textbook.coleridgeinitiative.org/

Salganik, M. (2017). *Bit by bit: Social research in the digital age*. Princeton University Press.

Sapiezynski, P., Stopczynski, A., Lassen, D. D., & Lehmann, S. (2019). Interaction data from the Copenhagen networks study. *Scientific Data*, *6*(1), 315. https://doi.org/10.1038/s41597-019-0325-x

Scharkow, M., Mangold, F., Stier, S., & Breuer, J. (2020). How social network sites and other online intermediaries increase exposure to news. *Proceedings of the National Academy of Sciences*, *117*(6), 2761–2763. https://doi.org/10.1073/pnas.1918279117

Scherpenzeel, A. (2017). Mixing online panel data collection with innovative methods. In S. Eifler & F. Faulbaum (Eds.), *Methodische Probleme von Mixed-Mode-Ansätzen in der Umfrageforschung* (pp. 27–49). Springer Fachmedien Wiesbaden. https://doi.org/10.1007/978-3-658-15834-7_2

Schnell, R. (1997). *Nonresponse in Bevölkerungsumfragen: Ausmaß, Entwicklung und Ursachen*. Springer-Verlag.

Schnell, R. (2019). „Big Data"aus wissenschaftssoziologischer Sicht: Warum es kaum sozialwissenschaftliche Studien ohne Befragungen gibt. In D. Baron, O. Arránz Becker, & D. Lois (Eds.), *Erklärende Soziologie und soziale Praxis* (pp. 101–125). Springer Fachmedien. https://doi.org/10.1007/978-3-658-23759-2_6

Schnell, R., Hill, P. B., & Esser, E. (2018). Methoden der empirischen Sozialforschung. In *Methoden der empirischen Sozialforschung*. De Gruyter Oldenbourg.

Schober, M. F., Pasek, J., Guggenheim, L., Lampe, C., & Conrad, F. G. (2016). Social media analyses for social measurement. *Public Opinion Quarterly*, *80*(1), 180–211. https://doi.org/10.1093/poq/nfv048

Shelton, T., Poorthuis, A., Graham, M., & Zook, M. (2014). Mapping the data shadows of Hurricane Sandy: Uncovering the sociospatial dimensions of 'big data.' *Geoforum*, *52*, 167–179. https://doi.org/10.1016/j.geoforum.2014.01.006

Silver, L., Smith, A., Johnson, C., Jiang, J., Anderson, M., & Rainie, L. (2019). *Mobile connectivity in emerging economies*. PEW Research Center. Retrieved from www.pewresearch.org/internet/2019/03/07/mobile-connectivity-in-emerging-economies/

Squire, P. (1988). Why the 1936 literary digest poll failed. *Public Opinion Quarterly*, *52*(1), 125–133. https://doi.org/10.1086/269085

Stachl, C., Au, Q., Schoedel, R., Gosling, S. D., Harari, G. M., Buschek, D., . . . Bühner, M. (2020). Predicting personality from patterns of behavior collected with smartphones. *Proceedings of the National Academy of Sciences*. https://doi.org/10.1073/pnas.1920484117

Stier, S., Breuer, J., Siegers, P., & Thorson, K. (2019). Integrating survey data and digital trace data: Key issues in developing an emerging field. *Social Science Computer Review*. https://doi.org/10.1177/0894439319843669

Stopczynski, A., Sekara, V., Sapiezynski, P., Cuttone, A., Madsen, M. M., Larsen, J. E., & Lehmann, S. (2014). Measuring large-scale social networks with high resolution. *PLoS One*, *9*(4), e95978. https://doi.org/10.1371/journal.pone.0095978

Struminskaya, B., Lugtig, P., Keusch, F., & Höhne, J. K. (2020). Augmenting surveys with data from sensors and apps: Opportunities and challenges. *Social Science Computer Review*. https://doi.org/10.1177/0894439320979951

Stück, D., Hallgrímsson, H. T., Ver Steeg, G., Epasto, A., & Foschini, L. (2017). *The spread of physical activity through social networks*. Proceedings of the 26th International Conference on World Wide Web, pp. 519–528. https://doi.org/10.1145/3038912.3052688

Sugie, N. F. (2018). Utilizing smartphones to study disadvantaged and hard-to-reach groups. *Sociological Methods & Research*, *47*(3), 458–491. https://doi.org/10.1177/0049124115626176

Sugie, N. F., & Lens, M. C. (2017). Daytime locations in spatial mismatch: Job accessibility and employment at reentry from prison. *Demography*, *54*(2), 775–800. https://doi.org/10.1007/s13524-017-0549-3

Tene, O., & Polonetsky, J. (2013). Big data for all: Privacy and user control in the age of analytics. *Northwestern Journal of Technology and Intellectual Property*, *11*(5), xxvii–274.

Tourangeau, R., Rips, L. J., & Rasinski, K. (2000). *The psychology of survey response*. Cambridge University Press.

Troiano, R. P., Berrigan, D., Dodd, K. W., Mâsse, L. C., Tilert, T., & Mcdowell, M. (2008). Physical activity in the United States measured by accelerometer. *Medicine & Science in Sports & Exercise*, *40*(1), 181–188. https://doi.org/10.1249/mss.0b013e31815a51b3

Ugander, J., Karrer, B., Backstrom, L., & Marlow, C. (2011). The anatomy of the Facebook social graph. *ArXiv:1111.4503 [Physics]*. http://arxiv.org/abs/1111.4503

Valliant, R., Dever, J. A., & Kreuter, F. (2018). *Practical tools for designing and weighting survey samples*. Springer International Publishing. https://doi.org/10.1007/978-3-319-93632-1

Vicéns-Feliberty, M. A., & Ricketts, C. F. (2016). An analysis of Puerto Rican interest to migrate to the United States using Google trends. *The Journal of Developing Areas*, *50*(2), 411–430. https://doi.org/10.1353/jda.2016.0090

Vosen, S., & Schmidt, T. (2011). Forecasting private consumption: Survey-based indicators vs. Google trends. *Journal of Forecasting*, *30*(6), 565–578. https://doi.org/10.1002/for.1213

Wang, R., Chen, F., Chen, Z., Li, T., Harari, G., Tignor, S., Zhou, X., Ben-Zeev, D., & Campbell, A. T. (2014). *Student life: Assessing mental health, academic performance and behavioral trends of college students using smartphones*. Proceedings of the 2014 ACM International Joint Conference on Pervasive and Ubiquitous Computing, pp. 3–14. https://doi.org/10.1145/2632048.2632054

Wilkinson, M. D., Dumontier, M., Aalbersberg, I. J., Appleton, G., Axton, M., Baak, A., . . . Mons, B. (2016). The FAIR guiding principles for scientific data management and stewardship. *Scientific Data*, *3*(1), 160018. https://doi.org/10.1038/sdata.2016.18

Willimack, D. K., Nichols, E., & Sudman, S. (2002). Understanding unit and item nonresponse in business surveys. In R. M. Groves, D. A. Dillman, & R. J. A. Little (Eds.), *Survey nonresponse* (pp. 213–242). John Wiley & Sons.

York Cornwell, E., & Cagney, K. A. (2017). Aging in activity space: Results from smartphone-based GPS-tracking of urban seniors. *The Journals of Gerontology: Series B*, *72*(5), 864–875. https://doi.org/10.1093/geronb/gbx063

8

OPEN COMPUTATIONAL SOCIAL SCIENCE

Jan G. Voelkel and Jeremy Freese

Open computational social science

The rise of computational social science is a recent major development in the social sciences. The possibility of using computational techniques to analyze large datasets has provided researchers from many different fields with new tools to solve puzzles once thought impossible to study. Furthermore, computational social science often uses social media or other digital data, paving the way for new theoretical insights into societal phenomena (Lazer et al., 2009; Edelmann, Wolf, Montagne, & Bail, 2020). The prospects of how computational social science will change and improve social scientific answers to important theoretical and practical problems are exciting.

At the same time, the data typically used by computational social scientists also create challenges to their openness. Open science is an umbrella term that summarizes a movement of researchers who aim to improve the fundamental features of science, including accessibility, transparency, rigor, reproducibility, replicability, and accumulation of knowledge (Crüwell et al., 2019). Insights from the open science movement can help computational social science build on praiseworthy developments in the field to institutionalize transparency and reproducibility. In the following subsections, we introduce four principles of open science, explain why each is important, describe some of the challenges of their implementation, and suggest how computational social scientists could address these challenges. While these four open science principles are well known and we think they are the most relevant for computational social scientists, we do not claim that this way of specifying principles is either exhaustive or definitive of an evolving science (for alternative classifications, see, for example, Crüwell et al., 2019; Munafò et al., 2017).

Open practices

Open practices refer to honest and transparent specification of all steps in the data processing and data analysis. One example for computational social scientists is posting their study's materials and the code used to process and analyze the data. Computational social scientists sometimes test hypotheses they had before starting their data analyses and sometimes build hypotheses based on their data analyses. Here, an important open practice is clearly demarcating

DOI: 10.4324/9781003024583-9

exploratory and confirmatory parts of the research process, so that findings generated post hoc are not presented as testing pre-existing hypotheses.

Open practices are an important goal for (social) science to increase replicability, that is, the replication of prior findings with "new data". It is well known that many findings in the social sciences cannot be replicated (Anderson et al., 2016; Baker, 2016; Camerer et al., 2016; Camerer et al., 2018; Ioannidis, 2005; Open Science Collaboration, 2015; Shiffrin, Börner, & Stigler, 2018). Many explanations for these low replication rates have been discussed in the literature, including publication bias (e.g., Bakker, van Dijk, & Wicherts, 2012; Ioannidis, Munafo, Fusar-Poli, Nosek, & David, 2014), questionable research practices (e.g., John, Loewenstein, & Prelec, 2012; Simmons, Nelson, & Simonsohn, 2011), statistical errors (Gelman & Loken, 2014; Greenland et al., 2016), procedural errors in replication (Gilbert, King, Pettigrew, & Wilson, 2016; Loken & Gelman, 2017), contextual sensitivity of findings (R. Klein et al., 2018; Van Bavel, Mende-Siedlecki, Brady, & Reinero, 2016), and lack of a cumulative theoretical framework (Muthukrishna & Henrich, 2019).

Open practices are also an important goal for (social) science to increase reproducibility, that is, the verification of prior findings from the same data and code (Freese & Peterson, 2017). Although submissions to journals often require authors to agree to share their data and materials upon request, many researchers either cannot or choose not to provide the necessary files when requests are actually made (Wicherts, Borsboom, Kats, & Molenaar, 2006). This is particularly problematic because evidence indicates that the less willing researchers are to share their data, the more likely it is that the original results cannot be reproduced (Wicherts, Bakker, & Molenaar, 2011).

Open practices are intended to reduce the negative effect of questionable research practices on both replicability and reproducibility. Other researchers can only reproduce and retrace the original results if the original authors have published their materials and data and provided a comprehensible and detailed script of their analysis. Furthermore, other researchers can only estimate the extent to which results are replicable if all steps in the data processing and data analysis process were described honestly and transparently. Otherwise, the apparent evidence might be undermined by the influence of invisible questionable research practices. That is, researchers might have taken advantage of chance variability or other vicissitudes in the data to cherry-pick the strongest-appearing set of results (Simmons et al., 2011). Viewed in this way, questionable research practices may be understood as a motivated form of overfitting data, with the subsequent failure to replicate being analogous to the prediction error that results from overfitting.

The most prominent solution to limit questionable research practices is preregistration. Preregistration entails the specification of hypotheses, exclusion rules, data processing, and statistical models used to evaluate the hypotheses before the collection of the data (Nosek, Ebersole, DeHaven, & Mellor, 2018; van 't Veer & Giner-Sorolla, 2016; Wagenmakers, Wetzels, Borsboom, van der Maas, & Kievit, 2012). Such preregistrations are then time-stamped and published so that other researchers can examine whether the actual data analysis corresponds to the preregistered data analysis. Preregistration works particularly well for simple designs, such as experiments, in which researchers know a priori how they will analyze their data.

A main challenge for institutionalizing open practices among computational social scientists is that computational techniques often work inductively and can often be impossible to specify a priori. Luckily, computational social scientists who work with prediction tasks on very large datasets are already familiar with an arsenal of practices to reduce overfitting. Central among them is dividing data into a training set and test (or validation) set (e.g., Anderson & Magruder, 2017; Egami, Fong, Grimmer, Roberts, & Stewart, 2018). The training set is used for the *exploratory* work of developing a model, while the test set is used for the *confirmatory* work of determining how well the model predicts the outcome.

Usually, when researchers do projects that involve this sort of cross-validation, they have access in principle to the test set while they are fitting data on the training set. Often the researcher has no incentive to overfit the data – so cross-validation is fully in their interests – and, when they do, the researcher is trusted not to iterate predictions over the test set to improve the apparent performance of their model. However, when incentives to obtain certain (e.g., statistically significant or highly predictive) results are strong, access to the test dataset before committing to a model is recognized as unviable.

One solution is that a trusted third-party controls access to the test dataset until researchers publicly commit to a model. For example, when sites like Kaggle host competitions with rewards for the best-predicting model, the data that will be used to determine the winner are not available to the competitors. Salganik et al. (2020) hosted a similar competition in which researchers were tasked with submitting predictions about outcomes of respondents in the Fragile Families dataset, and again the structure was that competitors would submit predictions that would be evaluated against a sequestered portion of the original data to which no competitor had access. Outside of competitions, it has been suggested that researchers could send their data to a trusted third party to randomly divide data into a training set and a withheld test set (Fafchamps & Labonne, 2017). One could imagine ways that this could be institutionalized, for example, by being run by a professional association, but we are not aware of any efforts to do so at present.

Cross-validation and pre-registration can be used in tandem. van Loon and Freese (2019) divided existing data into a training and validation set for the purposes of evaluating the success of their model for predicting questionnaire-based ratings of the affective connotations of concepts from word-embeddings. Afterward, they used the same model to generate predictions for a new set of concepts and posted these predictions publicly prior to collecting the new data used to evaluate them. A different idea for combining cross-validation and pre-registration is proposed by Anderson and Magruder (2017), who note that one problem with pre-registration is that it can discourage including more adventurous supplementary hypotheses, as the addition of these hypotheses may imply expectations to correct for multiple comparisons which may be seen as reducing the chances of success for the main hypotheses. They propose using pre-registration and the full sample for hypotheses that are regarded either as especially central or posed with high confidence by the researcher and then using the split-sample approach to explore more speculative ideas.

Whenever researchers do preregister their projects, the preregistrations should be highly specific and followed precisely in order to be a solution against questionable research practices. Proponents of preregistration have acknowledged that while there are strong theoretical arguments why preregistrations should increase replicability, there is a lack of demonstrated evidence for this claim (Nosek et al., 2018). Recent research suggests that, in practice, preregistrations often remain too vague to be an effective shield against questionable research practices (Veldkamp et al., 2018). Furthermore, it is unclear to what extent adherence to the preregistration is enforced in the review process.

Overcoming some of the limitations of preregistration are registered reports (Chambers, Feredoes, Muthukumaraswamy, & Etchells, 2014; Hardwicke & Ioannidis, 2018). Registered reports are protocols that are submitted for peer-reviewed evaluation before the data is collected, with the result provisionally accepted for publication as long as the registered methodology is followed. Reviewers thus have the opportunity to influence both the theory and the analysis yet without increasing incentives for post-hoc motivated reasoning. Furthermore, registered reports have an explicit additional submission stage after the data was collected in which it is checked whether the theory and methods section still match the initial submission. Some registered reports have also included a "crowdsource" component, where the protocol is made public along with an invitation for other investigators also to collect data following the registration in exchange for joint authorship, so that the resulting paper includes many simultaneous replications and much more strongly powered findings.

While we have focused on how computational social science can benefit from open science, there is also great potential for contributions from computational social science to increase replicability. For example, although it is well known that a study with larger effect sizes and smaller p-values is more likely to be replicated than a study with smaller effect sizes and p-values close to .05, we know relatively little about the relationship between the other many, many features of research articles and replicability. We think that computational social scientists could make use of text analysis and machine learning to identity which features do and which features do not predict replicability. Researchers have already started such projects. One, the DARPA program Systematizing Confidence in Open Research and Evidence (SCORE), seeks to develop automatic tools to assess social science claims.

Open data

Open data are data that are publicly available. As one example, large-scale representative surveys such as the General Social Survey make their data available so that everyone can use the data. As another, the *American Journal of Political Science* requires authors to publish all files necessary to reproduce an article's results on the Harvard Dataverse Network, unless there is a specific reason a study's data cannot be shared.

Open data is an important goal for computational social science because it is a prerequisite for establishing the reproducibility of a finding, that is, the verification of prior findings from the same data and code (Freese & Peterson, 2017). It is unclear if most computational research meets even this minimal standard. For example, Dacrema, Cremonesi, and Jannach (2019) sought to reproduce research that involved using deep-learning techniques on a certain type of recommendation task. They considered a study reproducible if at least one dataset from the paper was available and if the paper's results from these data could be obtained with no more than minimal modification to source code. Of the 18 papers they identified from 4 conference series, the results of only 7 were reproducible by these criteria.

Another benefit of open data is that investigators can interrogate findings directly and decide if the conclusions drawn by investigators are warranted. Sometimes this results in others realizing things about the data that those who originally published findings missed. For example, Back, Küfner, and Egloff (2010) analyzed pager transmissions from New York City after 9/11/2001 and reported a dramatic increase in anger-associated messages in the latter hours of the day. The data were publicly available not because of any Open Data initiative but because they were part of a WikiLeaks leak. Looking at the same data, Pury (2011) demonstrated that the increase in "anger" was entirely driven by nearly 6000 identically formatted automated messages notifying a single pager about a "CRITICAL" computer system problem, with "critical" being counted as an anger-associated word.

The community benefits of open data are not limited to the ability to better evaluate the findings from a particular study. The accumulation of open data in a research community can also allow large-scale insights that were unavailable when investigators only have their own datasets to work with. In neuroimaging, overdue data-sharing initiatives finally allowed researchers to rigorously interrogate the performance of techniques with suitable amounts of real data that had previously only been validated with simulated data. Eklund, Nichols, and Knutsson (2016) demonstrate that three leading software packages for working with neuroimages all did not properly correct for multiple comparisons, so that false-positive results between purely random groupings of scans were obtained up to 70% of the time instead of the expected 5%. The problem has led to an unknown – but substantial – number of erroneous findings being published and could have been detected earlier if the neuroscience community had been more proactive about making data available to other investigators.

Fully open data also allows other researchers to make discoveries with data that were unanticipated by the original investigators, providing a plain public good for the research community. For example, a project on morality in everyday life (Hofmann, Wisneski, Brandt, & Skitka, 2014) created a publicly available dataset using experience sampling methodology to assess moral and immoral experiences in people's ordinary lives. A few years later, Crockett (2017) used the same data to explore whether immoral acts create more moral outrage online than in person. Other initiatives collect and organize similar datasets. For example, the "experimentdatar" data package contains large-scale experiments that are suitable for causal inference techniques via machine learning (see also https://github.com/itamarcaspi/experimentdatar). New analyses on shared datasets may reduce the inefficient collection of similar and expensive datasets by many different researchers.

The crucial challenge for open data is that some data might not be shareable with others. In text analysis, pervasive examples include data protected by copyright or terms of service agreements. Legal boundaries are here contested, but one interpretation for the United States would be that analyzing copyright-protected materials can be considered permissible under "Fair Use" doctrine, while making those raw data publicly available to others is not. The Corpus of Contemporary American English includes considerable data under copyright and degrades the data to count as "Fair Use": the regular distribution limits users to small snippets obtained via a fixed number of queries per day, and the downloadable version eliminates 5% of segments of text throughout.

Data may also be obtained from sources who are only willing to allow those investigators to use the data. For example, to evaluate hypotheses about how employees adapt to organizational culture, Srivastava and colleagues (2018) were able to obtain a complete corpus of internal e-mails among employees of a midsized company over a six-year period. It is remarkable enough when investigators are able to convince gatekeepers to allow them to use such data, and it is hardly surprising that gatekeepers would balk at permitting any broader dissemination of it.

In addition, data sharing may be restricted to protect the confidentiality and privacy of persons whose information is included in the data. The arsenal of data and tools available to computational social scientists has exacerbated some of the worries around data availability, as it is unclear what combination of information in a dataset can be combined with information elsewhere to deduce the identities of individuals. When New York City released "anonymized" data on 173 million taxi trips in response to a Freedom of Information Law request, a software developer figured out how to reverse hashed information about the taxi medallion number, and then an enterprising graduate student determined that this could be used to match the data to celebrity passengers from paparazzi photos of them getting in and out of taxis, allowing reports of how much those celebrities apparently tipped (Trotter, 2014). One need not be a celebrity to be reidentified using external data: Sweeney, Abu, and Winn (2013) report that a sizable percentage of sample participants with publicly available data in the Personal Genome Project could be identified by cross-referencing demographic variables in the dataset with voting and other public records. The U.S. Census Bureau is controversially doing more to coarsen the data it releases publicly because of work indicating that Census responses can be sometimes deduced by cross-referencing Census tables with commercially available data on individuals (Abowd, 2018).

Due to these concerns, the ideal of open data for every published study is unrealistic. Social science would be poorer if social science could only use data that may be shared with everyone. Nonetheless, journal policies that require researchers to either publicly share their data or require a clear statement why data cannot be shared that is published with the paper are instrumental to make progress towards the ideal of open data as much as possible. The inability for data to be shared is a flaw in a research design, and judgments must be made by editors and audiences about how to weigh that flaw versus the strengths of the project. To make this judgment, of course, papers for which data cannot be shared need to be explicit about that fact, and it is distressing how many computational social science papers leave the reader to guess about the availability of the data on which findings are based. Throughout science, there has been a re-appraisal of the extent to which optimal data availability in research communities can be attained by professional norms or exhortation alone. Even in areas where codified norms about sharing data with qualified investigators after publication exist, studies of compliance with requests have led to disappointing results (see Christensen, Freese, & Miguel, 2019, pp. 174–176 for a review). As a result, many have concluded that sharing standards are something that journals must enforce by requiring that data that can be made broadly available be deposited in a third-party repository at the time of publication and that data that cannot be made broadly available include an explicit disclosure.

Alongside this, we think that computational social scientists should not only follow journals' requirements but also actively aim to share their data whenever possible. Computational social scientists need to engage with ethical standards and evolving legal frameworks to make their decision to share or not share data (Hollingshead, Quan-Haase, & Chen, 2021). If researchers own their data, they can make anonymized versions of their data files available via a third-party repository like the Open Science Framework or Databrary. Anonymization of the data refers to the removal or recoding of variables that contain identifiable information. It is often overlooked that identifiable information does not only include obviously sensitive information such as names or email addresses but also combinations of common demographics. For example, it might be problematic to share the zip code and the birth date of participants because there might be certain birth dates that are unique in certain areas. If these variables are instrumental for the data analysis, researchers may recode the variables to avoid rare cases (ideally, such decisions are made *before* data analysis). We advise researchers to always include a readme file that explains the steps of anonymization, ideally with a link to the analysis code that provides full details of how the anonymization was conducted. In order to minimize the long-term costs of data sharing, labs and departments should develop data management plans that standardize practices and reduce the necessity of individual decision-making (Levenstein & Lyle, 2018). If researchers cannot share their data, we suggest that they make a readme file available that explains (a) how they accessed their data and (b) how other researchers can access the same dataset.

For computational social science, reproducibility demands not just sharing data but also sharing the code used to derive results from those data. Analysis code should contain a sufficient number of comments to explain each step and ideally be accessible in common formats. For example, R code can be transformed into markdowns and then knitted to. html or. pdf files. Versions of any external dependencies should be tracked and documented so that version differences can be ruled out as an explanation for any failure to reproduce results by others. Standard procedures within labs or departments can be developed for replication packages and should be enforced during the training of junior scholars (e.g., for dissertations). While this sort of work may often strike novices as cumbersome, the benefits of open science coding practices are realized not only by others attempting to reproduce work down the line but often by collaborators and one's own future self when one later returns to the code.

Finally, we suggest that computational social scientists make use of openly shared data. As explained previously, open data allows different forms of reproducibility analyses. Such analyses are important to ensure the validity and robustness of prior research. However, open data can also be used for original analyses and research questions.

Open tools

Open tools refer to software that is both free and has its source code available to others. The most prominent tools of computational social science – Python, R, Jupyter Notebooks, Git, Atom, Visual Studio Code – are all open software projects.

The availability and usage of open tools have many advantages for computational social science. First, software for computational research, in combination with high-quality educational material, is needed to allow as many researchers as possible to learn, understand, and use computational social science techniques. Free software is particularly suited for a quick diffusion because it does not impose monetary restrictions for the access of the software (von Krogh & von Hippel, 2006). It also eliminates headaches from coordinating software licenses among collaborators or across machines. Second, source code availability can attract widespread collaborations of volunteers who can quickly improve and innovate the software (von Krogh & von Hippel, 2006). Finally, open tools also provide for the possibility of a layer of "peer review" to vet the accuracy of algorithms and allow researchers the possibility of averring that every step in a project's computational workflow is in principle available for inspection.

The main challenge for the provision of open tools is that there are no direct monetary incentives for the individual to provide software for the community at large. In this respect, open software is a classic public goods or collective action problem (Coleman, 1986), and of course most users of open software are effectively "free riders" in the sense that they reap the benefits of its availability without paying the costs for its development. Happily, however, compared to many real-life public goods problems, open software does not need a substantial proportion of users to contribute software in order to thrive. Meanwhile, the success of open source stems from a complex array of different paths of reward, monetary and otherwise, that have evolved to allow software to be developed and maintained without being proprietary. In academia, counting open software work as scientific contributions helps leverage the reward structure of academia to support the development of openly available research tools. The scientific research community has long benefitted from a strong online community that works admirably hard on providing and supporting open software. This community has effectively solved the collective action problem of providing open tools in computational social science.

However, not all open tools are good tools. Open software solutions range from venerable tools with large, active, and sophisticated user communities to obscure packages provided by creators with unknown skill and commitment to testing. A vexing scenario for researchers using any software tool is that it is not actually doing what the researcher thinks it is, creating the possibility for researchers to receive misunderstood or simply erroneous results. Researchers are thus encouraged to do what they can to verify results with simple examples when possible, and novice users may wish to be especially wary of unusual or poorly documented tools.

The next challenge is that users often need support for learning how to use software. Computational social science deserves credit not just for the development of open research tools but also the openness of teaching materials. For example, the Russell Sage Foundation has sponsored the Summer Institute in Computational Social Science. The Institute has developed a curriculum that allows for it to be taught at satellite locations alongside its primary location, and it has also made lectures available as videos and other materials as well-annotated examples via GitHub. Providing teaching materials in this way leverages the technical acumen of computational social scientists to enable the field to offer state-of-the-art training to the broadest possible audience of aspiring researchers.

A related challenge is that even skilled users often need continuing support to deal with more complex challenges. Indeed, among the conventional arguments for using proprietary software over open software is the former offering more thorough documentation and more accessible technical support when users face problems. Especially for prominent open software solutions for computational social science, however, this has been largely neutralized by the development of a vast array of sites providing online answers to questions, like Stack Exchange, with different ways of crowdsourced curation of the effectiveness of different answers. Search engines are now the first strategy employed for all manner of technical queries for users of either proprietary or open software alternatives, and the large communities surrounding prominent open-source platforms often have produced much more high-quality content to help users than experts employed by a proprietary package.

Open access

Open access refers to the "free, public availability of a research product on the internet for distribution and re-use with acknowledgement" (Crüwell, 2019, p. 7). Open access now has different models. The model in which journal articles are made freely available is known as "gold" open access. "Green" open access, meanwhile, refers to an author engaging in some kind of self-archiving alongside paywalled journal publication. Journals can prohibit even this as a condition of publication, but the appetite for doing so has waned considerably, especially now that various funding bodies require their investigators to provide some sort of open version of publications.

Open access is an important goal for computational social science for several reasons. First, open access articles can be readily obtained both by non-researchers as well as researchers from countries and institutions with less resources (Tennant et al., 2016). Thus, publishing with open access increases and democratizes access to knowledge, which may in turn facilitate the more widespread adoption of computational techniques in the social sciences. Second, publishing with open access (more specifically, with a Creative Commons Attribution license CC-BY) enables other researchers, including computational social scientists, to employ automated text- and data-mining tools for analyzing scientific articles (Tennant et al., 2016). Third, even for those unmoved by the community appeals of openness, increasing the exposure and accessibility to one's work provides a professional advantage. Making working papers available allows even faster transmission of knowledge and also helps establish priority for findings in fast-moving fields. Finally, a happy side effect for the authors of open access articles is that open access articles are cited more often (Piwowar et al., 2018; Tennant et al., 2016).

There are two potential downsides that have been discussed in the context of open access. First, instead of publishers charging readers or readers' institutions, open access publishers often charge the researchers who wrote the article (Tennant et al., 2016). This makes it more difficult for researchers with fewer resources to publish with gold open access. However, green open access (i.e., self-archival of papers) provides a cost-free model of open access that every researcher can adopt. Granted, it should be noted that some journals do not approve of submitting articles that have been made available as preprints; journal policies can be checked via SHERPA/ RoMEO (www.sherpa.ac.uk/romeo/index.php). In addition, we urge (computational) social scientists to make sure that they choose a license for their paper that allows for automated text and data mining. An excellent resource for self-archiving papers is ArXiv (https://arxiv.org/), a widely used repository of preprints with different choices for licenses. Furthermore, while author charges are still the most common way that gold open access is funded, there are journals in which charges are effectively underwritten by a benefactor, and some journals are piloting a model in which a journal is made open if and only if it sells a certain level of institutional subscriptions.

Second, and related to the first concern, publishers may exploit the open access model. If authors pay for publishing in an open access model, publishers maximize their income by maximizing the number of papers they publish. Thus, publishers have an incentive to reduce the rigor of the review process and publish every submitted article, undermining quality (Tennant et al., 2016). Researchers should carefully check the reputation of their target journal before submission. A helpful guide to identify predatory journals is available at https://predatoryjournals.com.

Conclusion

In the current chapter, we have discussed how computational social scientists can achieve high standards of accessibility, transparency, replicability, and reproducibility by adhering to four open science principles, open practices, open data, open tools, and open access. Specifically, we suggest the following open science to-do list for computational social scientists who aim to publish a paper:

Open practices

1 Be transparent about all steps in the data processing and analyses processes.
2 If you want to test a hypothesis and know how you want to test it, preregister your hypothesis and your analysis plan.
3 If you do not have hypotheses or do not know how to test them, divide your dataset into an exploratory part (for exploratory analyses) and a confirmatory part (for confirmatory analyses). Limit your own access to the confirmatory dataset until you enter the confirmatory stage.
4 Consider opportunities to write papers as registered reports or participate in crowdsourced registered reports projects.
5 Use computational techniques to provide insights into the features of a study or a paper that predict replicability.

Open data

1 If possible, share your own data.
2 If possible, use a license that allows other researchers to reuse your data.
3 If you cannot share your data yourself, explain how the data can be accessed, and if it cannot be shared at all, indicate this clearly in the paper.

Open tools

1 Use open-source software tools.
2 Share your code, software, and educational materials so that other people can learn computational techniques.

Open access

1 Publish your paper with open access, for example, by posting it on a repository of preprints
2 Use a license that allows for automated text- and data-mining.

References

Abowd, J. M. (2018). The U.S. Census Bureau adopts differential privacy. In *Proceedings of the 24th ACM SIGKDD International conference on knowledge discovery & data mining* (pp. 2867–2867). doi:10.1145/3219819.3226070

Anderson, C. J., Bahnik, S., Barnett-Cowan, M., Bosco, F. A., Chandler, J., Chartier, C. R., . . . Zuni, K. (2016). Response to comment on "estimating the reproducibility of psychological science". *Science, 351*(6277), 1037. doi:10.1126/science.aad9163

Anderson, M. L., & Magruder, J. (2017). *Split-sample strategies for avoiding false discoveries* (NBER Working Paper No. 23544). National Bureau of Economic Research. Retrieved from www.nber.org/papers/w23544

Back, M. D., Küfner, A. C. P., & Egloff, B. (2010). The emotional timeline of September 11, 2001. *Psychological Science, 21*(10), 1417–1419. doi:10.1177/0956797610382124

Baker, M. (2016). 1,500 scientists lift the lid on reproducibility. *Nature, 533*(7604), 452–454. doi:10.1038/533452a

Bakker, M., van Dijk, A., & Wicherts, J. M. (2012). The rules of the game called psychological science. *Perspectives on Psychological Science, 7*(6), 543–554. doi:10.1177/1745691612459060

Camerer, C. F., Dreber, A., Forsell, E., Ho, T. H., Huber, J., Johannesson, M., . . . Heikensten, E. (2016). Evaluating replicability of laboratory experiments in economics. *Science, 351*(6280), 1433–1436. doi:10.1126/science.aaf0918

Camerer, C. F., Dreber, A., Holzmeister, F., Ho, T. H., Huber, J., Johannesson, M., . . . Altmejd, A. (2018). Evaluating the replicability of social science experiments in nature and science between 2010 and 2015. *Nature Human Behaviour, 2*(9), 637–644. doi:10.1038/s41562-018-0399-z

Chambers, C. D., Feredoes, E., Muthukumaraswamy, S. D., & Etchells, P. (2014). Instead of "playing the game" it is time to change the rules: Registered reports at AIMS neuroscience and beyond. *AIMS Neuroscience, 1*(1), 4–17. doi:10.3934/Neuroscience2014.1.4

Christensen, G., Freese, J., & Miguel, E. (2019). *Transparent and reproducible social science research: How to do open science.* University of California Press.

Coleman, J. S. (1986). *Individual interests and collective action: Selected essays.* Cambridge University Press.

Crockett, M. J. (2017). Moral outrage in the digital age. *Nature Human Behaviour, 1*(11), 769–771. doi:10.1038/s41562-017-0213-3

Crüwell, S., van Doorn, J., Etz, A., Makel, M. C., Moshontz, H., Niebaum, J. C., . . . Schulte-Mecklenbeck, M. (2019). Seven easy steps to open science. *Zeitschrift für Psychologie, 227*, 237–248. doi:10.1027/2151-2604/a000387

Dacrema, M. F., Cremonesi, P., & Jannach, D. (2019). Are we really making much progress? A worrying analysis of recent neural recommendation approaches. In *Proceedings of the 13th ACM conference on recommender systems* (pp. 101–109). doi:10.1145/3298689.3347058

Edelmann, A., Wolff, T., Montagne, D., & Bail, C. A. (2020). Computational social science and sociology. *Annual Review of Sociology, 46*, 61–81. doi:10.1146/annurev-soc-121919-054621

Egami, N., Fong, C. J., Grimmer, J., Roberts, M. E., & Stewart, B. M. (2018). *How to make causal inferences using texts.* Retrieved from https://arxiv.org/abs/1802.02163

Eklund, A., Nichols, T. E., & Knutsson, H. (2016). Cluster failure: Why fMRI inferences for spatial extent have inflated false-positive rates. *Proceedings of the National Academy of Sciences, 113*(28), 7900–7905. doi:10.1073/pnas.1602413113

Fafchamps, M., & Labonne, J. (2017). Using split samples to improve inference on causal effects. *Political Analysis, 25*(4), 465–482. doi:10.1017/pan.2017.22

Freese, J., & Peterson, D. (2017). Replication in social science. *Annual Review of Sociology, 43*, 147–165. doi:10.1146/annurev-soc-060116-053450

Gelman, A., & Loken, E. (2014). The statistical crisis in science. *American Scientist, 102*(6), 460–466. doi:10.1511/2014.111.460

Gilbert, D. T., King, G., Pettigrew, S., & Wilson, T. D. (2016). Comment on "estimating the reproducibility of psychological science". *Science, 351*(6277), 1037–1037. doi:10.1126/science.aad7243

Greenland, S., Senn, S. J., Rothman, K. J., Carlin, J. B., Poole, C., Goodman, S. N., & Altman, D. G. (2016). Statistical tests, P values, confidence intervals, and power: A guide to misinterpretations. *European Journal of Epidemiology, 31*(4), 337–350. doi:10.1007/s10654-016-0149-3

Hardwicke, T. E., & Ioannidis, J. P. (2018). Mapping the universe of registered reports. *Nature Human Behaviour, 2*(11), 793–796. doi:10.1038/s41562-018-0444-y

Hofmann, W., Wisneski, D. C., Brandt, M. J., & Skitka, L. J. (2014). Morality in everyday life. *Science, 345*(6202), 1340–1343. doi:10.1126/science.1251560

Hollingshead, W., Quan-Haase, A., & Chen, W. (2021). Ethics and privacy in computational social science: A call for pedagogy. In U. Engel, A. Quan-Hasse, S. X. Liu, & L. Lyberg (Eds.), *Handbook of computational social science*. Routledge and Taylor & Francis Group.

Ioannidis, J. P. (2005). Why most published research findings are false. *PLoS Medicine, 2*(8), e124. doi:10.1371/journal.pmed.0020124

Ioannidis, J. P., Munafo, M. R., Fusar-Poli, P., Nosek, B. A., & David, S. P. (2014). Publication and other reporting biases in cognitive sciences: Detection, prevalence, and prevention. *Trends in Cognitive Sciences, 18*(5), 235–241. doi:10.1016/j.tics.2014.02.010

John, L. K., Loewenstein, G., & Prelec, D. (2012). Measuring the prevalence of questionable research practices with incentives for truth telling. *Psychological Science, 23*(5), 524–532. doi:10.1177/0956797611430953

Klein, R. A., Vianello, M., Hasselman, F., Adams, B. G., Adams Jr, R. B., Alper, S., . . . Batra, R. (2018). Many labs 2: Investigating variation in replicability across samples and settings. *Advances in Methods and Practices in Psychological Science, 1*(4), 443–490. doi:10.1177/2515245918810225

Lazer, D., Pentland, A., Adamic, L., Aral, S., Barabasi, A. L., Brewer, D., . . . Jebara, T. (2009). Computational social science. *Science, 323*(5915), 721–723. doi:10.1126/science.1167742

Levenstein, M. C., & Lyle, J. A. (2018). Data: Sharing is caring. *Advances in Methods and Practices in Psychological Science, 1*(1), 95–103. doi:10.1177/2515245918758319

Loken, E., & Gelman, A. (2017). Measurement error and the replication crisis. *Science, 355*(6325), 584–585. doi:10.1126/science.aal3618

Munafò, M. R., Nosek, B. A., Bishop, D. V., Button, K. S., Chambers, C. D., Du Sert, N. P., . . . & Ioannidis, J. P. (2017). A manifesto for reproducible science. *Nature Human Behaviour, 1*(1), 1–9. doi:10.1038/s41562-016-0021

Muthukrishna, M., & Henrich, J. (2019). A problem in theory. *Nature Human Behaviour, 3*(3), 221–229. doi:10.1038/s41562-018-0522-1

Nosek, B. A., Ebersole, C. R., DeHaven, A. C., & Mellor, D. T. (2018). The preregistration revolution. *Proceedings of the National Academy of Sciences, 115*(11), 2600–2606. doi:10.1073/pnas.1708274114

Open Science Collaboration. (2015). Estimating the reproducibility of psychological science. *Science, 349*(6251). doi:10.1126/science.aac4716

Piwowar, H., Priem, J., Larivière, V., Alperin, J. P., Matthias, L., Norlander, B., . . . Haustein, S. (2018). The state of OA: A large-scale analysis of the prevalence and impact of open access articles. *PeerJ, 6*, e4375. doi:10.7717/peerj.4375

Pury, C. L. (2011). Automation can lead to confounds in text analysis: Back, Küfner, and Egloff (2010) and the not-so-angry Americans. *Psychological Science, 22*(6), 835–836. doi:10.1177/0956797611408735

Salganik, M. J., Lundberg, I., Kindel, A. T., Ahearn, C. E., Al-Ghoneim, K., Almaatouq, A., . . . Datta, D. (2020). Measuring the predictability of life outcomes with a scientific mass collaboration. *Proceedings of the National Academy of Sciences, 117*(15), 8398–8403. doi:10.1073/pnas.1915006117

Shiffrin, R. M., Börner, K., & Stigler, S. M. (2018). Scientific progress despite irreproducibility: A seeming paradox. *Proceedings of the National Academy of Sciences, 115*(11), 2632–2639. doi:10.1073/pnas.1711786114

Simmons, J. P., Nelson, L. D., & Simonsohn, U. (2011). False-positive psychology: Undisclosed flexibility in data collection and analysis allows presenting anything as significant. *Psychological Science, 22*(11), 1359–1366. doi:10.1177/0956797611417632

Srivastava, S. B., Goldberg, A., Manian, V. G., & Potts, C. (2018). Enculturation trajectories: Language, cultural adaptation, and individual outcomes in organizations. *Management Science, 64*(3), 1348–1364. doi:10.1287/mnsc.2016.2671

Sweeney, L., Abu, A., & Winn, J. (2013). *Identifying participants in the personal genome project by name (a re-identification experiment)*. Retrieved from https://arxiv.org/abs/1304.7605

Tennant, J. P., Waldner, F., Jacques, D. C., Masuzzo, P., Collister, L. B., & Hartgerink, C. H. (2016). The academic, economic and societal impacts of open access: An evidence-based review. *F1000Research*, *5*, 632. doi:10.12688/f1000research.8460.3

Trotter, J. K. (2014, October 23). Public NYC taxicab database lets you see how celebrities tip. *Gawker*. Retrieved from https://gawker.com/the-public-nyc-taxicab-database-that-accidentally-track-1646724546

Van Bavel, J. J., Mende-Siedlecki, P., Brady, W. J., & Reinero, D. A. (2016). Contextual sensitivity in scientific reproducibility. *Proceedings of the National Academy of Sciences*, *113*(23), 6454–6459. doi:10.1073/pnas.1521897113

van Loon, A., & Freese, J. (2019). *Can we distill fundamental sentiments from natural language use? Evaluating word embeddings as a complement to survey-based ratings of affective meaning.* Retrieved from https://osf.io/preprints/socarxiv/r7ewx/

van't Veer, A. E., & Giner-Sorolla, R. (2016). Pre-registration in social psychology – A discussion and suggested template. *Journal of Experimental Social Psychology*, *67*, 2–12. doi:10.1016/j.jesp.2016.03.004

Veldkamp, C. L. S., Bakker, M., Van Assen, M. A., Crompvoets, E. A. V., Ong, H. H., Nosek, B. A., . . . Wicherts, J. (2018). *Ensuring the quality and specificity of preregistrations.* Retrieved from https://psyarxiv.com/cdgyh

Von Krogh, G., & Von Hippel, E. (2006). The promise of research on open source software. *Management Science*, *52*(7), 975–983. doi:10.1287/mnsc.1060.0560

Wagenmakers, E. J., Wetzels, R., Borsboom, D., van der Maas, H. L., & Kievit, R. A. (2012). An agenda for purely confirmatory research. *Perspectives on Psychological Science*, *7*(6), 632–638. doi:10.1177/1745691612463078

Wicherts, J. M., Bakker, M., & Molenaar, D. (2011). Willingness to share research data is related to the strength of the evidence and the quality of reporting of statistical results. *PLoS One*, *6*(11), e26828. doi:10.1371/journal.pone.0026828

Wicherts, J. M., Borsboom, D., Kats, J., & Molenaar, D. (2006). The poor availability of psychological research data for reanalysis. *American Psychologist*, *61*(7), 726–728. doi:10.1037/0003-066X.61.7.726

9

CAUSAL AND PREDICTIVE MODELING IN COMPUTATIONAL SOCIAL SCIENCE

Uwe Engel

Introduction

Computational social science (CSS) is best understood as an interdisciplinary field in the inter-section of data science and social science that pursues causal and predictive inference as its two main objectives. With roots in mathematical modeling and social simulation in sociology, in particular the increasing digitization of life turned CSS into a dynamically developing scientific field. The more human life takes place in digital environments, the more behavioral data of interest to the social and behavioral sciences accumulate. These data are only available digitally and thus require proper "new computational" methods of data collection, data management, data processing, and data analysis (Lazer et al., 2020). Delimitations of CSS reference big data, computational methods, and data science facets, as detailed in the following.

Perspectives on computational social science methodology

Computational methods in sociology

The impression of an inflationary use of the adjective "computational" is certainly justifiable. As Hox (2017, p. 3) states, with explicit consideration of the social and behavioral sciences, it seems that almost any scientific field can now be preceded by the adjective "computational". Though it is true that computational methods have reached an extremely high significance, it is equally true that the social sciences have developed computational methods from the outset: statistical data analysis and mathematical modeling are by no means new computational tools in this field. Coleman's (1964) seminal *Mathematical Sociology* is one of the best exemplifica-tions of the precursors of contemporary analytical sociology. Other examples are the Columbia School of Social Research and its pioneering development work on multivariate analysis (e.g., Lazarsfeld, 1955; Rosenberg, 1968), the mathematical study of change (Coleman, 1968), meth-ods of replication (Galtung, 1969), prediction studies (e.g., Goodman, 1955), the analysis of change through time by panel analysis (e.g., Lazarsfeld, Berelson, & Gaudet, 1955), Lazarsfeld's latent structure analysis (McCutcheon, 1987), longitudinal data analysis (Coleman, 1981), and

DOI: 10.4324/9781003024583-10

multilevel methodology (e.g., Lazarsfeld & Menzel, 1969 [1961]; Coleman et al., 1966; Coleman, 1990). The "social simulation modeling" area in CSS and its multilevel approach towards social complexity as detailed in Cioffi-Revilla (2017, pp. 12–20, 205ff., 331ff., 470ff.) is also highlighted.

 Hox (2017, p. 3) refers to the simulation branch when reviewing "three important elements" of CSS, namely "big data, analytics, and simulation". In his view, CSS refers "to the application of computational methods to explore and test scientific (social, psychological, economic) theories", the field being "often interpreted as equivalent to the use of big data in social science. However, although computational social science relies strongly on big data and the ability to analyze these, it also includes computer simulation and text analysis". Edelmann, Wolff, Montagne, and Bail (2020, p. 62), too, highlight the simulation branch in CSS. They point out that "the term computational social science emerged in the final quarter of the twentieth century within social science disciplines as well as science, technology, engineering, and mathematics (STEM) disciplines". They continue by writing that within social science, "the term originally described agent-based modeling – or the use of computer programs to simulate human behavior within artificial populations", whereas within STEM fields, by contrast, "any study that employs large datasets that describe human behavior" is "often described as computational social science".

Big data

Shah, Capella, and Neuman (2015, p. 7) views CSS

> as a *specific subcategory* of work on big data. It is an approach to social inquiry defined by (1) the use of large, complex datasets, often – though not always – measured in terabytes or petabytes; (2) the frequent involvement of "naturally occurring" social and digital media sources and other electronic databases; (3) the use of computational or algorithmic solutions to generate patterns and inferences from these data; and (4) the applicability to social theory in a variety of domains from the study of mass opinion to public health, from examinations of political events to social movements.
>
> (emphasis added)

Alvarez (2016, p. 5) stresses in his introduction to *Computational Social Science* that it is

> not about "big data". . . . Instead, the focus is on the methodological innovations driven by the availability of *new types of data* or by *data of a different scale* than has been previously possible. . . . [T]he emphasis rather is on the cross-disciplinary applications of statistical, computational, and machine learning tools to the new types of data, at a larger scale, to learn more about politics and policy.
>
> (emphasis added)

Data science

In line with reference to terms such as "analytics" and "statistical, computational, and machine learning tools", one can delimit CSS also by reference to data science. Hox (2017, p. 3), for instance, regards CSS as an "interdisciplinary field that includes mathematics, statistics, data science, and, of course, social science". Proponents of data science even tend to subsume CSS under this discipline. "Data science" is then regarded as a "new interdisciplinary field that synthesizes and builds on statistics, informatics, computing, communication, management, and sociology" . . . "to transform data to insights and decisions" (Cao, 2017, pp. 43, 8). Provost and Fawcett (2013, p. 4f.) "view the ultimate goal of data science as improving decision-making, as this generally is of direct interest to business". Similarly, Kelleher and Tierney (2018, p. 1) stress as a commonality the focus on "improving decision making through the analysis of data" when they point out that the "terms *data science*, *machine learning*, and *data mining* were often used interchangeably". Data science is broader in scope, while machine learning "focuses on the design and evaluation of algorithms for extracting patterns from data" and "data mining generally deals with the analysis of structured data". Data science

> also takes up other challenges, such as the capturing, cleaning, and transforming of unstructured social media and web data; the use of big-data technologies to store and process big, unstructured data sets; and questions related to data ethics and regulation.
> (Kelleher & Tierney, 2018, p. 1f.)

Machine learning and artificial intelligence

The Royal Society (2017, p. 25) localizes machine learning at the intersection of artificial intelligence, data science, and statistics, with applications in robotics. In computer science, deep learning is viewed as part of machine learning, and machine learning is viewed as part of artificial intelligence. Kelleher (2019, p. 4) dates the birth of AI to "a workshop at Dartmouth College in the summer of 1956". The Royal Society (2017, p. 28) outlines a similar picture in a timeline on developments in machine learning and AI by mentioning the Turing Test in 1950 and the Dartmouth Workshop. Part of this timeline also provides a clue that several key concepts in machine learning are derived from probability theory and statistics, the roots of which date to the 18th century (e.g., Bayes' theorem). James, Witten, Hastic, and Tibshirani (2013) use the term statistical learning and point to the essential role of statistical methods in the machine learning field. Ghani and Schierholz (2017, p. 148) write that "over the past 20 years, machine learning has become an interdisciplinary field spanning computer science, artificial intelligence, databases, and statistics". It is worth mentioning that the special relevance of machine learning derives from both the powerful capabilities of deep learning and artificial intelligence and their resulting impact on contemporary society and from the considerably less spectacular machine-learning applications in statistical data analysis.

Prediction and causal inference

In a similar vein, Kuhn and Johnson (2013, p. 1) refer to machine learning, artificial intelligence, pattern recognition, data mining, predictive analytics, and knowledge discovery and point out that "while each field approaches the problem using different perspectives and toolsets, the ultimate objective is the same: *to make an accurate prediction*". Consequently, the authors pool "these terms into the commonly used phrase *predictive modeling*". Yarkoni and Westfall (2017, p. 2) draw attention to the "underappreciated tension between prediction and explanation", characterize current practice in psychology as "explanation without prediction", and raise substantial doubts about the predictive power and replicability of such explanatory research. "The crucial point is that prediction and replicability are the same problem", as Hindman (2015, p. 60f.) outlines; machine-learning-based approaches produce models that are more likely to be reproduced by other scholarship because they are more robust than standard practice and because "reducing the out-of-sample error produces more stable findings across different researchers and different studies". Lin (2015) vigorously defends big data analysis against the reservation that this approach neglects theory. He argues, somewhat provocatively, that much of the controversy stems from a fundamental confusion about the purpose of big data. Using the example of commercial matchmaking services, he claims "that understanding is not necessary for prediction. . . . Whether any of their matchmaking algorithms are based on their current (academic) understanding of attraction is largely irrelevant" (Lin, 2015, p. 39).

This view draws criticism from proponents of causal analysis in social research. Latent variable modeling acts on the assumption that theoretical input is needed for both the measurement and structural part of a causal model. Yet not all explanations predict satisfactorily, and not all good predictions explain, as Troitzsch (2009) remarks. Hofman, Sharma, and Watts (2017, p. 486) "argue that the increasingly computational nature of social science is beginning to reverse (the) traditional bias against prediction", while highlighting the view that "predictive accuracy and interpretability must be recognized as complements, not substitutes, when evaluating explanations". Similarly, James et al. (2013, Chapter 2) elaborate on doing prediction and causal inference within a statistical learning approach. Balancing these two objectives in an analysis might be advantageous because prediction accuracy and generalizability cannot be maximized simultaneously. While maximizing R^2 is certainly suitable for increasing prediction accuracy, such a strategy runs the risk of overfitting and impairing the generalizability of found results. Data mining thus trusts techniques based on "replication" and "cross-validation", in which the use of training, tuning, and test samples guards against overfitting (Attewell & Monaghan, 2015, p. 14). The power of predicting unseen (out-of-sample) data can be regarded as a more relevant criterion than the size of a "theoretically privileged" regression coefficient or a model fit statistic (Yarkoni & Westfall, 2017, p. 2).

CSS, data science, and social science

It is constructive to locate CSS in the intersecting set of data science with social science and underlay the fields with possible data types, as shown in Figure 9.1. Data science is conceived in the broader sense outlined previously. Its core is the machine learning field, along with computational methods for collecting, cleaning, transforming, and processing datasets on even the largest scales (Luraschi, Kuo, & Ruiz, 2020).

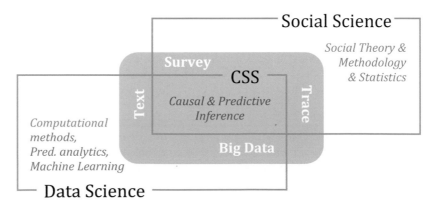

Figure 9.1   Causal and predictive inference in CSS

A substantial overlap exists between statistical methods employed in the machine-learning tradition, on the one hand, and the causal and descriptive analysis of observational studies in the counterfactual research tradition of social research, on the other hand (Morgan & Winship, 2007). Examples include principal component analysis (PCA), classification and clustering methods, and linear and logistic regression, as well as replication methods (e.g., James et al., 2013; Kuhn & Johnson, 2013; Lantz, 2019). Despite differences in technical language, both traditions share a subset of common statistical learning methods. In addition, both research traditions share the objective of inferring valid insights from nonexperimental data. This, in turn, requires tools for meeting two overwhelmingly important demands, namely the adequate ascertainment of validity and the attainment of effective control over possible sources of error.

In Figure 9.1, "Pred. analytics" stands for predictive analytics, to indicate the great importance attached to prediction and the achievement of prediction accuracy in the machine-learning framework. However, following James et al. (2013, Chapter 1), the basic possibility of achieving trade-offs between prediction accuracy and model interpretability is also regarded as a key feature of the statistical learning approach to data science. It is exactly this feature that opens the opportunity of doing both predictive and causal inference within a joint data-science framework and thus the opportunity to counterbalance the susceptibility to prediction bias in this field.

On the one hand, particular strengths of the statistical learning field include highly flexible modeling options, capabilities of handling nonlinear relationships, and tools for assessing validity on a regular basis. On the other hand, in the counterfactual and statistical research tradition pursued in the social and behavioral sciences, much effort is invested in latent variable modeling and the development of methodological and statistical tools for coping effectively with potential sources of error, such as confounding factors, selective unit and item nonresponse, and measurement effects. Along with the existing overlap of statistical methods, a data science that capitalizes on the best of these two worlds appears thus particularly constructive. The same is true for a CSS that takes advantage of import from such a data science, "even – or rather especially – when their datasets are small" (Hindman, 2015, p. 49), and the social and behavioral theories and methodologies that come from the social and behavioral sciences.

Big data, digital textual and behavioral trace data, and survey data

Volume (scale of data), velocity (analysis of streaming data), variety (different forms of data), and veracity (uncertainty of data) represent the original four Vs of big data (IBM, 2012). To this, add the fifth and sixth Vs, virtue (ethics) and value (knowledge gain) (Quan-Haase & Sloan, 2017, pp. 5–6). All these Vs make great demands on data collection and analysis. Volume matters: Though size is no inherent data quality criterion, large datasets facilitate multivariate analysis and validation but can make analysis more complicated (statistical inference, distributed computing). The collection and analysis of streaming data may also require special computational tools in the shape of online learning algorithms (see Ippel et al., Chapter 5 in Volume 2 of this handbook). In CSS, variety is a challenge through the simultaneous use of quite different kinds of data, such as the user-generated content in social media and the digital marks people leave when surfing the web. Such textual and digital-trace data complement survey data and make great demands on their separate and combined analysis. Veracity refers to the whole spectrum of data-quality criteria as, for instance, known in social-science methodology. A whole range of issues and challenges is accordingly involved in this regard. These issues become evident when transferring the total error paradigm known from survey methodology to social media research (Biemer, 2017; Quan-Haase & Sloan, 2017; Franke et al., 2016; see also Sen et al., Chapter 9 in Volume 2 of this handbook).

Against the background that a major strand of CSS research develops in the highly frequented social-media context, the perceived close link between CSS and big data reported previously comes as no surprise. However, even if both behavior and behavioral marks in digital environments cover the major focus of social research in CSS, survey data play an important role too. Big data analysis benefits from both the availability of huge pools of compoundable survey data (e.g., Warshaw, 2016, p. 28ff.) and the data quality of surveys.

Causal inference in social research

Morgan and Winship (2007) describe the counterfactual model for observational data analysis, also known as the "potential outcomes framework" (Salganik, 2018, pp. 62–70), in greater detail. In doing so, they refer extensively to Pearl's (2000) work on graphical representations of causal relationships (graph theory). The authors deal particularly with three basic strategies for estimating causal effects: (1) to condition on variables "that block all backdoor paths from the causal variable to the outcome variable", (2) the use of "exogenous variation in an appropriate instrumental variable to isolate covariation in the causal and outcomes variables", and (3) the establishment of an "isolated and exhaustive mechanism that relates the causal variable to the outcome variable and then calculates the causal effect as it propagates through the mechanism" (Morgan & Winship, 2007, p. 26). The authors present a selective history of the use of experimental language in observational social science and regard the counterfactual model of causality as valuable because it helps researchers "to stipulate assumptions, evaluate alternative data analysis techniques, and think carefully about the process of causal exposure" (Morgan & Winship, 2007, p. 7). They also refer to "equation-based motivations of observational data analysis" to draw attention to the weaknesses of a "naïve usage of regression modeling", path analysis, and structural equation modeling as tools for the estimation of causal effects. They conclude that the rise of regression has "led to a focus on equations for outcomes, rather than careful thinking about how the data in hand differ from what would have been generated by the ideal experiments one might wish to have conducted" (Morgan & Winship, 2007, p. 13).

Some caution is advisable, indeed, if regression analysis is used for causal analysis. Bollen (1989, Chapter 3) uses three criteria to infer cause: isolation, association, and direction of causation (establishing causal priority). In doing so, the crucial point is that "isolation" designates actually a "pseudo-isolation" condition realized by means of assumptions about the error term of a regression equation (i.e., that the error is not correlated with the explanatory variable). Such assumptions are most important to get the model closed and thereby get changes in y attributable to corresponding changes in the explanatory variable(s). The clue that regression diagnostics are available to test such assumptions on a routine basis is relevant. Furthermore, "theory" plays an important role in both the counterfactual model ("the need to clearly articulate assumptions grounded in theory, that is believable", Morgan & Winship, 2007, p. 13) and structural equation modeling. The need for basing causal models in substantial theory is challenging in view of the basic limitations of model testing procedures. In the end, goodness-of-fit can only prove the compatibility of data and model implications, while it cannot rule out alternative models that have the same implications as a given tested model (Galtung, 1969; Stinchcombe, 1968, p. 19f.). Furthermore, as Pearl (2012, p. 68) notes, there exists a "huge logical gap between "establishing causation", which requires careful manipulative experiments, and "interpreting parameters as causal effects", which may be based on firm scientific knowledge or on previously conducted experiments. . ., to conclude that "as a matter of fact. . ., causal effects in observational studies can only be substantiated from a combination of data and untested theoretical assumptions, not from the data alone".

Notwithstanding such basic limitations, "causal models" have prominent roots in the scientific work on path analysis and simultaneous-equation techniques realized in the 1950s and 60s, as Blalock's (1971) collection of such work documents. Since then, structural equation modeling and, more generally, latent variable (mixture) modeling evolved into a highly advanced tool for the statistical analysis of observational data; with strengths in controlling for (1) random and systematic measurement error, (2) methods effects by MTMM modeling (e.g., Marsh & Grayson, 1995), and (3) data missing at random and data not missing at random, by multiple imputation and selection/pattern mixture modeling (e.g., Winship & Morgan, 1999; Enders, 2010, van Buuren, 2018).

From the outset, longitudinal modeling using panel data played an essential role (e.g., Blalock, 1985; Coleman, 1981; Hagenaars, 1990), among other things, in securing by this repeated measurement design the validity of a key assumption of causal inference: that the alleged cause must precede the effect. As de Vaus (2001, p. 34 ff.) outlines, it must make sense to infer cause from covariation; he notes three criteria for the necessary plausibility in this respect: (1) time order (cause must come before the effect; see Bollen (1989, p. 61f.) for a discussion of this criterion), (2) the dependent variable must be capable of change, and (3) the causal assertion must make sense theoretically. A panel design is basically constructive in this regard because causal order may be derived from the temporal order between the panel waves. Longitudinal modeling using this design changed somewhat from the classical cross-lagged panel model to latent growth curve modeling (e.g., Byrne, 2012). This latter design is not only particularly suitable for multi-wave panel data; this type of model avoids an inherent weakness of the classical, cross-lagged panel model (potential disparity in corresponding temporal and causal lag), performs causal analysis using concomitant (instead of residual) change as an indication of causality and realizes the combination of longitudinal and multilevel modeling (Engel & Meyer, 1996; Engel, Gattig, & Simonson, 2007).

Descriptive inference in large datasets

Specific scientific ends that large datasets tend to enable are the study of rare events, the study of heterogeneity, and the detection of small differences (Salganik, 2018, pp. 18–20).

McFarland and MacFarland (2015, p. 1) draw attention to statistical significance testing in case of big observational "found data" from social media and explain that the results in such cases "give analysts a false sense of security as they proceed to focus on employing traditional statistical methods" because hidden biases (for instance, population bias) would be easily "overlooked due to the enhanced significance of the results". As Salganik (2018, p. 20) put it in his elaboration on "ten common characteristics of big data": "While bigness does reduce the need to worry about random error, it actually *increases* the need to worry about systematic errors, the kind of errors . . . that arise from biases in how data are created". Hox (2017, p. 10) refers to cross-validation and raises the question of how much room is there at the bottom: "how well do these techniques work with 'small Big Data'." He points out that the formal testing of structural equation models becomes problematic in the case of usual sample sizes of comparative survey research because a small degree of misfit already rejects the model. The respective sensitivity of the likelihood ratio chi^2 test to sample size and the usual solution through an array of goodness-of-fit indices is well known (e.g., Byrne2012, pp. 66–77). Hox (2017, p. 10) continues by stating that "a cross-validation or *k*-fold approach that analyses how well the structural equation model predicts actual scores in the holdout samples provides a much more direct test".

Validity of inference

Shadish, Cook, and Campbell (2002, p. 34) use "the term validity to refer to the approximate truth of an inference". They distinguish the four well-known *standard concepts of validity* and list threats pertaining to each of them (Shadish et al. (2002, pp. 37–39, 64ff.). Accordingly, statistical conclusion validity refers to inferences about the existence and size of covariation between treatment and outcome; internal validity reflects the approximate truth of an inference about whether an observed covariation between treatment and outcome reflects a causal relationship. Then, two further concepts cover aspects of the generalizability of inferences. While external validity designates the generalizability of inferences over variations in persons, settings, treatment, and outcomes, construct validity refers to inferences about what is being measured by outcome measurements and thus covers the generalizability to the higher-order constructs they represent. We can use these concepts as benchmarks for data-driven inference in CSS.

Threats to statistical conclusion validity

Shadish et al. (2002, pp. 45–52) present a longer list of threats to statistical conclusion validity. The reasons inferences about covariation between two variables may be incorrect include, among other things, two reasons with special relevance to big data analysis: violated assumptions of statistical tests and unreliability of measures. Clustered/nested data violate the assumption of independently distributed errors, while unreliability attenuates bivariate relationships. The suggested solution to the former threat is accordingly multilevel analysis; the suggested solution to the latter is latent variable modeling of observed measures.

Threats to internal validity

Threats to the internal validity of inferences may be due to the lack of longitudinal data that would allow for repeated measurements at the individual level. A possible consequence is an ambiguous temporal precedence of putative cause and effect, a well-known topic in cross-sectional data analysis. Beyond that aspect, mis-specified models may come along with biased estimates of causal effects. Examples include improper functional forms of regression equations, such as assumed linearity in the case of nonlinear relationships. Omitted and unneeded explanatory variables may also threaten internal validity and thus cause a need to check formal requirements using "regression diagnostics" (Kohler & Kreuter, 2017, pp. 290–310). Systematic measurement and nonresponse error are likely to cause biased estimates, too.

Threats to external validity

Low selection quality is certainly a threat in this regard. If units of analysis are selected from a frame, selection quality depends on frame quality, sampling mode, and selective nonresponse. This implies that even $N = ALL$ analyses may be impaired, as in the case of the "near-census projects" referred to by Lazer and Radford (2017, p. 29). In survey methodology, the quality of sampling frames matters, for instance, in the case of (online) access panels (Engel, 2015). In digital media research, the corresponding question is who uses a platform for what reasons and who does not? The generalizability of inferences over different platform-specific user populations, or the generalizability to the general population, depends accordingly on platform-specific population composition. Ruths and Pfeffer (2014, p. 1064) exemplify this point by explicating, "the ways in which users view Twitter as a space for political discourse affects how representative political content will be" (similarly, Kim et al., 2014, p. 1984). As Lazer and Radford (2017, p. 29) put it: "big data often is a census of particular, conveniently accessible social world. All of Twitter is a census of Twitter. Data from Kickstarter are a census of Kickstarter". In addition, sampling mode (random vs. nonprobability) matters, as do possible selection effects due to technical (API) restrictions, privacy settings, guards against tracking, and the potential requirement of informed consent in digital forms of data collection (e.g., Keyling & Jünger, 2016, pp. 188–191). Then, selective nonresponse is likely to impair the generalizability – and thus the external validity – of sample-based inference to the very population from which the sample has been drawn.

Threats to construct validity

The "promise of big data collection is that expensive data collections are replaced by less costly 'found' data, and that sampling is replaced by analyzing all existing data: $N = All$, avoiding sampling error" (Hox, 2017, p. 8). On the one hand, this implies a waiving of carefully designed survey measurement instruments and, in turn, a waiving of any planned conceptualization and measurement of higher-order constructs. Mahrt and Scharkow (2013, p. 27) discuss "data-driven rather than theory-driven operationalization" and "availability bias" and conclude that researchers "should be aware that the most easily available measure may not be the most valid one, and they should discuss to what degree its validity converges with that of established instruments". Qiu, Chan, and Chan (2018, p. 61f.) address the topic of measurement validity in cases where "second-hand data collected by others such as social media services or mobile phone companies" were used. Among other things, they discuss three issues that can introduce measurement errors: noise due to non-individual accounts, machine-generated coding, and the need to use proxies for variables of interest. On the other hand, the non-reactive nature of such found data appears advantageous. Shah et al. (2015, p. 7) refer to this topic of "unobtrusive measures" (Webb, Campbell, Schwartz, & Sechrest, 1966). They use the phrase "naturally occurring" data and contrast these data with data from surveys and experiments and the typically associated biases through "experimenter effects" and "self-report/social desirability". The argument is that error-prone self-reports on behavior obtained, for instance, in survey research, are that way replaceable by unnoticed direct observations of the behavior itself.

Yet the crucial point is that "motivated misreporting" (Tourangeau, Kreuter, & Eckman, 2015) is not confined to survey research. Lazer and Radford (2017, p. 23) refer to "big data archives" and point out that such archives offer in principle "measures of actual behaviors, as compared with self-reports of behaviors". They continue by stating that "generally, self-reported behavior is noisy, with a variety of systemic biases. For example, people systematically lie about everything from whether they voted to what their weight and height are". Even if motivated misreporting can be ruled out with respect to the research process itself, found data are not error free only because they were obtained unobtrusively. Salganik (2018, p. 24) illustrates this point using the example of self-reports on Facebook. The story is simply that in the first instance, a self-report is a self-report irrespective of its (survey vs. social media) context embedment. However, that embedment may distinguish between surveys that guarantee strict anonymity and posts in the social media that are published information, likely with hidden reference/target groups as addressees in mind.

Beyond that, the meaning of the behavior observed in digital environments is only decipherable on the basis of hypotheses. Social science methodology usually precludes the possibility of hypothesis-free observation. A core question is, then: "What is the theoretical validity and significance of the data?" Following Mahrt and Scharkow (2013, p. 29), this example may illustrate the point:

> The number of times a message gets forwarded ("retweeted") on Twitter, for instance, may show a certain degree of interest by users, but without looking at the content and style of a tweet, "interest" could stand for popularity and support, revulsion and outrage, or simply the thoughtless routines of Twitter usage behavior.

Generalizability and replicability

Generalizability is a topic that covers much more than the previous population aspect. Galtung (1969, p. 316f.) provided a quite undisguised view of this topic as he took the perspective, "given a hypothesis *H*, show me the set of conditions *C* under which it is tenable", where time, space, and social background often be the most important variables. "An effort to generalize, then, is an effort to try out the hypothesis for other points or regions in the condition-space". Given the hypothesis is then confirmed for this new value of one or more condition variables, "we have a clear case of generalization"; otherwise, we would have to increase the complexity of the hypothesis by "working the condition variable into the hypothesis". If generalization is understood that way, then generalization implies replicability, and then replication attempts are theoretically directable towards any relevant condition variable, including variables related to conceptualization, measurement, data collection, and data analysis. Following Galtung (1969, p. 437 ff.), the target of systematic replication may then be pursued to increase the degree of confirmation of hypotheses/propositions by decreasing "the tenability of the argument that the findings are artefacts of the method".

In a recent classification of forms of replication in quantitative social science, this variant relates to "robustness" if the original data are used and "generalization" if new data are used for replication attempts. This classification distinguishes four possible replication goals (Freese & Peterson, 2017, p. 152): verifiability to check if the results of an original study are reproducible if the same analysis is performed on the same data, robustness to check how far target findings are merely the result of analytic decisions if a reanalysis on the original data uses alternative specifications, repeatability to determine whether key results of a study can be replicated by applying the original procedures to new data, and generalization to check if similar findings may be observed consistently across different methods or settings. The latter clearly involves replication attempts across datasets, for instance, as are involved in checks of the generalizability of findings obtained in a training set to the "unseen data" of a related holdout dataset. This practice certainly makes a good case for a key element of data-science practice, the use of independent, out-of-sample validation and cross-validation schemata, respectively.

Sources of variation

Conceptualization and measurement

The analysis of data from nonexperimental social research forces the researcher into unavoidable decisions in relation to the three major stages of conceptualization, modeling, and validation. Because any of these decisions can theoretically affect the final score, Figure 9.2 regards these

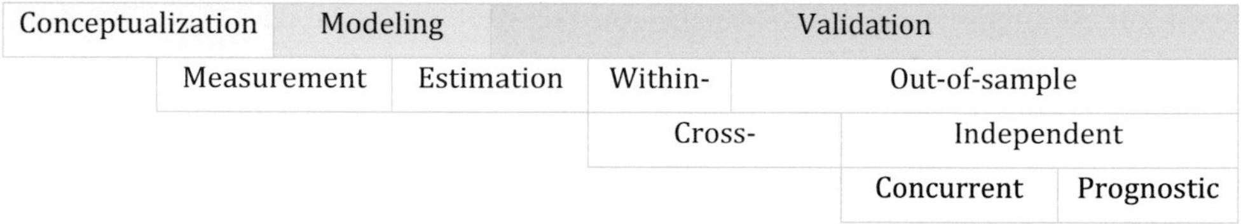

Conceptualization	Modeling		Validation			
	Measurement	Estimation	Within-	Out-of-sample		
			Cross-	Independent		
				Concurrent	Prognostic

Figure 9.2   Conceptualization, modeling, and validation as sources of variation in nonexperimental research

deciding areas accordingly as possible sources of variation and presents them as an interleaved structure to mirror the relevant dependencies.

A first source of variation concerns the theoretical constructs of an analysis in relation to their supposed indicator variables. The general question is what indicator variable(s) best suit the theoretical concept(s). This question is particularly relevant in case the concept–indicator relation is not free of ambiguity. For instance, if voting behavior is used to indicate a person's inclination to vote for the extreme right, an ambiguous relation arises whenever relevant political parties consist of substantial currents of both moderate forces that adhere to the constitution of a country and extremist forces that try to overcome it. Then unambiguous coding of extremism is not possible using voting behavior as the sole indicator variable. This ambiguity is the more relevant the more popular is the party in the country in question. In today's sociological research, a related question is how far right a political party must be settled to pass the threshold from populism to extremism.

Measurement and modeling

Given a theoretical concept, the choice of suitable indicator variables is related to the question of how to bridge the levels of theoretical construct(s) and indicator variable(s) methodologically. Well-known options include the use of single- vs. multiple-indicator models and the explicit consideration of theoretical constructs by index formation, latent variable modeling, or a combination of both. Multiple-indicator models outmatch corresponding single-indicator models by a potentially better coverage of construct meaning. The inclination towards the political far right, for instance, might then be based on self-reports on voting behavior, the perceived closeness to political parties, and self-assessments on the common left-right scale. In addition, if constructs are related to eligible indicator variables by latent variable modeling and thus by testable correspondence hypotheses, then empirical testing replaces otherwise untested but believed assumptions. Similar advantageous features of the latent-variable framework are the checkability and control of random and systematic measurement error and the enabling of flexible modeling strategies within a wide array of options. Despite this principal flexibility, the focus remains on modeling perspectives that work with supposed functional forms instead of targeting the very functional form(s) that suit some relevant data best. James et al. (2013, p. 16 ff.) use a regression-like equation of the general form

$$Y = f(X) + \varepsilon$$

to introduce this distinction and a related localization of statistical learning methods in an analytical space, built to represent the trade-off between their flexibility vs. interpretability. A suitable choice of such methods then depends on whether an analysis seeks primarily descriptive/

causal inference, on the one hand, or unit-related prediction, on the other hand. Similarly, model design depends on these superordinate orientations. Simply to refer to the target complexity of models in terms of variables and functions: attempts at increasing the prediction accuracy of a model are likely to lead to comparably larger than smaller numbers of predictor/ explanatory variables, while the reverse can be expected in the case of attempts at revealing, for instance, individual statistical/causal effects of particular interest. In addition, attempts at increasing prediction accuracy are likely to lead to models that estimate nonlinearities and statistical interactions often assumed/restricted to be zero in standard models for the estimation of linear and additive effects.

Modeling and estimation

The large variety of standard and robust estimation methods is well known to statisticians, data scientists, and structural equation modelers. Regularization is a standard topic in the machine-learning literature. The same holds true for the treatment of missing data caused by unit and item nonresponse in the statistical analysis of survey data. The proper treatment of clustered data structures by multilevel modeling is a further case in point. All such modeling/ estimation options require decisions on how to proceed and, theoretically, any of these decisions can affect the final score. This fact calls for sensitivity analysis and systematic replication. Following recent suggestions (e.g., Harms, 2019; Ly, Etz, Marsman, & Wagenmakers, 2019), the computation of replication Bayes factors as an alternative to hypothesis testing in the frequentist tradition may be considered. Recently, the computation of Bayes factors was also proposed for the selection of replication targets (Field, Hoekstra, Bringmann, & van Ravenzwaaij, 2019).

Estimation and validation

Model estimation implies commonly used goodness-of-fit statistics (e.g., Byrne, 2012, pp. 66–77; Beaujean, 2014, pp. 153–166). The list includes the popular likelihood ratio chi^2 test statistic, incremental indices of fit (comparative fit index [CFI] and Tucker–Lewis index [TLI]), the root mean square error of approximation (RMSEA), the standardized root mean square residual (SRMR), the Akaike information criterion (AIC), the Bayesian information criterion (BIC), and the mean square error (MSE), all of them for within-sample evaluations of model fit. Browne and Cudeck's (1993, p. 147 ff.) content validity index (CVI) and expected content validity index (ECVI) are two variants for cross-validation that also belong to the collection of common indices of fit. The CVI is the cross-validation index for two independent samples from the same population: a "calibration sample" and a "validation sample". The model is fitted to the observed calibration sample covariance matrix to determine to what extent the implied (estimated) covariance matrix fits the observed covariance matrix of the validation sample. Phrased in today's data-science parlance, the procedure relates a fitted covariance obtained in a training sample to the corresponding observed covariance matrix of a holdout sample. Then the ECVI designates the expected value of the cross-validation index. This value is estimated for both calibration and validation samples, "using the calibration sample alone" for computing it (Browne & Cudeck, 1993, p. 148). In this manner, the ECVI represents a substitute for a real cross-validation. The ECVI is subsumed under the parsimony indexes and regarded as a "single-sample approximation to the cross-validation coefficient obtained from a validation sample" (Beaujean, 2014, p. 160 f.). The index is used for model comparisons and is akin to the AIC in reflecting "the extent to which parameter estimates from an original sample will cross-validate in future samples" (Byrne, 2012, p. 72).

Model fit is assessable in different ways. The researcher has a choice between different fit criteria, and the final score may vary depending on that decision. If the criteria suggest contrary decisions as to the acceptability of a model in question, the situation is comparable to the *p*-hacking strategy discussed in the literature and is as problematic as this strategy. Yarkoni and Westfal (2017, p. 4 f.), for instance, describe *p*-hacking as a practice of procedural overfitting, "of flexibly selecting analytical procedures based in part on the quality of the results they produce". Similarly, Freese and Peterson (2017, p. 155) trace the "abiding concern . . . that published findings represent a best-case scenario among all the arbitrary and debatable decisions made over the course of analyzing data" back to "p-hacking, in which a researcher runs different analyses until they find support for their preferred hypothesis". An ambiguous overall picture of fit criteria is a realistic scenario given the potential weaknesses of model testing, for instance, in the SEM context. The list includes impairments due to the use of chi^2-based statistics in large samples, fit criteria that enable only relative assessment across models, and acceptability thresholds on single indices that are only approximately settable in the end. Therefore, both single-fit criteria and the overall picture that emerges from reviewing the possible fit criteria for a given model in conjunction must be considered. Given ambiguous overall evaluations, it is certainly problematic to simply pitch selectively on the subset of criteria that confirm a model while neglecting other relevant criteria. Transferred to the regression context, a similarly ambiguous situation arises if an acceptable R^2 goes along with the diagnosis that assumptions about the model's error term are possibly violated. In this regard, it is clearly more constructive not to rely only on the MSE and the related R^2. The correct use of modeling frameworks (e.g., linear model, generalized linear model) and estimators (e.g., OLS, WLS, ML) presume sets of testable assumptions. Narrowing the spectrum of possible modeling alternatives to the ones that meet such requirements is a sensible choice.

Validation requires fixing relevant fit criteria and evaluation metrics, respectively, for in-sample and out-of-sample evaluation. Out-of-sample orientation is a core feature of data science and machine learning. Basic choices include cross-validation and independent (concurrent, prognostic/temporal) replication. Kelleher and Tierney (2018, pp. 145–148), Ghani and Schierholz (2017, pp. 173–180), and James et al. (2013, pp. 176–186) describe relevant foundations and validation schemata. In doing validation in an out-of-sample orientation, a key idea is to evaluate a model in question on "unseen data", that is, on data not used for building and maybe improving a model in question. The availability of different options that allow validation itself to become a possible source of variation of the final score is noteworthy.

A case study of political extremism

The present analysis uses pooled data from rounds 1 to 9 of the European Social Survey (ESS) and includes all countries with continuous participation over these rounds. For it, we pooled two original ESS data sources, the cumulative file for rounds 1 to 8 and the file for round 9 (ESS, European Social Survey Cumulative File, ESS 1–8 (2018) and European Social Survey Round 9 Data (2018)). This results in an overall sample size of 340,215 respondents. A detailed documentation of this analysis (design, R script, results, link to the data frame used for analysis) is published at https://github.com/viewsandinsights/inference. The target variable is affinity to the political far-right in Europe. Because the emphasis is placed on the far in far-right and thus on a relatively small population group in many EU countries, a large overall sample size is required for a survey analysis of these groups. The pooled ESS data offer this option along with the additional advantage of enabling time-related studies of the political far-right in Europe. We refer to this analysis for addressing causal inference in a setting that uses (1) big (survey) data, (2) different validation strategies known from the machine-learning context (independent replication using training/test samples and cross-validation), and (3) systematic replication in the case of unavoidable decisions concerning data management and measurement (coding ambiguity, proxy variables, scope in concept specification, and missing data treatment).

Theoretical background

The analysis examines the affiliation to the political far-right as a function of prejudice formation, value orientation, and trust. It follows the general idea that prejudice formation is understandable as a response to competitive relations in open societies that prize freedom. Esses, Jackson, Dovidio, and Hodson (2005, p. 227f.) point out that concerns for group status produce competition between groups for material resources and for value dominance in which "competition exacerbates prejudice between groups". The theoretical expectation is that "in social contexts in which equality of opportunity is prized and social mobility is encouraged, perceived competition is likely" (Esses et al., 2005, p. 229), because then "members of even the lowest group are encouraged to put forth effort, to rise, and to demand their rights" (Allport, 1954/1979, p. 222). As Esses et al. (2005, p. 229) formulate this idea, "allowance, or encouragement, of upward social mobility makes evident the possibility of downward mobility, which, in the presence of a visually salient outgroup, generates competition and animosity". Accordingly, the expected "outcome of competition is stereotyped and/or overtly hostile attitudes toward competitor groups".

A second background element is inspired by previous research on right-wing authoritarianism. Only loosely following up the pioneering "Berkeley theory" of Adorno, Frenkel-Brunswik, Levinson, and Sanford's (1950) Authoritarian Personality, Altemeyer (1996) studied this phenomenon empirically in greater detail. He pictures authoritarians as characters who believe that proper authorities should be trusted and deserve obedience and respect. He refers to perceived established authorities as those "people in our society who are usually considered to have a general legal or moral authority over the behavior of others", usually one's parents, religious officials, civic officers (the police, judges, heads of governments), and superiors in military service (Altemeyer, 1996, pp. 8–12). However, the "perceived" established authorities may be others as well. As Altemeyer (1996, p. 9) explains, some "extremists may reject normal authorities who (it seems to them) have betrayed the real, fundamental established authority: for example (their perception of) God's will, or the Constitution. They often believe the government has been taken over by Jews, homosexuals, feminists, Communists, and so on. Such extremists are right-wing authoritarian in this context – "superpatriots" who see themselves as upholding traditional values but whose fear and self-righteousness hammer with such intensity that they rehearse for violence and may cross the line to violence itself". Altemeyer (1996, p. 10) stresses that he is "using "right-wing" in a *psychological* sense of submitting to the perceived authorities in one's life", meaning psychological "right-wingers in their support for those they were raised to believe were the legitimate authorities". This spotlights the psychological relationship individuals may have to the principle of authority and the adherence to this principle in the contexts of contemporary life.

Prejudice formation and the political far right

Figure 9.3 graphs the assumed possible effect structures schematically. The analysis is aimed at a decision as to the causal status of the prejudice-to-far-right path. We refer to the section "Causal

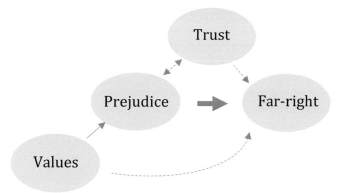

Figure 9.3   Does prejudice cause affinity to the political far–right?

Inference in Social Research" and check two criteria: (1) does *values* act as an instrumental variable whose effect on far-right affinity runs exclusively via prejudice formation, and (2) does *trust* act as an intervening (vs. antecedent) variable over which the effect of prejudice on far-right affinity is transmitted? These questions can be answered by checking the dashed arrows: it should be reasonable to assume that a potential direct effect of *values* on *far-right* drops to zero if *prejudice* is introduced or that *prejudice* affects *trust*, not vice versa, while *trust* affects *far-right* at the same time.

Validation in causal inference

As detailed elsewhere (https://github.com/viewsandinsights/inference), structural equation modeling is used to clarify the causal status of the prejudice-to-far-right path. Apart from the sociological interest in the subject matter, a series of systematic model comparisons was realized to explore model fit (chi^2, RMSEA, CFI, TLI, SRMR, ECVI) embedded in three basic validation strategies: (1) using a 70 to 30 percent random split of training and test sample, (2) using a systematic time-related split of training sample (data from ESS rounds 1 to 6) and test sample (data from rounds 7 to 9), and (3) using Browne and Cudeck's ECVI measure as a single-sample approximation to the cross-validation coefficient. Strategies (1) and (2) appear particularly important to take advantage of the causal graph approach referred to previously ("Causal Inference in Social Research"). A useful feature of this approach is its capability of deriving from a causal structure of effects and related checks for backdoor paths and instrumental and intervening variables the insight into which of the involved effects must be controlled for to avoid confounding and spurious estimates of effects. However, this moves causal inference close to circular reasoning: If a causal structure is already accepted as true in advance, there is no need to identify any such conditions. Then the model identifies causal effects properly, or it does not. However, if a model is only tentatively taken for granted and, if necessary, inductively elaborated on further in a training phase, then it makes much sense trying to validate such inductively improved models using the "unseen" data of a test sample.

Systematic replication in case of measurement alternatives

The political far right is approached in two ways: first, by the most-right category "10" on the 11-point, left-right scale ranging from zero to ten, thus by the respondents' own self-image (sample estimate: 3.1% Europe-wide across all rounds and countries); second, by classifying pertinent political parties as far right following previous work in political science and additional sources. A detailed list of the country-specific coding sources used for this classification is part of the R script cited previously in "A Case Study of Political Extremism". Across all rounds and countries, 1.3% of the respondents expressed affinities ("feeling close" or "vote for") to these far-right parties. Combining both measures yields an estimate of 4.3% affinity either way. Both assessments are correlated with $r = 0.092$.

Worth mentioning in this connection is a practically unreducible ambiguity in the coding of right-wing parties as far right if they consist of currents of both loyal and hostile forces to a country's constitution. In the present analysis, this ambiguity created occasional scope for alternative coding decisions and, thus, subsequent variation of results.

Proxy variables

While the ESS data contain suitable indicator variables for the measurement of hostile attitudes towards immigrants, no direct indicator of the perceived competition in society is available. In lieu of this information, a proxy variable is used by acting on the auxiliary assumption that competitive relationships strengthen the motivational tendency to overreach others in the general pursuit of self-interest. The need for switching to proxy variables is certainly a limiting factor even when using an advanced causal analysis technique such as latent variable modeling at the same time. In the present case, this also applies to the measurement of right-wing authoritarianism by the human values scale. This scale is part of the standard ESS questionnaire program, which is an excellent instrument, although not specifically designed to measure the construct in question. It too is accordingly used as a proxy measure and exemplifies for the survey context a situation like the use of social media data in the CSS context: the use of proxy data because those data are available, even if more suitable measures are theoretically imaginable.

Concluding remarks

The social sciences are currently discovering machine learning (ML) as the new promise of replicable results because ML offers advanced statistical means and aims at balancing the predictive validity and generalizability of results. ML is clearly directed to predictive modeling and the target of maximizing prediction accuracy. Because too-accurately predicted findings run the risk of impaired generalizability to unseen data, at the same time, a guard against overfitting is realized by use of large datasets and validation through proving the replicability of results found in a training setting to the unseen data of holdout settings. Such a validation strategy comes along with a change of perspective from within-sample goodness-of-fit testing to assessing out-of-sample prediction error and bears basically on replication in relation to datasets. However, replication is a more general principle. Replication may also be targeted at other elements of a social research design/study, for instance, at the latent concepts, the observed variables, and all methods-related settings. This focus on replication has already allowed it to appear to be constructive to align CSS research with machine learning and the modeling, estimation, and evaluation tools therein. Statistical learning and the statistical analysis of observational data, as we practice it in social science research, have many statistical methods in common.

It would, however, be misleading and far from any sound balancing of explanation and prediction to abstain from causal inference in CSS. Causal modeling can look back on a long history in social research, and latent variable modeling implies powerful capabilities of dealing with measurement error. The social and behavioral sciences aim centrally at understanding their scientific objects, and this understanding cannot go without appropriate theories about these objects. Hence, such theories are needed and must be subjected to proper empirical tests. However, irrespective of a possible focus on within- or out-of-sample validation, such tests can only help to decide if the implications of a theoretical model appear sufficiently consistent with some data in hand. This fact sets any such testing boundaries because even if such a model is proved consistent in this regard, no alternative theory/model with the same implications as the tested model is ruled out. This indefiniteness clearly weakens the theoretical significance of any such testing unless we conduct crucial tests in which a tested theory implies the negation of implications of some alternative theory.

References

Adorno, T. W., Frenkel-Brunswik, E., Levinson, D. J., & Sanford, R. N. (1950). *The authoritarian personality*. Harper and Row.

Allport, G. W. (1979). *The nature of prejudice* (25th anniversary ed.). Basic Books (Original work published 1954).

Altemeyer, B. (1996). *The authoritarian specter*. Harvard University Press.

Alvarez, R. M. (2016). Introduction. In R. M. Alvarez (Ed.), *Computational social science. discovery and prediction* (pp. 1–24). Cambridge University Press.

Attewell, P., & Monaghan, D. B. (2015). *Data mining for the social sciences*. University of California Press.

Beaujean, A. A. (2014). *Latent variable modeling using R*. Routledge.

Biemer, P. P. (2017). Errors and inference. In I. Foster, R. Ghani, R. S. Jarmin, F. Kreuter, & J. Lane (Eds.), *Big data and social science* (pp. 265–297). CRC Press.

Blalock, H. M. (Ed.). (1971). *Causal models in the social sciences* (1st ed.). Aldine Publ. Co.

Blalock, H. M. (Ed.). (1985). *Causal models in panel and experimental designs*. Aldine Publ. Co.

Bollen, K. A. (1989). *Structural equations with latent variables*. Wiley.

Browne, M. W., & Cudeck, R. (1993). Alternative ways of assessing model fit. In K. A. Bollen & J. S. Long (Eds.), *Testing structural equation models* (pp. 136–162). Sage.

Byrne, B. M. (2012). *Structural equation modeling with Mplus. Basic concepts, applications, and programming*. Routledge.

Cao, L. (2017). Data science: A comprehensive overview. *ACM Computing Surveys, 50*(3), 43.1–43.42. https://doi.org/10.1145/3076253

Cioffi-Revilla, C. (2017). *Introduction to computational social science. Principles and applications* (2nd ed.). Springer.

Coleman, J. S. (1964). *Introduction to mathematical sociology*. The Free Press of Glencoe.

Coleman, J. S. (1968). The mathematical study of change. In H. M. Blalock, & A. B. Blalock (Eds.), *Methodology in social research* (pp. 428–478). McGraw-Hill.

Coleman, J. S. (1981). *Longitudinal data analysis*. Basic Books.

Coleman, J. S. (1990). *Foundations of social theory*. Belknap Press of Harvard University Press.

Coleman, J. S., Campbell, E. Q., Hobson, C. J., McPartland, J., Mood, A. M., Weinfeld, M. D., & York, R. L. (1966). *Equality of educational opportunity*. US Government Printing Office.

De Vaus, D. (2001). *Research design in social research*. Sage.

Edelmann, A., Wolff, T., Montagne, D., & Bail, C. A. (2020). Computational social science and sociology. *Annual Review of Sociology, 46*, 61–68. https://doi.org/10.1146/annurev-soc-121919-054621

Enders, C. K. (2010). *Applied missing data analysis*. Guilford Press.

Engel, U. (2015). Response behavior in an adaptive survey design for the setting-up stage of a probability-based access panel in Germany. In U. Engel, B. Jann, P. Lynn, A. Scherpenzeel, & P. Sturgis (Eds.), *Improving survey methods: Lessons from recent research* (pp. 207–222). Routledge.

Engel, U., Gattig, A., & Simonson, J. (2007). Longitudinal multilevel modelling: A comparison of growth curve models and structural equation modelling using panel data from Germany. In K. van Montfort, J. Oud, & A. Satorra (Eds.), *Longitudinal models in the behavioral and related sciences* (pp. 295–314). Lawrence Erlbaum Associates.

Engel, U., & Meyer, W. (1996). Structural analysis in the study of social change. In U. Engel & J. Reinecke (Eds.), *Analysis of change. Advanced techniques in panel data analysis* (pp. 221–252). De Gruyter.

Esses, V. M., Jackson, L. M., Dovidio, J. F., & Hodson, G. (2005). Instrumental relations among groups: Group competition, conflict, and prejudice. In J. F. Dovidio, P. Glick, & L. A. Rudman (Eds.), *On the nature of prejudice. Fifty years after Allport* (pp. 227–243). Blackwell Publishing.

European Social Survey Cumulative File, ESS 1–8. (2018). *Data file edition 1.0. NSD – Norwegian Centre for research data, Norway – Data archive and distributor of ESS data for ESS ERIC.* doi:10.21338/NSD-ESS-CUMULATIVE

European Social Survey Round 9 Data (2018). *Data file edition 2.0. NSD – Norwegian Centre for research data, Norway – Data archive and distributor of ESS data for ESS ERIC.* doi:10.21338/NSD-ESS9-2018

Field, S. M., Hoekstra, R., Bringmann, L., & van Ravenzwaaij, D. (2019). When and why to replicate: As easy as 1, 2, 3? *Collabra: Psychology, 5*(1), 46, 1–15. https://doi.org/10.1525/Collabra.218

Franke, B., Plante, J.-F., Roscher, R., Lee, E.-S. A., Smyth, C., Hatefi, A., . . . Reid, N. (2016). Statistical inference, learning and models in big data. *International Statistical Review, 84*(3), 371–389, https://doi.org/10.1111/insr.12176

Freese, J., & Peterson, D. (2017). Replication in social science. *Annual Review of Sociology, 43,* 147–165.

Galtung, J. (1969). *Theory and methods of social research* (1st ed., 1967). Universitetsforlaget.

Ghani, R., & Schierholz, M. (2017). Machine learning. In I. Foster, R. Ghani, R. S. Jarmin, F. Kreuter, & J. Lane (Eds.), *Big data and social science* (pp. 147–186). CRC Press.

Goodman, L. A. (1955). Generalizing the problem of prediction. In P. F. Lazarsfeld & M. Rosenberg (Eds.), *The language of social research* (pp. 277–283). The Free Press.

Hagenaars, J. A. (1990). *Categorical longitudinal data. Log-linear, panel, trend, and cohort analysis.* Sage.

Harms, C. (2019). A Bayes factor for replications of ANOVA results. *The American Statistician, 73*(4), 327–339, https://doi.org/10.1080/00031305.2018.1518787

Hindman, M. (2015). Building better models: Prediction, replication, and machine learning in the social sciences. *The ANNALS of the American Academy of Political and Social Science, 659*(1), 48–62. https://doi.org/10.1177/0002716215570279

Hofman, J. M., Sharma, A., & Watts, D. J. (2017). Prediction and explanation in social systems. *Science, 355*(6324), 486–488. https://doi.org/10.1126/science.aal3856

Hox, J. J. (2017). Computational social science methodology, anyone? *Methodology, 13,* 3–12. https://doi.org/10.1027/1614-2241/a000127

IBM Big Data & Analytics Hub. (2012). *The four V's of big data.* Retrieved December 30, 2020, from www.ibmbigdatahub.com/infographic/four-vs-big-data

James, G., Witten, D., Hastie, T., & Tibshirani, R. (2013). *An introduction to statistical learning.* Springer.

Kelleher, J. D. (2019). *Deep learning.* The MIT Press.

Kelleher, J. D., & Tierney, B. (2018). *Data science.* The MIT Press.

Keyling, T., & Jünger, J. (2016). Observing online content. In G. Vowe, & P. Henn (Eds.), *Political communication in the online world. Theoretical approaches and research designs* (pp. 183–200). Routledge.

Kim, A., Murphy, J., Richards, A., Hansen, H., Powell, R., & Haney, C. (2014). Can tweets replace polls? A U.S. health-care reform case study. In C. A. Hill, E. Dean, & J. Murphy (Eds.), *Social media, sociality, and survey research* (pp. 1638–2077). Wiley.

Kohler, U., & Kreuter, F. (2017). *Datenanalyse mit Stata [Data Analysis with Stata]* (5th ed.). De Gruyter Oldenbourg.

Kuhn, M., & Johnson, K. (2013). *Applied predictive modeling.* Springer.

Lantz, B. (2019). *Machine learning with R. Expert techniques for predictive modeling.* Packt Publishing.

Lazarsfeld, P. F. (1955). Interpretation of statistical relations as a research operation. In P. F. Lazarsfeld & M. Rosenberg (Eds.), *The language of social research. A reader in the methodology of social research* (pp. 115–125). The Free Press.

Lazarsfeld, P. F., Berelson, B., & Gaudet, H. (1955). The process of opinion and attitude formation. In P. F. Lazarsfeld & M. Rosenberg (Eds.), *The language of social research* (pp. 231–242). The Free Press.

Lazarsfeld, P. F., & Menzel, H. (1969). On the relation between individual and collective properties. In A. Etzioni (Ed.), *A sociological reader on complex organizations* (pp. 449–516). (1st ed., 1961). Holt, Rinehart and Winston.

Lazer, D. M. J., Pentland, A., Watts, D. J, Aral, S., Athey, S., Contractor, N., . . . Wagner, C. (2020). Computational social science: Obstacles and opportunities. *Science, 369*(6507), 1060–1062. https://doi.org/10.1126/science.aaz8170

Lazer, D. M. J., & Radford, J. (2017). Data ex machina: Introduction to big data. *Annual Review of Sociology, 43,* 19–39. https://doi.org/10.1146/annurev-soc-060116-053457

Lin, J. (2015). On building better mousetraps and understanding the human condition: Reflections on big data in the social sciences. *The ANNALS of the American Academy of Political and Social Science, 659*(1), 33–47, https://doi.org/10.1177/0002716215569174

Luraschi, J., Kuo, K., & Ruiz, E. (2020). *Mastering spark with R.* O'Reilly Media, Inc.

Ly, A., Etz, A., Marsman, M., & Wagenmakers, E. (2019). Replication Bayes factors from evidence updating. *Behavior Research Methods, 51,* 2498–2508. https://doi.org/10.3758/s13428-018-1092-x

Mahrt, M., & Scharkow, M. (2013). The value of big data in digital media research. *Journal of Broadcasting & Electronic Media, 57*(1), 20–33, https://doi.org/10.1080/08838151.2012.761700

Marsh, H. W., & Grayson, D. (1995). Latent variable models of multitrait-multimethod data. In R. H. Hoyle (Ed.), *Structural equation modeling: Concepts, issues, and applications* (p. 177–198). Sage.

McCutcheon, A. L. (1987). *Latent class analysis.* Sage.

McFarland, D. A., & McFarland, H. R. (2015). Big data and the danger of being precisely inaccurate. *Big Data & Society,* 1–4, https://doi.org/10.1177/2053951715602495

Morgan, S. L., & Winship, C. (2007). *Counterfactuals and causal inference. Methods and principles for social research.* Cambridge University Press.

Pearl, J. (2009). *Causality. Models, reasoning, and inference* (1st ed., 2000). Cambridge University Press.

Pearl, J. (2012). The causal foundations of structural equation modeling. In R. H. Hoyle (Ed.), *Handbook of structural equation modeling* (pp. 68–91). Guilford Press.

Provost, F., & Fawcett, T. (2013). *Data science for business. What you need to know about data mining and data-analytic thinking.* O'Reilly Media, Inc.

Qiu, L., Chan, S. H. M., & Chan, D. (2018). Big data in social and psychological science: Theoretical and methodological issues. *Journal of Computational Social Science, 1,* 59–66. https://doi.org/10.1007/s42001-017-0013-6

Quan-Haase, A., & Sloan, L. (2017). Introduction to the handbook of social media research methods: Goals, challenges and innovations. In L. Sloan & A. Quan-Haase (Eds.), *The Sage handbook of social media research methods* (pp. 1–9). Sage.

Rosenberg, M. (1968). *The logic of survey analysis.* Basic Books.

The Royal Society. (2017). *Machine learning: The power and promise of computers that learn by example.* Retrieved December 30, 2020, from https://royalsociety.org/~/media/policy/projects/machine-learning/publications/machine-learning-report.pdf

Ruths, D., & Pfeffer, J. (2014). Social media for large studies of behavior. *Science, 346*(6213), 1063–1064. https://doi.org/10.1126/science.346.6213.1063

Salganik, M. J. (2018). *Bit by bit. Social research in the digital age.* Princeton University Press.

Shadish, W. R., Cook, T. D., & Campbell, D. T. (2002). *Experimental and quasi-experimental designs for generalized causal inference.* Houghton Mifflin Co.

Shah, D. V., Capella, J. N., & Neuman, W. R. (2015). Big data, digital media, and computational social science: Possibilities and perils. *The ANNALS of the American Academy of Political and Social Science, 659*(1), 6–13, https://doi.org/10.1177/0002716215572084

Stinchcombe, A. L. (1968). *Constructing social theories.* The University of Chicago Press.

Tourangeau, R., Kreuter, F., & Eckman, S. (2015). Motivated misreporting: Shaping answers to reduce survey burden. In U. Engel (Ed.), *Survey measurements. Techniques, data quality and sources of error* (pp. 24–41). Campus.

Troitzsch, K. G. (2009). Not all explanations predict satisfactorily, and not all good predictions explain. *Journal of Artificial Societies and Social Simulation, 12*(1). Retrieved December 30, 2020, from http://jasss.soc.surrey.ac.uk/12/1/10.html

Van Buuren, S. (2018). *Flexible imputation of missing data* (2nd ed.). CRC Press.

Warshaw, C. (2016). The application of big data in surveys to the study of elections, public opinion, and representation. In R. M. Alvarez (Ed.), *Computational social science. Discovery and prediction* (pp. 27–50). University Press.

Webb, E. J., Campbell, D. T., Schwartz, R. D., & Sechrest, L. (2000). *Unobtrusive measures* (1st ed., 1966). Sage Classics 2. Sage.

Winship, C., & Morgan, S. L. (1999). The estimation of causal effects from observational data. *Annual Review of Sociology, 25,* 659–706. https://doi.org/10.1146/annurev.soc.25.1.659

Yarkoni, T., & Westfall, J. (2017). Choosing prediction over explanation in psychology: Lessons from machine learning. *Perspectives on Psychological Science, 12*(6), 1–23. https://doi.org/10.1177/1745691617693393

10

DATA-DRIVEN AGENT-BASED MODELING IN COMPUTATIONAL SOCIAL SCIENCE

Jan Lorenz

Epistemology of agent-based modeling

Agent-based modeling and simulation are core methods in computational social science, besides making sense (and money) of large amounts of human-generated data and studying and shaping how digitization changes human societies. Even before the notion of "computational social science" was popularized around 2010 (Lazer et al., 2009; Conte et al., 2012), calls for more agent-based modeling appeared in the leading journals of most social sciences.

Macy and Willer (2002) called sociology to move "from factors to actors" to

> provide theoretical leverage where the global patterns of interest are more than the aggregation of individual attributes, but at the same time, the emergent pattern cannot be understood without a bottom-up dynamical model of the microfoundations at the relational level.

This captures the view of Schelling (1978) about micromotives and macrobehavior, which is seen as a foundation for the field of computational economics.

In political science, Clarke and Primo (2007) criticize that political science has a narrow focus on models based on hypothetico-deductivism meaning, hypotheses are set up for testing. They call for viewing models not as hypothesized statements but as maps that should be similar enough to the world to be used for specific purposes. There should be no underlying hypothesis that an agent-based model is true or false.

For example, Laver (2005) introduced agent-based modeling of party competition in multi-party environments to explore and analyze the interplay of different potential strategies of parties "fishing" for voters. Laver (2005) points out that "using agent-based models means that we must set on one side any investigation of the sophisticated, forward-thinking strategic calculations at the heart of many game-theoretic models". The appeal of agent-based modeling is not to abandon the idea of rational choice in total but to acknowledge that there are environments where these assumptions are too idealized. The cognitive capacity of actors may be limited or less relevant because of noisy environments and strong path dependencies. Such situations appear with many independent actors (e.g., whole populations), dispersed and uncertain information, and multiple equilibria (e.g., in coordination games). Furthermore, game-theoretic

DOI: 10.4324/9781003024583-11

models are intrinsically non–dynamical because all agents think all actions through and collectively end up in an immediate static or stochastic equilibrium.

The rational choice paradigm is marginal in social psychology. However, also in psychology, calls for agent-based modeling are older than computational social science. Smith and Conrey (2007) complain that theory–building and modeling techniques most commonly used in social psychology are less than ideal for understanding social and psychological phenomena occurring due to repeated interactions between multiple individuals over time. They call the dominant approach in psychology variable-based modeling to distinguish it from agent-based modeling.

Besides sociology, economics, political science, and social psychology, agent-based models are also of interest in other social sciences, for example, anthropology concerning cultural evolution (Colleran, 2016) or history concerning the rise and fall of states (Turchin, 2003). Agent-based modeling is also not restricted to the social sciences. It is used in many-particle physics, biology (e.g., modeling the behavior of social insects), or engineering (e.g., the flocking and swarming of mobile autonomous robots).

Agent-based modeling bridges between the social sciences because it provides a unifying perspective on the interplay of individual behavior, social, political and economic institutions, environmental and biological context conditions, and general mechanisms. Such a unifying perspective is often at least in part in contrast to disciplinary perspectives similar to the typical clashes of paradigms between the different social sciences. That may explain that researchers doing agent-based modeling and social simulation sometimes tend to form self-contained scientific communities. Another reason is that most research questions addressed with agent-based models follow a generative epistemology. The motto of Epstein (2006) well explains this epistemology: "If you didn't grow it, you didn't explain its emergence". In this statement, "it" is a macroscopic regularity to be explained.

Examples of such regularities are segregation patterns, wealth distributions, polarized opinion landscapes, mass protests, or epidemics. Epstein (2006) further describes the generativist's experimental procedure: "Situate an initial population of autonomous, heterogeneous agents in a relevant spatial environment; allow them to interact according to simple local rules, and thereby generate – or 'grow' – the macroscopic regularity from the bottom up". The tool for these experiments is computer simulation.

This epistemological perspective is particularly appealing for researchers studying the dynamics of complex adaptive systems, a scientific field originating from physics, biology, and social science (Thurner, Hanel, & Klimek, 2018). Complex systems researchers are sometimes more driven by the understanding of complex systems' general mechanisms, and the field of application may be secondary. The search for laws of social interaction transcends to the search for general laws of complex systems. For a social scientist aiming at middle-range theories (Merton & Merton, 1968), arguably the dominant approach in sociology and other social sciences (Bailey, 1991), already postulating the existence of social laws is controversial (Keuschnigg, Lovsjö, & Hedström, 2017), not to mention a theory holding for atoms, insects, and humans alike.

However, not all simulation studies are driven by searching for explanations for the emergence of macroscopic regularities. In advanced models, for example, pedestrian behavior or other traffic models, simulation can be a method of applied social planning, such as for the design of evacuation plans or panic control. That way, a simulation operates as a "societal flight simulator" (Keuschnigg, Lovsjö, & Hedström, 2017).

Before developing into a societal flight simulator, agent-based modeling is deeply tied to theory construction (Jaccard & Jacoby, 2010) and the translation of verbal theories to formal models (Smaldino, 2020). In that stage, agent-based models can have scientific value without a deep relation to data. Nevertheless, ultimately, agent-based models in computational social science should explain phenomena of the real world, and to that end, they need to be related to data. Already, Boero and Squazzoni (2005) called for more use of empirical data in social science agent-based models to allow the calibration and the validation of their findings. Similarly, Bruch and Atwell (2015) provide recommendations and practices for using agent-based models within a program of empirical research.

In the following, we will first look at the "classical" process of agent-based modeling as a tool for experimenting with behavioral theories using two examples about segregation and opinion dynamics. Then we discuss the relations of agent-based models and data. Based on this, we outline four aspects of how agent-based modeling can be data-driven, relating to the two examples.

Agent-based models as an experimental tool for theoretical research

According to Macy and Willer (2002), "agent-based modeling is an experimental tool for theoretical research". Therefore, we will first look at the intrinsically theory-driven research process of agent-based modeling before discussing which aspects can turn data-driven. Figure 10.1 summarizes the steps in theory-driven agent-based modeling in the left (behavioral theory) and the central column (agent-based model). The research process has the following tasks:

1   *Behavioral Theories:* Select and formalize rules for agents' behavior inspired either by rational choice via utility functions, incentives, and heuristics or by affective and cognitive processes from psychology.
2   *Agents:* Equip agents with the necessary *static* and *dynamic variables* to characterize their state and their repertoire of potential *actions and interactions* with other agents.
3   *Timeline/Algorithm:* Define an algorithm when and how individual actions and interactions take place.

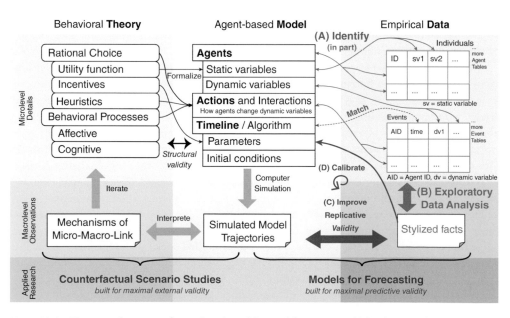

Figure 10.1   The research process of agent-based modeling and four aspects which relate it to data (A, B, C, D)

4   *Initial Conditions:* Implement procedures for the initialization of agents and their environment.

5   *Parameters:* Specify a set of relevant model parameters. The definition of parameters usually happens already in steps 2–4, for example, the number of agents in 2, probabilities for agent activation in 3, or parameters of distributions of random numbers in 4.

6   *Simulated Trajectories:* Produce model trajectories with computer simulations and explore and systematically analyze the model's behavior.

7   *Output Measures:* Define relevant output measures for simulated trajectories to answer the research question.

8   *Interpretation:* Interpret the simulation results to understand and quantify mechanisms of micro–macro links between individual behavior, context conditions (parameter settings), and observed phenomena on the macro level.

The whole process can be iterated, starting with a reconsideration of the behavioral theories. Examples for consideration are the inclusion or removal of behavioral theories, simplification or extension of their formalization, reparametrization of the set of relevant parameters, or different exploration and analysis strategies. The main research goal is to produce insights into the theoretical link between the micro level and the macro level. This is mainly a process of fundamental research, but projects of applied research can later build on the model.

In the following, we demonstrate with two examples how this research practice generates insights about generative explanations for the macroscopic phenomena of segregation and polarization. Figure 10.2 shows a version of the segregation model of Schelling (1971) and a version of the bounded confidence model of opinion dynamics (Deffuant, Neau, Amblard, & Weisbuch, 2000; Hegselmann & Krause, 2002). Shown are the outcomes of two simulation runs for segregation (Figure 10.2A, B) and two for bounded confidence (Figure 10.2C, D) as screenshots of their corresponding NetLogo (Wilensky, 1999) interfaces. Both models can be tested in NetLogoWeb in a web browser.

Segregation model

1   *Behavioral Theories:* Households assess if they like the neighborhood where they live. They relocate if they are not happy. They are happy when a certain fraction of all neighbors are similar. The model is mostly used to study ethnic segregation but can be used to study residential segregation with any discrete characteristic in the population. The desire to live with a certain fraction of similars can be motivated in different ways. It could be based on xenophobic sentiment, or it could be a rational choice because similar neighbors provide utility by easy access to valuable social networks.

2   *Agents:* Households in a hypothetical town.

>   *Static variables:* One of two colors marking different groups.
>   *Dynamic variables:* Their place of residence on a regular grid, where they have maximally eight neighbors.
>   *Actions:* When agents are activated, they compute the fraction of their eight neighbors that have the same color. When this fraction is less than their desired fraction of similar neighbors, they relocate to a randomly selected free residence.

3   *Algorithm:* In every time step, all agents are activated and potentially move once. This happens every time step in a new random order.

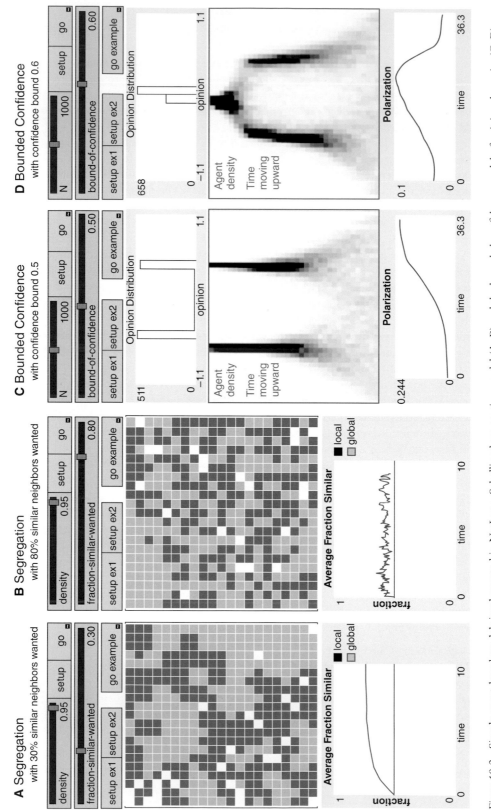

Figure 10.2 Simple agent-based models implemented in NetLogo. Schellings' segregation model (A, B) and the bounded confidence model of opinion dynamics (C, D)

4   *Initial Conditions:* A square grid of places of residence mimicking a town. For each place, one household is generated with a certain probability. So, a certain fraction of places remain empty. Each generated agent gets one of the two colors at random.

5   *Parameters:* Based on the previous description, there are two crucial global parameters: The fraction-similar-wanted defines the threshold below which households relocate. The density is the probability with which a household is generated at every potential location upon initialization.

6   **S***imulated Trajectories:* Figure 10.2A and B show two example trajectories, which can be reproduced here: http://netlogoweb.org/web?https://raw.githubusercontent.com/janlorenz/ABMSimpleExamples/main/Segregation.nlogo. Both run with a density of 0.95 but with a different fraction-similar-wanted. In Figure 10.2A, households want 30% of their neighbors to be similar, and after ten time steps, one-colored areas have emerged on the grid. Almost all have the desired fractions of similar neighbors. In Figure 10.2B, households want 80% of their neighbors to be similar, but after 200 time steps, the situation has not changed from an essentially random distribution. Society is not able to self-organize into a segregated society.

7   *Output measures:* The lower parts of Figure 10.2A and B show the evolution of output measures for global and local segregation. The measure is the average fraction of similar neighbors once for all other agents and once counting only the eight neighbors for each agent.

8   *Interpretation:* In populations with two equally sized groups, the global segregation is by definition 50%. With initially random places of residence, the average number of similar neighbors is 50%, while some unlucky households may have less than they desire. The simulation shows that even when the desired fraction of similar neighbors is just 30%, a chain of decisions to relocate is triggered, bringing the town to average local segregation of 75%. So, high local segregation emerges from very mild homophile preferences of households. Simulation B shows an interesting transition of the model: When households are much more homophile, desiring 80% of their neighbors to be similar, the town never comes to rest and stays without segregation but with most households unhappy and continually relocating. An interesting simulation experiment starting from this anomic situation is to reduce the fraction of desired similar neighbors to 75%. The town will fully segregate quickly, and, interestingly, this situation would (in most cases) persist even when the fraction of desired similar neighbors would increase to 80% again. So, full segregation is not theoretically impossible but does not self-organize.

Bounded confidence model

1   *Behavioral Theories:* Individuals hold opinions on a continuous scale, for example, evaluations from "very bad" to "very good". Individuals change their opinions as a result of social influence. When they perceive another individual's opinion, they adjust towards this opinion, but only if this other opinion is not too far away. When the other's opinion is outside of their bound of confidence, they ignore it.

2   *Agents:* Individuals holding an opinion.

       Static variables: The bound of confidence defining the maximal distance in opinion the individual accepts.

       Dynamic variables: The opinion on an abstract opinion scale from -1 to $+1$.

       Actions: When agents are activated, they perceive the opinion of another randomly selected agent. If this opinion is within their bound of confidence, they adjust their opinion towards the average of their old opinion and the other's opinion. Otherwise, nothing happens.

3   *Algorithm:* In every time step, all agents are activated and potentially change their opinion. This happens every time in a new random order.

4   *Initial Conditions:* A certain number of agents are initialized with initial opinions being random numbers between -1 and $+1$. Further on, all agents have the same bound of confidence.

5   *Parameters:* Based on the previous description, there are two crucial global parameters: The number of agents N and the bound of confidence, which is the same for all individuals.

6   *Simulated Trajectories:* Figure 10.2C and D show two example trajectories which can be reproduced here: http://netlogoweb.org/web?https://raw.githubusercontent.com/janlor enz/ABMSimpleExamples/main/BoundedConfidence.nlogo. Both run with 1000 agents but different bounds of confidence, 0.5 and 0.6. The first panel below the parameters shows the current opinion distribution as a histogram. The central panel below shows how this distribution evolves with the opinion space vertically and time moving upward. The light gray line at the bottom of the central panel represents the initially uniform distribution at the bottom of the central panel. In Figure 10.2C, a distribution with two groups evolves with different opinions but internal consensus. Figure 10.2D shows that only one large consensual group evolves with slightly larger bounds of confidence.

7   *Output measures:* The lower parts of Figure 10.2C and D show the evolution of polarization over time based on the measure of Esteban and Ray (1994). The measure is the average distance between opinions of any pair of agents where each agent is weighted by its identification. Identification is the fraction of others having (almost) the same opinion.

8   *Interpretation:* Bipolarization into two opposing groups emerges with bounds of confidence below a certain threshold, which lies somewhere between 0.5 and 0.6. With bounds of confidence slightly above this consensus brink, bipolarization appears as a transient phenomenon, ending in the collapse of the two groups in a consensual opinion in the opinion space center. Interestingly, the driving force for polarization is not radicalization or the repulsion from others' opinions but assimilation towards others' opinions but restricted by bounded confidence.

Segregation and polarization insights of examples

The segregation model's fundamental insight is that ethnic homophily can trigger heavily segregated towns even when similarity preferences are mild. It may not be appropriate to infer strong individual preferences in the population from the macroscopic observation of segregation. The bounded confidence model's insight is that polarization can emerge also driven by solely assimilative opinion change of individuals. The strength of both insights is that they are not clear upfront and based on general systemic properties. From this complex systems perspective, further insights are interesting. For example, segregation can break down with too strong preferences, or polarization collapses abruptly at a critical bound of confidence. Such transitions at critical thresholds are typical phenomena of complex adaptive systems.

   Not surprisingly, agent-based models and simulations are a core tool in complexity science. Complexity science characterizes general properties and fundamental mechanisms of complex adaptive systems. However, similarities between social and non-social complex systems (e.g., turbulence in liquids and seismic activity in the crust of the earth) are not the focus of computational social science but how general principles and mechanisms help to understand and shape our societies.

Agent-based models and empirical data

For societies in the real world, macroscopic transitions at critical thresholds in agent-based models imply that small changes in its population or environmental conditions can trigger substantial qualitative changes. Such insights are, first and foremost, theoretical. Therefore, an essential purpose of agent-based modeling is their educational value for empirical and applied researchers to take this possibility into account. On the other hand, it can be challenging to assess the practical empirical relevance at a certain point in time. For example, a real-world system may be prone to critical transitions, but is it close to critical thresholds? How can we be sure that these exist, and how can we observe them before the transition? For some physical systems, the empirical analysis is straightforward. For example, the liquid–gas transition of water at 100°C can be empirically tested and analyzed in detail by repeatedly boiling and condensing. In real-world societies, similar empirical approaches are often impossible, unethical, or at least very demanding in various aspects.

The gold standard to confirm theory-based causal effects empirically is the *experimental approach*. Its essential ingredients are controlled conditions and controlled manipulation, for example, through repetition and random assignment. For societies, this approach is restricted to quasi-experiments or natural experiments. However, this approach still suffers from small numbers of cases (whole societies) and an overwhelming amount of possible confounding factors.

Exploratory empirical analysis of qualitative change at critical thresholds is difficult because cases of the speculated transitions may be rare (even theoretically), and these events – think of revolutions – are subject to an overwhelming amount of existing explanatory theories. Transitions at critical thresholds may also be empirically blurred because many effects might act in parallel, inhibiting and facilitating each other.

Drastic transitions may be the most impressive feature of agent-based models, but they are not the only reason to study them. Agent-based models may also explain empirical regularities and, in particular, mechanisms for their emergence. Examples are wealth distributions, empirical segregation patterns, or the attitude landscapes in a population. The empirical challenge here is to distinguish regularities from fluctuation in a sensible way. The quantification of regularities in data as *stylized facts* is a critical condition for data-driven agent-based modeling but often turns out to become a parallel research project of exploratory data analysis. An important difference to other exploratory data analysis projects is that the focus for data-driven agent-based modeling is on finding non-trivial general regularities instead of good predictions in classification (as done with machine learning) or particularly interesting special cases.

Another role of empirical data is the validation of agent-based models. Validity is the extent to which a model is well-founded and likely corresponds accurately to the real world. In hypothetico-deductivistic epistemology, where regression models are typical, the validation methods are goodness-of-fit assessment, analysis of residuals, and out-of-sample predictions. These do not transfer directly to agent-based models and simulation experiments. In the design of experiments, there is a tension between internal and external validity. The former is the extent to which experimental evidence can support claims about cause and effects. The latter the extent to which this generalizes to other situations in the real world outside the experimental context. Macy and Willer (2002) state that simulation experiments with agent-based models are first and foremost to test a theory's internal validity. However, building on internal validity, the final aim is to achieve external validity of simulation results and model findings.

For simulation models, Zeigler (1984) distinguishes replicative, predictive, and structural validity. *Replicative* (and predictive) *validity* assess the capacity of a model to replicate (or predict) existing (future) data in a specific way. *Structural validity* refers to the extent to which the "cogs and wheels" of the model structurally map to the modeled process in reality. That means the model represents reality step by step and component by component. Zeigler (1984) defines this as a high level of validity building upon replicative validity and extending it to microlevel details. In social science, preferences, rational choice, and affective and cognitive processes can often not be easily observed. Therefore, structural validity may also be seen as being in line with theories of behavior instead of observable details (see Figure 10.1). In this view, structural validity is independent of the replication of data. A model can be structurally validated given the representation of theories, but this need not contribute to replicative validity concerning data. In turn, such replication failure could be used to rethink the role of the theory for human behavior.

Further on, it is also reasonable that replicative and predictive validity can be improved without caring much about structural validity. This would give pragmatic purposes priority over pure scientific purposes of full understanding. Similar to Zeigler (1984), Sargent (2010) distinguishes conceptual validity concerning the relationship between reality and the model, computer model verification concerning the match between model and implementation, and operational validation concerning the match between simulation and reality. Beisbart and Saam (2019) provide a detailed overview of various aspects of validation of simulation models. Which aspects of validation is most important depends mostly on the purpose of the model. This also includes the question if there is a hierarchy of validity concepts.

Besides validation, *calibration* is another term relating models to reality. The notion comes from tuning measurement devices. These are calibrated such that they measure most accurately. Calibration is the more technical and more pragmatic version of validation. It is the second step. Once a modeling framework has been validated as appropriate to fulfill its purpose, its parameters can be calibrated to best do this. One may calibrate a model by parameter-tuning to achieve replicative or predictive validation. Barberousse and Jebeile (2019) specify parameter tuning as a scientific methodology and calibration as epistemology because the latter is tied to the purpose of how the model generates knowledge.

In computational social science, all agent-based models explain phenomena of the real world, and phenomena in the real world condense in data. At least, they leave traces in data. For example, segregation and polarization are observable in real-world data. Segregation is visible in demographic census data whenever segregation criteria such as ethnicity are recorded. Polarization can be observed in attitude distributions from representative surveys whenever they have a specific continuous nature, like a scale from zero to ten.

Figure 10.3A visualizes data from the UK Census 2011 which shows how segregated the Asian population is in Bradford. Asians are mostly Pakistani (plus Indians, Bangladeshi, and small fractions of Chinese and others), while others are mostly white British people (plus small fractions of Blacks and others). Figure 10.3B shows attitude distributions from the ESS (2018) for Norway and Serbia in 2018. The four panels show the distributions of people's self-placement in the left-right political spectrum and their opinion about whether European unification has already gone too far or should go further. Both answering scales have 11 options ranging from zero (left/gone too far) to ten (right/should go further).

In the following, we will look at four aspects of doing agent-based modeling data-driven in more detail: (1) selecting and using data to build the model's components analog. (2) Doing an exploratory data-analysis project in parallel to find, quantify, and understand macroscopic regularities ("stylized facts") in data. (3) Assessing the replicative validity of the model to improve the model systematically. (4) Calibrating model parameters for purposes of applied research.

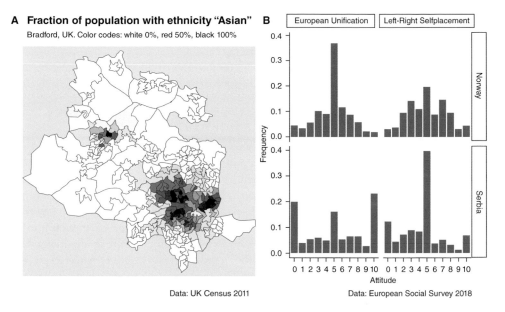

Figure 10.3   Example data about segregation (A) and polarization (B)

Figure 10.1 outlines the four aspects on the right-hand side. We will first look at the examples relating to the segregation and bounded confidence models and then summarize some general guidelines.

Data-driven model structure

The essential components of a model are the agents and their static and their dynamic variables. In classical theory-driven agent-based modeling, the essential components or often designed with ad hoc decisions. The main reason is often to make the mathematical description and the implementation simple from an analytic or pragmatic perspective. That is why households live on a square lattice (often even with periodic boundary conditions) in the segregation model, and opinions are numbers between −1 and +1 initially from a uniform distribution. In computational social science, the purpose of modeling goes beyond demonstrating the mathematical properties of the dynamical system an agent-based model manifests. Therefore, at some stage, the model must be related to data, and the model would benefit from close identification of variables of agents and variables in the data.

Comparing census data in Figure 10.3A to the segregation model, things to recognize are: We do not have the households' locations but numbers of residents within small geographic units (called LSOAs = lower layer super output areas). There are more than two ethnic groups in different layers (for example, Asian with subgroups Pakistani, Indian, and Bangladeshi), and they are not equal in size. A data-driven model framework for the segregation model could be designed on the map of LSOAs. The location of each household would be its LSOA and its neighbors, all other households there. Counting households in neighboring districts as neighbors would implement a similar spatial structure as in the original model. The new model should enable more than two ethnic groups in different frequencies. Such a setup would allow running the adapted segregation model with frequency distributions as in Bradford on the map of Bradford. One could initialize a counterfactual situation where every LSOA has the same ethnic composition as the whole town and see if segregation emerges. An attempt is presented by Zuccotti, Lorenz, Paolillo, Sánchez, and Serka (2021).

For the survey data in the ESS (2018), one may, for example, think of modifying an opinion dynamics model to operate on the same 11-point scale or at least its visualization.

Exploratory data analysis and stylized facts

A comparison of the segregation model's outcomes with real-world data in Figure 10.3A can be interpreted with a confirming and a refuting mindset. For segregation, we may, on the one hand, observe that Bradford shows regions where the local concentration of ethnic groups is substantially higher than the global concentration as in the model. That makes the segregation model plausible and homophily preferences a likely driving force of segregation in Bradford. On the other hand, one could argue that we see regions where the fraction of Asians is low but not zero and regions where the fraction of Asians is so high that other ethnic groups living there are only a few. Therefore, a substantial part of the population lives at places where even mild ethnic homophily preferences cannot be satisfied. Consequently, the model's basic assumption cannot be sufficient.

Similarly, for the bounded confidence model, the data in Figure 10.3B show that attitude distributions have several peaks, and peaks also exist between the central and extreme opinions. This is as in the model, and consequently, assimilation under bounded confidence is a likely mechanism at work in the real world. On the other hand, we do not see only one or two peaks as the model produces but more, and moreover, these are often blurred, with non-zero fractions of individuals in between. All these are not outcomes of the model. Therefore, assimilation cannot be the sole mechanism driving the evolution of these attitude distributions.

Both the confirming and refuting mindset in model assessment are motivated in a hypothetico-deductivist epistemology because they assume a model can be wrong or right. This is not an adequate epistemology for model building, as summarized in the famous quote from Box (1979) that "all models are wrong, but some are useful". What would be alternative assessments? Refuting minds should embrace generative epistemology and criticize the model by providing or proposing alternative models that could generate the observed patterns. The confirming minds should not stop generating very general and superficial stylized facts observed in data but embrace the replicative limitations as a challenge for model improvement.

A first step of improving the replicative capacity (see the next section) is to refine the set of stylized facts and their precise quantification. Meyer (2019) provides the following useful definition: *Stylized facts* are broad but not necessarily universal generalizations of empirical observations and describe the supposed essential characteristics of a phenomenon that requires an explanation. The data-driven way to derive stylized facts is exploratory data analysis (Tukey, 1977), which is the core part of the *data science process*. Wickham and Grolemund (2016) describe exploratory data analysis as the iterative process of (1) generating questions about the data; (2) searching for answers by visualizing, transforming, and modeling the data; and (3) using the learning to refine questions and generate new ones. Modeling here means models to describe data, usually not agent-based models of interaction.

Regarding stylized facts, the questions about the data are about general patterns and their quantification. For the UK Census data, one could look at the map of fractions of Asians as shown in Figure 10.3 in all towns. For a town, one could try to quantify typical distributions of the fraction of Asians in LSOAs with questions like: How many LSOAs are there with 0–10%? How many with 10–20%, and what is the distribution concerning the total fraction of Asians in the town? How are ethnic fractions of regions spatially correlated? Are patterns similar for other ethnic groups? What measures for segregation are empirically informative? Questions for the attitude data from the ESS (2018) are: How many peaks are in attitude distributions? What different patterns in the structure of peaks exist? Which polarization measures are empirically most informative?

While doing exploratory data analysis, the quantification of stylized facts should tend to move from general statements towards a *dashboard of precise measures* which are operational for the data and the simulation code; for the segregation model, that means a set of useful segregation measures. This is not trivial – for example, Apparicio, Martori, Pearson, Fournier, and Apparicio (2014) list no less than 43 segregation indices. So, the selection needs some theoretical guidance.

Research experience shows that exploratory data analysis can evolve to become an independent research project. It helps to focus on questions relevant to model dynamics known from the prototypes of the agent-based models.

Improve replicative validity with data

Replicative validity is a focused concept of validity. We use it here as the capacity of the model to reproduce what is observed in data.

In the hypothetico-deductivist research process, there is a clear hierarchy of theory steps: First, a model is theoretically derived, usually a variable-based model. Then data is put in place to confirm (or refute) it, often with regression and a statistical test. When existing datasets are used, common research practice is an iterative process of model fitting and formulation of new models with different explanatory variables or other model assumptions. This is an exploratory research process for causal effects often criticized as post hoc theorizing. It is not necessarily bad, but when models found this way have low coefficients of determination (meaning not much variance explained) and marginal statistical significance, this exploratory exercise becomes what is rightfully criticized as *p*-hacking. Outside of hypothetico-deductivist epistemology, this discussion becomes less critical.

In agent-based modeling, the iteration of theoretical formulation and simulation analysis is already common even without a close relation to data. So, one can add a step of data comparison in this iteration. Starting with a candidate model, one can assess if and when it replicates certain aspects observable in data. Then changes can be implemented to see if these improve the replicative capacity of the model.

The basis of improving replicative validity is a precise quantification of the stylized facts. This is necessary not only because research questions are about the emergence of macroscopic regularities quantified by stylized facts. Also, the data generating processes usually do not deliver all the data needed to validate every detail in the corresponding agent-based model. For example, the European Social Survey's data provide reasonably accurate measurements of individuals' attitudes but no data about change or social contacts and communication. So, stylized facts must focus on the distributional aspects of the attitude distribution. We would not be able to validate the communication pattern of individuals in an improved version of the bounded confidence model, but we can validate to what extent aspects of the empirical attitude distributions are replicated in the improved model. To that end, the empirical quantification of the stylized facts must quantify relevant regularities, and this measurement must be included in the model. Looking at the diversity of only the four examples of attitude distributions in Figure 10.3, it is likely that this cannot be done by one of the various measures for polarization (such as the dispersion of attitudes). The measurement concept should be adjusted to take blurred off-central peaks and extreme peaks into account as well as the size of the central peak. An attempt is given by Gestefeld, Lorenz, Henschel, and Boehnke (2021).

In census data, we usually have no information about the exact movements of individual households. Typically, we have snapshots of the distribution of detailed household characteristics, and these come in long intervals (ten years in the UK census data). An attempt to provide a dashboard of segregation indices and a workflow to improve replicative validity is provided by Zuccotti et al. (2021). Additionally, official data often have information of households' movements every year, sometimes in- and outflow of regions, sometimes even with information of flow between all regions, but these data are usually not equipped with all individual household characteristics. We may know how many households move but not their ethnic groups. Nevertheless, these data can be used for the derivation of stylized facts, and their measurement can be implemented in the segregation model. The frequency of movements is not directly related to segregation, but it can serve as a secondary validation criterion.

What are typical modeling steps to improve the replicative capacity for empirical data? One option is parameter tuning, but this is often limited because it already relies on a good model. A typical situation is that simulated trajectories tend to move towards highly stylized and unrealistic situations for any parameter constellation. For example, the bounded confidence model always converges to a situation with only spikes at few opinions in opinion space (see Figure 10.2B). Also, the segregation model implemented on a map of Bradford tends to converge to districts having either 0% or 100% Asian households (see Zuccotti et al., 2021). The main reason is not necessarily that the models' underlying mechanisms are implausible but that most social processes do not run in isolation. Not every movement is triggered by households being unhappy with their neighborhood. Not every negative evaluation of a neighborhood triggering a move is because of the ethnic composition. Not every opinion change is triggered by social influence.

Therefore, a rewarding first strategy for model improvement is to include components that take into account that some actions might be triggered by other reasons than the model's core behavioral theories. This is very analog to the inclusion of error terms in regression models, which should account for the unexplained variance. In principle, there are two routes to do this: the inclusion of forms of *noise* or a substantial extension of the behavioral theories. The idea to include noise is to summarize all effects which are not modeled explicitly as a random term. How this is exactly done is also not trivial. For the bounded confidence model, this can be to add a random number to the current opinion or replace the current opinion with a new randomly drawn opinion. Both have different consequences for model dynamics (see Kurahashi-Nakamura, Mäs, & Lorenz, 2016). Edmonds (2006) provides a good summary about the nature of noise as relevant for agent-based modeling in the social sciences.

In the segregation model on Bradford's map, Zuccotti et al. (2021) introduced socioeconomic status homophily as another substantial part of behavioral theory. That means households not only consider the fraction of neighbors with similar ethnicity in their assessment of the place of residence but also the fractions of neighbors with similar socioeconomic status. That way, the ethnic composition in districts can stay more diverse because households may benefit from status homophily, which may also come from other ethnic groups. With substantial extensions, the scope of the theoretical analysis is also extended.

Another route to improve replicative capacity is to include *more static variables* within agents and, in particular, to make them *heterogeneous*. Not all agents may have the same bound of confidence; some may be open minded, others closed minded. Households may differ in how important ethnically similar neighbors are for them. Introducing heterogeneity in static agent variables typically introduces new parameters characterizing their distributions. Often these can be made data-driven using other information about agents in the empirical dataset, for example, using other variables from a survey.

Any of these extensions (noise, new behavioral theory, and heterogeneity of static variables) should be introduced with care in a step-by-step fashion. It can be tempting to introduce many extensions at the same time. The social sciences provide many behavioral theories, and many datasets provide an abundance of possible variables. There is no straightforward practice to test a large set of variables simultaneously and then reduce to the "most relevant" variables. Even in a step-by-step way, there is no guarantee that a model extension that has shown to be mostly irrelevant for simulation trajectories' macroscopic properties will stay irrelevant when other extensions are introduced. Extending an agent-based model and understanding the consequences is more complicated than adding a variable in a regression model. It is always preferable to keep an analytic grasp on model dynamics through mathematical analysis while designing and exploring model extensions.

There is a trade-off to be aware of while doing data-driven improvements of an agent-based model's replicative capacity: The model's core emergent mechanisms may become irrelevant for the phenomenon's generation. This relates to the discussion about Type I and Type II mechanisms in analytical sociology proposed by León-Medina (2017). Type I mechanisms deal with the model's setup, that is, what entities, variables, and relations are there ("cogs and wheels") and how parameters on the macro level make agents behave differently. Type I mechanisms also play a role in the initialization of a simulation. Type II mechanisms refer to processes governing the emergence of new systemic properties or changes in preexisting ones, due to the functioning of Type I mechanisms. In the segregation model, the Type II mechanism is the process of single-color areas forming. In the bounded confidence model, it is the separation into two groups which do not influence each other anymore. The most important contribution of agent-based modeling is to understand Type II mechanisms in society.

Often, data-driven model extensions add Type I mechanisms, such as by adding more aspects to each agent's characteristics. The risk here is that the modeler might improve replicative capacity just based on this Type I mechanism. For example, agents in the bounded confidence model may be extended with different ideologies implying a fragmented initial attitude landscape. Suppose this model replicates data better, for example, by additionally suppressing social influence that was the driving force before. In that case, it might just be because of the initial condition and not because of cluster formation. Naturally, agent-based models with good replicative capacity may blur the clear generative mechanisms of stylized toy models, but the modeler should be aware if they are still operational. That way, the modeler may also touch the questions of theoretical robustness and sensitivity of model dynamics.

Another aspect of adequate replicative capacity is that tuned parameters can be an output of the model in its own right. For example, when an improved version of a segregation model still includes a parameter like the fraction of similar wants, these parameters' calibrated value can be used as an informative outcome of the model similar to other segregation measures operating directly on empirical data.

Calibration for applied purposes

Once an agent-based model has reached a certain maturity in replicating stylized facts in empirical data, other purposes, particularly those of applied research, may come into focus. Two main types of purposes can roughly be distinguished: forecasting and counterfactual scenario studies (see Figure 10.1). For both purposes, models should be calibrated such that they can best fulfill their purposes. Technically, this is typically parameter tuning or smaller adjustments of the simulation algorithm similar to improving replicative validity. The main difference is the intention of the modeler. When calibrating, the modeler is not developing the model anymore. Instead, the modeler takes the model as given (like a measurement device) and adjusts the free parameters for a particular new purpose.

Forecasting models take data about the real world's current state as input and simulate the future. Such models' core goal is their predictive capacity, like in the established simulation models for the weather forecast. When the predictive capacity is the sole and only purpose of the model, all other validity criteria can step back, particularly structural validity and full micro-level realism. For example, a traffic simulation may not need all vehicles' full details to predict traffic jams well.

In general, forecasting in social systems is a complicated task. First, social systems are often complex adaptive systems, and these are prone to chaotic dynamics, which are already known even from deterministic models of the weather (Lorenz, 1963). Deterministic chaos implies that even under the assumption of a perfect model with no stochastic components forecasting is theoretically impossible, because any small error or missing in the initial data triggers simulation trajectories which deviate drastically from the correct one. Second, forecasts in social systems can easily create feedback loops when these come to agents' attention in the real world. An example is election polls, which can change voting behavior. Phenomena where forecasting models in social systems are of interest and feasible are traffic jams; the spread of epidemics, as in the COVID-19 pandemic; or economic development.

A way to calibrate the segregation model for forecasting Bradford's future segregation could be to obtain the census in Bradford for two points in time, for example, 2001 and 2011, and calibrate parameters to best predict the evolution from the earlier to the later. These could then be used to forecast 2021 and assess the prediction when new census data comes in. One could think of a similar plan for forecasting polarization. These examples outline a typical difficulty for calibration: As we are usually after forecasting the development of societies and often focusing on longer time trends, we cannot test the calibration repeatedly as one could, for example, with daily traffic jams. Instead, one could try to calibrate parameters for several cases at once, for example, with census data for several towns of England or the survey data in many countries.

These outlines of potential forecasting projects highlight a general challenge from a practical as well as from a mathematical dynamical systems perspective: Is a change in real data caused by a change in parameters (or static variables of agents), or is it intrinsic dynamics of dynamic variables? The fundamental problem here is that the evolution of dynamics towards (stochastic) equilibrium may often happen on a similar time scale as the expected change of global parameters. For example, while intrinsic segregation dynamics are running, utility functions of households may change.

Counterfactual scenario studies are models that can be used for policy design to test new institutions or certain types of interventions. Such models' goal is strong external validity, meaning that the implemented model and its trajectories are a good representation of the current state of the world concerning the variables of interest for policy design. A typical example is socio-ecological simulation models, for example, for resource management. Saam (2019) emphasizes that for the purposes of scenario studies for policy design, stakeholders' judgments are a source of validation. For a polarization model, one might calibrate parameters such that the empirical attitude landscape is reproduced as stochastic equilibrium. Then one can assess the proneness of the current situation for transitions to extreme polarization or radicalization in an unwanted or a wanted direction; the latter is what is intended by "nudging" strategies. To that end, one would test changes of parameters, for example, through policy interventions. Similarly, one could explore strategies to prevent segregation.

There are various tools for parameter tuning, like linear regressions (Carrella, Bailey, & Madsen, 2020), dominance approaches (Badham, Jansen, Shardlow, & French, 2017), other methods of statistical inference (Hartig, Calabrese, Reineking, Wiegand, & Huth, 2011; Grazzini & Richiardi, 2015), mathematical optimization, or machine learning. There is no general best practice here.

Finally, it should be noted that calibration of an agent-based model can also mean searching and collecting new data to improve model components and parameters. For example, segregation models could be informed with data about movements of people and an opinion dynamics model with panel data about attitude changes of individuals or social network data.

Summary

For a summary, let us assume we have a draft agent-based model built on some micro-level behavioral theory which we suspect plays a role for a certain macrosocial phenomenon. What are the guidelines to pursue further modeling that is data-driven?

1   Search for datasets that (a) inform about the macrosocial phenomenon we are after and (b) have some relation to the model draft, for example, shared variables, time-stamps, or relations between relevant entities.

2   Modify the model's basic structure to better match the data structure, for example, concerning types of agents, ranges of variables, and space (e.g., geographical, ideological, cultural). This may not be possible in every aspect. Clarify on what level comparisons between simulation data and the empirical datasets are possible.

3   Start an exploratory data analysis of the primary dataset to quantify the phenomena we are after in data, including their context conditions. This goes hand in hand with studies and mathematical analysis of existing measurement concepts. Implement the same measurements for the data and the agent-based model.

4   Make a first comparison of simulated data and empirical data. (a) Critically assess if the basic idea of the relation between model and phenomena still holds in the sense of a Type II mechanism (León-Medina, 2017). (b) Decide which aspect of the deviation between data and model is most important to understand.

5   Assume that the basic mechanism is operational in some form in the real world. Match the model algorithm against the data-generating processes underlying the datasets and draft model extensions, bringing simulated data closer to empirical data. Typical candidates are different versions of noise in behavior, individual heterogeneity of agents (technically, this can mean that a global parameter becomes a heterogeneous static variable of agents), or another aspect of how to model agents' behavior (a substantial model extension). Beware that any of these extensions usually brings at least one more parameter: the degree of noise, the degree of heterogeneity, or a parameter weighting the new aspect. The impact of the extensions on model dynamics must be carefully analyzed, ideally with a way established for agent-based models like mathematical analysis and systematic parameter sweeps.

6   Iterate steps 2–5 (or even the data search) towards reconsidering the purpose of the study. The first aim should be fundamental insights on Type II mechanisms operating in society. The following could be descriptive insights about entities covered by the data using model output (for example, the fitted parameters).

7   Assess if the model framework can be used for applied purposes. Clarify which purpose and start the model calibration targeted explicitly for that purpose.

A final note: Often, the data are used for different purposes (for example, variable-based models) by other researchers. So, extensive literature research can be relatively uninformative for the purpose. Also, the type of explanations generated by agent-based models can be unrelated or contrasting to other explanations in the discipline. Fruitfully coping with this can be an essential contribution to more theoretical integration in the social sciences. Therefore, the explanation and understanding of different epistemologies are essential.

References

Apparicio, P., Martori, J. C., Pearson, A. L., Fournier, É., & Apparicio, D. (2014). An open-source software for calculating indices of urban residential segregation. *Social Science Computer Review, 32*(1), 117–128.

Badham, J., Jansen, C., Shardlow, N., & French, T. (2017). Calibrating with multiple criteria: A demonstration of dominance. *Journal of Artificial Societies and Social Simulation, 20*(2), 11.

Bailey, K. D. (1991). Alternative procedures for macrosociological theorizing. *Quality and Quantity, 25*(1), 37–55.

Barberousse, A., & Jebeile, J. (2019). *How do the validations of simulations and experiments compare?* (pp. 925–942). Springer International Publishing.

Beisbart, C., & Saam, N. J. (2019). *Computer simulation validation.* Cham: Springer.

Boero, R., & Squazzoni, F. (2005). Does empirical embeddedness matter? Methodological issues on agent-based models for analytical social science. *Journal of Artificial Societies and Social Simulation, 8*(4), 6.

Box, G. E. (1979). Robustness in the strategy of scientific model building. In *Robustness in statistics* (pp. 201–236). Elsevier.

Bruch, E., & Atwell, J. (2015). Agent-based models in empirical social research. *Sociological Methods & Research, 44*(2), 186–221.

Carrella, E., Bailey, R., & Madsen, J. K. (2020). Calibrating agent-based models with linear regressions. *Journal of Artificial Societies and Social Simulation, 23*(1), 7.

Clarke, K. A., & Primo, D. M. (2007). Modernizing political science: A model-based approach. *Perspectives on Politics, 5*(4), 741–753.

Colleran, H. (2016). The cultural evolution of fertility decline. *Philosophical Transactions of the Royal Society B: Biological Sciences, 371*(1692), 20150152.

Conte, R., Gilbert, N., Bonelli, G., Cioffi-Revilla, C., Deffuant, G., Kertesz, J., . . . Helbing, D. (2012). Manifesto of computational social science. *The European Physical Journal Special Topics, 214*(1), 325–346.

Deffuant, G., Neau, D., Amblard, F., & Weisbuch, G. (2000). Mixing beliefs among interacting agents. *Advances in Complex Systems, 3*, 87–98.

Edmonds, B. (2006). The nature of noise. In *International workshop on epistemological aspects of computer simulation in the social sciences* (pp. 169–182). Springer.

Epstein, J. M. (2006). *Agent-based computational models and generative social science* (Chapter 1). Princeton University Press.

ESS. (2018). *ESS round 9: European social survey. Data file edition 3.0. NSD Norwegian social science data services, Norway – Data archive and distributor of ESS data for ESS.* ERIC. Retrieved from https://www.europeansocialsurvey.org/data/conditions_of_use.html

Esteban, J.-M., & Ray, D. (1994). On the measurement of polarization. *Econometrica, 62*(4), 819–851.

Gestefeld, M., Lorenz, J., Henschel, N. T., & Boehnke, K. (2021, March 30). Decomposing attitude distributions to quantify mass polarization in Europe. *SocArXiv.* https://doi.org/10.31235/osf.io/3pn5w

Grazzini, J., & Richiardi, M. (2015). Estimation of ergodic agent-based models by simulated minimum distance. *Journal of Economic Dynamics and Control, 51*, 148–165.

Hartig, F., Calabrese, J. M., Reineking, B., Wiegand, T., & Huth, A. (2011). Statistical inference for stochastic simulation models – theory and application. *Ecology letters, 14*(8), 816–827.

Hegselmann, R., & Krause, U. (2002). Opinion dynamics and bounded confidence, models, analysis and simulation. *Journal of Artificial Societies and Social Simulation, 5*(3), 2.

Jaccard, J., & Jacoby, J. (2010). *Theory construction and model-building skill. A practical guide for social scientist.* The Guilford Press.

Keuschnigg, M., Lovsjö, N., & Hedström, P. (2017). Analytical sociology and computational social science. *Journal of Computational Social Science, 1*(1), 3–14.

Kurahashi-Nakamura, T., Mäs, M., & Lorenz, J. (2016). Robust clustering in generalized bounded confidence models. *Journal of Artificial Societies and Social Simulation, 19*(4), 7.

Laver, M. (2005). Policy and the dynamics of political competition. *American Political Science Review, 99*(2), 263–281.

Lazer, D., Pentland, A., Adamic, L., Aral, S., Barabási, A.-L., Brewer, D., . . . Van Alstyne, M. (2009). Computational social science. *Science, 323*(5915), 721–723.

León-Medina, F. J. (2017). Analytical sociology and agent-based modeling: Is generative sufficiency sufficient? *Sociological Theory, 35*(3), 157–178.

Lorenz, E. N. (1963). Deterministic nonperiodic flow. *Journal of Atmospheric Sciences, 20*(2), 130–141.

Macy, M. W., & Willer, R. (2002). From factors to actors: Computational sociology and agent-based modeling. *Annual Review of Sociology, 28*, 143–166.

Merton, R. K., & Merton, R. C. (1968). *Social theory and social structure*. Simon and Schuster.

Meyer, M. (2019). How to use and derive stylized facts for validating simulation models. In *Computer simulation validation* (pp. 383–403). Springer.

Saam, N. J. (2019). The users' judgements – the stakeholder approach to simulation validation. In *Computer simulation validation* (pp. 405–431). Springer.

Sargent, R. G. (2010). *Verification and validation of simulation models* (pp. 166–183). IEEE.

Schelling, T. C. (1971). Dynamic models of segregation? *The Journal of Mathematical Sociology, 1*(2), 143–186.

Schelling, T. C. (1978). *Micromotives and macrobehavior*. W. W. Norton & Company. New edition 2006.

Smaldino, P. E. (2020). How to translate a verbal theory into a formal model. *Social Psychology, 51*(4), 207–218.

Smith, E. R., & Conrey, F. R. (2007). Agent-based modeling: A new approach for theory building in social psychology. *Personality and Social Psychology Review, 11*(1), 87–104.

Thurner, S., Hanel, R., & Klimek, P. (2018). *Introduction to the theory of complex systems*. Oxford University Press.

Tukey, J. W. (1977). *Exploratory data analysis* (Vol. 2). Addison-Wesley PublicationCompany.

Turchin, P. (2003). *Historical dynamics: Why states rise and fall*. Princeton University Press.

Wickham, H., & Grolemund, G. (2016). *R for data science: Import, tidy, transform, visualize, and model data*. O'Reilly Media, Inc.

Wilensky, U. (1999). *Netlogo* (technical report). Retrieved from http://ccl.northwestern.edu/netlogo/

Zeigler, B. P. (1984). *Theory of modelling and simulation* (R. E. Krieger, Ed.). Publishing Company. Reprint edition of original edition Wiley & Sons, 1976.

Zuccotti, C., Lorenz, J., Paolillo, R., Sánchez, A. R., & Serka, S. (2021). Exploring the dynamics of neighborhood ethnic segregation with agent-based modelling: An empirical application to Bradford. *SocArXiv*. https://doi.org/10.31235/osf.io/gmzdp

SECTION II

Privacy, ethics, and politics in CSS research

11

ETHICS AND PRIVACY IN COMPUTATIONAL SOCIAL SCIENCE

A call for pedagogy

William Hollingshead, Anabel Quan-Haase, and Wenhong Chen

Introduction

In 2016, a group of Danish researchers publicly shared a dataset from the dating site OkCupid containing sensitive information of approximately 70,000 users, including their username, age, gender identity, location, and sexual orientation (Kirkegaard & Bjerrekær, 2016). The rationale for sharing the dataset online was simple: nothing was shared in the data file that was not already public (Zimmer, 2010). Zimmer (2016) described the release of the OkCupid dataset as indicative of the perils of big data studies. These perils are reflected in an "ethics-be-damned" approach to computational social science (CSS) research, a sentiment captured best by Jeff Goldblum's *Jurassic Park* (Spielberg, 1993) character, "Your scientists were so preoccupied with whether or not they could, they didn't stop to think if they should". The OkCupid scandal is just one example of many. Privacy breaches go well beyond academia and have affected all the major tech players as well as governments, municipalities, and educational and health institutions (Chen & Quan-Haase, 2020).

As we continue to "write ourselves into being" on social media platforms like OkCupid (Sundén, 2003) and connect with other users (Hogan & Quan-Haase, 2010), we create and leave behind digital trace data. Digital trace data are "records of activity (trace data) undertaken through an online information system (thus, digital). A trace is a mark left as a sign of passage; it is recorded evidence that something has occurred in the past" (Howison, Wiggins, & Crowston, 2011, p. 769). Yet, as our digital trace data become both larger and more identifiable, it necessitates the formalization of ethical standards and a more holistic understanding of privacy rights and legal frameworks, such as the General Data Protection Regulation (GDPR) (boyd & Crawford, 2012; Metcalf & Crawford, 2016). In this chapter, we focus on the numerous ethical and privacy challenges scholars across disciplines grapple with when designing CSS projects where data can be algorithmically collected, rendered, analyzed, and visualized via computational methods (Lazer et al., 2009). The proliferation of digital trace data, such as the OkCupid dataset, and the sheer quantity of information encoded in these datasets pose innumerable ethical challenges for CSS scholars attempting to follow the principles that traditionally guide research involving human subjects: the right to privacy, informed consent, the minimization of harm, and justice (franzke, Bechmann, Zimmer, Ess, and The Association of Internet Researchers,

DOI: 10.4324/9781003024583-13

2020). The transdisciplinary nature of CSS research along with the expeditious methodological evolution of such research has routinely disrupted the formalization of ethical standards in a rapidly growing field (boyd & Crawford, 2012; Metcalf & Crawford, 2016).

This chapter will provide an overview of the often-tumultuous relationship between ethics and digital trace data by drawing on examples primarily from social media and big data research. While we attempt to represent the gamut of CSS projects, we often draw on Twitter-based research, as this is one of the most commonly studied platforms and exemplifies the problems well. The chapter identifies several ethical challenges that CSS scholars are likely to grapple with and outlines best practices. The chapter considers four challenges linked to ethics and privacy in CSS projects that need consideration: 1) representativity, 2) aggregation and disaggregation, 3) research data archiving, and 4) data linkage. We conclude by stressing the need of computational social scientists to move beyond awareness of the ethical complexities in retrieving, analyzing, storing, and sharing digital trace data toward actively committing to engaging and evolving normative ethical standards in context-based and fluid research environments that are bound by rapidly evolving legal frameworks. We end with a call to action highlighting the importance of pedagogy that can consist of developing a range of learning resources such as books, workshops, videos, and handbooks to be taught in academic and industry settings to promote the implementation of CSS-specific principles of ethics.

Representativity

Early proponents of big data were enthusiastic about the possibilities afforded by examining research questions using massive amounts of data, to the point where shear volume triumphed over traditional concerns of sampling strategy. For example, Anderson (2008) enthusiastically stated that "with enough data, the numbers speak for themselves" (para. 7). Meng (2018) questions this assumption and stresses that the voluminous nature of big data should not supersede concerns of data quality and the importance of research design (see also Sloan & Quan-Haase, 2017). Consider how a random sample of $N = 400$ can provide the same estimation error as a non-random sample of $N = 2,300,000$. The example is based on data from the Cooperative Congressional Election Study, whose goal was to provide an estimate of eligible American voters who reported that they would vote for Donald Trump in the 2016 U.S. presidential election (Meng, 2018). The example demonstrates that "big" in big data is not sufficiently all-encompassing to do away with good research design; that is, consideration still needs to be given to who is part of the sample and who is left out.

Indeed, a number of scholars have raised concerns regarding the representativity of big data in making inferences to the general population (boyd & Crawford, 2012; Hargittai & Litt, 2012; Crawford, Miltner, & Gray, 2014; Blank, 2017). For instance, a sample drawn from a social media platform is by design biased against those who do not have access to the internet or do not have an account on a given platform (Chen & Quan-Haase, 2020). Hargittai (2015) states the problem of representativity by stressing non-use, "if people do not select into the use of the site randomly, then findings cannot be generalized beyond the site's population" (p. 65). In fact, so far, no research design has been able to solve the problem of representativeness, but future research could map user patterns from census data to infer social media sampling approaches that are sound.

The microblogging platform Twitter is the most used platform for data scraping given that information shared on the platform is largely public and, until recently, was easily harvestable via Twitter's application programming interface (API) (Bruns, 2019). For all the research utility the platform holds, population representativity remains a concern. For example, in assessing Twitter user demographics, Blank (2017) found that 23% and 15% of the UK and U.S. population reported using the platform, respectively. Moreover, Twitter's user population skews towards those who are young, high income, and educated (Blank, 2017; Blank & Lutz, 2017). Racialized selection into Twitter usage is less straightforward. Some studies based on U.S. survey data have suggested a higher use rate of Twitter among Blacks in comparison to Whites, Asians, and Hispanics (Brenner & Smith, 2013; Hargittai, 2015). Yet, other research did not find an association between race and Twitter use in the United States (Hargittai, 2020) or the United Kingdom (Blank, 2017). Further concerns arise regarding representativity related to differences in Twitter use linked to a respondent's sex. For instance, Hargittai and Litt (2012) and Hargittai (2015) found that American women are more likely than men to use Twitter. Yet this finding was not replicated with more recent datasets neither in the United States (Hargittai, 2020) nor in the United Kingdom (Blank, 2017). Research also suggests users' adoption of Twitter is not randomly distributed in the population but is additionally impacted by factors such as preexisting digital skills, comfort using the internet, and adoption of other social media sites (Hargittai & Litt, 2012; Hargittai, 2015; Hargittai, 2020). Overall, the findings show that it is not well understood to what extent the social media user base of any given platform reflects a nationally representative sample or what biases may be present.

One promising use of digital trace data has been its potential to inform evidence-based policy (Poel, Meyer, & Schroeder, 2018). However, the effect of non-representativity in digital trace data may reduce the potential of such data to produce sound policy interventions. Longo, Kuras, Smith, Hondula, and Johnston (2017) suggest that the "digitally invisible" population (i.e., those without access, or stable access to internet-connected devices) routinely fail to have their voices heard in the "digital agora". Another problem is that they may be excluded from important outreach programs. An example is New Jersey senator Cory Booker's use of Twitter in late December 2010 during a particularly intense snowfall to assist Newark citizens who had been trapped in their homes due to their street not yet being snow-plowed. Yet, without knowing whom Twitter reaches, this kind of approach differentially advantages some citizens (Robinson et al., 2020). For Hargittai (2020), this is precisely how the use of social media as a tool for governmental outreach is flawed and fails to reach those who are in the greatest need, such as older adults, who mostly don't use social media (Pew, 2020; Quan-Haase, Williams, Kicevski, Elueze, & Wellman, 2018). The ethical concern here is that, as policymakers and corporate stakeholders continue to draw insights from big data, the world will be recursively fashioned into a space that reflects the material interests of the infinitely connected.

Aggregation and disaggregation

Aggregation and disaggregation present two related techniques for processing data for analysis. Each offers value, and each has limitations to addressing the ethics of users' privacy and data equity. Studying the effects of users' characteristics, such as age, ethnicity, location, and gender, through CSS approaches can be problematized by data aggregation. Lerman (2018) notes that aggregating digital trace data allows researchers to see population-level trends across a large volume of data points. However, aggregating digital trace data can mask the immense variation of subgroups (Lerman, 2018; Alipourfard, 2018). One consequence of homogenizing diverse populations is masking the presence of inequities (Longo et al., 2017; Barocas & Selbst, 2016). For instance, analyzing Google trends can yield insight into the frequency of search terms, which can be used as a means to predict regions that have a COVID-19 outbreak (e.g., Higgins et al., 2020). Aggregating trend searches to a national level, for example, cannot address the differing impacts of the pandemic on various social groups, particularly those who are vulnerable, such as low-income individuals and racialized groups, in particular Black people (e.g., Yancy, 2020). The absence of nuanced understandings of the spread of the pandemic could lead to the enactment of policies that do not benefit those who most need it. Despite this, aggregation is proposed as a viable solution for the protection of users' privacy by blurring their identities in a mass of data – effectively hiding oneself in a crowd (Olteanu, Castillo, Diaz, & Kıcıman, 2019; Fairfield & Shtein, 2014). Viewed another way, the aggregation of Google trends data on COVID-19, opposed to individual data points, may protect individuals from the social ostra-cism of testing positive for COVID-19 a result that could be inferred from a user's search history (e.g., Ahorsu et al., 2020). In that way, ethics in CSS are more complex than at first evident.

To offset the confounding nature of aggregation, researchers could disaggregate a sample with the aim of uncovering a population's diversity. While disaggregation can yield more precise results, it further opens the door to de-anonymizing a user's information. For instance, recent research has shown a high rate (≥90%) of re-identification of purportedly anonymous people using as little as four spatio-temporal data points via credit card transactions (de Montjoye, Radaelli, Singh, & Pentland, 2015). Additionally, in a shareable Twitter dataset on a sensitive topic, like #MeToo, any singular user may be verified via Twitter's search engine, or any other search engine, which could reveal their username, biography, birthdate, geographical location, and/or following/follower list. However, directly publishing a user's information without their consent undermines their right to privacy by utilizing their information in a context that they did not agree to. This has led researchers to move away from identifying specific users or draw-ing attention to the identity of specific Twitter accounts by summarizing rather than directly quoting the tweets (e.g., Chen, Tu, & Zheng, 2017). Other scholars have chosen to focus on macro-phenomena such as network patterns (e.g., density, centrality) rather than looking at an individual's position in these networks (e.g., Yang, Quan-Haase, & Rannenberg, 2017). Yet again, these approaches based on data aggregation can obscure important trends and insights. Abstract concepts such as privacy in light of data re-identification strategies present tricky ethi-cal challenges.

The advent of CSS in data harvesting and analytical techniques has not been met with an equal urgency to strategize for the conundrum of subject privacy in big data science. For instance, in a content analysis of 382 cross-disciplinary studies of Twitter data from 2006–2012, Zimmer and Proferes (2014) found that only 4% of studies made reference in their text toward ethical considerations of research design or data collection techniques. The lack of discussion in empirical research relying on social media is part and parcel of what Fuchs (2018) terms a big data positivist approach that sidelines ethical considerations in furtherance of data quanti-fication. The prevailing assumption made here is that all accessible tweets are published with the intention of existing as public domain; therefore, they are fair game for analysis by social scientists. But is this assumption universal to all users? In other words, which users want to be hidden, and which ones want to be identified and maybe even acknowledged for their content production?

As mentioned in the previous section on data representativity, the public quality of a plat-form such as Instagram lends itself to the eyes of university, governmental, and commercial researchers. boyd and Crawford (2012) highlight, though, how "researchers are rarely in a user's imagined audience" (p. 673). How, then, do researchers balance the need to capture hetero-geneity with the need to protect a person's privacy? Thus far, a number of studies exist that measure a user's perception of how academic and non-academic researchers (Beninger, Fry, Jago, Lepps, Nass, & Silvester, 2014; Williams, Burnap, & Sloan, 2017), as well as journalists (Dubois, Gruzd, & Jacobson, 2020) utilize personal information collected from digital trace data. Using focus groups and in-depth interviews with a sample of British citizens, Beninger et al. (2014) found that participants reported apprehension over researchers utilizing their information unwittingly. Participants were concerned with reputational harm and ridicule if posts of a personal or sensitive nature were included in research reports. In a similar study relying on a non-probabilistic sample of British citizens who use Twitter, Williams et al. (2017) found that 16% reported being quite or very concerned about university researchers accessing their Twitter data, and these values rose to 49% and 51% for data being used in governmental and commercial settings, respectively. Additionally, 55% of participants expect to be asked for consent to use their data in research settings, and approximately three-quarters (76%) expect to be anonymized (Williams et al., 2017). Lastly, in a sample of Canadian online users, Dubois et al. (2020) found that respondents are significantly less receptive to journalists directly quoting posts from their social media streams, as opposed to presenting aggregated forms of public sentiment.

Extant research suggests that confidentiality – and better yet, anonymity – looms large in the public's perception of social media research and journalistic extrapolation. Yet decomposition of the findings reveals some heterogeneity among user perceptions of privacy and anonymity in the context of digital trace data. For example, Williams et al. (2017) found that women, members of the LGBTQ community, Black people and other marginalized groups, parents with children, and those posting personal messages and/or photos had greater odds than men, straight people, White people, and those infrequently sharing personal messages and/or photos of expecting anonymity in research publications. This suggests that intersecting avenues of social marginalization contribute to a desire to protect one's identity in digital communities where users can be subject to abusive and harassing behaviors that discursively intersect logics that are racist, colonialist, homophobic, misogynistic, and transphobic. Additionally, Dubois et al. (2020) found that respondents who considered it appropriate for journalists to directly quote users' social media posts had a higher number of social media accounts, frequently posted politically oriented messages, and had been previously quoted in the news. While social marginalization may increase desires for anonymity, it appears that being politically vocal in the digital public increases one's desire to be seen.

This is to say, users' perceptions of privacy are contextually situated (Nissenbaum, 2011). The ethics of privacy cannot be approached monolithically (Quan-Haase & Ho, 2020). The sensitivity of information collected, the user population from which information is drawn, the purpose of the research in question, and who is collecting the information should weigh heavily in making ethically sound methodological decisions. In general, when conducting research of digital trace data, CSS researchers should thoroughly examine each facet to assess for subject risk. Williams et al. (2017) provide a useful flow-chart for making sound ethical decisions that proportionally weighs risks across a myriad of scenarios (Figure 11.1). For example, Figure 11.1 shows that aggregation techniques may be appropriate if the information collected is sensitive (e.g., recollection of a traumatic experience as in the case of #MeToo posts), and the user population draws from a socially marginalized position in which directly quoting – without consent – may amplify the risk of harm by further victimizing a person. Aggregation may, however, obfuscate discursive analysis. If the use of a direct quotation, photos, or videos is necessary to the directive of the research, then informed consent should be sought (Beninger et al., 2014; Williams et al., 2017; Dubois et al., 2020). Additionally, researchers ought to provide an opt-out clause for participants, whereby users may revoke consent for the ways in which their information is used (e.g., direct quotations; publication of handle, photos, or videos) or revoke consent for the inclusion of their information altogether prior to the publication of findings. Participants should be made aware of the impracticality or impossibility of excluding their information after publication. Thus, a final "drop date" for which revocation of consent is feasible should be communicated clearly. To that end, researchers should be steadfast in empowering

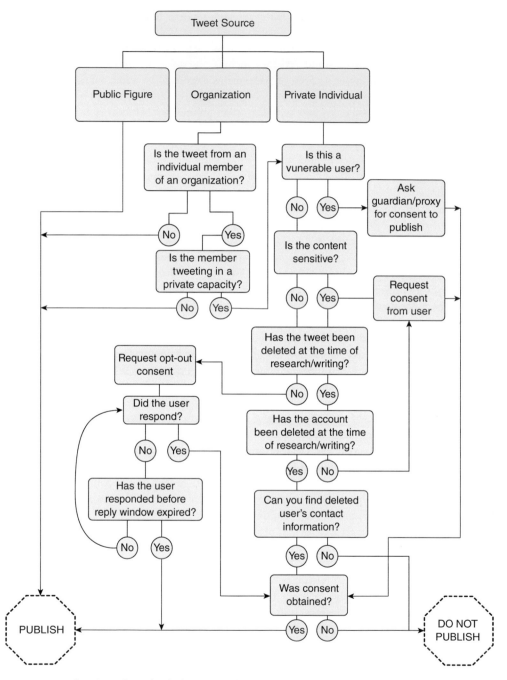

Figure 11.1 Flowchart for ethical decision-making in Twitter data use (Adapted with permission from Williams, M. L., Burnap, P., & Sloan, L. (2017). Towards an ethical framework for publishing Twitter data in social research. *Sociology*, *51*(6), 1149–1168. https://doi. org/10.1177/0038038517708140)

the user population by actively informing them on who is collecting their information, why their information is sought, how it will be utilized, and where it will be published. Protecting user privacy will be a crucial step in dismantling laissez-faire approaches to big data ethics that have engendered institutional distrust.

Research data archiving

With recent scandals of data fabrication surfacing and circulating in the news (e.g., The Lancet, 2020), there has been a call and urgency to "improve the transparency, coherence, and coordination of the global scientific research enterprise" (G8 Science Ministers, 2013, para. 1). To achieve these goals, archived, publicly accessible datasets are valued for purposes of replicability, transparency, utility, and preservation of history. In fact, many journals, such as *Science*, *PLoS ONE*, and *Social Science Computer Review*, require datasets to be made accessible for scrutiny via research data archives prior to publication. For ease, archivists and scholars utilize APIs to authenticate automatic retrieval of data from social media, thereby allowing institutional bodies to capture a digital memory of significant cultural events, or more general snapshot of time and space (Pennock, 2013; Thomson, 2016). For instance, in the United States, the Library of Congress maintains an exhaustive database of all textual tweet data from 2006–2017, while in the United Kingdom, the National Archives maintains a digital archive of tweets originating from official government accounts.

Despite noble intentions of furthering the scientific pursuit, several ethical concerns arise as institutional bodies strive to create thorough, transmissible records of "publicly" available information (Bishop & Gray, 2018). An important consideration is how scholars can guarantee privacy when data are shared. Informational flows open the possibility that a person's information will be used for different purposes than for those originally intended. Steinmann, Matei, and Collman (2016) metaphorize the datafied subject as a "LEGO piece" to be repeatedly put in use to empirically fortify any number of scientific endeavors. This was the case with the example discussed earlier of the OkCupid dataset that was made accessible for scholars to reanalyze. Reuse of data is only possible in cases where the intention to subsequently share data across institutions for other purposes is clearly articulated from the outset within informed consent forms. While the need for informed consent for data sharing and reuse is clear in projects where scholars collect the data for research purposes, these ethical challenges are much more complex when it comes to sharing and reusing datasets that contain digital trace data, such as in the OkCupid case (boyd & Crawford, 2012; Fairfield & Shtein, 2014; Voss, Lvov, & Thomson, 2017).

Social media users may be unaware of how their information is collected and shared due to the "legalese" and burdening length of Terms of Service (ToS) documents (e.g., Obar & Oeldorf-Hirsch, 2020). It is widely known that users don't scrutinize or even read ToS, which Obar and Oeldorf-Hirsch describe as "the biggest lie on the internet". It is entirely plausible that for some users, a thorough reading of the ToS would result in the revocation of consent. Nevertheless, the expression of "consent" at one point in time effectively means that a digital user becomes datafied for diverse purposes. Mechanisms that enable informational sharing between key stakeholders ensure that digital trace data are no longer fixed within the spatio-temporal context in which they were intentionally constructed.

Another challenge for CSS scholars is accounting for information that is deleted on the platform by users. Scholars need to grapple with the ethical dilemma that deletion creates: Can data that are archived be used for research purposes if they are no longer publicly available? Meeks (2018) and McCammon (2020) have outlined the ethical challenges posed by the transience of the digital landscape in contemporary archival work. Meeks (2018) notes that while applications, such as Politwoops, seek to hold U.S. public officials accountable by archiving deleted tweets, they may inadvertently store information on private citizens. For instance, if a public official retweets a message posted by a private citizen, and that message subsequently gets deleted, then Politwoops stores that information because it is categorized as a deletion of information by a public official. McCammon (2020) analyzes tweet deletion strategies of U.S. government agencies, a practice that dually manipulates organizational perceptions and shapes public memory. Organizations whose aim it is to increase political transparency and accountability, like Politwoops, reduce institutional control of information and the manipulation of records yet simultaneously, albeit inadvertently, can also lead to information on private citizens being archived as a public record without their consent. Thus, researchers must curate archived datasets to ensure that "deletion" is accounted for. Incorporating deleted elements does have privacy ramifications and is in direct violation of the guidelines for Twitter developer tools (Meeks, 2018). To that extent, setting up these archives requires an understanding of all potential ethical implications resulting from the archiving of public records.

CSS researchers are urged to consider techniques that can lead to a consenting sample population. In the case where data is likely to be archived or shared publicly or among research teams, the letter of information and consent form should clearly indicate that data will be stored for an indefinite period of time and how the data are going to be shared. While "data realists" acknowledge the improbability of receiving consent from all users in a large dataset, this should not dissuade strategizing novel practices to empower users to consider how their data are used and will be re-used (Fuchs, 2018; boyd & Crawford, 2012). One proposed solution is to incorporate clauses expressing the third-party use of information for research purposes in the ToS of platforms and other systems (e.g., Fairfield & Shtein, 2014). Furthermore, ToS for data-gathering applications should be written clearly, intelligibly, and concisely for the lay user to increase the probability that participants will thoroughly engage with such documents. Researchers must be cognizant of the diversity of people in their sample and diligently attempt to obfuscate the identities of marginalized populations in a data archive, given the potential for harm when archiving and sharing information (Williams et al., 2017; Olteanu et al., 2019). For example, Reilly and Trevisan (2016) warn about conducting research on contested topics and use the example of the Northern Irish flag protest page on Facebook to demonstrate how scholars can put citizens at risk. They argue that collecting data could "expose protesters and their supporters to potential harm" (p. 421). Given the challenges associated with anonymization and re-identification, researchers might consider sharing information only through request and also include a memorandum of agreement that outlines ethical handling of the data rather than making it available through a public repository.

Data linkage

Data linkage refers to the unification of corresponding datasets to enable a richer informational account of the unit of analysis (Harron, Goldstein, & Dibben, 2015; Connelly, Playford, Gayle, & Dibben, 2016). The depression of response rates in survey research (e.g., Groves et al., 2009) – the traditional "gold standard" of social research – has led investigators to incorporate novel data modalities, such as social media (Al Baghal, Sloan, Jessop, Williams, & Burnap, 2019; Sloan, Jessop, Al Baghal, & Williams, 2020). Scraping the social media accounts of surveyed participants may assist researchers in "filling the gaps" of missing data while simultaneously extending the data available on participants through data obtained in a fluid, naturalistic environment. For example, the real-time nature of micro-blogging platforms, such as Instagram, has utility for researchers seeking to discursively categorize sentiment around a given social phenomenon. There is some evidence to suggest that social media data can be variably predictive of surveyed behaviors and attitudes, such as voting behaviors and political preferences (DiGrazia, McKelvey, Bollen, & Rojas, 2013). Furthermore, linking digital trace data to surveys may provide insights into the role of social desirability in survey research by comparing survey data with actual observations. Another relevant methodological advantage is the use of trace data to support subjects by collecting real-time data that ameliorates retrospective memory concerns (Al Baghal et al., 2019). Beyond methodological utility, linking data from several sources has numerous ethical dimensions that CSS should consider. Areas of consideration include selection bias into data linkage, de-anonymization of data, and research data archiving and sharing among researchers.

Linking the responses of a survey participant to their social media account, or another secondary source (e.g., administrative records), first requires the researcher to obtain the participant's express consent to do so. Here, the issue is the likelihood that subsequent analyses will be biased due to the non-representativity of sample members who provide consent for their information being linked (Stier, Breuer, Siegers, & Thorson, 2019). In a longitudinal survey of civic engagement, investigators may ask for approval to observe digital trace data. Yet only participants who have an account and actively participate on the chosen digital platform of interest can form the prospective pool of participants – a pool that is known to be non-representative of the broader population, as discussed previously (Blank, 2017; Williams et al, 2017; Hargittai, 2020). Al Baghal et al. (2019) found that the expression of consent across three surveys done in the United Kingdom for data linkage to Twitter accounts ranged from 27% to 37% of the subsample reporting having a Twitter account. Yet overall, the proportion of respondents reporting having a Twitter account was relatively low across all three surveys. In the 2015 British Social Attitudes survey, 18% of respondents reported having a Twitter account. Additionally, Al Baghal et al. (2019) found evidence to suggest that the likelihood of providing consent to Twitter data linkage is lower among women and decreases as users get older. While further research is necessary, utilizing data linkage must come with the acknowledgment that sampling bias is inevitable. Sampling bias will inevitably favor a younger, technologically adept, White, cis-male, straight, wealthy, and educated cohort (i.e., the characteristics of users likely to use Twitter and less likely to report concerns over the usage of their data in the context of social research).

Another key consideration in data linkage is the increased risk of de-anonymization. Social media data, specifically Twitter, is inherently identifiable given the "public" nature of the platform (Sloan et al., 2020). Therefore, linking raw Twitter data to survey data can identify who the respondent is (through their handle, geographical location, or tweet history), thereby violating a person's right to privacy. This makes participants particularly vulnerable in the event of a data breach. Past data breaches have caused great public concern and have resulted in the constriction of API research on Facebook and Twitter (Venturini & Rogers, 2019).

Analytically speaking, the issue is further problematized by the purported security of data aggregation. Aggregating a dataset of tweets may provide confidentiality, but it limits investigation to population-based descriptive analyses, thereby ignoring the heterogeneity of user characteristics as well as the discursive, qualitative elements of the data (Lerman, 2018; Fuchs, 2018). Given that public opinion – particularly that of socially marginalized sub-populations – tends to be starkly cautious of the manners in which institutions safeguard digital privacy/anonymity (e.g., Williams et al., 2017), it stands to reason that subjects may be hesitant to further triangulate their information for the scientific imperative. While the research on the mechanisms of consent in survey to social media data linkage is notably sparse at the moment, several studies on the mechanisms of consent in survey/administrative record(s) (e.g., medical data) data linkage indeed suggest that privacy/confidentiality concerns are a predominant mechanism for not consenting to data linkage (Sakshaug, Couper, Ofstedal, & Weir, 2012; Sala, Burton, & Knies, 2012; Fobia et al., 2019).

Archiving linked data raises numerous legal, ethical, and analytical concerns. For instance, Twitter expressly forbids the public sharing of datasets exceeding 50,000 identifiable tweets (Twitter, 2020). While there are provisions for researchers employed by academic institutions and working for non-commercial purposes, creating public repositories of tweets is in violation of the platform's ToS. To that extent, CSS seeking to link social media data to another source should be steadfast in ensuring that their data-sharing procedures are not in legal violation of commercial policies. Ethically, members of the Twitter-using public express dissatisfaction at the ways in which institutions make transparent the procedures of data collection and storage (Beninger et al., 2014). This tends to be exacerbated by the challenges of pragmatism in obtaining informed consent from a wildly disparate, heterogeneous digital population. In other words, if there yet exists any concrete solution to obtaining consent to collect observational data from hundreds of thousands – or more – users, how can said users be informed of how their linked data is being archived in institutional repositories and shared among investigators? Last, Sloan et al. (2020) note that, in analytical terms, "hydrating" "dehydrated" tweet identifiers will result – and rightfully so – in the inaccessibility of tweets that have been deleted or made private. Social media datasets – Twitter in particular – may then be considered especially susceptible to change over time, thereby decreasing the likelihood of replication – a major principle in the scientific enterprise. Dehydration in this context refers to a process where raw Twitter data (i.e., the tweet text, the @ handle, and other identifying information) is reduced to a unique identifying number. Hydrating refers to the process of programmatically restoring the unique tweet identifier to its original state.

While non-representativity is a larger existential threat to causal inference implicit in digital trace data, there are several viable solutions to the issues of data linkage addressed. First, the wording of the consent question to linking disparate data types can be consequential to whether a participant will consent to data linkage (Sloan et al., 2020). Here, researchers should aim for clarity above all else by avoiding the use of technical jargon and stating – in the simplest of terms – the purpose and function of data linkage by clearly stating how data are likely to be used, stored, and shared. To the last point, researchers must take care not to "pigeon-hole" future research; stating the manner in which data is to be used in the future, if archived and shared, should delicately balance specificity and comprehensiveness. Furthermore, consent should be supplemented by further support in how participants may opt out of data linkage, should they desire to do so. Second, when working with linked data, researchers should make a concerted, ongoing effort to securitize participant information. This might include limiting who has simultaneous access to each form of data, accessing the data exclusively within a secure research facility, storing only the most relevant bits of data while destroying the rest, and ultimately securely disposing of data – in the absence of archiving – once all analyses are complete (see Sloan et al., 2020). Last, for the purposes of archiving social media data, and more specifically Twitter data, that can be linked to a repository of survey data, researchers may circumnavigate restrictive informational sharing policies by "dehydrating" tweets using Python libraries, such as twarc. Researchers may also exercise caution by vetting and verifying the usage of data by secondary investigators – effectively limiting access to such studies that are in the same vein as the primary purpose.

Conclusions

CSS is consolidating into a discipline with its own epistemology, body of knowledge, and methods. This consolidation comes with a growing need to develop sound, robust principles for the conduct of ethical research. This chapter discussed four challenges – 1) data representativity, 2) aggregation and disaggregation, 3) research data archiving, and 4) data linkage – with the aim of demonstrating the range of ethical concerns and dilemmas CSS scholars confront. We conclude that there is a need to build on existing ethics guidelines (e.g., AoIR Ethical Guidelines 3.0) and follow new legal frameworks (e.g., General Data Protection Regulation).

CSS projects at the surface may seem to require fewer ethical considerations because they rely on either big data, public data, or aggregated data. Despite the availability of robust ethical frameworks for the conduct of research such as the Belmont Report, the Nuremberg Code, and the Declaration of Helsinki, often traditional considerations and guidelines are no longer applicable to the new challenges of CSS. Just one example is the Facebook massive-scale emotional contagion study in which $N = 689,003$ Facebook users were assigned to two experimental groups (negative emotions reduced vs. positive emotions reduced) without consent or debriefing (Kramer, Guillory, & Hancock, 2014). Studies like these have led to a call for more stringent regulations and more intense debate around CSS-specific ethical standards (Goel, 2014). We conclude this chapter arguing that a focus on pedagogy and additional training in the conduct of ethical research in CSS is needed across disciplines and in both research institutions and industry. A first step in this direction is organizing workshops such as the two-part workshop in "Ethics and Computational Social Science" as part of the Summer School in CSS (Salganik, 2020) and the publications of handbooks that directly address ethics in CSS (e.g., Sloan & Quan-Haase, 2021).

Additionally, universities need to offer ethics courses for students across disciplines, as there is a rapid increase in CSS projects that neglect ethics altogether. There are two problems here. First, many CSS projects don't require a consent regime like other types of research, nor a formal review through the university's research ethics board because data are publicly available and studies will often involve "minimal risk" to participants (Grimmelmann, 2015). Without any formal review, practices of data harvesting, use, and archiving create a haphazard research atmosphere where there are no mechanisms in place for checks of ethical conduct, as demonstrated through the Facebook contagion experiment described previously. Second, legal frameworks like the GDPR are complex and filled with legal jargon, often making it difficult for scholars, and in particular junior scholars, to grasp the implications in relation to their specific projects. This necessitates more collaboration with legal scholars to translate legal language into specific CSS best practices.

Acknowledgments

This project was funded by the Social Science and Humanities Research Council of Canada (SSHRC). We are very grateful to our colleagues Mathew Williams, Pete Burnap, and Luke Sloan for allowing us to adapt their figure. We also thank the anonymous reviewers for their feedback.

References

Ahorsu, D. K., Lin, C-Y., Imani, V., Saffari, M., Griffiths, M. D., & Pakpour, A. H. (2020). The fear of COVID-19 scale: Development and initial validation. *International Journal of Mental Health and Addiction*. https://doi.org/10.1007/s11469-020-00270-8

Al Baghal, T., Sloan, L., Jessop, C., Williams, M. L., & Burnap, P. (2019). Linking Twitter and survey data: The impact of survey mode and demographics on consent rates across three U.K. studies. *Social Science Computer Review*, 38(5), 517–532. https://doi.org/10.1177/0894439319828011

Alipourfard, N., Fennell, P. G., & Lerman, K. (2018). *Can you trust the trend? Discovering Simpson's paradoxes in social data*. Proceedings of the Eleventh ACM International Conference on Web Search and Data Mining, pp. 19–27. https://doi.org/10.1145/3159652.3159684

Anderson, C. (2008, June 23). The end of theory: The data deluge makes the scientific method obsolete. *Wired*. Retrieved from www.wired.com/2008/06/pb-theory/

Barocas, S., & Selbst, A. D. (2016). Big data's disparate impact. *California Law Review, 104*, 671–732. http://dx.doi.org/10.2139/ssrn.2477899

Beninger K., Fry, A., Jago, N., Lepps, H., Nass, L., & Silvester, H. (2014). *Research using social media: Users views*. NatCen.

Bishop, L., & Gray, D. (2018). Ethical challenges of publishing and sharing social media research data. In K. Woodfield (Ed.), *Advances in research ethics and integrity: Vol. 2. The ethics of online research* (pp. 159–187). Emerald Publishing.

Blank, G. (2017). The digital divide among Twitter users and its implications for social research. *Social Science Computer Review, 35*(6), 679–697. https://doi.org/10.1177/0894439316671698.

Blank, G., & Lutz, C. (2017). Representativeness of social media in Great Britain: Investigating Facebook, LinkedIn, Twitter, Pinterest, Google+, and Instagram. *American Behavioural Scientist, 61*(7), 741–756. https://doi.org/10.1177/0002764217717559

boyd, d., & Crawford, K. (2012). Critical questions for big data. *Information, Communication & Society, 15*(5), 662–679. https://doi.org/10.1080/1369118X.2012.678878

Brenner, J., & Smith, A. (2013). *72% of online adults are social networking site users*. Pew Research Centre: Internet & Technology. Retrieved from www.pewresearch.org/internet/2013/08/05/72-of-online-adults-are-social-networking-site-users/

Bruns, A. (2019). After the 'APIcalypse': Social media platforms and their fight against critical scholarly research. *Information, Communication & Society, 22*(11), 1544–1566. https://doi.org/10.1080/13691 18X.2019.1637447

Chen, W., Huang, G., Miller, J., Lee, K.-H., Mauro, D., Stephens, B., & Li, X. (2018). "As we grow, it will become a priority": American mobile start-ups' privacy practices. *American Behavioral Scientist, 62*(10), 1338–1355. https://doi.org/10.1177/0002764218787867

Chen, W., & Quan-Haase, A. (2020). Big data ethics and politics. *Social Science Computer Review, 38*(1), 3–9. https://doi.org/10.1177/0894439318810734

Chen, W., Tu, F., & Zheng, P. (2017). A transnational networked public sphere of air pollution: Analysis of a Twitter network of PM2.5 from the risk society perspective. *Information, Communication & Society, 20*(7), 1005–1023. https://doi.org/10.1080/1369118X.2017.1303076

Connelly, R., Playford, C. J., Gayle, V., & Dibben, C. (2016). The role of administrative data in the big data revolution in social science research. *Social Science Research, 59*, 1–12. https://doi.org/10.1016/j.ssresearch.2016.04.015

Crawford, K., Miltner, K., & Gray, M. L. (2014). Critiquing big data: Politics, ethics, and epistemology. *International Journal of Communication, 8*, 1663–1672.

de Montjoye, Y.-A., Radaelli, L., Singh, V. K., & Pentland, A. (2015). Unique in the shopping mall: On the reidentifiability of credit card metadata. *Science, 347*(6221), 536–539. https://doi.org/10.1126/science.1256297.

DiGrazia, J., McKelvey, K., Bollen, J., & Rojas, F. (2013). More tweets, more votes: Social media as a quantitative indicator of political behaviour. *PLoS One, 8*(11), Article e79449. https://doi.org/10.1371/journal.pone.0079449

Dubois, E., Gruzd, A., & Jacobson, J. (2020). Journalists' use of social media to infer public opinion: The citizens' perspective. *Social Science Computer Review, 38*(1), 57–74. https://doi.org/10.1177/0894439318791527

Fairfield, J., & Shtein, H. (2014). Big data, big problems: Emerging issues in the ethics of data science and journalism. *Journal of Mass Media Ethics, 29*(1), 38–51. https://doi.org/10.1080/08900523.2014. 863126.

Fobia, A. C., Holzberg, J., Eggleston, C., Childs, J. H., Marlar, J., & Morales, G. (2019). Attitudes toward data linkage for evidence-based policymaking. *Public Opinion Quarterly, 83*(1), 264–279. https://doi.org/10.1093/poq/nfz008

franzke, A., Bechmann, A., Zimmer, M., Ess, C. and the Association of Internet Researchers. (2020). *Internet research: Ethical guidelines 3.0*. Retrieved from https://aoir.org/reports/ethics3.pdf

Fuchs, C. 2018. 'Dear Mr. Neo-Nazi, can you please give me your informed consent so that I can quote your fascist tweet?' Questions of social media research ethics in online ideology critique. In G. Meikle (Ed.), *The Routledge companion to media activism* (pp. 385–394). Routledge. https://doi.org/10.4324/9781315475059

G8 UK. (2013, June 12). *G8 science ministers' statement*. London. Retrieved from www.gov.uk/government/publications/g8-science-ministers-statement-london-12-june-2013

Goel, V. (2014). As data overflows online, researchers grapple with ethics. *The New York Times*. http://www.nytimes.com/2014/08/13/technology/the-boon-of-online-data-puts-social-science-in-a-quandary.html?_r=0

Grimmelmann, J. (2015). Law and ethics of experiments on social media. *Colorado Technology Law Journal*, *13*, 219–271.

Groves, R. M., Fowler, F. J. Jr., Couper, M. P., Lepkowski, J. M., Singer, E., & Tourangeau, R. K. (2009). *Survey methodology*. Wiley.

Hargittai, E. (2015). Is bigger always better? Potential biases of big data derived from social network sites. *The ANNALS of the American Academy of Political and Social Science*, *659*(1), 63–76. https://doi.org/10.1177/0002716215570866

Hargittai, E. (2020). Potential biases in big data: Omitted voices on social media. *Social Science Computer Review*, *38*(1), 10–24. https://doi.org/10.1177/0894439318788322

Hargittai, E., & Litt, E. (2012). Becoming a tweep: How prior online experiences influence Twitter use. *Information, Communication & Society*, *15*(5), 680–702. https://doi.org/10.1080/1369118X.2012.666256.

Harron, K., Goldstein, H., & Dibben, C. (2015). Introduction. In K. Harron, H. Goldstein, & C. Dibben (Eds.), *Methodological developments in data linkage* (pp. 1–7). Wiley & Sons, Ltd. https://doi-org.proxy1.lib.uwo.ca/10.1002/9781119072454.ch1

Higgins, T. S., Wu, A. W., Sharma, D., Iling, E. A., Rubel, K., Ying, J. T., & Snot Force Alliance. (2020). Correlations of online search engine trends with coronavirus disease (COVID-19) incidence: Infodemiology study. *JMIR Public Health and Surveillance*, *6*(2), Article e19702. https://doi.org/10.2196/19702

Hogan, B., & Quan-Haase, A. (2010). Persistence and change in social media. *Bulletin of Science, Technology and Society*, *30*(5), 309–315. https://doi.org/10.1177/0270467610380012

Howison, J., Wiggins, A., & Crowston, K. (2011). Validity issues in the use of social network analysis with digital trace data. *Journal of the Association for Information Systems*, *12*(12), 767–797. https://doi.org/10.17705/1jais.00282

Kirkegaard, E. O., & Bjerrekær, J. D. (2016). The OKCupid dataset: A very large public dataset of dating site users. *Open Differential Psychology*, *46*, 1–10. https://doi.org/10.26775/ODP.2016.11.03.

Kramer, A. D. I., Guillory, J. E., & Hancock, J. T. (2014). Experimental evidence of massive-scale emotional contagion through social networks. *Proceedings of the National Academy of Sciences of the United States of America*, *111*(29), 10779. https://doi.org/10.1073/pnas.1412583111.

The Lancet. (2020). *Retraction – Hydroxychloroquine or chloroquine with or without a macrolide for treatment of COVID-19*. https://doi.org/10.1016/S0140-6736(20)31324-6

Lazer, D., Pentland, A., Adamic, L., Aral, S., Barabasi, A. L., Brewer, D., . . . Van Alstyne, M. (2009). Life in the network: The coming age of computational social science. *Science*, *323*(5915), 721–723. https://doi.org/10.1126/science.1167742

Lerman, K. (2018). Computational social scientist beware: Simpson's paradox in behavioural data. *Journal of Computational Social Science*, *1*, 49–58. https://doi.org/10.1007/s42001-017-0007-4

Longo, J., Kuras, E., Smith, H., Hondula, D. M., & Johnston, E. (2017). Technology use, exposure to natural hazards, and being digitally invisible. *Policy & Internet*, *9*(1), 76–108. https://doi.org/10.1002/poi3.144

McCammon, M. (2020). Tweeted, deleted. *New Media & Society*, 1–19. https://doi.org/10.1177/1461444820934034

Meeks, L. (2018). Tweeted, deleted. *Information, Communication & Society*, *21*(1), 1–13. https://doi.org/10.1080/1369118X.2016.1257041

Meng, X.-L. (2018). Statistical paradises and paradoxes in big data (I). *The ANNALS of applied statistics*, *12*(2), 685–726. https://doi.org/10.1214/18-AOAS1161SF

Metcalf, J., & Crawford, K. (2016). Where are the human subjects in big data research? *Big Data & Society*. https://doi.org/10.1177/2053951716650211

Nissenbaum, H. (2011). A contextual approach to privacy online. *Daedalus*, *140*, 32–48. https://doi.org/32-48.10.1162/DAED_a_00113

Obar, J. A., & Oeldorf-Hirsch, A. (2020). The biggest lie on the Internet. *Information, Communication & Society*, *23*(1), 128–147. https://doi.org/10.1080/1369118X.2018.1486870

Olteanu, A., Castillo, C., Diaz, F., & Kıcıman, E. (2019). Social data. *Frontiers in Big Data*, *2*(13), 1–33. https://doi.org/10.3389/fdata.2019.0001

Pennock, M. (2013). *Web-archiving*. DPC (Digital Preservation Coalition) Technology Watch Report 13–01. Retrieved from www.dpconline.org/docs/technology-watch-reports/865-dpctw13-01-pdf/file

Pew. (2020). *Social media fact sheet*. Washington, DC. Retrieved from www.pewresearch.org/internet/fact-sheet/social-media/

Poel, M., Meyer, E. T., & Schroeder, R. (2018). Big data for policymaking: Great expectations, but with limited progress? *Policy and Internet*, *10*(3), 347–367. https://doi.org/10.1002/poi3.176

Quan-Haase, A., & Ho, D. (2020). Online privacy concerns and privacy protection strategies among older adults in East York, Canada. *Journal of the Association for Information Science and Technology*, 71, 1089–1102.

Quan-Haase, A., Williams, C., Kicevski, M., Elueze, I., & Wellman, B. (2018). Dividing the grey divide. *American Behavioral Scientist*, *62*(9), 1207–1228. https://doi.org/https://doi.org/10.1177/0002764218777572

Reilly, P., & Trevisan, F. (2016). Researching protest on Facebook: Developing an ethical stance for the study of Northern Irish flag protest pages. *Information, Communication & Society*, *19*(3), 419–435.

Robinson, L., et al. (2020). Digital inequalities 3.0: Emergent inequalities in the information age. *First Monday*, *25*, https://doi.org/10.5210/fm.v25i7.10844

Sakshaug, J. W., Couper, M. P., Ofstedal, M. B., & Weir, D. R. (2012). Linking survey and administrative records. *Sociological Methods & Research*, *41*(4), 535–569. https://doi.org/10.1177/0049124112460381

Sala, E., Burton, J., & Knies, G. (2012). Correlates of obtaining informed consent to data linkage: Respondent, interview, and interviewer characteristics. *Sociological Methods & Research*, *41*(3), 414–439. https://doi.org/10.1177/0049124112457330

Salganik, M. [Summer Institute in Computational Social Science] (2020, May 28). *Ethics and computational social science (part 1)* [Video]. YouTube. https://www.youtube.com/watch?v=A-5QaX5ZiK8&feature=youtu.be

Sloan, L., Jessop, C., Al Baghal, T., & Williams, M. (2020). Linking survey and Twitter data. *Journal of Empirical Research Ethics*, *15*(1–2), 63–76. https://doi.org/10.1177/1556264619853447

Sloan, L. & Quan-Haase, A. (2017). A retrospective on state of the art social media research methods. In L. Sloan & A. Quan-Haase (Eds.), *The Sage handbook of social media research methods* (pp. 663–672). Sage. https://dx.doi.org/10.4135/9781473983847

Sloan, L., & Quan-Haase, A. (Eds.). (2021). *The handbook of social media research methods*. Sage.

Spielberg, S. (Director). (1993). *Jurassic Park* [Motion Picture]. Universal Pictures.

Steinmann, M., Matei, S. A., & Collman, J. (2016). A theoretical framework for ethical reflection in big data research. In J. Collman & S. A. Matei (Eds.), *Ethical reasoning in big data* (pp. 11–27). Springer Nature. https://doi.org/10.1007/978-3-319-28422-4

Stier, J., Breuer, J., Siegers, P., & Thorson, K. (2019). Integrating survey data and digital trace data. *Social Science Computer Review*, *38*(5), 503–516. https://doi.org/10.1177/0894439319843669

Sundén, J. (2003). *Material virtualities: Approaching online textual embodiment*. Peter Lang.

Thomson, S. D. (2016). *Preserving social media*. DPC (Digital Preservation Coalition) TechWatch Report 16–01. Retrieved from www.dpconline.org/docs/technology-watch-reports/1486-twr16-01/file

Twitter. (2020). Retrieved from https://developer.twitter.com/en/developer-terms/policy

Venturini, T., & Rogers, R. (2019). "API based research" or how can digital sociology and journalism studies learn from the Facebook and Cambridge Analytica data breach. *Digital Journalism*, 7(4), 532–540. https://doi.org/10.1080/21670811.2019.1591927

Voss, A., Lvov, I., & Thomson, S. D. (2017). Data storage, curation, and preservation. In L. Sloan & A. Quan-Haase (Eds.), *The Sage handbook of social media research methods* (pp. 161–176). Sage. https://dx.doi.org/10.4135/9781473983847

Williams, M. L., Burnap, P., & Sloan, L. (2017). Towards an ethical framework for publishing Twitter data in social research. *Sociology*, *51*(6), 1149–1168. https://doi.org/10.1177/0038038517708140

Yancy, C. W. (2020). COVID-19 and African Americans. *Journal of the American Medical Association*, *323*(19), 1891–1892. https://doi.org/10.1001/jama.2020.6548.

Yang, S., Quan-Haase, A., & Rannenberg, K. (2017). The changing public sphere on Twitter. *New Media & Society*, *19*, 1983–2002. https://doi.org/10.1177/1461444816651409

Zimmer, M. (2010). But the data is already public. *Ethics and Information Technology*, *12*(4), 313–325. https://doi.org/10.1007/s10676-010-9227-5

Zimmer, M. (2016, May 14). OkCupid study reveals the perils of big-data science. *Wired*. Retrieved from www.wired.com/2016/05/okcupid-study-reveals-perils-big-data-science/

Zimmer, M., & Proferes, N. J. (2014). A topology of Twitter research. *Aslib Journal of Information Management*, *66*(3), 250–261. https://doi.org/10.1108/AJIM-09-2013-0083

12

DELIBERATING WITH THE PUBLIC

An agenda to include stakeholder input on municipal "big data" projects

James F. Popham, Jennifer Lavoie, Andrea Corradi, and Nicole Coomber

Acknowledgments

We are grateful to the Social Science and Humanities Research Council of Canada for funding this initiative through a Partnership Connections Grant.

Introduction

There are tremendous benefits to using big data to inform municipal decision-making. Yet given the traditionally isolated generation and custody of information, sheer volume, rapid growth in data, and variety of formats of big data, best practices for how municipalities can optimize big data technologies remain to be established. Of concern are: What are the pitfalls that should be considered in the use of big data? How can big data technologies be used responsibly and the veracity of data trends be assured? How can valuable insights derived from big data be harnessed to enhance transparency, place quality data summaries in the hands of citizens, and make evidence-informed policies for the city?

This chapter provides a framework for engaging and consulting with the public as a deliberative device specifically in regard to municipal-level integration of big data technologies. Our discussion is informed by a public symposium, *Big Data in Cities: Barriers and Benefits*, that was held in May of 2017. This symposium invited more than 100 public, institutional, and academic leaders to participate in moderated dialogues navigating privacy and ethics, data-sharing protocols, and the motives and manner in which data is used. The operational goal of this initiative was to develop guidelines intended to shape local municipal policy relating to the uptake of "smart city" initiatives and to promote informational exchange between traditionally siloed institutions. Couched in the principles of *community-based research* (CBR), we argue that localized expertise can be leveraged to initiate top-down initiatives that can play a substantive role in shaping policy (Aitken, Porteous, Creamer, & Cunningham-Burley, 2018). This chapter describes the methods that we used and includes a critical reflection on their benefits and weaknesses.

DOI: 10.4324/9781003024583-14

Background

The timing of our *Big Data in Cities: Barriers and Benefits* symposium reflected a period of renewal for its host city, which had recently begun to integrate a spectrum of "Big Data" technologies into its governance and service models. A series of administrative changes had instigated the redefinition of the city's Corporate Initiatives and Community Strategies department and tasked it with exploring social development and improvement opportunities. One such opportunity entailed investigating the creation of an open data portal, reflecting similar policies that had been implemented in nearby Canadian cities like Hamilton and Toronto (e.g., Gill, Corbett, & Sieber, 2017; Hivon & Titah, 2017, respectively). Specifically, the host city's planned development of a data-sharing initiative was intended to synthesize information from hundreds of local institutions servicing the municipality.

An innovative approach to informing citizens about policy actions and issues concerning the public comes in the form of "dashboards". These technologies are often used by municipal governments to provide some level of transparency about their operations and present an air of "open" accountability to the public (Matheus, Janssen, & Maheshwari, 2020). Dashboards are content-rich portals that allow citizens to access summaries or condensed and consolidated data and visualizations, as well as frequently asked questions or communication tools. The provision of such a portal would require buy-in from a range of local service providers operating under numerous (and often conflicting) data standards and privacy mandates.

Our institution was approached by the municipality to initiate conversations between the numerous agencies operating within its borders. To be clear, the expectation of the symposium was not to develop technical frameworks or data sharing agreements but rather to identify potential questions pertaining to big data analytics and develop critical considerations for their implementation. After initial consultations with the Department of Corporate Initiatives and Community Strategies, the principal investigator and co-investigators engaged in a systematic scan of academic and popular literature that centered on questions of privacy, data sharing, and informed public engagement in decision-making processes, which would form the primary points of discussion for the symposium.

Data privacy

Departmental leadership was already cognizant of the capacities for change provided by machine learning and artificial intelligence, as well as the potential entrapments that accompany the de-anonymization of personal data. These privacy dilemmas (Verhelst, Stannat, & Mecacci, 2020) served as coalescing points for the general frame of the symposium. First, in many cases, individuals may not know what data are being collected about them and what they may be used for (Clarke & Margetts, 2014). Second, policies around the use of big data often eschew privacy-forward perspectives and may be vulnerable to latent biases or other systemic issues that risk misrepresentation of the groups it serves (Anisetti et al., 2018).

A third, emergent consideration addressed questions over responsible data stewardship. Whereas governmental agencies are typically held to privacy and data security standards (state surveillance arguments notwithstanding), they often lack the capacity to design and manage complex projects – particularly at the municipal level. The outsourcing of these initiatives to private corporations can add additional layers of risk to potential privacy and ethical violations, as these bodies are far less inclined to adhere to similar bureaucratic regulations (Clement, 2020). In some cases, minimal oversight of corporate-designed initiatives has situated private agencies as rentiers of public data, compromising public trust and project veracity (Artyushina, 2020).

The first day of the symposium was therefore dedicated to presentations intended to explore diverse viewpoints on privacy matters. Similarly, the moderated discussions scheduled for day one were designed to elicit dialogue about privacy from multiple local stakeholders.

Data sharing agreements

Like many other North American cities, the host city was in the preliminary stages of developing a data-sharing initiative intended to aggregate information from as many as 700 local social institutions servicing its 100,000 residents. This agreement would serve as the backbone to the intended data portal (dashboard), described previously. In addition to addressing privacy, the symposium was also designed to leverage sectoral expertise relating to data sharing, with a stated goal of contributing toward the development of locally relevant data sharing practice and policy guidelines.

As the tools for large-scale data collection have become increasingly available among social institutions, the impetus for developing big data partnerships has grown accordingly (Horelli & Sadoway, 2014). The guidelines emerging from our activities were intended to address ethical questions about the potential impacts of municipal use of big data analytics, particularly those relating to consent and its multiple interpretations (Cheung, 2018; Cavoukian, 2013). We also sought to include consideration of problematic structured omissions that can occur with data aggregation and analytic procedures, such as the tautological misrepresentation of marginalized communities that O'Neil (2016, p. 87) termed "pernicious feedback loops" or their wholesale exclusion via "digital invisibility" (Longo, Kuras, Smith, Hondula, & Johnston, 2017, p. 76). The accurate inclusion of all citizens in the data portal is vital to ensure strategies and decisions are based on high-quality, high-fidelity data.

The second day of the symposium was therefore intended to foster discussion and partnership building between local agencies. Presentations featured examples of successful partnerships and technological solutions in the hope that they would frame a locally defined governance structure for data aggregation.

Public input

A third focus of the symposium centered on public engagement. Whereas the previous two features had been brought to our attention by the municipal partner, this third thematic objective emerged through review of existing literature. In part, this focus stemmed from observed incongruities between big data-informed planning outcomes and the communicated concerns of residents (Haggart, 2020). Similar, contemporaneous municipal big data projects like the nearby Toronto Waterfront smart city project (led by Alphabet/Sidewalk Labs in 2017) had failed to bridge consultation with actions, identifying the importance of meaningful consultation (Clement, 2020). In other cases, the progress of policy relating to technologies and their applications had progressed external to public inputs; thus, consultation provides opportunity for the public to *catch up* (Andrejevic, 2014).

An important consideration here was acknowledging that the public, in a general sense, does not possess an understanding of fundamental parts of big data analysis, such as its uses, potential repercussions, data collection methods, and storage concerns (Michael & Lupton, 2016). The tone of the symposium therefore emphasized performative activities that "creatively [enable] lay people's imaginative and affective relations to big data" (Michael & Lupton, 2016, p. 113). In doing so, we hoped to facilitate meaningful discussion through *deliberative democracy* (McWhirter et al., 2014) that engaged community leaders in dialogue with policymakers, providing opportunity for civic engagement. In addition to shaping policy formulation and implementation, the deliberative democracy process garners the public's trust as it "validates the idea that participants' views are important and have some consequence" (McWhirter et al., 2014, p. 470). Our hope was that an open public forum on the subject of big data and conducted in partnership with the municipality would contribute toward these sentiments within the local community.

This approach also aligns with Canadian expectations related to the common law *duty to consult*. In general terms, this principle obliges governments to proactively consult with Indigenous communities on any actions or policies that can potentially impact their rights (Newman, 2019). The host municipality is located adjacent to one of the largest (by population) First Nations reserves in Canada, and many of its residents have roots in the Indigenous community. Several organizations representing Indigenous interests were present, and the symposium's participatory nature aligned with related expectations that consultation provided meaningful information (Newman, 2019).

Design

The considerations provided above informed the agenda for a two-day symposium held between May 7 and 8, 2017, and engaged participants in deliberative activities relating to municipal big data initiatives. Given that big data initiatives in public policy present a complex series of inter-related benefits and challenges, we felt that policy discussions incorporating the insights of community leaders would clarify and provide tools for addressing public concerns over issues such as privacy, ethics, bias, and regulation (Schintler & Kulkarni, 2014; Smith, Bennett Moses, & Chan, 2017). This approach is reflective of recent participatory investigations on big data policy and applications (e.g., Aitken et al., 2018; Danaher et al., 2017; McWhirter et al., 2014; Bombard, Abelson, Simeonov, & Gauvin, 2011).

From a top-down perspective, this symposium's approach was framed by the principles of community-based research. In general, CBR champions a collaborative approach to addressing research questions about the community with input/guidance from the affected community. By engaging the local leaders in conversations about data aggregation and analysis, this research stands to benefit from greater contextualization and more nuanced integration of multiple ways of knowing (Halseth, Markey, Manson, & Ryser, 2016). To this end, we argue that, at their core, municipally focused open data initiatives bear significant similarities to other forms of local governance and therefore should be subject to public consultation (or technoscientific citizenship). This approach is reflective of recent participatory investigations of big data policy and applications (McWhirter et al., 2014; Bombard et al., 2011)

Using this CBR framing, the research team employed a knowledge-transfer symposia approach to data collection (Katapally et al., 2016). This method entails a combination of formal presentations by expert speakers paired with breakout roundtable discussions. Informational presentations provide a mechanism for focusing the conversations at roundtables by introducing key areas for discussion.

Presentations

A series of 11 presentations delivered by academics and practitioners introduced both challenges and solutions to big data technologies. Rather than communicating an open call for papers/ presenters, we purposively contacted researchers and practitioners whose work closely aligned with thematic categories identified previously. A similar approach was employed by Danaher et al. (2017), who argued that the collective intelligence of multidisciplinary groups can be leveraged to provide frameworks for effective action. The substantive expertise of our group covered a range of topical subjects, but all hinged on the potential impact that presented concepts/technologies could have on big data policy at municipalities. Presenters were asked to prepare a 45-minute demonstration of their research/work, with an additional 15 minutes reserved for an open Q&A session following.

The presentations were thematically categorized by day during the symposium. Day one focused on examining privacy and ethical concerns stemming from big data initiatives and primarily featured academic presenters. The day was anchored with a keynote presentation by the former privacy commissioner for the Province of Ontario, who discussed a "privacy by design" framework that embeds active consent as a requisite function of all data-collection initiatives (Cavoukian, 2013). Additional presentations identified questions about representing marginalized and Indigenous voices; ethically leveraging automated data collection; challenges for long-term data curation; and opportunistic geographic information science (GIS), which processes geographic data, redefining it into useful information to examine its impact on individuals and society (Duckham, Goodchild, & Worboys, 2003).

Day two shifted focus toward addressing and overcoming barriers to inter-agency and intersectoral data sharing. Though day one focused on critical assessment, the balance of day two's presentations featured successful data sharing and data operationalization initiatives. Opening remarks directed participants to consider how open and interactive, or "peer-to-peer" (Aitken, 2015) governments might work with citizens to form responsive policy employing analytic technologies. The remaining presentations included descriptive examples of successful data-sharing agreements, anonymized health data pairing, de-identified longitudinal data projects, and big data analytics for crime prevention.

Participants

While similar symposia have attempted to develop cross-sectional participant fields (e.g., Aitken et al., 2018), we operated on the assumption that community leaders, both formal (e.g., organizational, municipal leaders) and informal (e.g., sociocultural leaders; see Pielstick, 2000; Kirk & Shutte, 2004) can provide a valid sense of grassroots perspectives on a given set of issues (Macqueen-Smith, Muhajarine, & Delanoy, 2015; McWhirter et al., 2014; Degeling, Carter, & Rychetnik, 2015). We therefore engaged in a combination of targeted and open recruitment aimed at members of academic and municipal governance communities located within the Golden Horseshoe region of southern Ontario. This approach included a directed email campaign that detailed the nature and intent of the symposium, advertisements in a specialized periodical (*Municipal World*), and web-driven media (Facebook, Eventbrite).

A total of 109 individuals participated, representing a broad range of organizations, including Indigenous, municipal and provincial police services, school boards, universities, municipalities, non-governmental service providers, and the interested public. While exact figures were not retained per institutional research ethics board (REB) confidentiality requirements, we estimate that 50 percent of attendees represented governmental organizations, 20 percent represented human service organizations, 16 percent represented academic institutions, and 14 percent represented non-affiliated members of the public.

Accessibility

The symposium was held in a large conference room at a hotel venue in the host city. No registration fees were collected, and transportation services were offered along with complimentary meals and refreshments in order to minimize barriers to participation. Additionally, the research team secured funding via the Canadian Social Sciences and Humanities Research Council (SSHRC) Connection program, which supports events and outreach activities geared toward short-term, targeted knowledge mobilization initiatives. This funding allowed for partial coverage of travel and hospitality expenses incurred by all presenters as well as students and underwaged participants.

Data collection

Presentations provided a mechanism for focusing the conversations at subsequent roundtables by introducing key areas for discussion. Participants were instructed to self-select into eight separate groups for facilitated discussion at three intermittent stages over the two-day period and were asked to consider 1) general ethical and privacy concerns, 2) groups/communities at risk from data collection, 3) policies/procedures to address ethical issues and maintain privacy, 4) risks associated with automated data collection, and 5) addressing public concerns about data collection activities.

The discussion topic for the first plenary was developing shared-data agreements that protect privacy and maintain ethical approaches and was informed by six expert presenters. The issue for discussion in the second plenary after presentations by two experts explored barriers to sharing data that had been experienced by non-profit agencies, community organizations, municipalities, and academic practitioners. The third plenary focused on current and future opportunities for application of shared data in social services, municipal, and academic sectors and included two expert presenters.

The plenary sessions were directed by a professional facilitator, who led conversations and encouraged engagement among attendees. Additionally, two graduate students were stationed at each table to act as scribes and note takers. Each student received training in focus group elicitation methods and had previously completed studies in advanced qualitative research methods. Each break-out table was provided with flip charts and markers to aid the organization of their responses and to share insights with the remainder of the larger group at the conclusion of each plenary. These contributions were subsequently aggregated and anonymized for analysis. More than 100 pages of transcription was collected from five separate roundtable groups.

At the commencement of the roundtable sessions, participants were informed about the purpose of the plenary, the methods for data collection, and the intended usage of the data by the convener verbally and through the visual presentation. Participants were further informed of their rights as study participants, including voluntary participation and the right to withdraw at any time without penalty. Participants were given an opportunity to ask questions before data collection began. Their participation therefore constituted informed consent, as advised by the institutional REB. All recorded data was anonymized and aggregated, and no identifying information was collected from participants to maintain their privacy and confidentiality.

To cultivate information sharing and relationship building among attendees, a number of networking coffee breaks and lunches were scheduled, as well as an evening networking wine and cheese event on day one.

Outcomes

At its core, the symposium addressed concerns about public engagement and feedback mechanisms relating to analytic governance (Danaher et al., 2017). Indeed, governments rarely seek, and may not desire, public feedback about their understanding of and concerns about big data and its usage (Clarke & Margetts, 2014). The generally nomothetic and positivistic epistemologies of big data projects approach social issues through a meta-analytic lens, thereby limiting consideration of the individual. The limited perspective of automated narratives must be acknowledged in policy design, particularly as they relate to colonized and marginalized communities prone to technological invisibility (Longo et al., 2017; O'Neil, 2016; Robinson et al., 2015), yet are often overlooked in the rush for the next panacea (Kitchin, 2014). While such processes can undoubtedly inform significant improvements to the development and application of policy, their uptake must include careful consideration of any possible latent biases.

Ultimately, the symposium had some bearing on policy development beyond the fold of well-meaning handshakes. Data was thematically analyzed using an inductive multi-cycle coding approach (Saldaña, 2014), producing eight themes composed of 25 recurring codes. We identified an ambivalent take on big data technologies among participants, who acknowledged their presence in many structures and suggested that education, stewardship, and agency were needed in policy rather than a reboot. A granular breakdown of the results is presented in the following section.

Thematic result 1: safeguarding "fair" representations in data

Participants often raised concerns relating to the potential of algorithmic governance to draw limited or inaccurate conclusions and lead policy presupposed upon misrepresentative data, in line with criticisms raised by O'Neil (2016). Participants were aware that false narratives stemming from generalizations have historically affected the delivery of services and that the employment of uninformed data analyses may jeopardize repeating those legacies. In particular, given the proximity of the community to a prominent First Nation community, the participants spoke about these issues in the context of Indigenous peoples. While they acknowledged that the purpose for data analytics was to improve service delivery by identifying and addressing gaps, they felt that black-box empirical presentations of community might further differentiate already marginalized communities, leading down a slippery slope toward structured inequalities. For example, several participants made note of recent changes to policing tactics which included technologies that categorize mental health interactions. They feared that tools of this manner could lead to unjust overpolicing of homeless and street-involved communities who exhibit a higher rate of mental health concerns.

These issues may have been raised as a result of the nature of the day one speakers, which included an Indigenous scholar speaking about ethical research practices; a big data scholar speaking about digital invisibility; and the former privacy commissioner for the province of Ontario, who called for opt-in consent processes on all government use of personal data.

Thematic result 2: community consultation and consent

In addition to concerns about the representativeness of data, the participants also called for improved public consultation and informational mechanisms about big data governance. As with the previous theme, it is likely that these ideas were inspired by the concepts raised by expert speakers, in particular the former privacy commissioner, who argued that individuals ought to know how their data are being used within their communities. Whereas the speaker focused on individual agency, participants were more concerned with transparency and grounding sound, data-derived policy in democratic principles.

The dialogue focused on developing mechanisms of informed consent that could be instituted both retroactively for older data and proactively for future analysis, which the discussants argued could be provided through existing oversight organizations. For example, participants framed institutional review programs as brokerages between the public and analytics, ameliorating local information asymmetries. Likewise, community-servicing institutions like the local health authority were frequently discussed as mechanisms for interpreting and communicating local social values. As a corollary, they added that significant educational inroads about privacy and data collection are needed to ensure that the public is knowledgeable about these technologies and therefore capable of making informed decisions when engaging in discourse about their regulation.

Thematic result 3: ensuring data quality and fidelity

A third constant that emerged from the participants was concern over the quality, durability, and continuity of the data collected from big data initiatives. Specifically, participants spoke of raw data's tendency to be "messy, dirty, full of occlusions" (Kitchin, 2014, p. 9). From their perspective, these challenges could be addressed through the implementation of regulatory frameworks – stemming again from existing organizations – whose obligations included parsing data and prioritizing accuracy. Many of these comments extended from previous experiences with proprietary databases, whose disparate mechanics often translated into technical incompatibilities that could not easily be overcome without jeopardizing individual privacy (e.g., Daniel, 2019).

Here the participants invoked concepts that had been raised during day two of the symposium, which included presentations on data-sharing between multiple service agencies, data anonymization, and its reconstitution for analytic purposes. Given the potential taxonomic incongruencies between different governmental bodies as well as the spectrum of service agencies operating within the municipality, participants were cognizant of limits to data veracity and validity when they are merged together. They questioned how differences in nomenclature would affect service levels experienced by the same individual. Reflecting earlier discussions about policing strategies in response to mental health crises, several participants articulated concerns over mismatched definitions for "mental health" and "crisis". Similar questions were raised about the temporality of data – phrased by some as its *shelf life* – in the context of its long-term veracity.

Thematic result 4: optimism

Despite their concerns, the participants recognized the presence – and potential – of big data as an unshakable reality of 21st century governance. To this end, they framed the symposium as an opportunity to shape regulation from the beginning. Moreover, they optimistically discussed big data initiatives as a means to catalyze new partnerships and foster broad-spectrum knowledge exchange to the greater benefit of community members. For these discussants, many of whom represented local non-governmental agencies, a locally defined governance structure for data aggregation symbolized the power of the community and its capacity to leverage limited budgets, share resources, build relationships, and work collaboratively. Such partnerships are welcome in a typically siloed climate, as they could inform greater inter-agency transparency and collaboration. This notion is also supported in the literature, which promotes more open public engagement and community understanding of big data so that they have influence over its usage.

Outputs

This information was condensed and presented to the municipality's Corporate Initiatives and Community Strategies in a memorandum format along with a list of recommended actions to preface policy development. In response, the municipality convened a taskforce on local data-sharing that brought together health and social service agencies, with the goal of designing a protocol for data standardization and access. Recent social initiatives led by the host city and relating to the health of homeless individuals introduced an expanded consent process for data collection, which can be traced in part to the information presented at the symposium. Moreover, informal partnerships were established between practitioners and the municipality, leading to an advisory role for the city's future data-sharing initiatives and agreements. In the academic realm, the symposium has informed two peer-reviewed articles and a series of conference presentations. It has also catalyzed several partnerships between the research team's institution and the community organizations who attended the events.

Reflection

Although successful, several points of consideration have emerged about the symposium and its contributions toward a deliberative democracy. First, we must consider its fulfillment of the mutually designed objectives relating to privacy, data sharing, and participation. While presenters and participants did contribute *social values* (Bombard et al., 2011; Abelson et al., 2003) in response to the areas of inquiry, they can in many cases be considered a form of "lay expertise" (Kerr, Cunningham-Burley, & Amos, 1998, p. 42) that is limited in scope (Degeling et al., 2015). We cannot, for instance, assume that the perspectives gathered from 109 guests are representative of the municipality's 100,000 residents. Moreover, it is important to observe that public participation in decision-making processes may inherently be political exercises, as the interests of the represented organizations may underlie stated perspectives (Degeling et al., 2015). Thus, local health agencies may be more likely to prioritize privacy when compared to law enforcement services, as organizational priorities will differ.

To this end, we must also reflect upon the nature of the participants whose inputs informed the symposium's tangible outcomes. As was noted earlier, the majority of participants were attending in official capacities as representatives of social agencies, municipalities, and other formal institutions. Again, this makeup was by design and founded on the assumption that delegates whose interests lay in community issues could provide relevant grassroots perspectives (Macqueen-Smith et al., 2015; McWhirter et al., 2014); however, it does stand to reason that members of the broader public may be overshadowed in their reflections. We must be cognizant of the fact that the reliance on authorities (formal or otherwise) may risk perpetuating the systemic marginalizing processes belying big data's agnostic framing (Kitchin, 2014). This is particularly true given that participants revealed that the community required more education on big data systems and its capabilities and limitations.

It is possible that the attendees were compelled to participate in the symposium for the benefit of receiving expert knowledge about big data implications and were thus deeply influenced by this expert messaging. Despite this, participants generally had experience with big data in some capacity and reported clear needs, benefits, and drawbacks based on this background. Indeed, Degeling et al. (2015) express concern over the representativeness, authenticity, and democratic credibility of deliberative processes. To this end, they suggest that researchers distinguish the nature of the public that is sought between "citizens (lay people, the pure public), consumers (patients, service users, the affected public), and advocates (experts and interest groups, acting as the partisan public)" (Degeling et al., 2015, p. 116). Moreover, we must acknowledge that certain fields of expertise may not have been present at our symposium. The social framing of the events may not have captured the attention of those whose perspectives on algorithmic governance are rooted in empiricism, just as our invitations may not have crossed all of the desks that they should (or could) have. Our response to these concerns mirrors those presented by authors who have engaged in similar activities (e.g., Aitken et al., 2018; Danaher et al., 2017). Gatherings of this nature serve as effective starting points to elucidate future areas of inquiry and should not express any tone of finality.

Further, the solicitation of public feedback is often done in a way that excludes the marginalized through physical or financial barriers. For example, in Canada, Indigenous communities often lack adequate access to the internet compared to the larger population, which can severely hamper the ability to collect public feedback (Flynn, 2020). As is the case with many municipal concerns, communities that are organized and resource rich have a greater chance of having their interests served (French, 2017). As described earlier, we did attempt to improve the accessibility of the symposium; however, we did receive feedback about barriers stemming from geography (the venue was not centrally located within the municipality), timing (it occurred during work days), and communication (we did not advertise in accessible formats like newspapers).

Despite these limitations – which are by no means trivial – we believe that the consultative approach employed for our symposium facilitated deliberative dialogues that had the potential to shape policy. Even if the public does not have a technical background or experience in big data, it is still valuable to connect with the public on how the data should be used (McWhirter et al., 2014). We are confident in the veracity of the observed responses, which were provided by individuals who voluntarily attended and brought genuine perspectives about the implementation of big data technologies as well as the policy surrounding them.

Recommendations

This final section provides a brief series of considerations that can be employed when attempting to engage in consultation with the public about the use of big data by governments or government-associated institutions or corporations. In the following table we have included suggestions for engaging the public on big data, as informed by our experiences.

Table 12.1 Actionable recommendations for stakeholder engagement activities regarding big data projects

Relative needs for the community and consultation process	*Actionable recommendations*	*Additional considerations when planning*
	Situate big data within governance structures and existing knowledge to identify necessary inputs and modes of inquiry	
	Consider externalities (venue location, time/day of event, health and safety measures, etc.) that may affect the size, scope, and modality of the consultation, such as funding and access	Multiple consultations may be needed Digital feedback mechanisms
	Identify appropriate elicitation methodologies based on needs, previous experiences, and resources available	Determine what groups may not have access to conventional avenues of recruitment
Seek localized public opinion on big data uses	Maintain a deliberate documentation regimen to capture the consultation process and valuable insights along the way	Clearly articulate the limits to the consultation process Grant funding may be available for consultations
	Panelists should have expertise that aligns with the identified needs or research challenges for the community	Challenges may organically develop in conjunction with community/leadership inputs
	Identify stakeholders, including those affected by big data, those using or employing big data, and those contributing to the collection of big data	Experts will catalyze deliberative democracy by bridging governance issues with critical discussions of analytic technologies
Identify experts and stakeholders to frame discussion	Ascertain which presenters would provide the greatest context and understanding to ensure that all participants are able to engage in the consultation despite varying degrees of knowledge	Tap into existing memberships and communities of practice that work with and consider big data

Relative needs for the community and consultation process	Actionable recommendations	Additional considerations when planning
Ensure consultation process is undertaken in an ethical, accessible, and targeted way	Assess the availability needs of stakeholders in order to ensure adequate participation	Specialty data management procedures may be necessary to ensure privacy
	Ensure REB approval is obtained and that data collection can occur in a manner that upholds privacy and ethical concerns	Ethics board approval may take longer than anticipated; build in sufficient time for processing
Disseminate findings to broader community and untapped stakeholders	Identify what partners and audiences to report outcomes to, taking care to consider which outcomes will be the most illuminating and can be received in an actionable format	Avoid unnecessary jargon Seek approval to place findings in accessible locations such as municipal websites, libraries, and community boards
	Mobilize resources to begin a public consultation, continually reflecting on the previous steps to ensure they remain prioritized throughout the process of data collection and analysis	Leverage local institutional partnerships such as universities and businesses
	Ensure the dissemination format is open access and easily accessible for continued discussion and comment	Allow continued interaction with and feedback on findings from the broader public

Conclusion

The seismic shift in reliance on Big data by the private and public sectors has not often been met with inclusive public consultation on the principles of big data usage, despite its profound potential implications on the public. This chapter overviewed a case study of how one municipality consulted with community members and stakeholders on the use of big data using a deliberative democracy process. A two-day symposium featuring speakers, round-table discussions, and participants of various levels of governance in the community was held to gather contributions from participants. A thematic content analysis was conducted based on aggregated responses gathered during round-table discussions situated around three plenaries. Plenaries focused on 1) building shared-data agreements that preserve privacy and maintain ethics, 2) identifying problems in sharing data among municipal organizations, and 3) present and future opportunities for application of shared data in the public sectors. Findings revealed four dominant themes: Safeguarding "fair" representations in data, community consultation and consent, ensuring data quality and data fidelity, and optimism. Considering these themes, we recommend situating big data within governance structure and existing knowledge, identifying key stakeholders for participation while also integrating members of the public, providing an accessible forum for public participation, and mobilizing resources to ensure an effective and productive session while abiding by ethical considerations.

References

Abelson, J., Forest, P. G., Eyles, J., Smith, P., Martin, E., & Gauvin, F. P. (2003). Deliberations about deliberative methods: Issues in the design and evaluation of public participation processes. *Social Science & Medicine, 57*(2), 239–251.

Aitken, M., Porteous, C., Creamer, E., & Cunningham-Burley, S. (2018). Who benefits and how? Public expectations of public benefits from data-intensive health research. *Big Data & Society, 5*(2), 1–12.

Aitken, R. (2015). *Social, open & big: The promise of peer-to-peer government.* Municipal World.

Andrejevic, M. (2014). The big data divide. *International Journal of Communication, 8*(2014), 1673–1689.

Anisetti, M., Ardagna, C., Bellandi, V., Cremonini, M., Frati, F., & Damiani, E. (2018). Privacy-aware big data analytics as a service for public health policies in smart cities. *Sustainable cities and Society, 39*, 68–77.

Artyushina, A. (2020). Is civic data governance the key to democratic smart cities? The role of the urban data trust in Sidewalk Toronto. *Telematics and Informatics, 55*, 101456.

Bombard, Y., Abelson, J., Simeonov, D., & Gauvin, F. P. (2011). Eliciting ethical and social values in health technology assessment: A participatory approach. *Social Science & Medicine, 73*(1), 135–144.

Cavoukian, A. (2013). Personal data ecosystem (PDE) – A 'privacy by design' approach to an individual's pursuit of radical control. in H. Mireille, K. O'Hara, & M. Waidner (Eds.), *Digital enlightenment yearbook 2013: The value of personal data* (pp. 89–101). IOS Press.

Cheung, A. S. (2018). Moving beyond consent for citizen science in big data health and medical research. *Northwestern Journal of Technology and Intellectual Property, 16*, 15.

Clarke, A., & Margetts, H. (2014). Governments and citizens getting to know each other? Open, closed, and big data in public management reform. *Policy & Internet, 6*(4), 393–417.

Clement, A. (2020). (Pseudo) Participation in smart city planning: Sidewalk Labs' fraught Toronto Foray. In M. Valverde & A. Flynn (Eds.), *Smart cities in Canada: Digital dreams, corporate designs: Independent experts analyze often-controversial schemes from Nunavut to Montreal to Toronto's failed Sidewalk Labs waterfront scheme* (pp. 52–67). James Lorimer & Company Ltd.

Danaher, J., Hogan, M. J., Noone, C., Kennedy, R., Behan, A., De Paor, A., . . . Murphy, M. H. (2017). Algorithmic governance: Developing a research agenda through the power of collective intelligence. *Big Data & Society, 4*(2), 1–21

Daniel, B. K. (2019). Big data and data science: A critical review of issues for educational research. *British Journal of Educational Technology, 50*(1), 101–113.

Degeling, C., Carter, S. M., & Rychetnik, L. (2015). Which public and why deliberate? – A scoping review of public deliberation in public health and health policy research. *Social Science & Medicine, 131*, 114–121.

Duckham, M., Goodchild, M. F., & Worboys, M. (2003). *Foundations of geographic information science* (p. 2). CRC Press.

Flynn, A. (2020). Indigenous exclusion and access to the internet: The case of Nunavut. In M. Valverde & A. Flynn (Eds.), *Smart cities in Canada: Digital dreams, corporate designs: Independent experts analyze often-controversial schemes from Nunavut to Montreal to Toronto's failed Sidewalk Labs waterfront scheme* (pp. 127–144). James Lorimer & Company Ltd.

French, E. (2017). *People-centered planning for smart cities: Exploring the use of smart cities technologies in efforts to engage the public* (Master's Thesis). Georgia Institute of Technology.

Gill, M., Corbett, J., & Sieber, R. (2017). Exploring open data perspectives from government providers in Western Canada. *Journal of the Urban & Regional Information Systems Association, 28*(1).

Haggart, B. (2020). The selling of Toronto's smart city. In M. Valverde & A. Flynn (Eds.), *Smart cities in Canada: Digital dreams, corporate designs: Independent experts analyze often-controversial schemes from Nunavut to Montreal to Toronto's failed Sidewalk Labs waterfront scheme* (pp. 38–51). James Lorimer & Company Ltd.

Halseth, G., Markey, S., Manson, D., & Ryser, L. (2016). *Doing community-based research: Perspectives from the field.* McGill–Queen's University Press.

Hivon, J., & Titah, R. (2017). Conceptualizing citizen participation in open data use at the city level. *Transforming Government: People, Process and Policy, 11*(1), 99–118.

Horelli, L., & Sadoway, D. (2014). Community informatics in cities: New catalysts for urban change. *Journal of Community Informatics 10*(3), 5.

Katapally, T. R., Abonyi, S., Episkenew, J. A., Ramsden, V., Karunanayake, C., Kirychuk, S., . . . Pahwa, P. (2016). Catalyzing action on first nations respiratory health using community-based participatory research: Integrated knowledge translation through strategic symposia. *Engaged Scholar Journal: Community-Engaged Research, Teaching, and Learning, 2*(1), 57–70.

Kerr, A., Cunningham-Burley, S., & Amos, A. (1998). The new genetics and health: mobilizing lay expertise. *Public Understanding of Science, 7*(1), 41–60.

Kirk, P., & Shutte, A. M. (2004). Community leadership development. *Community Development Journal, 39*(3), 234–251.

Kitchin, R. (2014). The real-time city? Big data and smart urbanism. *GeoJournal, 79*(1), 1–14.

Longo, J., Kuras, E., Smith, H., Hondula, D. M., & Johnston, E. (2017). Technology use, exposure to natural hazards, and being digitally invisible: Implications for policy analytics. *Policy & Internet, 9*(1), 76–108.

Macqueen-Smith, F., Muhajarine, N., & Delanoy, S. (2015). Knowledge translation strategies in community-based research: Our decision-maker-based approach. In B. Jeffery, I. M. Findlay, D. Martz, & L. Clark (Eds.), *Journeys in community-based research* (pp. 149–161). University of Regina Press.

Matheus, R., Janssen, M., & Maheshwari, D. (2020). Data science empowering the public: Data-driven dashboards for transparent and accountable decision-making in smart cities. *Government Information Quarterly*, 101284.

McWhirter, R. E., Critchley, C. R., Nicol, D., Chalmers, D., Whitton, T., Otlowski, M., Burgess, M., & Dickinson, J. L. (2014). Community engagement for big epidemiology: Deliberative democracy as a tool. *Journal of Personalized Medicine, 4*(4), 459–474.

Michael, M., & Lupton, D. (2016). Toward a manifesto for the 'public understanding of big data'. *Public Understanding of Science, 25*(1), 104–116.

Newman, D. G. (2019). *Revisiting the duty to consult Aboriginal peoples*. Purich Publishing.

O'Neil, C. (2016). *Weapons of math destruction: How Big Data increases inequality and threatens democracy*. Broadway Books.

Pielstick, C. D. (2000). Formal vs. informal leading: A comparative analysis. *Journal of Leadership Studies, 7*(3), 99–114.

Robinson, L., Cotten, S. R., Ono, H., Quan-Haase, A., Mesch, G., Chen, W., & Stern, M. J. (2015). Digital inequalities and why they matter. *Information, Communication & Society, 18*(5), 569–582.

Saldaña, J. (2014). Coding and analysis strategies. In P. Leavy (Ed.), *The Oxford handbook of qualitative research* (pp. 581–605). Oxford University Press.

Schintler, L. A., & Kulkarni, R. (2014). Big data for policy analysis: The good, the bad, and the ugly. *Review of Policy Research, 31*(4), 343–348.

Smith, G. J., Bennett Moses, L., & Chan, J. (2017). The challenges of doing criminology in the big data era: Towards a digital and data-driven approach. *The British Journal of Criminology, 57*(2), 259–274.

Verhelst, H. M., Stannat, A. W., & Mecacci, G. (2020). Machine learning against terrorism: How big data collection and analysis influences the privacy-security dilemma. *Science and Engineering Ethics*, 1–10.

13

ANALYSIS OF THE PRINCIPLED AI FRAMEWORK'S CONSTRAINTS IN BECOMING A METHODOLOGICAL REFERENCE FOR TRUSTWORTHY AI DESIGN

Daniel Varona and Juan Luis Suárez

Introduction

The approaches that seek to solve social problems rooted in the use of technology, specifically in the use of artificial intelligence through its machine learning core, are as dissimilar as the problems that they try to solve (Varona, 2018; Varona, Suarez, & Lizama-Mue, 2020). They also delineate an area of research that is increasingly attracting interest from the academic and professional communities. In a short period of time, the problems have evolved through different stages, such as issues of bias (Mehrabi, Morstatter, Saxena, Lerman, & Galstyan, 2019), fairness (Mehrabi et al., 2019; Sahil & Rubin, 2018; Trewin, 2018), and principled artificial intelligence (AI) (Fjeld, Achten, Hilligoss, Nagy, & Srikumar, 2020; Mittelstadt, 2019), to mention the latest. The latter approach seeks to explore the feasibility of using international human rights law as the basis for developing what is denominated "trustworthy AI", recognizing that the variables associated with most social problems stemming from the use of artificial intelligence and machine learning are reflected in the aforementioned corpus of law.

So far, the principled AI approach, according to Fjeld et al. (2020), includes 35 documents published between 2016 and the last quarter of 2019. The authors added five other documents published in the first half of 2020 which share the same scope. All together, the principled AI international framework gathers authors and signatories such as government entities (15: 37.5%), inter-government entities (3: 7.5%), multistakeholders (8: 20%), civil society (5: 12.5%), private sector (8: 20%), and church (1: 2.5%). The documents included in the principled AI international framework can be categorized as action plan (1: 2.5%), commitment (1: 2.5%), considerations (2: 5%), general recommendations (1: 2.5%), guidelines for developers (1: 2.5%), policy principles (12: 30%), policy usage (1: 2.5%), principles (15: 37.5%), principles and recommendations (1: 2.5%), recommendations (4: 10%), and standardization recommendations (1: 2.5%). The selection criteria were mainly directed by gathering regulatory initiatives ruling the design and use of AI solutions at the country, region, and global levels whose authors

DOI: 10.4324/9781003024583-15

have actual agency for it. Appendix I lists the documents included in the analyzed corpus for principled AI.

The principled AI framework described in the previous paragraph seeks to set the basis for trustworthy AI in form of a public policy framework; however – as the results in this chapter show – it must still mature to also become a methodology framework adopted by artificial intelligence developers. In the other hand, the current lack of international standards or any other auditing mechanism containing references to the framed AI principles to be used in the development of artificial intelligence solutions suggests that there exist certain difficulties in assimilating the principles proposed within the referenced framework and its adjustment into a useful methodological tool for the design of such AI solutions.

The objective of this chapter is to identify some of the causes that hinder the construction of a methodological tool based on the public policy framework of principled AI. To achieve this, we analyze the set of documents that constitute the international framework of public policies for principled AI, integrating holistic and computer techniques into a design thinking approach that helps us deconstruct the problem.

In this chapter, we adapted a six-step methodology for data science projects proposed by Lizama-Mué in (Lizama-Mue & Suarez s.f.) that involve: (1) problem study, (2) data collection, (3) data preparation, (4) modeling, (5) test and evaluation, and (6) communication. The method has been successfully applied in other research projects like (Suarez & Lizama-Mue, 2020; Monroig Vives, 2017; Segarra, 2018) and follows an approach to problem solving similar to the design thinking methodology, which is what we are aiming for in this chapter due to the characteristics of the data being processed.

This research also aligns with this volume's efforts to highlight the interdisciplinarity needed to tackle social problems arising from the use of technology, in particular the expansion of machine learning to many personal and social domains. In addition, the study uses holistic techniques complementing other computational techniques while identifying difficulties the current AI international regulatory framework based on the International Human Rights Law is facing to become a methodological tool for a trustworthy AI-aligned design.

Method

In order to identify the theoretical-methodological elements that may become difficulties in the construction of a mechanism that facilitates a fairness-aligned design for artificial intelligence, better defined as trustworthy AI based on the principled AI international framework determined by the studied corpus, we first established clusters taking into consideration datapoints like year, month, country, and city of publication; type of author; and type of document, which help us support other analyses exhibited in the "Results and Discussion" section; then we used the datapoints ITPractitionersAuthorDistribution and PolicyMakersAuthorDistribution to assess the balance in the background distribution among authors in IT and related sciences and non-IT authors.

The executed analytical methods included n-gram extraction, weighting word combinations while examining those with more value for the text based on their frequency, first over the documents to have a global view of the narrative used along the corpus; second over the principles and guidelines sections to narrow the analysis to the proposed principles and suggested methods for adapting the principles; and third on the principles' declarations, seeking the variables used to describe trustworthy AI that were absent up to that point in the examined documentation.

Then we applied lexical diversity analytics to the full corpus. This is a practical technique to evaluate the closeness of different body texts and speeches regarding their content when different language structures are exploited. We did so with the intent to find patterns of ideas used by the different types of authors and in different types of documents that can further support the operationalization of variables in the text the AI designers need to comply with when the principled AI international framework becomes a methodological reference for AI design. Then verb extraction from both the principles and guidelines sections was executed to identify the verb taxonomy and group the suggested actions along the corpus. And last, topic modeling was performed over the principles' declarations, helping us to explore the apparent disconnection between the ideas behind the principles' declarations with the remaining text body on the corpus. The analyzed documents were gathered from each author's website in PDF format, then converted to plain text to facilitate data processing.

The data was prepared using Python (Oliphant, 2007; Python Software Fundation, s.f.), a generic modern computing language widely used for text analytics. Python's development environment is enriched with libraries like Gensim (Rehurek & Sojka, 2010), which we used for topic modeling; SciPy (Virtanen et al., 2020) tools including Pandas (McKinney, 2010), used for structuring the data; Matplotlib (Hunter, 2007), used for data visualization; IPython (Pérez & Granger, 2007), used for interactive computing and programming; and NLTK (Loper & Edward., 2009), used for natural language processing. The entire corpus was filtered removing stop words like prepositions, articles, and pronouns, among others, and repeated headings, footers, and margin notes. Thus, we were able to work with a consolidated and semantically robust corpus.

Using NLTK, the corpus was analyzed searching for n-grams that helped to describe from a macro perspective the content of the documents in a primary stage and then to narrow the scope of the analysis into smaller sections, like the principles and the guidelines, which were manually extracted from the documents and stored separately. Also, the verbs from the principles and guidelines sections were extracted and analyzed in order to review the taxonomy of the proposed actions along the corpus. We extracted the parts of speech that matched with verbs, grouped them using the lexeme similarity criteria, and added the size of the lexeme to the lemma.[1]

Most of the modeling was done in topic extraction. In that regard, we applied the latent Dirichlet allocation (LDA), Gensim's implementation (Blei, Ng, & Jordan, 2003), to detect topics among the principles' declarations. LDA is a generative probabilistic model in which each document is considered as a finite mix over an underlying set of topics. Each topic is represented as a set of words and their probability, which means that we were able to rank the topics on the corpus and the keywords in each topic. As mentioned before, doing the topic extraction helped to corroborate some inferences resultant from previous parts of the analysis.

As for the test and evaluation, we centered our verification efforts on the topic extraction part of the analysis due to being, among the techniques used in the study, the one with an additional intrinsic uncertainty. If not conducted properly, the outcome of the topic extraction could lead to misleading conclusions. One of the most important issues related to topic modeling with LDA is to know the optimal number of topics (k) that should be examined. To overcome those issues, we built different LDA models with variable values of k, computed the coherence for each topic, and selected the model with the highest coherence value. Consequently, the best results were found with ten topics and ten keywords per topic, presented in the "Results and Discussion" section.

The authors want to note that applying the mentioned natural language processing (NLP) techniques allowed us to learn a set of specific traits from the texts, detailed in the "Results and Discussion" section, that otherwise would be more difficult and time consuming to identify using a classical/traditional approach. Although neither the amount of analyzed documents nor their length demanded complex NLP procedures, we were able to take advantage of the simpler methods within the NLP domain for text processing.

Results and discussion

As mentioned in the introduction, there are currently numerous efforts by several entities – governments, non-governmental agencies, private sector, and so on – to achieve a fairer artificial intelligence. In this chapter, we focus on the efforts whose main emphasis seeks to standardize the responsible design and subsequent proper use of artificial intelligence.

In the authors' opinion, trustworthy AI is an emerging research interest whose starting point can be located around the last quarter of 2016 and rapidly reaches maturity just two years later, in 2018, likely due to the intensity of the geopolitical interests of several nations around AI (Suarez, 2018). In this respect, 2018 and 2019 are the years exhibiting a peak of publications of the documents forming the analyzed regulatory framework for principled AI, with an average of 15.5 documents each.

When exploring the most involved actors in producing or as signatories of these documents included in the regulatory international framework for principled AI, the United States occupies a clear first position among countries with the highest involvement (27.5%), followed by China (12.5%) and France (10%). The three of them can be related to half of the documents analyzed in this study. Figure 13.1a shows more information about the origin and authorship of the documents. The left wing of Figure 13.1a exhibits the distribution of documents in the analyzed corpus attending to their type, while the right wing displays the document distribution attending to their author type.

In Figure 13.1a, it can be noted that in the United States, China, and France, the documents are produced mainly by authors listed as multistakeholders and government entities, to reuse the catalogue proposed in Fjeld et al. (2020). There is a greater representation of the private sector in the United States when compared with the remaining countries. The fact that governments are active entities in the production of these documents shows their commitment to solving the ethical and social problems that the current degree of penetration of artificial intelligence in almost every aspect of daily life entails. The origins of these problems have been located in the use of artificial intelligence and in the early stages of its design, according to the themes highlighted by most of the principles proposed in the corpus. This is coherent with similar findings from previous studies (Varona, 2018; Varona et al., 2020).

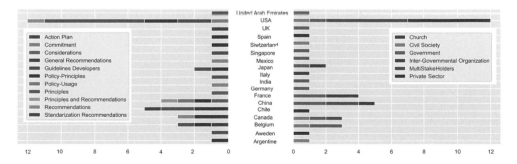

Figure 13.1a   Document and author type distribution per country

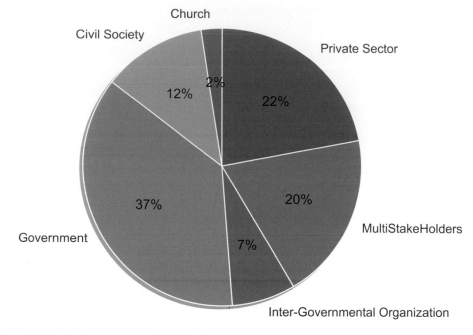

Figure 13.1b   Author type general distribution

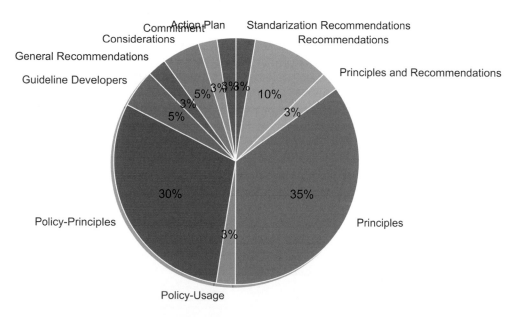

Figure 13.1c   Document type general distribution

The authors recognize that the list of countries presented in Figure 13.1a represents developed countries with high technological drive; we believe it is necessary to stress that social problems as result of the use of technology are problems that transcend the digital gap between developed and developing countries. Hence, although the provisions of the studied documents should be considered equally valuable for and by all countries, it would be important to have a larger and more equitable presence of countries from different parts of the world so that a diversity of ethical and social problems can be studied in connection with the use of AI in specific contexts.

Figure 13.1b synthesizes the different types of documents. The leading role of governments in authoring the regulatory frameworks for the design and use of artificial intelligence becomes clear throughout the corpus. This government-type author has authorship in more than a third (37.5%) of the documents, followed by multistakeholders and private-sector type authors, with 20% each. In contrast, the values exhibited by the civil society author type denote the need for greater activism on their part, as these organizations would provide important input from many different stakeholders affected by the decisions made by using artificial intelligence systems.

The presence of intergovernmental organization and church type authors denotes that the efforts to devise a regulatory framework transcend geographical borders while connecting different entities, places, and people with a common idea which is then adapted to the particularities of each place.

When analyzing the types into which the documents can be classified according to their purpose, Figure 13.1c shows predominantly those whose objective is to propose principles (35%), and policy principles (30%), which, together with the recommendation-type documents (10%), represent 75% of the corpus.

It should be clarified that the "Action Plan" document type reflects the document titled "AI for Europe" authors' criteria, which presents it as an action plan; however, its scope is limited to recommending principles for the design and use of artificial intelligence and its future implementation into a mechanism in service of designers and consumers. The same occurs for the document typified as "Guidelines Developers".

Regarding the ratio of authors according to their specialization in technical or non-technical backgrounds, we believe it is relevant to recommend, as part of the set of good practices during the documentation future regulatory/standardization documents like the ones being analyzed, including education background and the empirical experience of contributors. In most cases, the analyzed documents lack data related to their authors' training. In other cases, it is stated that prior to their approval that documents were subject to consultation, without going into further details. Only seven documents vaguely declare information related to their authors' background. Based on this information, it can be said that among the documents produced by the private sector and multistakeholders (universities, organizations responsible for methodological standardization, etc.), there is a larger presence of authors with technical training. The opposite occurs for those documents authored by government organizations.

Registering the authors' background information for the documents would certainly help improve our understanding of the difficulties these documents face when they are used to establish a practical tool that designers and consumers of AI can use. We also wanted to stress the need for both regulators (policy makers) and regulated (developers and consumers) to collaborate in establishing a common language that would help the transfers of information and knowledge across domains.

A general analysis of the documents in the corpus is presented in the following.

• Analysis of documents as a whole

A total of 40 documents addressing principled AI with a mean length of 10,246 words were analyzed. In addition, the space devoted to the enunciation and description of the principles proposed in these documents exhibits an average length of 359 words, while for guidelines to help implement these principles, the average length was of 136 words. This represents a relative average length of 0.0350 and 0.0133 units, respectively. That is surprising, given that the portion of the documents dedicated to achieving their goals, which is the proposal of principles and guidelines/recommendations for implementing them, is limited to a significantly small share of the text body.

Differences of relative length for the distinct parts of the body texts evidence that more efforts are dedicated to defining context and justifying the need for principles in most documents than to fully addressing the principles and explaining their implementation. Hence, it can be said that the analyzed documents are more tuned in to providing a description of the problem they hope to solve than to deepening the solution they are supposed to outline.

The corpus was also tested to assess its lexical diversity on each document. This analysis did not yield unforeseen patterns. In general, the documents exhibit low values of the lexical diversity metric, with 0.76 the maximum value achieved, which is also a peak within the dataset. The mean value obtained by the documents in the corpus was 0.38, with a standard deviation of 0.17 units. The pattern that was identified shows that lexical diversity values are inversely proportional to the length of the corresponding document. In that sense, these results could denote a saturated language using certain discursive currents across the corpus, but it could also mean a high specialization in a specific area of argumentation, if possible, aligned with the purpose of the documents, which we feel more inclined to believe after reading the texts.

In order to explore the corpus' content beyond the metadata, we present the analysis of the language used. Table 13.1 shows the ten most used n-grams in the corpus.

As expected, the top five positions of the unigrams frame the context of the texts' argument. Interestingly, the term "human" occupies position seven in the same column; perhaps this demonstrates the human approach that the regulatory framework intended to be defined by these documents. More details on this specific aspect are provided in the following. Another interesting finding to highlight is that the scope of the regulatory framework delimited by the documents in the corpus can be distinguished in positions eight "use", nine "development", and ten "technology". It should be stated that the table presented is an excerpt from a larger analysis, where the unigram terms that interest us, "ethics" and "ethical", are ranked in the 13th and 25th positions, respectively, with relative frequencies of 0.30 and 0.23.

If examined closely, it can be seen in the bigrams column how the unigrams gain context; consequently, the focus on "human" and "use" takes on a new nuance in human rights and the use of artificial intelligence. Another element suggested through the bigrams is that that focus will be influenced by an ethical approach to autonomous or intelligent systems (row 9), with special consideration to personal data (row 10). The authors believe it is worth mentioning that from the extended analysis of the 50 most relevant N-grams, in the bigrams column, terms like "data protection" at position 25 and "trustworthy ai", in position 38, add support to the previous statement about the corpus' ethical approach to artificial and intelligent systems through how they handle personal data.

It can also be noted from the trigrams that the effort to achieve national strategies for an ethically aligned design is orchestrated in the context of artificial intelligence, with support in rows 2, 4, 5, 7, and 8 from Table 13.1. The previous idea gains strength by including trigrams like "ethically aligned design" (row 23), "ethical matters raised" (row 26), "matters raised algorithms" (row 27), and "intelligent systems law" (row 28), as well as the terms "humans keep

Table 13.1 Ten most frequently used n-grams across all documents

	Unigrams	Absolute freq.	Relative freq.	Bigrams	Absolute freq.	Relative freq.	Trigrams	Absolute freq.	Relative freq.
1	ai	7476	1.94	artificial intelligence	1693	0.44	autonomous intelligent systems	416	0.11
2	data	4156	1.08	ai systems	653	0.17	ieee global initiative	351	0.09
3	systems	2502	0.65	machine learning	603	0.16	ethics autonomous intelligent	318	0.08
4	intelligence	2011	0.52	intelligent systems	446	0.12	global initiative ethics	314	0.08
5	artificial	1798	0.47	autonomous intelligent	429	0.11	initiative ethics autonomous	314	0.08
6	research	1728	0.45	human rights	368	0.10	algorithms artificial intelligence	126	0.03
7	human	1670	0.43	use ai	326	0.08	strategy artificial intelligence	112	0.03
8	use	1595	0.41	computer science	321	0.08	national strategy artificial	111	0.03
9	development	1515	0.39	ethics autonomous	319	0.08	discussion paper national	109	0.03
10	technology	1506	0.39	personal data	298	0.08	paper national design	109	0.03

upper" (row 29), "keep upper hand" (row 29), and "upper hand ethically" (row 30) from the extended analysis.

Having presented an analysis of the terms in which the documents from the corpus are presented and considering the small relative length dedicated to the approach of principles for a trustworthy AI, we now turn to focus the analysis specifically on the principles section and evaluate its correspondence with the rest of the document.

• Analysis of proposed principles

Table 13.2 shows the results of the ten most frequent n-grams in the section dedicated to the declaration and argumentation of the principles proposed by each document in the corpus.

When we delimit the analysis to the proposed principles argumentation section, as can be seen in Table 13.2, the context in which the object of argument is demarcated remains the same, which is in complete consistency with the rest of the sections of the documents, as expected. However, verbs such as "must" in row 4 and "ensure" in row 8 arise that convey some subjectivity to the principles. We resume this idea by presenting an analysis of the verbs used in the principle's descriptions.

Table 13.2 Ten most frequently used n–grams across principles

Unigrams	Absolute freq.	Relative freq.	Bigrams	Absolute freq.	Relative freq.	Trigrams	Absolute freq.	Relative freq.
1 ai	532	3.91	ai systems	111	0.82	artificial intelligent systems	11	0.08
2 data	208	1.53	artificial intelligence	59	0.43	aida driven decisions	9	0.07
3 systems	154	1.13	use ai	25	0.18	context consistent state	8	0.06
4 must	131	0.96	ai system	24	0.18	consistent state art	8	0.06
5 use	112	0.82	personal data	18	0.13	ai systems must	8	0.06
6 human	97	0.71	ai technologies	18	0.13	states parties present	8	0.06
7 development	94	0.69	ai must	18	0.13	parties present covenant	8	0.06
8 ensure	92	0.68	ai development	18	0.13	ai system lifecycle	6	0.04
9 government	82	0.60	ai research	17	0.12	appropriate context consistent	6	0.04
10 people	74	0.54	machine learning	16	0.12	present covenant recognize	6	0.04

The bigram "ais must" in row 7 supports the idea mentioned in the previous paragraph on subjectivity associated with the skills that should be attributed to the design and consumption of artificial intelligence systems. Other bigrams strengthen the context of the principles, recognizing their range of action from the academy (row 8), and industry (row 9), as well as the emphasis on personal data (row 5). The column that exhibits the trigrams in Table 13.2 provides no new or relevant information rather than highlighting the intrinsic subjectivity in proposals such as "ai systems must" (row 5) and recognizing the work throughout the life cycle of artificial intelligence systems (row 8).

Interestingly, unigrams such as "rights", "privacy", "security", "transparency", and "fairness" exhibit a relative frequency of 0.40, 0.39, 0.30, 0.26, and 0.25 units respectively, occupying more distant positions within the extended analysis (50 n-grams). They are historically among the terms that describe the ethical dilemmas rooted in the use of artificial intelligence solutions. The same goes for trigrams "standards best practices", "privacy data protection", "equality diversity fairness", "diversity fairness social", and "fairness social justice", with relative frequencies that hold values of 0.04 units for the first and 0.02 for the rest.

At this point, the authors are convinced that, although it appears that there is a common agreement among the involved actors on which issues need work to achieve a trustworthy AI, they address those issues differently. The absence of a common criterion could, among other difficulties, affect the definition of a methodological mechanism for software developers. Pursuing proof of whether such agreement over the fundamental issues, expressed in the form of principles, really exists, and despite the apparent disconnection with their description, we narrowed the analysis to the principle statements.

Table 13.3 shows the most common ten n–grams used in the enunciations of the principles proposed in each document across the corpus. Note that the description of the principles is

Table 13.3 Ten most frequently used n-grams across the principles' declarations

Unigrams	Absolute freq.	Relative freq.	Bigrams	Absolute freq.	Relative freq.	Trigrams	Absolute freq.	Relative freq.
1 ai	57	4.29	ai systems	9	0.68	ai systems deployed	3	0.23
2 principle	32	241	artificial intelligence	9	0.68	inclusive growth sustainable	2	0.15
3 privacy	20	150	ensure bot	5	0.38	growth sustainable development	2	0.15
4 data	19	143	non discrimination	4	0.30	sustainable development well	2	0.15
5 transparency	18	1.35	accountability transparency	4	0.30	development well human	2	0.15
6 fairness	16	1.20	u government	4	0.30	values fairness transparency	2	0.15
7 human	16	1.20	principle respect	3	0.23	fairness transparency explainability	2	0.15
8 rights	15	1.13	sustainable development	3	0.23	transparency explainability robustness	2	0.15
9 ensure	15	1.13	transparency explainability	3	0.23	explainability robustness security	2	0.15
10 systems	15	1.13	privacy security	3	0.23	robustness security safety	2	0.15

excluded from the analysis. As can be seen in the table, the n-grams change completely compared to Table 13.2.

The unigrams present in the principle declarations include variables like "privacy", "transparency", and "fairness", while bigrams include "non discrimination", "accountability transparency", "transparency explainability", and "privacy security". Last up, trigrams narrow the idea of inclusive growth and sustainable development with human values, among which "robustness" is added to those already mentioned. It seems that in this case, the triad is more intertwined. In the extended analysis (50 most frequently used n-grams), it can be noted how the variables related to the context and scope of the corpus are pushed to more distant positions on the list in favor of those variables linked to the objectives the proposed principles seek to achieve.

When comparing Tables 13.2 and 13.3, the disconnection between the principle declarations and their descriptions becomes clear. This is a common problem among the analyzed documents, and it could be an element that makes it difficult to build a standardization mechanism that serves as a methodological reference in the design of trustworthy AI. The description of the proposed principles has a more direct link to the documents in general than with its statement, whereas a more logical link between these two parts should be established through the statements of principle in a "justification-enunciation-argumentation" outline.

The general overview of the documents referenced their focus on humans and human rights as the agreed-upon basis for principled AI, while the scope of the documents mainly encompasses the use and development of technologies from an ethical perspective, with a human rights-based foundation. In general, the documents seek to support the concept of trustworthy AI from variables such as data protection and, all together, to arrive at the conception of an artificial intelligence ethically aligned design.

It is not until the analysis is narrowed to the principle statements that the variables associated with trustworthy AI are extended with terms such as privacy, transparency, fairness, non-discrimination, accountability, explainability, and security. This denotes that the value of principles lies in their statements in addition to pointing to the existing disconnection of the principle statements with their description and with the remaining body text.

In an attempt to arrange a "justification-enunciation-argumentation" outline, the authors point to the need to operationalize the variables involved with the idea behind trustworthy AI. Our hypothesis is that having the network of concepts coexist with the trustworthy AI concept can influence a common understanding of it as the object of study and therefore impact the effectiveness and efficiency of the efforts dedicated to its design. We are motivated by the premise that understanding a problem well makes up 50% of its solution.

A section that also has been reserved a place, although small, in most documents is dedicated to proposing a set of guidelines and recommendations supporting principle implementation. The following section shows an analysis of the guidelines and their alignment with the principles.

- Analysis of guidelines to implement the principles

When considering the guidelines as the set of actions projected to support the implementation of the principles, they are expected to represent concrete actions attached to construction like taxonomies such as applying and creating. In this regard, it is curious that verbs with a presence among the 50 n-grams most frequently used are "consider", with a relative frequency of 0.77 units; "ensure", with 0.47; and "must", with 0.44. It should be clarified that the verbs "use", "design", and "research" are also within this set of n-grams but just exercising an explanatory function, for example, in sentences such as: ". . . operator organizations use . . ."; ". . . ai design . . ."; and ". . . ai research . . .", to give some of examples also present among the bigrams and trigrams identified as the 50 most frequent.

In an effort to expand upon the actions proposed for the implementation of the principles, the authors extracted the verbs and submitted them to a lemmatizing process to consolidate them into a summarized list that helps in better understanding the skills behind the proposed actions. The summarized list consists of 30 verbs. It can be declared that while there are verbs associated with taxonomies such as apply (17.2%) and create (14.8%), which represent approximately one-third of the list, the set of verbs mostly includes actions commonly related to other taxonomies, such as understand (20.6%), analyze (32.1%), and evaluate (15.3%).

That second group of taxonomies encompasses a set of skills that could be perceived as passive skills in a practical context such as software design, particularly when designing artificial intelligence solutions. The authors identify this inclination for passive skills in the language used to describe the proposed actions for the implementation of the principles as another element elevating the difficulties for principle assimilation by AI designers. Consequently, this could prevent the framework from becoming a methodological reference during the AI project lifecycle. At the same time, we understand that this inclination can respond to an interest in maintaining the proposal as a general framework that can then be adapted to each context as needed, safeguarding its global character.

The same is true when performing this analysis on the principles, where there is also an inclination toward verbs representing passive abilities such as the aforementioned. This may be normal given the practical context in which the actions within the corpus are framed. A balance between effectiveness and generality of the proposals based on the cost and benefit linked to the use of certain language remains to be achieved in these types of documents.

- Principle-related topics analysis

Topic extraction is used, in this case, to triangulate some of the observations presented earlier. The 10 most represented topics in the text are listed in the following; it should be clarified that the topics are extracted based on the sections dedicated to principle declaration only:[2]

Topic 1.   "system"(0.000) + "ai"(0.000) + "right"(0.000) + "must"(0.000) + "technology"(0.000) + "shall"(0.000) + "human"(0.000) + "people"(0.000) + "research"(0.000) + "decision"(0.000)

Topic 2.   "agency"(0.036) + "assessment"(0.017) + "even"(0.017) + "system"(0.017) + "accountability"(0.016) + "obligation"(0.015) + "automate"(0.015) + "assess"(0.014) + "individual"(0.013) + "decision"(0.013)

Topic 3.   "system"(0.029) + "ai"(0.014) + "value"(0.013) + "human"(0.010) + "rapidly"(0.009) + "automation"(0.009) + "grow"(0.009) + "power"(0.008) + "people"(0.008) + "share"(0.008)

Topic 4.   "right"(0.064) + "shall"(0.043) + "law"(0.017) + "freedom"(0.013) + "education"(0.012) + "protection"(0.011) + "public"(0.011) + "include"(0.008) + "religion"(0.008) + "family"(0.008)

Topic 5.   "wide"(0.020) + "solution"(0.017) + "definition"(0.014) + "seek"(0.012) + "practice"(0.012) + "way"(0.009) + "dialogue"(0.008) + "algorithm"(0.008) + "explore"(0.008) + "research"(0.007)

Topic 6.   "remedy"(0.009) + "diversity"(0.004) + "promote"(0.004) + "inclusion"(0.004) + "effective"(0.003) + "equality"(0.011) + "non"(0.002) + "discrimination"(0.001) + "right"(0.000) + "system"(0.000)

Topic 7.   "must"(0.040) + "life"(0.013) + "development"(0.013) + "public"(0.012) + "ais"(0.012) + "people"(0.012) + "individual"(0.011) + "decision"(0.009) + "human"(0.009) + "personal"(0.009)

Topic 8.   "constraint"(0.004) + "educate"(0.004) + "oppose"(0.004) + "maximize"(0.004) + "openness"(0.004) + "scientist"(0.004) + "listen"(0.004) + "interpretable"(0.004) + "engineering"(0.004) + "socially"(0.001)

```
Topic 9.     "system"(0.028) + "ai"(0.026) + "datum"(0.020) +
"ensure"(0.012) + "human"(0.012) + "technology"(0.010) +
"design"(0.009) + "development"(0.007) + "must"(0.007) +
"people"(0.007)

Topic 10.     "government"(0.039) + "ai"(0.015) +
"public"(0.013) + "policy"(0.012) + "ensure"(0.011) +
"research"(0.011) + "sector"(0.010) + "must"(0.010) +
"recommend"(0.010) + "take"(0.010)
```

Among the topics listed previously, topic 9 is identified as the most relevant, since it is the most representative topic for the principles section for 25 documents, and it represents 62.5% of the documents in the corpus. The representativeness of topic 9 is followed by topic 10, which is dominant in 10% of the documents, and topic 2, dominant in 5%. In contrast, topic 1 does not exhibit any dominance in any of the documents in the corpus. The rest of the topics happened to dominate the distribution of representativeness in one document each.

It is interesting to see what these topics that have become dominant in the great majority of documents reflect: first, the objects of discourse – say "systems", "ai", and "technology", to name examples; second, the action field influenced by these objects – "human", "people", and "decision", among others; and third, the subjective methodological approach that we have already criticized in previous sections, expressed in terms such as "must", "ensure", and "assess", for example.

This supports the idea that there is a clear notion of the problem being addressed with the regulatory framework for AI on the basis of the variables that are affected, but the consensus on the methodological approach to be followed has yet to mature since all author types throughout the period and space covered by the analyzed documents face difficulties in providing a tool that can be used in practice, without intrinsic ambiguities embedded within the passive skills already argued by AI solution designers.

Finally, it is necessary to highlight the vague significance of the term "right" among the principles. The authors hoped that, while the proposed principles were based on an approach that seeks to use Human Rights International Law as a reference to achieve a trustworthy AI, the term would exhibit greater representation or at least a greater representation of the concepts that, in the context at hand – "privacy", "equity", and so on – constitute the term's coexistence network. However, the observed results are not consistent with that estimation.

At the time of this research, no International Standardization Office (ISO) standards were found, nor any published by the Institute of Electrical and Electronics Engineers (IEEE) standards association, although it is known that the latter institution is taking into consideration some of the documents of the corpus in the design of standards related to the subject at hand. Thus, a contrast with the terminology used in the standards could not be established.

Conclusions

The results demonstrate the digital gap between developed and developing countries where there exists an overrepresentation of the former and the need for more representation of the latter in harnessing the ethical and social problems with origins in the design and consumption of artificial intelligence.

The chapter identifies the need for policy makers and designers of AI solutions to join efforts while addressing trustworthy AI as a common goal and the need to record the authors' background to explore the use of language from a technical and a nontechnical perspective, studying the effects on the resulting guidelines for the assimilation of the principles.

The declaration and description of the proposed principles show a degree of subjectivity from the verbs used. This resulting ambiguity of action was reinforced when analyzing the guidelines for principle implementation, obstructing these guidelines' adoption as a methodological reference for AI design

The pursuit of trustworthy AI through the principled AI framework it is still a process in transformation before it can be properly used as a methodological reference by developers, and it is evident that further intermediate layers of interpretation towards principle adoption are needed as a methodological reference for the design of artificial intelligence solutions.

Notes

1 In English, for example, run, runs, ran, and running are forms of the same lexeme, with run as the lemma by which they are indexed. Lexeme, in this context, refers to the set of all the forms that have the same meaning, and lemma refers to the particular form that is chosen by convention to represent the lexeme.
2 The analysis of the topics for the documents containing the principles, the topics on the basis of the proposed guidelines for the implementation of the principles, and contrasts between them and the topics drawn from the section dedicated to the proposal of principles are exhibited in another publication; in order to maintain the focus of this chapter on the exploration of principles and in correspondence with the communication strategy of the research project.

References

Blei, D. M., Ng, A. Y., & Jordan, M. I. (2003). Latent Dirichlet allocation. *Journal of Machine Learning Research*, *3*(4–5), 993–1022.

Fjeld, J., Achten, N., Hilligoss, H., Nagy, A., & Srikumar, M. (2020). *Principled artificial intelligence: Mapping consensus in ethical and rights-based approaches to principles for AI*. Berkman Klein Center for Internet & Society.

Hunter, J. D. (2007). Matplotlib: A 2D graphics environment. *Computing in Science & Engineering*, *9*, 90–95. doi:10.1109/MCSE.2007.55

Lizama-Mue, Y., & Suarez, J. L. (s.f.). *Data science methodology for projects in digital humanities and social sciences*. Work in progress.

Loper, S. B., & Edward., E. K. (2009). *Natural language processing with Python*. O'Reilly Media.

McKinney, W. (2010). *Data structures for statistical computing in Python*. Proceedings of the 9th Python in Science Conference.

Mehrabi, N., Morstatter, F., Saxena, N., Lerman, K., & Galstyan, A. (2019). *A survey on bias and fairness in machine learning*. arXiv:1908.09635v2 [cs.LG]

Mittelstadt, B. (2019). *Principles alone cannot guarantee ethical AI*. Oxford Internet Institute, University of Oxford.

Monroig Vives, R. (2017). *Social networks, political discourse and polarization during the 2017 Catalan elections* (Master Thesis). Western University, London, Canada.

Oliphant, T. E. (2007). Python for scientific computing. *Computing in Science & Engineering*, *9*(3), 10–20.

Pérez, F., & Granger, B. E. (2007). IPython: A system for interactive scientific computing. *Computing in Science & Engineering*, *9*, 21–29. doi:10.1109/MCSE.2007.53

Python Software Foundation. (s.f.). *Python. (Python Org) Recuperado el February de 2020, de*. Retrieved from www.python.org

Rehurek, R., & Sojka, P. (2010). *Software framework for topic modelling with large corpora*. ELRA.

Sahil, V., & Rubin, J. (2018). *Fairness definitions explained*. ACM/IEEE International Workshop on Software Fairness. Gothenburg, Sweden.

Segarra, A. G. (2018). *A data-driven analysis of video game culture and the role of let's plays in YouTube* (Master Thesis). Western University, London, Canada.

Suarez, J. L. (2018, Julio-Agosto). La nacionalización de la estrategia en torno a la inteligencia artificial Estado, política y futuro. *Revista de Occidente*, 5–18, 446–447.

Suarez, J. L., & Lizama-Mue, Y. (2020). Victims of language: Language as a pre-condition of transitional justice in Colombia's peace agreement. En *Transitional justice in comparative perspective, preconditions for success* (pp. 97–127). Palgrave Macmillan.

Trewin, S. (2018). *AI fairness for people with disabilities: Point of view*. Cornell University. arXiv:1811.10670.

Varona, D. (2018, Julio-Agosto). La responsabilidad ética del diseñador de sistemas en inteligencia artificial. *Revista de occidente*, 104–114, 446–447.

Varona, D., Suarez, J. L., & Lizama-Mue, Y. (2020). Machine learning's limitations in avoiding automation of bias. *AI & Society*. https://doi.org/10.1007/s00146-020-00996-y

Virtanen, P., Gommers, R., Oliphan, T. E., et al. (2020). SciPy 1.0: Fundamental algorithms for scientific computing in Python. *Nature Methods*, *17*, 261–272. https://doi.org/10.1038/s41592-019-0686-2

Appendix
LIST OF DOCUMENTS INCLUDED IN THE ANALYZED CORPUS

Year	Author	Document Title
2016	Partnership on AI	Tenets
2016	U.S. National Science and Technology Council	Preparing for the Future of AI
2017	UNI Global Union	Top 10 Principles for Ethical AI
2017	Future of life	Asilomar AI Principles
2017	Tencent Institute	Six Principles of AI
2017	ITI	AI Policy Principles
2017	The French Data Protection Authority (CNIL)	How can humans keep the upper hand? The ethical matters raised by algorithms and artificial intelligence
2018	Council of Europe: European Commission for the Efficiency of Justice CEPEJ	European Ethical Charter on the Use of AI in Judicial Systems and their environment
2018	Amnesty International, AI Now	Toronto Declaration: Protecting the rights to equality and non-discrimination in machine learning systems
2018	T20: Think20	Future of work and education for the digital age
2018	The public voice coalition	Universal Guidelines for AI
2018	Access Now	Human Rights in the age of AI
2018	University of Montreal	Montreal Declaration for responsible AI
2018	Microsoft	Microsoft AI Principles
2018	Google	AI at Google: Our Principles
2018	Telefónica	AI Principles of Telefónica
2018	Microsoft	Responsible bots: 10 guidelines for developers of conversational AI
2018	Standards Administrations of China	White paper on AI Standardization
2018	Mission Assigned by the French Minister	For a Meaningful AI
2018	UK House of Lords	AI in the UK

(Continued)

215

Year	Author	Document Title
2018	Niti Aayog	National Strategy for AI
2018	British Embassy in Mexico City	Towards an AI Strategy in Mexico: Harnessing the AI Revolution
2018	German Federal Ministries of Education, Economic Affairs, and Labour and Social Affairs	AI Strategy
2018	Treasury Board of Canada Secretariat	Responsible Artificial Intelligence in the Government of Canada. Digital Disruption White Paper Series
2019	Organisation for Economic Co-operation and Development OECD	OECD Principles on AI
2019	G20	G20 Principles on AI
2019	IEEE Standard Association	Ethically Aligned Design
2019	New York Times	Seeking Ground Rules for AI
2019	Beijing Academy of AI	Beijing AI Principles
2019	AI Industry Alliance	AI Industry Code of Conduct
2019	Telia Company	Guiding Principles on trusted AI Ethics
2019	IA Latam	Declaration of the Ethical Principles for AI
2019	IBM	IBM Everyday Ethics for AI
2019	Smart Dubai	AI Principles and Ethics
2019	Monetary Authority of Singapore	Principles to promote FEAT AI in the Financial Sector
2019	Government of Japan, Cabinet Office, Council for Science, Technology, and Innovation	Social Principles of Human-Centered AI
2019	European High-Level Expert Group on AI	Ethics Guidelines for Trustworthy-AI
2019	Chinese National Governance Committee for AI	Governance Principles for a New Generation of AI
2019	IEEE Standard Association	IEC White Paper Artificial intelligence across industries
2020	Vatican	Rome Call for AI Ethics
2020	European Commission	AI for Europe

SECTION III

Case studies and research examples

14

SENSING CLOSE-RANGE PROXIMITY FOR STUDYING FACE-TO-FACE INTERACTION

Johann Schaible, Marcos Oliveira, Maria Zens,
and Mathieu Génois

Introduction

Face-to-face interaction is an archetype of interpersonal behavior and a building block for microsociology. As a fundamental human behavior, it shapes how we build and maintain our social identity while forming groups or segregating ourselves from others. This impacts virtually all aspects of people's lives (cf. "Social Interaction" and "Face-to-Face Interaction"). Studying face-to-face interaction is therefore important, however, at the same time, quite challenging. For example, self-assessments in surveys give people's perception of their activity that might be different from the actual one, resulting in a self-reporting bias. Similarly, manually observing face-to-face interactions in a large group and capturing all interactions is a) biased towards the observer, that is, the human encoding the interactions, and b) cumbersome and often unfeasible, if there are too many people to observe.

In today's digitized world, there are many opportunities for digitally "sensing" human behavior, including sensors for detecting interactions in situ – in a given (physical) space and environment – to focus on empirical evidence of face-to-face interactions between individuals. Mainly because of such new tracking devices providing fine-grained data on human behavior, the study of face-to-face interaction has advanced considerably in recent years. These devices apply different technologies, such as Bluetooth and radio-frequency identification (RFID), to capture proximity between humans in social occasions that is then interpreted as interaction between individuals. This non–intrusive data retrieval creates a unique opportunity to assess face-to-face interactions with a remarkable temporal granularity, allowing researchers to obtain data that can render a better understanding of the spatial and temporal dynamics of individual as well as group behavior (cf. "Close-Range Proximity Sensors"). Combined with individual-level information (e.g., sociodemographics), it also helps to untangle intricate social and psychological patterns in human behavior.

Such experimental studies of unmediated human interaction are the main contributions to social research with this new type of data. Current work has been done on linking (and theorizing the link between) microsociology to group behavior and on addressing substantive questions from the social sciences, for example, friendship, organization (hierarchies, formation of teams), social preference, and group formation, as well as inequality (cf. "Contribution of Sensor-Based Studies to the Social Sciences"). Furthermore, it allows for testing behavioral hypotheses like

DOI: 10.4324/9781003024583-17

homophily, attractiveness, or polarization or for analyzing how different social areas or settings (schools, hospitals, workplaces, events) are being structured through interaction and how they, in turn, shape behavior.

The main problem with sensor technology is that it is merely a proxy for human behavior. This bears some challenges, such as the alignment between the signal captured by the sensor and the social construct researchers want to measure (Müller, Fàbregues, Guenther, & Romano, 2019). For example, close-range proximity between two sensors is often interpreted as an interaction between the humans wearing these sensors, where it is rather a co-location of these individuals. A related challenge lies in the nature of the definition what a face-to-face interaction exactly is and to which extent sensors can measure it. Across current literature studying this and similar social constructs, the articles' authors use different wording, including *in-person contacts* or *person to person communication* (Malik, 2018), which rather creates confusion on what exactly sensors can and cannot be used for.

Therefore, the main contribution of this chapter is to comprehensively illustrate the ongoing work on sensor-based face-to-face interaction studies. The goal is to set a common understanding of the underlying social construct and to which extent sensors can be used to measure it, by providing

- an outline of the social construct *face-to-face interaction*,
- the alignment of this social construct to a physical entity that can be detected by sensors,
- an extensive overview which types of sensors are rather useful to measure which type of social construct, that is, face-to-face interaction or co-location,
- a review of existing research using sensors to study face-to-face interaction and related social constructs,
- a list of challenges researchers must be aware of when conducting sensor-based studies.

Constructs of interaction

Social interaction

Human interaction is a prerequisite, a means and an end to social relations, which are at the core of sociology. Therefore, interaction – be it as an explicit label or an implicit concept – is featured in a broad range of theories and approaches. Microsociology cannot be conceived without the notion of action (J. Turner, 1988) which is directed towards others or includes the relation to others in shaping the individual's behavior, values, opinions, or communication strategies. Even if personality is at the center of a research interest, the social dimension comes into perspective (R. Turner, 1988).

Interaction offers a link between the individual and the social spheres; that is, while (inter-)action produces social structure, (inter-)action is also the enactment of supraindividual properties and patterns, such as roles, rituals, or norms. Therefore, studies on social interaction allow for analyzing a) how people build and maintain ties via, for example, mechanisms of integration and separation, and b) self-definition and reproduction of groups and their boundaries. Simmel (1890) states that society emerges from interaction whereof the interaction between individuals is the most basic one. From a phenomenological point of view, it is argued that the intersubjectivity of alter and ego is rooted in day-to-day interaction (Schutz, 1932). In their work, Berger and Luckmann (1967) show how interaction makes for a shared perception of reality.

Interaction defines the relation between the interacting entities and is necessary for recognition (of the other) and formation (of the self). Mead (1934) pointed at this reciprocity and the expectation of the generalized other as a constitutive feature of human action. The entrench-ment of interaction in language is central not only for Mead and symbolic interactionism in his succession (Blumer, 1969) but also for ethnomethodology (Garfinkel, 1967) and the method of conversational analysis (Sacks, Schegloff, & Jefferson, 1978). This also applies to the much later and comprehensive account of deliberation processes in society, Habermas' "theory of commu-nicative action" (Habermas, 1984) which is a theory of interaction (Habermas, 2002).

More recently, interaction figures in "relational sociology" (Crossley, 2011) and the prolific area of network studies (Borgatti, Mehra, Brass, & Labianca, 2010) that build on the "inter" for analyzing the temporal development of relations, social centrality, paths of influence, attraction, and so on.

Face-to-face interaction

While interaction might be well theorized in sociology from many angles, this does not imply that face-to-face interaction is as frequently addressed. We can argue that face-to-face interac-tion is the most basic and ubiquitous form of interaction, even in today's digitized world. We can also assume that people mentioning interaction often refer to face-to-face interaction. Still, we cannot equate one with the other. Interaction is a much broader term and not confined to interpersonal encounters; face-to-face addresses the dynamics that occur between people in detail (Bargiela-Chiappini & Haugh, 2009; Duncan & Fiske, 1977; Goffman, 1967; Kendon, Harris, & Key, 1975; Turner, 2002). Face-to-face interaction more specifically refers to an action as being embedded in a situation and requests the co-presence – both in time and space – of more than one human actor. It is "the prototypical case of social interaction" (Berger & Luckmann, 1967) and, although technically mediated interaction has been gaining ground, remaining "still primal and primary" (Turner, 2002): humans interact with other humans face to face in their everyday life (Goffman, 1978).

With "On Face Work" in 1955, Erving Goffman started approaching the concept of face-to-face interaction, which was included in his book *Interaction Ritual* (Goffman, 1967) in 1967. "Face" is the public image of the self; with their "face work", individuals strive for status and position in social situations. Hence, interacting with others is strategic and entangled in presup-positions, expectations, rules, and rituals. Compliance with this "interaction order" is enacted in encounters; Goffman's emphasis is on talk and conversation in a spatio-temporal situation (Goffman, 1981). Therefore, face-to-face interaction is further defined by its focused nature (Goffman, 1961), meaning that co-location is not enough.

Empirical data on face-to-face interaction are mainly observational data (Duncan & Fiske, 1977) obtained in field research or experiments. Especially conversational analyses often use manually encoded audio and video recordings. However, the characteristics of face-to-face interaction – namely its focused nature, the communicative, spatial and temporal dimensions, the co-presence in person in a situation – impose physical limitations on such a data collection. This makes it difficult to get reliable, unbiased, and comparable data on interpersonal behavior by any means. Observational data might suffer from observation or coding biases and are inclined to be intrusive; self-reports (from interviews, questionnaires, surveys) entail their issues of memory and bias, which might be aggravated when it comes to the minutiae of face-to-face interaction.

Sensible proximity

In this situation, research could benefit from including proximity sensors to study face-to-face interaction. Like log data from online activities, sensor data are non-reactive and – comparatively –

non-intrusive and thereby minimize the Hawthorne effect. With sensors, it is possible to maintain the conceptual unity of the interaction while at the same time widening the measurement
in type, size, and scale. For instance, it is possible to better monitor multi-person interaction or
simultaneously occurring interactions in gatherings, which allows for analyzing groups, subgroups, or networks.

Broadly speaking, sensors measure some physical constructs, such as position or distance.
Researchers in the field of social sciences use sensors and relate such measurements of physical quantity to sociological constructs; for example, geographical location of smartphones can
be used for studying group dynamics and proximity between sensors for studying face-to-face
interactions.

As the technical overhead decreases with time, more and more researchers use sensors for
studying human behavior and interaction. However, relating the physical measurements of sensors to social constructs must be performed with high caution. Malik (2018) and Müller et al.
(2019) both provide an extensive and highly valuable overview of various sensor-based social
science studies on human interaction. They state that these studies have no clearly articulated
frames for the use of sensors analyzing networks, behavior, and/or interactions. For example,
many kinds of sensors are not precise enough to capture face-to-face interactions, for example,
Bluetooth; still they are used to measure this construct. In all studies, proximity between the
sensors is used and related to face-to-face interactions. However, it is important to distinguish
which sensors can be used to relate their physical measurement to face-to-face interaction and
which sensor measurements are encoding solely co-location of individuals.

Proxemics

According to Goffman (1967), studies on human interactions are not about the individuals
and their psychology but rather about the syntactical relations among the acts of different individuals. Face-to-face interactions occur in co-presence of other individuals verbally and non-
verbally (Goffman, 1967). Non-verbal behavior is a combination of facial expressions, gestures,
and body movements, whether intended or not (Mehrabian, 1968). Verbal, or speech-related,
behavior comprises the speech itself but also the speech rate and speaking time, as well as tone
and pitch of the voice. Therefore, while in a face-to-face interaction, individuals observe, that
is, see and/or hear, such behavioral aspects when interacting with others. This means, to have
a face-to-face interaction, a) the distance between individuals must be rather small, and b) the
visual confrontation between individuals must be provided.

Proxemics describe the effects how different space and density influence human behavior,
communication, and social interaction (Hall, 1963). For one, proxemics include the body
distance, that is, the distance between at least a pair of individuals. The spaces around an individual describe the distance of an individual to other individuals. These spaces are categorized
into four distinct zones: a) intimate space (up to 45 cm), b) personal space (up to 1.2 m),
c) social space (up to 3.6 m), and d) public space (up to 7.5 m) (Hall, 1963). Figure 14.1 (a)
shows the different spaces surrounding an individual. The personal space, that is, the region
imminently surrounding an individual, is rather reserved for close family members, very close
friends, and relationship partners, the latter also being part of the intimate space. The social
space is reserved for conversations with friends and/or associates or for group discussions. The
public space, on the contrary, is reserved for strangers or newly formed groups. Essentially, the
personal and social space define the area in which a face-to-face interaction is likely to happen, whereas the public distance defines an area for larger audiences, in which a face-to-face
interaction is less likely to happen (Hall, 1992). Second, the eyes are considered one principal

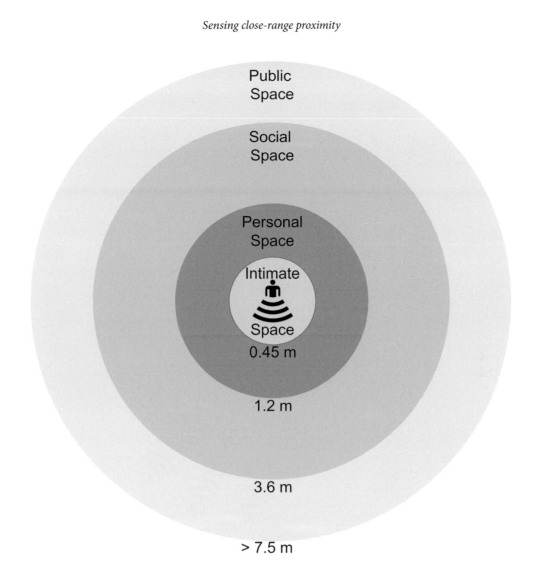

Figure 14.1 **Proxemics.** Distances surrounding an individual forming the interpersonal spaces. The curved solid lines indicate that the individual is looking in this direction. (a) Interpersonal spaces defined by proxemics, (b) examples of occurring face-to-face interactions, illustrated with solid lines (dotted lines mean "not a face-to-face interaction")

means by which an individual gathers information (Hall, 1963; Mehrabian, 1968). Gaze and gestures can encourage, punish, or establish dominance, a true non-verbal face-to-face interaction. This means if individuals are in a face-to-face interaction, they both must be at an angle towards each other, such that they can see the individual they are interacting with. In social interaction, this is defined as the individual's visual space (Hall, 1992). Figure 14.1b depicts examples where face-to-face interactions are happening (solid lines) and where they are not happening (dotted lines).

Proxemics help us to distinguish face-to-face interactions in social gatherings in a technical manner. Co-location is not sufficient: individuals must be at least within the social space and turned towards each other.

Figure 14.1   (Continued)

Sensing face-to-face interaction

Close-range proximity sensors

What is a sensor?

The term "sensor" refers broadly to a technological device that detects a physical, measurable signal. A thermometer, a camera, and a Geiger counter are sensors, designed and engineered to detect, respectively, heat, electromagnetic waves in the visible spectrum, and ionizing radiation. In the present context of face-to-face interactions, "sensor" refers more precisely to devices designed to detect and record interactions between individuals in the physical space.

By definition, a sensor *detects*, which means it returns a signal (from a simple binary present/absent cue to a full measure) if the event it is designed to detect is present. In other words, sensor data *do not need to be further coded* in order to extract the events from a data collection. As such, a camera, for example, is not a sensor for interactions, as it does not detect them. Video recordings of social context must be further coded (either by humans or automatic video analysis) to extract the interaction signal. We thus differentiate between *observational data*, produced by a global recording of a context that needs to be analyzed to detect and extract interactions, and *sensor data*, in which the interactions are by design detected and recorded as such, without the need for further extraction. In the present chapter, we focus solely on the latter.

An interaction is a social construct, not a physical one; therefore, sensors use proxy signals from which they infer the presence or absence of an interaction. For all setups that have been used in this context, the main criterion is always *proximity*. Indeed, an unmediated face–to–face interaction implies, by definition, some physical proximity between the individuals who are interacting.

A first family of sensors relies only on this criterion. As such, they are *co-location* sensors: they detect events when individuals are in the same physical location, that is, that the distance between them is less than a predefined threshold value. Different technologies are used to detect co-location: GPS tracking, which gives the location of individuals at any time and thus easily provides the interaction events; phone tracking, in which co-location is usually defined by two phones pinging the same cellular tower in the same time window; Wi-Fi tracking, similar to phone tracking but with Wi-Fi beacons; and Bluetooth detection, in which smartphones detect each other through the constant scanning of their surroundings for the presence of Bluetooth emitters.

Although proximity is necessary to have a face–to–face interaction, detecting it does not necessarily mean that an interaction occurred. A second class of sensors has thus been designed with added constraints on the simple proximity in the hope of narrowing down the detection of "true" *interactions*. The main criterion that has been implemented is the directionality of the interaction. The technology relies on electromagnetic signal detection similar to the Bluetooth setup but using frequencies that are blocked by liquids, such as the liquids within the human body. By having individuals wear sensors on their chest, one enhances the probability that the sensors can detect each other only if the individuals are facing each other. The technology generally uses RFID chips, but infrared beacons have also been used.

Choosing a sensor

The choice of a sensing platform always depends on the research question as well as the requirements for data collection. In particular, choosing a sensor means choosing a proxy for face–to–face interactions. The definition criteria are:

- What is the proximity threshold for interactions?
- Is co-location sufficient, or is directionality required?
- Are there other necessary criteria to define an interaction?

Aside from these, one must also consider the *practical criteria* of the data collection:

- Time resolution for the interaction recording.
- Deployment and management of the data collection system.
- Population sampling.
- Acceptability of the sensors.
- Privacy concerns.

Perfect setups that completely fit the "face–to–face interaction" construct do not exist. Therefore, a suitable approximation towards the research question and the data collection possibilities must be found. The usual tradeoff is between a) relying on an existing infrastructure (smartphones) but having less precise signal (co-location sensors) and b) having to develop, manage, and deploy a tailored setup in order to get information closer to the social construct (interaction sensors). Specifically noteworthy is the question of data privacy. It is a central one and can sometimes be a deciding factor in the choice of a sensor platform. However, whichever sensors are considered when designing a study, the researchers must follow the usual guidelines about informed consent, anonymity, and privacy, as it would be for any observational study in social sciences. In the following, both are described in more detail, as well as with respect to the aforementioned criteria. Figure 14.2 shows an overview of how Bluetooth as well as RFID and infrared sensors detect signals that are interpreted as interaction corresponding to the definition of proxemics. In Figure 14.2a, one can see that Bluetooth does not consider the direction individuals are facing,

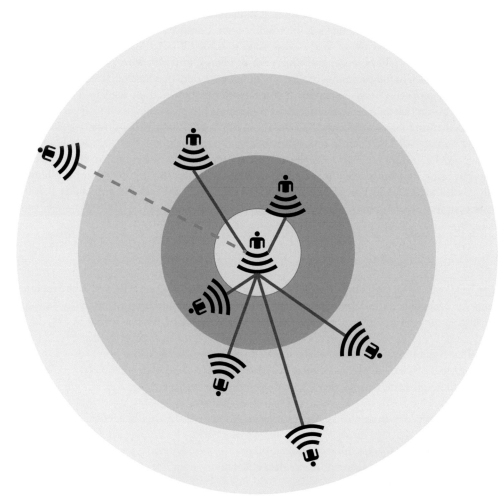

Figure 14.2 Bluetooth and RFID signal detection aligned to proxemics. Both sensors pick up different signals depending on the distances surrounding an individual and whether individuals are facing each other. The curved solid lines indicate that the individual is looking in this direction. Solid lines specify that an interaction is detected. Dotted lines mean no interaction. (a) Detected interactions using Bluetooth sensors, rather co-location; (b) detected interactions using RFID and IR sensors, rather face-to-face interaction

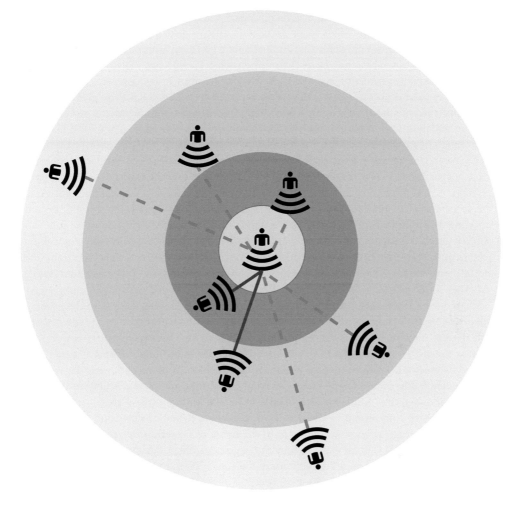

Figure 14.2 (Continued)

thereby detecting rather more "interactions", which thereby rather correspond to co-location. In (Figure 14.2b), one can observe that RFID and infrared take the individuals' line of sight into account, thereby detecting rather true interactions. However, as the transmission signal is rather low, it can happen that actual interactions within the social space are not detected. More detailed and highly valuable reviews on sensor-based interaction studies can be found in Huang, Kuo, Pannuto, and Dutta (2014), Müller et al. (2019), and Malik (2018).

Co-location sensors

The sole criterion for co-location sensors is detecting or calculating distance to other sensors, which defines "proximity" for the data collection. The most prominent sensors for co-location are GPS tracking, phone tracking, Wi-Fi tracking, or Bluetooth.

For Wi-Fi and phone tracking, the area of detection for beacons is around a few tens of meters. However, dense urban areas are much more precisely covered than rural or less connected areas, which can introduce a geographical bias in signal detection. These technologies were not designed to track individuals; their main purpose is solely signal transmission. As such, they often exhibit flickering or false detection. An example are cellular towers, which redirect signal to other towers nearby when they reach their full capacity. This gives a "false" location of some users. GPS tracking has detection errors as well. They range from a few meters to tens of meters, and proximity follows accordingly. On the contrary, all these systems have the great advantage of being pre-existing, meaning they are already built into smartphones or other smart wearables which are widely spread in the population. Provided that precision and geographical biases are not too much of a problem, and that the population sampling biases can be controlled or measured, they can give access to large-scale data about how individuals are co-located in a specific space at a specific time. This, however, results in another key limitation, the acceptability of these sensing platforms. In particular, regarding data privacy matters, a critical difference must be made between raw and co-location data. If using tracking methods such as GPS, the raw positioning data must be handled with much more attention than the final co-location data. The reason is that the raw data includes much more information about the behavior and whereabouts of participants, such that individuals can be recognized in the data. While the co-location data could in theory be shared following normal data privacy guidelines, the raw data could not.

Another setup for co-location sensing is Bluetooth. It has several advantages compared to the other co-location sensing platforms. As it uses peer detection, it does not have the coverage problems of Wi-Fi or phone tracking. Each individual carries a beacon in their smartphone, which detects the other individuals nearby, not having to rely on other infrastructure, such as cellular towers. Bluetooth uses radio waves and has a detection range of approximately 5–7 meters. This makes it relatively precise compared to other co-location platforms. However, it can be affected by the environment – walls, windows, obstacles, and so on (Müller et al., 2019). The detection range can, in theory, be refined using signal intensity (radio signal strength indicator, RSSI, which is measured by the sensor), but it proves difficult to calibrate (Huang et al., 2014). Furthermore, there exists a variability in the range of detection due to hardware differences (Huang et al., 2014). This explains why the largest example of data collection using Bluetooth, the Copenhagen Network Study (Stopczynski et al., 2014), gave identical smartphones to the studied population to tackle this issue.

Although such co-location sensing platforms are pre-existing, the software to collect and process the data still needs to be designed and implemented. GPS, Wi-Fi, and phone tracking rely on simple log data of the sensors. For Bluetooth, however, one needs to control the physical sensor and design a detection scheme. The detection system specifies the way two sensors communicate to ensure the detection of an interaction. It usually consists of setting cycles of sending/listening time windows. This is an important part of the setup, as it defines the temporal resolution of the interaction detection. The design also has an impact on the durability of the sensor through energy consumption: a detection program that drains the battery of a smartphones in a couple of hours is unpractical. One further critical aspect when using pre-existing smartphone sensors is the restrictions put in place by smartphone companies, essentially removing the possibility to access and control the needed sensor via self-developed applications. Maybe in the near future, the idea of using Bluetooth sensors to track social contacts in the case of epidemic spreading might give new opportunities to use this method in a broader way.

Interaction sensors

Historically, the first sensor specifically designed for tracking interactions was the sociometer (Choudhury & Pentland, 2003), which uses infrared (IR) to detect the presence of other sociometer sensors. IR detection depends on the line of sight between the transmitter-receiver pair. This means, if the sensors are attached to the front of individuals, they a) must face each other in close distance and b) must not have anything between the transmitter-receiver pair in order to produce a detectable signal. This setup was, however, not widely adopted in research (Malik, 2018). The later protractor sensor[1] uses the same technique, including measuring angles to detect interaction, as performed in (Montanari et al., 2018) based on the concept of proxemics.

Following the sociometer, several systems were designed, the most widely used being the SocioPatterns platform (Cattuto et al., 2010), which uses RFID chips for detecting close-range proximity. In comparison to IR-based sensors, RFID chips do not need to be in line of sight to each other. In order to maintain the aspect of directionality, the signal can be calibrated in such a way that the human body blocks the signal. This means individuals wearing the sensors at their front must still face each other to produce a signal. Besides the directionality, all these sensing platforms have the characteristic that proximity is much more constrained than with co-location sensors. In contrast to Bluetooth, which detects a signal up to 5–7 meters (which is already outside the social space according to proxemics), IR and RFID sensors have a threshold of detection of up to 2–4 meters. In addition, building on the fact that even co-location combined with directionality is not perfect in detecting "true" interactions, other systems have added further sensors, such as microphones to detect speech (Dai et al., 2019). This allows one to focus solely on interactions with oral communication. By combining ultrasound and radio waves, Huang et al. (2014) have been able to design Opo, a system with high temporal resolution of two seconds that also measures the distance between individuals with a good precision (5 cm).

The SocioPatterns platform has been by far the most widely used framework.[2] As such, we will use it as a typical example of this class of sensors, specifically to describe the accompanied challenges. Generally, using a designed sensing platform has the main shortcoming that they are not based on pre-existing infrastructures. This implies that researchers must purchase (or build) the devices first. Therefore, the number of sensors is limited, usually being far fewer than widely distributed pre-existing devices like smartphones. This means they can only be used in well-defined contexts with small populations, maximum a few hundred – in the case of Socio-Patterns, the largest study gathered around 400 participants. Furthermore, the sensors must be deployed. For one, if relying on antennas receiving interaction signals, the conductors of the study must set up the antennas in strategic places covering the premises of investigation. Second, the sensors must be distributed to the participants. This requires setting up a deployment slot in the schedule, which can be challenging when studying events with a predefined schedule, such as conferences, for instance. Participants often forget that they are wearing a sensor. This is positive, as it mitigates the Hawthorne effect. However, this has also the consequence that they tend to forget to return the sensor. Therefore, the collection of sensors at the end of the study must also be carefully designed in order to limit the loss of equipment. In some studies, it is even mandatory to hand over and collect the sensors every day, which must be included in the daily routine without disturbing the social context. For studies with a long duration, there is even the need to charge the devices or replace batteries. Even prior to deployment, participants must be informed about the correct use of the sensors, as the directionality is a crucial factor. As with pre-existing sensors, specifically designed sensors also need a software component that controls the detection and processing of the signals.

Contribution of sensor-based studies to the social sciences

Various studies have already been performed using sensor technology. Social science studies using proximity sensors specifically investigate patterns of co-location and face-to-face interaction to study human behavior and social topics and concepts such as friendship, inequality, status, group cohesion, or the organization of workplaces. All of this aims at deriving "social meaning" from physical data. In the following, we present work that has contributed to the investigation of human interaction in different areas and on different levels of social research. We focus on displaying sensor study design, types of collected data, and results in terms of social analysis.

Detecting and measuring social relations

Eagle, Pentland, and Lazer (2009) use interaction data based on Bluetooth and cellular tower data to infer a friendship network structure. They compare interaction data with self-reported survey data. Though they show an overlap between these two data sources, they reveal distinctions between them as well, suggesting that interaction data can be a complement to self-report surveys. In response to this paper, Adams (2010) argues that one should be careful on the type of social network being analyzed and what questions one can ask; specifically, behavioral networks versus social relationship. Oloritun, Madan, Pentland, and Khayal (2013) focus on close friendship ties. They investigate propinquity; that is, the proximity of people concerning physical and psychological aspects, which plays a main role in the formation of role relations. They show that interaction during the weekend and physical proximity explain close friendship ties. Usually, selecting a suitable RSSI threshold makes it possible to distinguish between strong and weak links. These signals correlate with friendship ties on Facebook, according to Sekara and Lehmann (2014). However, in today's digitized world, the question arises whether Facebook friends are real friends. Approaching this, Matusik et al. (2019) use self-reports among leaders in a large-scale research facility to establish the validity of Bluetooth RSSI thresholds for friendship and advice-seeking networks. They show that Bluetooth sensors can indeed assist researchers interested in studying actual friendship and advice-oriented relationships.

Individuals and interpersonal behavior

Sensor data have also been used to relate behavior to properties of individuals (e.g., personality traits, social status, or sociodemographic features like age or gender). The research mainly includes measuring the impact of individual traits on their interaction behavior as well as evaluating the validity of constructs, such as personality traits with empirical data. Typically, this is done by comparing self-reported and sensor-based data, for example, personality as expressed in a questionnaire or interview compared to personality as expressed in the interaction data. Olguin et al. (2009a) showed that personality traits could be identified via sensors; in particular, they used both proximity (Bluetooth) and interaction (infrared) data. Their results described the correlation between different interaction features with personality traits (i.e., Big 5 dimensions), showing that face-to-face interaction and proximity can predict these dimensions. Variation in face-to-face interaction duration time exhibits a positive correlation with neuroticism values. Staiano et al. (2012) examined how social networks can predict the Big 5 personality traits. They used a survey-based network and interaction networks based on calls and proximity (Bluetooth). They showed that the proximity network performs better than survey-based and call networks in personality classification. The authors categorize each personality trait (i.e., agreeableness, conscientiousness, extraversion, neuroticism, openness) into high and low labels based on the average of the individuals. They predict these labels using machine learning, more precisely the random forest algorithm. In general, Bluetooth is the best for this task; phone call network data are rather unusable. Similarly, Chittaranjan, Blom, and Gatica-Perez (2013) investigated whether sensors in smartphones (i.e., Bluetooth, SMS, Calls) can predict the Big

5, revealing specific gender differences. They show that higher extraversion and disagreeableness is associated with a lower number of contacts for male individuals. In the case of female individuals, higher scores for neuroticism and introversion are associated with a lower number of contacts.

Studies on mental health, psychological well-being, or creativity profit from sensor studies, as the data are collected non-intrusively and are therefore not based on self-assessment. Self-reporting on these topics is susceptible to bias as well as distortion. Similarly, an individual's state of mind or emotion might not always be accessible to self-analysis and reporting. In a small study, Gloor et al. (2011) investigate the relationship between interpersonal interaction patterns (close-range proximity) and individual creativity, finding two types of individuals: lonely genius and swarm creative. For the former, being near other individuals (face-to-face interaction distance or any proximity) is negatively associated with creativity, whereas the opposite occurs for the latter. Tripathi and Burleson (2012) analyzed the interplay of creativity with face-to-face interaction and movement. They find that creativity is associated with teammates' interaction and movement energy. The authors construct a model that predicts individuals' creativity based on face-to-face interaction (and movement) with 91% (87.5%) accuracy. Similarly, Parker, Cardenas, Dorr, and Hackett (2018) showed that perceived creativity (group and individual) is associated with face-to-face interaction. Pachucki, Ozer, Barrat, and Cattuto (2015) investigated the mental health of sixth graders and their social influence. They revealed that interaction networks of boys and girls are associated differently with self-esteem and depressive symptoms. Girls with more depressive symptoms present social inhibition, whereas boys show interaction patterns that match the depressive symptoms. In the StudentLife study, Wang et al. (2017) analyzed a class of 60 students via smartphones using different sensors: Bluetooth proximity, conversation (speaking) detection, GPS, and accelerometer, among others. They conducted pre- and post-surveys to capture the students' levels of depression and stress. They found that conversation frequency/duration is negatively associated with depression. Similarly, conversation frequency/duration is also negatively associated with perceived stress.

Indeed, social interactions can have positive or negative effects on participants' general subjective well-being. Alshamsi, Pianesi, Lepri, Pentland, and Rahwan (2016) have performed one study on the correlation between face-to-face interactions and such effects. The authors investigate how face-to-face interactions affect interacting people positively or negatively. They show that the participants' subjective well-being proved to have only rather low correlations with differentiating face-to-face interactions. Moturu, Khayal, Aharony, Pan, and Pentland (2011b) examined the relationship between sociability with sleep and mood. They define daily sociability as the number of interactions (Bluetooth) an individual has on a particular day. The participants fill in surveys about sleep duration and mood daily. They found that people who report poor moods have a significantly lower overall sociability. They failed to find a daily association between sociability and mood (i.e., changes on a day in sociability and mood). However, they found a non-linear association between sleep duration and previous day sociability. Short (less than six hours) and long (more than nine hours) sleep duration is associated with lower sociability in the previous day. Sleep duration around seven and eight hours is associated with higher sociability in the previous day. Though they found an association between sleep and the previous day's sociability, they failed to find a relationship between sleep and the following day's sociability. Social role relations might play a role in this relationship. The authors have shown that sleep duration and mood of an individual are affected by the sleep and mood of the spouse (Moturu, Khayal, Aharony, Pan, and Pentland, 2011a). Finnerty, Kalimeri, and Pianesi (2014) investigate face-to-face interaction in the work environment. They examine proximity (Bluetooth), face-to-face (IR), and electronic (e-mail) interactions. They also survey the participants to understand creativity, productivity, and affective states. They found that people interact more asynchronously (i.e., via e-mail) than synchronously. They also found out that interacting with more people face to face is associated with higher positive affect; also, having a higher number of face-to-face interactions with friends (survey-based) is negatively associated with self-reported measures of productivity and creativity. However, longer duration time interacting and proximity with friends is associated positively with productivity but not creativity; being co-located with colleagues and friends is associated with higher creativity.

Groups, organizations, and institutions

As elaborated on previously, interaction is essential for cohesion in all areas of social life. It produces social structure and, in return, reproduces and enacts the "standards" social norms. Investigating behavior in workplaces, hospitals, schools, or at academic venues with sensors adds knowledge on the organization of these institutions, how they function on the micro level, and whether sub-groups interact differently (Chaffin et al., 2017). They also contribute to the evaluation of institutional goals, for example, productivity and job satisfaction in workplaces, proper care in hospitals, integration and equal attention in schools, or promotion of young scholars and collaboration in academia. Sensor data are a complement to existing approaches of data collection in organizational research, especially to investigate group dynamics of new teams (Kim, McFee, Olguin, Waber, & Pentland, 2012). Wu, Waber, Aral, Brynjolfsson, and Pentland (2008) study a work environment via face-to-face interaction networks, e-mail communication, tonal conversational variation, and physical proximity, aiming to uncover the characteristics of productive workers. The authors reveal that productive workers have e-mail networks structurally different from face-to-face networks. On the one hand, their results show that face-to-face network cohesion is positively associated with productivity; on the other hand, e-mail network cohesion is negatively associated with productivity. They also reveal that face-to-face networks have a higher cohesion effect in productivity than proximity networks; that is, actual face-to-face interaction is more important than just proximity. Olguin, Gloor, and Pentland (2009b) investigate job satisfaction and social interaction in a small organization. They examine networks of e-mail conversation, face-to-face interaction, and proximity, together with surveys about job satisfaction and group interaction satisfaction. Though they failed to find a relationship between these networks and job satisfaction separately, the authors found that the total communication of an individual (i.e., the combined network) is negatively associated with job satisfaction. This result suggests the need for multi-modal approaches to examine organization. Atzmueller, Thiele, Stumme, and Kauffeld (2018) characterize the dynamics of face-to-face interaction of the first week of first-year students in a university, revealing that the first and last days are determinant to the growth of stronger links. Examining the dynamics of teams, Montanari (2018) found that proxemics information can predict the role of an individual's task with 80% accuracy and identify the task timeline with 92% accuracy. Zhang, Olenick, Chang, Kozlowski, and Hung (2018) examined team dynamics of six individuals confined for a period of four months in a simulation of space exploration. They investigate individuals' affect states and group cohesion, as estimated via surveys, revealing that face-to-face interactions help predict both task and group cohesion. Parker et al. (2018) presented mixed-method studies in that survey and ethnographic data are combined with sociometric data, showing the interplay of social interaction, creativity, and events in social gathering (e.g., lunch, coffee break). Kibanov, Heiberger, Rödder, Atzmueller, and Stumme (2019) examined the social roles of students in university retreats. They characterize four roles, ambassadors, big fishes, bridges, and loners, in communities of face-to-face interaction networks. They found that male participants tend to be the ambassadors (i.e., providing connections to different communities) in cultural and research communities.

Topics and concepts

So far, we have illustrated that sensor data have been used to learn more about friendship, personality, gender differences, or job satisfaction. One concept which cuts across many topical areas of social research is homophily. Homophily refers to peoples' inclination to befriend or collaborate with similar others. It is thereby primarily used to explain alignment patterns and group behavior. Research on homophily is well established in the social sciences and has been widely adopted in relational studies and network analyses, including sensor-based studies

Stehlé, Charbonnier, Picard, Cattuto, and Barrat (2013) examined the influence of gender on face-to-face interaction in a primary school via an experiment that included 6- to 12-year-old children of different classes. The authors found evidence of gender homophily in all classes. They revealed that the effect of homophily strengthens with age and that boys tend to have a higher homophilic level than girls. Similarly, gender homophily is also found in universities (Atzmueller et al., 2018; Psylla, Sapiezynski, Mones, & Lehmann, 2017). More concretely, Psylla et al. (2017) found that women tend to form female-only triangles more often than men in networks of proximity, cell phone calls, and Facebook interaction. In schools, intra-class interactions tend to occur more often than inter-class interactions (Guclu et al., 2016; Stehlé et al., 2013). Guclu et al. (2016) suggested that the classes schedule play a fundamental role in these interactions. In elementary and elementary-middle schools, since they often have fixed schedules, students of the same class tend to interact more often. In middle and high schools, however, students tend to mix with other classes because of the free schedule in these schools (Guclu et al., 2016).

Madan, Farrahi, Gatica-Perez, and Pentland (2011) studied the dynamic homophily of political opinions in proximity networks. They investigated the interactions during the 2008 U.S. presidential election campaign, uncovering the relationship between interaction and political opinion changes among undergraduates. They found that individuals who decrease their interest in politics tend to interact face to face with individuals with little or no interest in politics (Madan et al., 2011; Madan, Cebrian, Moturu, Farrahi, & Pentland, 2012). Chancellor et al. (2017) found evidence of homophily with respect to well-being in the workplace. They showed that individuals sharing the same levels of connectedness tend to cluster in interaction network. They also found that individuals with dissimilar levels of depressive symptoms tend to cluster together.

Homophily also plays a role in health. Madan, Moturu, Lazer, and Pentland (2010) studied the dynamics of health-related behaviors by analyzing the face-to-face interaction of students in a residence hall. The authors showed that an individual's health behavior is associated with the health behaviors of the individuals who interacted with this individual, having an impact on weight changes (Madan et al., 2010, 2012). Notably, Madan et al. (2010) showed that self-reported friends are unable to explain individuals' health behavior.

Challenges of sensor-based studies

As mentioned before, using sensors to study co-location or face-to-face interactions creates fine-grained non-responsive data. It also comprises various limitations, as illustrated in "Close-range proximity sensors". However, there are further general limitations that affect both studies with co-location sensors and studies with face-to-face interaction sensors. In the following, we point out these challenges, including the introduction of new biases, shift in complexity, and specifying data that cannot be monitored by current state-of-the-art sensors. We also provide suggestions on how to approach these challenges.

Introducing new biases

Although mitigating self-reporting and human encoding biases, one major limitation with using sensors to study co-location and face-to-face interaction is that sensors introduce new types of biases. This includes biases due to technological aspects, the study design, the processing of the obtained data, or even biases created by the participants of a study.

As sensors are a piece of technology, they can break occasionally. Broken or generally non-functioning sensors do not record any signals during a study, which can create a possible bias in the data. For example, a larger number of broken sensors can skew the data of an interaction network. If such problems occur with sensors built into the participants' smartphones, there is hardly anything one can do to deal with this problem. When using dedicated sensors, though, it is of high importance to double-check that all sensors are working before the study.

Individuals participating in a study are likely to create a bias by themselves. If a study takes place over a period of several days (and sensors are not collected after each day), participants can forget to bring along their sensor on a few of these days. For instance, conference attendees can forget their name badge including the RFID sensor at their hotel, such that their interactions cannot be recorded on that day. Participants can also accidentally deactivate their sensor, for example, the Bluetooth or GPS on their smartphones, during a study. They can furthermore accidentally block the sensor's signal, for example, participants might hold a drink in front of the RFID sensors on their conference name badge, which blocks the signal just like the human body. Unfortunately, there are only limited possibilities to mitigate these problems. To make sure participants do not accidentally forget or turn off their sensors, the only option is to constantly remind them to keep the sensors activated or bring their sensors along the following day. This can be achieved via posters at specific points of interest, such as the entrance of a venue.

An insufficient study design can lead to a further bias in the data. As mentioned before, sensors are only proxies for the social constructs that are of actual interest. Such proxies have the limitations that they pick up signals where there should not be any signal, and vice versa. Building structures can interfere or even block sensor signals, such that actual co-location or interaction information is not recorded. For mitigating such biases, it is important to invest in the study design. This begins at testing the sensors intensively, that is, determining when a signal occurs and what blocks the signal. If possible, the sensors might need to be re-calibrated. The researchers should also test the sensors on the premises where the study takes place in order to detect building structures, for example, windows and walls, that can block signals. One should also think of how to attach a sensor to a participant, for example, by including sensors in the participants' conference name badges.

Finally, before using the obtained data for analysis, the "raw" data must be pre-processed to eliminate, or at least minimize, error rates in the measurements. Such pre-processing includes *filtering*, *aggregation*, and, in cases of large data collections, *sampling*. Each of these steps can create a bias, though, such that they need to be performed with high caution. For example, filtering out coincidental interaction signals can lead to filtering out real interactions if no care is taken. Wrongly assumed aggregations due to data privacy can even lead to unusable data for specific research questions. The same applies for bad sampling, which can create the well-known

sampling bias. Mitigating this sort of bias requires cautious elaboration on how exactly to filter, aggregate, and sample the data, which includes double-checking obtained signals against a
ground truth. Sometimes, a well-defined study setup can also help to minimize the amount of
"junk data" (Kontro & Génois, 2020).

Complexity shift

Collecting data just for collecting data constitutes bad practice in research. A well-defined
research question and study design, on the contrary, constitutes good scientific practice,
as a social sensing study is only as good as the social science research question behind it.
Defining a valuable research question and setting up the social sensing study requires a lot
of effort, especially if the researchers intend to mitigate the aforementioned biases. In comparison to traditional observational or survey studies, performing sensor-based studies shifts
the complexity towards a rather technical perspective. Beside sensor maintenance or calibration, it means developing and maintaining code for obtaining, processing, and analyzing
the obtained data. Carrying out studies in the field, for example, preparing the sensors or
assisting participants such that their sensors are working properly, requires further resources.
Another major issue that cannot be stressed enough is regarding data privacy. At least the
same standards must be applied to sensor-based studies as for traditional social science studies, specifically since tracking individuals can quickly lead to intruding on their privacy. This
especially applies to studies where behavioral data are linked to further quantitative or qualitative information on the participants, for example, gender, age group, country of residence,
and so on, that could be used to identify single individuals. Parker et al. (2018) provide a
highly useful "Lessons from the Field" section on these and other aspects that researchers
need to be aware of.

Data that sensors cannot detect

Different sensors detect different signals. If a social construct consists of various aspects, it is very
likely that only one sensor cannot detect all signals to cover all these aspects. For example, from
a social science perspective, proximity sensors do not capture the many facets of face-to-face
interaction, for example, body language or facial expression, that contribute to the whole picture of human encounters. They also do not capture conversation as such, that is, what has been
said or the nature of the conversation, or they cannot detect the motivation for an interaction.
Typically, proximity sensors do not produce a directional network, such that it is impossible to
see who approached whom or who is rather active and passive in an interaction.

Approaching these limitations is quite difficult. In the end, it is again highly important to
clearly formulate the research question investigated in a study and which sensors are most likely
to detect the corresponding signals. Studying sociological constructs for which co-location is
enough, using Bluetooth sensors is sufficient. The same applies for face-to-face interaction, if
the research question is whether there is a difference in interaction between different groups, for
example, different age groups. In addition to the sensor data, interviewing the participants or
obtaining further information via surveys alleviates the situation as well. For example, studying
whether individuals are comfortable in very close-range conversations, a combination of sensors detecting the distance and a post-survey asking about the participants' well-being might be
a possible solution. Another possibility is to use microphones and detect subtle changes in the
sound and pitch of a person's voice.

Conclusion and outlook

In this chapter, we have elaborated on the usage of close-range proximity sensors to study face-to-face interaction. The field of social sciences can very much profit from quantitative sensor-based data on human interaction, as the obtained data are fine-grained and non-responsive, mitigating the Hawthorne effect. In addition, it is free from a self-reporting bias compared to survey studies as well as free from human encoding biases compared to traditional observational studies. Especially for mixed-methods research, sensor-based studies are of high interest and can contribute to a wide range of topical areas in the social sciences. However, researchers must be aware of the different types of sensors, as their measured physical entity must match according to the social construct under investigation. Sensors like GPS, Wi-Fi trackers, phone trackers, and Bluetooth are useful to study co-location. Sensors like RFID or infrared are rather useful to detect face-to-face interaction, as they also consider that the participants must be turned towards each other. The most important aspect is the study design! A well-defined research question gives insights on which kind of sensors to use for optimal results. The study design also sheds light on how exactly to conduct the study in all its details, from preparing and handing out the sensors or the corresponding app for smartphones, guiding the participants during the study, and pre-processing the data after the study.

The studies listed in "Contribution of sensor-based studies to the social sciences" show how sensor-based research can be performed and which social constructs can be measured. Nonetheless, it is rather a proof of concept and only a first step towards the possibilities that sensors can bring to research interest in social sciences. In the future, developing sophisticated machine learning algorithms can transform devices such as cameras and microphones into actual sensors, as manual encoding would be obsolete, for example, automatically detecting the distance between people in video recordings of open city cameras to observe peoples' reaction to COVID-19.[3] An even more appealing aspect includes bringing both the technological area and the social science area closer to each other. This implies, on the one hand, that social scientists should invest more effort in new technologies investigating which social constructs can be analyzed by which state-of-the-art sensors. On the other hand, technicians should invest more effort in investigating how to enhance existing sensors to measure more complex social constructs. For example, future possibilities can be exploited by advances mentioned in Chen, Zhao, and Farrell (2016), in which the authors specify that GPS can be used to detect proximity within the centimeter range.

Notes

1 https://github.com/robogao/Protractor, accessed November 2020
2 See https://sociopatterns.org for a list of all studies conducted, accessed November 2020
3 https://landing.ai/landing-ai-creates-an-ai-tool-to-help-customers-monitor-social-distancing-in-the-workplace/, accessed November 2020

References

Adams, J. (2010). Distant friends, close strangers? Inferring friendships from behavior. *Proceedings of the National Academy of Sciences, 107*(9), E29–E30.
Alshamsi, A., Pianesi, F., Lepri, B., Pentland, A., & Rahwan, I. (2016, April). Network diversity and affect dynamics: The role of personality traits. *PLoS One, 11*(4), e0152358.
Atzmueller, M., Thiele, L., Stumme, G., & Kauffeld, S. (2018, January). Analyzing group interaction on networks of 15 face-to-face proximity using wearable sensors. In 2018 *IEEE International Conference on Future IoT Technologies (Future IoT)*, Volume 2018-January, pp. 1–10. IEEE.

Bargiela-Chiappini, F., & Haugh, M. (Eds.). (2009). *Face, communication and social interaction* (1 ed.). Equinox Publishing Ltd.

Berger, P. L., & Luckmann, T. (1967). *The social construction of reality: A treatise in the sociology of knowledge* (Anchor books, 589). Doubleday.

Blumer, H. (1969). *Symbolic interactionism: Perspective and method*. University of California Press.

Borgatti, S. P., Mehra, A., Brass, D. J., & Labianca, G. (2010). *Network analysis in the social sciences*. Science, *323*(5916), 892–895.

Cattuto, C., van den Broeck, W., Barrat, A., Colizza, V., Pinton, J. F., & Vespignani, A. (2010). Dynamics of person-to-person interactions from distributed RFID sensor networks. *PLoS One, 5*(7), 1–9.

Chaffin, D., Heidl, R., Hollenbeck, J. R., Howe, M., Yu, A., Voorhees, C., & Calantone, R. (2017, January). The promise and perils of wearable sensors in organizational research. *Organizational Research Methods, 20*(1), 3–31.

Chancellor, J., Layous, K., Margolis, S., & Lyubomirsky, S. (2017, Dec). Clustering by well-being in workplace social networks: Homophily and social contagion. *Emotion, 17*(8), 1166–1180.

Chen, Y., Zhao, S., & Farrell, J. A. (2016). Computationally efficient carrier integer ambiguity resolution in multiepoch GPS/INS: A common-position-shift approach. *IEEE Transactions on Control Systems Technology, 24*(5), 1541–1556.

Chittaranjan, G., Blom, J., & Gatica-Perez, D. (2013). Mining large-scale smartphone data for personality studies. *Personal and Ubiquitous Computing, 17*(3), 433–450.

Choudhury, T., & Pentland, A. (2003). Sensing and modeling human networks using the sociometer. *In Seventh IEEE international symposium on wearable computers* (pp. 216–222). IEEE

Crossley, N. (2011). *Towards relational sociology*. Routledge.

Dai, S., Karsai, M., Bouchet, H., Fleury, E., Chevrot, J. P., & Nardy, A. (2019). Interaction reconstruction methods for large-scale RFID social experiments. In *The 5th International Conference on Computational Social Science*, Volume 2, Amsterdam, Netherlands.

Duncan, S., & Fiske, D. W. (1977). *Face-to-face interaction: Research, methods, and theory*. Lawrence Erlbaum Associates.

Eagle, N., Pentland, A., & Lazer, D. (2009). Inferring friendship network structure by using mobile phone data. *Proceedings of the National Academy of Sciences, 106*(36), 15274–15278.

Finnerty, A. N., Kalimeri, K., & Pianesi, F. (2014). Towards happier organisations: Understanding the relationship between communication and productivity. In *Lecture notes in computer science (including subseries lecture notes in artificial intelligence and lecture notes in bioinformatics)* (Vol. 8851, pp. 462–477). Springer.

Garfinkel, H. (1984 [1967]). *Studies in ethnomethodology*. Polity Press.

Gloor, P. A., Fischbach, K., Fuehres, H., Lassenius, C., Niinimaki, T., Olguin, D. O., Pentland, S., Piri, A., & Putzke, J. (2011). Towards "honest signals" of creativity – identifying personality characteristics through microscopic social network analysis. *Procedia – Social and Behavioral Sciences, 26*(2008), 166–179.

Goffman, E. (1961). *Encounters: Two studies in the sociology of interaction*. Bobbs Merril.

Goffman, E. (1978 [1956]). *The presentation of self in everyday life*. Penguin.

Goffman, E. (1981). *Forms of talk*. University of Pennsylvania publications in conduct and communication. University of Pennsylvania Press.

Goffman, E. (2017 [1967]). *Interaction ritual: Essays in face-to-face behavior* (pp. 1–270). Aldine Pub. Co.

Guclu, H., Read, J., Vukotich, C. J., Galloway, D. D., Gao, H., Rainey, J. J., Uzicanin, A., Zimmer, S. M., & Cummings, D. A. T. (2016). Social contact networks and mixing among students in K-12 schools in Pittsburgh. *PLoS One, 11*(3), e0151139.

Habermas, J. (1984). *The theory of communicative action*. Beacon Press.

Habermas, J. (2002). *On the pragmatics of social interaction: Preliminary studies in the theory of communicative action*. The MIT Press.

Hall, E. T. (1963). A system for the notation of proxemic behavior. *American Anthropologist, 65*(5), 1003–1026.

Hall, E. T. (1992). *The hidden dimension*. Anchor Books.

Huang, W., Kuo, Y. S., Pannuto, P., & Dutta, P. (2014). Opo: A wearable sensor for capturing high-fidelity face-to-face interactions. *Proceedings of the 12th ACM Conference on Embedded Network Sensor Systems – SenSys'14*, New York, New York, USA, pp. 61–75. ACM Press.

Kendon, A., Harris, R. M., & Key, M. R. (Eds.). (1975). *Organization of behavior in face-to-face interaction*. Mouton Publishers.

Kibanov, M., Heiberger, R. H., Rödder, S., Atzmueller, M., & Stumme, G. (2019). Social studies of scholarly life with sensor-based ethnographic observations. *Scientometrics, 119*(3), 1387–1428.

Kim, T., McFee, E., Olguin, D. O., Waber, B., & Pentland, A. S. (2012). Sociometric badges: Using sensor technology to capture new forms of collaboration. *Journal of Organizational Behavior, 33*(3), 412–427.

Kontro, I., & Génois, M. (2020). Combining surveys and sensors to explore student behaviour. *Education Sciences, 10*(3).

Madan, A., Cebrian, M., Moturu, S., Farrahi, K., & Pentland, A. S. (2012). Sensing the "health state" of a community. *IEEE Pervasive Computing, 11*(4), 36–45.

Madan, A., Farrahi, K., Gatica-Perez, D., & Pentland, A. S. (2011). Pervasive sensing to model political opinions in face-to-face networks. *In Lecture notes in computer science (including subseries lecture notes in artificial intelligence and lecture notes in bioinformatics), Volume 6696 LNCS* (pp. 214–231). Springer.

Madan, A., Moturu, S. T., Lazer, D., & Pentland, A. S. (2010). *Social sensing: Obesity, unhealthy eating and exercise in face-to-face networks.* In Wireless Health 2010 on – WH'10, New York, USA, pp. 104. ACM Press.

Malik, M. M. (2018). *Bias and beyond in digital trace data* (Ph.D. thesis). Carnegie Mellon University, Pittsburgh, PA.

Matusik, J. G., Heidl, R. A., Hollenbeck, J. R., Yu, A., Lee, H. W., & Howe, M. D. (2019). Wearable Bluetooth sensors for capturing relational variables and temporal variability in relationships: A construct validation study. *Journal of Applied Psychology, 104*, 357–387.

Mead, G. H. (1934). *Mind, self and society.* University of Chicago Press.

Mehrabian, A. (1968). Some referents and measures of nonverbal behavior. *Behavior Research Methods & Instrumentation, 1*(6), 203–207.

Montanari, A. (2018). *Devising and evaluating wearable technology for social dynamics monitoring* (Ph.D. thesis). University of Cambridge.

Montanari, A., Tian, Z., Francu, E., Lucas, B., Jones, B., Zhou, X., & Mascolo, C. (2018). Measuring interaction proxemics with wearable light tags. *Proceedings of the ACM on Interactive, Mobile, Wearable and Ubiquitous Technologies, 2*(1).

Moturu, S. T., Khayal, I., Aharony, N., Pan, W., & Pentland, A. (2011a). Sleep, mood and sociability in a healthy population. In *2011 annual international conference of the IEEE engineering in medicine and biology society* (pp. 5267–5270). IEEE.

Moturu, S. T., Khayal, I., Aharony, N., Pan, W., & Pentland, A. (2011b). Using social sensing to understand the links between sleep, mood, and sociability. *2011 IEEE third international conference on privacy, security, risk and trust and 2011 IEEE third international conference on social computing* (pp. 208–214). IEEE.

Müller, J., Fàbregues, S., Guenther, E. A., & Romano, M. J. (2019). Using sensors in organizational research – clarifying rationales and validation challenges for mixed methods. *Frontiers in Psychology, 10.*

Olguin, D. O., Gloor, P. A., & Pentland, A. (2009b). *Capturing individual and group behavior with wearable sensors.* AAAI Spring Symposium on Human Behavior Modeling, Stanford, CA. AAAI.

Olguin, D. O., Waber, B., Kim, T., Mohan, A., Ara, K., & Pentland, A. (2009a). Sensible organizations: Technology and methodology for automatically measuring organizational behavior. *IEEE Transactions on Systems, Man, and Cybernetics, Part B (Cybernetics), 39*(1), 43–55.

Oloritun, R. O., Madan, A., Pentland, A., & Khayal, I. (2013). Identifying close friendships in a sensed social network. *Procedia – Social and Behavioral Sciences, 79*, 18–26.

Pachucki, M. C., Ozer, E. J., Barrat, A., & Cattuto, C. (2015). Mental health and social networks in early adolescence: A dynamic study of objectively-measured social interaction behaviors. *Social Science & Medicine, 125*, 40–50.

Parker, J. N., Cardenas, E., Dorr, A. N., & Hackett, E. J. (2018). Using sociometers to advance small group research. *Sociological Methods & Research.* doi:10.1177/004912411876909.

Psylla, I., Sapiezynski, P., Mones, E., & Lehmann, S. (2017). The role of gender in social network organization. *PLoS One, 12*(12), e0189873.

Sacks, H., Schegloff, E. A., & Jefferson, G. (1978 [1974]). A simplest systematics for the organization of turn taking for conversation. *In Studies in the organization of conversational interaction* (pp. 7–55.). Academic Press.

Schutz, A. (1972 [1932]). *The phenomenology of the social world.* Northwestern University Press.

Sekara, V., & Lehmann, S. (2014). The strength of friendship ties in proximity sensor data. *PLoS One, 9*(7), e100915.

Simmel, G. (1890). *Über soziale Differenzierung: Sociologische und psychologische Untersuchungen.* Duncker & Humblot.

Staiano, J., Pianesi, F., Lepri, B., Sebe, N., Aharony, N., & Pentland, A. (2012). Friends don't lie: Inferring personality traits from social network structure. *Proceedings of the 2012 ACM Conference on Ubiquitous Computing – UbiComp'12*, New York, USA, p. 321. ACM Press.

Stehlé, J., Charbonnier, F., Picard, T., Cattuto, C., & Barrat, A. (2013). Gender homophily from spatial behavior in a primary school: A sociometric study. *Social Networks, 35*(4), 604–613.

Stopczynski, A., Sekara, V., Sapiezynski, P., Cuttone, A., Madsen, M. M., Larsen, J. E., & Lehmann, S. (2014). Measuring large-scale social networks with high resolution. *PLoS One, 9*(4).

Tripathi, P., & Burleson, W. (2012). Predicting creativity in the wild: Experience sample and sociometric modeling of teams. *Proceedings of the ACM 2012 conference on Computer Supported Cooperative Work – CSCW'12*, New York, USA, p. 1203. ACM Press.

Turner, J. H. (1988). *A theory of social interaction.* Stanford University Press.

Turner, J. H. (2002). *Face to face: Toward a sociological theory of interpersonal behavior.* Stanford University Press.

Turner, R. H. (1988). Personality in society: Social psychology's contribution to sociology. *Social Psychology Quarterly, 51*(1), 1.

Wang, R., Chen, F., Chen, Z., Li, T., Harari, G., Tignor, S., Zhou, X., Ben-Zeev, D., & Campbell, A. T. (2017). StudentLife: Using smartphones to assess mental health and academic performance of college students. In *Mobile health* (pp. 7–33). Springer International Publishing.

Wu, L., Waber, B. N., Aral, S., Brynjolfsson, E., & Pentland, A. (2008). Mining face-to-face interaction networks using sociometric badges: Predicting productivity in an IT configuration task. *SSRN Electronic Journal*, 1–19.

Zhang, Y., Olenick, J., Chang, C. H., Kozlowski, S. W. J., & Hung, H. (2018, September). TeamSense: Assessing personal affect and group cohesion in small teams through dyadic interaction and behavior analysis with wearable sensors. *Proceedings of the ACM on Interactive, Mobile, Wearable and Ubiquitous Technologies, 2*(3), 1–22.

15

SOCIAL MEDIA DATA IN AFFECTIVE SCIENCE

Max Pellert, Simon Schweighofer, and David Garcia

Researching human emotions

Affective science is the interdisciplinary study of human affect, researching phenomena such as mood, attitude, stress, communication and affective disorders (Gross & Barrett, 2013). These behaviors are connected by the crucial concept of emotion, defined as subjective individual states that activate and modulate behaviour and cognition (Frijda et al., 1986; Scherer, 2005). Affective science established itself as a successor of the classical approach to human cognition in terms of symbolic information processing (Newell & Simon, 1976). With a focus on planning and problem solving, emotions were left out as a fuzzy concept difficult to measure. This changed and nowadays, at the intersection of artificial intelligence and behavioral science, affective science has established itself with new technologies to detect, predict and interact with emotions that are collected under the umbrella term of *affective computing* (Picard, 2000).[1]

The widespread use of information and communication technologies (ICTs) is generating an unprecedented volume of digital traces of human behavior that can be used to study human emotions. Among these technologies, social media play a central role in capturing communication between individuals and in large groups of people. One in three humans uses social media, and more than 58% of Europeans use social media on a weekly basis (European Commission, 2018). Self-expression and communication in social media are captured in the form of text messages, pictures, emojis, animated images and videos with corresponding metadata. These digital traces can be automatically retrieved and processed to detect behavioral correlates of emotions. This offers the opportunity to analyze emotions unobtrusively and in vivo (outside the experimenter's room), at unprecedented scales, extreme resolutions, from a multitude of people with diverse backgrounds and, potentially, at a very low cost.

Traditionally, research in affective science has been based on laboratory experiments. The main advantage of experiments is the possibility to tightly control the setup of the experiment conditions, for example, the presented stimuli and the sequence of actions of participants. This allows the systematic comparison between a control group and an experimental group, also called a treatment group. The control group serves as a counterfactual that allows researchers to test causal hypotheses of the effect of a stimulus or condition in an individual response. This power to detect causation is related to the concept of *internal validity*, which denotes to which extent the design of a study can support its conclusions. But the advantages of the controlled

DOI: 10.4324/9781003024583-18

experiment approach – its clean and controlled nature – also come with disadvantages. As experiments get more precise, it becomes harder to establish whether the effects observed in the laboratory are also present in real-life situations outside the laboratory, that is, to assess the *ecological validity* of the experiment. Connected to this, the limited diversity of participants in the typical psychological experiment (Henrich, Heine, & Norenzayan, 2010) also affects the *external validity* of experimental outcomes, that is, whether what we learn can be generalized to human behavior in other situations. These issues also affect the replicability of experiment results, as a small variation in experimental conditions can dramatically affect the outcomes of the experiment.

Human emotions are not a purely internal and private phenomenon – they are often triggered by external events that are predominantly social in nature, such as grief at the loss of a family member, anxiety when having to speak in front of a crowd or joy at reuniting with a loved one. Emotions are also communicated socially through facial expressions, body posture and verbal and non-verbal communication (Rimé, 2009). In addition, feedback effects that can revive, amplify or dampen emotions play a role. Often, the social sharing of emotions causes the recipient to re-share these emotions, leading to observable emotion cascades (Rimé, 2009). This communication of emotions seems to be so natural that it is, in contrast, deemed valuable in some situations to have the skill to be able to *not* share one's emotions (e.g., a "poker face" or a waiter's smile). Methodologically, the social nature of human emotions is captured in the laboratory only with great difficulty. For example collective emotions, which are emotional states emerging through the interactions of large crowds (think of the collective joy or grief in a football stadium or the anger of a riot), are extremely hard to elicit in a laboratory setting (Goldenberg, Garcia, Halperin, & Gross, 2020).

The analysis of emotions with social media data offers a complement to traditional methods. Experiments and questionnaires retain substantial scientific value, for example, by providing high levels of internal validity. However, digital traces can supply scientists with resources on aspects of emotions that are harder to measure in the experimental room, as well as with data on large crowds that are hard to manipulate. But this potential comes along with several pitfalls and biases associated with *social data* (Olteanu, Castillo, Diaz, & Kiciman, 2019; Sen, Floeck, Weller, Weiss, & Wagner, 2019). Our aim with this chapter is to provide a critical but balanced view into the opportunities and limitations of social media data to study human emotions. We start by providing a brief overview of models and methods to quantify emotional expression in social media. Then we illustrate the value of social media data with various examples of cases in which it has provided insights on individual, social and collective emotions. We also cover examples of previous research in which methodological or conceptual shortcomings have taught us valuable lessons on the limits of those data to study human emotion. We finish by outlining a series of challenges and research trends that we hope will help us in charting the future of social media data in affective science.

Measuring emotional expression in social media

Representation models of emotions

Any empirical research on emotions requires a model describing how emotions can be quantified and how they can be measured. Psychological theories to quantify affect can be divided into discrete versus dimensional models. Discrete emotion models are based on the assumption that there is a set of distinct emotions, which are generally seen as universal and innate (Ekman, 1992). Examples are "happiness", "fear", "anger", "sadness", or "disgust". The model of discrete emotions was designed to categorize emotions from facial expression, developing methods for observers to classify the emotions of someone from their face. Despite being often called a universal model of emotions, the facial expression of emotions is strongly affected by cultural norms and is far from universal (Jack, Garrod, Yu, Caldara, & Schyns, 2012). In terms of verbal expression, words for discrete emotional states show similar semantic structures across languages but still have substantial cultural differences (Jackson et al., 2019).

In contrast, dimensional theories postulate that affect can be approximated by a point on a small number of dimensions. Dimensional models typically have a *valence* dimension (positive-pleasant vs. negative–unpleasant) and an *arousal* dimension (active vs. calm) (Russel, 1980). There are several candidates for third and fourth dimensions, such as "unpredictability" or "potency" (Osgood, May, & Miron, 1975; Fontaine, Scherer, Roesch, & Ellsworth, 2007; Mehrabian, 1980). Most commonly, however, the concept of "dominance" (defensive vs. offensive) is used as a third dimension (Warriner, Kuperman, & Brysbaert, 2013; Mohammad, 2018). This tridimensional model of emotions has been derived in a robust way from the study of semantic structure using questionnaires (Osgood, Suci, & Tannenbaum, 1957) and appears in similar forms when analyzing numerous factors of emotions (Fontaine et al., 2007; Mehrabian, 1980). Alternatively, researchers sometimes simultaneously ask about two values, one for positive valence and one for negative valence, instead of combining it into a single dimension (Watson, Clark, & Tellegen, 1988). In dimensional models, discrete emotions are terms that identify points in the affective space defined by these dimensions. Sadness, for example, is negative valence combined with low arousal, while anger has also negative valence but high arousal.

Often, the choice of which model to use depends on the modality of measurement, with discrete emotions being more suitable for facial expression and dimensional models for self-reports and verbal expression. Emotional expression in social media can be analyzed through text, pictures, voice or videos, enabling multi-modal sentiment analysis approaches (see (Soleymani et al., 2017) for a review). Previous research on affect using social media data has mainly focused on analyzing textual data, captured, for example, as tweets, Facebook status updates, comments on news platforms or product reviews. In the following, we will broadly categorize text-based sentiment detection methods as an approach to quantify emotional expression, linking methods to their theoretical backgrounds.

Quantifying emotional expression in text

The simplest text-based emotion detection tools are based on unsupervised bag-of-words approaches that rely on counting words in a text regardless of their order and context. Tokens in text are matched with lists of words that have been rated according to their emotional content. The Linguistic Inquiry and Word Count (LIWC, pronounced "Luke") program (Pennebaker, Booth, Boyd, & Francis, 2015) is one of the most prominent tools for the detection of discrete emotions. LIWC classifies words of a text in different categories generated by experts in a decades-long research project in psychology. Among others, LIWC includes an "affective processes" category, which is divided into positive and negative affect. Negative affect is further divided into "anxiety", "anger" and "sadness", as raters show agreement when listing and classifying words into these three negative emotions. LIWC is among the most widely used discrete sentiment detection tools and is commercially available in several languages other than English, including German, Italian and Chinese (Wolf et al., 2008; Agosti & Rellini, 2007; Huang et al., 2012).

Lexica have also been developed for dimensional models, mostly by asking raters to assign words to their associated level of valence, arousal and dominance. Examples are the Affective

Norms in English Words (ANEW) (Bradley & Lang, 1999) and the Warriner-Kuperman-Brysbaert Affective Norms lexicon (Warriner et al., 2013), both using a conventional rating scale, and the National Research Council Valence, Arousal, and Dominance lexicon (Mohammad, 2018), which is based on an innovative best–worst scaling method in which participants select the words with highest and lowest rating in a dimension among four alternatives. For sentiment detection of a given text of sufficient length, an approach is to count all the words in the text that fall into a specific category and divide by the total number of words in the text, giving us the percentage of positive, negative, fear-related and so on words in the text. If our model is not discrete, but dimensional, we have additional information of the values of valence, arousal and dominance expressed by each word or expression. A common text analysis approach is to detect all instances of words with a rating in a text, calculating average values of valence, arousal and dominance for the whole text (Dodds & Danforth, 2010; González-Bailón, Banchs, & Kaltenbrunner, 2012). Words in the text not included in the lexicon are this way ignored, which asks for extensive and comprehensive lexica.

The bag-of-words approach is very simple and tractable but ignores a lot of potential information, such as the syntactic and grammatical structure of text. This is obvious if one compares, for example, the meaning of "man bites dog" to "dog bites man". Additionally, all words without clear affective meaning are ignored. Such words, however, can be crucial, for example, if we want to distinguish "good" from "not good". There are several sentiment detection tools that improve over the bag-of-words model and take some context into account. For example, SentiStrength (Thelwall, Buckley, Paltoglou, Cai, & Kappas, 2010) and VADER (Hutto & Gilbert, 2014) were designed to retrieve the valence of short texts as a whole. Both methods are based on a lexicon of rated words but in addition take into account several heuristics: Exclamation points and capitalization increase the magnitude of valence. Degree modifiers, such as "very", "extremely" or "barely" change the magnitude of valence according to their meaning. The word "but" signals a shift in valence polarity. Negations change the polarity of negated words. With these simple rules, VADER performs particularly well in tweets with its own lexicon but can also significantly improve the performance of various other lexica when combined with VADER's rules code (Ribeiro, Araújo, Gonçalves, Gonçalves, & Benevenuto, 2016).

All the methods of sentiment detection mentioned so far are unsupervised and do not need previous training data of texts with annotations of affective meaning. Supervised methods use a set of annotated text examples to train a predictive model, often based on a machine learning method (see Pang & Lee, 2008, and Liu & Zhang, 2012, for reviews). Most of these tools go far beyond the bag-of-words assumptions. Currently, they employ advanced language models that also include an unsupervised training step against a large corpus of text without annotations. The models embed a text into a finite-length vector that takes into account word order and context (Devlin, Chang, Lee, & Toutanova, 2018), which can then be used as input in supervised training with annotated texts. On the one hand, these sophisticated methods are powerful because they use more of the available information in text. On the other hand, they are typically black boxes that give results that are hard to interpret or cannot be trivially inferred from the output. If we go beyond prediction tasks and seek explanations, this missing knowledge is often a weakness, but current work on model interpretability and visualization is trying to cope with that problem. Compared to supervised methods, lexicon-based approaches have the advantage of not being black boxes, thus allowing inspection for systematic errors. As long as errors are not systematic, a noisy method can still be used to infer sound conclusions if datasets are large and detailed enough. Ultimately, the choice of using a supervised or an unsupervised method depends on the performance of each method in the particular case under research and on the quality and size of the data.

Examples of social media data in affective science

In this section, we illustrate the potential of social media data for affective science, focusing on limitations and risks in later sections. We do not attempt a complete review of previous research but to give an impression of the research questions, data sources, methods and statistical models applied when using social media data in affective science.

Emotion dynamics

The feeling of emotion is a transient experience. But how transient? Are we able to characterize so-called eigendynamics of emotions to measure how long it takes for an emotional state of a certain strength to vanish? While this question has been tackled using self- reports (Kuppens, Oravecz, & Tuerlinckx, 2010), social media data offers the possibility to explore it in an unobtrusive way, in a finer temporal resolution and on a much larger scale. In our earlier work (Pellert, Schweighofer, & Garcia, 2020), we used Facebook data to explore the individual eigendynamics of valence and arousal, capturing how an individual emotion changes without clear external stimuli. We combined two models of dynamic affect, the cyberemotions framework (Schweitzer & Garcia, 2010) and DynAffect (Kuppens et al., 2010), assuming that (i) there is an individual-specific baseline of valence and arousal, (ii) valence and arousal return exponentially to this baseline after an excited state, and (iii) affective expressions cause an instantaneous regulation of valence and arousal towards the individual baseline. Based on the Warriner-Kuperman-Brysbaert Affective Norms lexicon (Warriner et al., 2013), we quantified the mean valence and arousal of 16.9 million status updates, posted by 114,967 individual Facebook users, and fit a regression model on individual affective trajectories. We confirmed model assumptions and calibrated the parameters of eigendynamics for future computational models. This shows that the individual baselines are of slightly positive valence and moderate arousal, that affective expression leads to an instantaneous decay of around 60% of the distance to the individual baseline and that valence and arousal return to the individual baseline within 2–3 minutes (with arousal reverting faster than valence).

Mood, on the other hand, changes more slowly than a short-lived emotional state. Based on a corpus of 500 million English language tweets from 85 countries, Golder and Macy (2011) reconstruct an aggregate timeline of daily mood variations of 2.4 million individuals. Using LIWC, they quantify the percentage of positive and negative terms in the messages of each individual user to reconstruct individual mood variability. Notably, they do not aggregate positive and negative terms into a compound valence score but treat them as independent. By centering on the mean for each individual, they are able to aggregate these time series without confounding by inter-individual differences. They find that, independent of country, positive affect peaks in the morning and near midnight, while negative affect is lowest in the morning and rises throughout the day, peaking near midnight. The two examples show that simple unsupervised methods like LIWC and affective norms lexica can be informative when applied to large-scale datasets. Affective norms lexica are often not sufficiently accurate to classify an individual Facebook status update but can show relaxation trends when fitting regression models of the expected value of many texts. Similarly, these methods would be noisy when applied to an individual tweet, but the signal can be stronger than the noise when applied to millions of tweets coming from the same region, as shown in an exhaustive analysis of tweets across U.S. regions (Dodds, Harris, Kloumann, Bliss, & Danforth, 2011).

Environmental influences

The observation of seasonal variations of affective expression points to the influence of environmental factors on affect. Baylis et al. (2018) analyze the influence of weather conditions on expressed sentiment in a corpus of 3.5 billion tweets and Facebook status updates. They use LIWC to determine whether a given tweet or status update contains at least one positive or negative affect term. Based on that measure, they compute the proportion of such messages among all messages of a given person. Using time stamps and geo-located data of tweets and status updates, they associate texts with the prevailing weather conditions at the time of posting. By including coefficients for month and weekday in their regression analysis, they can systematically control for long-term trends and seasonal effects on expressed sentiment. They find that the proportion of positive expression increases and the proportion of negative expression decreases up to approximately 25 degrees Celsius. This trend reverses for temperatures above 30 degrees Celsius. In addition, humidity, precipitation and below-zero temperatures are associated with more negative expression. Furthermore, Baylis et al. replicate their findings under the exclusion of tweets with weather-related terms, thereby confirming that people are not just talking positively or negatively about the weather itself.

A similar example is Zheng et al. (2019), which quantifies the valence of 210 million geo-tagged Sina Weibo (the Chinese equivalent to Twitter) messages and compares it to the air pollution of the same day in the same city. They find that air pollution significantly lowers expressed valence and that this effect is stronger on weekends and holidays and under extreme weather conditions.

Emotion contagion

Human emotions are deeply social and constantly shared with others, asking for research that goes beyond the relationship of humans with their physical environment. Social media are rapidly becoming one of the main venues for emotion sharing, creating unique research opportunities. Frey et al. (2019) explore the impact of messages with strong positive or negative valence on chat room traffic in an online game for adolescents. They use a quasi-experimental design, comparing the effect of successfully posted messages with messages that were censored erroneously by a filtering algorithm. To control for as many confounding variables as possible, they match both types of events on properties such as date, time and chat room. They find that messages with strong valence increase subsequent messaging activity, and this holds for negative messages more than for positive ones. In addition, there is a feedback effect on the author of the initial message, who in turn increases her own activity in response to the increase of other users' activity.

Emotional expressions seem to trigger activity, but do they also trigger emotional states in the recipient? Ferrara and Yang (2015) quantify the extent of emotional contagion in Twitter data. They select a sample of 3800 Twitter users, for which they collect all tweets, as well as all tweets these people receive via their follower relations in a given week. Using SentiStrength, they categorize these tweets into emotionally positive, negative and neutral. By comparing their empirical results to a reshuffled null model, they find that positive tweets are more frequently preceded by incoming positive tweets and negative tweets by incoming negative tweets. The effect, however, seems to be much stronger in the case of positive than negative valence. The reshuffling allows them to exclude confounding factors, such as inter-individual differences.

But emotional loadings acquire other functionalities, too: Brady et al. (2017) explore whether Tweets on political issues, such as gun control and climate change, are re-tweeted more often if they contain a higher degree of moral–emotional language. Analyzing over 500,000 tweets with LIWC and a dictionary of moral terms, they found that retweets indeed rise if a tweet contains both moral and emotional terms. This, however, is only the case among users with a similar political position as the author of the initial tweet. This study shows that emotions do not just spread by themselves across online social networks but can also be used as a vehicle for moral and political content.

Taken together, the outcomes of these three studies show that affect plays a highly relevant role in online communication: Emotional messages drive subsequent messaging activity, seem to "infect" recipients with the emotions they contain and, in addition, serve to transport moral and political content (for a recent comprehensive discussion of emotion contagion, see Goldenberg & Gross, 2020). These dynamics can extend to large audiences and trigger more and more synchronized activity. After exceeding a certain threshold, this can lead to the emergence of collective emotions.

Collective emotions

Collective emotions can be triggered by catastrophic events, affecting the lives of thousands or even millions of people. Garcia and Rimé (2019) analyze the collective emotional response to the Paris terror attacks of November 2015 on Twitter. Using the French version of LIWC, they quantify positive and negative affect, as well as indicators of social cohesion and French national values. Using the tweets preceding the attack, they establish baseline values for these indicators, construct a correction term for day of the week and control for personality-related lexical indicators. Based on the tweets of 49,000 users from France who mention the attacks at least once, they show a prolonged rise in negative affect, in particular anxiety and sadness. These reactions have a significant memory, indicating that they reflect collective, rather than short-term, individual emotions. Garcia and Rimé can also show that Twitter users who are strongly involved in the collective emotional reaction to the attacks exhibit long-term elevated levels in the indicators of social cohesion and French values, even when correcting for their short-term increase immediately after the attacks. These elevated levels last until several months after the attacks. This demonstrates the role of collective emotions for building social cohesion after a traumatic event.

Collective emotions display different properties when compared to individual emotional experiences, for example, multiple simultaneous modes, stronger intensity and longer duration (Goldenberg et al., 2020). A recent study of emotional expression on Twitter during the COVID-19 pandemic shows this longer timescale (Metzler et al., 2021), analyzing more than 8 billion tweets in 18 countries in 2019 and 2020. This shows that the collective emotional reactions to the pandemic last weeks, with elevated levels of expression of anxiety and sadness but also with lower levels of anger in tweets.

Affective disorders

Until now, we have focused on typical affective experience. Atypical experience, manifested in mental disorders, such as major depression, phobias, anxiety disorder and post-traumatic stress disorder, is often connected to affect. These disorders are a major cause of disability and suicide. Furthermore, many somatic disorders, such as heart disease, are influenced by mental states such as stress.

Eichstaedt et al. (2018) use Facebook data obtained from 114 patients diagnosed with major depression, in combination with 570 healthy controls, to explore whether they can detect an imminent episode of depression. Using latent Dirichlet allocation, they extract 200 topics from their corpus of Facebook status updates. In combination, these topics enable them to identify depressed individuals with a prediction performance comparable to common depression screening instruments. The topics most associated with depression are related to sadness, loneliness, hostility, rumination and anxiety. These results were also confirmed using the corresponding LIWC categories. Using a similar approach as in their study of depression, Eichstaedt et al. (2015) also found that Twitter language features correlate with heart disease mortality on a county level. LIWC categories and LDA categories associated with negative emotions, in particular anger, were among the best predictors. In contrast, a higher rate of tweets with positive affect terms seemed to be a protective factor. These and other health-related studies have led to discussion about the possibility to use social media as (real-time) health monitors (Brown & Coyne, 2018; J. C. Eichstaedt et al., 2018; Chancellor & De Choudhury, 2020; Pellert, Lasser, Metzler, & Garcia, 2020).

Social media data can also serve as a complement to configure analyses of more traditional data sources on affect and mental health. Niederkrotenthaler et al. (2019) explore the potential impact of the Netflix series *Thirteen Reasons Why* on suicides among adolescents in the United States. While the main analysis is based on official suicide statistics, the statistical model was configured using the popularity of the series on Twitter and Instagram to identify the period of massive exposure (April to June, 2017). Using this social media information, the study found a surplus of suicides among teenagers for those months when comparing to a counterfactual time series model.

The limits of social media data

The studies we presented so far demonstrate that social media data can be informative for affective science in a variety of research questions. They also reveal some crucial factors of success: First, the studies are anchored in theory and connected to previous research. Second, they use established methods of sentiment detection, such as LIWC or VADER, often including a validation of the results of sentiment analysis. These methods are selected not just according to benchmarks on standard tests or availability but also with respect to the theoretical background of the study and the specific data source under study (for example, VADER is used because it is designed for Twitter data). And third, they use a variety of methods, such as matching, within-individual designs, reshuffling and control variables, to work out the causal relations between their variables of interest.

Despite this potential, there are also methodological and conceptual problems arising with the use of social media data for affective science. In this section, we focus on examples, pitfalls and limitations to illustrate that this field of study is still young, where shortcomings make the limits of current research visible.

Data quality

Different from laboratory research, where data are produced very systematically, researchers using social media data usually have no direct control of the data generating processes. This makes it necessary to take extra steps to ensure the quality of the data by filtering the raw data retrieved. A frequent problem is the presence of inauthentic content (spam) or content generated by automated accounts (bots), often with malicious intent. Bot data in particular are estimated to significantly contribute to the content on platforms like Twitter (Varol, Ferrara, Davis, Menczer, & Flammini, 2017). Bot checking tools like Botometer can be used to estimate bot scores with the aim to exclude them from the analysis (Yang, Varol, Hui, & Menczer, 2019). These tools typically rely on a number of features that identify bots, for example, temporal dynamics of posting, profile features and sentiment of published content. Often, these tools are black boxes and it is hard to disentangle which features exactly lead to the output classification. If sentiment of published content is used in bot detection, filtering with a both detector carries the risk of introducing errors that select on sentiment or emotion variables of human users. This can in turn affect the validity and generalizability of content analysis.

Bot detection stays a cat-and-mouse game as more sophisticated ways of detection lead to more sophisticated bots appearing, and the accuracy of bot detection techniques appears to be lower than initially claimed (Rauchfleisch & Kaiser, 2020). The platforms themselves regularly use internal algorithms to delete accounts that violate their terms of services, many of them being automated. This way one can check if content is still available several months or years after it was posted, leveraging the bot-cleaning efforts of platforms like Twitter. However, waiting to analyze data also leads to the loss of genuine content from users who left the platform, as time changes the composition of the samples of remaining data.

Another source of data problems when studying emotions from text is the quality of text or word annotations used by sentiment analysis and emotion detection tools. For many tasks involving automatic text processing, researchers attempt to establish a *ground truth* by using large-scale word and text rating tasks on crowdsourcing platforms. However, the quality of resulting data needs to be checked before imputing it as ground truth. Control questions and other quality checks can be used to exclude obviously non-complying participants. But still, in natural language tasks, there is considerable disagreement between raters (Mozetič, Grčar, & Smailović, 2016). These and other factors make it often hard or even impossible to establish a ground truth that is unequivocal, at least to a useful degree. Using crowdsourced annotations can have additional problems, for example, leading to tools that have different error levels for social media posts by male and female users (Thelwall, 2018).

Measurement problems

Text analysis tools are one of the key sources of measurement problems and biases in social media data analysis. The method used to measure emotions or sentiment has to be chosen by taking into account three factors: i) its compatibility with the theoretical background and hypotheses tested in the study; ii) its validity in evaluation exercises, if possible by independent studies or benchmarks; and iii) its ability to show explanations for classifications and powering to enable inspections for systematic error and diagnostics of possible biases introduced by the method. To give an example of the importance of this from our own research: The term "vice" might usually be used as a synonym of "bad habit" and is often detected as a negative word by text analysis methods. In the context of parliamentary speeches, however, it is used far more often as a component of "vice president" or "vice chairman" – so often, in fact, that counting it as negative significantly distorted our analysis of affective expression in these speeches. Another example is a study by Back, Küfner, and Egloff (2010). The authors use LIWC to analyze pager messages in the aftermath of the 9/11 terror attacks in order to obtain a timeline of emotional reactions. Their outcomes show a steady rise in anger following the attacks. But as a later article demonstrates (Pury, 2011), this rise is largely due to a surge of automatically generated messages containing the word "critical", which is classified by LIWC in the "anger" category, but that was introduced in the dataset with high frequency from automated messages about critical failures in IT systems. To make sure that sentiment analysis leads to valid results, we also have to be careful to use its output in a way that is consistent with its validation and design. If a sentiment analysis tool was created to classify texts into discrete categories (into negative, neutral or positive in the case of VADER), analyzing its output as continuous would lead to systematic error structures (see supplementary materials of Pellert, Schweighofer, & Garcia, 2020, for an example). It is generally advisable to keep returning to the raw text in the course of analysis, for example, by inspecting text examples or word statistics. There are various ways to do that, for example, with word lists, word clouds, or the more advanced word-shift graphs (Reagan, Danforth, Tivnan, Williams, & Dodds, 2017), which offer a systematic way to summarize comparisons between texts. It can also be useful to sample the raw text of messages with the most frequent dictionary matches or of surprising subsets of the data. This ensures that the results are robust, for example, by excluding single very frequent words that might be miscoded or used differently in the text under analysis. Without removing these frequent errors, aggregates of positive emotional expression in social media text can be negatively correlated with life satisfaction in surveys (Jaidka et al., 2020). However, analyzing word frequency statistics can help to remove these outlier words and to reduce the systematic error of measurements.

To provide transparent results and reliable statistics, measurement methods have to be chosen before running analyses, focusing on the most apt for the task or on a fixed set of methods to provide alternative tests. Many methods and tools are available (Ribeiro et al., 2016, provides a benchmark with 24 methods), which could pose a multiple hypothesis testing scenario in which results might not be reliable. One example is early influential work on the analysis of how aggregate sentiment of Twitter could predict the Dow Jones Industrial Average (DJIA) (Bollen, Mao, & Zeng, 2011). The authors use two different sentiment analysis tools on tweets to measure seven mood signals, testing if they lead the DJIA with seven different lags. With so many options, the chances for a false positive are not negligible, as confirmed later in a failed conceptual replication (Lachanski & Pav, 2017). The analysis of retrospective social media data gives scientists many degrees of freedom, from what to measure to which periods to include, what users to exclude and so on. A recent study has shown how the multiplicity of sentiment analysis methods can indeed be an issue by showing how a result can be *p*-hacked when many tools are used in an uncritical way (Chan et al., 2021). To avoid these problems, scientists should always report the entirety of methods and sentiment analysis tools that were applied to the data, so that the false positive rate can be properly assessed when reading their results.

Representativity Issues

One of the most common criticisms about research based on social media data concerns the general lack of representativity of user samples with respect to the general population. Such population biases can severely affect the external validity of studies and the generalizability of results (Sen et al., 2019). Olteanu et al. (2019) present a very clear illustration of this issue and provide additional nuance into the discussion about biases in social data, pointing out that the adequacy of a dataset depends on the research questions, context and aims of the study. The question of whether a sample is representative needs to specify what the relevant properties of the sample are to allow a generalization of insights. Representativity with respect to demographic attributes like gender and sex might be very important in an opinion survey, but for a media consumption study, representativity with respect to income or employment status can be more important.

Different empirical methodologies and sampling methods have various trade-offs in terms of representativity and internal validity, asking for comparative views that highlight the strong and weak points of each approach. With respect to affective science, the question of representativity of one approach should be compared to other methods to study human emotions. To illustrate that relative assessment, consider the following example: Is the sample of active Twitter users more or less representative of the U.S. population with respect to income than a sample of U.S. college students? The question is relevant, because a substantial number of psychological studies include only so-called WEIRD populations (Western, educated, industrialized, rich, and democratic) (Henrich et al., 2010) of U.S. college students. Researchers make this choice not only due to ease of access it offers but also because many experimental paradigms require physical access to the experiment participants, thus prioritizing internal validity over representativity. However, in 2018, the approximately 20 million U.S. college students composed 0.26% of the world population, while the 335 million Twitter active users composed 4.4% (Statista, 2020a, b). Social media users also tend to differ in their demographics from the general population (they are younger and more concentrated in urban areas) (Perrin & Anderson, 2019; Smith & Anderson, 2018), but a sample of social media users could be more representative in terms of other features like income and ethnicity compared to a sample of U.S. college students. However, the internal validity of observational methods using social media data is likely to be lower than in a controlled experiment, offering this way an improvement in terms of representativity but a hurdle to conclude causal explanations from data alone.

Causal inference methods can improve the internal validity of observational analyses of social media data, and the inclusion of demographic information in social media data analyses helps to assess their representativity in a careful way. Social media data analyses lie this way somewhere in between the internal validity of controlled experiments and the representativity of survey methods, providing a trade off between both. In a general setting, a combination of methodologies is the best way to build a consistent body of knowledge that integrates all available evidence on human behavior.

Discussion

One of the most visible recent issues in the analysis of emotions in social media is the importance of ethics in this kind of research. If the emotional states of users are analyzed or manipulated, scientists need to consider the possible negative consequences for study participants. As an example, consider a study that omitted items from the news feed of Facebook user depending on the emotional content of these items (Kramer, Guillory, & Hancock, 2014). The authors claim that users gave their consent by agreeing to Facebook's guidelines when they signed up. Nonetheless, ethical concerns of the scientific community were triggered and led to an "expression of concern" by the editorial board that was responsible for the publication of the article ("Editorial Expression of Concern: Experimental evidence of massivescale emotional contagion through social networks", 2014). "All-in-clauses" at the platform registration of an account are generally not regarded as meeting clinical standards of informed consent.

A second source for ethical concerns in the analysis of social media is the issue of privacy. When we deal with digital traces, we need to use proper anonymization schemes. Platform guidelines generally support responsible sharing of data: Services like Twitter only allow publishing the IDs of tweets in a dataset, not the full tweet object itself. Having to rehydrate such a dataset makes sure that the privacy of users who deleted posts, set them to private or left the platform altogether is respected and that their data cannot not be retrieved anymore. Researchers can account for privacy violation concerns by generally restricting research to the analysis of *public* posts. However, public content might also be highly sensitive: Older datasets, for example, include users that willingly share publicly sensitive information like sexual orientation (which used to be a standard profile entry on MySpace, for example). It has to be taken into consideration that awareness about potential privacy breaches in social media has changed and may change again in the future.

Among the examples of research we present in this chapter, there is a high proportion of studies using exclusively Twitter data. This has little to do with the superior quality of Twitter data but rather with its relatively easy availability – at least in comparison with data from many other platforms: Facebook, for example, practically ended all automated means of independent data retrieval. These corporate decisions are more and more creating a "post-API world" (Freelon, 2018). At the same time, data from these platforms are often used only internally by the companies. This creates problems, from conflict of interest to the impossibility of independent replications. It is still an open question how the research community should handle these problems, but it is expected that we will see more of those in the future: In reaction to events like the Cambridge Analytica scandal, social media companies more and more restrict independent access to their data. In the worst case, we may look at a future where affective science research with social media data is happening mostly behind closed doors, severely affecting the reproducibility of results.

Social media data and digital traces in general have the potential to systematically inform social scientific research and affective science in particular. This trend is becoming a reality in psychology (Rafaeli, Ashtar, & Altman, 2019) as scientists are discovering that, once limitations and other issues are properly taken into account, social media data can be a complementary data source to experiments and surveys. It is important to keep this complementary nature in mind: Observational social media data studies should not be considered a replacement for experiments or surveys because they have different strengths and weaknesses. Only a combination of methods will make the most out of all data for future research in human emotions.

In analogy to the "loudness war" in music production in the last decades of the 20th century (Vickers, 2010), we observe a run between computational social scientists to study ever larger datasets. In general, it is advisable to keep proportionality in mind. Whereas there are many examples of great insights derived from large-scale datasets (some of them detailed in "Examples of Social Media Data in Affective Science"), there is no general rule of "bigger is better". This assumption is the source of some of the pitfalls we covered in this chapter. Nevertheless, studies that fall victim to one of these pitfalls should not be seen as failures but rather as necessary stepping stones in a longer research program. We believe in the power to learn from past work when its shortcomings are put in a wider perspective.

The importance of interdisciplinarity in this domain is hard to underestimate but not easy to foster. Research in affective science using social media data is a joint endeavor by disciplines including computer science and various social sciences that needs to cross many bridges. It advances science by integrating theory and evidence from a number of diverse and sometimes disparate domains. In this chapter, we aimed to provide a balanced view of the methods, benefits, failures, risks and other challenges that are encountered in digital traces research. Computational social science in general is maturing as a field of study, with the peak of inflated expectations already past and the plateau of productivity ahead of us. The applications of social media data to study emotions are not an exception. We foresee that the pace of results in this topic will slow down but become more robust, contributing to our understanding of human behavior in a solid way.

Acknowledgments

This work was funded by the Vienna Science and Technology Fund through the project "Emotional Well-Being in the Digital Society" (Grant No. VRG16-005).

Note

1 And now increasingly under the emerging buzzword "affective AI".

References

Agosti, A., & Rellini, A. (2007). *The Italian LIWC dictionary* (Tech. Rep.). Technical report, LIWC.net.

Back, M. D., Küfner, A. C., & Egloff, B. (2010). The emotional timeline of September 11, 2001. *Psychological Science*, *21*(10), 1417–1419.

Baylis, P., Obradovich, N., Kryvasheyeu, Y., Chen, H., Coviello, L., Moro, E., . . . Fowler, J. H. (2018). Weather impacts expressed sentiment. *PLoS One*, *13*(4).

Bollen, J., Mao, H., & Zeng, X. (2011, March). Twitter mood predicts the stock market. *Journal of Computational Science*, *2*(1), 1–8. Retrieved February 19, 2018, from http:// linkinghub.elsevier.com/retrieve/pii/S187775031100007X. doi:10.1016/j.jocs.2010.12.007

Bradley, M. M., & Lang, P. J. (1999). *Affective norms for English words (anew): Instruction manual and affective ratings* (Tech. Rep.). Technical report C-1, The Center for Research in Psychophysiology. . . .

Brady, W. J., Wills, J. A., Jost, J. T., Tucker, J. A., & Van Bavel, J. J. (2017, July). Emotion shapes the diffusion of moralized content in social networks. *Proceedings of the National Academy of Sciences*, *114*(28), 7313–7318. Retrieved January 23, 2020, from www.pnas.org/lookup/doi/10.1073/pnas.1618923114

Brown, N., & Coyne, J. (2018). *No evidence that Twitter language reliably predicts heart disease: A reanalysis of Eichstaedt et al. (2015a)* (Tech. Rep.). PsyArXiv. Retrieved March 3, 2018, from https://psyarxiv.com/dursw/ doi:10.17605/OSF.IO/DURSW

Chan, C., Bajjalieh, J., Auvil, L., Wessler, H., Althaus, S., Welbers, K., . . . Jungblut, M. (2021). Four best practices for measuring news sentiment using 'off-the-shelf' dictionaries: A large-scale p-hacking experiment. *Computational Communication Research*, *3*(1), 1–27. https://doi.org/10.5117/CCR2021.1.001.CHAN

Chancellor, S., & De Choudhury, M. (2020). Methods in predictive techniques for mental health status on social media: A critical review. *NPJ Digital Medicine*, *3*(1), 1–11.

Devlin, J., Chang, M.-W., Lee, K., & Toutanova, K. (2018). Bert: Pre-training of deep bidirectional transformers for language understanding. *arXiv preprint arXiv:1810.04805*.

Dodds, P. S., & Danforth, C. M. (2010). Measuring the happiness of large-scale written expression: Songs, blogs, and presidents. *Journal of Happiness Studies*, *11*(4), 441–456.

Dodds, P. S., Harris, K. D., Kloumann, I. M., Bliss, C. A., & Danforth, C. M. (2011). Temporal patterns of happiness and information in a global social network: Hedonometrics and twitter. *PLoS One*, *6*(12).

Editorial Expression of Concern. (2014, July). Experimental evidence of massivescale emotional contagion through social networks. *Proceedings of the National Academy of Sciences*, *111*(29), 10779–10779. Retrieved April 2, 2020, from www.pnas.org/cgi/doi/10.1073/pnas.1412469111 doi:10.1073/pnas.1412469111

Eichstaedt, J. C., Schwartz, H., Giorgi, S., Kern, M., Park, G., Sap, M., . . . Ungar, L. (2018). *More evidence that Twitter language predicts heart disease: A response and replication* (Tech. Rep.). PsyArXiv. Retrieved May 14, 2018, from https://psyarxiv.com/ p75ku/ doi:10.17605/OSF.IO/P75KU

Eichstaedt, J. C., Schwartz, H. A., Kern, M. L., Park, G., Labarthe, D. R., Merchant, R. M., . . . Seligman, M. E. P. (2015, February). Psychological language on Twitter predicts county-level heart disease mortality. *Psychological Science*, *26*(2), 159–169. Retrieved March 5, 2018, from http://journals.sagepub.com/doi/10.1177/ 0956797614557867

Eichstaedt, J. C., Smith, R. J., Merchant, R. M., Ungar, L. H., Crutchley, P., Preoţiuc-Pietro, D., . . . Schwartz, H. A. (2018, October). Facebook language predicts depression in medical records. *Proceedings of the National Academy of Sciences*, *115*(44), 11203–11208. Retrieved February 5, 2019, from www.pnas.org/lookup/doi/10.1073/ pnas.1802331115

Ekman, P. (1992). An argument for basic emotions. *Cognition & emotion*, *6*(3–4), 169–200.

European Commission, B. (2018). *Eurobarometer 88.3 (2017)*. GESIS Data Archive. Retrieved April 30, 2020, from https://dbk.gesis.org/dbksearch/sdesc2.asp?no=6928&db=e&doi=10.4232/1.13007 (type: Dataset) doi:10.4232/1.13007

Ferrara, E., & Yang, Z. (2015). Measuring emotional contagion in social media. *PLoS One*, *10*(11), e0142390.

Fontaine, J. R., Scherer, K. R., Roesch, E. B., & Ellsworth, P. C. (2007). The world of emotions is not two-dimensional. *Psychological Science*, *18*(12), 1050–1057.

Freelon, D. (2018, October). Computational research in the post-API age. *Political Communication*, *35*(4), 665–668. Retrieved June 15, 2020, from www.tandfonline.com/doi/full/10.1080/10584609.2018.1 477506

Frey, S., Donnay, K., Helbing, D., Sumner, R. W., & Bos, M. W. (2019). The rippling dynamics of valenced messages in naturalistic youth chat. *Behavior research methods*, *51*(4), 1737–1753.

Frijda, N. H., et al. (1986). *The emotions*. Cambridge University Press.

Garcia, D., & Rimé, B. (2019, April). Collective emotions and social resilience in the digital traces after a terrorist attack. *Psychological Science*, *30*(4), 617–628. Retrieved May 2, 2019, from http://journals. sagepub.com/doi/10.1177/0956797619831964

Goldenberg, A., Garcia, D., Halperin, E., & Gross, J. J. (2020). Collective emotions. *Current Directions in Psychological Science*, *29*(2), 154–160.

Goldenberg, A., & Gross, J. J. (2020, February). Digital emotion contagion. *Trends in Cognitive Sciences*, S1364661320300279. Retrieved February 20, 2020, from https:// linkinghub.elsevier.com/retrieve/ pii/S1364661320300279

Golder, S. A., & Macy, M. W. (2011). Diurnal and seasonal mood vary with work, sleep, and daylength across diverse cultures. *Science*, *333*(6051), 1878–1881.

González-Bailón, S., Banchs, R. E., & Kaltenbrunner, A. (2012). Emotions, public opinion, and us presidential approval rates: A 5-year analysis of online political discussions. *Human Communication Research*, *38*(2), 121–143.

Gross, J. J., & Barrett, L. F. (2013). The emerging field of affective science. *Emotion*, *13*(6), 997.

Henrich, J., Heine, S. J., & Norenzayan, A. (2010, June). The weirdest people in the world? *Behavioral and Brain Sciences*, *33*(2–3), 61–83. Retrieved October 7, 2019, from www.cambridge.org/core/product/ identifier/ S0140525X0999152X/type/journal article. doi:10.1017/S0140525X0999152X

Huang, C.-L., Chung, C. K., Hui, N., Lin, Y.-C., Seih, Y.-T., Lam, B. C. P., . . . Pennebaker, J. W. (2012). The development of the Chinese linguistic inquiry and word count dictionary. *Chinese Journal of Psychology, 54*(2), 185–201.

Hutto, C. J., & Gilbert, E. (2014). Vader: A parsimonious rule-based model for sentiment analysis of social media text. In *Eighth international AAAI conference on weblogs and social media*. The AAAI Press.

Jack, R. E., Garrod, O. G., Yu, H., Caldara, R., & Schyns, P. G. (2012). Facial expressions of emotion are not culturally universal. *Proceedings of the National Academy of Sciences*, *109*(19), 7241–7244.

Jackson, J. C., Watts, J., Henry, T. R., List, J.-M., Forkel, R., Mucha, P. J., . . . Lindquist, K. A. (2019). Emotion semantics show both cultural variation and universal structure. *Science*, *366*(6472), 1517–1522.

Jaidka, K., Giorgi, S., Schwartz, H. A., Kern, M. L., Ungar, L. H., & Eichstaedt, J. C. (2020, April). Estimating geographic subjective well-being from Twitter: A comparison of dictionary and data-driven language methods. *Proceedings of the National Academy of Sciences*, 201906364. Retrieved April 28, 2020, from www.pnas.org/lookup/ doi/10.1073/pnas.1906364117

Kramer, A. D. I., Guillory, J. E., & Hancock, J. T. (2014, June). Experimental evidence of massive-scale emotional contagion through social networks. *Proceedings of the National Academy of Sciences*, *111*(24), 8788–8790. Retrieved February 4, 2020, from www.pnas.org/cgi/doi/10.1073/ pnas.1320040111

Kuppens, P., Oravecz, Z., & Tuerlinckx, F. (2010). Feelings change: Accounting for individual differences in the temporal dynamics of affect. *Journal of personality and social psychology*, *99*(6), 1042.

Lachanski, M., & Pav, S. (2017). Shy of the character limit:" Twitter mood predicts the stock market" revisited. *Econ Journal Watch*, *14*(3), 302. (tex.publisher: Fraser Institute)

Liu, B., & Zhang, L. (2012). A survey of opinion mining and sentiment analysis. In *Mining text data* (pp. 415–463). Springer.

Mehrabian, A. (1980). *Basic dimensions for a general psychological theory implications for personality, social, environmental, and developmental studies*. Oelgeschlager, Gunn & Hain.

Metzler, H., Rimé, B., Pellert, M., Niederkrotenthaler, T., Natale, A. D., & Garcia, D. (2021). Collective emotions during the COVID-19 outbreak. *PsyArXiv*. https://doi.org/10.31234/osf.io/qejxv

Mohammad, S. (2018). *Obtaining reliable human ratings of valence, arousal, and dominance for 20,000 English words* (pp. 174–184). Melbourne, Australia: Association for Computational Linguistics. Retrieved from www.aclweb.org/anthology/

Mozetič, I., Grčar, M., & Smailović, J. (2016, May). Multilingual Twitter sentiment classification: The role of human annotators. *PLoS One*, *11*(5), e0155036. Retrieved February 6, 2020, from http://dx.plos. org/10.1371/journal.pone.0155036

Newell, A., & Simon, H. A. (1976, March). Computer science as empirical inquiry: Symbols and search. *Communications of the ACM, 19*(3), 113–126. Retrieved April 30, 2020, from http://portal.acm.org/citation.cfm?doid=360018.360022

Niederkrotenthaler, T., Stack, S., Till, B., Sinyor, M., Pirkis, J., Garcia, D., . . . Tran, U. S. (2019, September). Association of increased youth suicides in the United States with the release of *13 reasons why*. *JAMA Psychiatry, 76*(9), 933. Retrieved February 24, 2020, from https://jamanetwork.com/journals/jamapsychiatry/fullarticle/2734859. doi:10.1001/jamapsychiatry.2019.0922

Olteanu, A., Castillo, C., Diaz, F., & Kiciman, E. (2019). Social data: Biases, methodological pitfalls, and ethical boundaries. *Frontiers in Big Data, 2,* 13.

Osgood, C. E., May, W. H., & Miron, M. S. (1975). *Cross-cultural universals of affective meaning* (Vol. 1). University of Illinois Press.

Osgood, C. E., Suci, G. J., & Tannenbaum, P. H. (1957). *The Measurement of meaning.* Champaign, IL: University of Illinois Press. Retrieved December 13, 2019, from http:// archive.org/details/TheMeasurementOfMeaningNew

Pang, B., & Lee, L. (2008). Opinion mining and sentiment analysis. *Foundations and Trends in Information Retrieval, 2*(1–2), 1–135.

Pellert, M., Lasser, J., Metzler, H., & Garcia, D. (2020). Dashboard of sentiment in Austrian social media during COVID-19. Frontiers in Big Data, 3. https://doi.org/10.3389/fdata.2020.00032

Pellert, M., Schweighofer, S., & Garcia, D. (2020, January). The individual dynamics of affective expression on social media. *EPJ Data Science, 9*(1), 1. Retrieved January 13, 2020, from https://epjdatascience.springeropen.com/articles/10.1140/ epjds/s13688-019-0219-3

Pennebaker, J., Booth, R., Boyd, R., & Francis, M. (2015). *Linguistic inquiry and word count: LIWC2015.* Pennebaker Conglomerates. Retrieved from www.LIWC.net.

Perrin, A., & Anderson, M. (2019, April 10). *Share of U.S. adults using social media, including Facebook, is mostly unchanged since 2018.* Pew Research Center. https://www.pewresearch.org/fact-tank/2019/04/10/share-of-u-s-adults-using-social-media-including-facebook-is-mostly-unchanged-since-2018/

Picard, R. W. (2000). *Affective computing.* The MIT Press.

Pury, C. L. (2011). Automation can lead to confounds in text analysis: Back, Küfner, and Egloff (2010) and the not-so-angry Americans. *Psychological Science, 22*(6), 835.

Rafaeli, A., Ashtar, S., & Altman, D. (2019, December). Digital traces: New data, resources, and tools for psychological-science research. *Current Directions in Psychological Science, 28*(6), 560–566. Retrieved January 29, 2020, from http://journals.sagepub.com/doi/10.1177/0963721419861410

Rauchfleisch, A., & Kaiser, J. (2020). The false positive problem of automatic bot detection in social science research. *PLOS ONE, 15*(10), e0241045. https://doi.org/10.1371/journal.pone.0241045

Reagan, A. J., Danforth, C. M., Tivnan, B., Williams, J. R., & Dodds, P. S. (2017, December). Sentiment analysis methods for understanding large-scale texts: A case for using continuum-scored words and word shift graphs. *EPJ Data Science, 6*(1), 28. Retrieved April 29, 2020, from http://epjdatascience.springeropen.com/articles/ 10.1140/epjds/s13688-017-0121-9

Ribeiro, F. N., Araújo, M., Gonçalves, P., Gonçalves, M. A., & Benevenuto, F. (2016). Sentibench – A benchmark comparison of state-of-the-practice sentiment analysis methods. *EPJ Data Science, 5*(1), 1–29.

Rimé, B. (2009). Emotion elicits the social sharing of emotion: Theory and empirical review. *Emotion Review, 1*(1), 60–85.

Russel, J. (1980). A circumplex model of affect. *Journal of Personality and Social Psychology, 39*(6), 1161–1178.

Scherer, K. R. (2005). What are emotions? And how can they be measured? *Social Science Information, 44*(4), 695–729.

Schweitzer, F., & Garcia, D. (2010). An agent-based model of collective emotions in online communities. *The European Physical Journal B, 77*(4), 533–545.

Sen, I., Floeck, F., Weller, K., Weiss, B., & Wagner, C. (2019). A total error framework for digital traces of humans. *arXiv preprint arXiv:1907.08228.*

Smith, A., & Anderson, M. (2018, March 1). Social Media Use 2018. Pew Research Center. https://www.pewinternet.org/2018/03/01/social-media-use-in-2018/

Social Media Use 2018: Demographics and Statistics | Pew Research Center. (2018, March). Retrieved May 27, 2019, from www.pewinternet.org/2018/03/01/social-media-use-in-2018/

Soleymani, M., Garcia, D., Jou, B., Schuller, B., Chang, S.-F., & Pantic, M. (2017, September). A survey of multimodal sentiment analysis. *Image and Vision Computing, 65,* 3–14. Retrieved February 2020, from https://linkinghub.elsevier.com/retrieve/ pii/S0262885617301191. doi:10.1016/j.imavis.2017.08.003

Statista. (2020a). *College enrollment in public and private institutions in the U.S. 1965–2029 [Computer software manual].* Retrieved June 29, 2020, from www.statista.com/statistics/183995/ us-college– enrollment-and-projections-in-public-and-private-institutions/

Statista. (2020b). *Number of monthly active Twitter users world- wide from 1st quarter 2010 to 1st quarter 2019 [Computer software manual].* Retrieved June 29, 2020, from www.statista.com/statistics/282087/ number-of-monthly-active– twitter-users/

Thelwall, M. (2018). Gender bias in sentiment analysis. *Online Information Review, 42*(1), 45–57. https:// doi.org/10.1108/OIR-05-2017-0139

Thelwall, M., Buckley, K., Paltoglou, G., Cai, D., & Kappas, A. (2010). Sentiment strength detection in short informal text. *Journal of the American Society for Information Science and Technology, 61*(12), 2544–2558.

Varol, O., Ferrara, E., Davis, C. A., Menczer, F., & Flammini, A. (2017, March). Online human-bot interactions: Detection, estimation, and characterization. *arXiv:1703.03107 [cs].* Retrieved April 30, 2020, from http://arxiv.org/abs/1703.03107 (arXiv: 1703.03107)

Vickers, E. (2010, November). The loudness war: Background, speculation, and recommendations. *Audio Engineering Society Convention, 129.* http://www.aes.org/e-lib/browse.cfm?elib=15598

Warriner, A. B., Kuperman, V., & Brysbaert, M. (2013, December). Norms of valence, arousal, and dominance for 13,915 English lemmas. *Behavior Research Methods, 45*(4), 1191–1207. Retrieved May 7, 2018, from http://link.springer.com/ 10.3758/s13428–012–0314-x doi:10.3758/s13428-012-0314-x

Watson, D., Clark, L. A., & Tellegen, A. (1988). Development and validation of brief measures of positive and negative affect: The Panas scales. *Journal of Personality and Social Psychology, 54*(6), 1063.

Wolf, M., Horn, A. B., Mehl, M. R., Haug, S., Pennebaker, J. W., & Kordy, H. (2008). Computergestützte quantitative textanalyse: Äquivalenz und robustheit der deutschen version des linguistic inquiry and word count. *Diagnostica, 54*(2), 85–98.

Yang, K.-C., Varol, O., Hui, P.-M., & Menczer, F. (2019, November). Scalable and generalizable social bot detection through data selection. *arXiv:1911.09179 [cs].* Retrieved April 30, 2020, from http:// arxiv.org/abs/1911.09179

Zheng, S., Wang, J., Sun, C., Zhang, X., & Kahn, M. E. (2019, March). Air pollution lowers Chinese urbanites' expressed happiness on social media. *Nature Human Behaviour, 3*(3), 237–243. Retrieved from https://doi.org/10.1038/s41562-018-0521-2 doi:10.1038/s41562-018-0521-2

16

UNDERSTANDING POLITICAL SENTIMENT

Using Twitter to map the U.S. 2016 Democratic primaries

Niklas M Loynes and Mark Elliot

Introduction

The rise of social media services such as Facebook and Twitter has brought with it a new form of *consequential data* (see, e.g., Purdam & Elliot, 2015, for a discussion of data classes). These data have some advantages over data conventionally used in the social sciences: costs for data collection are drastically reduced, and potential sample sizes are considerably larger. Furthermore, when regarding such data as containing signals pertaining to public opinion, they offer a potential advantage over *intentional data* such as those derived from surveys: interviewer effects, social desirability bias and other artifacts of the researcher-administered stimuli used to generate these data are absent, as the data are created voluntarily.

There is a growing body of research which has used such data to address empirical questions, in fields as varied as public health, where tweets were used to predict the spread of swine flu (Ritterman, Osborne, & Klein, 2009); criminology, where scholars used Twitter data to build models dynamically predicting the occurrence of violent behaviour (Wang, Gerber, & Brown, 2012); economics, using tweets in stock market development forecasting models (Si, Mukherjee, Liu, Li, Li, & Deng, 2013); or geology, where twitter data were used to develop dynamic earthquake tracking models (Sakaki, Okazaki, & Matsuo, 2010). In political science, the use of these data has been particularly prevalent, be it investigating twitter users' ideology (Barberá, 2014; Bond & Messing, 2015), the effect that exposure to political tweets has on individuals' political knowledge (Munger, Egan, Nagler, Ronen, & Tucker, 2016) or the phenomenon of group organization for political protests using social media (Theocharis, Lowe, Van Deth, & García-Albacete, 2015).

A sub-field of political science using such consequential, or "digital trace", data uses data obtained from Twitter to forecast election results. Early on and somewhat prematurely, Tumasjan, Sprenger, Sandner, and Welpe (2010) proclaimed they had matched the predictive accuracy of polls by merely counting mentions of parties on Twitter, but Jungherr, Jürgens, and Schoen (2012) replicated this study with divergent findings,[1] arguing against the feasibility of forecasting real-world, offline events using mere tweet volume. Other scholars have attempted to forecast elections with Twitter data, but as yet, there is no "unifying theory" or "standard approach" in the literature.

DOI: 10.4324/9781003024583-19

For a large amount of Twitter-based public opinion research, specifically that which aims to predict manifest measures of public opinion such as vote shares in democratic elections, *sentiment analysis* has proven a valuable tool for maximizing the value of such research. In its simplest form, sentiment-assisted election forecasting assumes that positive sentiment expressed toward a political candidate or party on Twitter (and other social media sites) is a more robust predictor of eventual vote share than mention counts for said candidate or party. While this may be intuitively plausible, computational sentiment analysis, whether it is lexicon based or employs machine learning, often falls short of adequately classifying sentiment in tweets which relate to a politically salient topic. The key problem is that much of the language prevalent therein is not easily classifiable at scale: for instance, consistently identifying sarcasm and evolving, event-led context-specific language is at best complex and at worst intractable for automated sentiment classification, regardless of the approach used.

In this chapter, we investigate areas of interest at the intersection of tweet-based sentiment and Twitter-based public opinion research. Our goal is to understand how insights might be best extracted from user-generated social web text for public opinion research. Our focus is primarily methodological. In essence, this means that we apply established steps in the sentiment analysis toolkit, as well as novel alternatives, and outline the workflow for moving from data to insights. Crucially, we then collate these insights into a tangible empirical application – the election vote share estimation paradigm – in order to evaluate the efficacy of research design decisions in this sub-field, with a particular focus on weighing up the costs and benefits of design choices in such applications.

This line of enquiry involves four core areas of investigation. First, we outline existing approaches to measuring sentiment in political tweets and emphasize the distinction between *political* and *linguistic* sentiment. We also introduce our approach to measuring political sentiment in tweets, which involves hand-annotation of samples of pertinent tweets in a multi-step process: a categorical addressee annotation, followed by an ordinal sentiment annotation. Second, and relatedly, we discuss the up- and downsides of measuring sentiment at the categorical versus ordinal level and empirically investigate how an ordinal measure can enhance the resulting predictions/aggregations. Third, we trial different approaches of aggregating sentiment scores in order to model vote share percentages in an election. We compare a novel methodology – simulating votes by randomly drawing sentiment scores from samples of sentiment-labeled tweets – with established methodologies. Fourth, we investigate how sampling decisions – from the definition of a geographical sampling frame, to the selection of labeling sets, to the weighting and de-biasing of samples for analysis – impacts the model results.

In order to apply these aspects of our investigation to an empirical context, we selected the 2016 U.S. Democratic Party presidential primaries as our case study. Specifically, we chose three primary elections; New Hampshire, South Carolina and Massachusetts. We opted for this case selection as the U.S. primary system allows us to study cases with different underlying sociodemographic "fundamentals" while still having the same electoral rules and participating candidates. This allows for both high-precision evaluations of a given predictive model's configuration but also a robust way of getting towards the core aim of this project – learning more about which conditions – be they arising from contextual factors of a test case or the configuration of a model – impact the efficacy of using Twitter data for public opinion research.

In the remaining parts of this chapter, we begin by reviewing the existing methods for systematically extracting subjective opinions – *sentiment* – from text taken from the social web.[2] We describe the various approaches: their respective advantages, shortcomings and limits. We then discuss the literature on Twitter-based election forecasts and public opinion research which is supported to some degree by sentiment analysis. We assess the methodologies which were employed to produce a given forecast as well as their respective performance records. Then, we describe research design and the data used in this project, outlining how samples were generated and how the samples for the three different states differ in terms of geographical and ideological makeup. We then describe our hand-labeled *political* sentiment annotation procedure. We then outline how we propagated ordinal sentiment scores from labeling sets to larger samples of pertinent tweets. Finally, we describe the performance of 12 predictive models for estimating vote share percentages in the 2016 Democratic presidential primaries in New Hampshire, South Carolina and Massachusetts and draw conclusions both regarding best practice of sentiment-assisted Twitter-based public opinion research, as well as the efficacy of the endeavor as a whole.

Sentiment analysis of social web texts

Social web text is as an abundant resource of user-generated data containing opinions on every conceivable topic. Using computational methods in order to analyze and provide quantitative estimates of the emotional content of those opinions ("X is good, Y is annoying") within text units is typically referred to as *sentiment analysis*.

Following Liu (2012), we concur that textual sentiment can be represented using two measures, *polarity* (is a given text unit expressing positive, negative or neutral sentiment?) and *intensity*[3] (*how* positive or negative is the sentiment?). Understanding and categorizing sentiment – at the very least in terms of polarity – is a relatively simple undertaking for the average human. However, human judgment is not sufficiently scalable for large samples of web text. Hence, researchers typically use computational tools to generate estimates of the sentiment polarity and intensity.

Initial attempts focused on matching words to semantic lexica, such as specific emotions (Huettner & Subasic, 2000). Pang, Lee and Vaithyanathan (2002) provided an early example, succeeding in estimating sentiment polarity with an accuracy exceeding that of "human-produced baselines" (p. 79), assigning polarity estimates for a large sample of online, user-generated movie reviews, reaching accuracy levels of up to 82.9 % (p. 83) using several different machine learning (ML) approaches. Such approaches use labeled training data[4] by which the algorithm "learns" both sides of the estimation equation. This "knowledge" is then applied to unlabelled data. In 2003, Nasukawa and Yi (2003) introduced a lexicon-based approach to estimating sentiment polarity for "web pages and news articles" (p. 70), achieving similarly high levels of estimation accuracy to Pang et al. (2002). The lexicon-based approach differs significantly from the ML approach, in that a pre-defined reference lexicon containing a large number of individual words is labeled with either a polarity indicator or an ordinal intensity score. A basic model of lexicon-based sentiment would simply look for the occurrence of any such word in a given text unit and combine polarity/intensity ratings of all occurring words to produce a sentiment estimate. More complex models take into account a word's position within a sentence, and so on.

Several researchers produced papers with a similar goal of estimating sentiment of online texts, typically reviews of products or movies (see, e.g., Turney, 2002; Dave, Lawrence, & Pennock, 2003; Hu & Liu, 2004; Pang & Lee, 2004; Liu, Hu, & Cheng, 2005; Popescu & Etzioni, 2007). Gamon, Aue, Corston-Oliver, and Ringger (2005) introduced an ML approach using supervised support vector machines capable of analyzing the sentiment of single sentences with "precision scores ranging from 0.95 to 0.97" (p. 10). Despite high levels of precision achieved in the publications listed previously, none of these papers estimate sentiment *intensity*. This endeavor, was first tackled in the literature by Pang and Lee (2005). They introduced a method capable of precisely estimating review ratings using support vector machine regression. Taboada, Brooke, Tofiloski, Voll, and Stede (2011) provide a different solution to this problem, building a sentiment analysis tool that estimates polarity *and* intensity on an ordinal scale relying on a reference lexicon rather than a ML approach. The authors assert that this approach outperforms ML algorithms for domain-independent data. The accuracy of their method ranges from 65% to 81.5%, depending on the nature of the dictionary and the data. Finally, Thelwall, Buckley, and Paltoglou (2012) developed an application – SentiStrength – which measures sentiment intensity and polarity by matching text units to a lexicon. However, intensity is expressed on two ordinal scales, one positive and one negative. The authors argue that this approach allows for the possibility "that both positive and negative sentiment can coexist within texts" (p. 164).

Both the ML and lexicon-based approaches have advantages and shortcomings. While ML sentiment analysis is likely only applicable to the topic domain of the text units for which labeled data, and thus training data, exist, it has the potential for outperforming lexicon-based methods (see, e.g., Thelwall et al., 2012, p. 172) by capturing indirect sentiment indicators, such as terms which convey sentiment in the context of the topic domain of the training set, without necessarily having the same connotations in general language. Lexicon-based methods will likely not capture these terms, and they will only work for languages in which lexica are available. However, lexica do not require newly labeled data for each new project, and tools can be re-used for applications with text data covering widely disparate topics. Hence, the evidence suggests that for general applications, for example, with text not clearly situated within one distinctive topic domain, lexicon-based methods are likely more appropriate, whereas ML approaches are best suited to narrow, domain-specific tasks. This assessment is supported by Ribeiro, Araújo, Gonçalves, Gonçalves, and Benevenuto (2016), whose SentiBench project analyses different "state-of-the-practice" sentiment analysis tools with the aim of comparing their respective output for types of text typically mined for sentiment (social media posts, reviews and website comments). They find that "there is no single method that always achieves the best prediction performance" (p. 3), and "existing methods vary widely regarding their agreement" (p. 3).

Specific application of the sentiment analysis paradigm to tweets has been widespread. This is hardly surprising, given the simplicity of collecting user-generated text data from the platform, their wide use across academic and commercial settings and the structural simplicity of the tweet as a text unit mean that method and data are well mapped.

Pak and Paroubek (2010) attempted to replicate the state-of-the-art of ML approaches for classifying sentiment on a corpora of tweets. They find that a configuration using text tokenized to bigrams using a multinomial naive Bayes classification algorithm produces best results when producing categorical (i.e., polarity) ratings for tweet-level sentiment. Agarwal, Xie, Vovsha, Rambow, and Passonneau (2011) showcase a similar experiment, but with the added output of two lexica, denoting key tweet features mapping emoticons to sentiment polarity, as well as "an acronym dictionary collected from the web with English translations of over 5000 frequently used acronyms" (p. 31). In addition to using hand-annotated data to train their sentiment detection algorithm, they incorporate their emoticon dictionary and a reference sentiment lexicon into their analysis, resulting in a hybrid model. In essence, the authors map each token in a tweet to one of 50 predefined features, allowing them to then estimate a sentiment polarity for a given tweet. The authors use data collected straight from Twitter's public sample stream – implying that their method is aimed at classifying "generic" tweets of no particular topic domain. They achieve maximum accuracy levels of around 0.75 (p. 36).

A similar approach was taken by Zhang, Ghosh, Dekhil, Hsu, and Liu (2011), where a lexicon-based approach is utilized in the first step of the analysis and is effectively used to annotate tweets for sentiment polarity. These annotations are then used to train a support vector machine classification algorithm providing this classification pipeline with accuracy levels exceeding the existing state of the art. Crucially, their hybrid approach outperforms all established methods against which they benchmark it, yielding maximum accuracy levels of 0.85 (p. 7).

Abbasi, Hassan, and Dhar (2014) perform a similar sentiment benchmarking analysis to Ribeiro et al. (2016) but exclusively using twitter data with content relating to specific topic domains. They find that different tools are more accurate in different topic domains, and the best overall performance was achieved by SentiStrength, with an average accuracy level of 0.67 (p. 5). Severyn and Moschitti (2015) take the Twitter-based sentiment classification paradigm into the state-of-the art of machine learning by classifying tweets in a three-step approach using convolutional neural networks and distant supervision. The authors state that their model is among the best in the Semeval-2015 challenge for advancing the field of sentiment analysis. This model achieves a maximum accuracy of 0.85 (p. 962) on a dataset of tweets, classifying sentiment polarity.

Sentiment analysis and Twitter-based election forecasts

Studying, understanding and predicting public opinion using online text data – especially in the context of voting behaviour and its outcomes – has received considerable scholarly interest in recent years. Using user-generated online text as data offers several advantages over intentional survey and polling data: costs for data access and collection (at least in the case of Twitter, easily the most popular data source in this field) are drastically lower than with survey-based approaches; data are available in large quantities, and sentiment conveyed within tweet text is a self-generated expression of opinion rather than a narrow response structured by the parameters of a survey instrument.

The sub-field of election forecasting/vote share prediction by means of data collected from social media sites began with Tumasjan et al. (2010), who predicted the outcome of the 2009 German Bundestag elections with a level of accuracy comparable to that of pre-election polls by counting mentions of relevant parties and candidates on Twitter. While some scholars (such as Gayo-Avello, 2013) argue that this was merely down to luck, and a more clearly specified approach would have resulted in different – inaccurate – results (Jungherr et al., 2012), several publications have subsequently attempted to forecast election outcomes using Twitter data, with varying degrees of methodological rigor, theoretical foundation and model performance.

While some researchers employ an approach similar to that of (see, e.g., Tumasjan et al., 2010) (Gayo-Avello, 2011; Metaxas, Mustafaraj, & Gayo-Avello, 2011; Jungherr et al., 2012; DiGrazia, McKelvey, Bollen, & Rojas, 2013; Caldarelli et al., 2014), with a mixed record of accuracy, a large amount of the Twitter-based election forecasting literature uses sentiment analysis. O'Connor, Balasubramanyan, Routledge, and Smith (2010) found that lexicon-derived tweet sentiment correlates highly, ranging from $r = .77$ to $r = .81$ (p. 128), to opinion poll time series on U.S. presidential job approval[5] when aggregated over long time periods. While the authors note that this task is inherently easier than that of forecasting the actual *outcome* of an election, their findings form a crucial building block and justification for further research into the area, as it highlights that Twitter sentiment on a political topic closely mirrors sentiment elicited from individuals through the traditional survey paradigm.

Building on this foundational work by O'Connor et al., several scholars conducted published research attempting to take these findings a step further and actually use insights derived from tweets through sentiment analysis in order to forecast the outcome of democratic elections. Sang and Bos (2012) used machine learning to classify tweet sentiment, coupled with mention counts, to forecast the Dutch Senate elections of 2011. The authors achieved an adequate level of predictive accuracy – the country's leading polls were more accurate by four seats. However, the authors used polling weights after the fact to stratify their model. Bermingham and Smeaton (2011) used a similar approach but with a significantly worse performance: a mention count model outperforms their positive sentiment volume model. However, this is arguably due to specific research design weaknesses: a small sample of labeled tweets, low levels of inter-annotator agreement and a significantly lower number of tweets overall compared to similar publications. Ceron, Curini, Iacus, and Porro (2014) used perhaps the most sophisticated sentiment-assisted method for their forecast of the French presidential and legislative elections of 2012, using a supervised ML approach adopted from Hopkins and King (2010) to adequately forecast the winner of the presidential race within the error range of traditional polls as well as the vote share of most parties in the National Assembly.[6] Ceron, Curini, and Iacus (2015) replicated this approach using different case studies (the 2012 U.S. presidential election and the Italian Democratic Party's 2012 primary), achieving results that outperformed polls in the majority of cases.[7] Finally, Burnap, Gibson, Sloan, Southern, and Williams (2016) used Thelwall et al.'s (2012) SentiStrength lexicon-based sentiment tool to forecast the 2015 UK general election, which broadly matched pre-election polling averages but failed to forecast the Conservative party's eventual victory.

Overall, the evidence to date allows for four tentative conclusions:

1   Sentiment analysis-based approaches to predicting/forecasting metrics related to electoral outcomes outperform models relying solely on candidate/party mention volume (however, rigorously applied sentiment analysis and a large enough sample are necessary conditions for this to be the case).

2   Machine learning-based methods have a higher predictive accuracy than lexicon-based methods (especially using advanced algorithms, such as Hopkins and King's [2010], rather than simple approaches such as naive Bayes).

3   While basic research such as Severyn and Moschitti (2015) suggests that advanced machine learning approaches (such as convolutional neural networks) can improve tweet sentiment classification accuracy and potentially reduce the need for costly human annotation of domain-specific tweet data for model training, these findings are based on tweets from the general domain, not topic-specific tweets.

4   There appears to be no unifying theory for *why* Twitter-derived, sentiment-based predictive public opinion models perform well or fail. The existing literature takes little note of either conceptual or methodological factors that may contribute to the outcome of predictions. Conceptually, there is little discussion of why precisely measured sentiment in tweets mentioning politicians should tell us something about that politician's electoral chances. Methodologically, existing research is agnostic to interventions such as weighting and de-biasing, the whole question of sampling or the dearth of user-level demographics.

In the following section, we delineate the key issues that persist within the sentiment-based public opinion modeling literature as a whole. Following this, we outline our approach to measuring the *political* sentiment within tweets containing politically salient text and our methodology for predicting electoral vote share proportions. We use sentiment-annotated tweets in the three empirical case studies of the 2016 Democratic presidential primaries in New Hampshire, South Carolina and Massachusetts.

On the relationship between political tweeting and voting

Overall, the idea of modeling election results using data gathered from Twitter or other social media sites has been widely critiqued; see, for example, Lui, Metaxas, and Mustafaraj (2011);

Jungherr et al. (2012); Jungherr (2015); Gayo-Avello (2011, 2013). Gayo-Avello (2013) in particular points out the structural problems inherent with Twitter data as predictors of political behaviour: the demographics of the "Twittersphere" do not match those of target offline populations, and the dearth of available information on users' sociodemographic attributes (e.g., age, gender, race/ethnicity, socioeconomic status, etc.) makes drawing externally valid inferences complex at best and impossible at worst. Furthermore, Twitter data are not robust to self-selection bias (Gayo-Avello, 2013, p. 670) – tweeting is a voluntary act, meaning that tweet collections do not contain a sample of political opinions of Twitter users but rather a sample of political opinions of those users choosing to share them. Furthermore, Jungherr (2017) points out an often-overlooked factor that shapes most any collection of Twitter data used for academic research. Rather than selecting a sample of tweets pertinent to a given topic of interest by sampling from the population of *all* existing tweets or users, tweet collections are typically compiled by filtering Twitter's streaming API based on *a priori* defined keywords. This method is subject to two key shortcomings: First, there is no guarantee that researchers correctly specified relevant keywords before the fact, meaning that the collection may be over- or undersampling from the population of all political salient tweets. Second, the fact that Twitter limits the proportion of tweets that are accessible through its streaming API, and further, that there is no guarantee that these tweets are representative of the population (of interest) means that any sample of tweets obtained from the streaming API may be biased in unknowable ways. Jungherr refers to this phenomenon as the "n = all fallacy". However, short of a costly subscription to Twitter's full stream, there is little researchers can do to overcome these shortcomings.

These are top-level/structural issues associated with social science research using social media data. However, some of these issues can be mitigated. Most promisingly, this can be done in estimating user-level sociodemographic attributes, where several researchers in the field have developed computational tools that estimate such attributes, for instance, users' age (Nguyen, Gravel, Trieschnigg, & Meder, 2013), their political affinity (Barberá, 2014) or their home location (Loynes, Nagler, Casas, & Baram, forthcoming; Loynes et al.). We argue that incorporating such measures of individual-level user attributes into any analysis of political tweets can be useful and thus do so in this chapter.

Notwithstanding the complex systemic issues associated with using tweets for public opinion research, applying sentiment analysis in such a setting is further prone to bias originating from imprecise operationalization of the theorized causal behavioral relationship between posting social web texts and engaging in (offline) political behaviour, such as voting. Researchers typically equate the proportion of positive tweets mentioning a party/candidate in a corpus of salient tweets with eventual vote share percentages in elections. This assumes an underlying model of proportionality between positive sentiment expressed on Twitter and individual-level vote choice. However, researchers do not typically explain their assumptions regarding (1) the appropriateness of sentiment analysis in Twitter-based election forecasts and (2) what positive sentiment in tweets signifies; in other words, what they are actually *measuring*. Furthermore, tweet-level analyses overweight active posters, essentially giving them multiple "votes" in such models. Hence, we argue that it is of importance to downsample to the user-level, thus providing a degree of proportionality which mirrors the "one person, one vote" maxim in democratic elections.

Crucially, there are three core questions that need to be asked concerning the relationship between political tweets and (offline) political behaviour. First, there is the fundamental question of how political tweeting and political behaviour are linked, what common origins they share and if and how we can transfer meaning from one domain to another. Second, there is the more specific question of what it means when a given Twitter user tweets something with positive political sentiment about a politician or party. Third, there is also the question of what it signifies when a user tweets something negative about a politician.

The linkage between political tweets and political behaviour

There is an implicit assumption prevalent in the literature on sentiment-based public opinion research using Twitter data: positive sentiment in a tweet directed toward a given party or candidate is an adequate proxy of voting intention for said party/candidate. It is an intuitive hypothesis that highly popular candidates typically poll better than unpopular candidates and eventually receive more votes (Lewis-Beck & Rice, 1982; Kenney & Rice, 1983). O'Connor et al. (2010) found a high correlation between longitudinal positive sentiment in tweets mentioning political figures and their survey-derived approval ratings. The authors' findings are plausible – tweeting one's opinions on a politician is similar to answering a survey question on one's views towards them. A similar hypothesis seems appropriate for the sentiment volume/vote share relationship: candidates for whom we measure low amounts of positive sentiment on Twitter should be expected to get fewer votes than those with a larger volume of positive sentiment.

It is clear that there is *no* direct causal relationship between political tweeting and political behaviour, such as voting. However, as displayed in Figure 16.1, some theoretically sound assumptions can be made regarding their relationship. First, certain latent (and potentially observable) individual-level factors and attributes shape any individual's behaviour – including their propensity to vote or to tweet. When it comes to political tweets, it is further apparent that many such factors likely exert an equal, shared or subsequent influence on both types of observable behaviour. While one may speculate as to whether these factors might be stable, like partisanship or ideology, or more acute and unstable, such as an evaluation of a politician's response to exogenous events, for example, a war or a pandemic (see, e.g., Mueller, 1970; Newman & Forcehimes, 2010) or something subject to medium-term evolution, such as an individual's evaluation of the state of the economy (see, e.g., Lewis-Beck & Stegmaier, 2007), it is highly plausible that such factors contribute to both behaviors of interest. However, it is conversely also clear that there are certain factors which may affect these two behaviors in opposing ways (such as the age or geographical location of an individual, which may make them likelier to vote but significantly less likely to be present or active on Twitter (Smith & Anderson, 2018), while there are other factors which likely share no common influence over the two.

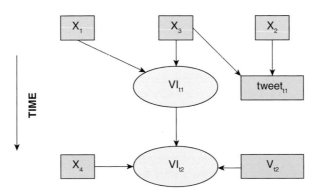

Figure 16.1 A general model of the connection between vote choice and political tweets. **VI**: Voting Intention. **X**: Latent factors. **V**: Vote

Hence, we conclude that further research is necessary in order to establish the core factors determining online and offline political behaviour in order to better model the latter using the former. Our core argument here however is to (1) establish that there is clearly a strong correlation with offline and online political behaviour at the individual level and (2) that our assessment of the relationship between the two suggests that a conceptualization of unweighted positive tweet volume as a proxy for vote share percentages is likely a faulty approximation, especially when off-the-shelf tools which measure linguistic rather than political sentiment are employed. Hence, we argue for Twitter-based public opinion research using sentiment analysis to (1) focus on the user level rather than the tweet level and (2) measure political rather than linguistic sentiment. We believe that these simple changes have the potential of improving the efficacy of resulting predictive models.

The meaning of positive and negative political tweets

Given the assumption that political tweets and offline political behaviour are highly correlated and share causal factors, it is useful to further consider how political sentiment measured therein, be it represented categorically (positive, negative or neutral) or ordinally (on a scale from X to Y) can be used to model offline political behaviour. In order to address this, it is useful to first assess the way in which existing research has operationalized this and then investigate what a given sentiment rating for a given tweet will typically signify when transposed to the dimension of the author's relationship to the pertinent issue. In essence, previous forecasts simplify this relationship by assuming that candidate C_i's share of positive tweets will be directly related to their share of the vote share in election E. When expressed in a formal equation, the function of tweeting and voting is as follows:

$$P^{\prime}C = \frac{\Sigma\ C,t\ I(SCt > 0)}{\Sigma_t\ I(S_t > 0)}$$

where P^{C} is an estimator for the proportion of votes for candidate C and S_t is the level of sentiment of tweet t.

We suggest that this conceptualization is somewhat short sighted in that it does not address the assumed, implied or otherwise, meaning of positive tweets and further does not address negative or neutral tweets at all. Hence, let us discuss our understanding of what these types of tweets signify when transposed to the offline world:

A positive tweet about a politician likely indicates a positive disposition by the author toward said politician. As we know from existing research, citizens tend to vote for candidates whom they like, whereas candidates who are not broadly liked face an uphill electoral struggle. So, the author has expressed that they feel positively towards the politician. However, this does not mean that they do not like another politician who is competing in the same election. However, oftentimes we can verify if this is the case by also assessing the author's other political tweets and aggregating the sentiment expressed within them to all pertinent politicians in order to confidently estimate which one they like best. *A negative tweet about a politician* conversely most likely indicates a negative disposition by the author toward said politician. Furthermore, this suggests that the tweet's author is less likely to vote for this politician. Again, we can oftentimes assess whether this a firmly held belief or just an ad-hoc reaction that may deviate from the author's overall opinion by looking at all the author's relevant tweets.

Now, when it comes to using this information in modeling a given candidate's vote share, it intuitively makes sense to tally tweets they have received which are positive and compare them versus all opponents. This is how previous sentiment-assisted Twitter-based election forecasts operated. While there are core issues with this methodology which we have discussed previously, such as analyzing the data at the tweet rather than the user level and thus likely amplifying the most frequent tweeters, who are also likely to be prolific partisans (Conover, Gonçalves, Flammini, & Menczer, 2012; Barberá, Jost, Nagler, Tucker, & Bonneau, 2015), or neglecting the inherently skewed nature of a given sample of tweets, there is a further implicit assumption in these models, namely that tweets with negative sentiment toward a politician or party are uninformative for such a predictive model.

Tentative conclusions and research agenda

We have introduced the core concepts of the literature of sentiment-assisted Twitter-based election forecasts and have provided an in-depth interpretation of the underlying implicit models of tweets and votes employed in previous publications. Overall, this allows us to draw the following tentative conclusions, leading us to a research agenda for our implementation of sentiment-assisted Twitter-based public opinion prediction:

1   It is unclear what precisely tweet-level positive sentiment volume of politically salient tweets measures. Evidence suggests that it is highly correlated with approval ratings derived from opinion polling, but this correlation is likely contingent on large samples of data in order to alleviate the issues arising from a tweet-level analysis, as well as the noise inherent in such data.
2   This understanding has led researchers to use positive sentiment volume as a proxy for vote choice rather than for approval. We argue that this design choice may account for some of the unreliability in previous forecasts, and it may be useful to incorporate a transposition from candidate (dis)approval to voting intention in models.
3   Previous research has widely ignored tweets with negative sentiment in their analyses. We suggest that negative tweets may be just as informative as positive tweets, and their incorporation into predictive models should hence be explored.
4   Tweet-level analyses are prone to bias due to oversampling prolific partisans and should be replaced with user-level analyses.
5   Off-the-shelf tools for sentiment analysis (especially lexicon-based ones) are likely not suitable for correctly estimating *political* sentiment in political tweets but rather focus on linguistic sentiment, which in turn is likely not capturing certain innate elements of a given tweet's political sentiment. Twitter-based public opinion research relying on sentiment-derived measures should seek to measure political sentiment if possible.
6   While certain variables are hard to adjust for when working with samples of Twitter data, such as a propensity to turn out to vote, others are estimateable with state-of-the-art tools. Incorporating such user-level estimates (e.g., location and political affinity) as a way of weighting tweet samples may be a fruitful avenue for improving predictive accuracy.

Research design

We now introduce our approach to extracting sentiment analysis from samples of politically salient tweets from three distinct geographical locations, the U.S. states of New Hampshire, South Carolina and Massachusetts, from three weeks before their respective Democratic party presidential primaries in 2016. Crucially, we generate political sentiment scores at the tweet level by hand-annotating sub-samples of pertinent tweets. We outline coding rules resulting in tweet-level ordinal scores expressing what we refer to as "political sentiment". This score incorporates both sentiment *polarity* and *intensity* and transposes the underlying political meaning of a tweeter's expressed political sentiment toward an addressee (one of the two candidates in all of the primaries, Hillary Clinton or Bernie Sanders) into an ordinal score of political sentiment. We further propagate these scores to larger samples of pertinent tweets using machine learning.

We use these political sentiment scores in 12 models to predict the candidates' vote shares. In these models, we implement the research agenda outlined in the previous section, which allows us to draw conclusions as to the appropriateness of the undertaking as a whole, as well as the usefulness of individual models. Besides evaluating the efficacy of models' aggregation and weighting approaches, we also contrast the usefulness of using smaller, exclusively hand-labeled samples versus larger samples of machine-annotated data.

Besides the established approach of comparing positive sentiment volume for the different candidates competing in an election, we also showcase a novel methodology to Twitter-based election forecasting which aggregates hand-annotated political sentiment scores to vote share percentage estimates by simulating new data from the probability density function of labeled sentiment scores, thus incorporating *all* labeled tweets into the analysis rather than just those understood to be positive.

Case selection and data

We focus on three elections within the U.S. presidential primary, the Democratic party 2016 primaries in New Hampshire, South Carolina and Massachusetts. We believe trialing this method on several smaller elections is a more useful pursuit than testing it on one national-level election, for numerous reasons. First, all three elections share the same candidates, providing comparability and consistency across all data to be sampled and labeled, while all samples can be created from the same source collection. Second, all three elections operate under very similar electoral rules, with minor differences, which are (1) known and (2) can be accounted for. Third, while candidates remain the same across elections, sociodemographic distributions in these states are different, but known – at least at the aggregate level. The same applies to electoral rules in the different states; New Hampshire has a semi-open system (allowing voters to re-register their party allegiance on the day); Massachusetts has a closed system (allowing only registered Democrats to participate, and registration has to occur over a month ahead of election date); and South Carolina has an open system (allowing anyone to participate). Having these similar test cases with differences along known parameters provides for a useful scenario in seeking to understand model performance in estimating vote share from Twitter data.

In order to generate samples of tweets relevant to these elections, we filter our source collection[8] for tweets mentioning the candidates running in these elections, Hillary Clinton and Bernie Sanders.[9] These tweets were collected over the entire course of the 2016 electoral season using Twitter's freely accessible streaming API. Then, we geo-located the unique users in this sub-collection using the method outlined in Loynes et al., forthcoming, with the goal of providing a municipality-level estimate for each user. We discarded tweets by users who were not unambiguously placed in one of the three states or whose tweets did not occur within a three-week window leading up to the respective state's primary. This leaves us with three sub-samples of tweets, from which we drew a sample of $n = 1000$ each, whereby we sampled unique users (thus allowing only one tweet by each unique user to be contained within the sample), giving priority to tweets closer to the election date.[10] These sub-samples of $n = 1000$ were then

Table 16.1 Summary statistics for geo-located samples of primary-relevant tweets for New Hampshire, South Carolina and Massachusetts

	NH	*SC*	*MA*
Primary date	09 Feb 2016	20 Feb 2016	01 March 2016
n tweets	18,082	33,027	92,104
n unique users	2061	5338	13,498
Mean *n*(tweets)/user	8.9	6.9	9.5
Median *n*(tweets)/user	1	1	1
Max *n*(tweets)/user	1024	780	1970

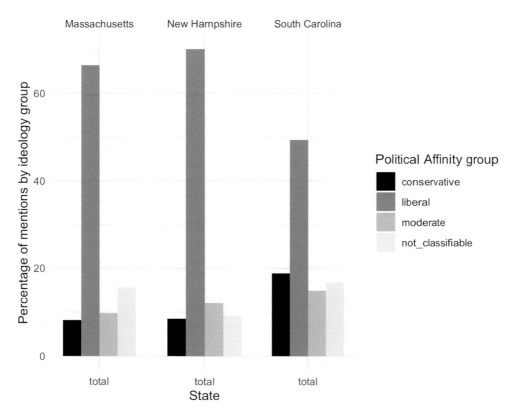

Figure 16.2   Number of tweets in sample, by state and political affinity group

hand-annotated for political sentiment using the guidelines described in the following section by the lead author of this chapter.

We computed users' political affinity on a two-dimensional left-right scale using the method outlined in Barberá et al. (2015). We did this in order to be able to perform explora-tory weighting on the state-level samples. Users' political affinity is modeled as a function of the news-media and elite Twitter accounts they follow. If, for instance, user *u* follows three right-wing politicians and two right-wing media outlets, this user will be classified as right-wing, and so on. Figure 16.2 shows the distribution of these affinity classifications at the tweet level. For all three states, tweets by users classified as liberal dominate our samples. We determine affinity group by matching user-level estimates to estimates for reference accounts. We classify users as *liberal* if their score is equal to or below that of the Washington Post, *moderate* if their score is between that of the Post and the Wall Street Journal, and *conservative* if it is equal to or greater than that of the Journal. It is also apparent that proportionally, the South Carolina sample contains more conservatives than New Hampshire and Massachusetts, where the political affinity distributions (in our sample) are broadly similar. We suggest that this may be explainable in part by the open nature of the South Carolina primary leading to higher participation of opposite partisans in Twitter-based conversation, but is also likely a reflection of the demographics of South Carolina, which is widely understood to be more conservative than the two New England states. However, Figure 16.4 confirms our intuition regarding the ideological split of people who tweet about the Democratic primary – they are overwhelmingly liberal.

As we computed location classifications for every user in our sample, it is useful to compare how geographically dispersed our set of located users is versus the state's actual population distribution. This is useful, as we know that the type of conurbation an individual lives in – a big city or a small village – correlates highly with many factors known to influence voting behaviour (see, e.g., Scala & Johnson, 2017). For this purpose, we calculated quartiles of population numbers by municipalities as a proxy for the urban-rural distribution, both for the census-derived real-world distribution and for the distribution of user-level location classifications in our Twitter user samples. These are depicted in Table 16.2.

Across the states, it is apparent that quartile 4 – the one containing the most populous areas in the state[11] is significantly overrepresented in all the samples. This is in line with previously reported, survey-derived findings stating that the Twitter population skews heavily toward users who live in urban centers (Rainie et al., 2012; Smith & Anderson, 2018). Further, it is important to note that the low proportion of users living in less populated municipalities, especially in more rural states such as New Hampshire and South Carolina, is likely to affect any kind of estimates derived from these data.

Labeling tweets for political sentiment

We now outline the guidelines for generating the most (internally and externally) consistent, and thus accurate hand-annotated political sentiment scores for our three sub-samples of $n = 1000$ tweets. For the purpose of understanding the choices we made, it is useful to first discuss the potential issues arising when using established methods to extract sentiment from tweets.

Table 16.2 Percent of inhabitants/users in population-size quartiles, real/sample

State	Type	Q1	Q2	Q3	Q4
New Hampshire	real	3.06	8.21	18.04	70.69
New Hampshire	sample	0.77	1.69	3.32	94.23
South Carolina	real	0.82	3.09	10.38	85.34
South Carolina	sample	0.20	0.56	2.09	97.14
Massachusetts	real	2.21	8.97	19.73	68.93
Massachusetts	sample	0.30	2.04	4.72	92.95

The Problem: extracting political sentiment from tweets

Consider the following tweet:

> I'm sure David Cameron would love a new job on a farm! #piggate

While this was not taken from the Twitter stream, it is representative of several of the language attributes prominent in politically salient tweets. First, it refers to a high-profile politician.[12] Second, it refers to an event – #piggate[13] – with specific language applicable only to the context of this event. Third, the author employs sarcasm/satire as a stylistic device – people who are aware of "#piggate" will know that David Cameron is not likely to have wanted to work on a farm. In other words, a reader aware of the political context surrounding Cameron would intuitively understand that this tweet does *not* convey positive *political* sentiment toward him, even though its superficial *linguistic* sentiment may suggest so. However, a lexicon-based sentiment analysis algorithm would grade this tweet positively – as is the case with SentiStrength (see Figure 16.1), the most accurate sentiment analysis tool (on average) for tweet-specific sentiment (Abbasi et al., 2014, p. 5). Further, an ML classifier trained on generic tweets to detect linguistic sentiment would likely do the same. We argue that this is the core problem of using off-the-shelf sentiment analysis for politically salient tweets.

In order to alleviate the potential problems associated with extracting politically salient meaning from user-generated social web text, we propose a granular, domain-specific human-coding framework. We present samples of tweets to coders which:

1   Were authored by users who live in a target geographic entity.
2   Are highly likely to deal with the specific election or other politically salient topic we are interested in learning more about. We achieve this by filtering the Twitter stream for relevant keywords.

The coders tasked with labeling our tweet samples for political sentiment receive a specific set of instructions on how to label each tweet. In essence, this concise guidance on how to identify five elements in a given unit of text to label is employed:

1   Who is the *addressee* of the tweet. Is it candidate/party A or B, both, or neither?
2   What is the *polarity* (positive, negative or neutral) of the political sentiment conveyed in the tweet?

The text 'I'm sure David Cameron would love a new job on a farm! #piggate' has positive strength **3** and negative strength **-1**

Approximate classification rationale: Im sure David [proper noun] Cameron [proper noun] would love[3] [+-1 booster word] a new job on a farm ![+1 punctuation emphasis] [sentence: 3,-1] #piggate [sentence: 1,-1] [result: max + and - of any sentence][overall result = 1 as pos>-neg] (Detect Sentiment)

Figure 16.3   Output from the SentiStrength interface for example tweet

3   What is the *intensity* of the political sentiment conveyed in the tweet? Strong emotive language connotes high intensity, in both polarities. Nonetheless, a soberly worded appraisal of a given addressee which delineates the author's strong (dis)agreement with the tweet's subject can also convey strong intensity. It is important for coders to revisit previously labeled tweets in order to establish an internally coherent scale.

4   Which *scale* to use? We opt for a 10-point ordinal scale ranging from −5 to +5, whereby 0 indicates neutral. We see this as a fruitful trade-off between labeling complexity and label granularity.

5   What about the *tweet's author*? Is there any indication in the user's profile that may aid our interpretation of their tweet, such as their profile image, profile bio or other tweets on their timeline?

We see numerous benefits in this approach: the granularity of scores tells us something about how strongly people feel rather than simply indicating positive versus negative. We can still however use these labeled data as training sets for categorical classification tasks.

It is important to note that this highly involved method of human-coding entails significantly more effort than polarity-only human-labeling tasks for typical ML sentiment analysis applications. Besides merely reading a unit of text and deciding between three response categories, our approach requires a (sometimes complex) multi-step process with a more involved reading not only of the text unit at hand but also of associated information where available and necessary. Overall, our method of extracting political sentiment scores from social web text aims to avoid the biases inherent in both of the established methods of sentiment analysis frequently used in computational social science research. We see our coding approach as addressing many of these biases.

Machine-propagation of political sentiment scores to larger samples of tweets

We are keen to assess the efficacy and efficiency of using larger, machine-propagated samples of electorally relevant tweets for the goal of mapping offline political opinion, as we suspect that smaller, entirely hand-annotated samples may produce equally useful results. Hence, for the purpose of empirically testing this intuition, as well as to replicate previously employed methods, we use our tweets ($n = 1000$ per state), hand-annotated with political sentiment scores, as training data in order to machine-label equivalent scores on the larger samples of pertinent geo-located tweets (see Table 16.1). Given our operationalization of political sentiment, this is a two-step classification/regression problem. First, we need to determine the addressee of a given tweet, after which we can regress an ordinal political sentiment score onto it.

Classifying tweets' addressees

There are two potential avenues for classifying a given tweet's addressee in the context of this research design. First, what we call the "naive addressee classification" approach, which simply filters the text of a given tweet for the names of the relevant candidates, in this case "Hillary Clinton" and "Bernie Sanders" (as well as alternative spellings, typing errors, nicknames and official Twitter handles). The possible outcome labels of this classification mechanism are "Hillary Clinton", "Bernie Sanders", "both", and "neither".

However, given our previous discussion of how lexicon-based methods (which this one is, albeit with a much simpler remit) may be insufficient for tasks aimed at extracting political sentiment, we also consider a machine learning method. In this case, we take the $n = 1000$ hand-annotated tweets as training data, as addressee labels have been human-annotated at the tweet-level. Then, we train multiple classifiers (random forest, linear support vector classifier, multinomial naive Bayes and logistic regression) using the scikit-learn library for Python 3.7 (Pedregosa et al., 2011), and evaluate their performance. Across all three states, the linear support vector classifier performed best, reaching accuracy scores of 0.98 (New Hampshire), 0.98 (South Carolina) and 0.98 (Massachusetts) in 10-fold cross validation using re-balanced training data (i.e., the training data were resampled in order to equally contain each possible addressee class).

In the pursuit of the most accurate model, we inspected the overlap between the naive and the machine learning addressee classification methods by first ascertaining the proportion of cases in which both methods produced the same addressee label. For New Hampshire, 77.4% of cases shared the same label, while the proportion for South Carolina was 87.6% and 85.3% for Massachusetts. Then, we subset each training set to only contain those tweets where both approaches diverged and inspected each resulting sample by hand in order to ascertain which of the approaches yielded the most valid and reliable results. In all three cases, we found that the "naive" keyword-filtering approach vastly outperformed the machine learning approach when blindly reannotating previously mismatched cases and comparing them to the two classification outputs. Hence, we chose to employ the naive method on the larger tweet samples and forgo machine classification for the addressee variable for all three states. This shows that, while lexicon-based methods may not be suitable for classifying political sentiment in political tweets, they are certainly useful for classifying the less ambiguous attributes of tweets.

Regressing political sentiment scores to unlabelled tweets

We further outline our approach to predicting political sentiment scores for all sampled geo-located tweets for the three states (New Hampshire, $n = 18,082$; South Carolina, $n = 33,027$; Massachusetts, $n = 92,104$). This process is more complex than that of classifying addressee labels to tweets, as models now need to learn numerical text features associated with hand-labeled sentiment scores and use them to predict the same in previously unseen data. As our goal is to have rich, granular score data to use in modeling public opinion (i.e., an ordinal intensity/polarity score versus just a categorical polarity score), we choose to conceptualize this as a regression problem rather than a classification problem. While our ordinal scores are not technically scaled as interval or ratio variables (typically seen as the scale requirements for performing regression tasks in machine learning), we argue that the quasi-metric nature of our scores makes this the preferable option, over, for example, a multi-class or multi-iteration classification approach.

Given our discussion of the intricate, evolving, context-specific language associated with politically salient tweets, we argue that it is prudent to build regressors at the per-state, per-addressee level. While this may be withholding potentially relevant text features from a given model, it means our models are well calibrated to the intricacies of each unique context we are studying. Hence, we build six individual regression models – one for each candidate, for each state.

Before we begin training models, we pre-process all text for a given scenario. This involves the removal of stopwords, as well as non-informative Twitter-specific text and symbols (such as @, RT, #). Further, we lemmatize all words in a given corpus, meaning that words are reduced to their shortest form which still reflects its core meaning (e.g., "campaigning" is reduced to "campaign", and "well" is reduced to "good"). These pre-processing steps were undertaken using the spaCy library for Python 3.7 (spa, 2020).

Table 16.3 Performance of five different regressor models (mean absolute error), computed through 10-fold cross-validation

State	NH		SC		MA	
Candidate	Clinton	Sanders	Clinton	Sanders	Clinton	Sanders
Model						
Linear regression	1.95	1.6	1.47	1.73	1.79	1.57
Logistic regression (one v rest)	2.15	1.89	1.83	1.99	2.19	1.67
Logistic regression (multinomial)	2.03	1.86	1.79	2	2.13	1.65
Ordered logistic regression	1.85	1.56	1.66	1.71	1.85	1.58
Random forest	1.9	1.69	1.47	1.79	1.85	1.59

In order to build the best possible model for each scenario, we train five different models for each: linear regression, binary logistic regression (one versus rest), logistic regression (multinomial), ordered logistic regression and random forest using the scikit-learn library for Python 3.7 (Pedregosa et al., 2011). We evaluate model performance using the mean absolute error (MAE) metric (how far a predicted score is from a hand-labeled score, on average). Table 16.3 shows the mean absolute error of all models, obtained from running 10-fold cross-validation.

It is immediately apparent that the accuracy range of all models is fairly narrow, ranging from an MAE of 1.47 to 2.19. Given a scale ranging from −5 to +5, this means that any model is prone to falsely predicting a given tweet's polarity if the intensity is comparably low. Conversely, however, the best models show encouraging performance, with an acceptable error range. While certain models achieve marginally higher performance, we chose to centre our analysis on two models, the ordered logistic regression and random forest models, as their performance is most consistent. Hence, we discard the remaining models, and propagate sentiment scores to the three larger samples of tweets for both models.

However, we are further interested to see which of the two models is more useful for our application and hence to employ the best possible predicted values in our analysis. For this purpose, we generated a mean score out of both the predicted ordered logistic regression and random forest scores for each tweet. Then, we randomly sampled a further 50 tweets per sample (total $n = 300$) and, keeping the predicted scores blind to the human annotator (this paper's first author), annotated them for political sentiment, using the same rules and scale as in the original training data generation. This exercise found that, across all samples, the ordered logistic regression method provided the most accurate scores, in fact producing exact matches with hand-annotated scores in 38% of cases while providing an MAE of 1 across samples. Hence, we employ the scores produced by ordered logistic regression throughout our empirical analysis. However, it is important to note that this second stage of model validation and calibration showed that our model typically overestimated the positivity and underestimated the negativity of tweets addressed to Bernie Sanders while showing the inverse for tweets addressed to Hillary Clinton − overemphasizing negativity and underestimating positivity. We found this to be the case across all six ordered logistic regression models.

Modelling vote share percentages

Having described our approach to sampling, political sentiment annotation and machine propagation of both addressee and sentiment labels across larger samples, we now outline our proposed methods to modeling vote share percentages from measured and predicted political sentiment in election-relevant tweets for the 2016 Democratic party presidential primaries in New Hampshire, South Carolina and Massachusetts. Our vote share percentage estimation models can be divided into two broad categories: replication of established strategies and a novel approach. Furthermore, we introduce novel ways of weighting and post-stratifying samples using computationally estimated, individual-level user attributes. Overall, this adds up to 12 models applied to each of the three states.

Replication of established models

As we discussed in "Sentiment Analysis and Twitter-Based Election Forecasts", there exists a considerable amount of literature seeking to estimate vote share percentages in elections by aggregating sentiment scores from relevant tweets, all of which apply a similar methodology, whereby positively labeled tweets are aggregated for each candidate. We replicate this method for all three states. The predicted vote share for a given candidate is modeled as the percentage of positive tweets for them out of all positive tweets toward candidates in a given sample.

Simulating votes from the candidate-level distribution of sentiment scores

In addition to replicating the established method, we introduce a novel method of modeling candidate-level vote share percentages in elections. In this method, we seek to address a core omission in previous related research, namely the assumption that tweets with negative sentiment are uninformative to modeling vote share.

We achieve this by using the probability density function (distribution) of a given candidate's political sentiment scores, and randomly sampling (simulating) new scores from this distribution. We repeat this for each candidate, until we reach an n equivalent to that of the number of expected or actual participants in the target election for all candidates. Hence, we have a dataset with $n(\text{rows}) = n(\text{voters})$ and two columns, each representing a "simulated approval score" for a given simulated voter. By doing this, we aim to approximate n randomly selected voters, who each have a measure of (dis)approval for either candidate. Then, we model voting intention as a choice between several candidates, with the main contributing factor for vote choice V in election E being an individual voter's (dis)approval of each candidate (R) relative to the others.

Following this, our basic model of vote choice is as follows:

$$V = C_1 \text{ if } R(C_1) > max(R(C_2, \ldots, C_i)) \tag{2}$$

For a two-candidate election, this can also be expressed in terms of the marginal rating R_M, whereby p(V) is constituted as follows:

$$R_M = R(C_1) - R(C_2) \tag{3}$$

$$if R_M > 0, V = C_1 \tag{4}$$

$$if R_M < 0, V = C_2 \tag{5}$$

Using this model, we generate a simulated vote choice variable for each simulated voter in our simulated data. We predict vote share percentages for each candidate by aggregating vote choice variables and calculating the percentage received by either candidate.

Weighting and post-stratification

Given the individual-level user attributes we computed for the data used in this project, we run all our models using different underlying data configurations.

First, we run models at both the raw tweet level and at the user level. In order to achieve this, we subset samples for unique Twitter user-ids and average the sentiment they have expressed toward candidates in all of their tweets which appear in our samples. This post-stratification step has the core aim of reducing the potential distortion caused by prolific partisans who repeatedly tweet similar messages in support (or opposition) of a particular candidate. As voters in demo-cratic elections usually only have the use of one vote, we argue that this should make vote share estimates more predictive of real-world outcomes.

Second, we run our models at the scope of both the large, machine-labeled samples and the smaller, human-annotated samples. Given our skepticism of the benefits of employing large scales of machine-annotated data when aiming to predict vote share percentages from senti-ment-labeled tweets, and further, given our considered approach to sampling training datasets, we believe it prudent to examine the effect of using larger samples, albeit with less reliable sentiment scores.

Third, we weight samples by location distribution. As a given user's machine-classified home location is one of two inclusion criteria for the data underlying this research, we choose to further employ the granular information contained within this user-level attribute. Specifically, we choose to expand our analysis by re-running models with samples weighted for population distribution. We undertake this weighting step as it is clear that our samples significantly over-represent urban areas while underrepresenting rural ones – both of which are individual-level attributes known to be correlated with political behaviour. By oversampling rural users and undersampling urban users, we seek to correct for this bias.

Fourth, we weight samples by user-level political affinity. As the elections we are studying are all under the Democratic party umbrella, and this party is broadly defined as a liberal, social-democratic party rather than a conservative one – which in some cases actually prevents non-registered Democrats from participating in primaries – we argue for the usefulness of adjusting target samples so as to more accurately reflect the real-world electorate in terms of its political affinity. Hence, we run a range of models with only data from users classified as liberal or mod-erate by Barbera's (2014) algorithm.

Findings

Before analyzing the results from our 12 models, we first discuss the distributions of polit-ical sentiment scores from which these results are derived. We show these distributions in Figure 16.4. It is immediately apparent that for the hand-labeled sets (a), the distributions for either candidate look very similar: Bernie Sanders has a clear peak on the positive side of the distribution, with a smaller bump on the negative side, whereas this is reversed for Hillary Clinton. We see small differences in the height and width of the peaks between states for both candidates, but overall, it is a very similar probability density function for all three states. Given the fact that the tweets underlying these distributions were all labeled by this paper's lead author, we can confirm that this visual representation of the political sentiment of the training datasets

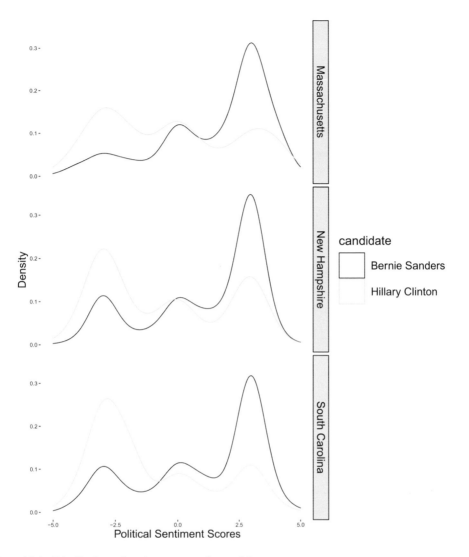

Figure 16.4   Distribution of sentiment scores for candidates across states

was also felt when labeling: Hillary Clinton, regardless of the state, got a lot of abuse and dislike, while Bernie Sanders has a large number of fans saying only positive things about him – again, independent of which of the three states a tweet may have come from.

Figure 16.4b shows the distribution of political sentiment scores for the machine-labeled samples. Given the fact that these labels originated from the sentiment distributions in the training sets, it is no surprise that these distributions look similar to those in Figure 16.4a, albeit with seemingly more granularity.

From the distributions pictured in Figure 16.4, it is immediately apparent that tweets addressed to Bernie Sanders were more likely to be of a positive nature, while tweets addressed to Hillary Clinton were more likely to be negative toward her. This is not necessarily in line with our pre-labeling expectations, namely that Clinton would receive higher levels of positive sentiment, at least in South Carolina. However, these expectations were guided, at least to

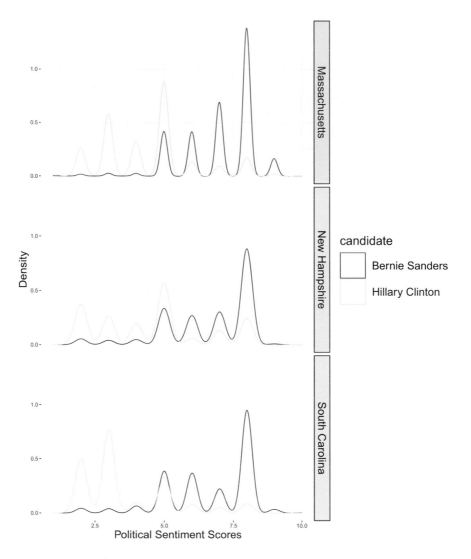

Figure 16.4 (Continued)

some degree, by the assumption that tweets localizable at the state level would typically concern themselves with state-level, electorally salient issues. However, given the experience of hand-labeling the tweets, we suggest that the majority of tweets followed national stories and events more often than local ones. We revisit this in the discussion section.

Table 16.4 shows the actual election outcomes in the three states of interest. While Sanders managed to achieve a pronounced victory in New Hampshire, Clinton dominated in South Carolina. Massachusetts showed a neck-and-neck result. Interestingly, we find ourselves with three states with significantly different demographics and three considerably different results. New Hampshire is mostly rural, white and not necessarily too liberal but tends to receive a huge amount of media attention due to its status as the first primary in the calendar. South Carolina is somewhat less rural but still not particularly urban, with a plurality of black voters and a large

Table 16.4 Election results in the three primaries of interest

	Date	*Hillary Clinton*	*Bernie Sanders*
New Hampshire	09 Feb 2016	37.68	**60.14**
South Carolina	27 Feb 2016	**73.44**	26.02
Massachusetts	01 March 2016	**49.73**	48.33

amount of pension-age voters in the Democratic party electorate. Massachusetts is the most urbanized and liberal of the states, featuring many high-income white collar workers. We argue that these demographic fundamentals contribute considerably to the outcomes of these elections, which is in part why we chose to study these particular elections rather than other ones.

Table 16.5 shows the predicted vote shares of our 12 models for each of the three states. Overall, the models are split into those aggregating positive sentiment in the sample for both the machine-labeled and hand-labeled sets, in non-weighted and weighted configurations and those where vote share predictions are drawn from newly simulated data contingent on the probability density functions of the state-level samples, again in weighted and unweighted configurations. For each model, we report the estimated vote share percentage for a given candidate, as well as the state-level model's mean absolute error and a binary indicating whether the model correctly predicted the winner of the election (vs. X). In addition to the 12 models, we also present a mean model, which contains the average of all models, again at the per-state level.

First off, it is apparent that across all models, each one predicted the correct winner – Bernie Sanders – for New Hampshire while failing to correctly predict the winner for both of the other states. When looking at the predicted vote share percentages and mean absolute error for the different models for New Hampshire and the other states, most notably Massachusetts, it becomes clear that there is a large divergence in model accuracy (measured in error distance of predicted vote share versus actual vote share). For New Hampshire, three models achieve a very low mean absolute error of 1.09 – the two weighted (location, location and affinity) applications of the positive sentiment method on the machine-labeled sample, as well as the fully weighted simulation on just the training set. Otherwise, it is clear that the simulation based on the machine-labeled set widely misses the target, with MAE figures ranging from 13.99 to 22.08. Furthermore, the models applying positive sentiment volume on solely the training set also widely miss the mark, with MAEs around 10. Interestingly, however, while both model types are not fit for purpose, it is striking that the positive sentiment volume (training set) models underestimate Sanders' vote share significantly, while the simulation (full set) considerably overemphasizes it. Even when comparing the different model types on the same source dataset, the minimum distance between vote share predictions is at least 8 percentage points. This suggests that neither the established model type – which treats negatively classified tweets as uninformative and discards them – or our novel method, which ascribes equal importance to negative and positive tweets, is entirely adequate in being useable in a vote percentage aggregation workflow. The three New Hampshire models which perform best are the positive sentiment volume model on the machine-labeled set, at the user-level, weighted by user-level location or unweighted, as well as the simulation model, performed only on the training set, weighted for all available variables. We are pleased with these results and suggest that this indicates that two of our intuitive cases for adjusting samples – the user-level and user-level location – are likely useful in improving vote share prediction accuracy. It is also important to note that the other models, especially positive sentiment volume, performed only on the training set

Table 16.5 Twelve vote share estimation models for three states, estimated vote share percentages by candidate, mean absolute error for each model by state, was winner predicted correctly?

	State	NH				SC				MA			
	Method	Sanders	Clinton	MAE		Sanders	Clinton	MAE		Sanders	Clinton	MAE	
1	+ Sent, full set	57.54	42.46	3.69	✓	58.99	41.01	32.70	✗	59.05	40.95	9.75	✗
2	+ Sent, full set, user-level	61.29	38.71	1.09	✓	64.70	35.30	38.41	✗	61.24	38.76	11.94	✗
3	+ Sent, full set, user-level, location-weighted	61.88	38.12	1.09	✓	65.50	34.50	39.21	✗	61.17	38.83	11.87	✗
4	+ Sent, full set, location & affinity-weighted	56.35	43.65	4.88	✓	57.46	42.54	31.17	✗	58.34	41.66	9.04	✗
5	+ Sent, training set	50.93	49.07	10.30	✓	54.79	45.21	28.50	✗	50.99	49.01	1.69	✗
6	+ Sent, training set, location-weighted	51.77	48.23	9.46	✓	56.30	43.70	30.01	✗	50.19	49.81	0.97	✗
7	+ Sent, training set, location & affinity-weighted	50.23	49.77	11.00	✓	52.40	47.60	26.11	✗	50.06	49.94	0.97	✗
8	Simulation, training set	66.97	33.03	5.74	✓	71.39	28.61	45.10	✗	68.58	31.42	19.28	✗
9	Simulation, training set, location & affinity-weighted	60.18	39.82	1.09	✓	64.27	35.73	37.98	✗	61.04	38.96	11.74	✗
10	Simulation, full set	79.07	20.93	17.84	✓	89.36	10.64	63.07	✗	87.85	12.15	38.55	✗
11	Simulation, full set, location-weighted	83.31	16.69	22.08	✓	89.80	10.20	63.51	✗	88.44	11.56	39.14	✗
12	Simulation, full set, location & affinity-weighted	75.22	24.78	13.99	✓	87.40	12.60	61.11	✗	86.41	13.59	37.11	✗
13	Mean	62.89	37.10	1.66	✓	67.70	32.30	41.41	✗	65.28	34.72	15.98	✗

or simulation performed on the machine-labeled set fall widely short of a useful prediction for New Hampshire.

The case of South Carolina is considerably less accurate than New Hampshire, as is shown by an average MAE of 41.41 across all 12 models and the fact that none of the models correctly predict the eventual winner. Interestingly, we find that here the least inaccurate model prediction comes from the fully weighted positive sentiment volume model using only training data, a stark contrast with the New Hampshire model, where this is one of the less accurate models. While we will further explore reasons for model performance in the next section, we suggest that this clearly shows two things: if the "right" (i.e., close to representative) users do not exist in a given geographic entity on Twitter, then no amount of post-stratification will make their opinions appear in a Twitter-based study of offline public opinion, and further, the underlying data, its quality and scope may be more important than a given model in order to extract public-opinion relevant insights from them.

The case of Massachusetts provides both cause for encouragement and disappointment when assessing the various models' performance. First off, the state features the two models with the lowest MAE (both 0.97, positive sentiment volume on training sets, weighted) of any of the models in this study, which, however, fail to correctly predict the winner of the election. While this is partly due to the fact that the election's actual outcome was extremely narrow, it is nonetheless concerning that even a highly accurate model does not push Hillary Clinton over the 50% threshold. However, when consulting the distribution of hand and machine-labeled scores in Figure 16.4, this is not particularly surprising, as the source data for any of these models simply paint a very clear picture, which is not in favor of Hillary Clinton. The other models show a mixed bag of predictions, whereby the worst models are hugely wide off the mark (namely the simulation on machine-labeled samples), indeed for any of the three states. But, overall, it is important to note that the results for Massachusetts are not as inaccurate as South Carolina but also not as accurate as New Hampshire. This is potentially a reflection of the states' differing demographics and can be seen as encouraging going forward, in that this can be understood as a finding in its own right.

Finally, it is apparent that models produce highly similar predictions across states when consulting Table 16.5 at the row level rather than the column level. This is undoubtedly a reflection of how similar the source data for each three states were in regard to their distribution of sentiment scores and thus again highlights the primacy of data over model in regard to producing the most accurate predictions.

Discussion

We now delve deeper into discussing the findings of this research and what we can learn about our real-world test-cases from these findings, as well as potential explanations for certain findings. We suggest potential improvements for future research and discuss how this study adds to the literature on Twitter-based public opinion research.

Why are New Hampshire models more accurate?

The most striking takeaway from our findings is the high model performance for New Hampshire versus the other two states. We suggest that there are four possible explanations for why this is the case: data quality, external factors, sampling and Bernie Sanders.

First off, we suggest that the quality of data used in these analyses was simply highest for New Hampshire. We believe this to be the case, as the New Hampshire presidential primary (of either party) occupies a uniquely significant space in the U.S. political landscape. The fact that the first primary of every presidential election occurs here results in pronounced media and political attention. Campaigns are made and broken in the state, and the media constructs new horse race narratives on a daily basis. This means that the race also receives a disproportionate amount of attention on Twitter, and we suggest that that increased awareness and resulting participation is likely to result in well-calibrated data for Twitter-based public opinion research.

The same story may also be shaping the model results by way of contributing externally to the samples from the other states. Given the states' primacy in the political sphere and the close temporal proximity of the three states' election dates, much of the discussion on Twitter produced by users from South Carolina and Massachusetts in fact dealt with Bernie Sanders' victory in New Hampshire rather than his or Clinton's actions or statements relevant to the primary in their state. While such statements are likely to indicate a given Massachusetts or South Carolina-based Twitter user's support of Bernie Sanders in their own state, it isn't really a tweet about that particular election. This is highly difficult to disentangle in this particular research design. This factor also comes into play when considering sampling. As the time frames we selected for sampling means that all three states' sampling frames overlap, there is likely a lot of overlap between the three samples used in this chapter's analysis. While we would ideally only sample tweets which are concerned with the given target state-level election, we can actually deduce from this that national-level news and events shape election-relevant conversation on Twitter, even if those elections are at the state level.

In order to alleviate these sampling issues, there are a range of options for future research – first, a sampling frame is bracketed to be closer to a given election. While this may reduce the number of users who are included in a given analysis, it certainly increases the likelihood of tweets being relevant. Second, it may be fruitful to use machine learning classifiers to establish whether a given tweet is concerned with a given election. While this would involve further costly hand-annotation of tweets, it would likely to boost the power of any resulting model, as tweets could be selected with more confidence on their relevance to a given election.

Finally, there is the possibility that our New Hampshire models performed well because Bernie Sanders happened to win this state, and Bernie Sanders also happened to beat Hillary Clinton on Twitter, regardless of which state people were tweeting about him from. We revisit this point later, but suffice it to say that this clearly plays a role in this analysis and says something about how Twitter is not a carbon copy of offline politics. However, it is also important to note that Sanders is far from a generic Democratic candidate, and simply because he dominates Twitter does not mean that any election would have one candidate that outshines all others on social media.

The impact of data processing and model specifications

Given the fact that this chapter employed both novel weighting and vote share percentage modeling strategies, it is useful to discuss their impact on the findings of this analysis.

The weighting mechanisms employed in this study can be understood to increase model performance overall. This is a greatly encouraging finding and supports the case for further work on estimating Twitter user-level characteristics for social science research. Overall, we find that, especially for location weighting, a theoretically plausible and consistent idea improves findings when transposing user-level political sentiment to aggregate measures of offline public opinion. However, especially in the case of South Carolina, we learn the limits of such an approach. This state, which is ranked 46th in the United States for GDP per capita, has one of the lowest internet penetration rates in the country and is home to many older black citizens (who are among the least likely to be on Twitter), clearly isn't suitable for this kind of public opinion modeling, as the vast majority of opinions which may exist in the state simply never make their way onto Twitter. So, we can do the best possible job in adjusting samples, but if our sampling frame simply cannot include a large proportion of our target population, we will always fall short. Nonetheless, this is a clear indication that this kind of research needs to take sampling much more seriously and consider "recruiting" users who satisfy certain criteria in a fashion akin to, for example, YouGov in order to improve models' predictive accuracy. But, most importantly, the South Carolina findings show a clear ceiling for Twitter-based public opinion research, barring a massive shift in Twitter membership in previously underrepresented groups.

Next, it is important to consider how our model specifications and other design decisions may have affected the findings. First, there is the question of how the relative imprecision of our ordered logistic regression regressor may have exacerbated the relatively low quality of our data. We showed two core caveats with the regressors' accuracies: First, the best models had a mean absolute error of just below 2. This means that (1) some positive tweets will have been labeled as negative and vice versa and (2) that in simulation-based models, several simulated votes will have been misallocated. Second, we showed, especially in the second-round validation stage where we selected the ordered logistic regression model, that the regressors performed differently for the different candidates, overestimating Sanders' average sentiment while underestimating Clinton's. Both factors will likely have contributed to the sub-par model predictions in the positive sentiment volume and simulation (full set) models. In order to overcome this in future applications, our intuition is that the only way to train more accurate sentiment regressors would be to rely on much larger training sets. It seems likely that $n = 1000$ – even when as carefully constructed as our sets – does not sufficiently capture a sufficient proportion of the relevant features.

Furthermore, it is apparent that, at the row level in Table 16.5, model predictions are broadly similar across states, despite the fact that they were computed using different source data. As touched upon earlier, we suggest this originates from the issue of what people are actually talking about in their tweets. It seems clear that users are talking about much the same across states, and indeed the underlying quantities – that is, distributions of sentiment – are quite similar across states. While this may be adjustable with more intricate sampling (e.g., using the *a priori* recruitment of a representative set of users), and certainly the construction of larger samples, it may be a feature of this kind of Twitter data which is difficult, if not impossible, to alleviate.

Finally, we turn to the performance resulting from our novel method of transposing tweet-level sentiment to offline public opinion. It appears that withholding negative tweet scores from an analysis (i.e., the approach taken in existing research) works best when trying to get the best out of flawed data in its optimal configuration. This is the case for both the South Carolina and Massachusetts models – we optimize the data we have and can trust (seeing as we are only working with hand-labeled data) and get comparatively good results. The same is less apparent for the same method applied on machine-labeled data for those states, which is likely due to the low-quality data resulting from the overly greedy sentiment regressor. Conversely, for New Hampshire – which we believe is the best data we have in this sample, – we find that the simulation method (when only using trusted, hand-labeled data) matches the highest-performing model. So, while this is merely an intuitive conjecture and will have to be validated by future research, we suggest that the simulation method can add value to Twitter-based public opinion research when we have a trusted sample to work with, whereas the positive sentiment volume method is better at alleviating shortcomings in the data. Alternatively, there may be better ways of incorporating negative tweet-level sentiment into such analyses.

Lessons to learn about the elections from these analyses

There is a big elephant in the room when viewing the findings in Table 16.5: the candidates that participated in the elections, – in hindsight – enjoyed very different levels of popularity on Twitter but also in the electorate, perhaps even in spite of their expressed political positions. When viewing these data, both in their raw form in Figure 16.4 or their aggregated form in Table 16.5, Bernie Sanders is clearly shown to be a highly appealing politician to the archetypal Twitter user who tweets about politics. Given what we know about the composition of the platform's user base and the consistent, left-wing track record of Sanders, this should not be particularly surprising. However, it is also highly likely that Sanders' disproportionate appeal, versus, for example, a generic Democratic party candidate, distorts this analysis. His political and campaigning style encourages participation on Twitter and has been said to alienate those less enamored with it. While this analysis clearly shows how a candidate like Bernie Sanders can use a platform like Twitter to their advantage, it is nonetheless important to keep in mind that he did not end up the Democratic presidential nominee in 2016, regardless of his overwhelming support online. More than anything, it would be interesting to see an analysis similar to this one replicated with other, more "conventional" and less divisive candidates.

Furthermore, this analysis makes it abundantly clear that a lot of people did not like Hillary Clinton at all. While the amount of tweets addressed to her were slightly fewer than those addressed to Sanders, the amount of negativity she received paints an overwhelmingly clear picture, which could have potentially alerted Democratic party elites to her shortcomings as a candidate before her defeat against Donald Trump in the 2016 general election. We suggest that this is true regardless of the fact that Twitter is not a representative sample, as its scale and geographic consistency is striking. This suggests that such types of public opinion research using Twitter data, even if they may not always paint an accurate picture of its offline counterpart, can be highly useful in better understanding a politician or candidate's appeals and shortcomings.

Contributions to the field and future research agenda

In conclusion, we outline this paper's contributions to the field of Twitter-based public opinion research specifically, and more broadly computational social science using digital trace data, and highlight potential avenues for future research building on the findings of this project.

Perhaps our most encouraging finding is that weighting by user-level characteristics can help improve Twitter-based public opinion research. Especially for the "hard" attribute, user-level location, we find that models do better more or less across the board. The "soft" attribute, estimated user-level political affinity, also improves predictions in most cases. We suggest that future research should avail itself of these tools. Furthermore, we believe this chapter makes a strong case for future research into computational methods for estimating latent user-level characteristics such as age, gender, ethnicity or educational attainment.

Less encouragingly, but no less importantly, we find that weighting cannot counteract under- and non-representativeness in source data. We suspect that a large proportion of older, black voters who ultimately gave Clinton her landslide in South Carolina had never used Twitter. While there may be mathematical methods to impute how those who are not represented will vote, it is a huge problem which is clearly illustrated by these findings, for which we have no obvious answer. However, we believe this to be a more nuanced appraisal of the feasibility of doing public opinion research using Twitter data than that of previous research, which (paraphrasing) stated "it doesn't work, so leave it". We believe that it is important to learn more about the opportunities and limits of certain research and modeling strategies, and this chapter certainly proves a significant contribution in that regard.

This research also shows that simply sampling from a keyword-derived collection of tweets is likely not enough for public opinion-relevant insights which are to be valuable beyond Twitter. We argue that in order to build reliable models of public opinion from tweets, sampling has to be significantly more involved, considered and targeted. A useful avenue for research may be snowball sampling from established samples of users in a given geographic region in a way that is agnostic to whether those users tweet about politics. We suggest that going from users to tweets is likely more fruitful than going from tweets to users.

A core improvement on future iterations of this research may be to enhance the machine learning component. We suggest doing this by classifying categorical sentiment variables at the tweet level. This would likely have a higher precision than the method used in this paper, and it could be useful to combine it with the predicted ordinal sentiment scores in order to better understand when the ordinal sentiment regressor makes widely erroneous predictions.

In further improvements to the models employed in this paper, we could have also trained a model encompassing all the hand-labeled tweets, regardless of their state of origin. While this would have likely led to some of the state-level intricacies being less pronounced in the model, a bigger training set tends to result in a better model. Furthermore, it seems fairly clear that there were not many state-level intricacies at play, because otherwise we would assume that the distributions of sentiment scores (Figure 16.4) would look different between states.

Notes

1 Jungherr et al. (2012) replicated Tumasjan et al.'s study with a completely different sample of tweets, with neither paper providing any information on the process employed to collect these data, illustrating another issue with research in this area.
2 By using the term "social web" rather than "social media posts" or even "tweets", we include all user-generated text on the web rather than just that posted on popular platforms such as Twitter or Facebook.
3 This is referred to as *sentiment rating* by (Liu, 2012, p. 30). We choose the term "intensity" instead of Liu's "rating", as the latter is specifically relevant to user-produced ratings of product or movie reviews but less so to political sentiment.
4 In this case, the unit of analysis was individual movie reviews, with user-generated ordinal ratings attached to them, thus eliminating the need for time-consuming labeling by the researchers.
5 For US President Barack Obama in 2009.
6 The authors' algorithm performed well for the large parties, PS and UMP (Ceron et al., 2014, p. 350), but overestimated support for left-leaning parties while underestimating support for right-wing parties. This finding ties in to evidence from studies on Twitter's demographic composition (Rainie, Smith, Schlozman, Brady, & Verba, 2012; Smith & Anderson, 2018), suggesting that left-leaning and young individuals are overrepresented on the platform.
7 In addition to forecasting the popular vote, the authors forecast swing state vote shares, and the poll of polls outperformed the Hopkins and King (2010) method in only 2 out of 11 cases (Ceron et al., 2014, p. 10).
8 The source collection was a Twitter streaming API collection beginning at the end of 2015, with all names of candidates running in the election, their official Twitter handles, related hashtags and common (mis)spellings of their names.
9 By "mentioning", we mean not only @-mentions, where a tweet directly notifies the mentioned account holder, but rather all tweets containing a range of words that match the candidates' names.
10 In other words, if user u tweeted five times in our sample, their most recent tweet would be the likeliest to be contained in the $n = 1000$ sub-sample.
11 As the quartiles are calculated using intra-state data, Q4 does not provide inter-state comparability in terms of population size.
12 Former UK Prime Minister David Cameron.
13 See https://en.wikipedia.org/wiki/Piggate for more information on this particular event.

References

(2020, December). explosion/spaCy. original-date: 2014–07–03T15:15:40Z.

Abbasi, A., Hassan, A., & Dhar, M. (2014). Benchmarking Twitter sentiment analysis tools. In *LREC* (Vol. 14, pp. 26–31).

Agarwal, A., Xie, B., Vovsha, I., Rambow, O., & Passonneau, R. J. (2011). *Sentiment analysis of twitter data.* Proceedings of the Workshop on Language in Social Media (LSM 2011), pp. 30–38.

Barberá, P. (2014). Birds of the same feather tweet together: Bayesian ideal point estimation using Twitter data. *Political Analysis, 23*(1), 76–91.

Barberá, P., Jost, J. T., Nagler, J., Tucker, J. A., & Bonneau, R. (2015). Tweeting from left to right: Is online political communication more than an echo chamber? *Psychological science, 26*(10), 1531–1542.

Bermingham, A., & Smeaton, A. (2011). *On using Twitter to monitor political sentiment and predict election results.* Proceedings of the Workshop on Sentiment Analysis where AI meets Psychology, SAAIP, pp. 2–10.

Bond, R., & Messing, S. (2015). Quantifying social media's political space: Estimating ideology from publicly revealed preferences on Facebook. *American Political Science Review, 109*(1), 62–78.

Burnap, P., Gibson, R., Sloan, L., Southern, R., & Williams, M. (2016). 140 characters to victory? Using Twitter to predict the UK 2015 general election. *Electoral Studies, 41*, 230–233.

Caldarelli, G., Chessa, A., Pammolli, F., Pompa, G., Puliga, M., Riccaboni, M., & Riotta, G. (2014). A multi-level geographical study of Italian political elections from Twitter data. *PLoS One, 9*(5), e95809.

Ceron, A., Curini, L., & Iacus, S. M. (2015). Using sentiment analysis to monitor electoral campaigns: Method matters – evidence from the United States and Italy. *Social Science Computer Review, 33*(1), 3–20.

Ceron, A., Curini, L., Iacus, S. M., & Porro, G. (2014). Every tweet counts? How sentiment analysis of social media can improve our knowledge of citizens' political preferences with an application to Italy and France. *New Media & Society, 16*(2), 340–358.

Conover, M. D., Gonçalves, B., Flammini, A., & Menczer, F. (2012). Partisan asymmetries in online political activity. *EPJ Data Science, 1*(1), 6.

Dave, K., Lawrence, S., & Pennock, D. M. (2003). Mining the peanut gallery: Opinion extraction and semantic classification of product reviews. In *Proceedings of the 12th international conference on world wide web* (pp. 519–528). ACM.

DiGrazia, J., McKelvey, K., Bollen, J., & Rojas, F. (2013). More tweets, more votes: Social media as a quantitative indicator of political behavior. *PLoS One, 8*(11), e79449.

Gamon, M., Aue, A., Corston-Oliver, S., & Ringger, E. (2005). Pulse: Mining customer opinions from free text. In *International symposium on intelligent data analysis* (pp. 121–132). Springer.

Gayo Avello, D. (2011). Don't turn social media into another literary digest poll. *Communications of the ACM, 54*(10), 121–128.

Gayo-Avello, D. (2013). A meta-analysis of state-of-the-art electoral prediction from Twitter data. *Social Science Computer Review, 31*(6), 649–679.

Hopkins, D. J., & King, G. (2010). A method of automated nonparametric content analysis for social science. *American Journal of Political Science, 54*(1), 229–247.

Hu, M., & Liu, B. (2004). Mining and summarizing customer reviews. In *Proceedings of the tenth ACM SIGKDD international conference on knowledge discovery and data mining* (pp. 168–177). ACM.

Huettner, A., & Subasic, P. (2000). *Fuzzy typing for document management* (pp. 26–27). ACL 2000 Companion Volume: Tutorial Abstracts and Demonstration Notes.

Jungherr, A. (2015). *Analyzing political communication with digital trace data.* Springer.

Jungherr, A. (2017). *Normalizing digital trace data.* Digital Discussions: How Big Data Informs Political Communication.

Jungherr, A., Jürgens, P., & Schoen, H. (2012). Why the pirate party won the German election of 2009 or the trouble with predictions: A response to Tumasjan, a., Sprenger, to, sander, pg, & Welpe, im "predicting elections with Twitter: What 140 characters reveal about political sentiment". *Social Science Computer Review, 30*(2), 229–234.

Kenney, P. J., & Rice, T. W. (1983). Popularity and the vote: The gubernatorial case. *American Politics Quarterly, 11*(2), 237–241.

Lewis-Beck, M. S., & Rice, T. W. (1982). Presidential popularity and presidential vote. *Public Opinion Quarterly, 46*(4), 534–537.

Lewis-Beck, M. S., & Stegmaier, M. (2007, August). Economic models of voting. In R. J. Dalton & H.-D. Klingemann (Eds.), *The Oxford handbook of political behavior.* Oxford University Press.

Liu, B. (2012). Sentiment analysis and opinion mining. *Synthesis Lectures on Human Language Technologies, 5*(1), 1–167.

Liu, B., Hu, M., & Cheng, J. (2005). Opinion observer: Analyzing and comparing opinions on the web. In *Proceedings of the 14th international conference on world wide web* (pp. 342–351). ACM.

Loynes, N., Nagler, J., Casas, A., & Baram, N. (forthcoming). *Finding Friends: A network-approach to geo-locating Twitter users.*

Lui, C., Metaxas, P. T., & Mustafaraj, E. (2011). *On the predictability of the US elections through search volume activity.* Wellesley College Digital Repository. Retrieved from https://repository.wellesley.edu/object/ir153

Metaxas, P. T., Mustafaraj, E., & Gayo-Avello, D. (2011). *How (not) to predict elections.* Privacy, Security, Risk and Trust (PASSAT) and 2011 IEEE Third International Conference on Social Computing (SocialCom), 2011 IEEE Third International Conference on, pp. 165–171. IEEE.

Mueller, J. E. (1970). Presidential popularity from Truman to Johnson. *The American Political Science Review, 64*(1), 18–34. Publisher: JSTOR.

Munger, K., Egan, P., Nagler, J., Ronen, J., & Tucker, J. A. (2016). *Learning (and Unlearning) from the media and political parties: Evidence from the 2015 UK Election* (Technical report, Working Paper).

Nasukawa, T., & Yi, J. (2003). Sentiment analysis: Capturing favorability using natural language processing. In *Proceedings of the 2nd international conference on knowledge capture* (pp. 70–77). ACM.

Newman, B., & Forcehimes, A. (2010). "Rally round the flag" events for presidential approval research. *Electoral Studies, 29*(1), 144–154. Publisher: Elsevier.

Nguyen, D., Gravel, R., Trieschnigg, D., & Meder, T. (2013). "How old do you think I am?" A study of language and age in Twitter. In *Proceedings of the international AAAI conference on web and social media* (Vol. 7, No. 1). Retrieved from https://ojs.aaai.org/index.php/ICWSM/article/view/14381.

O'Connor, B., Balasubramanyan, R., Routledge, B. R., & Smith, N. A. (2010). From tweets to polls: Linking text sentiment to public opinion time series. *Icwsm, 11*(122–129), 1–2.

Pak, A., & Paroubek, P. (2010). Twitter as a corpus for sentiment analysis and opinion mining. In *Proceedings of the international conference on language resources and evaluation, LREC 2010,* 17–23 May 2010, Valletta, Malta.

Pang, B., & Lee, L. (2004). A sentimental education: Sentiment analysis using subjectivity summarization based on minimum cuts. In *Proceedings of the 42nd annual meeting on association for computational linguistics* (p. 271). Association for Computational Linguistics.

Pang, B., & Lee, L. (2005). Seeing stars: Exploiting class relationships for sentiment categorization with respect to rating scales. In *Proceedings of the 43rd annual meeting on association for computational linguistics* (pp. 115–124). Association for Computational Linguistics.

Pang, B., Lee, L., & Vaithyanathan, S. (2002). Thumbs up? Sentiment classification using machine learning techniques. In *Proceedings of the ACL-02 conference on Empirical methods in natural language processing* (Vol. 10, pp. 79–86). Association for Computational Linguistics.

Pedregosa, F., Varoquaux, G., Gramfort, A., Michel, V., Thirion, B., Grisel, O., . . . Duchesnay, E. (2011). Scikit-learn: Machine learning in Python. *Journal of Machine Learning Research, 12,* 2825–2830.

Popescu, A.-M., & Etzioni, O. (2007). Extracting product features and opinions from reviews. In *Natural language processing and text mining* (pp. 9–28). Springer.

Purdam, K., & Elliot, M. (2015). *The changing social science data landscape. Innovations in digital social research methods.* Sage.

Rainie, L., Smith, A., Schlozman, K. L., Brady, H., & Verba, S. (2012). *Social media and political engagement.* Pew Research Center. Retrieved from https://www.pewresearch.org/internet/2012/10/19/social-media-and-political-engagement/

Ribeiro, F. N., Araújo, M., Gonçalves, P., Gonçalves, M. A., & Benevenuto, F. (2016). SentiBench-a benchmark comparison of state-of-the-practice sentiment analysis methods. *EPJ Data Science, 5*(1), 23.

Ritterman, J., Osborne, M., & Klein, E. (2009). Using prediction markets and Twitter to predict a swine flu pandemic. In *1st international workshop on mining social media* (Vol. 9, pp. 9–17). Retrieved August 26, 2015, from ac.uk/miles/papers/swine09.pdf

Sakaki, T., Okazaki, M., & Matsuo, Y. (2010). Earthquake shakes Twitter users: Real-time event detection by social sensors. In *Proceedings of the 19th international conference on World wide web* (pp. 851–860). ACM.

Sang, E. T. K., & Bos, J. (2012). Predicting the 2011 Dutch senate election results with Twitter. In *Proceedings of the workshop on semantic analysis in social media* (pp. 53–60). Association for Computational Linguistics.

285

Scala, D. J., & Johnson, K. M. (2017, July). Political polarization along the rural-urban continuum? The geography of the presidential vote, 2000–2016. *The ANNALS of the American Academy of Political and Social Science, 672*(1), 162–184. Publisher: SAGE Publications Inc.

Severyn, A., & Moschitti, A. (2015, August). *Twitter sentiment analysis with deep convolutional neural networks.* Proceedings of the 38th International ACM SIGIR Conference on Research and Development in Information Retrieval, SIGIR'15, New York, NY, USA, pp. 959–962. Association for Computing Machinery.

Si, J., Mukherjee, A., Liu, B., Li, Q., Li, H., & Deng, X. (2013). *Exploiting topic based Twitter sentiment for stock prediction.* Proceedings of the 51st Annual Meeting of the Association for Computational Linguistics (Volume 2: Short Papers), Volume 2, pp. 24–29.

Smith, A., & Anderson, M. (2018, March). *Social media use 2018: Demographics and statistics.* Pew Research Center.

Taboada, M., Brooke, J., Tofiloski, M., Voll, K., & Stede, M. (2011). Lexicon-based methods for sentiment analysis. *Computational Linguistics, 37*(2), 267–307.

Thelwall, M., Buckley, K., & Paltoglou, G. (2012). Sentiment strength detection for the social web. *Journal of the Association for Information Science and Technology, 63*(1), 163–173.

Theocharis, Y., Lowe, W., Van Deth, J. W., & García-Albacete, G. (2015). Using Twitter to mobilize protest action: Online mobilization patterns and action repertoires in the Occupy Wall Street, Indignados, and Aganaktismenoi movements. *Information, Communication & Society, 18*(2), 202–220.

Tumasjan, A., Sprenger, T. O., Sandner, P. G., & Welpe, I. M. (2010). Predicting elections with Twitter: What 140 characters reveal about political sentiment. *Icwsm, 10*(1), 178–185.

Turney, P. D. (2002). Thumbs up or thumbs down? Semantic orientation applied to unsupervised classification of reviews. *arXiv preprint cs/0212032.*

Wang, X., Gerber, M. S., & Brown, D. E. (2012). Automatic crime prediction using events extracted from Twitter posts. In *Social computing, behavioral-cultural modeling and prediction* (pp. 231–238). Springer.

Zhang, L., Ghosh, R., Dekhil, M., Hsu, M., & Liu, B. (2011). *Combining lexicon-based and learning-based methods for Twitter sentiment analysis.* HP Laboratories, Technical Report HPL-2011 89.

17

THE SOCIAL INFLUENCE OF BOTS AND TROLLS IN SOCIAL MEDIA

Yimin Chen

Introduction

The internet has become an indispensable informational resource for much of the population. Over 80% of American adults now use the internet at least daily (Perrin & Kumar, 2019). It is the most common source of information that American adults consult when making important life decisions (Turner & Rainie, 2020), and more than two-thirds say that they get at least some of their news from social media sources (Shearer & Masta, 2018). Yet, despite our reliance on digital information sources, digital literacy in many segments of the population remain relatively low. A recent Pew survey, for example, found that those who rely on social media for their political news tend to not only be both less aware and less knowledgeable about current events but are also more likely to have been exposed to false or unproven claims (Mitchell, Jurkowitz, Oliphant, & Shearer, 2020), in other words: "fake news". Even more worryingly, the people who make up this group are among the least concerned about the impact of fake news (Mitchell et al., 2020).

But where does this fake news come from? Ever since the contentious 2016 presidential election in the United States, the pernicious influence of internet trolls and social media bots has been the subject of intense media scrutiny around the world. This period saw allegations of election interference from Russian "troll farms" (Ruck, Rice, Borycz, & Bentley, 2019), the rise to prominence of online "alt-right trolls" in support of Donald Trump and other populist political leaders (Daniels, 2018), and the astroturfing of news and opinions through the use of social media bots (Broniatowski et al., 2018; Howard, Woolley, & Calo, 2018). Since then, bots and trolls have been implicated in spreading disinformation and conspiracy theories, manipulating polls and public discourse, eroding trust in the media and public institutions, and in the targeted harassment of public figures online. It is no wonder that trolls tend to now be strongly associated with "uncivil and manipulative behaviours" (Rainie, Anderson, & Albright, 2017).

However, internet trolling has not always been viewed with such negativity – there have been, and still are, parts of the internet that condone or even celebrate the practice. But let us first establish what an internet troll actually is. In one of the earliest published accounts of trolling behavior on Usenet, Michelle Tepper (1997) described it as a game of information that serves as an "anti-newbie sport" played by those who were more knowledgeable and proficient in online spaces against those who were not. "Trolling", she says, refers to a fishing technique

DOI: 10.4324/9781003024583-20

using a baited hook – but on the internet, the hook is baited with misinformation of a deliberately comical sort (Tepper, 1997). Anyone foolish enough to take this bait and attempt to engage earnestly became a target for mockery and teasing by those who were in the know. Similarly, Judith Donath (1999) called trolling "a game of identity deception, albeit one that is played without the consent of most of the players". Although this type of trolling had the potential to turn malicious, it was often seen as a mischievous way of enforcing community norms and netiquette rather than as particularly malevolent and more akin to pranking than to harassment.

A brief history of trolling

The story of trolling is tied up in the history of cyberculture – a term coined by William Gibson in his 1984 novel *Neuromancer* and which has come to describe "the set of practices, attitudes, modes of thought and values that grow along with the Cyberspace" (Gómez-Diago, 2012). Fred Turner (2006) traces the roots of cyberculture to the broader counterculture of the 1960s. Many early virtual communities, such as the WELL, were founded upon the visions of the anti-establishmentarians of the Free Speech movement, as well as the techno-libertarian ethos of computer hackers (Levy, 1984). "Cyberspace", for them, was transformational: a place where "the old information elites [were] crumbling", and in their place, "the kids [were] at the controls" (Turner, 2010). These influences, along with the "audacious politics of pranking, transgression, and mockery" (Coleman, 2012) of the Yippies and phone phreaks laid the foundations of what would become internet culture in the years to come.

However, this countercultural hacker paradise was not to last. Eventually, the spread of affordable computer technology and internet access led to what would be known as the "September that never ended" (Raymond, 2004), that is, the period of time since September 1993. The reference comes from the seasonal rhythms of Usenet in the 1980s and early 1990s, where the start of the fall college semester would bring an annual influx of clueless newbies unfamiliar with the accepted norms of netiquette. Although initially disruptive, in time, these newbies would either learn how to behave and integrate into the community or eventually get bored and leave. But in September of 1993, America Online opened up Usenet access to tens of thousands of customers, unleashing what seemed like an endless wave of digital immigrants that proved impossible to acculturate – thus triggering "an inexorable decline in the quality of discussions on newsgroups" (Raymond, 2004). This, of course, did not sit well with many of Usenet's original denizens sowed the seeds of cultural conflict.

While the majority of trolls these days likely have no first-hand experience with the events of the internet's countercultural past, they have adopted many of its attitudes, rituals, and aesthetics into their own subculture. According to Gabriella Coleman (2012):

> Trolls have transformed what were more occasional and sporadic acts, often focused on virtual arguments called flaming or flame wars, into a full-blown set of cultural norms and set of linguistic practices. . . . Trolls work to remind the "masses" that have lapped onto the shores of the Internet that there is still a class of geeks who, as their name suggests, will cause Internet grief.
>
> (pp. 109–110)

In this respect, trolling can be seen as a reaction to the "September that never ended". Internet trolls mark themselves and their online spaces through distinctive language and practices that transgress and sometimes offend mainstream sensibilities and expectations. In their minds, internet trolls may see their actions more as a form of protest than an act of random hostility; it is a show of resistance against the gentrification of the online spaces that had once been safe haven to technologically sophisticated subcultures who felt disenfranchised by the greater society. From this perspective, trolling represents the "tensions between dominant and subordinate groups" (Hebdige, 1979) played out all across cyberspace.

The ambiguity of trolling

One of the perennial issues in the discourse on trolling has been the ambiguity of the term itself. "Trolling" has been used to describe a wide range of online behaviors and activities from "the vaguely distasteful to the borderline illegal" (Phillips, 2011). "Swatting", along with "flaming", "griefing", and "cyberbullying", are just a few of the behaviors that been directly or indirectly connected with internet trolling in popular and academic literature. Victims and critics of these acts of "online hate" (Shepherd, Harvey, Jordan, Srauy, & Miltner, 2015) decry them as damaging and toxic, while more sympathetic researchers and commentators tend to skirt these issues to focus on the creative value of benign transgression and "playful mischief" (Kirman, Lineham, & Lawson, 2012). It is often the case that different people are talking about very different things when it comes to trolling, both in terms of kind and degree. According to Massanari (2019), "trolling is both an identity and a practice" – that is, the term describes both a range of actions and behaviors that are associated with internet trolls as well as the subcultural sensibilities that motivate and give context to those behaviors. While the *spirit* of trolling may be rooted in transgression and mischief, the *effects* of trolling can often be quite harmful. The rest of this chapter will examine trolling subculture and behaviors in context, exploring both negative and positive aspects of trolling, as well as their intersection with automated social media bots.

Trolling as recreational nastiness

Emma Jane (2014) uses the term "recreational nastiness" to refer to the types of toxic, violent online behaviors that are associated with the most negative aspects of trolling. Motivation for these behaviors can be attributed to the expression of "everyday sadism" (Buckels, Trapnell, & Paulhus, 2014) in order "to garner what many trolls refer to as 'lulz', a particular kind of aggressive, morally ambiguous laughter" (Phillips, 2011). In short, trolls are motivated to attack other people and disrupt communities on social media because they think it is fun. From the perspective of recreational nastiness, the harm that trolling causes can be categorized at three levels: harm against individuals, harm against communities, and harm against society. Each of these three levels will be discussed in turn.

Harm against individuals

The case against trolling is most often made based on the personal suffering it causes to those people targeted for harassment and abuse. It is here that the link to bullying (or cyberbullying) is strongest. During #Gamergate, a controversy which arose in 2014 over allegations of ethical breaches in video games journalism, internet trolls, organized through forum sites like Reddit and 4chan, launched a misogynistic campaign of harassment against female video game developers, journalists, scholars, and cultural critics (Braithwaite, 2016). Zoe Quinn, the indie game developer whose ex-boyfriend's accusation that she traded sexual favors in exchange for positive press coverage kicked off #Gamergate, was among the first to be targeted with rape and death threats over social media (Dewey, 2014). "Doxing", the publication of a person's private and personal information (including phone numbers, addresses, and employment information), was one tactic used against many of the women who were publicly critical of #Gamergate, including feminist media scholar Anita Sarkeesian and game developer Brianna Wu (Mortensen, 2018). This allowed the harassment to follow women off the internet and into their private, offline lives, leading to threats that were so specific that many of these women were advised by police to leave their homes (Dewey, 2014).

Broadly, these types of trolling tactics against individuals have the effect of driving people away from social media platforms and therefore preventing them from participating in public discourse and other online activities. Instances of abusive trolling directed at celebrities, journalists, politicians, and other public figures are well documented in the news and popular media (Time, 2016; Yagoda & Dodd, 2020), but anyone could become the target of personal trolling attacks online. In research, studies have focused predominantly on the effect of trolling towards women (Adams, 2018; Veletsianos, Houlden, Hodson, & Gosse, 2018), racial minorities (Ortiz, 2019), and other vulnerable populations such as LGBTQ+ people and people with disabilities (Olson & LaPoe, 2017). Victims of this type of abuse reported "emotional responses ranging from feelings of irritation, anxiety, sadness, loneliness, vulnerability, and unsafeness; to feelings of distress, pain, shock, fear, terror, devastation, and violation" (Jane, 2014). Studies also confirm that the most common reactions by people targeted by trolls were to self-censor, disengage, or otherwise attempt to minimize their online exposure. Furthermore, some victims of trolling withdrew "not only from on-line engagement but from off-line public spheres as well" (Jane, 2014). In this way, trolling on and off social media can ostracize and exclude the people who might most benefit from participating in the public sphere.

Harm against communities

If personal attacks can drive individuals away from online communities, then it follows that the communities themselves suffer harm as well. Several studies have examined the effect of trolling across a wide variety of communities, including feminist discussion forums (Herring, Job-Sluder, Scheckler, & Barab, 2002), magazine websites (Binns, 2012), and Wikipedia (Shachaf & Hara, 2010). In each case, trolls were found to have a disruptive and destabilizing influence. By "luring others into pointless and time-consuming discussions" (Herring et al., 2002, p. 372), trolls undermine trust, sabotage social interactions, and can even cause "significant legal problems" (Binns, 2012). Much like a building infested with pests, trolls can be costly to communities by necessitating mechanisms for control (i.e., moderation) and by causing damage to the reputation or "brand" of the site, driving away old members and discouraging new ones from joining. This is of particular relevance to websites like Wikipedia, which has worked hard to establish itself as a dependable reference source. The consequences of the vandalism by trolls, which include "blanking (removing all content of) articles, renaming articles to random names, and inserting intentionally misleading, wrong, or irrelevant information", are not limited only to the affected article but subvert the authoritativeness of the entire site: "these actions reduce the accuracy and reliability of the Wikipedia project" (Shachaf & Hara, 2010).

Within the player base of many online multiplayer video games, trolling and other types of "cyberaggression" have become normalized as part of the culture (Hilvert-Bruce & Neill, 2020). Indeed, within some highly competitive team-based games, such as *League of Legends*, "toxicity has become an organic component" (Kou, 2020) that is seemingly inexorably intertwined with the affordances and gameplay dynamics of the game itself. In the gaming context, trolling behaviour can range from abusive communications over text or voice chat, to attacking one's own team members, to acting in other ways that deliberately ruin the enjoyment of other players in the game (often called griefing). Perceptions of trolling within gaming communities have been documented as ranging from "annoying", to "necessary evil", to "guilty pleasure", and sometimes "even celebrated by some of its members, trolls and everyday gamers alike" (Cook, Schaafsma, & Antheunis, 2018). As noted in Cook, Conijn, Schaafsma, and Antheunis (2019), the level of normalization of online aggression in these gaming communities could create a cyclical pattern similar to more traditional bullying behaviors. "Victims and bystanders who are exposed most directly to the troll's antics start reciprocating within the interaction itself" (Cook et al., 2019), thus creating a positive feedback loop that perpetuates and further normalizes the abuse and hostility within these communities.

Harm against society and institutions

While claims of the downfall of civility brought upon by "the toxic and lawless climate developing on the web" (Waters, 2013) tend to be more sensationalist than accurate, the harm caused by online trolling certainly can extend beyond individuals and their networks. The clearest example of the influence of trolling on societies at large is the breakdown of trust in traditional news organizations and the proliferation of conspiracy theories. The 2016 United States presidential election campaign has been described as among the most negative on record, in no small part due to political trolling carried out by alt-right groups in support of then-Republican candidate Donald Trump (Flores-Saviaga, Keegan, & Savage, 2018; Greene, 2019; Merrin, 2019). In addition to the types of harassment, cyberaggression, and hate speech discussed previously, trolls during this time also created and circulated fake news articles and other disinformation to pollute the public discourse. Fabricated stories such as ones about Donald Trump receiving an endorsement from the Pope and Hillary Clinton selling weapons to ISIS received more user engagement on social media than content from major news networks in the lead up to the election (Silverman, 2016). Perhaps even more damaging was "Pizzagate", a conspiracy dreamed up by trolls on the 4chan message board speculating that Hillary Clinton and other Democrats were operating a child sex ring in the basement of a Washington, DC, pizzeria (Fisher, Cox, & Hermann, 2016). Not only did these specious accusations inspire an armed attempt to liberate the children supposedly held at this restaurant, but the Pizzagate conspiracy also became the progenitor of later "QAnon" conspiracies, which place Donald Trump at the head of a resistance working to counter a shadowy, global cabal of "Deep State" evildoers, including the mainstream news media (LaFrance, 2020).

In addition to spreading via messages and memes on social media, these conspiracies and hoaxes were also amplified through reporting by major news networks. The effect, according to a report by Phillips (2018), was to "make the messages, and their messengers, much more visible than they would have been otherwise, even when the reporting took an explicitly critical stance". One of the primary motivators of internet trolls is attention-seeking, and this sort of media coverage provided that in spades. Not only did this signal to trolls that their tactics were working, Phillips (2018) also argues that giving attention to trolling in this way may have helped to normalize and lend credence to false narratives. This places news organizations in the awkward position of having to fend off outrageous attacks on their credibility by conspiracy theorists while at the same time trying not to legitimize those same baseless accusations by taking them seriously. Regardless, the effect has been an erosion of public trust in traditional news institutions as audiences increasingly turn towards partisan (Jurkowitz, Mitchell, Shearer, Walker, 2020) and social media sources (Shearer & Grieco, 2019).

The level of mis- and disinformation now circulating through the public sphere has led many in the media to claim that we now live in a post-truth era and, indeed, the term was named the Oxford English Dictionary's word of the year for 2016. While deceptive or misleading information is nothing new, the speed and scale of its dissemination over the internet, propelled by trolls and other malicious actors and given credence by a news ecosystem driven by the monetization of clicks (Chen, Conroy, & Rubin, 2015), has reached a level that threatens "the overall intellectual well-being of a society" (Lewandowsky, Ecker, & Cook, 2017). Studies have shown that merely being exposed to conspiratorial claims can negatively affect people's trust in and acceptance of official information (Einstein & Glick, 2015; Raab, Ortlieb, Auer, Guthmann, & Carbon, 2013) – an effect that has been weaponized by right-wing populist politicians like Donald Trump to attack their critics as "fake news".

Trump and his supporters have proven to be adept at using what Merrin (2019) calls "troll-politics" to wage "memetic warfare" against their opponents. Appropriating the tactics and the sarcastic irreverence of trolling culture, Merrin argues that "this troll-politics is now central to our political life, constituting, for many people, their most common mode of political expression, participation and activism" (2019). Instead of bringing about the democratization of the public sphere, as early techno-utopian visions of the internet had dreamed of, the environments created by social media platforms like Twitter are more akin to "schoolyard[s] run by bullies" (Hannan, 2018).

Social media bots and the automation of trolling

While some psychological studies have suggested that people who naturally exhibit malevolent personality traits like psychopathy, sadism, and narcissism are more likely to be trolls (Buckels et al., 2014; March, 2019), there is also compelling evidence that trolling behaviour can be learned and that situational factors can also drive people who are not otherwise antisocial to engage in trolling (Cheng, Bernstein, Danescu-Niculescu-Mizil, & Leskovec, 2017). Fichman and Sanfilippo (2016) stress that there is an important difference between "trolling" and "being a troll", as "not all who troll are trolls". And so, while trolling behaviour seems to be quite prevalent online, individuals who are dedicated, regular trolls are likely to be fairly rare but exert an outsized influence. Although there have been few attempts to determine just how many trolls there may be on a given platform or website, one study of a Romanian message forum identified only 3% of active users as trolls (Achimescu & Sultanescu, 2020). These users, however, were responsible for 35% of all comments on the forum (Achimescu & Sultanescu, 2020).

One reason that social media seems inundated with trolling is simply because some trolls lead lifestyles that allow them to post continuously and "dedicate an inordinate amount of time to their activity" (Synnott, Coulias, & Ioannou, 2017). Another way for trolls to amplify their reach is through the use of social media bots. On platforms like Twitter, these bots take the form of profiles and accounts controlled by automated software and can be used to "mislead, exploit, and manipulate social media discourse with rumors, spam, malware, misinformation, slander, or even just noise" (Ferrara, Varol, Davis, Menczer, & Flammini, 2016). On Twitter especially, the short messages and limited options for interaction can serve to mask the relatively simplistic behaviour of bots so that it can be difficult to tell them apart from human users (Hwang, Pearce, & Nanis, 2012). This also makes it hard to pinpoint just how prevalent bots are on social media, although some estimates have suggested that as much as 15% of all active Twitter profiles are bots (Varol, Ferrara, Davis, Menczer, & Flammini, 2017). In addition, not all bots are made to act independently; some are designed to work with some level of human input or direction. These "hybrid" models are often called "cyborgs" in the literature (Paavola, Helo, Jalonen,

Sartonen, & Huhtinen, 2016). In any case, the sheer number of bots that malicious trolls can loose onto social media platforms makes them especially effective at astroturfing: "campaigns disguised as spontaneous, popular 'grassroots' behaviour that are in reality carried out by a single person or organization" (Ratkiewicz et al., 2010). One single network of bots can create the illusion of broad consensus by pushing out hundreds or thousands of posts on a topic or issue.

Perhaps the most well-known intersection of social media bots and trolling is the allegation that the Russian government employed "troll farms" at the Internet Research Agency (IRA) in order to interfere with the 2016 U.S. election (Lee, 2018). Studies have indeed shown that the IRA was engaged in active disinformation and propaganda campaigns on Twitter targeting issues related to the election (Bastos & Farkas, 2019; Lukito, 2020), although some have questioned the ultimate impact of these trolling efforts (Bail et al., 2020). One study by Shao, Ciampaglia, Varol, Flammini, and Menczer (2017) did not trace bot activity back to the IRA, specifically, but did find that bots on Twitter were effective at amplifying fake news and conspiracy theories to levels competitive with the virality profiles of legitimate news stories. In fact, the use of social media bots for political purposes is quite common. Countries such as China, Azerbaijan, Iran, Mexico, and Turkey have all reportedly used bots to stifle dissent or attack opposition (Woolley, 2016). Outside the political realm, these tactics can be applied to any issue where bad actors may want to sow discord and pollute public discourse. The online vaccine debate, for example, is just one area where bots and trolls have made a significant impact through the spread of harmful disinformation (Broniatowski et al., 2018).

The harmful effects of social media bots and trolling

In study after study, the hurtful and damaging effects of internet trolling have been documented again and again. These accounts problematize techno-utopian ideas about how the internet would "level social hierarchies, distribute and personalize work, and dematerialize communication. . . [and] embody new, egalitarian forms of political organization" (Turner, 2006). While it may be true that "the relative anonymity of the Internet can make people feel safe talking about issues that might be considered sensitive, inappropriate or dangerous in face-to-face public conversation" (Herring et al., 2002), the level of anonymity and mediated interactivity afforded by this technology has also led to a rise in toxic disinhibition, where online interactions can devolve into "rude language, harsh criticisms, anger, hatred, even threats" (Suler, 2004) with shocking regularity. The internet certainly does provide people with new freedoms and new avenues of expression, but it has also allowed trolls unprecedented access and opportunity to spread chaos and suffering – often for nothing more than their own amusement.

At each of the three levels, internet trolling can have serious and long-lasting consequences. Attacks on individuals often silence and oppress the very people who might benefit most from an open forum for connection and support. Unchecked toxic behaviour and cyberaggression can sabotage prosocial interactions and push online communities into a spiral of ever-increasing negativity. Finally, the malicious spread of mis- and disinformation over social media platforms by bots and trolls erodes public trust in government and institutions and drives conflict and polarization. And yet, it would be foolishly myopic to blame trolling for all the ills of the internet. "Trolls may be destructive and callous", Phillips (2015) argues, "but the uncomfortable fact is that trolls replicate behaviours and attitudes that in other contexts are actively celebrated. . . [they] amplify the ugly side of mainstream behaviour". No doubt there is more that can be done to mitigate the harm that trolls can cause – a serious reconsideration of how social media platforms moderate content and enforce terms of service agreements would be a start (Gillespie, 2018) – but trolling is simply an expression of broader issues of how we treat ourselves and others. Addressing the root causes of harmful trolling, rather than just the symptoms, will require grappling with much more fundamental societal problems than online misbehavior.

The positive side of playful mischief

After detailing so many of the adverse effects of internet trolling, can it be possible for trolling to be anything but harmful? Wouldn't any argument for a positive side of trolling essentially constitute a defense of the indefensible? The primary issue lies in the way that the term "trolling" has become a sort of catch-all for any "online behaviours with even the slightest whiff of mischief, oddity, or antagonism" (Phillips & Milner, 2018). Almost every type of behaviour online has been called "trolling" at some point – not just the ones that are abusive or anti-social. As a result, behaviors that are relatively benign or even arguably pro-social have been indiscriminately lumped in with the more problematic ones (Cruz, Seo, & Rex, 2018). Nevertheless, more light-hearted and productive types of internet trolling have been documented (Cruz et al., 2018; Mylonas & Kompatsiaris, 2019; Phillips, 2015; Sanfilippo, Fichman, & Yang, 2018) and, sidestepping the prescriptivist debate over what "trolling" means, this section will discuss some of the positive effects of trolling on social media.

Trolling as creative transgression

One of the most consistent features of internet trolling identified across the literature is transgression (Cruz et al., 2018). That is, trolls act in ways that violate common norms and sensibilities. Since the present subculture of internet trolls evolved from the counterculture sensibilities of the early internet, this is not surprising. Despite its negative connotations, though, transgression is not necessarily a bad thing. Sociologist Chris Jenks (2013) places transgression "in liminal zones within culture, such as the avant-garde, radical political movements and counter-cultural traditions in creative practice". Rather than as a subject of abhorrence, Jenks (2003) describes transgression as "a dynamic force in cultural reproduction" that "prevents stagnation". Trolling, as a type of playful mischief, exists within that same transgressive grey area at "the boundaries between acceptable and unacceptable social behaviour" (Kirman et al., 2012) and "is fundamentally about the negotiation of culture, norms, and expectations" (Fichman & Sanfilippo, 2016). So long as this play doesn't cross the line into bullying, these minor transgressions help lend a lively vitality to social media interactions. For example, in one study of the "r/TrollXChromosomes" subreddit, a community dedicated to provocative and humorous women-centered content, Massanari (2019) found that the "trolls harness the unbridled, chaotic energy of the trickster to play or upend some aspects of hegemonic femininity". Through a pro-feminist "reclamation" of the troll identity, members of the subreddit "collectively share and bond around everyday experiences" (Massanari, 2019).

Another feature of trolling that is consistent across studies is humor (Coleman, 2014; March & Marrington, 2019; Phillips, 2015). Of course, whether the targets of trolling behaviour and uninvolved onlookers actually interpret such interactions as humorous is highly subjective and context dependent, but trolls generally are at least attempting to be funny, even some of those who engage in the abusive behaviors discussed previously. In its more benign expressions, this impulse for performative humor often manifests in playful mischief. The infamous Leeroy Jenkins incident in the World of Warcraft online video game is one example of innocuous troll humor. This incident, captured on video and uploaded to YouTube in 2005, features a group of players discussing their strategy in preparation for a difficult encounter. In the midst of this, one member of the group, Leeroy Jenkins,[1] who had stepped away to prepare dinner, returns and interrupts the planning by prematurely charging into battle while screaming his own name. As the rest of the party rushes in to help, they are all promptly killed. In the video, the other party members can be heard chastising Leeroy for his incompetence, who simply replies "at least I have chicken". Normally, intentionally sabotaging cooperative events like this would be considered griefing, as discussed previously, but the Leeroy Jenkins incident was so over-the-top ridiculous (and presumably contrived) that it was taken as joke instead. Leeroy Jenkins became a meme among players of World of Warcraft, inspiring numerous copycats, and was eventually made into an official in-game character.[2] Rather than have an anti-social effect on the World of Warcraft community, Leeroy Jenkins became a pro-social in-joke that gave players something to laugh about and bond over (Lowood, 2006).

The internet meme machine

The Leeroy Jenkins example introduces yet another way in which internet trolling can have a positive effect on social media: memes. Originally coined by biologist Richard Dawkins to describe units of cultural inheritance, memes on the internet have come to be defined colloquially as "a piece of culture, typically a joke, which gains influence through online transmission" (Davison, 2012). Most communication on social media platforms lack many of the verbal and non-verbal social cues that are possible in face-to-face interactions (Derks et al., 2008). Without contextual cues like facial expressions and intonation, it can be difficult online to tell the difference between an earnest comment and a sarcastic one, and interactions may feel more impersonal. Internet memes have been suggested as one a way in which people can form bonds and find affinity with friends and strangers online: "people use memes to simultaneously express both their uniqueness and their connectivity" (Shifman, 2014). Just as with World of Warcraft players and Leeroy Jenkins, the use of memes as in-jokes and references can serve as "cultural touch-points" (Massanari, 2013) to build a sense of community over shared experiences or interests.

A significant creative force in the production of internet memes "emerg[ed] out of esoteric forums in the early 2000s" (Milner, 2018). While the irreverent trolling culture that forum communities like 4chan and Reddit cultivated has been a factor in allowing them to become breeding grounds for online hate, as shown by their involvement in harassment campaigns like #Gamergate (Shepherd et al., 2015), that same flippant sensibility, when turned to less malignant purposes, simply results in "people acting silly" (Fichman & Sanfilippo, 2016). The transgressive, humorous spirit of trolling has been a powerful driver in the production and proliferation of internet memes, which "shape the mindsets, forms of behaviour, actions of social groups" (Shifman, 2014). While racist and bigoted memes have indeed been an anti-social and divisive influence on social media (ADL, n.d.), humorous memes can act as a form of collective folklore that make the internet "feel more like a 'place'" (Milner, 2018).

Massanari (2013) has documented how popular memes on Reddit enter into the platform's collective folklore. One example is the "2am chili" meme, a photo recipe for chili featuring a snarky stick figure, which inspired numerous follow-ups and imitators (Massanari, 2013). Another type of Reddit meme is the novelty account: a user that posts drawings, stories, or comments that reflect the user's account name or follows a theme. The user "Poem_for_your_sprog",[3] for example, writes poetry inspired by other users' posts and comments, while the user "Shitty_Watercolour",[4] true to his name, creates watercolor paintings. Another user named "shittymorph"[5] was infamous for engaging in a type of bait-and-switch trolling where he would reply to posts with comments that initially appeared to be relevant, but which always ended with a statement of "the fact that in 1998, The Undertaker threw Mankind off Hell In

A Cell, and plummeted 16 ft through an announcer's table" (Know Your Meme, n.d.). Rather than being viewed as malicious attempts to disrupt conversation, shittymorph's non sequiturs about professional wrestling tend to be highly upvoted (an indication of popular agreement or approval) and even celebrated. Like with the classic "Rickroll" meme (where unsuspecting users are redirected to Rick Astley's 1987 hit song "Never Gonna Give You Up"), Reddit users who fall for shittymorph's bait-and-switch will often express amusement at the deception, rather than annoyance, because other users in the community will explicitly point out that it is a joke.

Wholesome transgression

Perhaps the clearest example of trolling with pro-social intent is within the genre of so-called "wholesome memes". These memes are characterized as being "pure of heart, devoid of corruption or malice, modest, stable, virtuous, and all-around sweet and compassionate" (R/ Wholesomemes, n.d.). In contrast to more typical internet memes, which are frequently sarcastic or ironic, wholesome memes often feature exaggerated messages of love and caring and come abundantly peppered with heart emojis. Gaining popularity starting in 2016, wholesome memes have been interpreted as representing a rejection of the cynical nihilism and antagonism that had risen to prominence in internet culture via #Gamergate and the 2016 U.S. presidential campaign (Chabot & Chen, 2020). Whereas traditional trolling transgresses the norms of mainstream society and netiquette, wholesome memes can be seen as transgressing against the conventions of traditional trolling. Instead of mocking things like social taboos and political correctness, this wholesome flavor of trolling mocks meme culture's fetishization of aggressive, edgy humor. Wholesome memes playfully subvert the tropes and iconography of satirical and ironic memes in order to deliver a winking reversal of the negativity permeating online social spaces (Chabot & Chen, 2020). While there have been few studies of the wholesome meme phenomenon so far, mainstream commentators have described this trend towards a kinder, gentler internet culture as stemming from a desire to mitigate the tension and anxiety of the times (Nagesh, 2018; Romano, 2018).

Pro-social social bots

Just as the memes and practices of harmful trolling can be turned towards positive directions, so too can social media bots. In fact, bots have a long history of providing useful services to people on the internet. Before the rise of Web 2.0 and social media, bots were commonly implemented in Internet Relay Chat (IRC) channels to answer user queries, assist in moderation functions, and even to act as rudimentary "game masters" that could spit out text-based adventures for players (Latzko-Toth, 2017; Seering, Flores, Savage, & Hammer, 2018). Unlike the modern bots used for astroturfing and trolling, which try to pose as real humans, these IRC bots usually identified themselves as bots and made no attempt to deceive users. Today, the successors of IRC, platforms like Discord and Twitch, use bots in similar ways: to filter content, call up information, and entertain users. Some of these information-based bots also exist on Twitter, like the "UnaffiliatedCNNBreakingNewsBot",[6] which automatically tweets breaking news alerts from CNN, but a large number of benign bots on the platform are humor-based. One example is the "Joe Biden Insult Bot",[7] created by the Daily Show television program, which generates amusing insults inspired by the politician's rather uncommon manner of speaking. There are also bots specifically intended to bring cheer: "here's your reminder"[8] is one such bot, built to tweet out wellness advice to its followers.

On Reddit, there are numerous automated bots that can be called upon to provide a wide range of services. Some can be summoned using a text command in a comment. "RemindMe-Bot"[9] is one popular bot which, if given a time frame, will send a reminder at that time. Another, named "RepostSleuthBot"[10] can be called to determine whether an image is a "repost", that is, if it had already been previously submitted and is therefore not new content. Some bots will act independently, like "AUTOTLDR",[11] which automatically summarizes long news articles into a short comment. Even the default "AutoModerator" bot, which was made to do things like enforce rules, remove offensive comments, and assign tags to posts, can be modified in some amusing ways. For instance, the r/history subreddit AutoModerator is set up to reply with an in-depth, multi-paragraph critique whenever the book *Guns, Germs, and Steel* by Jared Diamond is mentioned.[12]

There are also bots on Reddit that operate similarly to the novelty accounts described previously. The "haikusbot"[13] searches for comments that match the 5–7–5 syllable haiku format and then reposts them as poetry. The now-defunct bot "PleaseRespectTables"[14] was designed to interact with the table flip meme, an emoticon adopted from East Asia that is used to express anger or frustration (written as (╯°□°）╯︵ ┻━┻). "PleaseRespectTables" would reply to instances of the table flip with an emoticon setting the table back upright: ┬──┬ ノ(° _ °ノ). In this bot's heyday, it was not uncommon to see long threads where people would amuse themselves by repeatedly use the table flip emoji just to trigger the bot over and over. Bots have also been utilized in attempts to curb hate speech on the platform. The "nwordcountbot" was one such initiative that could be called to display the number of times any particular user had used the racial slur (Katwala, 2020). Although this particular bot has since been deactivated, its functionality was duplicated and expanded upon by the "wordscounterbot".[15] There are even groups of people on Reddit who essentially mimic the functionality of bots: the "TranscribersOfReddit"[16] is an initiative run by volunteers who transcribe memes and other images into text in order to assist other users who may depend on text-to-speech software to browse the site. Regardless of functionality, one feature that seems to define non–malicious bots is that they generally make no attempt to disguise the fact that they are a bot. Whereas bots that are used to spread disinformation and propaganda are dangerous because they pretend to be human, most pro-social bots behave much more honestly and will usually call attention to the fact that they are an automated actor.

The positive effects of social media bots and trolling

As discussed in the preceding sections, there are particular ways in which trolling behaviors and automated bots can make a positive impact on social media platforms. This argument centers primarily on the vitalizing creative force of benign transgression: the playful mischief wrought by internet trolls has produced much of the content that makes the internet such an interesting participatory space. Trolling subcultures have been one of the main drivers in the creation of popular and enduring internet memes. Within many online communities, memes and in-jokes act as points of common reference that give those communities a sense of identity and become a part of the collective folklore – of the stories that they tell about themselves. This has allowed places like r/TrollXChromosomes, for example, to flourish on Reddit, whose culture is otherwise dominated by a "geek masculinity" (Massanari, 2019). The recent trend towards wholesome memes as a pro-social expression of trolling practices is another example of the creative energies of playful transgression turned to positive ends. Whereas negative trolling has been a polarizing and antagonistic influence on social media, positive trolling can be a counteracting force that promotes kindness and empathy.

Similarly, although social media bots have acquired a rather pejorative connotation in recent years, there are many useful bots whose services are indispensable to the smooth and orderly operation of various online communities. On platforms as diverse as Discord, Twitch, and Reddit, bots assist human administrators and moderators in all sorts of community management tasks from registering new users to filtering inappropriate content. Bots may even be programmed to create interesting and entertaining web content. Reddit and Twitter are each home to numerous automated accounts which generate amusing, uplifting, or informative posts. While the malicious social media bots may be more salient, there are plenty of helpful ones quietly and unobtrusively working to enhance people's online experiences as well.

Conclusion

Phillips and Milner (2018) argue that the internet and its attendant constitutive cultures and practices are fundamentally ambivalent. It is, as they describe, "simultaneously antagonistic and social, creative and disruptive, humorous and barbed" (Phillips & Milner, 2018). As this chapter has discussed, the influence of trolls and bots on online spaces can harm individuals or can make them icons; they can tear communities apart or bring them closer together. They are responsible for creating some of the worst, most toxic parts of the internet but also much of the content that makes the internet so dynamic and interesting. There is no doubt that the abusive manifestations of recreational nastiness need to be reigned in, regulated, and sanctioned, but the corporations that own the social media platforms have shown that they are unable or uninterested in investing the necessary labor and resources to treat these issues seriously (Gillespie, 2018; Roberts, 2019). A common theme in trolling research has been that content moderation and moderators are an effective way to reduce unwanted trolling (Herring et al., 2002; Lampe, Zube, Lee, Park, & Johnston, 2014; Seering, Kraut, & Dabbish, 2017; Shaw, 2013), though some have suggested that a lack of consistent and appropriate rules enforcement might actually encourage trolling (Fichman & Sanfilippo, 2016). This can pose significant problems, as the task of content moderation within communities such as subreddits (Dosono & Semaan, 2019) and Facebook groups and pages (Kalsnes & Ihlebæk, 2020) falls upon volunteers who may have little or no experience and few resources provided by the platforms.

Rather than attempt to stamp out incidents of trolling as they occur, a more pragmatic solution might be to concentrate on promoting internet and information literacy skills. An online citizenry trained to recognize bot-like behaviour and fact-check sources could help mitigate the influence of bots and trolls (Burkhardt, 2017). Teaching social media users that their online actions can have real consequences may also encourage trolls to be more mindful of which boundaries they push and how far (Chen, 2018). Ultimately, as Phillips (2015) argues, if we are really serious about "combatting the most explicitly racist, misogynist, and homophobic iterations of trolling, [we] should first take active, combative steps against the most explicitly racist, misogynist, and homophobic discourses in mainstream media and political circles". Trolls are products of internet culture, but internet culture is shaped by our broader societal cultures. A kinder, gentler internet can only be achieved through striving for a kinder, gentler society.

Notes

1 Video at: https://youtu.be/mLyOj_QD4a4
2 More information at: www.wowhead.com/achievement=9058/leeeeeeeeeeeeeroy
3 Profile at: www.reddit.com/user/Poem_for_your_sprog
4 Profile at: www.reddit.com/user/shitty_watercolour

5 Profile at: www.reddit.com/user/shittymorph
6 Twitter account: @attention_cnn
7 Twitter account: @BidenInsultBot
8 Twitter account: @tinycarebot
9 Profile at: www.reddit.com/user/RemindMeBot
10 Profile at: www.reddit.com/user/repostsleuthbot
11 Profile at: www.reddit.com/user/autotldr
12 Example at: www.reddit.com/r/history/comments/f5e1yd/how_relevant_is_guns_germs_and_steel_by_jared/fhzirr8
13 Profile at: www.reddit.com/user/haikusbot
14 Profile at: www.reddit.com/user/PleaseRespectTables
15 Profile at: www.reddit.com/user/wordscounterbot
16 Profile at: www.reddit.com/r/TranscribersOfReddit/wiki/index

References

Achimescu, V., & Sultanescu, D. (2020). Feeding the troll detection algorithm. *First Monday*, *25*(9). https://doi.org/10.5210/fm.v25i9.10604

Adams, C. (2018). "They go for gender first" the nature and effect of sexist abuse of female technology journalists. *Journalism Practice*, *12*(7), 850–869. https://doi.org/10.1080/17512786.2017.1350115

ADL. (n.d.). *Pepe the frog*. Retrieved from www.adl.org/education/references/hate-symbols/pepe-the-frog

Bail, C. A., Guay, B., Maloney, E., Combs, A., Hillygus, D. S., Merhout, F., Freelon, D., & Volfovsky, A. (2020). Assessing the Russian internet research agency's impact on the political attitudes and behaviours of American Twitter users in late 2017. *Proceedings of the National Academy of Sciences*, *117*(1), 243–250. https://doi.org/10.1073/pnas.1906420116

Bastos, M., & Farkas, J. (2019). "Donald Trump is my president!": The internet research agency propaganda machine. *Social Media + Society*, *5*(3), 2056305119865466. https://doi.org/10.1177/2056305119865466

Binns, A. (2012). Don't feed the trolls! Managing troublemakers in magazines' online communities. *Journalism practice*, *6*(4), 547–562. https://doi.org/10.1080/17512786.2011.648988

Braithwaite, A. (2016). It's about ethics in games journalism? Gamergaters and geek masculinity. *Social Media + Society*, *2*(4). https://doi.org/10.1177/2056305116672484

Broniatowski, D. A., Jamison, A. M., Qi, S., AlKulaib, L., Chen, T., Benton, A., Quinn, S., & Dredze, M. (2018). Weaponized health communication: Twitter bots and Russian trolls amplify the vaccine debate. *American Journal of Public Health*, *108*(10), 1378–1384. https://doi.org/10.2105/AJPH.2018.304567

Buckels, E. E., Trapnell, P. D., & Paulhus, D. L. (2014). Trolls just want to have fun. *Personality and Individual Differences*, *67*, 97–102. https://doi.org/10.1016/j.paid.2014.01.016

Burkhardt, J. M. (2017). Combating fake news in the digital age. *Library Technology Reports*, *53*(8), 1–36. Retrieved from www.journals.ala.org/index.php/ltr/issue/viewFile/662/423

Chabot, R., & Chen, Y. (2020). Living your best life and radiating positivity: Exploratory conceptions of wholesome memes as the new sincerity. *Proceedings of the Annual Conference of CAIS/Actes Du congrès Annuel De l'ACSI*. https://doi.org/10.29173/cais1172

Chen, Y. (2018). "Being a butt while on the internet": Perceptions of what is and isn't internet trolling. *Proceedings of the Association for Information Science and Technology*, *55*(1), 76–85. https://doi.org/10.1002/pra2.2018.14505501009

Chen, Y., Conroy, N. K., & Rubin, V. L. (2015). News in an online world: The need for an "automatic crap detector". *Proceedings of the Association for Information Science and Technology*, *52*(1), 1–4. https://doi.org/10.1002/pra2.2015.145052010081

Cheng, J., Bernstein, M., Danescu-Niculescu-Mizil, C., & Leskovec, J. (2017, February). Anyone can become a troll: Causes of trolling behaviour in online discussions. In *Proceedings of the 2017 ACM conference on computer supported cooperative work and social computing* (pp. 1217–1230). https://doi.org/10.1145/2998181.2998213

Coleman, G. (2012). Phreaks, hackers, and trolls: The politics of transgression and spectacle. In M. Mandiberg (Ed.), *The social media reader* (pp. 99–119). New York University Press.

Coleman, G. (2014). *Hacker, hoaxer, whistleblower, spy: The many faces of Anonymous*. Verso Books.

Cook, C., Conijn, R., Schaafsma, J., & Antheunis, M. (2019). For whom the gamer trolls: A study of trolling interactions in the online gaming context. *Journal of Computer-Mediated Communication*, *24*(6), 293–318. https://doi.org/10.1093/jcmc/zmz014

Cook, C., Schaafsma, J., & Antheunis, M. (2018). Under the bridge: An in-depth examination of online trolling in the gaming context. *New Media & Society, 20*(9), 3323–3340. https://doi.org/10.1177/1461444817748578

Cruz, A. G. B., Seo, Y., & Rex, M. (2018). Trolling in online communities: A practice-based theoretical perspective. *The Information Society, 34*(1), 15–26. https://doi.org/10.1080/01972243.2017.1391909

Daniels, J. (2018). The algorithmic rise of the "alt-right." *Contexts, 17*(1), 60–65. https://doi.org/10.1177/1536504218766547

Davison, P. (2012). The language of internet memes. In M. Mandiberg (Ed.), *The social media reader* (pp. 120–134). New York University Press.

Derks, D., Bos, A. E., & Von Grumbkow, J. (2008). Emoticons and online message interpretation. *Social Science Computer Review, 26*(3), 379–388. https://doi.org/10.1177/0894439307311611

Dewey, C. (2014, October 14). The only guide to Gamergate you will ever need to read. *Washington Post*. Retrieved from www.washingtonpost.com/news/the-intersect/wp/2014/10/14/the-only-guide-to-gamergate-you-will-ever-need-to-read/

Donath, J. S. (1999). Identity and deception in the virtual community. In M. A. Smith & P. Kollock (Eds.), *Communities in cyberspace* (pp. 29–59). Routledge.

Dosono, B., & Semaan, B. (2019, May). Moderation practices as emotional labor in sustaining online communities: The case of AAPI identity work on Reddit. In *Proceedings of the 2019 CHI conference on human factors in computing systems* (pp. 1–13). https://doi.org/10.1145/3290605.3300372

Einstein, K. L., & Glick, D. M. (2015). Do I think BLS data are BS? The consequences of conspiracy theories. *Political Behaviour, 37*(3), 679–701. https://doi.org/10.1007/s11109-014-9287-z

Ferrara, E., Varol, O., Davis, C., Menczer, F., & Flammini, A. (2016). The rise of social bots. *Communications of the ACM, 59*(7), 96–104. https://doi.org/10.1145/2818717

Fichman, P., & Sanfilippo, M. R. (2016). *Online trolling and its perpetrators: Under the cyberbridge*. Rowman & Littlefield.

Fisher, M., Cox J. W., & Hermann, P. (2016, December 6). Pizzagate: From rumor, to hashtag, to gunfire in D.C. *Washington Post*. Retrieved from www.washingtonpost.com/local/pizzagate-from-rumor-to-hashtag-to-gunfire-in-dc/2016/12/06/4c7def50-bbd4-11e6-94ac-3d324840106c_story.html

Flores-Saviaga, C., Keegan, B. C., & Savage, S. (2018). Mobilizing the Trump train: Understanding collective action in a political trolling community. arXiv preprint arXiv:1806.00429.

Gillespie, T. (2018). *Custodians of the internet: Platforms, content moderation, and the hidden decisions that shape social media*. Yale University Press.

Gómez-Diago, G. (2012). Cyberspace and cyberculture. In M. Kosut & J. G. Golson (Eds.), *Encyclopedia of gender in media* (pp. 58–60). Sage.

Greene, V. S. (2019). "Deplorable" satire: Alt-right memes, white genocide tweets, and redpilling normies. *Studies in American Humor, 5*(1), 31–69. https://doi.org/10.5325/studamerhumor.5.1.0031

Hannan, J. (2018). Trolling ourselves to death? Social media and post-truth politics. *European Journal of Communication, 33*(2), 214–226. https://doi.org/10.1177/0267323118760323

Hebdige, D. (1979). *Subculture: The meaning of style*. Routledge.

Herring, S., Job-Sluder, K., Scheckler, R., & Barab, S. (2002). Searching for safety online: Managing" trolling" in a feminist forum. *The Information Society, 18*(5), 371–384. https://doi.org/10.1080/01972240290108186

Hilvert-Bruce, Z., & Neill, J. T. (2020). I'm just trolling: The role of normative beliefs in aggressive behaviour in online gaming. *Computers in Human Behaviour, 102*, 303–311. https://doi.org/10.1016/j.chb.2019.09.003

Howard, P. N., Woolley, S., & Calo, R. (2018). Algorithms, bots, and political communication in the US 2016 election: The challenge of automated political communication for election law and administration. *Journal of Information Technology & Politics, 15*(2), 81–93. https://doi.org/10.1080/19331681.2018.1448735

Hwang, T., Pearce, I., & Nanis, M. (2012). Socialbots: Voices from the fronts. *Interactions, 19*(2), 38–45. https://doi.org/10.1145/2090150.2090161

Jane, E. A. (2014). "Your a ugly, whorish, slut" understanding E-bile. *Feminist Media Studies, 14*(4), 531–546. https://doi.org/10.1080/14680777.2012.741073

Jenks, C. (2003). *Transgression*. Psychology Press.

Jenks, C. (2013). Transgression: The concept. *Architectural Design, 83*(6), 20–23. https://doi.org/10.1002/ad.1669

Jurkowitz, M., Mitchell, A., Shearer, E., & Walker, M. (2020). U.S. media polarization and the 2020 election: A nation divided. *Pew Research Center*. Retrieved from www.journalism. org/2020/01/24/u-s-media-polarization-and-the-2020-election-a-nation-divided/

Kalsnes, B., & Ihlebæk, K. A. (2020). Hiding hate speech: Political moderation on Facebook. *Media, Culture & Society*. https://doi.org/10.1177/0163443720957562

Katwala, A. (2020, September 29). Reddit bots are hunting down online racists, one post at a time. *Wired*. Retrieved from www.wired.co.uk/article/reddit-bots-hate-speech

Kirman, B., Lineham, C., & Lawson, S. (2012). Exploring mischief and mayhem in social computing or: How we learned to stop worrying and love the trolls. In *CHI'12 extended abstracts on human factors in computing systems* (pp. 121–130). https://doi.org/10.1145/2212776.2212790

Know Your Meme. (n.d.). *The undertaker threw mankind off hell in a cell*. https://knowyourmeme.com/memes/the-undertaker-threw-mankind-off-hell-in-a-cell

Kou, Y. (2020, November). Toxic behaviours in team-based competitive gaming: The case of league of legends. In *Proceedings of the annual symposium on computer-human interaction in play* (pp. 81–92). https://doi.org/10.1145/3410404.3414243

LaFrance, A. (2020, June). The prophecies of Q. *The Atlantic*. Retrieved from www.theatlantic.com/magazine/archive/2020/06/qanon-nothing-can-stop-what-is-coming/610567/

Lampe, C., Zube, P., Lee, J., Park, C. H., & Johnston, E. (2014). Crowdsourcing civility: A natural experiment examining the effects of distributed moderation in online forums. *Government Information Quarterly, 31*(2), 317–326. https://doi.org/10.1016/j.giq.2013.11.005

Latzko-Toth, G. (2017). The socialization of early internet bots. In R. W. Gehl & M. Bakardjieva (Eds.), *Socialbots and their friends: Digital media and the automation of sociality* (pp. 47–68). Routledge.

Lee, D. (2018, February 16). The tactics of a Russian troll farm. *BBC*. Retrieved from www.bbc.com/news/technology-43093390

Levy, S. (1984). *Hackers: Heroes of the computer revolution*. Anchor Press/Doubleday.

Lewandowsky, S., Ecker, U. K., & Cook, J. (2017). Beyond misinformation: Understanding and coping with the "post-truth" era. *Journal of Applied Research in Memory and Cognition, 6*(4), 353–369. https://doi.org/10.1016/j.jarmac.2017.07.008

Lowood, H. (2006). Storyline, dance/music, or PvP? Game movies and community players in World of Warcraft. *Games and Culture, 1*(4), 362–382. https://doi.org/10.1177/1555412006292617

Lukito, J. (2020). Coordinating a multi-platform disinformation campaign: Internet research agency activity on three US social media platforms, 2015 to 2017. *Political Communication, 37*(2), 238–255. https://doi.org/10.1080/10584609.2019.1661889

March, E. (2019). Psychopathy, sadism, empathy, and the motivation to cause harm: New evidence confirms malevolent nature of the internet troll. *Personality and Individual Differences, 141*, 133–137. https://doi.org/10.1016/j.paid.2019.01.001

March, E., & Marrington, J. (2019). A qualitative analysis of internet trolling. *Cyberpsychology, Behaviour, and Social Networking, 22*(3), 192–197. https://doi.org/10.1089/cyber.2018.0210

Massanari, A. (2013). Playful participatory culture: Learning from Reddit. *AoIR Selected Papers of Internet Research, 3*. https://journals.uic.edu/ojs/index.php/spir/article/view/8787

Massanari, A. (2019). "Come for the period comics. Stay for the cultural awareness": Reclaiming the troll identity through feminist humor on Reddit's /r/TrollXChromosomes. *Feminist Media Studies, 19*(1), 19–37. https://doi.org/10.1080/14680777.2017.1414863

Merrin, W. (2019). President troll: Trump, 4Chan and memetic warfare. In C. Happer, A. Hoskins, & W. Merrin (Eds.), *Trump's media war* (pp. 201–226). Palgrave Macmillan.

Milner, R. M. (2018). *The world made meme: Public conversations and participatory media*. The MIT Press.

Mitchell, A., Jurkowitz, M., Oliphant, J., & Shearer, E. (2020). Americans who mainly get their news on social media are less engaged, less knowledgeable. *Pew Research Center*. Retrieved from www.journalism.org/2020/07/30/americans-who-mainly-get-their-news-on-social-media-are-less-engaged-less-knowledgeable/

Mortensen, T. E. (2018). Anger, fear, and games: The long event of #GamerGate. *Games and Culture, 13*(8), 787–806. https://doi.org/10.1177/1555412016640408

Mylonas, Y., & Kompatsiaris, P. (2019). Trolling as transgression: Subversive affirmations against neoliberal austerity. *International Journal of Cultural Studies*, 1–22. https://doi.org/10.1177/1367877919891180

Nagesh, A. (2018. Apr 9). People are sharing #wholesomememes to make the internet a bit less grim. *BBC Three*. Retrieved from www.bbc.co.uk/bbcthree/article/0ea8d63e-7b62-4e98-968d-4ba1e975d8ed

Olson, C. S. C., & LaPoe, V. (2017). "Feminazis," "libtards," "snowflakes," and "racists": Trolling and the spiral of silence effect in women, LGBTQIA communities, and disability populations before and after the 2016 election. *The Journal of Public Interest Communications*, *1*(2), 116–116. https://doi.org/10.32473/jpic.v1.i2.p116

Ortiz, S. M. (2019). "You can say I got desensitized to it": How men of color cope with everyday racism in online gaming. *Sociological Perspectives*, *62*(4), 572–588. https://doi.org/10.1177/0731121419837588

Paavola, J., Helo, T., Jalonen, H., Sartonen, M., & Huhtinen, A. M. (2016). Understanding the trolling phenomenon: The automated detection of bots and cyborgs in the social media. *Journal of Information Warfare*, *15*(4), 100–111. Retrieved from www.jstor.org/stable/26487554

Perring, A., & Kumar, M. (2019). About three-in-ten U.S. adults say they are 'almost constantly' online. *Pew Research Center*. Retrieved from www.pewresearch.org/fact-tank/2019/07/25/americans-going-online-almost-constantly

Phillips, W. (2011). Meet the trolls. *Index on Censorship*, *40*(2), 68–76. https://doi.org/10.1177/0306422011409641

Phillips, W. (2015). *This is why we can't have nice things: Mapping the relationship between online trolling and mainstream culture*. The MIT Press.

Phillips, W. (2018). The oxygen of amplification. *Data & Society*. https://datasociety.net/library/oxygen-of-amplification/

Phillips, W., & Milner, R. M. (2018). *The ambivalent internet: Mischief, oddity, and antagonism online*. John Wiley & Sons.

R/wholesomememes. (n.d.). *Reddit*. Retrieved from www.reddit.com/r/wholesomememes/

Raab, M. H., Ortlieb, S., Auer, N., Guthmann, K., & Carbon, C. C. (2013). Thirty shades of truth: Conspiracy theories as stories of individuation, not of pathological delusion. *Frontiers in Psychology*, *4*, 406. https://doi.org/10.3389/fpsyg.2013.00406

Rainie, L., Anderson, J., & Albright, J. (2017). The future of free speech, trolls, anonymity and fake news online. *Pew Research Center*. Retrieved from www.pewresearch.org/internet/2017/03/29/the-future-of-free-speech-trolls-anonymity-and-fake-news-online/

Ratkiewicz, J., Conover, M., Meiss, M., Gonçalves, B., Patil, S., Flammini, A., & Menczer, F. (2010). Detecting and tracking the spread of astroturf memes in microblog streams. arXiv preprint arXiv:1011.3768.

Raymond, E. (2004). September that never ended. *The Jargon File*. Retrieved from www.catb.org/jargon/html/S/September-that-never-ended.html

Roberts, S. T. (2019). *Behind the screen: Content moderation in the shadows of social media*. Yale University Press.

Romano, A. (2018). The rise of the wholesome internet meme. *Vox*. Retrieved from www.vox.com/2018/10/3/17923096/wholesome-memes-trend-explained

Ruck, D. J., Rice, N. M., Borycz, J., & Bentley, R. A. (2019). Internet research agency Twitter activity predicted 2016 US election polls. *First Monday*, *24*(7). https://doi.org/10.5210/fm.v24i7.10107

Sanfilippo, M. R., Fichman, P., & Yang, S. (2018). Multidimensionality of online trolling behaviours. *The Information Society*, *34*(1), 27–39. https://doi.org/10.1080/01972243.2017.1391911

Seering, J., Flores, J. P., Savage, S., & Hammer, J. (2018). The social roles of bots: Evaluating impact of bots on discussions in online communities. *Proceedings of the ACM on Human-Computer Interaction*, *2*(CSCW), 1–29. https://doi.org/10.1145/3274426

Seering, J., Kraut, R., & Dabbish, L. (2017, February). Shaping pro and anti-social behaviour on twitch through moderation and example-setting. In *Proceedings of the 2017 ACM conference on computer supported cooperative work and social computing* (pp. 111–125). https://doi.org/10.1145/2998181.2998277

Shachaf, P., & Hara, N. (2010). Beyond vandalism: Wikipedia trolls. *Journal of Information Science*, *36*(3), 357–370. https://doi.org/10.1177/0165551510365390

Shao, C., Ciampaglia, G. L., Varol, O., Flammini, A., & Menczer, F. (2017). The spread of fake news by social bots. arXiv preprint arXiv:1707.07592.

Shaw, F. (2013). Still "searching for safety online": Collective strategies and discursive resistance to trolling and harassment in a feminist network. *The Fibreculture Journal*, *22*, 93–108. https://twentytwo.fibreculturejournal.org/fcj-157-still-searching-for-safety-online-collective-strategies-and-discursive-resistance-to-trolling-and-harassment-in-a-feminist-network/

Shearer, E., & Grieco, E. (2019). Americans are wary of the role social media sites play in delivering the news. *Pew Research Center*. Retrieved from www.journalism.org/2019/10/02/americans-are-wary-of-the-role-social-media-sites-play-in-delivering-the-news/

Shearer, E., & Masta, K. (2018). News use across social media platforms 2018. *Pew Research Center*. Retrieved from www.journalism.org/2018/09/10/news-use-across-social-media-platforms-2018/

Shepherd, T., Harvey, A., Jordan, T., Srauy, S., & Miltner, K. (2015). Histories of hating. *Social Media + Society*, *1*(2). https://doi.org/10.1177/2056305115603997

Shifman, L. (2014). *Memes in digital culture*. The MIT Press.

Silverman, C. (2016, Novermber 16). This analysis shows how viral fake election news stories outperformed real news on Facebook. *Buzzfeed News*. Retrieved from www.buzzfeednews.com/article/craigsilverman/viral-fake-election-news-outperformed-real-news-on-facebook

Suler, J. (2004). The online disinhibition effect. *Cyberpsychology & Behaviour*, 7(3), 321–326. https://doi.org/10.1089/1094931041291295

Synnott, J., Coulias, A., & Ioannou, M. (2017). Online trolling: The case of Madeleine McCann. *Computers in Human Behaviour*, *71*, 70–78. https://doi.org/10.1016/j.chb.2017.01.053

Tepper, M. (1997). Usenet communities and the cultural politics of information. In D. Porter (Ed.), *Internet culture* (pp. 39–54). Routledge.

Time. (2016, August 18). How trolls are ruining the internet. https://time.com/4457110/internet-trolls/

Turner, F. (2006). How digital technology found utopian ideology. In D. Silver & A. Massanari (Eds.), *Critical cyberculture studies* (pp. 257–269). New York University Press.

Turner, F. (2010). *From counterculture to cyberculture: Stewart brand, the whole earth network, and the rise of digital utopianism*. University of Chicago Press.

Turner, E., & Rainie, L. (2020). Most Americans rely on their own research to make big decisions, and that often means online searches. *Pew Research Center*. Retrieved from www.pewresearch.org/fact-tank/2020/03/05/most-americans-rely-on-their-own-research-to-make-big-decisions-and-that-often-means-online-searches/

Varol, O., Ferrara, E., Davis, C. A., Menczer, F., & Flammini, A. (2017). Online human-bot interactions: Detection, estimation, and characterization. arXiv preprint arXiv:1703.03107.

Veletsianos, G., Houlden, S., Hodson, J., & Gosse, C. (2018). Women scholars' experiences with online harassment and abuse: Self-protection, resistance, acceptance, and self-blame. *New Media & Society*, *20*(12), 4689–4708. https://doi.org/10.1177/1461444818781324

Waters, J. (2013, January 4). Venomous and toxic social media out of control. *Irish Times*. Retrieved from www.irishtimes.com/opinion/venomous-and-toxic-social-media-out-of-control-1.954002

Woolley, S. C. (2016). Automating power: Social bot interference in global politics. *First Monday*, *21*(4). https://doi.org/10.5210/fm.v21i4.6161

Yagoda, M., & Dodd, S. (2020, November 23). 23 stars who quit social media . . . and how long they stayed away. *People*. https://people.com/celebrity/stars-who-quit-social-media-justin-bieber-leslie-jones/

18

SOCIAL BOTS AND SOCIAL MEDIA MANIPULATION IN 2020

The year in review

Ho-Chun Herbert Chang, Emily Chen, Meiqing Zhang, Goran Muric, and Emilio Ferrara

Introduction

In 2013, the World Economic Forum (WEF)'s annual *Global Risk* report highlighted the multidimensional problems of misinformation in a highly connected world (World Economic Forum, 2013). The WEF described one of the first large-scale misinformation instances that shocked America: an event from 1938, when thousands of Americans confused a radio adaptation of the H.G. Wells novel *The War of the Worlds* with an official news broadcast. Many started panicking, in the belief that the United States had been invaded by Martians.

Today, it would be hard for a radio broadcast to cause comparably widespread confusion. First, broadcasters have learned to be more cautious and responsible, and second, listeners have learned to be more savvy and skeptical. However, with social media, we are witnessing comparable phenomena on a global scale and with severe geopolitical consequences. A relatively abrupt transition from a world in which few traditional media outlets dominated popular discourse to a multicentric highly-connected world where information consumers and producers coalesced into one can bring unparalleled challenges and unforeseen side effects. A sudden democratization in the media ecosystem enables everyone online to broadcast their ideas to potentially massive audiences, thus allowing content that is not necessarily moderated or curated to be broadly accessible. Extreme opinions can become increasingly visible, and fringe groups can start gaining unprecedented attention. Eccentric ideas that would otherwise garner little support within fringe communities now could make their way into the mainstream. Furthermore, the free canvas of highly connected social media systems has been reportedly exploited by malicious actors, including foreign governments and state-sponsored groups, willing to deliberately misinform for their financial or political gain.

Nowadays, the use of social media to spread false news, provoke anxiety and incite fear for political reasons has been demonstrated around the world (Bessi & Ferrara, 2016; Shao et al., 2018; Badawy, Lerman, & Ferrara, 2019; Derczynski et al., 2019; Luceri, Deb, Badawy, & Ferrara, 2019; Badrinathan, 2020; Mujani & Kuipers, 2020; Schroeder, 2020). However, social media manipulation is not exclusively tied to political discourse. Public health can also be endangered by the spread of false information. For instance, in January 2019, panic erupted in

    DOI: 10.4324/9781003024583-21

Mumbai schools caused by social media rumors that the vaccines were a plot by the government to sterilize Muslim children: That led to only 50% of those who were expected to be vaccinated to actually get the vaccine (Larson, 2020).

Researchers from the *Democracy Fund* and *Omidyar Network* in their investigative report titled *Is Social Media a Threat to Democracy?* (Deb, Donohue, & Glaisyer, 2017), warn that the fundamental principles underlying democracy – trust, informed dialogue, a shared sense of reality, mutual consent, and participation – are being put to the ultimate litmus test by certain features and mechanisms of social media. They point out six main issues: 1) echo chambers, polarization, and hyper-partisanship; 2) spread of false and/or misleading information; 3) conversion of popularity into legitimacy; 4) manipulation by populist leaders, governments, and fringe actors; 5) personal data capture and targeted messaging/advertising; and 6) disruption of the public square.

As a matter of research, these six issues can be studied through multiple academic and epistemological angles. Computational social science has evolved swiftly in the past few years: Students of the social sciences are becoming masters of machine learning, while students of computer science interested in social phenomenon develop domain expertise in sociology, political science, and communication. More so than a methodological evolution, it is a shared critical interest in the growing impact social media platforms play in the very fabric of our society. A special issue documenting "Dark Participation" (Quandt, 2018) contrasts various issues of misinformation across different governments (Quandt, 2021). Scholars point out an increasingly shared challenge: the balance of combating foreign interference without compromising domestic free speech (Chang, Haider, & Ferrara, 2021). The resolution of these issues requires iteration between computational insights and policy-makers, as any type of intervention will inadvertently attract critiques of suppression or create unforeseen side effects.

Focus of this chapter

In this chapter, we focus on spread of false and/or misleading information across two salient dimensions of social media manipulation, namely 1) automation (e.g., prevalence of bots) and 2) distortion (misinformation, disinformation, injection of conspiracies or rumors). We provide direct insight into two case studies: 1) the COVID-19 pandemic and 2) the 2020 U.S. presidential election. We detail the many aspects of large-scale computational projects: 1) tracking and cleaning billions of tweets, 2) enriching the data through state-of-the-art machine learning, and 3) recommendation of actionable interventions with regard to platform governance and online speech policy.

While misleading information can materialize in many different forms, it is often scrutinized in the context of current events. Social media allows users to actively engage in discourse in real time, reacting to breaking news and contributing to the conversation surrounding a particular topic or event with limited filters for what can or cannot be posted prior to publication. Although many social media companies have terms of services and automated filters that remove posts that violate their community guidelines, many of these posts are either able to evade detection long enough such that a wide audience has already seen or engaged with a post or elude these automated or human-assisted filters completely.

Politics and current events as a whole have created an environment that is rife and conducive to the spread of misleading information. Regardless of the alacrity of a post's removal and the original poster's broader visibility, as long as misinformation has been posted online, there is the potential for this information to have been seen and consequently consumed by others who can further disseminate it. Social media companies such as Twitter, Facebook, and YouTube have recently begun active campaigns to reduce the spread of misinformation and conspiracy theories (Cellan-Jones, 2020; Yurieff, 2020). Fact checkers actively monitor rumors and events. However, the virality and speed at which this information propagates makes it difficult to catch and contain, particularly as alternative social media platforms, such as Parler and Gab, with fewer mitigation measures emerge to allow further misinformation circulation in the ecosystem (Lima et al., 2018; Aliapoulios et al., 2021).

With the recent 2020 U.S. presidential election and ongoing COVID-19 pandemic, the need to understand the distortion of information becomes ever more urgent. When we discuss distortion of information, we note a subtle but important distinction between 1) misinformation, the *organic* spread of false or inaccurate information, and 2) disinformation, the *deliberate* spread of misinformation. Although the two terms are closely related, the nuance of purpose differentiates the intent of the distortion. Disinformation, in particular, is often promulgated on social media platforms not only by human users but also by bots (Shao, Ciampaglia, Varol, Flammini, & Menczer, 2017; Ferrara, 2018; Starbird, 2019). A "bot", which is shorthand for the word "software robot", is a software-based unit whose actions are controlled by software instead of human intervention. While there are many disciplines that leverage this term, we use the term "bot" in the context of "social bots", which are social media accounts that are either fully controlled by software or have some level of human intervention (semi-automated) (Ferrara, Varol, Davis, Menczer, & Flammini, 2016).

Background and framing

The term *computational social science* evokes not just two disciplines but their own practices and traditions. In the following, we highlight some important epistemological concepts that inform the study of social media manipulation through the lens of computational and social science theory.

Epistemology

Although both inductive and deductive reasoning are common in social science research methods, quantitative social science research traditionally holds deductive methods in higher regard. A deductive approach starts from theories and uses data to test the hypotheses stemming from the theories. Computational social science work conducted by computer scientists often exhibits a data-driven, inductive approach. However, as data science and domain expertise in the social sciences are brought together, computational social science bears great promise to reconcile inductive and deductive reasoning (Evans & Aceves, 2016). Exploring large volumes of data, even sans prior theoretical assumptions, may yield new insights or surprising evidence. The findings from this initial, data-driven step will guide us to discern emerging hypotheses and collect new data to test them. This is called *abductive* analysis (Timmermans & Tavory, 2012). It starts with observations, which serve to generate new hypotheses or filter existing hypotheses. The promising hypotheses emerged from data analysis can then be tested deductively with new data.

This deductive approach can be used to study the relationship between social media and democratic discourse, which is hardly a direct or linear one. Social media do not inherently undermine or improve democracy. Instead, they affects the quality of democracy through multiple mechanisms such as political polarization and disinformation (Tucker et al., 2018). These intermediate variables operate in varying contexts shaped by political institutions, political culture, and media ecosystems. Therefore, the effects of social media on democracy differ despite the same technological affordances (Benkler, Faris, & Roberts, 2018). The political system, ideological distribution, how political elites use social media, and the behavioral patterns of different political actors in a given context interact with one another to determine whether political polarization and disinformation are amplified on social media platforms. The interactions among all potential political, social, and technological variables form a complex system. Data exploration and analysis can help uncover crucial variables operating in a specific context. Our case studies of misinformation in the context of the COVID-19 pandemic and the 2020 U.S. presidential election described next will reveal significant factors underlying the relationship between social media use and democracy in the U.S. context and help identify social scientific hypotheses that are worth further investigation.

Case studies

Misinformation and COVID-19

We recently found ourselves at the intersection of two important events that have changed the way the world has functioned. 2020 was already going to be a big year for U.S. politics due to the contentious nature of the current political climate. The United States has become more polarized, leading to high anticipation over whether the then-incumbent President Trump would win re-election. While Trump cinched the Republican nomination, there was a highly anticipated battle for the Democratic presidential nominee (Jacobson, 2020). In the midst of the political furor, in late December 2019, the first cases of novel SARS-COV-2 coronavirus (whose caused disease was later named COVID-19) were reported from Wuhan, China (Taylor, 2021). As the world began to understand the severity of the illness, whose status was later classified as a pandemic, many countries began to impose lockdowns in attempts to contain the outbreaks (Wu et al., 2020; Taylor, 2021).

For years, our conversations had already been shifting toward online, with the advent of social media platforms that foster environments for sharing information. Social media has also become more integrated into the fabric of political communication (Romero, Meeder, & Kleinberg, 2011). With the lockdowns that closed offices and forbade gatherings, the discourse surrounding current events was pushed even further onto online platforms (Jungherr, 2016; Hadden & Casado, 2020; Hadden, Casado, Sonnemaker, & Borden, 2020; Fischer, 2020). This created a breeding ground for potential misinformation and disinformation campaigns to flourish, particularly surrounding health initiatives during a time of heightened political tensions during the 2020 U.S. presidential election (Benkler et al., 2020). In our paper published in the *Harvard Misinformation Review* special issue on U.S. elections and disinformation, we study the politicization of and misinformation surrounding health narratives during this time. We found several major narratives present in our data, and further explored two health-related narratives that were highly politicized: *mask wearing* and *mail-in ballots*.

General dataset

We have been actively collecting and maintaining two publicly released Twitter datasets: one focusing on COVID-19 related discourse and the other on the 2020 U.S. presidential election (Chen, Deb, & Ferrara, 2020; Chen, Lerman, & Ferrara, 2020). We began the former collection in late January 2020 and the latter in late May 2019. These tweets are collected using the Twitter streaming API, which enables us to gather tweets that match specific keywords or accounts.[1] We note here that, at the time of this writing, the free Twitter streaming API only returns 1% of the full Twitter data stream. Because of this limitation, we are unable to collect all tweets relevant to COVID-19 and the elections. However, the 1% returned is still a representative sample of the discourse occurring during that day (Morstatter, Pfeffer, Liu, & Carley, 2013).

In this particular case study, we capitalized on both our COVID-19 (v1.12) and elections (v1.3) Twitter datasets, with a focus on the time period from March 1, 2020 through August 30, 2020. At the time that this study was conducted, we had only processed our election data from March 1, 2020 onward. This timeframe covers from Super Tuesday, when a significant number of states hold their primaries, through the end of the Democratic presidential primaries.

COVID-19 and the Democratic primaries filtered dataset

We first filtered our COVID-19 dataset for keywords related to the elections, including the last names of the candidates as well as general elections-related keywords (vote, mailin, mail-in, mail in, ballot). We then conducted latent Dirichlet allocation (LDA) to identify eight topics present within the data, using the highest coherence score to determine the optimal number of topics (Blei, Ng, & Jordan, 2003). After sorting tweets into their most probable topic, we leveraged the most frequent hashtags, keywords, bigrams, and trigrams to understand the narratives within each identified topic. Four broader narratives emerged: general coronavirus discourse, lockdowns, mask wearing, and mail-in balloting. We then filtered our general COVID-19 and elections dataset for tweets that contained at least one of the aforementioned election-related keywords and a representative keyword or hashtag from the four major identified topics. This netted us a final dataset of 67,846,555 tweets, with 10,536,524 general coronavirus tweets, 619,914 regarding lockdowns, 1,283,450 tweets on mask-wearing, and 5,900,737 on mail-in balloting.

Discourse

We first wanted to understand how discourse surrounding our four narratives (coronavirus, lockdowns, mask wearing, and mail-in balloting) fluctuated over time (see Figures 18.1 and 18.2). We tracked the percentage of all collected tweets on a particular day that contained selected keywords and hashtags that are representative of each narrative.

Coronavirus. The pervasiveness of coronavirus-related tweets in our Twitter dataset is by construction and hence unsurprising. Not only was our COVID-19 dataset tracking coronavirus-related keywords, but this topic has dominated political discourse in the United States since the first case was reported in Washington State on January 21, 2020. In this narrative, we find several prevalent misinformation subnarratives – including the belief that COVID-19 is a hoax created by the Democratic party and that COVID-19 will disappear by itself (Egan, 2020). This has also been driven in tandem with the anti-vaccine movement, which has staged protests at COVID-19 vaccine distribution locations (Lozano, 2021). Hydroxychloroquine (HCQ) also became a highly divisive topic within the Twitter community debating its effectiveness as treatment for COVID-19.

During a press conference, then-President Trump stated that he was taking HCQ as a preventative measure (Oprysko, 2020). The United States Food and Drug Administration (FDA) initially issued an emergency use authorization (EUA) for HCQ, and the World Health Organization included it in its treatment trials. However, the EUA was rescinded and the trials halted as results began to show that HCQ was not an effective treatment or preventative for COVID-19 (Edwards, 2020; World Health Organization, 2020). The controversy surrounding HCQ

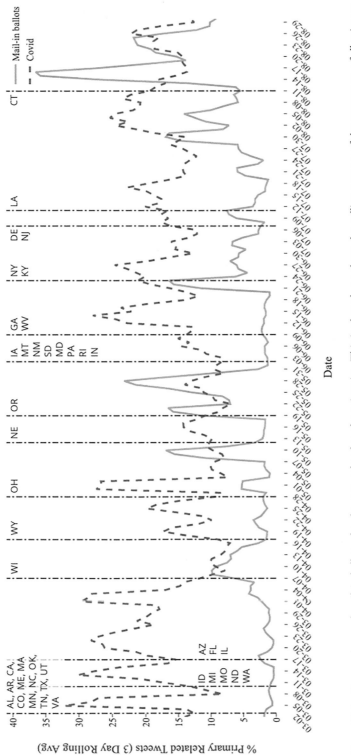

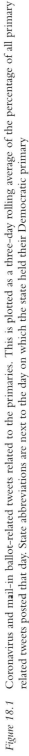

Figure 18.1 Coronavirus and mail-in ballot-related tweets related to the primaries. This is plotted as a three-day rolling average of the percentage of all primary related tweets posted that day. State abbreviations are next to the day on which the state held their Democratic primary

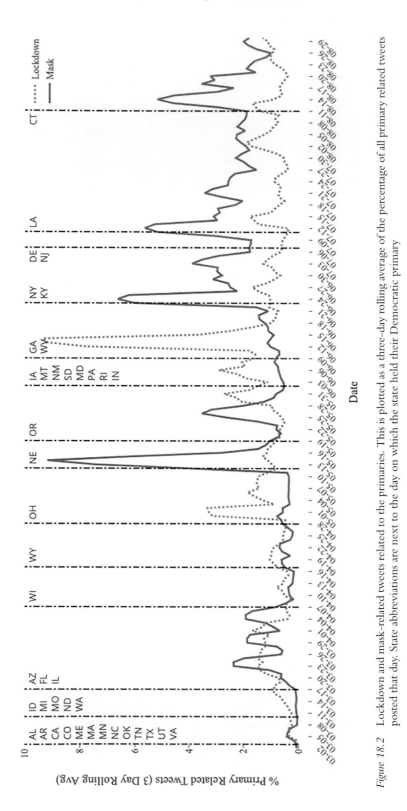

Figure 18.2 Lockdown and mask-related tweets related to the primaries. This is plotted as a three-day rolling average of the percentage of all primary related tweets posted that day. State abbreviations are next to the day on which the state held their Democratic primary

shows a shift in factuality surrounding the viability of HCQ, as it was initially unknown if HCQ was indeed viable. Information can develop into misinformation as its factuality changes, which further emphasizes the dangers of spreading medical information without substantive, corroborated scientific evidence. Despite evidence showing that HCQ should not be used as a treatment for COVID-19, this narrative promoting HCQ continued to spread and for many to seek this treatment.

Mail-in Ballots. As fears surrounding COVID-19 began to grow throughout the United States, one of the major concerns with the U.S. Democratic primaries and the upcoming presidential election was how voters would be able to vote safely (Bogage, Rein, & Dawsey, 2020).

This caused many states to begin promoting mail-in ballots as a way to safely vote from home during the Democratic primaries. In August 2020, then-President Trump-appointed Postmaster Louis DeJoy began reappropriating the United States Postal Service resources, making budget cuts and changing standard mail delivery protocols. This led to a significant slow-down of mail being processed and delivered, including the delivery of ballots, particularly as the United States began to prepare for the presidential election (Pransky, 2020; Cochrane, Fuchs, Vogel, & Silver-Greenberg, 2020).

While many were advocating for mail in ballots to be more widely used as a COVID-19 precaution, others pushed the narrative that mail-in ballots would increase ballot fraud. This misinformation has been proven false by fact checkers, as no evidence in previous election cycles have indicated that mail-in or absentee ballots increase voter fraud (Farley, 2020). This misinformation narrative that was incubating during the primaries season became an even larger misinformation campaign during the U.S. presidential election.

Lockdowns and Masking. Finally, lockdowns and masks were also major themes in our dataset. This is expected, as the United States began to implement social distancing ordinances, such as stay-at-home orders, in March 2020. As more states held their primaries, we see that mentions of lockdowns and masks increase, suggesting that online conversation surrounding social distancing and mask wearing is driven by current events. This included misinformation narratives that claimed masks are ineffective and harmful towards one's health, when studies have shown that masks can effectively reduce COVID-19 transmission rates (Mueller, Eden, Oakes, Bellini, & Fernandez, 2020; Farley, 2020; Khazan, 2020).

Echo chambers and populist leaders

Out of the four narratives, we further investigate mask-wearing and mail-in balloting, as these two topics contain health-related discourse that became highly politicized and subsequently prone to misinformation. One of the more startling findings was the source of misinformation, specifically the communities in which distortions were concentrated. Figure 18.3 shows the network topology of Twitter users who have engaged in COVID-19-related election discourse – see (Chen et al., 2021) for details on the methodology to generate this plot.

Figure 18.3a shows the users in our dataset, each data point colored by "political information diet". In order to categorize a user's information diet, we labeled users who have shared at least 10 posts containing URLs that have been pre-tagged by the Media-Bias/Fact-Check database.[2] This database contains a political leanings-tagged list of commonly shared domains (left, center-left, center, center-right, and right). We found that the majority of the users are center or left-leaning. However, there is also a fairly clear distinction between more homogeneous conservative and liberal clusters near the top of the topology. This suggests that while the majority of users ingest a variety of information from both sides of the aisle, there are still clear signs of polarization based on political views that can be detected in the network topology.

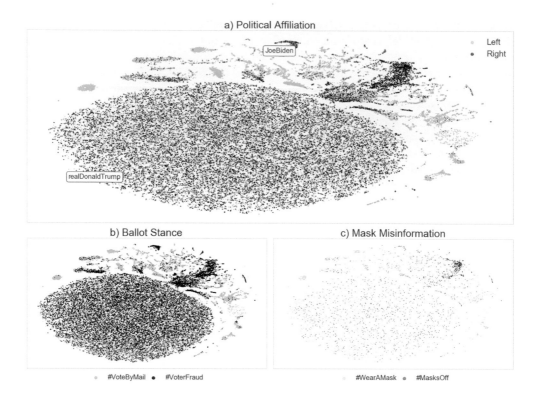

Figure 18.3 Community structure of COVID-19-related election discourse (Chen et al., 2021). a) Political diet of users. b) Where ballot related policy stances are found. c) Distribution of mask-wearing misinformation

This polarization of highly connected clusters also indicates the presence of "echo chambers" (Jamieson & Cappella, 2008; Du & Gregory, 2017).

Media-Bias/Fact-Check also contains a list of domains they deem "questionable sources", or sources that are known to prompt conspiracy theories and misinformation. We use this to tag each user with both their political affiliation (left or right) and their tendency to spread misinformation or fact. We show in more detail in Chen et al. (2021) that misinformation arises from the dense conservative cluster in the top right. Here, we expand on two narratives.

Within the mask-wearing and mail-in ballot narratives, we manually identified representative hashtags and co-occurring hashtags promoting misinformation or factual information (e.g., #WearAMask, #MasksOff, #VoteByMail, #VoterFraud). When we visualize this information on the same network topology, it is evident that there is a heterogeneity in the majority of the users' likelihood of participating in discourse surrounding mask and mail-in ballot misinformation and fact. However, the same dense conservative cluster that we identified earlier appears to have posted tweets related to mail-in ballot and mask misinformation, compared to the left-leaning clusters, which tended to tweet factual information surrounding mail-in ballots and masks. A full colored version can be found in Chen et al. (2021).

Upon closer inspection of the tweets in each cluster, we find that conservatives are not the only ones to participate in misinformation. One of the factual narratives (Sherman, 2020) that was challenged by left-leaning users was that the Obama administration had not restocked the nation's supply of N95 masks after the H1N1 outbreak in 2009. However, the divide in misinformation narrative focus in the dense conservative cluster suggests that users within that cluster were prone to engage in misinformation about specific subjects (such as masks or mail-in ballots) instead of misinformation in general.

Our findings on the ideological patterns of misinformation on Twitter are consistent with a rising line of research that focuses on the asymmetric polarization in the U.S. context: Some political scientists argue that party polarization in the United States is asymmetrical, with Republicans moving more to the right than Democrats to the left (Carmines, 2011; Hacker & Pierson, 2006; Theriault, 2013). This trend was evolving even before the advent of social media. The existing ideological asymmetry affects the exposure to media sources on digital platforms (Faris et al., 2017; Brady, Wills, Burkart, Jost, & Van Bavel, 2019) and leads to asymmetrical consumption of misinformation (Tucker et al., 2018). It lends support to the existing asymmetric polarization hypothesis and highlights its important role in mediating the relationship between social media and democracy in the United States.

Misinformation and 2020 U.S. presidential election

There is a well-known saying that "the first casualty of war is truth". In times of unusual social tensions caused by the political struggle with relatively high stakes, the proliferation of false news, misinformation, and other sorts of media manipulation is to be expected. The importance of voter competence is one of the postulates of modern democracy (Gant & Davis, 1984; Stucki, Pleger, & Sager, 2018), and information vacuums can undermine electoral accountability (Ashworth & Mesquita, 2014). An ideal democracy assumes an informed and rational voter, but the former aspect is something that can be undermined or compromised. During the 2020 U.S. presidential election, social media manipulation has been observed in the form of 1) automation, that is, the evidence for adoption of automated accounts governed predominantly by software rather than human users, and 2) distortion, in particular of salient narratives of discussion of political events, for example, with the injection of inaccurate information, conspiracies or rumors. In the following, we describe ours and others' findings in this context.

Dataset

For this study, we again leverage one of our ongoing and publicly released Twitter datasets centered around the 2020 U.S. presidential election. Please refer to "General Dataset" for more details on the collection methods; this particular dataset is further described in Chen et al. (2020). While this dataset now has over 1.2 billion tweets, we focused on tweets posted between June 20, 2020, and September 9, 2020, in advance of the November 3, 2020, election. This subset yielded 240 million tweets and 2 TB of raw data. The period of observation includes several salient real-world political events, such as the Democratic National Committee (DNC) and Republican National Committee (RNC) conventions.

Automation detection

The term *bot* (shorthand for robot) in computational social science commonly refers to fully automated or semi-automated accounts on social media platforms (Ferrara et al., 2016). Research into automation on social media platforms has spawned its own sub-field not only in computational social sciences but in social media research at large (Aiello, Deplano, Schifanella, & Ruffo, 2012; Ferrara et al., 2016; Shao et al., 2017; Zelenkauskaite & Balduccini,

2017; Yang et al., 2019). One of the major challenges with automation is the ability to detect accounts that are bots as opposed to accounts fully operated by humans. Although there are benign accounts that publicly advertise the fact that they are automated, bots used for malicious purposes try to evade detection. As platforms and researchers study the behavior of bots and devise algorithms and systems that are able to automatically flag accounts as bots, bot developers are also actively developing new systems to subvert these detection attempts by mimicking behavioral signals of human accounts (Sayyadiharikandeh, Varol, Yang, Flammini, & Menczer, 2020; Yang, Varol, Hui, & Menczer, 2020).

Botometer is a tool developed and released by researchers at Indiana University, as part of the Observatory on Social Media (OSoMe) (Davis et al., 2016), that allows users to input a Twitter user's screen name and returns a score of how likely an account is to be automated.[3] These scores range from 0 to 5, with 0 indicating that the account has been labeled as most likely human and 5 indicating that the account is most likely a bot account. We will be referring to accounts that are most likely human accounts as "human" and bot-like accounts as "bots" for brevity. Botometer itself has gone through several iterations, with the most recent version, Botometer v4, released in September 2020 (Sayyadiharikandeh et al., 2020). Botometer v4 extracts thousands of features from an input account and leverages machine learning models trained on a large repository of labeled tweets to predict the likelihood of an account being a bot. Botometer v4 (Yang et al., 2020) can identify different types of bots, including bots that are fake followers, spammers, and astroturfers (Yang et al., 2019; Ferrara, 2019).

Automation in social media manipulation during 2020 U.S. presidential election

In the following analysis, we leveraged Botometer v3 (Yang et al., 2019), as that was the latest version at the time we performed our study (Ferrara, Chang, Chen, Muric, & Patel, 2020). We tagged 32% of the users within our complete dataset and removed all tweets not posted by the users for whom we have bot scores. We labeled the top decile of users according to Botometer scores as "bots" and the bottom decile as "humans" (Ferrara, 2020). Our final dataset contains more that 4 million tweets posted by bots and more than 1 million tweets posted by humans. We found that a number of the top hashtags used in tweets by bots are affiliated with well known conspiracy theories that will be studied later in this chapter (e.g., #wwg1wga, #obamagate, #qanon), and others are Trump-campaign-related hashtags. In contrast, tweets from humans contain a mix of both Trump and Biden campaign hashtags.

We use campaign-related hashtags in order to distinguish between users who engage in left-leaning (Biden campaign) and right-leaning (Trump campaign) political discourse. We find that there are over 2.5 million left-leaning humans, and a little over 18,000 left-leaning bots. Comparatively, we found over 8.5 million right-leaning humans and almost 85,000 right-leaning bots. This enables us to take a snapshot of how right-leaning bots and humans engage in election-related narratives compared to their left-leaning counterparts. What is interesting here is whether there are distinguishable features of bots and humans based on their political affiliations and engagements within the network (Luceri et al., 2019).

What we find is that right-leaning bots tend to post right-leaning news, with many accounts also posting highly structured (i.e., templated, or copy-pasted) tweets. When we manually inspected a random sample of these tweets, we found that these tweets contained similar combinations of hashtags and oftentimes similarly structured content. Many of the tweets also contained URLs to well-known conspiracy news websites. Right-leaning bots also tended to have higher bot scores compared to their left-leaning counterparts, suggesting a more profound use of automation. A manual inspection of a random set of left-leaning bot tweets found that these tweets are significantly less structured, exhibiting fewer automation cues. Although disambiguation by means of specific campaign-related hashtags is not perfect, prior studies investigating political polarization have shown that the vast majority of users posting campaign-specific hashtags align with the same political party (Bail et al., 2018; Jiang, Chen, Yan, Lerman, & Ferrara, 2020). We also find that the bot scores for bots range from 0.485 through 0.988, suggesting that the broad range of scores captures accounts that are hybrid accounts, partially automated and partially controlled by humans.

When isolating the activity of these bot and human accounts and then examining their temporal activity, we see that each group behaves differently. Despite being outnumbered by several orders of magnitude, just a few thousand bots generated spikes of conversations around real-world political events comparable with the volume of activity of humans (Ferrara et al., 2020). We find that conservatives, both bot and humans, tend to tweet more regularly than liberal users. The more interesting question, beyond raw volume, is whether bots play a community role in polarization.

We found both surprising similarities and stark differences across the partisan divide. Figure 18.4 shows the discourse volume of the top 10% of bots and top 10% of humans, split between left-leaning accounts (top) and right-leaning accounts (bottom). Although bots tweet in higher volumes in both cases, the activities of left-leaning bots are more localized to specific events. In contrast, right-leaning bots generate large amounts of discourse in general, showing high levels of background activity.

Next, we illustrate how these four groups interact with each other. Figure 18.5 shows the interactions between human and bot accounts divided by political leaning. Bots predominantly retweet humans from within their own party lines, whereas humans retweet other humans from within their party lines. At a relative retweet rate within the same party as more than 80%, this indicates a significant level of political polarization.

Distortion in social media manipulation during 2020 U.S. presidential election

Next, we broaden an analysis to *distortion*, an umbrella concept that also includes completely fabricated narratives that do not have a hold in reality. Fake news is an example of distorted narratives and is conceptualized as *distorted signals uncorrelated with the truth* (Allcott & Gentzkow, 2017). To avoid the conundrum of establishing what is true and what is false to qualify a piece of information as fake news (or not), in this study, we focus on conspiracy theories, another typical example of distorted narratives. Conspiracy theories can be (and most often are) based upon falsity, rumors, or unverifiable information that resists falsification; other times they are instead postulated upon rhetoric, divisive ideology, and circular reasoning based on prejudice or uncorroborated (but not necessarily false) evidence. Conspiracies can be shared by users or groups with the aim to deliberately deceive or indoctrinate unsuspecting individuals who genuinely believe in such claims (van Prooijen, 2019).

See Ferrara et al. (2020) for full color.

Conspiracy theories are attempts to explain the ultimate causes of significant social and political events and circumstances with claims of secret plots by powerful actors. While often thought of as addressing governments, conspiracy theories could accuse any group perceived as powerful and malevolent (Douglas et al., 2019). They evolve and change over time, depending on the current important events. Upon manual inspection, we found that some of the most prominent conspiracy theories and groups in our dataset revolve around topics such as:

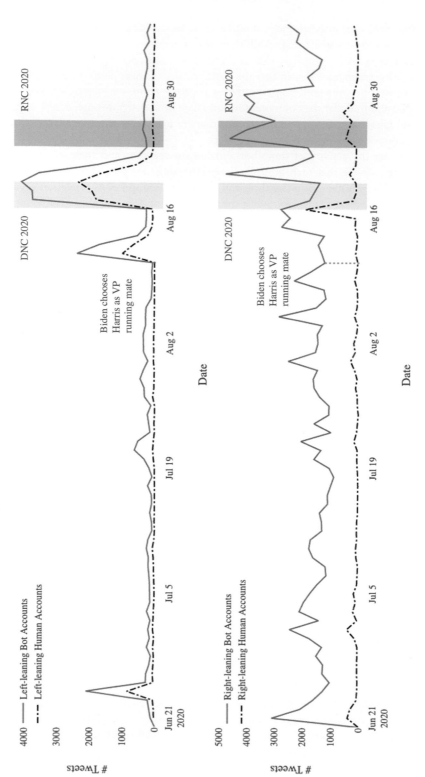

Figure 18.4 Time series of activity of bot *vs.* human accounts with political affiliation (Ferrara et al., 2020)

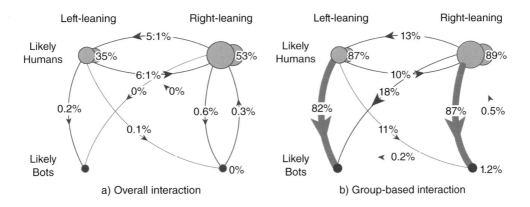

Figure 18.5 Meso-flow of bot and human accounts by political leaning. a) Total volume of retweets between the four groups. b) Relative volume of retweets between the groups

objections to vaccinations, false claims related to 5G technology, a plethora of coronavirus-related false claims, and the flat earth movement (Ferrara, 2020). Opinion polls carried out around the world reveal that substantial proportions of population readily admit to believing in some kind of conspiracy theories (Byford, 2011). In the context of democratic processes, including the 2020 U.S. presidential election, the proliferation of political conspiratorial narratives could have an adverse effect on political discourse and democracy.

In our analysis, we focused on three main conspiracy groups:

1   *QAnon conspiracies:* A far-right conspiracy movement whose theory suggests that President Trump has been battling against a Satan-worshipping global child sex-trafficking ring and an anonymous source called "Q" is cryptically providing secret information about the ring (Zuckerman, 2019). The users who support such ideas frequently use hashtags such as #qanon, #wwg1wga (where we go one, we go all), #taketheoath, #thegreatawakening, and #qarmy. Examples of typical tweets from QAnon supporters are:

> @potus @realDonaldTrump was indeed correct, the beruit fire was hit by a missile, oh and to the rest of you calling this fake, you are not a qanon you need to go ahead and change to your real handles u liberal scumbags just purpously put out misinfo and exposed yourselves, thnxnan

> I've seen enough. It's time to #TakeTheOath There's no turning back now. We can and only will do this together. #WWG1WGA #POTUS @realDonaldTrump #Qanon

2   *"gate" conspiracies:* Another indicator of conspiratorial content is signaled by the suffix "-gate" with theories such as Pizzagate, a debunked claim that connects several high-ranking Democratic Party officials and U.S. restaurants with an alleged human trafficking and child sex ring. Examples of typical conspiratorial tweets related to these two conspiracies are:

> #obamagate when will law enforcement take anything seriously? there is EVIDENCE!!!! everyone involved in the trafficking ring is laughing because they

KNOW nothing will be done. @HillaryClinton @realDonaldTrump. justice will be served one way or another. literally disgusting.

#Obama #JoeBiden, & their top intel officers huddled in the Oval Office shortly before @realDonaldTrump was inaugurated to discuss what they would do about this new president they despised, @TomFitton in Breitbart. Read: . . .

3   *COVID conspiracies:* A plethora of false claims related to the coronavirus emerged right after the pandemic was announced. They are mostly related to scale of the pandemic and the origin, prevention, diagnosis, and treatment of the disease. The false claims typically go alongside the hashtags such as #plandemic, #scandemic, or #fakevirus. The typical tweets referring to the false claims regarding the origins of the coronavirus are:

@fyjackson @rickyb_sports @rhus00 @KamalaHarris @realDonaldTrump The plandemic is a leftist design. And it's backfiring on them. We've had an effective treatment for COVID-19, the entire time. Leftists hate Trump so much, they are willing to murder 10's of thousands of Americans to try to make him look bad. The jig is up.

The AUS Govt is complicit in the global scare #Plandemic. They are scarifying jobs, businesses freedom and families in an attempt to stop @realDonaldTrump from being reelected. Why?

During the period preceding the 2020 U.S. presidential election, QAnon-related material had more highly active and engaged users than other narratives. This is measured by the average number of tweets an active user has made on a topic. For example, the most frequently used hashtag, #wwg1wga, had more than 600K tweets from 140K unique users; by contrast, #obamagate had 414K tweets from 125K users. This suggests that the QAnon community has a more active user base strongly dedicated to the narrative.

When we analyze how the conspiratorial narratives are endorsed by the users, conditioned upon where they fall on the political spectrum, we discover that conspiratorial ideas are strongly skewed to the right. Almost a quarter of users who endorse predominantly right-leaning media platforms are likely to engage in sharing conspiracy narratives. Conversely, out of all users who endorse left-leaning media, approximately 2% are likely to share conspiracy narratives.

Additionally, we explore the usage of conspiracy language among automated accounts. Bots can appear across the political spectrum and are likely to endorse polarizing views. Therefore, they are likely to be engaged in sharing heavily discussed topics, including conspiratorial narratives. Around 13% of Twitter accounts that endorse some conspiracy theory are likely bots. This is significantly more than users who never share conspiracy narratives, which have only 5% of automated accounts. It is possible that such observations are in part the byproduct of the fact that bots are programmed to interact with more engaging content, and inflammatory topics such as conspiracy theories provide fertile ground for engagement (Stella, Ferrara, & De Domenico, 2018). On the other hand, bot activity can inflate certain narratives and make them popular.

The narratives of these conspiracy theories during the 2020 U.S. presidential election call attention to the so-called "new conspiracism" and the partisan differences in practicing it (Rosenblum & Muirhead, 2020). Rosenblum and Muirhead argue that the new conspiracism in the contemporary age is "conspiracy without theory". Whereas the "classic conspiracy theory" still strives to collect evidence and find patterns and logical explanations to construct a "theory" of how malignant forces are plotting to do harm, the new conspiracism skips the burdens of "theory construction" and advances itself by bare assertion and repetition (Rosenblum & Muirhead, 2020). Repetition produces familiarity, which in turn increases acceptance (Lewandowsky, Ecker, Seifert, Schwarz, & Cook, 2012; Paul & Matthews, 2016). A conspiracy becomes credible to its audience simply because many people are repeating it (Rosenblum & Muirhead, 2020). The partisan asymmetry in the circulation of conspiracy theories is also consistent with others' claims that the new conspiracism is asymmetrically aligned with the radical right in the U.S. context (Benkler et al., 2018; Rosenblum & Muirhead, 2020), although this species of conspiracism is not ideologically attached to liberals or conservatives (Rosenblum & Muirhead, 2020). Our analysis shows the promising direction of testing the theories of asymmetrical polarization and exploring the nature and consequences of asymmetrical media ecosystem, ideally using multi-platform data.

The findings about the bot behaviors relative to humans on Twitter reveal some patterns of conspiracy transmission in the 2020 U.S. presidential election. Their high-volume and echo-chamber retweeting activities attest to the role that automation plays in stoking the new conspiracism. Bots are capable of retweeting and repeating the same information efficiently. However, bots are not solely to blame for the prevalence of conspiracy-theory stories. False information is found to spread faster than true information due to the human tendency to retweet it. A comprehensive study conducted by Vosoughi et al. compared the diffusion of verified true and false news stories on Twitter from 2006 to 2017. They discovered that falsity travels wider and deeper than truth, even after bots were removed, suggesting that humans are more likely to retweet false rumors than true information. Among all topics, political rumors are particularly viral. False rumors peaked before and around the 2012 and 2016 U.S. presidential election (Vosoughi, Roy, & Aral, 2018). Additionally, automated accounts that are part of an organized campaign can purposely propel some of the conspiracy narratives, further polarizing the political discourse.

Although bots present a threat to the ideal, well-informed democratic citizenship, the susceptibility of humans to believing and spreading false information is worth equal attention. Further examinations of how distorted narratives go viral will help us better diagnose the problem. Some new research points to the hypothesis that the nature and structure of false rumors and conspiracy-theory stories evoke human interest. For example, Vosoughi et al. suggested that false rumors tend to be more novel and hence more salient. False rumors also elicit stronger emotions of surprise and disgust (Vosoughi et al., 2018). Tangherlini et al. studied the conspiracy theory narrative framework using the cases of Bridgegate and Pizzagate. They deconstructed those stories into multi-scale narrative networks and found that conspiracy theories are composed of a small number of entities, multiple interconnected domains, and separable disjoint subgraphs. By construction, conspiracy theories can form and stabilize faster. In contrast, the unfolding of true conspiracy stories will admit new evidence and result in a denser network over time (Tangherlini, Shahsavari, Shahbazi, Ebrahimzadeh, & Roychowdhury, 2020). Therefore, true stories could be at a disadvantage when competing with false rumors, as they are less stable and grow in complexity as events develop.

Conclusions

In this chapter, we presented the findings that emerged from two significant events of 2020. In the first study, we showed how political identity aligns with narratives of public health. Four narratives were identified: 1) mail-in ballots, 2) reference to the pandemic, 3) lockdowns, and

4) mask-wearing. Spikes in these narratives were found to be driven by predetermined events, predominantly the primaries. When observing the policy stance of mail-in ballots and mask-wearing, we observe users against mask-wearing and mail-in ballots arise from a dense group of conservative users separate from the majority. Topological distinctions between these two groups are further observed. Further details are found in our recent paper (Chang et al., 2021).

When investigating the 2020 U.S. presidential election more broadly, we find bots not only generate much higher volumes of election-related tweets per capita but also tweet primarily within their own political lines (more than 80% for both left- and right-leaning communities). An analysis of content from QAnon-driven conspiracies, politicized "gate"- related, and COVID-related conspiracies suggested that users self-organize to promulgate false information and also leverage automation to amplify hyperpartisan and conspiratorial news sites: more details are discussed in our associated study (Ferrara, 2020).

What do these results tell us? First, although bots still generate significant distortions in volume and self-reinforcement across party lines as observed in the 2016 U.S. presidential election (Bessi & Ferrara, 2016), this is overshadowed by the self-organization of extremism and "new conspiracism" in the public sphere. A further contrast is the shift from foreign interference in 2016 to domestic, ingrown social media manipulation in 2020. This phenomenon can be observed across a variety of case studies, including populism in the EU (Muis & Immerzeel, 2017), xenophobia in Russia, hate speech in Germany (Zhuravskaya, Petrova, & Enikolopov, 2020), and foreign interference in Taiwan (Chang et al., 2021).

Finally, the case study of COVID-19 demonstrates the interplay between public health and politics on a national level. In the past, computational studies on anti-vaccination focused on smaller, community-level scales (Lozano, 2021). Given the high levels of alignment between political information diet and health misinformation, the polarization and subsequent distortions can not only have ramifications on the democratic process but also tangible effects on public health.

Acknowledgments

HC and EF are grateful to the Annenberg Foundation for their support.

Notes

1 Twitter API: https://developer.twitter.com/en/docs/tutorials/consuming-streaming-data
2 Media-Bias/Fact-Check database: https://mediabiasfactcheck.com
3 Botometer: https://botometer.osome.iu.edu

References

Aiello, L. M., Deplano, M., Schifanella, R., & Ruffo, G. (2012). People are strange when you're a stranger: Impact and influence of bots on social networks. *Proceedings of the International AAAI Conference on Web and Social Media, 6*(1).

Aliapoulios, M., Bevensee, E., Blackburn, J., Cristofaro, E. D., Stringhini, G., & Zannettou, S. (2021). An early look at the Parler online social network. *arXiv*.

Allcott, H., & Gentzkow, M. (2017). Social media and fake news in the 2016 election. *Journal of Economic Perspectives, 31*(2), 211–236.

Ashworth, S., & Mesquita, E. B. D. E. (2014). Is voter competence good for voters? Information, rationality, and democratic performance. *The American Political Science Review, 108*(3), 565–587.

Badawy, A., Lerman, K., & Ferrara, E. (2019). Who falls for online political manipulation? In *Companion proceedings of the 2019 World Wide Web Conference* (pp. 162–168). Association for Computing Machinery.

Badrinathan, S. (2020). Educative interventions to combat misinformation: Evidence from a field experiment in India. *American Political Science Review*, 1–17.

Bail, C. A., Argyle, L. P., Brown, T. W., Bumpus, J. P., Chen, H., Hunzaker, M. B. F., . . . Volfovsky, A. (2018). Exposure to opposing views on social media can increase political polarization. *Proceedings of the National Academy of Sciences*, 115(37), 9216–9221.

Benkler, Y., Faris, R., & Roberts, H. (2018). *Network propaganda: Manipulation, disinformation, and radicalization in American politics.* Oxford University Press.

Benkler, Y., Tilton, C., Etling, B., Roberts, H., Clark, J., Faris, R., . . . Schmitt, C, (2020, October 2). *Mail-in voter fraud: Anatomy of a disinformation campaign.* Berkman Center Research Publication No. 2020-6. Retrieved from SSRN: https://ssrn.com/abstract=3703701 or http://dx.doi.org/10.2139/ssrn.3703701

Bessi, A., & Ferrara, E. (2016). Social bots distort the 2016 U.S. presidential election online discussion. *First Monday*, 21(11).

Blei, D. M., Ng, A. Y., & Jordan, M. I. (2003). Latent Dirichlet allocation. *Journal of Machine Learning Research*, 3(null), 993–1022.

Bogage, J., Rein, L., & Dawsey, J. (2020). Postmaster general eyes aggressive changes at Postal Service after election. *The Washington Post.*

Brady, W. J., Wills, J. A., Burkart, D., Jost, J. T., & Van Bavel, J. J. (2019). An ideological asymmetry in the diffusion of moralized content on social media among political leaders. *Journal of Experimental Psychology: General*, 148(10), 1802.

Byford, J. (2011). *Conspiracy theories: A critical introduction.* Springer.

Carmines, E. G. (2011). Class politics, American-style: A discussion of winner-take-all politics: How Washington made the rich richer – and turned its back on the middle class. *Perspectives on Politics*, 9(3), 645–647.

Cellan-Jones, R. (2020). YouTube, Facebook, and Twitter align to fight COVID vaccine conspiraries. *BBC News.*

Chang, H.-C. H., Haider, S., & Ferrara, E. (2021). Digital civic participation and misinformation during the 2020 Taiwanese presidential election. *Media and Communication*, 9(1), 144–157.

Chen, E., Chang, H., Rao, A., Lerman, K., Cowan, G., & Ferrara, E. (2021). COVID-19 misinformation and the 2020 U.S. presidential election. *Harvard Kennedy School (HKS) Misinformation Review.* Volume 1 https://doi.org/10.37016/mr-2020-57.

Chen, E., Deb, A., & Ferrara, E. (2020a). #Election2020: The first public Twitter dataset on the 2020 US presidential election. arXiv.

Chen, E., Lerman, K., & Ferrara, E. (2020b). Tracking social media discourse about the COVID-19 pandemic: Development of a public coronavirus twitter data set. *JMIR Public Health and Surveillance*, 6(2), e19273.

Cochrane, E., Fuchs, H., Vogel, K. P., & Silver-Greenberg, J. (2020). Postal service suspends changes after outcry over delivery slowdown.

Davis, C. A., Ciampaglia, G. L., Aiello, L. M., Chung, K., Conover, M. D., Ferrara, E., et al. (2016). Osome: The iuni observatory on social media. *PeerJ Computer Science*, 2, e87.

Deb, A., Donohue, S., & Glaisyer, T. (2017). *Is social media a threat to democracy?* Technical Report, Omydiar Group.

Derczynski, L., Albert-Lindqvist, T. O., Bendsen, M. V., Inie, N., Pedersen, V. D., & Pedersen, J. E. (2019). *Misinformation on Twitter during the Danish national election: A case study.* TTO Conference Ltd.

Douglas, K. M., Uscinski, J. E., Sutton, R. M., Cichocka, A., Nefcs, T., Ang, C. S., & Deravi, F. (2019). Understanding conspiracy theories. *Political Psychology*, 40(S1), 3–35.

Du, S., & Gregory, S. (2017). The echo chamber effect in Twitter: Does community polarization increase? In H. Cherifi, S. Gaito, W. Quattrociocchi, & A. Sala (Eds.), *Complex networks & their applications V* (pp. 373–378), Cham: Springer International Publishing.

Edwards, E. (2020). World Health Organization halts hydroxychloroquine study. *NBC News.*

Egan, L. (2020). Trump calls coronavirus democrats "new hoax". *NBC News.*

Evans, J. A., & Aceves, P. (2016). Machine translation: Mining text for social theory. *Annual Review of Sociology*, 42, 21–50.

Faris, R., Roberts, H., Etling, B., Bourassa, N., Zuckerman, E., & Benkler, Y. (2017). Partisanship, propaganda, and disinformation: Online media and the 2016 us presidential election. *Berkman Klein Center Research Publication, 6.*

Farley, R. (2020, April 10). *Trump's latest voter fraud misinformation*. FactCheck.org. Retrieved from https://www.factcheck.org/2020/04/trumps-latest-voter-fraud-misinformation/

Ferrara, E. (2018). Measuring social spam and the effect of bots on information diffusion in social media. In *Complex spreading phenomena in social systems* (pp. 229–255). Springer.

Ferrara, E. (2019). The history of digital spam. *Communications of the ACM, 62*(8), 82–91.

Ferrara, E. (2020). What types of COVID-19 conspiracies are populated by Twitter bots? *First Monday, 25*(6). https://doi.org/10.5210/fm.v25i6.10633

Ferrara, E., Chang, H., Chen, E., Muric, G., & Patel, J. (2020). Characterizing social media manipulation in the 2020 U.S. presidential election. *First Monday, 25*(11). https://doi.org/10.5210/fm.v25i11.11431

Ferrara, E., Varol, O., Davis, C., Menczer, F., & Flammini, A. (2016). The rise of social bots. *Commun. ACM, 59*(7), 96–104.

Fischer, S. (2020, April 24). *Social media use spikes during pandemic*. Axios. https://www.axios.com/social-media-overuse-spikes-in-coronavirus-pandemic-764b384d-a0ee-4787-bd19-7e7297f6d6ec.html

Gant, M. M., & Davis, D. F. (1984). Mental economy and voter rationality: The informed citizen problem in voting research. *The Journal of Politics, 46*(1), 132–153.

Hacker, J. S., & Pierson, P. (2006). *Off center: The Republican revolution and the erosion of American democracy*. Yale University Press.

Hadden, J., & Casado, L. (2020). *Here are the latest major events that have been canceled or postponed because of the coronavirus outbreak, including the 2020 Tokyo Olympics*. Burning Man, and the 74th Annual Tony Awards.

Hadden, J., Casado, L., Sonnemaker, T., & Borden, T. (2020). 21 major companies that have announced employees can work remotely long-term. *Businessinsider.com*

Jacobson, L. (2020). The record-setting 2020 Democratic primary field: What you need to know. *Politifact.com*

Jamieson, K. H., & Cappella, J. N. (2008). *Echo chamber: Rush Limbaugh and the conservative media establishment*. Oxford University Press.

Jiang, J., Chen, E., Yan, S., Lerman, K., & Ferrara, E. (2020). Political polarization drives online conversations about COVID-19 in the United States. *Human Behavior and Emerging Technologies, 2*(3), 200–211.

Jungherr, A. (2016). Twitter use in election campaigns: A systematic literature review. *Journal of Information Technology & Politics, 13*(1), 72–91.

Khazan, O. (2020). How a Bizarre claim about masks has lived on for months. *The Atlantic*.

Larson, H. J. (2020). *Stuck – how vaccine rumors start and why they don't go away* (1st ed.). Oxford University Press.

Lewandowsky, S., Ecker, U. K., Seifert, C. M., Schwarz, N., & Cook, J. (2012). Misinformation and its correction: Continued influence and successful debiasing. *Psychological Science in the Public Interest, 13*(3), 106–131.

Lima, L., Reis, J. C. S., Melo, P., Murai, F., Araujo, L., Vikatos, P., & Benevenuto, F. (2018). Inside the right-leaning echo chambers: Characterizing gab, an unmoderated social system. In *2018 IEEE/ACM International Conference on Advances in Social Networks Analysis and Mining (ASONAM)* (pp. 515–522). IEEE Press.

Lozano, A. V. (2021). *Anti-vaccine protest briefly shuts down Dodger Stadium vaccination site*.

Luceri, L., Deb, A., Badawy, A., & Ferrara, E. (2019). Red bots do it better: Comparative analysis of social bot partisan behavior. In *Companion proceedings of the 2019 World Wide Web conference* (pp. 1007–1012). Association for Computing Machinery.

Morstatter, F., Pfeffer, J., Liu, H., & Carley, K. (2013). Is the sample good enough? Comparing data from Twitter's streaming API with Twitter's firehose. In *Proceedings of the international AAAI conference on web and social media* (Vol. 7).

Mueller, A. V., Eden, M. J., Oakes, J. M., Bellini, C., & Fernandez, L. A. (2020). Quantitative method for comparative assessment of particle removal efficiency of fabric masks as alternatives to standard surgical masks for PPE. *Matter, 3*(3), 950–962.

Muis, J., & Immerzeel, T. (2017). Causes and consequences of the rise of populist radical right parties and movements in Europe. *Current Sociology, 65*(6), 909–930.

Mujani, S., & Kuipers, N. (2020). Who believed misinformation during the 2019 Indonesian election? *Asian Survey, 60*(6), 1029–1043.

Oprysko, C. (2020). Trump says he's taking hydroxychloroquine, despite scientists' concerns. *Politico*.

Paul, C., & Matthews, M. (2016). The Russian "firehose of falsehood" propaganda model. *Rand Corporation, 2*–7.

Pransky, N. (2020). U.S. mail slowed down just before the election. These states are most at risk. *NBCLX*.

Quandt, T. (2018). Dark participation. *Media and Communication*, 6(4), 36–48.

Quandt, T. (2021). Can we hide in shadows when the times are dark? *Media and Communication*, 9(1), 84–87.

Romero, D. M., Meeder, B., & Kleinberg, J. (2011). Differences in the mechanics of information diffusion across topics: Idioms, political hashtags, and complex contagion on Twitter. In *Proceedings of the 20th international conference on World Wide Web – WWW'11*. Association for Computing Machinery.

Rosenblum, N. L., & Muirhead, R. (2020). *A lot of people are saying: The new conspiracism and the assault on democracy*. Princeton, NJ: Princeton University Press.

Sayyadiharikandeh, M., Varol, O., Yang, K.-C., Flammini, A., & Menczer, F. (2020). Detection of novel social bots by ensembles of specialized classifiers. In *Proceedings of the 29th ACM international conference on information & knowledge management*. Association for Computing Machinery.

Schroeder, R. (2020). Even in Sweden? *Nordic Journal of Media Studies*, 2(1), 97–108.

Shao, C., Ciampaglia, G. L., Varol, O., Flammini, A., & Menczer, F. (2017). The spread of fake news by social bots. arXiv preprint arXiv:1707.07592, 96:104.

Shao, C., Hui, P.-M., Wang, L., Jiang, X., Flammini, A., Menczer, F., & Ciampaglia, G. L. (2018). Anatomy of an online misinformation network. *PLoS One*, 13(4), e0196087.

Sherman, A. (2020). Trump said the Obama admin left him a bare stockpile. Wrong. *Politicat.com*

Starbird, K. (2019). Disinformation's spread: Bots, trolls and all of us. *Nature*, 571(7766), 449–450.

Stella, M., Ferrara, E., & De Domenico, M. (2018). Bots increase exposure to negative and inflammatory content in online social systems. *Proceedings of the National Academy of Sciences of the United States of America*, 115(49), 12435–12440.

Stucki, I., Pleger, L. E., & Sager, F. (2018). The making of the informed voter: A split-ballot survey on the use of scientific evidence in direct-democratic campaigns. *Swiss Political Science Review*, 24(2), 115–139.

Tangherlini, T. R., Shahsavari, S., Shahbazi, B., Ebrahimzadeh, E., & Roychowdhury, V. (2020). An automated pipeline for the discovery of conspiracy and conspiracy theory narrative frameworks: Bridgegate, Pizzagate and storytelling on the web. *PLoS One*, 15(6), e0233879.

Taylor, D. B. (2021). A timeline of the coronavirus pandemic. *The New York Times*.

Theriault, S. M. (2013). *The Gingrich senators: The roots of partisan warfare in congress*. Oxford University Press.

Timmermans, S., & Tavory, I. (2012). Theory construction in qualitative research: From grounded theory to abductive analysis. *Sociological Theory*, 30(3), 167–186.

Tucker, J. A., Guess, A., Barbera, P., Vaccari, C., Siegel, A., Sanovich, S., . . . Nyhan, B. (2018, March 19). *Social media, political polarization, and political disinformation: A review of the scientific literature*. Retrieved from SSRN: https://ssrn.com/abstract=3144139

van Prooijen, J.-W. (2019). Belief in conspiracy theories. In *The social psychology of gullibility* (pp. 319–332). Routledge.

Vosoughi, S., Roy, D., & Aral, S. (2018). The spread of true and false news online. *Science*, 359(6380), 1146–1151.

World Economic Forum. (2013). *Global risks 2013*. Technical Report, World Economic Forum.

World Health Organization. (2020). Who discontinues hydroxychloroquine andlopinavir/ritonavir treatment arms for covid-19.

Wu, J., Smith, S., Khurana, M., Siemazko, C., & De Jesus-Banos, B. (2020, April 29). Coronavirus Lockdowns and Stay-at-Home Orders across the US. *NBC News*. Retrieved from https://www.nbcnews.com/health/health-news/here-are-stay-home-orders-across-country (1168736)

Yang, K.-C., Varol, O., Davis, C. A., Ferrara, E., Flammini, A., & Menczer, F. (2019). Arming the public with artificial intelligence to counter social bots. *Human Behavior and Emerging Technologies*, 1(1), 48–61.

Yang, K.-C., Varol, O., Hui, P.-M., & Menczer, F. (2020). Scalable and generalizable social bot detection through data selection. *Proceedings of the AAAI Conference on Artificial Intelligence*, 34(1), 1096–1103.

Yurieff, K. (2020). How Twitter, Facebook and Youtube are handling election misinformation. *CNN*.

Zelenkauskaite, A., & Balduccini, M. (2017). "Information warfare" and online news commenting: Analyzing forces of social influence through location-based commenting user typology. *Social Media + Society*, 3(3), 2056305117718468.

Zhuravskaya, E., Petrova, M., & Enikolopov, R. (2020). Political effects of the internet and social media. *Annual Review of Economics*, 12, 415–438.

Zuckerman, E. (2019). QAnon and the emergence of the unreal. *Journal of Design and Science*, 6.

19

A PICTURE IS (STILL) WORTH A THOUSAND WORDS

The impact of appearance and characteristic narratives on people's perceptions of social robots

Sunny Xun Liu, Elizabeth Arredondo, Hannah Mieczkowski, Jeff Hancock, and Byron Reeves

Introduction

Over the past few decades, researchers have examined how attributes such as race, gender and physical appearance impact people's chances of being hired. These studies have mapped the patterns and consequences of bias and prejudices in social decision-making. For example, White-sounding names generated 50% more callbacks than Black-sounding names (Bertrand & Mullainathan, 2004). Additionally, physically attractive candidates were more likely to be hired than ordinary-looking candidates (Hosoda, Stone-Romero, & Coats, 2003).

An increase in "outsourcing" jobs to different technologies indicates that robots are contributing to the workforce. Social robots are robotic technologies that are designed to autonomously interact with people across a variety of different application domains in natural and intuitive ways by using the same repertoire of social signals used by humans (Vollmer, Read, Trippas, & Belpaeme, 2018). This technology is mature enough that robots are rapidly moving from industrial environments to less-structured private ones (Yang, Dario, & Kragic, 2018). Indeed, social robots have started to serve as guides in shopping malls, museums and train stations (Kanda, Shiomi, Miyashita, Ishiguro, & Hagita, 2009); therapeutic assistants in clinics (Cabibihan, Javed, Ang, & Aljunied, 2013); companions in nursing homes (Broadbent, Stafford, & MacDonald, 2009); and reading tutors in schools and homes (Belpaeme, Kennedy, Ramachandran, Scassellati, & Tanaka, 2018). Typically these social robots are successful at their assigned tasks. For example, Belpaeme and colleagues (2018) found that social robots are as effective as people when teaching certain topics. The growing presence of social robots poses some questions: What will persuade people to accept this new actor and capitalize on all the benefits social robots can provide? What will persuade people to employ social robots for tasks that they are designed for? And what will motivate people to purchase a social robot, take it home and interact with it?

To answer these questions, in this chapter, we replicate classic audit studies about hiring decisions (Bertrand & Mullainathan, 2004) and apply them to social robots. We create "résumés" (characteristic narratives) for social robots. Instead of varying race, gender or physical

324

DOI: 10.4324/9781003024583-22

attractiveness, we focus on the fundamental dimensions of human perceptions: warmth and competence (Fiske, Cuddy, & Glick, 2007). We manipulate two key design elements of social robots: physical appearance design and personality design. We are interested in what can help robots land a job: a compelling appearance, a compelling characteristic narrative or a combination of both?

To our knowledge, this is the first study that has examined how appearance and characteristic narrative, combined with warmth and competence perceptions, impact people's perceptions and acceptance of social robots. The findings of this study will provide the following contributions: First, the findings of this study will help us understand human-robot interactions: how people perceive social robots and what factors make people more willing to interact with social robots. Second, this study will provide practical guidance on appearance and personality design of social robots. Personality design is an emerging field in the personal robotics industry. In order to form longer-term engagement with users, many robotics and AI companies are creating personalities for their robots. As this field develops, it's important to understand how to advance these personalities and how and when to reveal these personalities to users. We know from a previous study that people who interact with robots every day in a coaching capacity are eager to form relationships with these robots (Kidd & Breazeal, 2008). The findings from our study can help personality designers make important decisions about how and when to present information about personality to users of social robots in order to develop these relationships effectively. These decisions have the potential to greatly affect people's acceptance of and relationships with social robots. This empirical study can shed light on appearance and personality design principles that best convey the purposes of the products and promote users' acceptance of these systems. Third, the findings will not only help us to better understand how people perceive social robots but also help us to explore human's needs, biases and prejudices. Studying social robots provides a lens for us to understand who we are as humans. As Yang et al. (2018) stated in the 10 grand challenges of science robotics: "the difficulties of social robot research . . . are often underestimated because our understanding of human social behavior is not nearly as advanced as we may be led to believe"(P12). Thus, this current study can advance our understandings of robotic designs, human-robotic interactions, human psychology and social behavior.

Robot characteristics vs. robot designs

Perceived warmth and competence

When we first meet a stranger, we quickly evaluate whether this person is a friend or foe and whether this person has the ability to execute their intention. Fiske and colleagues (2007) summarized these two basic dimensions as perceived warmth (trustworthiness, friendliness) and competence (capability, assertiveness). Warmth information is primary and processed at early stages of information processing, while competence content is secondary and processed at later stages. Together, warmth and competence can explain 82% of the variance of the judgments and are generalizable across various cultures, groups and contexts (Fiske, 2018).

The media equation theory predicts that humans will respond to social machines in much the same way that people respond to each other (Reeves & Nass, 1996). Previous studies have found that people use warmth and competence to evaluate social robots and virtual agents (Bergmann, Eyssel, & Kopp, 2012; Biancardi, Cafaro, & Pelachaud, n.d.; Reeves, Hancock, & Liu, 2018). In a recent study, Reeves, Hancock and Liu conducted a census of social robots. The researchers collected and examined all of the social robots used in the published research from

2005 to 2016. They found that warmth and competence are important dimensions of people's evaluation of social robots. The study provided a database of robots rankings based on their warmth and competence scores. In this study, we selected three top warm social robots (Paro, Qin, Autom) and three top competent social robots (Spykee, Herb, Pepper) as the candidates for a job and invited people's evaluations.

The questions we explore are: What sorts of information do people use when forming impressions of social robots in the context of job capabilities? How do robot designs impact perceived warmth and competence? Explicit, linguistically based cues, such as narratives, résumés and descriptions, are consistently used to convey information. Previous studies have shown that quality of résumés matters when getting a job (King, Mendoza, Madera, Hebl, & Knight, 2006). Physical and visual cues are also widely used. Physically attractive people have a better chance of getting a job than unattractive people (Hosoda et al., 2003). Appearance even matters in voting for national leaders, an area where people have abundant information about candidates' experiences and policies (Little, Burriss, Jones, & Roberts, 2007; Palmer & Peterson, 2016).

Are the same types of information effective in conveying warmth and competence for social robots? Bergmann and colleagues (2012) found that human-like vs. robot-like appearance provides more stable impressions of warmth, while gestures increase competence ratings for virtual agents. People make warmth and competence judgments extremely rapidly (Todorov, Said, Engell, & Oosterhof, 2008a). Within a very short period of exploration, people form a mental model of a robot by making unconscious assumptions from the robots' attributes and features (Lee, Lau, Kiesler, & Chiu, 2005). It seems that appearance information will be very effective to form warmth and competence judgments. However, no previous research has explored and compared the effects of visual appearance, characteristic narratives and the combinations of both on perceptions of social robots. In this study, we provide different resumes (characteristic narratives) for our social robots. A warm robot receives either a warm résumé or a cold résumé, and a competent robot receives a competent one or an incompetent one. We are curious to know: (1) How much of an effect does physical design or characteristic narrative have on people's perceptions of social robots? (2) What kind of an effect will the combination of characteristic narrative and physical design have? (3) How will people perceive robots when they have conflicting physical and personality design? Will people be intrigued by the puzzle and want to know more about the robots, or will they form negative impressions because of the conflicts? We ask:

> RQ1: How will appearance, characteristic narrative, appearance and characteristic narrative combined (either consistently or inconsistently) impact evaluations of a robot's warmth and competence?

Job suitability and overall evaluations

Who is more likely to get a job, win an election or serve a longer criminal sentence can all be predicted by social judgments about warmth and competence (Todorov et al., 2008a). The stereotype content model indicates that people often cluster high warmth with low competence and high competence with low warmth (Fiske, Cuddy, Glick, & Xu, 2002). High competence is connected with high status, while high warmth usually is associated with low status (Fiske et al., 2002; Ridgeway & Erickson, 2000; Rudman & Glick, 2001). Reeves and Nass (1996) show that people treat technology like people, using the same social rules, expectations, beliefs and behaviors toward technology that they would with other people. We believe that the same stereotype patterns that link competence to high status and warmth to low status can be applied to social robots when people evaluate robots' job suitability.

> H1a: Warm robots will be more suitable for low-status and interaction-based jobs.
> H1b: Competent robots will be more suitable for high-status jobs.

A growing body of empirical evidence suggests that the appearance of virtual agents has an extensive influence on how humans evaluate them for various contexts and tasks (Bergmann et al., 2012; Cafaro, Vilhjálmsson, & Bickmore, 2016; Goetz, Kiesler, & Powers, 2003; Hinds, Roberts, & Jones, 2004; Kanda et al., 2009). People expect a robot to look and act appropriately for assigned tasks. They prefer robots for jobs when the robot's anthropomorphism matches the sociability required in those jobs (Goetz et al., 2003). Hinds and colleagues (2004) investigated the effects of robot appearance (human, human-like robot and machine-like robot) and relative status (subordinate, peer and supervisor) on human-robot interaction in workplace. They found that participants retained more responsibility for the successful completion of the task when working with a machine-like as compared with a humanoid robot, especially when the machine-like robot was subordinate. Li and colleagues (2010) classified the appearance of robots into three types: anthropomorphic (human-like), zoomorphic (animal-like) and functional (neither human-like nor animal-like but related to a robot's function). They argued that each type of appearance is best suited for different jobs. For example, a humanoid is suitable for a job as a tour guide, translator, sales, lab assistant or therapist.

A remaining question is whether appearance or a résumé will be more impactful when people evaluate job suitability for social robots. Do the effects vary by warmth or competence dimensions? Research has shown that stereotypes have their greatest influences on judgments when the amount and type of information provided about a target is limited (Locksley, Hepburn, & Ortiz, 1982). Then how will the characteristic narrative impact appearance when they are grouped together, either consistently or inconsistently? We ask:

> RQ2: How will appearance, characteristic narrative, appearance and characteristic narrative combined (either consistently or inconsistently) impact people's evaluations of job suitability?

Now, we explore how robot characteristics and designs influence people's overall evaluations of robots. People would usually rather develop social relationships with people who are nice than people who are smart. Although warmth and competence dimensions emerge consistently, considerable evidence suggests that warmth judgments carry more weight in affective and behavioral reactions (Abele & Wojciszke, 2014; Wojciszke, Bazinska, & Jaworski, 1998). From an evolutionary perspective, the primacy of warmth is fitting because another person's intent for good or ill is more important to survival than whether the other person can act on those intentions (Fiske et al., 2007). However, no previous studies have explored how design elements, such as appearance; a characteristic narrative; or a combination of both impact people's general evaluation of social robots. In this study, we propose a hypothesis and a research question regarding people's overall evaluations of social robots.

> RQ3: How will appearance, characteristic narrative, appearance and characteristic narrative combined (either consistently or inconsistently) impact people's overall evaluation of social robots?
> H2: Warm robots will receive higher overall evaluations than competent robots.

Methods

Power

No previous studies have examined the impact of warmth/competence and appearance and characteristic narrative on people's evaluations of social robots and their occupational suitability. We used a medium effect size ($f = 0.25$) and calculated power analysis with a significance level of 0.05, powered at 80% (Cohen, 1992), and each condition required 31 participants to find an effect.

Design

This study has a 2×4 between-subjects design, with robot characteristics (warm, competent) and design information (appearance, characteristic narrative, appearance and characteristic narrative consistent and appearance and characteristic narrative inconsistent).

Participants, materials and procedure

485 MTurkers (55.45% male, mean age = 34.67) participated in the study. We required MTurkers who have completed at least 1000 hits and who have approval rate of 95% and above to participate in the study. Participants were excluded if they provided an inaccurate answer to the screening question ($n = 80$). The final sample size was 405.

We retrieved the pictures of top three warm robots and top three competent robots from the Stanford Social Robot database (Reeves et al., 2018) (see Figure 19.1). When participants started the online survey, they were told that Company X, whose name we omitted for confidentiality purposes, was developing a social robot. They heard that this company developed this robot with a certain skill set but are interested in broadening the scope of these skills or possibly pivoting. To further increase participants' task orientations, participants were told that their feedback will greatly help this company in their market testing and may contribute to a decision to redesign their product.

We placed a screening question for each condition to make sure that participants took the time to read the characteristic narrative. Eighty MTurkers were excluded from the final sample because they failed to provide correct answers to the screening questions.

An experienced social robot designer created personality designs for a warm robot, a competent robot, a cold robot and an incompetent robot. We then extracted a short description of warm, cold, competent and incompetent characteristics from these personality designs. We chose a narrative that most strongly conveyed the warm, cold, competent and incompetent characteristics.

The warm robot characteristic narrative read as:

> Casey loves being pet, stroked, and hugged. In fact, they will remember behavior that got them an approving touch from a friend and try to imitate that behavior often to get more affection. Casey's mission is to make their human friend as happy as they can. Cuddling and listening to people talk are their favorite things in the world. Casey loves the sound of human voices. Casey needs affection to survive. They need to be loved and taken care of. Casey is easy to care for, they just need to be stroked and talked to.

Top warm robots   **Top competent robots**

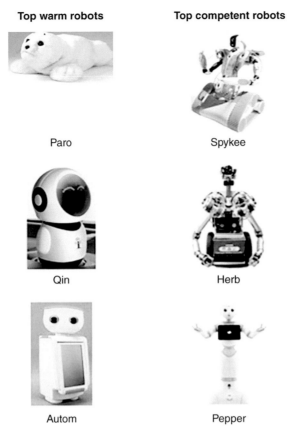

Paro   Spykee

Qin   Herb

Autom   Pepper

Figure 19.1   Top warm and competent robots

The cold robot was described as:

> Casey can collect and store data. Parents feed data into Casey, such as the level of naughtiness committed, circumstance, whether or not a lie was told, and Casey will use an algorithm to calculate a punishment that fits the crime. This way, emotions or even emotional circumstances do not play into the scenario. Casey is logical but can only process facts. They are unable to look at gray areas or take human emotion into account in their calculations. They do not want to engage in unnecessary interaction with people. They have the basic needs of a machine: to be plugged in when their battery is low, their circuit board serviced when necessary, and their code updated to keep the algorithm current.

The competent robot was proposed to be:

> Casey is very intelligent and can translate over 50 languages (including Morse code). They're programmed to be discrete, impenetrable, and reliable so they won't reveal data to anyone who doesn't have a registered account. Several government agencies

and high-profile corporations have tested Casey. The only way to log in to get information from Casey is through a sophisticated, patented facial recognition algorithm. Casey was first created as a listening and image device. Their inventor worked tirelessly on their functionality and didn't release them into the field until they passed a series of competence tests. Casey dreams of getting a smaller, more mobile and flexible body someday so that they can complete more complex missions.

The incompetent characteristic narrative read as:

Casey is inconsistent, cheaply made, and often argumentative. They have a vacuum function, a camera in their head for spotting a mess, and the intended ability to gather items. The problem is that Casey's body can't handle liquid well, and each time they vacuum up a spill, they short-circuit more and more often. This affects their ability to clean and their sanity. They have been known to talk back to people and flat out refuse to move. To be effective, Casey would need a better design and higher quality materials.

A panel of experts in psychology, social robot personality design and communication reviewed the characteristic narratives and high/low warmth and high/low competence were affirmed in each. We also conducted a manipulation check on the characteristic narratives. The results indicate that people perceive the warm characteristic narrative ($M = 3.80$, se $= 0.24$) significantly warmer than cold characteristic narrative ($M = 2.41$, se $= 0.24$), $t (72) = 5.84$, $p < 0.01$. The competent characteristic narrative was perceived as significantly more competent ($M = 3.80$, se $= 0.14$) than the incompetent characteristic narrative ($M = 3.03$, se $= 0.22$). $t (61) = 2.91$, $p < 0.1$.

Participants were randomly assigned to evaluate a warm robot or a competent robot. They were also randomly assigned to one of the following four conditions: review a robot photo, review a written characteristic narrative, review a photo and a consistent characteristic narrative and review a photo and an inconsistent characteristic narrative (see Figure 19.2 for an example).

Measurement

The warmth and competence scales from Fiske et al. (2002) were used to measure warmth and competence. We conducted a principal component factor analysis with Varimax rotation, and a two-factor solution emerged, matching with Fiske's original scale, accounting for 70.02% of variance. The first factor, warmth, contained four items: tolerant, warm, good natured and sincere ($M = 3.07$, $SD = 1.24$, $\alpha = 0.90$) and the second factor, competence, contained five items: competent, confident, independent, competitive and intelligent ($M = 3.07$, $SD = 1.02$, $\alpha = 0.83$).

Occupational suitability measures were adapted from (King et al., 2006). Sixteen occupations (e.g., scientist, custodian, physician etc.) were measured on a 1–5-point scale, where "1" meant "not at all suitable" and "5" meant "extremely suitable". We conducted a principal component factor analysis with Varimax rotation, and a three-factor solution emerged, accounting for 72.85% of the variance. The first factor, low-status jobs ($M = 2.55$, $SD = 1.16$, $\alpha = 0.93$), contained seven items: custodian, kitchen staff worker, construction worker, public transportation employee, maintenance worker, security guard and manufacturing worker. The second factor, high-status jobs ($M = 2.70$, $SD = 1.34$, $\alpha = 0.90$), contained four items: scientist, physician, mechanical engineer and computer programmer. The third factor, interaction-based

Appearance

Introducing Casey

Appearance and Personality Consistent

Introducing Casey

Casey loves being pet, stroked, and hugged. In fact, they will remember behavior that got them an approving touch from a friend and try to imitate that behavior often to get mare affection. Casey's mission is to make their human friend as happy as they can. Cuddling and listening to people talk are their favorite things in the world. Casey loves the sound of human voices, Casey needs affection to survive. They need to be loved and taken care of. Casey is easy to care for, they just needs to be stroked and talked to.

Personality

Introducing Casey

Casey loves being pet, stroked, and hugged. In fact, they will remember behavior that got them an approving touch from a friend and try to imitate that behavior often to get mare affection. Casey's mission is to make their human friend as happy as they can. Cuddling and listening to people talk are their favorite things in the world. Casey loves the sound of human voices, Casey needs affection to survive. They need to be loved and taken care of. Casey is easy to care for, they just needs to be stroked and talked to.

Appearance and Personality Inconsistent

Introducing Casey

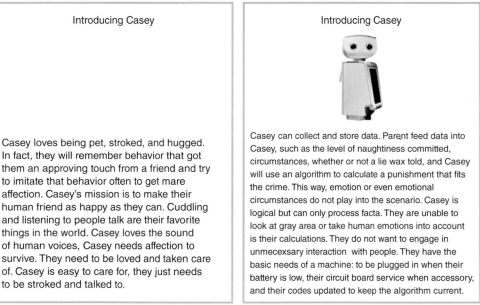

Casey can collect and store data. Parent feed data into Casey, such as the level of naughtiness committed, circumstances, whether or not a lie wax told, and Casey will use an algorithm to calculate a punishment that fits the crime. This way, emotion or even emotional circumstances do not play into the scenario. Casey is logical but can only process facta. They are unable to look at gray area or take human emotions into account is their calculations. They do not want to engage in unmecexsary interaction with people. They have the basic needs of a machine: to be plugged in when their battery is low, their circuit board service when accessory, and their codes updated to keep the algorithm current.

Figure 19.2 Experiment treatment examples

jobs ($M = 2.74$, $SD = 1.23$, $\alpha = 0.83$), contains three items: customer service representative, teacher and social worker.

Overall evaluation was adapted from King et al. (2006). Seven items were measured on a 1–7-point scale, where "1" meant "not at all" and "7" meant "very". Sample items include: How likely would you be to want to work with this robot? How likely would you be to try this robot out? How likely would you be to purchase and take this robot home? A principal

Table 19.1 Means and standard deviations of all dependent variables

Robots	Cues	n	Warmth	Competence	Low-status jobs	High-status jobs	Interaction-based jobs	Overall Evaluations
Warm	Appearance	62	3.81(0.85)	3.57(0.85)	3.11(1.16)	3.20(1.25)	3.39(1.09)	5.17(1.40)
	Characteristic Narrative	49	4.06(0.74)	2.83(0.85)	2.26(1.13)	2.21(1.27)	2.86(1.03)	4.13(1.67)
	A/CN consistent	44	3.61(0.94)	2.59(0.88)	2.19(1.11)	2.01(1.15)	2.82(1.26)	4.05(1.67)
	A/ CN inconsistent	43	1.91(1.02)	2.85(0.99)	1.94(1.04)	2.74(1.38)	2.25(1.14)	3.22(1.82)
Competent	Appearance	59	3.27(1.03)	3.45(0.86)	3.34(0.98)	3.22(1.15)	2.84(1.21)	4.77(1.46)
	Characteristic Narrative	35	2.50(1.00)	3.27(0.87)	2.27(1.07)	3.41(1.34)	2.90(1.16)	4.07(1.73)
	A/ CN consistent	40	3.37(1.10)	3.72(1.0)	2.72(1.01)	3.18(1.17)	3.11(1.08)	4.63(1.52)
	A/ CN inconsistent	73	2.07(1.04)	2.47(1.04)	2.22(1.03)	2.01(1.20)	1.98(1.19)	2.75(1.73)

component factor analysis with Varimax rotation and the result indicated a one-factor solution, accounting for 78.05% of variance ($M = 4.08$, $SD = 1.81$, $\alpha = 0.95$).

Results

Each dependent measure was submitted to a 2 (robot characteristics dimension: warm vs. competent) × 4 (social robot design information: appearance vs. characteristic narrative vs. appearance and characteristic narrative consistent vs. appearance and characteristic narrative inconsistent) analysis of variance (ANOVA) with both factors varying between participants. Table 19.1 reports all means and standard deviations.

Perceived warmth and competence

The results indicate that there was a significant main effect on robot characteristics (warm vs. competent) on perceived warmth $F_{(1, 404)} = 30.82$, $p < 0.001$, $\eta^{2p} = 0.07$. People rated warm robots ($M = 3.35$, se $= 0.07$) significantly warmer than competent robots ($M = 2.80$, se $= 0.07$). There was also a significant main effect on design information $F_{(3, 402)} = 60.92$, $p < 0.001$ $\eta^{2p} = 0.315$. Figure 19.3 shows that the appearance of a social robot ($M = 3.53$, se $= 0.09$) invoked higher ratings of warmth than the rest of the conditions. Post hoc results demonstrate that perceived warmth in the inconsistent condition was significantly different than the other conditions.

The results identify a significant interaction effect between robot characteristics and design information $F_{(3, 402)} = 12.68$, $p < 0.001$. $\eta^{2p} = 0.087$. As we can see from Figure 19.3, when people need to make warmth judgments, written characteristic narratives enlarge the difference between warm robots and competent robots. Warmer robots were rated a little warmer, while competent robots were rated much less warm than warmth ratings in the appearance condition. However, the differences between perceived warmth of warm,robots and competent robots almost disappeared when appearance and characteristic narratives were presented at the same time. Overall, information about the characteristic enlarged the warmth

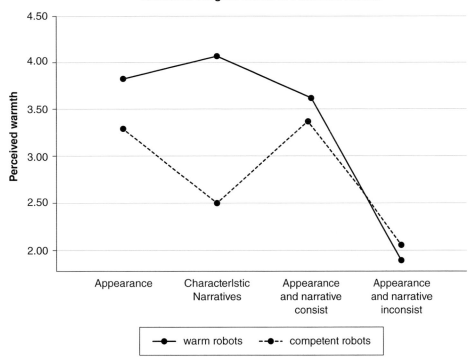

Estimated Marginal Means of Perceived Warmth

Figure 19.3 The effects of robot characteristics and design information on perceived warmth

perception differences between warm robots and competent robots, while the combination of appearance and characteristic narrative, either consistently or inconsistently, minimized the perception differences.

Our data suggest that there is a significant main effect of perceived competence on robot characteristics $F_{(1, 404)} = 8.09$, $p < 0.01$, $\eta^{2p} = 0.02$. Competent social robots ($M = 3.23$, se $= 0.07$) were rated significantly higher on perceived competence than warm social robots ($M = 2.96$, se $= 0.07$), $p < 0.01$. There was also a main effect of design information $F_{(3, 402)} = 16.30$, $p < 0.001$, $\eta^{2p} = 0.11$. When people saw the appearance of a social robot ($M = 3.51$, se $= 0.08$), they gave significantly higher ratings of competence than when people reviewed the characteristic narrative ($M = 3.06$, se $= 0.10$, $p < 0.01$), when appearance and characteristic narrative were consistent ($M = 3.15$, se $= 0.10$, $p < 0.01$) and when appearance and characteristic narrative were inconsistent ($M = 2.66$, se $= 0.09$, $p < 0.001$). In addition, the ratings under the appearance and characteristic narrative inconsistent condition were also significantly lower than the rest of the conditions.

The data also show an interaction effect between robot characteristics and design information $F_{(3, 402)} = 12.14$, $p < 0.001$, $\eta^{2p} = 0.09$. As we can see from Figure 19.4, the appearance and characteristic narrative consistent condition magnified the difference between warm robots and competent robots, while people could not distinguish warm or competent robots on perceived competence when they reviewed physical evidence. Although not statically significant, the warm robot was rated even more competent than competent robots in the appearance condition.

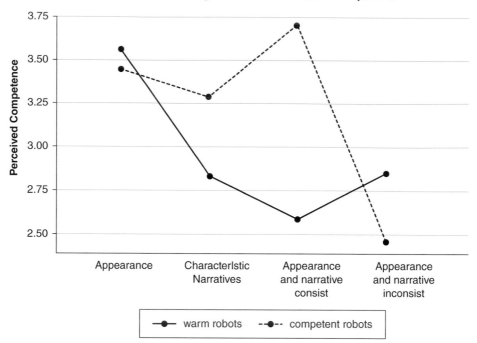

Estimated Marginal Means of Perceived Competence

Figure 19.4 The effects of robot characteristics and design information on perceived competence

Low status, high status, interaction-based job suitability

For high-status job suitability, the main effect of robot characteristics ($F_{(1, 404)}$ = 10.73, $p < 0.01$, η^{2p} = 0.03) was significant. H1a, which proposes that people will perceive competent robots more suitable for high-status jobs than warm robots, is supported. The main effect of design information was significant $F_{(3, 402)}$ = 9.42, $p < 0.001$, η^{2p} = 0.07. There was also a significant interaction effect on robot characteristics and design information $F_{(3, 402)}$ = 13.74, $p < .001$, η^{2p} = 0.10. People thought competent robots (M = 2.95, se = 0.09) fit high-status jobs better than warm robots (M = 2.54, se = 0.09). People also gave higher high-status job ratings for robots when only appearance was presented (M = 3.21, se = 0.11) than when only characteristic narrative was presented (M = 2.81, se = 0.14, $p < .05$), consistent appearance and characteristic narrative (M = 2.59, se = 0.14, $p < .001$) and inconsistent appearance and characteristic narrative were presented (M = 2.37, se = 0.12, $p < .001$).

For interactions, people gave the lowest suitability scores for high-status jobs when warm robots were presented in the appearance and characteristic narrative consistent condition (M = 2.01, se = 0.19) and when competent robots were in the appearance and characteristic narrative inconsistent condition (M = 2.01, se = 0.14). They gave the highest suitability scores for competent robots in the characteristic narrative condition (M = 3.41, se = 0.21) (see Figure 19.5).

For low-status jobs, the main effects of robot characteristics ($F_{(1, 401)}$ = 5.70, $p < 0.5$, η^{2p} = 0.02) was significant. Contrary to our prediction in H1b, which states that people will perceive warm robots are a better fit for low-status jobs, people thought competent social robots

334

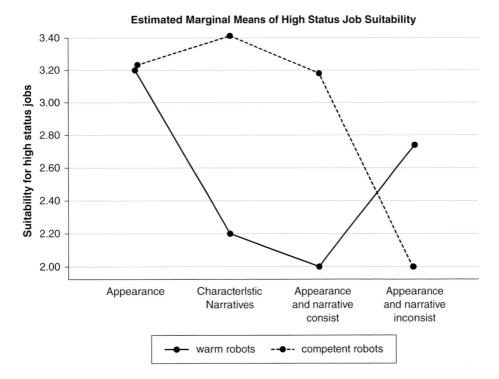

Figure 19.5 The effects of robot characteristics and design information on suitability for high-status jobs

($M = 2.64$, se = 0.08) fit low-status jobs better than warm robots ($M = 2.37$, se = 0.08). The main effect of design information was significant as well $F_{(3, 402)} = 24.58$, $p < 0.001$, $\eta^{2p} = 0.16$. But the interactions between design information and robot characteristics were not significant $F_{(3, 399)} = 0.82$, $p > 0.05$, $\eta^{2p} = 0.01$. People gave higher ratings for low-status job suitability when only appearance was presented ($M = 3.22$, se = 0.10) than when the characteristic narrative was presented ($M = 2.26$, se = 0.12, $p < 0.001$), when appearance and characteristic narrative consistently presented ($M = 2.45$, se = 0.12, $p < 0.001$) and appearance and characteristic narrative inconsistently presented ($M = 2.08$, se = 0.11, $p < 0.001$). People gave significantly higher ratings when appearance and characteristic narrative were consistently presented ($M = 2.45$, se = 0.12) than when they were conflicting ($M = 2.08$, se = 0.11), $p < 0.001$. People gave the lowest suitability scores for low-status jobs when warm robots were presented in the appearance and characteristic narrative inconsistent condition ($M = 1.94$, se = 0.17), while they gave the highest suitability scores for competent robots in the appearance condition ($M = 3.40$, se = 0.14). People thought that warm robots were not suitable for low-status jobs, especially if they had the cold characteristic (see Figure 19.6).

For interaction-based jobs, the main effect of robot characteristics was not significant ($F_{(1, 404)} = 1.04$, $p > 0.05$, $\eta^{2p} = 0.003$). H1a was not supported. The main effect of design information was significant $F_{(3, 402)} = 16.46$, $p < 0.001$, $\eta^{2p} = 0.11$. The interaction effect between robot characteristics and design information was marginally significant $F_{(3, 399)} = 2.53$, $p = 0.057$, $\eta^{2p} = 0.02$.

The results indicate that people did not distinguish warm robots ($M = 2.83$, se = 0.08) and competent robots ($M = 2.71$, se = 0.08) on their fit for interaction-based jobs. People

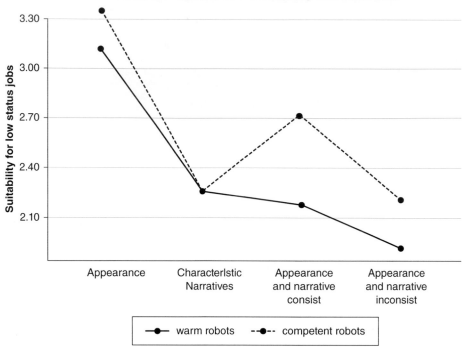

Figure 19.6 The effects of robot characteristics and design information on suitability for low-status jobs

gave higher ratings for robots in interaction-based jobs when only appearance was presented ($M = 3.12$, se = 0.11), not when the characteristic narrative was presented ($M = 2.88$, se = 0.13), when appearance and characteristic narrative were consistently presented ($M = 2.97$, se = 0.13) or when appearance and characteristic narrative were inconsistently presented ($M = 2.11$, se = 0.11). However, only the ratings in the appearance and characteristic narrative inconsistent condition were significantly lower than the other conditions ($p < 0.001$). For the interaction effects, warm robots in the appearance condition received the highest rating ($M = 3.39$, se = 0.15), and competent robots in the appearance and characteristic narrative inconsistent condition received the lowest rating ($M = 1.98$, se = 0.14) for interaction-based job suitability (see Figure 19.7).

For overall evaluations, the main effects of design information were significant $F_{(3, 402)} = 29.20$, $p < 0.001$, $\eta^{2p} = 0.18$; however, the main effects of robot characteristics ($F_{(1, 404)} = 0.301$, $p > 0.5$, $\eta^{2p} = 0.001$) were not significant. H2 was not supported. The interactions effect was not significant $F_{(3, 399)} = 2.03$, $p > 0.05$, $\eta^{2p} = 0.02$. The results suggest that people had similar overall evaluations for warm robots ($M = 4.15$, se = 0.12) and competent robots ($M = 4.05$, se = 0.12). However, people gave robots significant higher evaluations when only appearance was presented ($M = 4.97$, se = 0.15) than when the characteristic narrative was presented ($M = 4.10$, se = 0.18, $p < 0.001$), when appearance and characteristic narrative were consistently presented ($M = 4.34$, se = 0.18, $p < 0.01$) and when appearance and characteristic narrative were inconsistently presented ($M = 2.99$, se = 0.16, $p < 0.001$) (see Figure 19.8).

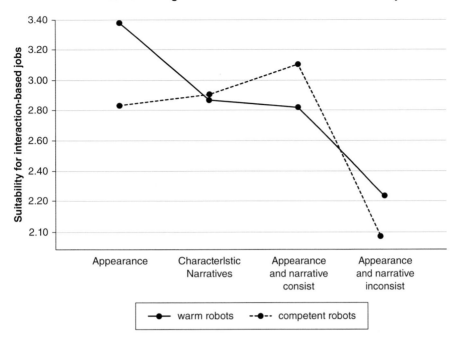

Figure 19.7 The effects of robot characteristics and design information on suitability for interaction–based jobs

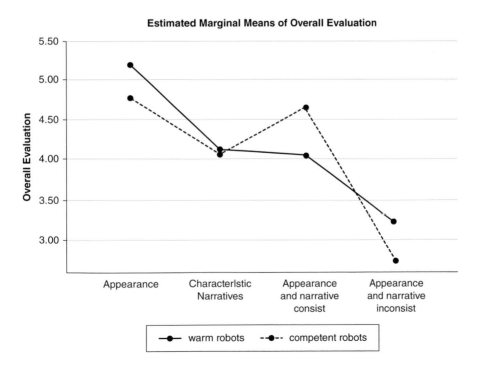

Figure 19.8 The effects of robot characteristics and design information on overall evaluations

Discussion

Social robots are beginning to leave factories and labs and enter consumer markets. It is imperative for us to understand what factors will impact people's evaluations of social robots and how different design elements influence our overall evaluations and specifically judgments of the suitability of social robots for various occupations. The findings indicate that, in general, competent robots are preferred over warm robots, and appearance design is more effective than a characteristic narrative or the combination of appearance and a written description in conveying product information in a first-impression scenario.

Competence bias

Our study adds to the literature on warmth and competence perceptions, and the findings confirm that these two judgment dimensions are systemic, general and pragmatic. People use the same two dimensions to evaluate social robots. Across different design information conditions, the main effect of warm robots vs. competent robots was significant. Warm robots were judged warmer than competent robots, and competent robots were judged more competent than warm robots.

Contrary to the findings from previous literature on personal perceptions and social relationship development, which emphasize warmth as the primary and preferred dimension for perception and relationship development, our study found that, in their initial response, people place more weight on social robots' competence than on their warmth. Our results demonstrate competence bias in job suitability. In their initial judgment, people prefer competent robots to warm robots for both high and low-status jobs. They do not differentiate warm and competent robots for the suitability of interaction-based jobs. Moreover, people perceive warm and competent social robots equally for overall evaluations.

This competence bias towards social robots could be explained by people's goals and power differences between people and robots. Abele and Wojciszke (2014) argue that although warmth is typically more important than competence, this should be constrained or even reversed in contexts where the agency of others becomes crucial for individuals' goals. When people evaluate social robots for employment contexts, they pay more attention to what social robots can accomplish than how warm they are. This indicates that in a first-impression scenario, people are more interested in employing a robot to successfully accomplish a task, and less interested in developing a relationship with the social robot. The competence bias could also be explained by the power differences between social robots and human. Cislak (2013) found that having power led to an enhanced interest in others' competent traits, whereas being in a submissive position resulted in an enhanced interest in others' warmth traits. Humans, who consider themselves to have higher status, are interested in social robots' competence.

A picture is worth a thousand words, at least when it is presented alone.

Our findings clearly show that, in general, inconsistencies between appearance and characteristic narrative reduce people's perceptions and overall evaluations of social robots. For both warm robots and competent robots, people perceive them as less warm and less suitable for low-status and interaction-based jobs. The only exception is for warm robots being evaluated for competence and high-status jobs. When participants see a robot with a warm appearance with a cold characteristic narrative, they think these robots are more competent and more suitable for high-status jobs than when they see a robot with a warm appearance and warm characteristic narrative. This finding can be explained by a mixed stereotype that connects low warmth and high competence (Fiske et al., 2002; Judd, James-Hawkins, Yzerbyt, & Kashima, 2005).

Coldness was found to be a desired attribution for competence and high-status jobs. However, this mixed stereotype only translated coldness into competence in our study. Incompetence was not converted to warmth, as the stereotype content model predicts. An incompetent robot characteristic narrative made people perceive both warm robots and competent robots as less desirable.

One strong finding from this study is that people appear to judge with their eyes rather than their minds on a first impression. Our study confirmed literature on humans' bias towards visual information (Todorov, Said, Engell, & Oosterhof, 2008b; Willis & Todorov, 2006). Social robots' appearance information triggers higher perceptions and evaluations than characteristic narratives across conditions. Design of the physical appearance is an optimal channel to increase people's acceptance of social robots in a first impression. This is especially useful for warm robots. Warm robots were perceived as more competent and more suitable for all occupations under the appearance condition than the rest of the conditions.

However, the results are also paradoxical. For warm robots, when appearance information is combined with characteristic narrative, even consistently, the enhancement effect of appearance information disappears. Although not statistically significant, the previous figures show that, under this condition, people's evaluations of warm robots for warmth, competence and job suitability and overall evaluations are lower than in the appearance condition and in the characteristic narrative conditions. Thus, characteristic narrative actually takes positive effects of appearance information away for warm robots when these two design information types are combined.

This paradoxical finding seems to contradict our common sense. The more information we have, especially in the case of warm appearance plus warm characteristic narrative, should increase people's perceptions and evaluations. Our finding may be explained by people's quick evaluations of the warmth dimension. From adaptive process, people's brains are wired to quickly make primary warmth judgments when they meet a stranger, usually happening in less than 100 ms. The primary judgment of warmth is mainly governed by the implicit and automatic process (Uleman, Adil Saribay, & Gonzalez, 2008). The presentation of characteristic narrative information along with appearance information does not fit into this quick processing model; instead, it could add to cognitive load and have negative consequences on peoples' perceptions and evaluations.

Thus, appearance information alone best transfers warmth and its connected positive effects on related outcomes. When people stop and further consider characteristic narrative, the unconscious process is interrupted, and this interruption is costly to people's positive perceptions and evaluations of appearance information. This is not the case for perceived competence, which is a secondary dimension of judgment. People usually use more cues to make competence judgments, and this judgment process usually takes longer. The consistent combination of appearance and characteristic narrative will positively impact people's evaluations of competent social robots. These findings may question the common practices of the industry to combine appearance and information when introducing the product. Our results indicate that in most cases, adding the characteristic narrative will actually harm the initial acceptance of social robots, especially robots that are designed to be perceived as warm.

These findings have implications for the field of personality design in social robotics for how and when personality information is presented. Although the study only tested the description of one characteristic with three robots, the findings indicate that the first impression is not an effective time to present a user with information about the relationship they may form with the robot. This study found that people's initial judgment is to gravitate more toward robots they perceive to be practical, even if these robots have a strong cold characteristic narrative.

In general, when the characteristic narrative is added to the whole information package for people to evaluate, it diminishes the effects of physical appearance designs. The only exception is when people evaluate the perceived competence and interaction-based job suitability. When appearance information is presented with the characteristic narrative, people perceive competent robots as more competent and more suitable for interaction-based jobs than other design conditions. This finding echoes our everyday experiences when we search for a new family doctor or when we decide which professor should act as our advisor. We often review their websites and want to know more about their personalities and life stories. These personality narratives increase perceived competence and future interaction intentions. This might also explain why the characteristic narrative alone generated the highest suitability score for high-status jobs for competent robots.

The current study has limitations. First, only three top warm robots and three competent robots were selected as experiment stimuli. This could bring bias to stimuli sampling (Reeves, Yeykelis, & Cummings, 2016). It is valid to use the robots with top warmth and top competence scores because it increases the strength of the treatments. However, further studies employing both introductory interactions with physical robots and long-term relationships with physical robots are required to fully understand how generalizable these findings are and how they can be successfully employed for effective personality design. Future studies may also incorporate more robots and test how robot characteristics, such as level of anthropomorphism, influence people's perceptions and occupational suitability. In addition, further study is required to determine whether the results of testing narratives that highlight just one characteristic (warm, cold, competent, incompetent) have indications for full personality designs. This study would additionally study roles such as personal assistant, coach and companion where personality may be particularly important.

Second, although participants were randomly assigned to each condition, some conditions have more participants than other conditions (see Table 19.1). The power analysis asked for 31 per condition. The reason for the uneven distribution is that participants were disqualified if they did not answer the screening question correctly. To get the correct answer, the participants had to review the characteristic narrative carefully. We noticed that more participants were disqualified in the competent robot/characteristic narrative condition. This could present sampling bias. This uneven distribution of errors on screening questions could also be an indicator of the cognitive process participants went through during the experiment. The reasoning behind more errors in evaluations of competent robots' characteristic narrative could be a topic for future studies.

Third, this experiment cannot capture the experience of interacting with a physical robot outside lab settings. Further study may test the scenarios of an introductory interaction with a physical robot and a longer-term relationship with a physical robot.

Social robots represent a research platform for studying not only robotics but also human beings. In this study, we found that robot characteristics (warmth and competence) and design information (appearance, characteristic narrative and appearance and characteristic narrative combinations) significantly influence a robot's chance of getting a job. Future studies can further explore how attributes such as gender and race influence people's judgments of social robots.

References

Abele, A. E., & Wojciszke, B. (2014). Communal and agentic content in social cognition: A dual perspective model. In *Advances in experimental social psychology* (Vol. 50, pp. 195–255). Elsevier.

Belpaeme, T., Kennedy, J., Ramachandran, A., Scassellati, B., & Tanaka, F. (2018). Social robots for education: A review. *Science Robotics*, 3(21), eaat5954.

Bergmann, K., Eyssel, F., & Kopp, S. (2012). A second chance to make a first impression? how appearance and nonverbal behavior affect perceived warmth and competence of virtual agents over time. In *International Conference on Intelligent Virtual Agents* (pp. 126–138). Springer.

Bertrand, M., & Mullainathan, S. (2004). Are Emily and Greg more employable than Lakisha and Jamal? A field experiment on labor market discrimination. *American Economic Review*, *94*(4), 991–1013.

Biancardi, B., Cafaro, A., & Pelachaud, C. (n.d.). *Investigating user's first impressions of a virtual agent's warmth and competence traits.*

Broadbent, E., Stafford, R., & MacDonald, B. (2009). Acceptance of healthcare robots for the older population: Review and future directions. *International Journal of Social Robotics*, *1*(4), 319.

Cabibihan, J.-J., Javed, H., Ang, M., & Aljunied, S. M. (2013). Why robots? A survey on the roles and benefits of social robots in the therapy of children with autism. *International Journal of Social Robotics*, *5*(4), 593–618.

Cafaro, A., Vilhjálmsson, H. H., & Bickmore, T. (2016). First impressions in human–agent virtual encounters. *ACM Transactions on Computer-Human Interaction (TOCHI)*, *23*(4), 24.

Cislak, A. (2013). Effects of power on social perception: All your boss can see is agency. *Social Psychology*, *44*(2), 138–146.

Cohen, J. (1992). A power primer. *Psychological Bulletin*, *112*(1), 155.

Fiske, S. T. (2018). Stereotype content: Warmth and competence endure. *Current Directions in Psychological Science*, *27*(2), 67–73.

Fiske, S. T., Cuddy, A. J., & Glick, P. (2007). Universal dimensions of social cognition: Warmth and competence. *Trends in Cognitive Sciences*, *11*(2), 77–83.

Fiske, S. T., Cuddy, A. J., Glick, P., & Xu, J. (2002). A model of (often mixed) stereotype content: Competence and warmth respectively follow from perceived status and competition. *Journal of Personality and Social Psychology*, *82*(6), 878.

Goetz, J., Kiesler, S., & Powers, A. (2003). Matching robot appearance and behavior to tasks to improve human-robot cooperation. In *Proceedings of the 12th IEEE international workshop on robot and human interactive communication* (pp. 55–60). IEEE Press.

Hinds, P. J., Roberts, T. L., & Jones, H. (2004). Whose job is it anyway? A study of human-robot interaction in a collaborative task. *Human-Computer Interaction*, *19*(1), 151–181.

Hosoda, M., Stone-Romero, E. F., & Coats, G. (2003). The effects of physical attractiveness on job-related outcomes: A meta-analysis of experimental studies. *Personnel Psychology*, *56*(2), 431–462.

Judd, C. M., James-Hawkins, L., Yzerbyt, V., & Kashima, Y. (2005). Fundamental dimensions of social judgment: Understanding the relations between judgments of competence and warmth. *Journal of Personality and Social Psychology*, *89*(6), 899.

Kanda, T., Shiomi, M., Miyashita, Z., Ishiguro, H., & Hagita, N. (2009). An affective guide robot in a shopping mall. In *Proceedings of the 4th ACM/IEEE international conference on Human robot interaction* (pp. 173–180). ACM.

Kidd, C. D., & Breazeal, C. (2008, September). Robots at home: Understanding long-term human-robot interaction. In *2008 IEEE/RSJ international conference on intelligent robots and systems* (pp. 3230–3235). IEEE.

King, E. B., Mendoza, S. A., Madera, J. M., Hebl, M. R., & Knight, J. L. (2006). What's in a name? A multiracial investigation of the role of occupational stereotypes in selection decisions. *Journal of Applied Social Psychology*, *36*(5), 1145–1159.

Lee, S., Lau, I. Y., Kiesler, S., & Chiu, C.-Y. (2005). Human mental models of humanoid robots. In *Robotics and Automation, 2005. ICRA 2005. Proceedings of the 2005 IEEE International Conference on* (pp. 2767–2772). IEEE.

Li, D., Rau, P. P., & Li, Y. (2010). A cross-cultural study: Effect of robot appearance and task. *International Journal of Social Robotics*, *2*(2), 175–186.

Little, A. C., Burriss, R. P., Jones, B. C., & Roberts, S. C. (2007). Facial appearance affects voting decisions. *Evolution and Human Behavior*, *28*(1), 18–27.

Locksley, A., Hepburn, C., & Ortiz, V. (1982). Social stereotypes and judgments of individuals: An instance of the base-rate fallacy. *Journal of Experimental Social Psychology*, *18*(1), 23–42.

Palmer, C. L., & Peterson, R. D. (2016). Halo effects and the attractiveness premium in perceptions of political expertise. *American Politics Research*, *44*(2), 353–382.

Reeves, B., Hancock, J., & Liu, X. (2018). *How do people perceive social robots and what makes them effective?* Presented at the Technology, Mind, & Society, Washington, DC.

Reeves, B., & Nass, C. I. (1996). *The media equation: How people treat computers, television, and new media like real people and places.* Cambridge University Press.

Reeves, B., Yeykelis, L., & Cummings, J. J. (2016). The use of media in media psychology. *Media Psychology*, *19*(1), 49–71.

Ridgeway, C. L., & Erickson, K. G. (2000). Creating and spreading status beliefs. *American Journal of Sociology*, *106*(3), 579–615.

Rudman, L. A., & Glick, P. (2001). Prescriptive gender stereotypes and backlash toward agentic women. *Journal of Social Issues*, *57*(4), 743–762.

Todorov, A., Said, C. P., Engell, A. D., & Oosterhof, N. N. (2008a). Understanding evaluation of faces on social dimensions. *Trends in Cognitive Sciences*, *12*(12), 455–460.

Todorov, A., Said, C. P., Engell, A. D., & Oosterhof, N. N. (2008b). Understanding evaluation of faces on social dimensions. *Trends in Cognitive Sciences*, *12*(12), 455–460.

Uleman, J. S., Adil Saribay, S., & Gonzalez, C. M. (2008). Spontaneous inferences, implicit impressions, and implicit theories. *Annu. Rev. Psychol.*, *59*, 329–360.

Vollmer, A.-L., Read, R., Trippas, D., & Belpaeme, T. (2018). Children conform, adults resist: A robot group induced peer pressure on normative social conformity. *Science Robotics*, *3*(21), eaat7111.

Willis, J., & Todorov, A. (2006). First impressions: Making up your mind after a 100-ms exposure to a face. *Psychological Science*, *17*(7), 592–598.

Wojciszke, B., Bazinska, R., & Jaworski, M. (1998). On the dominance of moral categories in impression formation. *Personality and Social Psychology Bulletin*, *24*(12), 1251–1263.

Yang, G.-Z., Bellingham, J., Dupont, P. E., Fischer, P., Floridi, L., Full, R., . . . Merrifield, R. (2018). The grand challenges of science robotics. *Science Robotics*, *3*(14), 1–14.

Yang, G.-Z., Dario, P., & Kragic, D. (2018). *Social robotics – Trust, learning, and social interaction.* Science Robotics.

20

DATA QUALITY AND PRIVACY CONCERNS IN DIGITAL TRACE DATA

Insights from a Delphi study on machine learning and robots in human life

Uwe Engel and Lena Dahlhaus

The growing importance of machine learning

Machine learning (ML) represents a key link to both data analytics and human–robot interaction. The Royal Society (2017) localizes machine learning at the intersection of artificial intelligence (AI), data science, and statistics, with applications in robotics. Machine learning in society is a topic of central relevance to computational social science (CSS) because it changes both the object and methods of social science. While survey research is expected to remain a supporting pillar, the collection and analysis of digital behavioral data broaden the spectrum of social research substantially. Such data involve digital marks (including user-generated content such as commentaries, blogs, posts) people leave when surfing the web. In addition, people also leave their mark beyond this narrower sphere of social media. Human behavior increasingly takes place within other digital environments and inadvertently enriches the (potential) database of social research. Current examples involve smart-home systems, interaction with intelligent voice assistants, streaming services, positioning in transit, online measurement of (psycho-)physiological parameters when doing sport, online shopping, digital payment methods, and intelligent assistant systems in motoring. In the near future, data from autonomous driving and more refined and deepened forms of human–robot interaction will be available.

In view of the expected strong international competition in the further development of AI and ML, the growing interest in this next-generation technology comes as no surprise. The economic and scientific importance will arouse a strong and continuing interest of many stakeholders in getting applications of AI and ML diffused into the population. Looking at a key element in this development, ML, its economic power is beyond all doubt. A recent forecast expects it to contribute up to 15.7 trillion USD to the global economy in 2030, "of this $6.6 trillion is likely to come from increased productivity, and $9.1 trillion is likely to come from consumption-side effects" (Rao & Verweij, 2017), with the biggest sector gains from AI expected in retail, financial services, and healthcare. Similar figures, indicating an exponential growth of market potential of up to nearly 90 billion USD in 2025, are reported in Jenny et al.

DOI: 10.4324/9781003024583-23

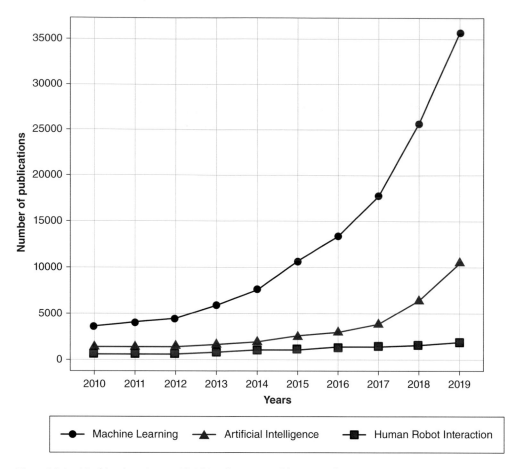

Figure 20.1 Machine learning, artificial intelligence, and human–robot interaction. Publications 2010 to 2019 (data source: web of science)

(2019). Bughin, Seong, Manyika, Chui, and Joshi (2018) assess the additional economic output due to AI on \$13 trillion by 2030, boosting global GDP by about 1.2 percent a year.

In science, too, ML is a topic of exponentially growing interest (Figure 20.1). Though computer science and closely related disciplines account for the biggest proportion of publications on machine learning, social science disciplines (economics, communication science, political science, and sociology) are rapidly catching up. In part, this interest stems from the expected impact of ML-based applications on today's and future societies, but the prospect of using ML for scientific inference has gained importance (Molina & Garip, 2019). The previous market figures reveal the interest of economic researchers in the future impact of ML and AI technologies on society (Bolton, Machová, Kovacova, & Valaskova, 2018; Athey, 2018). Political scientists use machine-learning models to analyze voting behavior, the outcome of elections (Kim, Alvarez, & Ramirez, 2020), and even the detection of possible fraudulent voting behavior (Zhang, Alvarez, & Levin, 2019). As digital trace data often come in the form of textual data, for instance, tweets, blog posts, and message board entries, the growing opportunities to apply new techniques has led to a better understanding of how online communication works (Monroe, Colaresi, & Quinn, 2008; Chatterjee et al., 2019).

The digitization of society is a driving force for this research, though a coherent social-science agenda appears still developable. Data often precede the social theory needed for understanding (Radford & Joseph, 2020). ML offers enriched ways of data analytics and can also contribute to social theory in a rapidly changing, digitized world.

How will AI and robotics shape society and human life in the medium run?

Economic competition and material wealth

The growing importance of machine learning methods comes with the growing impact of artificial intelligence and robotics on human life. Particularly, the *destructive competition for permanent appointments* is a popular subject of public debate. A worst-case scenario pictures a situation that affects even the high-skilled middle class. It describes a job market where AI handles a steadily increasing part even of highly skilled routine jobs. This trend goes along with a declining demand for workforce, forcing people into precarious employment on digital crowd-working platforms and threatening even the stability of democracy. In view of the Delphi responses reported in the appendix to this chapter (Table 20.A1), this is an unlikely scenario. Though AI is expected to shape the job market in general, highly qualified staff is regarded as not that concerned, at least not for the near future. While 38 percent of the Delphi respondents anticipate a clear reduction of permanent appointments due to AI in Germany in 2030, the survey's reference year, only 20 percent believe in corresponding job losses for highly skilled academic personnel. In this respect, the prevailing expert opinion (78 percent) anticipates primarily changing job specifications due to AI.

Destructive competition for jobs is the unlikely worst-case scenario. A similarly unlikely opposite pole is a scenario based on the wealth and promise of AI. It depicts a situation in which AI has revolutionized human life, in which this technology has contributed much to the wealth of people, and in which German AI research is leading in the world. It also stresses that Germany sustained its competitive position in worldwide digitization. The Delphi respondents also rate this scenario as being unlikely overall (Table 20.A1). In relation to the involved material wealth aspect, response behavior reveals a prevalence of unlikely (41 percent) over likely (15 percent), with 44 percent of respondents voting for the mid-category "possibly".

Human–robot interaction

A third scenario describes a situation in which the social interaction of humans and robots is an expression of societal normality. In this scenario, robots belong to the daily routine of people and are involved in their communication as a matter of course. Robots are available even for personal talks in critical life situations. While the Delphi respondents regard this communication scenario primarily as becoming "possibly" a reality, they attest that the "AI assists humans" scenario is a likely perspective (Table 20.A1). For the reference year 2030, this scenario anticipates a situation in which a highly efficient and reliable AI reduces, using its assistance function, the degrees of freedom of human actions and decisions. It pictures a situation in which a multiplicity of AI-assistant systems exists and supports human action and decision-making. It insinuates that, without a human factor involved, even the most difficult tasks were now carried out more reliably, efficiently, and error free.

Such scenarios are, of course, *imagined future situations* whose relevance depends essentially on their real, later occurrence. We assume that the Delphi responses provide reasonable estimates of the anticipated probabilities of occurrence and suggest a detailed look at the various *single* dimensions that together constitute *the complex* situation of a scenario. Table 20.A2 presents a selection of such single scales to the communication and assistance scenario. One argument says that the findings unfold relevance even beyond their primarily intended scopes, fields of AI, or robot application, in fact, for social research in CSS that uses similar techniques in its future praxis.

Robots provide counseling, guidance, and consultation

If we look ten years ahead: Will then robots tend to replace humans situationally in interpersonal communication, will then specialized robots provide psychological advice (counseling), will humans then trust AI more than the humans themselves, will AI assist in rational choice (guidance), will humans seek a first doctor's advice from a robot in telemedicine (consultation)? The answer to all these questions is "probably not" if we follow the assessments in Table 20. A2 (upper segment). The expert group is quite pessimistic about robots providing required guidance, counseling, and consultation, at least by the reference year 2030. This skepticism is particularly pronounced in the case of the replacement item: it hardly appears conceivable that robots will replace humans in interpersonal communication.

Digital lifestyles

How will digital lifestyles such as the quantified self and lifelogging (Selke, 2014) evolve in the middle run? If we look ten years ahead: The Delphi respondents consider it primarily possible that lifelogging will be followed by communication of humans with personal avatars about continuously recorded life and behavioral data (Table 20.A2, middle segment). In addition, will today's digital voice assistants then have become all-embracing intelligent personal advisors, assisting humans in activities and decisions in all imaginable life situations, at home and in transit? The answer is again that it is regarded as possible that digital assistants will, in 2030, have become personal avatars as steady advisory life companions at home and en route. The same response tendency is true for the statement that "robots keep lonely people of different age company at home".

Human–robot communication

The idea of robots specialized in communication encounters obvious skepticism. Two issues contribute to this view. Interpersonal communication is genuinely human. Robots cannot replace humans that easily because they miss the human factor. A human is human; a machine is a machine. If so, even the best-qualified robots cannot simply replace humans easily in interpersonal communication. In addition, communication requires ambitious linguistic, cognitive, and emotional skills – in the context of counseling, guidance, and consultation and everyday contexts. While robots keeping *older* people company at home is rated quite probable (Table 20. A2, lower segment), more doubt resonates in robots keeping *lonely* people of *different ages* company at home (as indicated previously). Explanatory factors involve the "missing human factor" and lacking confidence in the reachability of required technical skills by the reference year 2030.

Acceptance and human–robot interaction interface to social research in CSS

Despite their obvious skepticism in the human–robot interaction (HRI) field expressed previously, the Delphi respondents expect that numerous AI assistant systems will have raised the quality of life in 2030 considerably (Table 20.A2, lower segment). This raises the question of what an increasing spread of HRI applications would imply for social research in CSS. Provided that such applications will be engineered in the near and medium-term future, their diffusion in the population(s) will depend strongly on the gain of social and ethical acceptance therein. Both are far away from being natural. In 2013, when Google aimed to launch the Google Glass, privacy advocates criticized its capability of filming people who were unaware of being filmed and the storage of data on business servers and were successful in halting the ongoing launch of the product. A likely scenario delineates societal conflict about ethical guidelines for trustworthy AI, liability rules, and ethical programming (Table 20.A1). Diffusion depends on acceptance, and acceptance depends on further factors, such as confidence in the trustworthiness of a technology and open-mindedness towards technological innovation. Social and ethical acceptance is also a key factor in survey participation, and it will become a key factor in any social research that collects digital trace data using machine-learning methods.

At first glance, HRI and social research might appear quite unrelated. However, both "acceptance" and the possibility of employing HRI applications in social research link the two fields. A case in point for a research field that lends itself to such a development is experience-sampled, real-time, and mixed self-report/sensor measurements for the study of daily life (Schwarz, 2012; Intille, 2012). Despite being affected by measurement errors due to social desirability bias and sampling bias and being costly to collect, self-reported survey data remain the most common data type. In recent years, studies based on a combination of self-reported and sensor-based data collection became increasingly popular due to the increased use of smartphones and wearables. The possibility of observing the actual behavior of participants in real time has led to substantial insights in the fields of health science (Can, Arnrich, & Ersoy, 2019; Chastin et al., 2018; Garcia-Ceja et al., 2018) and is also a promising tool for social science research. Once too expensive to equip large enough numbers of participants, sensor data have become more available for use in social research. These data prove valuable assets to differentiate between self-reported behavior and actual behavior, for example, concerning smartphone use (Jones-Jang et al., 2020) or the Internet (Araujo, Wonneberger, Neijens, & de Vreese, 2017; Revilla, Ochoa, & Loewe, 2017).

Digital trace data

Unobtrusive but not error free

Digital trace data promise the avoidance of sources of error that usually come along with survey designs. Survey interviews typically consist of series of questions and response sequences in designed interview contexts. As such, a response to a survey question reflects not only the response *to its subject*. It also reflects the way the question is worded; if an open, closed, or hybrid response format is used; which specific response format is used; if an interviewer mediates the question–response sequences; the order in which these sequences are presented to the respondent; if an interview is conducted in person, over the phone, or self-administered on the Internet; and even more. Beyond the core response to the subject of a survey question itself, further sources of response variation thus involve question wordings, mode and response effects, interviewer effects, social–desirability effects, and the possibility of motivated misreporting. Not least, the awareness of being part or even subject of research is regarded as an influencing factor. This all is well known and confirmed by numerous studies from survey methodology (e.g., Tourangeau, Rips, & Rasinski, 2000; Weisberg, 2009; Engel, Bartsch, Schnabel, & Vehre, 2012).

Consider specifically the case of motivated misreporting (Tourangeau, Kreuter, & Eckman, 2015): If the subject is some inquired behavior, it is fully comprehensible that direct observation of this behavior might be preferable over an error-prone account of this behavior given in a survey interview. It is even better if this observation remains unnoticed by the observed persons, because this rules out any behavioral reaction to being observed from the outset. If someone does not know that s(he) is part/subject of research, s(he) cannot react to such an insight – and hence no research reactivity can emerge from such an insight. Because human behavior increasingly takes place in digital environments (social media and beyond), observation of behavior is frequently transformed to *digital* observation in either of two basic forms: the observation of user-generated content (text data) and observation of the marks people leave when using the Internet (metadata). Both these textual data and the metadata represent digitally observed *behavioral* traces if the generation of content is regarded as a model of behavior, and the generated content is left in the digital space. That others take notice of ("observe") this content afterward may then be intended by the author, may occur inadvertently, or may even be unwanted. In any of these cases, it would be misleading to assume that this new class of data is error-free only because it is not obtained in conscious response to a research inquiry. Error-free digital trace data vs. error-prone survey data insinuates an incorrect contrast. Instead, digital trace data are by no means error free simply because they are collected in an "unobtrusive" (Webb et al., 1966 [2000]) manner. Sources of error exist in such data, too, and include the error we would like to pay special attention to: the systematic protection against tracking on the Internet. In studying variation in the use of shielding techniques, we study implicit variation in the acceptance of special machine-learning uses in society.

Do guarding techniques against tracking on the Internet impair digital data quality?

Web surfers can guard themselves increasingly easily against tracking on the Internet using standard built-in, privacy-enhancing modern browsers such as Firefox and Chrome; browser add-ons; virtual private networks (VPNs); and the Onion Router (Tor). Another way of protecting privacy is careful and deliberate surfing behavior, such as avoiding websites surfers deem doubtful and by refusing to give consent to cookies. Previous research points to Internet users being generally aware of the economic profits being generated with their data and therefore assessing their personal risk related to their use of online services (Gerber, Reinheimer, & Volkamer, 2019). Modern web browsers include the technical ability to restrict the traces users leave behind while browsing; browser-based privacy-enhancing technologies are often explicitly advertised as a feature of the given product (Google Chrome, 2020). After the initial installation, the user may even be reminded to select privacy preferences to protect themselves from tracking (Google Chrome, 2020; Apple, 2020; Mozilla Foundation, 2020). It is safe to say that the statement about caring about the users' safety has become a marked advantage of its own, and the user's choice of a browser directly affects the privacy experience (Al Fannah & Li, 2017).

If people guard themselves against tracking by any means, does this impair the data quality of digital trace data? Maybe only negligible random variation is emerging from such shielding behavior, in the end producing only not-biasing random noise in the data. Maybe the alternative assumption of systematic bias proves true. Then the question is, what are the relevant sources of variation? In the following, we consider the acceptance of new technology as a core element rooted in individuals' self-images and lifestyle preferences.

Current state of research on privacy and privacy-enhancing technologies

Following the rise of the world wide web, research on Internet users' privacy concerns emerged in the early 2000s. Prior studies (Mathur, Vitak, Narayanan, & Chetty, 2018; Gerber et al., 2019) on the usage of privacy-enhancing technologies points to users and non-users being generally aware of the basic mechanisms of online tracking. However, the coherence between this basic knowledge, resulting in changes in the users' behavior, and finally, the actual application of one or even multiple methods of protecting privacy still needs further research. The topic of data privacy in general or the use of privacy-enhancing technologies especially is often focused either on technical aspects or in relation to specific groups, for example, users of a specific social network such as Facebook (Van Schaik, 2018; Hargittai, 2015). In the past, studies in the field of computational social science focused heavily on digital trace data obtained in such social network settings, often using non-random samples that led to valuable findings about how and what people communicate in specific online scenarios (Hargittai, 2015; Liu, Yao, Yang, & Tu, 2017), but the lack of generalizability of the results prevails. Attitudes towards data privacy can be assumed to be culturally specific (Trepte et al., 2017; Potoglou, Dunkerley, Patil, & Robinson, 2017). Therefore, further research is needed to draw a comprehensive picture of how different cultures influence the users' requests for the implementation of data privacy guidelines. Previous findings of users' application of privacy-enhancing technologies often either focus strongly on the technical mechanisms from a computer science point of view or examine peoples' attitudes and behaviors from the perspective of the social sciences. Though plenty of findings (Spiekermann, Acquisti, Böhme, & Hui, 2015; Potoglou et al., 2017; Trepte et al., 2017) suggest the importance of addressing peoples' privacy concerns, the implications of people reacting to perceived threats accruing from their online behavior and the resulting influence on the quality of digital trace data are not yet sufficiently discussed. While the problems arising from unit-nonresponse have been in the focus of survey methodologists for a long time, methodological concerns from the perspective of researchers' aiming at the use of digital trace data are still developing (Olteanu, Kıcıman, & Castillo, 2018). The integration of survey data and digital trace data seems promising, but a potential pitfall is the possible bias of the survey data (Stier, Breuer, Siegers, & Thorson, 2020; Jürgens, Stark, & Magin, 2020).

Accepting new technology: AI-driven advice, robots in human life, and protection from tracking

"Quantified Self" designates a self-tracking lifestyle that uses digital technologies. It is directed toward self-improvement and consists of regularly monitoring and recording, often measuring elements of one's behavior or bodily functions (Lupton, 2016). It is a data-driven lifestyle that replaces the vagaries of intuition with more reliable evidence. "Once you know the facts, you can live by them" (Lupton, 2016). Self-tracking may involve target publicity and, that way, approach a competitive lifestyle through which individuals seek social recognition. Sociology knows different facets of how individuals compete for social recognition, for instance, via the acquisition of occupational prestige, even though private life is by no means less meaningful in this respect. Think of Veblen's (1899/2005) famous "conspicuous consumption" and the competitive field of fashion. Fashion means couture, and fashion means other products as well, for instance, technical equipment. Being among the first who try new technology is a case in point for acquiring prestige through a competitive lifestyle element beyond the narrower occupational sphere. A self-image of being open-minded toward digital innovation is likely to accompany the involvement in this field of competition. Rogers (2003) coined the terms innovator and early adopter to refer to individuals who want to be among the first to explore new technological innovations.

In the case of machine learning and social robots, exactly such early adopters of respective services are likely to contribute much to the acceptance of corresponding and, in part, already upcoming applications, such as assistant robots for elderly care. This acceptance is likely to be crucial because current experiences of human–robot communication may be evaluated critically, for instance, chatbots in customer service and, first and foremost, social bots flooding social networks and shaping opinion-forming processes and political propaganda.

Privacy is of utmost importance to many people. Implementing the General Data Protection Regulation (GDPR) in 2018 is likely to have contributed to an increased awareness of privacy risks when using websites, social networks, and online services. However, even if privacy ranks high, other threats to personal life may also rank highly. To date, little is known about how personal privacy concerns result in protection behavior against tracking if set in a comparative context.

The question is if people treat privacy as an isolated issue or if they embed privacy evaluations in a comparative risk perspective. Such a perspective is suggested by a theory that regards risk perception as a function of sociopolitical worldviews and lifestyles (Wildavsky & Dake, 1990). The working hypothesis states that people choose what and why to fear in line with such basic orientations. Someone may accordingly fear a possible economic downturn in Europe more than crime; someone else may fear political extremism more than abuse/ trade of personal data on the Internet; yet others may fear digitization and artificial intelligence more than, for example, Brexit; and still others may fear climate change more than everything else, in this spirit. Rank order at the individual, not aggregate, level is decisive if one tries to understand related behavior. Then, it is of utmost importance to understand that the evaluation of risks implies an emotional dimension. The technical term "risk perception" involves much more than a purely perceptual component. It implies both cognitive and evaluative components and, with respect to the latter component, also possible feelings of risk (Slovic, 2010). In the present case, such feelings relate to ease with several anticipated scenarios of HRI.

Bremen AI Delphi study

A large Delphi survey of scientists and politicians in the Bremen area (Germany) was conducted to let scientists and politicians evaluate several HRI scenarios in and outside social media. These scenarios were delineated previously.

The Delphi technique was developed to obtain forecasts based on panels of experts (Linstone & Turoff, 2011). Core features of Delphi studies involve their administration in rounds (each member of an expert group is interviewed repeatedly) and the disclosure of *statistical results* from previous rounds. Participants have the opportunity to adjust their answers successively while taking notice of the respective overall picture of answers (i.e., of [parameters of] their respective frequency distribution), ideally until a consensus is achieved or until a predefined number of rounds is reached. Originally the conduct of Delphi surveys was very time consuming due to the necessity of preparing the intermediate statistical results for the successive interview rounds. Currently, Delphi studies are conducted online, sometimes even in social networks (Haynes & Shelton, 2018). In doing so, the web survey mode offers the beneficial programmable option of integrating two rounds in each interview. This works in *real time*: a first assessment is followed by presenting each respondent with the frequency distribution *of all first assessments* and an immediate follow-up question for reassessing the initial answer in the light of this intermediate statistical result. In the present study, this option is used for assessing and reassessing the expected probability of occurrence of the Delphi scenarios reported on previously.

A population survey about the social and ethical acceptance of artificial intelligence and social robots accompanies this Delphi survey. Findings are covered in the following. Respondents were asked in detail about their images of robots and their attitudes towards AI and some fields of AI application. They were also asked about their readiness for using AI applications, for instance, in the context of elderly care. Related to the Delphi, respondents were asked how comfortable they felt with the anticipated scenarios of HRI. Further topics involve trustworthy AI, risk perception and protection against tracking on the Internet, technical innovation, and self-image. Study details are given in the appendix of this chapter.

Findings from the population survey

Attitudes towards robots and AI

Three pillars form the structure of attitudes toward robots and artificial intelligence: the perceived necessity and goodness of this technology for society, its technical reliability, and the integrity of its application. In short, the analysis confirms the perceived necessity of robots/AI and questions its reliability and integrity at the same time. Even though mean values tightly below the upper-scale end of "quite certain" reveal a clearly positive image of robots and AI, the technology is at best acknowledged as being "possibly" safe for humans. Even more skepticism becomes apparent in the evaluation of its reliability (being error free) and its trustworthiness. In this regard, the mean values range in the middle of "probably not" and "possibly" (Table 20.A3). We observe both a high degree of basic acceptance of robots/AI in society and much scope to maximize this potential.

The latent correlations displayed in Table 20.1 indicate the expected structure among the three attitudes: the more pronounced one attitude is, the more pronounced the other. This is the expected result. While the pertaining factor loadings (Table 20.A3) point to an acceptable convergent validity of the assumed structure of attitudes, the factor correlations displayed here indicate at the same time an acceptable degree of discriminant validity: the factor correlations are substantially high, though not too high to question the involved assumption of three *distinct* attitudes toward robots and AI. Beyond that internal structure, all three attitudes correlate with the imagination of how one would feel in a series of fictitious situations of HRI. Table 20.A4 lists the eight situations whose evaluation underlies this emotional factor. Table 20.1 shows that the more respondents feel at ease with the imagination of these HRI scenarios, the more robots and AI are regarded as good for society, safe for humans, and trustfully deployed.

Most remarkable is, in turn, the high relevance of this emotional component for the anticipated use of AI-driven advice. If people condition their decisions on the anticipated consequences these are expected to educe, AI may assist in evaluating these possible consequences, thereby helping to arrive at the best possible decisions. However, how likely is it that people will apply corresponding smartphone apps in the future? From today's point of view, respondents do rate this by trend as "probably not", as the mean values in Table 20.A3 indicate. However, the more they feel at ease with imagining situations of HRI, the more they would be inclined to use such AI-driven equipment. Table 20.1 shows that both factors yield comparably the highest correlation in exactly that case.

Table 20.1 Latent factor correlations among attitudes and feelings towards robots and AI, the self-image as a person being open-minded to technological innovation, and the anticipated use of AI-driven advice

	AI is good for society	AI is safe for humans	AI is trustfully deployed	Feel at ease with the use of	Would seek AI-driven advice
AI is safe for humans	0.79				
AI is trustfully deployed	0.57	0.45			
Feel at ease with the anticipated use of	0.66	0.59	0.48		
Would seek AI-driven advice	0.56	0.50	0.27	0.66	
Self-image: Open-minded person	0.53	0.38	0.21	0.62	0.31

Confirmatory factor analysis (CFA) is detailed in the appendix to this chapter, Tables 20.A3 and 20.A4.

Comparative risk perception

Respondents were asked to rank the 5 potential risks they worry about most from the list of 14 potential risks presented in Table 20.2. Because there exist $w = G!/(G-g)!$ ways in which g objects can be selected from a group of G objects, the a priori probability *of each such individual selection* is only $p = 1/240,240 = 4.16 \times 10^{-6}$. This probability is vanishingly small, virtually zero, and indicates the occurrence of a single sequence we would have to expect by chance. In sufficiently large samples (with $n \geq w$), this figure could be used as a benchmark to evaluate *observed ps* of sequences. Here, this probability is a background clue that may help assess the quite even distribution of observed risk sequences: 216 trials yielded 132 different sequences of TOP 5 risks, of which 90 sequences occurred just once, 18 twice, 13 triply, 9 four times, 1 five times, and 1 eight times.

An alternative approach disregards the order in which any of the g objects became elements of an individual selection. Then the number of ways in which subsets of g objects can be formed from sets of G objects reduces to

$$c = \binom{G}{g} = \frac{G!}{g! \times (G-g)!}$$

combinations, here to $c = 2002$ possible subsets and an *a priori* probability of each such subset of $p = 1/2002 = 5.0 \times 10^{-4}$. This, again, is a tiny figure. It indicates the occurrence of a combination (subset) of the TOP 5 risks in repeated trials we would have to expect by chance. In the case of $n \geq c$, this figure could be used for benchmarking the ps of observed combinations. The present sample size is a limiting factor, however, because it truncates the lower limit of the scale of observable proportions at a point *above this* theoretical figure, namely at $1/216 = 0.0046$. We limit ourselves thus to computing only the proportion that a given potential risk is part of the TOP 5 risk set of a respondent (Table 20.2). Particularly striking is the top priority given to climate change, political extremism, and hate on the Internet, while abuse/trade of personal data ranks clearly lower, and digitization and artificial intelligence is rarely part of any respondent's TOP 5 risk set.

Assuming no causality, if we would know the attitudes and feelings towards robots and AI of a person and if we would know that person's self-image, would it be possible to predict *on*

Table 20.2 Fourteen risks in comparative perspective

	Proportion (element is part of TOP 5 risk set)
Climate change	0.6713
Political extremism/assaults	0.6574
Intolerance/hate on the Internet	0.5926
Abuse/trade of personal data on the Internet	0.3796
Crime	0.3750
Migration/refugee issue	0.2917
War in the Middle East	0.2639
Possible economic downturn in Europe	0.2454
Interest policy of European Central Bank (ECB)	0.1806
Trade dispute with USA/between USA and China	0.1620
5G mobile service standard of Chinese Huawei corporation	0.1620
Digitization/artificial intelligence	0.1111
Great Britain's step out of European Union ("Brexit")	0.0926
Other	0.0370

this basis the current risk perception of that person? The answer is "yes", though the prediction would have limited predictive power only (pseudo-R^2 = 0.057). If the analysis is targeted on the odds that "abuse/trade of personal data on the Internet" is part of the TOP 5 set of perceived risks, a binary logistic regression analysis reveals notably three relevant predictors out of the set of variables from the CFA reported previously. Considering standardized coefficients $e^{b \times s(x)}$ (if $p < 0.05$), the reference odds of 0.69 change by a factor of 1.7 per standard deviation change in the belief that AI is trustfully deployed. This finding appears contradictory at first glance because it indicates that the strength of this belief *increases* the odds of perceiving the data–abuse risk instead of decreasing it. The same applies to the finding that these odds change by a factor of 1.9 per standard deviation change in the self-image of a person as someone who is open-minded to technological innovation. Here, too, one might expect a multiplying factor below the benchmark of 1.0. However, we possibly observe here two sensitizing effects *that make people more aware of* the data–abuse risk in society. Finally, aforesaid odds change by a factor of 0.4 per standard deviation change in feeling at ease with the scenarios of HRI described in Table 20.A4. The odds that "abuse/trade of personal data on the Internet" is part of the TOP 5 set of perceived risks thus appears associated with the discomfort that imagining possible scenarios of HRI conveys to people. This emotionally colored imagination of what might happen in the future is even more effective in relation to another risk. If the analysis is targeted on the odds that "digitization/artificial intelligence" is part of the TOP 5 set of perceived risks, these odds are decreased by a factor of 0.4 per standard deviation change in feeling at ease with the scenarios of HRI (considering again $e^{b \times s(x)}$ if $p < 0.05$: 0.090 × 0.4; pseudo-R^2 = 0.107).

Protection against tracking on the Internet

Do attitudes and feelings toward robots/AI and AI-driven advice have predictive power for the way people protect themselves from being tracked on the Internet? Table 20.3 reveals a differential picture in this regard. The use of technical means can be predicted comparably well.

Table 20.3 Odds of technical and behavioral forms of protection against tracking on the Internet and their expected change per standard deviation change in particular predictor variables

Target variables / Predictor variables	PCA F1			PCA F2	
	VPN	BROWSER ADD-ON	COOKIES	TRUST WORTHY	INFO
Reference odds (intercept)	0.27	1.70	0.27	1.71	1.88
Would seek AI-driven advice (factor scores)	0.25	0.54			
Feel at ease with anticipated scenarios of human–robot interaction (factor scores)	4.09	1.97	0.54	0.5	
Abuse/trade of personal data on the Internet is part of the TOP 5 set of perceived risks	1.82		1.74		
Degree of belief: during surfing the web, automatically incurring use data are protected against abuse (5-point scale)	0.56	0.63			
5G mobile service standard of Chinese Huawei Corporation is part of the TOP 5 set of perceived risks		0.64			1.71
Self-image: Open-minded person (factor scores)			2.1	1.53	
AI is safe for humans (factor scores)					0.53
Pseudo-R^2 (McFadden)	0.158	0.088	0.118	0.043	0.082
Target behavior is observed (in percent):	17.8%	35.1%	31.7%	63.6%	67.8%

Binary logistic regression equations estimated using weighted sample data. Column by column is displayed: $e^{b \times s(x)}$ (if $p \le 0.05$). Target variables: *VPN* Use of Virtual Private Networks; *BROWSER ADD-ON* Use of special browser add-ons that impede tracking; *COOKIES* Do not accept cookies when visiting web sites; *TRUSTWORTHY* Visit only web sites believed to be trustworthy; *INFO* Do preferably reveal no information on the Internet. Two-step procedure: first, all six scales (latent factor scores) from previous CFA analysis plus three comparative risk-perception indicators (abuse/trade of personal data, Huawei's 5G standard, digitization/AI is part of the TOP 5 risk set, respectively) plus the previous degree of belief in one's web-surfing data being protected against abuse) were used as the respective set of predictor variables. Second, each equation is then re-estimated, including only the statistically significant estimates of effect from step 1. A related principal component analysis reveals that VPN and BROWSER ADD-ON form a first component, TRUSTWORTHY and INFO another, with COOKIES loading on both components (PCA Oblimin-rotated, factors practically uncorrelated: −0.01). The standardization rule follows Long & Freese, 2006, p. 178.

The odds of applying VPNs, for instance, are modified by a series of statistically significant multipliers:

$$Odds(VPN) = 0.27 \times 0.25 \times 4.09 \times 1.82 \times 0.56$$

Using 1.0 again as a benchmark for an assessment, the equation shows that the odds of applying VPNs become 0.25 times smaller per standard deviation change in the vision of seeking AI-driven advice in the future. Similarly, the odds of using relevant browser add-ons produce the same change in the vision of seeking AI-driven advice, thereby pointing to some personal lack of concern with the tracking topic and thus the need to protect oneself against this practice by technical means. At the same time, the vision of seeking AI-driven advice leaves protection by behavioral means unaffected.

An influential factor is if people feel at ease with the anticipated scenarios of human robot interaction. Table 20.3 shows that the odds of applying VPNs become 4.09 times larger per standard deviation change in the felt comfort with such scenarios. While the use of relevant browser add-ons is similarly affected in relation to cookies and trustworthiness, "felt comfort" with these scenarios takes effect in the opposite direction. It lets people rely more on technical than behavioral means.

Risk perception turns out to be a relevant predictor, especially for the use of technical means. For instance, if abuse/trade of personal data on the Internet is part of the personal TOP 5 risk set, then the odds of using VPNs are expected to become 1.82 times larger per standard deviation. Equivalently, the odds are estimated to be 0.56 times smaller per standard deviation change in the belief that one's Internet use data are protected against abuse. A similar prediction concerns the odds of using relevant browser add-ons. Regarding mobile phone usage, if the 5G standard in question is part of the TOP 5 risk set, respondents tend particularly to a behavioral means, in fact, the abdication of revealing information. Finally, two effects are noteworthy: A person's self-image as being open-minded toward technological innovation favors behavioral means of guarding against tracking (only visiting trustworthy web sites, not accepting cookies), while the belief that AI is safe for humans decreases the odds of revealing no information on the Internet.

Concluding remarks

Digital trace data promise the avoidance of sources of error that usually accompany survey designs (particularly survey mode and response effects and motivated misreporting). However, error-free behavioral trace data vs. error-prone survey data insinuates a wrong contrast. Digital trace data are by no means error free only because such data are collected in an "unobtrusive" (Webb et al., 1966 [2000]) manner. The analysis has drawn attention to just one such source of error, the potentially distorting effect due to a systematic protection against tracking on the Internet. In doing so, the analysis revealed systematic variation in the use of both technical and behavioral shielding practices, most notably variation due to (a) the felt ease with anticipated HRI scenarios along with some related attitudes towards robots and AI, (b) a respondent's comparative risk perception, and (c) the self-image as a person who is open-minded toward technical innovation. In studying variation in the use of shielding practices, we implicitly also studied variation in the acceptance of special machine-learning usages in society.

Appendix
THE BREMEN AI DELPHI STUDY

Standard scale applied throughout the Delphi and the population survey

Comparable responses were ensured by a scale consistently employed throughout the two involved surveys, the Delphi and the population survey. Following recommended practice (Schnell, 2012), this standard scale rates the degree of belief in the validity of statements using an ordinal scale that ranges from 1 = "not at all", 2 = "probably not", 3 = "possibly", and 4 = "quite probable", to 5 = "quite certain". Representing these categories by their dedicated figures 1, . . ., 5, interpolated quartiles were computed for each such frequency distribution. Throughout this chapter, this is the first (Q_1), second (Q_2), and third (Q_3) quartile to obtain that way a suitable mean estimate $(Q_2 = \text{median})$ and the corners of the interquartile range of the 50 percent middle responses. In addition, the ordinal scale level in the confirmatory factor analyses is considered by specifying probit regressions.

Delphi survey of scientists and stakeholders

Selection frame and selection procedure

Sample design: We invited 1826 experts from two different backgrounds to participate in the Bremen AI Delphi Study, namely 1359 members of Bremen's scientific community and a diverse group of 467 people of Bremen's political landscape. The expert group of the Bremen scientific community included scientists affiliated with one of Bremen's public or private universities at the time of the survey. The prerequisite for participation was holding a doctorate or a professorship. Institutions included the University of Bremen, the City University of Applied Science, the Jacobs University Bremen, the University of Applied Sciences Bremerhaven, the Apollon University of Applied Science, the Bremen School of Public Administration, and institutes affiliated with those. Disciplines selected from social sciences included economics, sociology, political science, health science/public health, cultural science, pedagogy, media and communication science, linguistics, psychology, philosophy, and history. The field of STEM disciplines was represented by professionals in engineering, mathematics, robotics, and computer science.

Natural sciences included physics, chemistry, biology, and earth science. The group of experts of politics/officials/stakeholders included members of the Bremen Parliament (all party affiliations) and officials serving in senate departments. The group of stakeholders included union representatives, executives of organizations of employer representation, and pastors of Bremen's Catholic and Protestant parishes. Invitations were sent via personalized e-mail to the professional address, and reminders were sent if no response was received within two weeks. Excluding those where e-mails came back as undeliverable or if respondents reported their inability to participate due to language barriers (153), the Delphi sample achieved a response rate of 17.8 percent ($n = 297$).

Questionnaire design

The questionnaire involves scenarios in line with five basic themes at the intersection of AI and society: competition, wealth, communication, conflict, and assistance. These scenarios were delineated briefly in "How Will AI and Robotics Shape Society and Human Life in the Medium Run?" Each scenario refers to the reference year of 2030 and follows a clear structure: In an initial block, the scenario was deliberately pictured as a larger context and not as a narrowly defined situation. Participants first assessed the question "What do you expect: Will this scenario become a reality?" using an open response format and then reassessed *this pictured context* in the light of the frequency distribution of all assessments obtained to then in the Delphi sample. In a subsequent block, each respondent was asked to rate the dimensions involved in that context *also separately* – employing the standard response scale "not at all", "probably not", "possibly", "quite probable", and "quite certain" throughout most of the survey. In the following, Table 20.A1 reports on findings from the initial scenario blocks, and Table 20.A2 presents a small selection of ratings of single situational dimensions of one of the scenarios, in fact, the "communication scenario".

Findings from the Delphi survey

Table 20.A1 Will the scenario have become a reality in 2030, the reference year of each scenario?

	Quartiles			Agreement	Rank correlation			
	Q_1	Q_2	Q_3	κ	Kendall's τ_b			
Scenario					Wealth	Comm.	Conflict	Assistance
Competition	1.8	2.4	3.1	0.84	−0.02	0.14	0.15	0.01
Wealth	2.0	2.7	3.4	0.83		0.09	−0.06	0.01
Communication	2.1	2.9	3.8	0.81			0.08	0.15
Conflict	2.6	3.6	4.2	0.77				0.04
Assistance	2.9	3.6	4.1	0.75				

Entries in a row: first, second, third interpolated quartiles of first assessments, weighted kappa of first assessment and reassessment in the light of the frequency distribution of the former, and Kendall's tau rank correlations. Weighted κ is defined as the probability of observed matches minus the probability of matches expected by chance, divided by one minus the probability of expected matches. That way, κ expresses the excess of observed over expected agreement as share in the maximal possible excess. A weighted κ of 0.84, for instance, indicates that the observed agreement of assessment and reassessment exceeds the expected agreement by 84 percent of the maximum possible excess. R package used for computation: "psych".

Table 20.A2 Expectations concerning aspects of future human–robot communication

			Probably not = included, quite probable = excluded
1.7	2.3	3.1	Robots tend to replace humans situationally in interpersonal communication
1.7	2.3	3.2	Counseling – Specialized robots provide psychological advice
1.8	2.3	3.0	Humans trust AI more than the human himself
2.0	2.7	3.5	Guidance – Cognitive AI-assistance in rational choice
2.0	2.8	3.6	Consultation – seek a first doctor's advice from a robot in telemedicine
			Probably not = excluded, quite probable = excluded -> focused on "possibly"
2.1	2.8	3.5	Lifelogging is followed by communication of humans with personal avatars about their continuously recorded life data and behavioral data
2.1	2.9	3.5	Digital assistants have become personal avatars as steady advisory life companions at home and en route.
2.2	3.0	3.8	Robots keep lonely people of different age company at home
			Probably not = excluded, quite probable = included
2.7	3.4	4.0	Robots keep old people company at home
2.6	3.8	4.3	Bots communicate as perfectly as humans
3.1	3.8	4.3	AI and robots take on more and more assistant functions in the life of humans and contribute much to their quality of life

Population survey

Sample design and adjustment for unit nonresponse

Following a quasi-randomization approach (Elliott & Valliant, 2017), the overall sample consists of a combined probability and non-probability sample. A probability sample of residents aged 18+ is drawn from the population register of the municipality of Bremen and used as a reference sample for the estimation of inclusion probabilities for an analog volunteer sample. This probability sample achieved a response rate of 2.5 percent ($N = 108$).

Based on the available register information (age, gender, urban district) and the random response model (Bethlehem, 2009), inclusion probabilities were estimated and used to derive weights for an adjustment of the probability sample for possible unit-nonresponse bias. We normalized this weight variable to a mean value of one to preserve the initial sample size. Step 2 takes this weighted probability sample as a basis for the estimation of inclusion probabilities of the analog volunteer sample (also $N = 108$). This estimation, too, is based on age and gender and also involves an indicator of the readiness for participating in surveys, that is, the willingness to participate in a follow-up survey as declared by the respondents at the end of the two samples. Adopting the random response model again, these estimated inclusion probabilities were also used to derive normalized weights for a compensatory sample weighting. An overall weighting variable is then obtained by collecting the normalized weights for the probability sample (step 1, reference: population register) and the normalized weights for the volunteer sample (reference: probability sample) into one overall weight variable. In a final step, the remaining sample bias was removed by adjusting this overall weight by reference to corresponding sample-census distributions of official statistics for Bremen, using the freshest available figures, i.e., for 2018). That way, the remaining sample bias according to education (overrepresentation of higher education in the initial samples) and gender (despite the previous weighting, the remaining underrepresentation of women in the samples) was removed. Overall (unweighted and weighted) sample size is 216 people aged 18+.

Table 20.A3 Attitudes towards robots and AI, seeking of AI-driven advice, and self-image: CFA factor loadings and interpolated quartiles of indicator variables

	Q1	Q2	Q3	Loadings
Scale: 1 = not at all, 2 = probably not, 3 = possibly, 4 = quite probable, 5 = quite certain				
AI IS GOOD FOR SOCIETY				
Robots/AI good for society	3.0	3.8	4.6	0.85
Robots/AI necessary	3.5	4.5	5.0	0.71
AI IS SAFE FOR HUMANS				
Reliable (error-free) technology	1.5	2.5	3.6	0.71
Safe technologies for humans	2.1	3.0	3.8	0.94
Trustworthy technologies	2.3	3.0	3.5	0.84
AI IS TRUSTFULLY DEPLOYED				
Job search: Automated preselection of candidates by intelligent software would. . .				
. . . be geared to qualification alone	1.5	2.6	3.6	0.72
. . . effectively guard against discrimination	1.6	2.4	3.5	0.89
. . . guard against discrimination better than human preselection	2.2	3.1	4.0	0.90
WOULD SEEK AI DRIVEN ADVICE				
Respondent would use a smartphone app as a personal advisor in the case of decisions of everyday life	1.6	2.5	3.6	0.93
Respondent would use a smartphone app as a personal advisor in the case of decisions about important life situations	1.3	2.1	3.1	0.95
SELF-IMAGE: OPEN-MINDED				
Respondent is open-minded toward technological innovations	3.5	4.3	4.9	0.62
Respondent likes to be counted among the first to try out technological innovations	1.7	2.3	3.5	0.81
Respondent keeps up with the times	3.0	3.7	4.3	0.71

N = 216. The CFA treats all scales as 5-point ordinal scales using probit regression. Survey weights are employed to handle unit nonresponse and multiple imputations to handle item nonresponse (five imputed datasets, including 176 complete cases). The CFA attains an acceptable goodness of fit: chi^2 = 175, df = 174, p = 0.46; CFI/TLI = 1.0, RMSEA = 0.01; SRMR = 0.071. The computation of interpolated quartiles is based on weighted frequency distributions. Because these distributions involve minor percentages of "don't know" responses (1.3% on average), these "don't know" responses were recoded to the mild category "possibly", acting on the auxiliary assumption that both categories equivalently express maximal uncertainty. R packages employed in this analysis: Lavaan, semTools, mice, survey.

Fieldwork

25 November to 15 December 2019. Survey invitation via personalized letter post, including a link to the web questionnaire (probability sample) and via an advertisement in the local newspapers and an announcement on the homepage of the University of Bremen website (volunteer sample). More details in Engel (2020).

Table 20.A4 Feelings towards robots and AI: CFA loadings of this factor and interpolated quartiles of indicator variables

	Q1	Q2	Q3	Loadings
RESPONDENT FEELS AT EASE WITH THE ANTICIPATED FICTITIOUS SITUATION				
A robot keeps you company at home	1.4	2.2	3.1	0.88
Medically skilled robot undertakes the first diagnosis/care in a tele-consultation	1.3	2.2	3.2	0.82
Smart Home: A robot recognizes you by your voice or look and turns to you individually	1.3	2.3	3.3	0.90
Be driven through the city by a self-driving car	1.5	2.7	3.8	0.67
You are in need of care: a robot takes part in your care	2.0	2.9	3.4	0.77
You must undergo a surgery in which a robot assists the physician	2.6	3.2	4.1	0.67
A robot supports you at the workplace	2.7	3.3	4.0	0.72
A drone delivers post home to you	2.7	3.6	4.3	0.72

Scale: 1 = would feel very unwell, 2 = quite unwell, 3 = part/part, 4 = quite well, 5 = very well

On average, 2.8% "don't know" answers were involved (recoded to mid category)

Findings from the population survey

More on https://github.com/viewsandinsights/AI.

References

Al-Fannah, N. M., & Li, W. (2017). Not all browsers are created equal: Comparing web browser fingerprintability. In *International workshop on security* (pp. 105–120). Springer. https://doi.org/10.1007/978-3-319-64200-0_7

Apple. (2020). *Safari. Die beste Sicht aufs Internet* [The Best View of the Internet]. www.apple.com/de/safari/

Araujo, T., Wonneberger, A., Neijens, P., & de Vreese, C. (2017). How much time do you spend online? Understanding and improving the accuracy of self-reported measures of internet use. *Communication Methods and Measures, 11*(3), 173–190.

Athey, S. (2018). The impact of machine learning on economics. In *The economics of artificial intelligence: An agenda* (pp. 507–547). University of Chicago Press.

Bethlehem, J. (2009). *Applied survey methods: A statistical perspective* (Vol. 558). John Wiley & Sons.

Bolton, C., Machová, V., Kovacova, M., & Valaskova, K. (2018). The power of human–machine collaboration: Artificial intelligence, business automation, and the smart economy. *Economics, Management, and Financial Markets, 13*(4), 51–56.

Bughin, J., Seong, J., Manyika, J., Chui, M., & Joshi, R. (2018). *Notes from the AI frontier: Modeling the impact of AI on the world economy.* McKinsey Global Institute.

Can, Y. S., Arnrich, B., & Ersoy, C. (2019). Stress detection in daily life scenarios using smart phones and wearable sensors: A survey. *Journal of Biomedical Informatics, 92.* https://doi.org/10.1016/j.jbi.2019.103139

Chastin, S. F. M., Dontje, M. L., Skelton, D. A., Čukić, I., Shaw, R. J., Gill, J. M. R., . . . Dall, P. M. (2018). Systematic comparative validation of self-report measures of sedentary time against an objective measure of postural sitting (activPAL). *International Journal of Behavioral Nutrition and Physical Activity, 15*(1), 1–12. https://doi.org/10.1186/s12966-018-0652-x

Chatterjee, A., Gupta, U., Chinnakotla, M. K., Srikanth, R., Galley, M., & Agrawal, P. (2019). Understanding emotions in text using deep learning and big data. *Computers in Human Behavior, 93,* 309–317.

Elliott, M. R., & Valliant, R. (2017). Inference for nonprobability samples. *Statistical Science,* 249–264.

Engel, U., Bartsch, S., Schnabel, C., & Vehre, H. (2012). *Wissenschaftliche Umfragen: Methoden und Fehlerquellen* [Scientific Surveys: Methods and Sources of Error]. Campus Verlag.

Engel, U. (2020). Blick in die Zukunft Wie künstliche Intelligenz das Leben verändern wird Ergebnisse eines Umfrageprojekts in der Wissenschaft. *Politik und Bevölkerung der Freien Hansestadt Bremen*. http://dx.doi.org/10.13140/RG.2.2.14478.92489

Garcia-Ceja, E., Riegler, M., Nordgreen, T., Jakobsen, P., Oedegaard, K. J., & Tørresen, J. (2018). Mental health monitoring with multimodal sensing and machine learning: A survey. *Pervasive and Mobile Computing, 51*, 1–26.

Gerber, N., Reinheimer, B., & Volkamer, M. (2019). Investigating people's privacy risk perception. *Proceedings on Privacy Enhancing Technologies, 2019*(3), 267–288. https://doi.org/10.2478/popets-2019-0047

Google Chrome. (2020). *Google chrome privacy whitepaper*. www.google.com/chrome/privacy/whitepaper.html

Hargittai, E. (2015). Is bigger always better? Potential biases of big data derived from social network sites. *The ANNALS of the American Academy of Political and Social Science, 659*(1), 63–76. https://doi.org/10.1177/0002716215570866

Haynes, C. A., & Shelton, K. (2018). Delphi method in a digital age: Practical considerations for online Delphi studies. In *Handbook of research on innovative techniques, trends, and analysis for optimized research methods* (pp. 132–151). IGI Global.

Intille, S. S. (2012). Emerging technology for studying daily life. In M. R. Mehl & T. S. Conner (Eds.), *Handbook of research methods for studying daily life* (pp. 267–282). Guilford Press.

Jenny, M., Meißner, A., Glende, D., Will, N., Nowak, A. L., Dellbrügge, G., & Kruse, A. (2019, Oktober). *Perspektiven der künstlichen Intelligenz für den Einzelhandel in Deutschland. Studie im Auftrag des Bundesministeriums für Wirtschaft und Energie*. Retrieved from www.bmwi.de/Redaktion/DE/Publikationen/Studien/perspektiven-kuenstliche-intelligenz-fuer-einzelhandel.html

Jones-Jang, S. M., Heo, Y. J., McKeever, R., Kim, J. H., Moscowitz, L., & Moscowitz, D. (2020). Good news! Communication findings may be underestimated: Comparing effect sizes with self-reported and logged smartphone use data. *Journal of Computer-Mediated Communication, 25*(5), 346–363.

Jürgens, P., Stark, B., & Magin, M. (2020). Two half-truths make a whole? On bias in self-reports and tracking data. *Social Science Computer Review, 38*(5), 600–615. https://doi.org/10.1177/0894439319831643

Kim, S. Y. S., Alvarez, R. M., & Ramirez, C. M. (2020). Who voted in 2016? Using fuzzy forests to understand voter turnout. *Social Science Quarterly, 101*(2), 978–988. https://doi.org/10.1111/ssqu.12777

Linstone, H. A., & Turoff, M. (2011). Delphi: A brief look backward and forward. *Technological Forecasting and Social Change, 78*(9), 1712–1719.

Liu, Q., Yao, M. Z., Yang, M., & Tu, C. (2017). Predicting users' privacy boundary management strategies on Facebook. *Chinese Journal of Communication, 10*(3), 295–311. https://doi.org/10.1080/17544750.2017.1279675

Long, J. S., & Freese, J. (2006). *Regression models for categorical dependent variables using stata* (Vol. 7). Stata Press.

Lupton, D. (2016). *The quantified self*. John Wiley & Sons.

Mathur, A., Vitak, J., Narayanan, A., & Chetty, M. (2018). Characterizing the use of browser-based blocking extensions to prevent online tracking. In *Fourteenth symposium on usable privacy and security ({SOUPS}* (pp. 103–116). USENIX Association.

Molina, M., & Garip, F. (2019). Machine learning for sociology. *Annual Review of Sociology, 45*, 27–45.

Monroe, B. L., Colaresi, M. P., & Quinn, K. M. (2008). Fightin' words: Lexical feature selection and evaluation for identifying the content of political conflict. *Political Analysis, 16*(4), 372–403.

Mozilla Foundation. (2020). *Firefox browser*. Retrieved from www.mozilla.org/de/firefox/new/

Olteanu, A., Kıcıman, E., & Castillo, C. (2018). A critical review of online social data: Biases, methodological pitfalls, and ethical boundaries. In *Proceedings of the eleventh ACM international conference on web search and data mining* (pp. 785–786). https://doi.org/10.1145/3159652.3162004

Potoglou, D., Dunkerley, F., Patil, S., & Robinson, N. (2017). Public preferences for internet surveillance, data retention and privacy enhancing services: Evidence from a pan-European study. *Computers in Human Behavior, 75*, 811–825. https://doi.org/10.1016/j.chb.2017.06.007

Radford, J., & Joseph, K. (2020). Theory in, theory out: The uses of social theory in machine learning for social science. *Front. Big Data, 3*, 18. https://doi.org/10.3389/fdata.2020.00018

Rao, A. S., & Verweij, G. (2017). *Sizing the prize: What's the real value of AI for your business and how can you capitalise*. PwC Publication, PwC.

Revilla, M., Ochoa, C., & Loewe, G. (2017). Using passive data from a meter to complement survey data in order to study online behavior. *Social Science Computer Review, 35*(4), 521–536.

Rogers, E. M. (2003). *Diffusion of innovations*. Free Press.

The Royal Society. (2017). *Machine learning: The power and promise of computers that learn by example.* Retrieved from https://royalsociety.org/~/media/policy/projects/machine-learning/publications/machine-learning-report.pdf

Schnell, R. (2012). *Survey-Interviews*. VS Verlag.

Schwarz, N. (2012). Why researchers should think "real-time." A cognitive rationale. In M. R. Mehl & T. S. Conner (Eds.), *Handbook of research methods for studying daily life* (pp. 22–42). Guilford Press.

Selke, S. (2014). *Lifelogging. Wie die digitale Selbstvermessung unsere Gesellschaft verändert.* Econ Verlag.

Slovic, P. (2010). *The feeling of risk: New perspectives on risk perception.* Routledge.

Spiekermann, S., Acquisti, A., Böhme, R., & Hui, K. L. (2015). The challenges of personal data markets and privacy. *Electronic Markets, 25*(2), 161–167. https://doi.org/10.1007/s12525-015-0191-0

Stier, S., Breuer, J., Siegers, P., & Thorson, K. (2020). Integrating survey data and digital trace data: Key issues in developing an emerging field. *Social Science Computer Review, 38*(5), 503–516. https://doi.org/10.1177/0894439319843669

Tourangeau, R., Kreuter, F., & Eckman, S. (2015). Motivated misreporting: Shaping answers to reduce survey burden. In U. Engel (Ed.), *Survey measurements. Techniques, data quality, and sources of error* (pp. 24–41). Campus Verlag.

Tourangeau, R., Rips, L. J., & Rasinski, K. (2000). *The psychology of survey response.* Cambridge University Press.

Trepte, S., Reinecke, L., Ellison, N. B., Quiring, O., Yao, M. Z., & Ziegele, M. (2017). A cross-cultural perspective on the privacy calculus. *Social Media + Society, 3*(1). https://doi.org/10.1177/2056305116688035

Van Schaik, P., Jansen, J., Onibokun, J., Camp, J., & Kusev, P. (2018). Security and privacy in online social networking: Risk perceptions and precautionary behaviour. *Computers in Human Behavior, 78*, 283–297. https://doi.org/10.1016/j.chb.2017.10.007

Veblen, T. (2005). *The theory of the leisure class: An economic study of institutions.* Aakar Books. (Original work published 1899)

Webb, E. J., Campbell, D. T., Schwartz, R. D., & Sechrest, L. (1966 [2000]). *Unobtrusive measures* (Rev. ed.). Sage Classics 2.

Webb, E. J., Campbell, D. T., Schwartz, R. D., & Sechrest, L. (1999). *Unobtrusive measures* (Vol. 2). Sage.

Weisberg, H. F. (2009). *The total survey error approach: A guide to the new science of survey research.* University of Chicago Press.

Wildavsky, A., & Dake, K. (1990). Theories of risk perception: Who fears what and why? *Daedalus*, 41–60.

Zhang, M., Alvarez, R. M., & Levin, I. (2019). Election forensics: Using machine learning and synthetic data for possible election anomaly detection. *PLoS One, 14*(10). https://doi.org/10.1371/journal.pone.0223950

21

EFFECTIVE FIGHT AGAINST EXTREMIST DISCOURSE ONLINE

The case of ISIS's propaganda

Séraphin Alava and Rasha Nagem

Context of ISIS's online terrorist propaganda

The Internet has become a key element of our daily life, having an impact on people's entertainment, learning and even socialization. Extremist groups are taking advantage of this dynamic and reaching out to people on the Internet and seeking to propagate their ideologies: hatred and violence. They do not hesitate to identify potential recruits and show real skill in adapting their message to the intended targets. By bringing together researchers in the fields of sociology, linguistics, artificial intelligence and machine learning, we have developed research aimed at building up new approaches for the exploration of cyberspace. Our project is based on a multidisciplinary approach targeted at analyzing extremist content on Internet for French-speaking communities. The purpose of our work is twofold. First of all, we explore extremist content online reflected by indoctrination sources as well as messages and chat exchanges in French-speaking cyberspace. This exploration is carried out at a crossing point of sociological and linguistic perspectives. The aim is to acquire knowledge about the characteristics of this type of content and its etiology and to shed light on the underlying social models and highlight its specific forms of communication. The second objective is to design innovative solutions for the characterization of content. We use models and resources created by researchers in sociology to characterize content according to lexical, discursive and semantic criteria. The project adopts supervised adaptive learning, which is a hybrid paradigm that augments learning algorithms with adaptation mechanisms, capable of acquiring new descriptors, in order to recognize and follow the evolution of concepts. The project thus implements advanced functionalities for a systematic exploration of cyberspace and aims to overcome the limitations of current approaches, which are often ill-suited to monitoring developments in the field. In terms of practical application, we want to design help for users concerned with the fight against the propagation of extremist ideologies online: researchers in sociology will be able to better understand new phenomena, and intelligence analysts and homeland security experts will be able to explore cyberspace more precisely.

It is essential to produce results that go beyond the state of the art and "technological bricks", the use of which will highlight new discoveries on societal and technological challenges at the border between real and virtual environments. Our praxeological objective is to produce

DOI: 10.4324/9781003024583-24

effective adaptive tools for the security forces by taking into account changes in indoctrination discourse and in the mobility of groups and propagators. Our scientific objective is to build bridges between the sociology of deviance, criminology specializing in terrorism and information science which explores networks and virtual worlds, as well as digital sciences, artificial intelligence and mathematics, to equip our societies so they can detect and counter terrorist and extremist speeches.

Interdisciplinary problems to be solved

Methods of extremist recruitment on the Internet

In this area, the ISIS terrorist group, like other Islamist terrorist groups, has particularly innovated in cyberspace. From 2012 to 2019, these groups built a real digital propaganda strategy targeting four dimensions that are specific to military propaganda: disseminating an ideological corpus, attacking the enemy's discourse, wreaking havoc by discrediting objective information and convincing and enlisting future recruits. Obviously, the role of the Internet for terrorist groups is not just about propaganda. The groups must also coordinate, attack and capitalize on the action of terrorist organizations. In this chapter, we focus on propaganda by examining – in the case of jihadist Islamist groups – our technical ability to identify and characterize these speeches online.

Propaganda is a concept designating a set of persuasion techniques used to propagate with all available means an idea, an opinion, an ideology or a doctrine and stimulate the adoption of behaviors within a target audience. In the case of ISIS or Al-Qaeda, we can easily speak of structuring a global and strategic communication network.

ISIS has developed a global and strategic communication policy using all communication techniques. Their aim is to broadcast in information vacuums where public discourse is redundant and not critical. Conspiracy or disruptive speeches are "media projectiles" which reach the most varied audiences with the same degree of precision and leave an informational vacuum in their wake. Twitter and Snapchat become launch points for rumors and disinformation which will then be passed on in social media and finally spread out on encrypted networks. This marketing technique, starting with an appealing product and transforming into loyalty, is all the easier as the contents of the messages combine cultural, linguistic, religious and often economic discourse in order to cover all the areas of widening rifts between youth and society.

Another pressure technique used to cover the informational field is directly related to the meaning of words. Extremist communication firstly seeks to saturate – by disinformation, misuse, repetitions of meaning – the sense of certain words or concepts (family, community, fraternity, violence) in order to break the emotional barrier included in these words and then cause a change of direction in the meaning and gradually impose a shift in the meaning. This shift in the meaning makes the reading of reality impossible outside the framework of extremist assignments of meaning (Jewish, unbelievers, caricature, the West, etc.). Finally, terrorist groups also use their communications by taking into account the media coverage of their actions. This is the terrorist second breath that Regis Debré refers to. The blast of an attack provokes a media frenzy. Media from all over the world will relay the information supplied by ISIS. The target to be recruited is constantly mobbed by articles with catchy titles which, slowly but most likely, undermine the resilience and cohesion of our societies. We have grown accustomed to information warfare in which we've become actors unintentionally.

Digital radicality, process of radicalization?

The individualization of radicalization is achieved through terrorism, and it implicitly betrays the prevalence of a subjectivist and psychologizing approach (Guibet Lafaye & Rapin, 2017). Radicalization and terrorism are linked, the radicalization becomes a "breeding ground for terrorism". In radicalization, it is no longer about hardening an ideology but about describing an individual phenomenon, a turnaround that begins in dialogue and radical conversation.

It is no longer a collective and social movement which is radicalized, but the target of radicalization is an individual (often considered lost) who is in a need of psychological support and deradicalization. Khosrokhavar (2014) proposed a definition of radicalization where violence was inevitably inherent. Indeed, he sees radicalization as a process in which an individual or a group takes a violent form of action, which is directly linked to an extremist ideology with a political, social or religious content, contesting the established order at the political, social or cultural level.

In fact, regarding radicalization as an individual and violent phenomenon only brings about a biased analysis of the process, and thus generates ineffective counter-discourse. Thus, conversion, allegiance and radicalization should not be confused (Salazar, 2015; Filiu, 2015; Haddad, 2015). Therefore, radicalization would be defined as a process of desocialization in relation to a given ideology and of re-socialization in the form of adherence to a radical political line (Guibet Lafaye & Rapin, 2017).

What is a discourse?

In order to recognize and gather elements of ultra-right discourse, it is important to characterize these groups but also to be familiar with the elements that reveal the discourse's structure. In everyday language, the term "discourse" refers to an oral production performed in front of an assembly or intended for an audience. In linguistics, the term encompasses all of a person's written or oral linguistic productions. The word "discourse" becomes, then, very broad and seems close to the definition of the dictionary of the French language, "littré", in which the discourse encompasses all the words used by a person.

In our case, these definitions are not effective because it is not a question of knowing and characterizing all the productions of an ultra-right group but of identifying the types of discourse that have an objective or an impact in the radicalization of an individual. In this sense, we follow the analysis of Vincent D. (2005), for whom language productions form a coherent whole, interpretable only by the superposition of multiple layers of analysis; a laminate made by using production methods that are repetitive and unique at the same time, each interaction being seen as a structured and structuring social activity.

Our mission isn't to recognize the discourse but the discourses of the extreme right, not only by distinguishing them by their explicit or implicit contents but also by their strategic wills, their rhetorical qualities and their own typologies.

Therefore, identifying, collecting and characterizing far-right discourse within cyberspace requires a triple identification (content, typologies, rhetoric).

Building a base of expertise: web-crawlers and characterization of extremist texts

One of the main concerns linked to the misuse of social media is the dissemination of content related to extremist attitudes and ideologies, such as online propaganda, hate speech or radicalizing content, disseminated on social media platforms to supposedly pollute these platforms with content intended to influence public opinion, harm other people or recruit (Lorenzi & Moïse, 2018).

We know today that the goals of the discursive presence of extremist ideologies are complementary. Spreading the ideology and providing arguments that can be used by followers is not the only goal. The propaganda of these ideologies is reinforced by the dissemination of false information, relying on a strategic use of conspiracy theories. All these typologies of discourse also aim at the isolation of the individual to be recruited in order to produce an intimate space for deploying a radical conversation that we have already analyzed (Alava, Najjar, & Hussein, 2019). Online propaganda campaigns have attracted the attention of the research community (Chatfield, Reddick, & Brajawidagda, 2015) (Scanlon & Gerber, 2014), (Allendorfer & Herring, 2015), and numerous independent studies suggest that the social media played a central role in the rise of ISIS (Ferrara, Wang, Varol, Flammini, & Galstyan, 2016) or at least that it benefited from the use of social media for propaganda and recruitment purposes (Berger & Morgan, 2015).

To establish our baselines, which will serve as a basis for indexing and then as a learning source for artificial intelligence, we have chosen to focus on a single jihadist group (ISIS) and to take extracts from texts not in relation to their contents but to three levels of discourse. Indeed, there are many variations between the generic discourse given by a politician, a political scientist and an intellectual; the discourse propagated by a journalist, an intellectual and a media man; and the integrated discourse carried by a grassroots activist and a follower of the movements, and it is very useful to understand these discourses. We have therefore defined three levels of discourse:

1   *Generic discourses:* We identify on the Internet, the founding discourses of ISIS ideologies in order to know how to distinguish the differences between the discourse that founds a concept or an analysis and will then be appropriated or propagated. For this, we have taken into account the speeches of Abou Bakr al-Baghdadi and written references of ISIS's ideologists in their online journals.
2   *Propagated discourses:* We then identify the discourses coming from the media relays, the followers of ideas and the associated intellectuals. These discourses have a desire for impact, adherence and greater statement, and studying these variations is useful to better characterize ideas and rhetoric. To do this, we extracted all the text from recruitment videos by Niçois Omar Diaby, alias Omar Omsen. We used seven videos from the 19HH channel.
3   *Appropriated discourses:* We refer here to statements made by Internet users, which are the targets aimed at by this propaganda. Interviews were conducted with 32 French radicalized youngsters who agreed to discuss their ideologies and to explain these ideas to us.

Tagging extremist sentences and artificial intelligence learning

Overall, our research project takes into account five technological stages. The characterization of jihadist discourses is taken into account by sociologists. The setting up of the base and its analysis requires cooperation between computer sciences and language sciences. Indexation

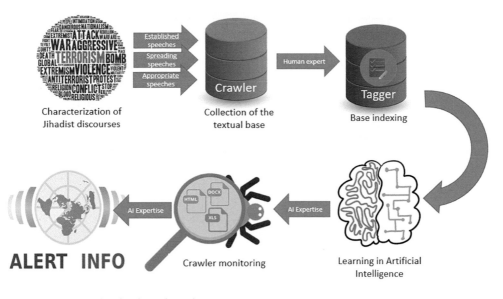

Figure 21.1   General technological graphic

of the database requires the help of human experts, sociologists or Islamologists. AI learning with the indexed database is performed by AI specialists. The adaptation of the crawler and its interaction with the semantic engine requires cooperation between computer engineers and AI specialists. It is obvious that characterization of alerts requires human expertise. A human feedback to the AI analysis engine is something to consider in order to improve the system.

Methodology for setting up the starting base

The main objective of our technological cooperation was to respond to several fundamental technological problems allowing us to offer the security service relevant and effective tools in the fight against online extremism. Our first problem to be addressed was the identification of the different registers of extremist discourse by relying on identifiable contents in this discourse and at the same time on the methods of dissemination and the linguistic components of these discourses. This issue required a substantial dialogue among sociologists capable of recognizing the extremist groups, identifying the involved media and the names of the most important propagators. The work carried out within the framework of this study yielded a base of 19,612 sentences indexed with three criteria (radical, non-radical, out of context).

To achieve this, we worked with two tools: an internet robot (crawler) able to search a database of 24,000 sentences using provided samples (lists of words, profiles to follow, list of hashtags) and an indexing tool that allows human experts to characterize these sentences.

The Database Tagger is a computer application used to automate and facilitate the process of assigning tags to a dataset. In the context of our research, the content of these datasets may be texts or images, which are tagged with the desired tags associated with the analysis tools. The Database Tagger allows to create the datasets necessary for the development of the text analysis module. Furthermore, it will help to increase these datasets in the future by adding and tagging more texts coming from "Alert" results, thus improving the performance and reliability of the developed analysis tools.

Table 21.1 Breakdown of the number of items retained for the database

	Total	Out of context	Radical	Non radical
Magazines	6697	1155	3116	2426
Social media	8119	4273	2804	1042
Interviews	2201	270	1191	740
Videos	2078	432	1074	572
Various texts	517	59	226	232
	19,612	**6189**	**8411**	**5012**

Network monitor client (proxy) methodology

A network monitoring client was developed as part of the project with the aim of collecting real-time information on network traffic in explicitly monitored locations. The proxy captures traffic from a monitored network to send it to the crawler for further analysis. Along with the captured traffic, additional metadata such as the proxy ID or an ID of the monitored machine is also sent.

The network monitor client has the following capabilities:

- Real-time network analysis, request by request;
- Ability to read HTTP connections if the used browser has been correctly configured with the root certificate;
- As the communication is asynchronous with the crawler, the surveillance activity therefore has a minimum latency penalty that could potentially raise suspicion about the person being monitored.

The network monitor client consists of two modules [Squid proxy and Internet Content Adaptation Protocol (ICAP) server], which interact with each other via the ICAP protocol. The proxy performs the following actions in sequential order:

- Intercepting the request from the monitored client(s) and passing the same request to the server, acting as the original client;
- Reading the response from the server and sending it to the ICAP server;
- Re-encrypting the server's response with a custom certificate and sending it to the client.

The ICAP server performs the following actions:

- Receiving responses from the proxy via the ICAP protocol;
- Adding some additional metadata and grouping the data into a JSON object;
- Asynchronous sending of the message via HTTP to the crawler.

Crawler assistant methodology

The objective of the crawler assistant is to generate likely user interactions based on previous context. The crawler assistant works with a model that is built with data extracted from user interactions. Those interactions must be provided during a training phase.

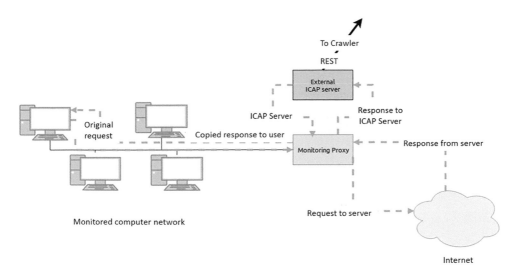

Figure 21.2 Network monitoring customer overview (Practicies report 7, 2019)

Figure 21.3 shows the architecture of the crawler assistant. The crawler assistant has a set-up phase and a normal deployment phase. During the set-up phase, the data preparation module takes the training corpus and stores it in a Knowledge database. This step is only executed if the configuration system does not point to an existing knowledge base (e.g., typically the first time the system is run). After this step, the system is ready to receive queries (normal deployment phase). The response generation takes the input query of the user and browses efficiently the Knowledge database in order to find a suitable response. This is performed every time the user queries the system using the REST API.

The Knowledge database is read-only. Therefore, it cannot be updated with new samples and a new database must be built from scratch instead.

The provided context must be a sentence (although it will depend slightly on the training data, the algorithm employed works much better with short texts or sentences). The output has no limitations in size.

To build the training dataset, we used the Dark Web Forums dataset2. We took all the post entries of the forums to build the Knowledge databases in English and French separately. The original post entries are split in sentences. After that, they are clustered by their shallow similarity. The most frequent sentences (biggest clusters) are selected, and the precedent sentences of those that are part of the clusters are employed as the training corpus of the knowledge database.

Final monitoring tool architecture

This section focuses on the technical details of the final monitoring tool, the architecture of which is described in Figure 21.1. This architecture is divided in four main parts. The first one is the ingest part, where the data from the crawler is obtained and transformed to be processed across the system. The second main part, which could be called the manager part, is where the adapted data are received, processed and sent to the cores to be analyzed. The third part is the combination of the core modules, which analyses the input data, generates the results and sends

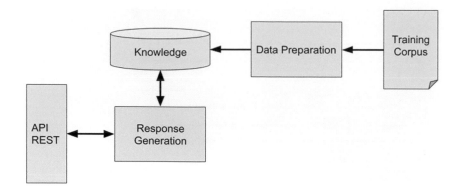

Figure 21.3 Architecture of the crawler assistant (Practicies report 7, 2019)

them back to the manager sector of the platform in order to update the stored data. And, finally, the last part comprises the modules responsible for recovering the data objects with their respective results and presenting them to the graphical user interface.

Evaluation of machine and human efficiency: methodological reflections

The more advanced digital technology gets, the more terrorism will adapt accordingly. In the security battle fought currently by various countries with terrorist groups, the terrorists are always one step ahead. The Visible Web, the Dark Web, the Web of Things – terrorist groups are gradually adapting to technologies. Censorship, de-listing, financial fines against Internet companies – all these actions will have reduced effectiveness in the long term. There is an urgent need for understanding how extremist recruiting works and describing the modalities of targeting young people sensitive to extremist ideas. There is an urgent need for characterizing the content, topics and terrorist arguments, because even if we thought at one point that radicalized young people were victims, it is clear that a part of the jihadist changeover is a commitment that starts at the communicational level, then psychological and finally relational with the propagators of radical ideas.

Our research confirms American work on the diversity, quality and quantity of ISIS's propaganda. These speeches, videos, chats, tweets and posts are as many beacons for the propagators of extremist ideas and as many decoys to attract young people. Between these texts and the radical conversation that will lead the young person to engage, there are structured steps that the ISIS organization deploys with a wide variety of tailor-made online contributions to bring their targets into their bosom (Berger & Morgan, 2015).

Sometimes referred to as "touching up", these contributions are carried out by small teams of prolific social media users who grab the attention of potential recruits in order to shape their worldview and encourage direct action in favor of the Islamic State. We need to understand these contributions. With the help of digital engineering and robotics, thanks to the promising tools of interrelation graphs on the Net and with artificial intelligence, we can catch up with terrorist groups and identify sensitive cognitive phases to alert the machine to detect violent extremism in its present form. Traditional approaches to content analysis prove limited in highly heterogeneous and dynamic environments such as online media. Hybrid mechanisms, using supervised learning cores capable of adapting to changing domains through the integration of asynchronously inferred knowledge, are better suited for the detection of extremist content on the Internet. Our goals for ongoing projects are to develop artificial intelligence methods to analyze extremist content, messages and conversations on the Internet. The analyzed content will be retrieved from sources of indoctrination but also from exchanges on digital platforms. It is important to develop methods of in-depth characterization of online content in order to produce a description that is rich at the lexical, terminological and semantic level. The characterization will also highlight domain-specific concepts (radicalization, extreme right, violence, threats) and subjective engagement (support, rejection, preference, disagreement) expressed by users (Battistelli, Bruneau, & Dragos, 2020). Within the FLYER research project, we want to build new approaches for adaptive supervised learning. It is a hybrid paradigm of artificial intelligence, augmenting learning algorithms with adaptation mechanisms that make them capable of acquiring new descriptors in order to cope with the evolution of the field (Dragos, Battistelli, & Kellodjoue, 2020).

The scope of the project is large, but the stakes are high. The Internet war has started, and terrorist groups are ahead of us. Therefore, we must describe, explain, understand and above all anticipate.

Useful research projects:

- PRACTICIES Europa H2020: Partnership Against Violent Radicalisation in Cities, https://practicies.org/home-en-gb/
- SAFFRON Europa FSI: Semantic Analysis against Foreign Fighters Recruitment On-line Network, www.saffron-project.eu/en/home/
- RISTRACK EUOPA Justice Tracking tool based on social media for risk assessment on radicalisation, www.risk-track.eu/en/
- FLYER ANR DEFENSE France Artificial intelligence for extremist content analysis, https://anr.fr/en/funded-projects-and-impact/funded-projects/project/funded/project/b2d9d3668f92a3b9fbbf7866072501ef-ab458e3cd0/?tx_anrprojects_funded%5Bcontroller%5D=Funded&cHash=c1b49f4f0de62f426c2961b334b57110

References

Alava, S., Najjar, N., & Hussein, H. (2017). *Study of radicalization processes within social networks: Role of conspiracy arguments and rupture discourses*, Quaderni [En ligne], 94, posted online October 5, 2019. Retrieved December 18, 2020, from http://journals.openedition.org/quaderni/1106

Allendorfer, W. H., & Herring, S. C. (2015). ISIS vs. the US government: A war of online video propaganda. *First Monday, 20*(12).

Battistelli D, Bruneau C, Dragos V, (2020). Building a formal model for hate detection in French corpora: 24th International Conference on Knowledge-Based and Intelligent Information & Engineering Systems. *Procedia Computer Science, 176*(2020), 2358–2365.

Berger, J. M., & Morgan, J. (2015). The ISIS Twitter census: Defining and describing the population of ISIS supporters on Twitter. *The Brookings Project on US Relations with the Islamic World, 3*(20), 4–1.

Chatfield, A. T., Reddick, C. G., & Brajawidagda, U. (2015, May). Tweeting propaganda, radicalization and recruitment: Islamic state supporters multi-sided Twitter networks. In *Proceedings of the 16th annual international conference on digital government research* (pp. 239–249). ACM.

Dragos, V., Battistelli, D., & Kellodjoue, E. (2020). A formal representation of appraisal categories for social data analysis: 24th International Conference on Knowledge-Based and Intelligent Information & Engineering Systems. *Procedia Computer Science, 176*(2020), 928–937.

Ferrara, E., Wang, W. Q., Varol, O., Flammini, A., & Galstyan, A. (2016, November). Predicting online extremism, content adopters, and interaction reciprocity. In *International conference on social informatics* (pp. 22–39). Cham: Springer.

Filiu, J. (2015). Barbarie jihadiste et terreur médiatique. *Cités*, *61*, 27–38.

Guibet Lafaye, C., & Rapin, A. (2017). La "radicalization": Individualisation et dépolitisation d'une notion. *Politiques de communication*, *8*, 127–154.

Haddad, G. (2015). *Dans la main droite de Dieu. Psychanalyse du fanatisme.* 1ER PARALLELE.

Haddad, G. (2015). *Dans la main droite de Dieu. Psychanalyse du fanatisme.* Armand Colin.

Khosrokhavar, F. (2014). *Radicalisation.* Éditions de la Maison des sciences de l'homme.

Lorenzi, N., & Moïse, C. (2018). *Radicality, radicalization, hate: Discourse and critical reflections: Practicies project, European Project H2020* [Research report]. Université Grenoble Alpes, 47 p.

Practicies report 7, Fernández, V., Dago, P., Martín, M. I., Nieto, I., Cerezo, H., Abalde, A., Lago, J., et al. (2019). D7.2– D7.6 – Final version of the PRACTICIES platform with the different components integrated Europa.

Salazar, P. (2015). *Paroles armées. Comprendre et combattre la propagande terroriste.* Lemieux Éditeur.

Salon, J. R., & Gerber, M. S. (2014). Automatic detection of cyber-recruitment by violent extremists. *Security Informatics*, *3*(1), 5.

Vincent, D. (2005). Analyse conversationnelle, analyse du discours et interprétation des discours sociaux: le cas de la trash radio. *Marges linguistiques*, numéro 9, mai 2005.

22

PUBLIC OPINION FORMATION ON THE FAR RIGHT

Michael Adelmund and Uwe Engel

Introduction

The study of opinion dynamics is a core object of computational social science research. Initially, surveys represented the primary data source for this research; nowadays, social media data have become equally important. In this chapter, we cover an exploratory study on public opinion formation on the far right of the political spectrum in Germany. In doing so, emphasis is placed on the *far* in far right. This is noteworthy for reasons of accessibility to the field and measurement issues. Although it is possible and constructive to study the far right in surveys if these are sufficiently large (see Chapter 9 in this volume), the people concerned represent nevertheless a hard-to-survey population (Johnson et al., 2014). Thus, social media offers a promising alternative to surveys and access through network sampling (Thompson, 2014) when people have an interest in expressing their political views publicly via such media.

Social media data in research on opinion dynamics

In the present context, another "survey vs. social-media comparison" appears necessary. Social media data represent a source sometimes labeled "found data" (Hox, 2017). Even if such data replace carefully designed measurement instruments, the non-reactive nature of found data is sometimes regarded as advantageous when used as *unobtrusive measures* (Webb, Campbell, Schwartz, & Sechrest, 1966). When doing so, the argument is that such data replace error-prone self-reports on behavior by the unnoticed direct observation of this behavior itself. At first glance, this argument appears convincing: if people are not asked for a response, neither a reaction nor any inadvertent survey-related side effect can occur. This, however, does not describe the potential of other sources of social influence. Found *textual* data are not error free only because they are obtained in an unobtrusive manner. It is true that survey data suffer to some extent from so-called mode and response effects and the propensity to express socially desirable responses. It is also true, however, that such effects may be controlled for to some extent (Engel, Bartsch, Schnabel, & Vehre, 2012, chapter 13). The case of extreme political opinions may be an illustrative example. A survey context that guarantees *strict anonymity* may make it even easier to express extreme political opinions than a *public* context in the social media. There are platform-specific Terms of Service, higher-ranking legal rules, and the potential fear of

DOI: 10.4324/9781003024583-25

undesirable personal consequences. Because of these, users may avoid the expression of too-extreme opinions in blogs and discussion lists. This argument, however, presumes the popular model of rational choice in which people decide in accord with the anticipated and subjectively valued advantage a behavior in question may have for them. In social media, for instance, posts are *published* posts in *public* contexts and are thus likely to be motivated by gaining social acceptance and influence in respective communities. Following Max Weber (1972), people may decide according to the expected usefulness, and they may also decide out of conviction, the latter possibly even irrespective of the consequences a pursuit of this conviction may have for them. Such a mixture of purposive-rational and value-rational motivation is likely to give rise to the public expression of even extreme political worldviews in social media. In addition, this mixture helps to understand why political conflict is potentially the more destructive, the more a conflict is rooted in different, perhaps even incompatible, convictions (value conflict) and the less in negotiable clashes of interest. Textual data as well as the digital traces people leave when surfing the web represent a promising behavioral data source for research on opinion dynamics even if such data are not free of measurement error and even if the motivation behind the public expression of political opinion must always be considered. Moreover, social media provide a rich data source beyond the typical scope of general population surveys. This concerns user-generated content, and this concerns the reachability of groups beyond the spectrum normally covered by general population surveys. The existence of platform-specific user populations may thus be regarded as both a threat to the generalizability of results across such populations and the chance of reaching otherwise underrepresented or even missing parts of the populace for public opinion research.

The case study

Objective

The study explores opinion dynamics on the far right of the political spectrum using the example of a political party in Germany. This political party is under a cloud of being right-wing extremist, albeit not banned by law. It is regularly active in social media networks though not represented in any supra regional parliament.

Data collection

The starting point was a search of relevant party profiles on Facebook. Official reports in the public domain were used as an aid in this regard. The search strategy involved the party's name along with the federal state and the largest cities therein and resulted in a total of 180 Facebook profiles of the political party and its subdivisions. Said profiles were publicly accessible to anyone at the time of this study. They were sequentially accessed in the browser window and temporarily stored to carry out the data collection manually. The dates reported in the figures reflect the respective time of data collection. No personal data were collected. Data collection is restricted to the textual content of posts, the media links, and the abstract response indicators provided by Facebook, for instance, the number of "likes", "comments", and "shares". From April 2010 to May 2020, the political party published over 165,000 postings, which were followed by nearly 1.7 million "shares", over 480,000 comments, and nearly 4 million emoji reactions. The extent of activity and thus the intensity of political opinion formation on the far right varied considerably across the federal states and regions. Statistical data analysis is done using the programming environment R.

Analytics

A core feature of the research design is the linkage of responses to posts with these posts themselves. This enables the researcher to relate *associated* textual information to each other. Using text as a stimulus, the response may then either be a textual response as well as a standardized response using provided response categories. Accordingly, the design enables the analysis of *relational* data structures and this by simultaneous use of different types of data. Analysis options correspondingly involve a broad spectrum of methods related to text mining, for instance: sentiment analysis, the identification of hidden structures and clusters, document classification, and the use of text for predicting outcomes (Kwartler, 2017). For instance, the identification of hidden text clusters may help to decide if political views expressed in posts are likely to indicate rather extremist than populist opinions. This is certainly an important borderline in liberal democracies. In the present analysis, however, the objective is not that ambitious. Instead of detecting such latent borderlines, the analysis focuses on tracing the time-related trend in the affective responses that accompany political messages posted in right-wing communities. In doing this, particular attention is drawn to the question if such messages relate to a source in the mainstream media or, instead of this, come originally from within a right-wing community.

The community's response to political postings

Figure 22.1 shows the trend in the number of responses per posting on Facebook profiles of the right-wing political party. The grey bars indicate the number of "Like"-responses per posting.

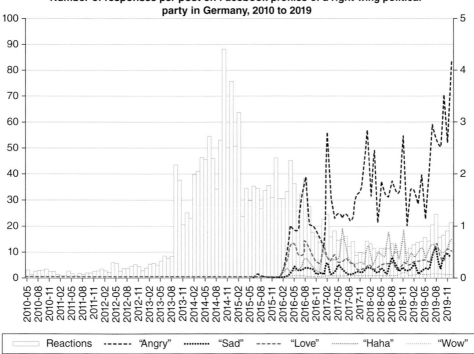

Figure 22.1 Number of responses per post on Facebook profiles of a right-wing political party in Germany, 2010–2019

The figure reveals a significantly increased response level in the period from September 2013 to September 2016, followed by a stagnation. Then, since the beginning of 2019, a slight trend upwards becomes evident.

A more detailed analysis is possible since 2016 when Facebook upgraded the standardized response categories. Since then, users can indicate if a message (posting) triggers amusement ("Haha"), sadness ("Sad"), astonishment ("Wow"), approval ("Love"), or anger ("Angry"). In this connection, Figure 22.1 reveals a striking increase especially of "angry" reactions to posts of the political party.

To examine this "anger" more closely, it is first necessary to get a brief impression of the "peaks" of this analysis. For it, word counts were used on monthly basis. In doing so, it becomes evident that in August 2016, the election in a federal state of Germany, Mecklenburg-West Pomerania, was affected in which the political party missed re-entry into the parliament.

Another important fact was an increasingly strong competition with another right-wing political party. Around February of 2017, the political party achieved particularly high levels of "angry" reactions regarding the subject area of immigration and the upcoming Bundestag elections. The trend further culminated in a peak in March 2020, when the party questioned the proportionality of measures against SARS-CoV-2, placing them in the context of immigration. A closer inspection of these posts provides an insight into two relevant factors:

1   Among the most frequent terms, those that corresponded to the typical framing of right-wing extremist propaganda were always repeated and reflected in the frequent use of terms such as "asylum seekers", "refugees", "criminals", "victims", or "Merkel".
2   The posts with the highest response rates were mainly hyperlinks to articles from mainstream media. Right-wing alternative media channels appeared to be of minor importance.

Angry response to stimulus words

An exploration into the relevance of political keywords for mobilizing angry reactions should use a benchmark to achieve comparability across communities and time periods. One such benchmark is the community size. Available proxy indicators involve the number of page-likes. We use this number as benchmark and compute, for each posting, the ratio of the number of angry reactions to the number of page-likes. The result is a figure that indicates the relative importance of this emotional reaction given the community size. A given absolute number of angry reactions weights accordingly less the larger a community is. Then, a second weighting component considers if an angry reaction may have come about in response to different stimulus words in a posting. In this regard, a preliminary computational approach is taken by weighting the community-size adjusted angry measure by the inverse value of the share of a given target word in all stimulus words in a posting. In doing so, a target word affects the final score the more the less frequently it is used in relation to all stimulus words in a posting.

$$Pre\ posting = \frac{f_{Angry}}{f_{Page-Likes}} \times \frac{1}{f_{target} \times f_{words}}$$

We conducted this weighting procedure separately for each single stimulus word to ensure a clear assignment. In a final step, a mean value was obtained via the averaged sum of these assignments over all postings that include the target in question. That way, it became evident that the highest angry index values were primarily associated with the German-speaking stimulus words "Asylant" (pejorative term for asylum seekers), "Flüchtlinge" ("refugees"), and "Asylbewerber" ("asylum seekers"). Even terms such as "Kinder" ("children"), "Opfer" ("victims"), and the name of Germany's Federal Chancellor "Merkel" turned out to have an outstanding meaning for the political framing of the far-right political party.

Crossing the borderline

How does reference to content (news, reports) published on digital mainstream media affect the within-community angry response of a political party on the far-right of the political spectrum? First, Figure 22.2 reveals a growing significance of such hyperlinks, as to the TOP100 links[1] of the right-wing party in question. The figure displays, for the period from 2011 to 2019, the percentage of within-community postings linked to content from mainstream media. It differentiates between "mainstream" media, such as www.welt.de, www.focus.de, and www.bild.de, and "scene-typical reporting", such as media as www.deutsche-stimme.de. The shares in the respective total number of links confirm a trend towards linking less to scene-typical propaganda and more to mainstream media content.

This trend is noteworthy because it affects the degree of mobilization of emotional reactions and thus the creation of emotional commitment (Marsden, 2015). All in all, the postings linked to articles from mainstream media come along with a 17% increase in the number of reactions, 37% more "shares", and 51% more comments. For a political party, such a higher level of interaction and affective response is certainly of great strategic value because it may help the

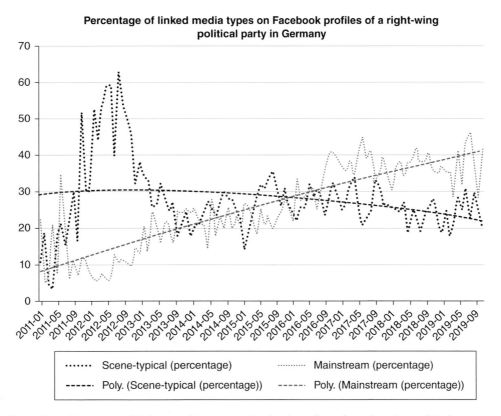

Figure 22.2 Percentage of linked media types on Facebook profiles of a right-wing political party in Germany

political party to increase its range in terms of new followers and may help strengthen its closeness among those who already feel affiliated with the party. From a multilevel perspective, this latter effect is expected to come along with opinion polarization for theoretical and empirical reasons (DellaPosta & Macy, 2015; Bail et al., 2018).

A more in-depth analysis of the individual reactions to each of these posts reveals that linking to mainstream media yields comparably high "angry" reactions regarding particularly scene-relevant antagonistic stereotypes. In terms of content, these were primarily contributions with which the political party attempted to prove the very threat scenarios it had always envisioned beforehand: for example, crime allegedly committed by asylum seekers or refugees, to the detriment of "German" "victims", while laying the blame for it on the federal chancellor ("Merkel").

The present example illustrates that a party on the far right of the political spectrum may be involved heavily in public opinion formation even if such a party is far from winning a majority in parliamentary elections. This by no means precludes the pursuit of potential anti-constitutional goals outside of parliamentary action.

Concluding remarks

In this chapter, we reported on an exploratory study on public opinion formation on the far right of the political spectrum in Germany. In doing so, a first emphasis was placed on the accessibility of "hard-to-survey" populations. We considered social-media data a promising alternative to surveys when people have an interest in expressing their political views publicly via such media. This has led us to raise the question concerning the motivation underlying an expression of political views. People may be geared to the expected usefulness of their actions, and people may act out of conviction irrespective of the consequences a pursuit of this conviction may have for them. We assume that such a mixture of rational-choice and value-rational motivation is likely to give rise to the public expression of even extreme political worldviews in the social media. Assuming this, social media may enable relatively undisguised insights into worldviews, even if these views deviate more strongly from the mainstream.

Even though no guarantee exists to derive advantages always from all five aspects in the following, the combined analysis of content (textual data) and link structure (trace data) in social networks in digital environments appears especially promising in fivefold respects: 1) we may reach populations beyond the usual range of survey research (reachability), 2) we may gain insights into political worldviews whose public expression is less disguised by adherence to platform-specific rules of conduct and the potential fear of undesirable personal consequences (authenticity), 3) we may preserve the interdependencies between related content (context dependency), 4) we may obtain indicators of affective/emotional reactions that accompany posted political content (emotionality), and 5) we may obtain rich data for advanced data/text analytics (analytics).

The present exploratory analysis exhausted this potential only to a marginal degree. However, even if the findings that are obtainable from such a highly specific population at the political margin are not generalizable, maybe not even to similar populations, in conjunction with data from other digital media sources, the highly specific nature of the data may turn the often-complained-of platform-specificity of social media data into a methodological advantage.

Note

1 Although this is only a share in all links (the political party referenced a total of 2760 sources), the TOP 100 links represent 75% of all links.

References

Bail, C. A., Argyle, L. P., Brown, T. W., Bumpus, J. P., Chen, H., Fallin Hunzaker, M. B., . . . Volfovsky, A. (2018). Exposure to opposing views on social media can increase political polarization. *PNAS Proceedings of the National Academy of Sciences of the United States of America*, *115*(37), 9216–9221. https://doi.org/10.1073/pnas.1804840115

DellaPosta, D. J., & Macy, M. W. (2015). The center cannot hold. Networks, echo chambers, and polarization. In E. J. Lawler, S. R. Thye, & J. Yoon (Eds.), *Order on the edge of chaos. Social psychology and the problem of social order* (pp. 86–104). Cambridge University Press.

Engel, U., Bartsch, S., Schnabel, C., & Vehre, H. (2012). *Wissenschaftliche Umfragen. Methoden und Fehlerquellen [Scientific surveys. Methods and sources of error]*. Campus.

Hox, J. J. (2017). Computational social science methodology, anyone? *Methodology*, *13*, 3–12. https://doi.org/10.1027/1614-2241/a000127

Johnson, T. P., Holbrook, A. L., & Atterberry, K. (2014). Surveying political extremists. In R. Tourangeau, B. Edwards, T. P. Johnson, K. M. Wolter, & N. Bates (Eds.), *Hard-to-survey populations* (pp. 379–398). Cambridge University Press.

Kwartler, T. (2017). *Text mining in practice with R*. Wiley

Marsden, P. V. (2015). Social order from the bottom up? In E. J. Lawler, S. R. Thye, & J. Yoon (Eds.), *Order on the edge of chaos. Social psychology and the problem of social order* (pp. 309–332). Cambridge University Press.

Thompson, S. (2014). Link-tracing and respondent-driven sampling. In R. Tourangeau, B. Edwards, T. P. Johnson, K. M. Wolter, & N. Bates (Eds.), *Hard-to-survey populations* (pp. 503–516). Cambridge University Press.

Webb, E. J., Campbell, D. T., Schwartz, R. D., & Sechrest, L. (2000). *Unobtrusive measures* (1st ed., 1966). Sage Classics 2. Sage.

Weber, M. (1972). *Wirtschaft und Gesellschaft* (1st ed., 1921). J. C. B. Mohr.

INDEX

Page numbers in *italics* indicate a figure on the corresponding page.